The Politics of
Modern Europe

The Politics of
Modern Europe

The State and Political Authority in
the Major Democracies

Michael Keating
Professor of Political Science,
University of Western Ontario,
Canada

Edward Elgar
Cheltenham, UK • Lyme, US

Published by
Edward Elgar Publishing Limited
8 Lansdown Place
Cheltenham
Glos GL50 2HU
UK

Edward Elgar Publishing, Inc.
1 Pinnacle Hill Road
Lyme
NH 03768
US

Reprinted 1994, 1997

British Library Cataloguing in Publication Data
Keating, Michael
    Politics of Modern Europe: State and
    Political Authority in the Major
    Democracies
    I. Title
    320.94

Library of Congress Cataloguing in Publication Data
Keating, Michael, 1950–
    The politics of modern Europe: the state and political authority
    in the major democracies / Michael Keating.
        p.   cm.
    Includes bibliographical references.
      1. Europe—Politics and government.   2. European Economic
    Community countries—Politics and government.   3. State, The.
    I. Title.
    JN94.A2K43   1993
    320.3'094—dc20   93–28613
                                        CIP

ISBN 1 85278 573 X
     1 85278 574 8 (paperback)

Printed and bound in Great Britain by
Hartnolls Limited, Bodmin, Cornwall

Contents

Tables

Figures

Preface

European politics is a large subject and one whose contours are rapidly changing. The distinction between western and eastern Europe which informed a generation of political science courses, may soon be irrelevant. The map of Europe itself is being altered by secessions and the growth of European institutions. So rapid and unexpected have been the changes in the late 1980s and early 1990s that books have been rendered out of date before they have appeared in print.

A textbook treatment of such a large subject must necessarily be selective. This imposes some difficult choices, of themes to cover, of material to include and analytical approaches. As always in the study of comparative politics, there is the dilemma of whether to approach the subject thematically or country by country. In favour of the thematic approach is that it is more scientific, it allows systematic comparisons and encourages students to think in terms of general theories and explanations. On the other hand, without the historical, cultural and institutional context provided by studying individual countries, the thematic approach can become very abstract, a mental exercise without application. In this study, I have tried to secure the advantages of both approaches. The first chapter is thematic, looking at European politics in general and raising a series of issues and problems. The following five chapters follow these issues through in individual national contexts. The broad theme of the book is to do with the state in Europe, its structures and policy capacity and its relation to civil society. This is indeed a broad theme, encompassing much of government and politics but does help the book to focus on some issues rather than others. There is not a great deal of political sociology here and politics is defined in relation to the activities of the state. There are some thirty countries in Europe, large and small, and selecting which ones to examine is a serious problem. In the event, I have opted for the four large democracies and have added Spain as an example of a historic state which has chosen Europe as the theme and guide for its efforts at political, economic and social modernisation. There is also a chapter on European integration, focusing on the European Community since this is a vital factor in the political life of each member state. There are no chapters on the smaller countries, on Scandinavia, on Greece or Portugal, Switzerland or Austria, not because these are unimportant, but because neither the length of the book nor that of a one-year course permit it.

It is important that students be introduced to data on politics and policy so as to encourage them to make their own judgements and learn to interpret and assess quantitative material. I have therefore included quite extensive data in the form of tables and charts in the text, with additional information in the statistical appendix.

This book reflects my teaching of European politics since 1985 at the University of Strathclyde (Scotland), Virginia Polytechnic Institute and State University (USA), University of Western Ontario (Canada) and *Institut d'Etudes Politiques de Paris* (France). Students at these institutions have been the testing ground for this material and have helped greatly in indicating by word or puzzled silence when they did not understand, making me formulate my thoughts in a comprehensible manner, and occasionally laughing at my class jokes. I am indebted also to colleagues who have helped me with information, discussed issues and read draft chapters, especially to Tom Mackie (Strathclyde University), Sean Loughlin (Erasmus University), Barry Jones (University of Wales), Antonio-Carlos Pereira Menaut (University of Santiago de Compostela), Francesc Pallarés and Francesc Morata (Autonomous University of Barcelona), Luis Moreno (CSIS, Madrid), Carlo Desideri and Enzo Santantonio (Istituto di Studi sulle Regioni, Rome), Odo Bullman, Hans Kastendiek and Dieter Eisel (University of Giessen), Otto Schiller (University of Marburg), Richard Balme (University of Bordeaux) and Jacques Leruez (FNSP, Paris). Stephanie Dobro, graduate student at the University of Western Ontario, read and corrected an earlier version of the manuscript. The University of Santiago de Compostela gave me a two-month visiting professorship in which I was able to work on Spain and the *Maison Suger* provided a base in Paris. The University of Strathclyde provided a base in the UK. Finally, I am grateful to the University of Western Ontario for a sabbatical year in 1991-2 in which much of the work was done and the Social Science and Humanities Research Council of Canada which provided a grant for travel in Europe.

The book was typed and set by myself with the occasional assistance of my fourteen-year-old son Patrick to whom, as to most of his generation, the mysteries of the computer hold no fears.

Michael Keating

London, Ontario

1 Politics and the State in Western Europe

Politics has been defined in many different ways and observed in a multitude of settings, from the United Nations to the local sports club. There is a danger in the more all-encompassing definitions that, by extending the notion of politics to the entire social reality, they fail to define the subject. In other words, if politics is everything, then perhaps it is nothing.

This book defines politics in a more restrictive manner, as the competition for power within the state. Power is sought in order to further the interests of individuals or social groups; or in order to put into effect political ideals. This enables us to distinguish politics from sociology, economics or the other social sciences, while recognizing that these divisions are merely for the sake of analysis and should not be mistaken for the social reality itself.

This focus on the state as the central element of political life helps define the subject matter and organize material. Yet the state itself is a complex idea. Americans and British, brought up in 'stateless' societies, rarely use the term, except, in the American case, to refer to the lower-tier units in the federal system, preferring the term government. In continental Europe, on the other hand, the state features constantly in legal, academic and political debate, often contrasted with the private world of civil society. There is a large and complex literature on conceptual definitions of the state. Here it will be used to refer to the domain of public power and authority and the institutions of constitutional government. It is characterized by the claim to sovereignty; by defined territorial boundaries; and by a defined citizenship which creates patterns of reciprocal claims and obligations between the citizen and the public authorities.

To understand the complexities of the state, it is helpful to break the subject down into distinct issues. In the following pages, the state is considered as a national or territorial unit. Then the functional scope of the state is examined, that is what the state in Europe actually does. Next, constitutional theories of the state are considered, drawing a distinction between state societies, which have a clear concept of the state as an entity above society and stateless or common law societies, in which the state merges with civil society itself. Then constitutional regimes and political systems are examined. The relationship of political power to bureaucratic power and the power of the state in relation to organized interests is considered. Finally, the challenges facing the

1

contemporary European state are explored.

The Nation State

In western Europe, and specifically the five countries studied here, the state has taken a specific form, that of the nation-state. By this is meant that the boundaries of the state correspond to a sense of common national identity which both legitimates government and allows it to make demands upon its citizens. The idea of the nation-state originated in western Europe between the sixteenth and nineteenth centuries, and such is the power of the idea that it has since been adopted throughout the world. Yet it still arouses scholarly controversy. Some people believe that nations are natural and unchanging entities going back into antiquity and insist that state boundaries must be drawn to correspond to these natural nations. This view has been drummed into countless generations of European schoolchildren by national education systems. Other observers insist, on the contrary, that nations are the invention of state builders in specific historical periods. To put the same point slightly differently, the argument centres on whether the nation precedes the state; or the state precedes and creates the nation. The experience of the nation states of Europe gives evidence for both schools of thought. There is a complex interplay of top-down state building by political elites, and bottom-up nation building through the development of a popular sense of national identity.

The actual process of nation-state formation in Europe has taken two forms. In most of eastern and central Europe and in a few west European examples such as Ireland and Norway, the state was created as a breakaway from a larger state or imperial system. This process of fragmentation, which resumed in the 1990s, is usually justified by the argument that the old state does not correspond to the nationality principle. The most comprehensive attempt to apply the nationality principle was at the Treaty of Versailles (1919) after the first world war. This was not a success since it has proved impossible to agree on what constitutes a nationality and what its boundaries are.

By contrast, in most of western Europe, including our five cases, states were built up from disparate territories in a process of consolidation. In France, Spain and the United Kingdom, the state was built up over centuries, by conquest, treaty and dynastic marriage. The state preceded the nation and governments have sought over the centuries, with more or less zeal and more or less success, to forge their peoples into a common sense of nationality. Germany and Italy were created as states quite rapidly in the late nineteenth century. These built upon existing ideas of nationality, the theory being that all Italians and all Germans should form a single state. The problem lay in defining just who was a German or an Italian. Germany has never occupied all the territories peopled by German-speakers. Nineteenth- and twentieth- century

Italian governments had to forge a nation from the diverse peoples of the peninsula.

The historical emergence of European nation states and the determination of their boundaries was often conflictual. France and Germany long fought over their mutual boundary and the status of Alsace and Lorraine, which have changed hands four times since 1870. Germany's eastern border on the Oder-Neisse line, finally confirmed only in 1991, excludes large parts of historic Germany. Nice and Savoy were transferred to France from Italy in 1860 and the national status of the Alpine regions of Val d'Aosta and Alto Adige (Sud Tirol in German) has given rise to local political movements. The French-Spanish border was fixed as long ago as 1648, though it cuts through the historic territories of Catalonia, the Basque Country and Navarre. The present boundaries of the United Kingdom date from 1922. Since the Second World War, boundaries have not often been an issue between west European states. Rather, governments have sought to transcend the nation state, through a new continental order. A range of international and supranational institutions has been established, the most important of which is the European Community.

If states now accept their mutual boundaries, there are still pressures within them for recognition of national minorities. In Northern Ireland, Scotland, the Basque Country and Corsica and elsewhere, separatist movements exist, dedicated to creating their own states out of one or more existing states, though they have not succeeded in converting a majority of the population to their view. Elsewhere, regional movements seek recognition as nationalities in their own right, with local autonomy but without necessarily having complete separation. Germany is the only one of the major European states to have been largely free of these tensions.

The Scope of the State

Europe has always possessed a stronger state tradition than the United States and a tendency to state regulation of social and economic affairs. European society also has a larger place than the United States for collectivist values, with less emphasis on individual responsibility and competition. Many Europeans see government both as a source of authority and as an agent for economic and social improvement. Underpinned by shared values and solidarities, the nation state has provided a framework for the development of a complex and interventionist apparatus of government, particularly since the second world war.

Measuring the size of government is a difficult exercise, since there are several yardsticks which could be used and it is not always possible to obtain comparable data. One measure is the proportion of Gross National Product taken by government in taxes, including social security contributions (Table

Table 1.1 Taxes and social security contributions as % of Gross National Product		
	1970	1989
France	38.5	44.5
W. Germany	38.3	44.6
Italy	30.4	41.1
Spain	22.5	35.0*
UK	40.2	39.7
USA	28.9	31.8
*1986 Source: OECD, Economic Outlook, 49 (Paris: OECD, 1991).		

1.1). This indicates that European governments take a larger proportion of the national wealth than does the United States. It also shows that the less advanced countries in southern Europe have taken a smaller proportion of national income in government spending, but that they are now catching up to their northern neighbours as they extend the range of public services.

Government can also be measured by the functions undertaken by the state. These expanded after the second world war, notably in economic and social matters. State intervention in the economy has a long history but after the war was placed on a new foundation. European governments assumed responsibility for full employment, rising living standards and balanced regional development. The political will for this stemmed from the postwar settlement, in which the working class were integrated into political society without the need for a radical redistribution of wealth. The method was provided by the Keynesian revolution in economic management, with its use of fiscal and monetary instruments for managing aggregate demand. In some countries, intervention was taken further, in the form of national and regional economic planning. While France led the way here, Britain, Italy and to some extent Spain, followed. States also intervened more directly through industrial policies, to encourage restructuring, development and regional relocation. State ownership of industry was used quite extensively in Britain, France, Italy and Spain. The state sector was expanded after the war, with the nationalization of utilities and basic industries, and again in the 1960s and 1970s (Britain and Italy) and the 1980s (France). Italy had already inherited a substantial state sector from the prewar Fascist regime. In Spain, a large state sector was inherited from the Franco regime. In Germany, on the other hand, state ownership in industry is more limited.

State involvement in the economy can also be measured through the amount of assistance to industry in various countries. Table 1.2 shows government support for industry as a proportion of GNP, although these figures should be taken with caution, given the problems of definition. In general, state industrial assistance has come down from a peak in the 1970s, except in Germany where the figure was already relatively low. This reflects a general tendency away from direct state intervention in industry as well as pressures from the European Community and international trading partners. Since the oil crises of the 1970s, Keynesianism as a method of economic management has been in

Table 1.2
Government aid to
industry as % of
GNP, 1988

France	2.5
W. Germany	2.3
Italy	3.0
Spain	2.0
UK	1.5
USA	0.6

Source: R. Ford and W.
Suyker, 'Les aides à
l'industrie dans les
économies de l'OCDE,
Revue économique de
l'OCDE, 15 (1990).

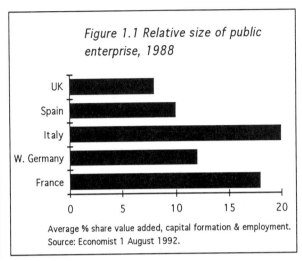

Figure 1.1 Relative size of public
enterprise, 1988

Average % share value added, capital formation & employment.
Source: Economist 1 August 1992.

retreat, in the face of a revived monetarist doctrine. The commitment to full employment has been abandoned. Nationalization has been widely rejected in favour of privatization, and planning has been challenged by a new belief in the market. An extensive programme of privatization reduced the public sector of the economy of Britain dramatically. In France, the short-lived conservative government of 1986-8 embarked on the same path, while in Italy there has been a slower process of divestment. Spanish governments have also reduced the state sector. Figure 1.1 shows the relative size of public enterprise in the economies of the five countries in 1988.

Another key element in the postwar settlement was the welfare state, a set of policies and instruments intended to provide comprehensive welfare coverage of citizens from the 'cradle to the grave'. Universal health care, provided directly by the state or demanded by law, has taken health care largely out of the market. Public provision for old age was introduced gradually into European countries from the early part of the twentieth century. Provision against unemployment was largely made after the second world war. European welfare states have most ambitiously aimed for a comprehensive welfare safety net, a minimum below which no-one should fall. This has largely been achieved in the wealthier European countries, though it has not eliminated the problem of poverty and poor living standards. Housing has also been regarded as a responsibility of the state in the last resort though the availability and quality of housing at the lower end of the market has often left a great deal to be desired.

Explanations for the growth of the welfare state and its more complete development in Europe than America vary. One factor was the extension of the franchise and the mobilization of the working class. There is no doubt that the rise of working-class parties and the need to compete for work-ing class votes was a factor. On the other hand, the welfare state has not led to a dramatic shift of income and wealth into working class families. It has generally taken the form of universal services, often used disproportionately by the middle classes. It can perhaps better be understood as a mutual insurance system, a mechanism for spreading risk across the population and the life cycle. It also serves the purpose of national consolidation, binding all social classes to the nation, as nation-building politicians have often been aware. In the last century, the German chancellor Bismarck saw social welfare as an important item in building the German nation. Under the Fifth Republic, French governments saw the welfare state as an aspect of nationalism rather than socialism. This collectivist, social conception of nation-building is one of the features which most sharply distinguishes European nations from the United States.

Development of the welfare state in the European context is also strongly correlated with levels of economic development. Table 1.3 shows the levels of spending on social welfare in the five European countries and the United States. It is the wealthier European states which have the most comprehensive and best-funded welfare systems, though the southern states are catching up. The figures also show the strong growth of welfare states in the 1960s and the stabilization of social expenditures as a share of national product in the 1980s.

Since the 1980s, the European welfare model has also come under strain. Fiscal problems have emerged, with resistance to taxes, although not to the same extent as in the United States. Neo-conservative politicians have begun to question the welfare state and sought to roll back provision. Control of costs, especially in health care, has become a serious problem. This is not peculiar to the European state but takes a specific form there because of the link with

Table 1.3 Expenditure on social protection as percentage of GDP

	1962	1975	1980	1987
France	13.1	22.9	25.5	28.3
W. Germany	14.5	27.8	28.6	28.2
Italy	11.9	22.7	19.8	22.9
Spain	3.7	11.7	17.0*	17.7
UK	11.2	20.6	21.6	23.6
USA	6.9	12.5	12.7	

*1982. Source: Basic Statistics of the European Community (Luxembourg, European Community, 1990).

Table 1.4 Military expenditure as percentage of GDP

	1960	1991
France	6.3	3.5
W. Germany	4.0	2.6
Italy	2.7	2.1
Spain	2.9	1.7
UK	6.4	4.2
USA	8.8	5.5

Sources: R.T. Sward, World Military and Social Expenditures
(Washington: World Priorities, 1989); Labour Research
Department, Fact Service, 54.31 (1992).

government finances. There is no consensus on how to ration health and social services but a continuous political debate. Complaints are also heard about the bureaucratization of the welfare state and its dependence on centrally-managed professional models of service delivery. Demands are heard for more decentralized approaches, tailored more to client needs.

The classic function of the nation state, national defence, has consumed smaller proportions of the national product in recent years (Table 1.4). Again, there is a contrast between the high spending northern and the low spending southern countries. The United Kingdom also stands out as devoting a relatively large proportion of its GNP to military expenditure, though less than the United States. France and Germany manage to reduce military expenditures by means of conscription, while Britain retains all-volunteer armed forces.

CONCEPTIONS OF THE STATE

A distinction is often made in Europe between state-societies, in which the state is recognized as an actor with its own powers, rights and duties, and non-state societies, in which government is conducted through a multiplicity of agencies and there is no theory of the state as an entity. Most continental European nations are state-societies. Britain and the United States are non-state societies. In both France and Germany, the state is regarded as a distinct entity, above and beyond the private world of civil society. Actions are taken in the name of the state and authority is conceived in rather rigid and legalistic terms. A large range of transaction is subject to legal regulation and state supervision. Visitors to France may be struck by the way in which private associations are described as being constituted under the law of 1901. French and German traditions differ, however, on the origins of state power and its relations to society.[1] In France, the state is exalted as an institution and mystified as the embodiment of national purpose and the general will. Its autonomy from private pressures is part of its very essence, as is its prestige and that of its officials. It is above and apart from civil society yet it remains the expression of popular sovereignty, created by the nation as its instrument.

German ideas of the state see it as more of an organic entity, growing along with civil society. It is above civil society but not apart from it. Rather, civil society is largely encompassed by the state. It is not the delegate of the nation but the entity which itself defines the nation. This is combined with a strong emphasis on the rule of law, the *Rechtsstaat* . This produces a unitary and organic view of the political system in which competing interests are managed or accommodated within the state but subordinated to the common purpose. Much German thinking also contains romantic or irrational elements, stressing the subordination of the individual to the greater whole. French thinking, by contrast, tends to be highly rational, seeing the state as an efficient machine and stressing the value of individual liberty alongside that of state power.

Other countries, including Spain and Italy, have borrowed freely from these models, adapting them to their own circumstances or combining them in various ways. The *Rechtsstaat* has become the *Stato di diritto* and the *Estado de derecho*. French ideas of uniformity and bureaucratic centralization have been imported but rarely applied successfully. In Italy, a whole range of activity requires the official *carta bollata*, or stamped form, evidence of the ubiquity of the state. This is accompanied by a resigned cynicism on the part of the citizens who know that their state does not live up to the model of machine-like efficiency implied by the theory.

In contradistinction to these state-society models, the United Kingdom is often presented as a stateless society in which the independent institutions of civil society and the unwritten understandings of the ages, underpinned by social consensus, remove the need for a formalized state.[2] There is no codified written constitution in the UK and no system of administrative law. Much of the civil and criminal law stems not from statute but from common law, evolved over the ages by judicial decisions. Governments are accountable not to the law but to the political authority of Parliament. It is not really correct to describe the UK as a stateless society, since that would imply an absence of political authority. Yet the state is rarely invoked as an entity and a great deal of activity which in other countries would be regulated by the state is dealt with by non-state organizations. These have traditionally included the professions, the universities and the financial system. Local governments exist not as arms of the state but as corporations.

These distinctions are important but should not be over-drawn. The vision of the all-powerful state, over and above civil society, owes a great deal to mythology or wishful thinking. In France, the state has constantly struggled to assert its prerogatives. Modern observers have begun to demythologize the state. Continental countries have seen a gradual strengthening of civil society and a lessened emphasis on the state. The abuses of state authority in Nazi Germany have led to a profound reconsideration of the nature of authority. Modernization, pluralism and democratization have produced independent groups and interests and a growth of external pressures on the state. At the same time, the British tradition of independent civil society has come under attack in the 1990s, with closer state regulation of local government, trade unions, universities and other independent institutions. As systems of government have stabilized in western Europe, there may be some tendency to convergence as all face similar problems of adaptation and change.

Constitutionalism and Liberal Democracy

Systems of government in western Europe evolved over a long time as countries passed through successive regimes. The term regime refers to the *system* of government in force in a country. This is to be distinguished from the government of the day which may change as a result of elections or party manoeuvring without affecting the system. Of the countries considered here, only the United Kingdom has had a stable regime going back through generations, evolving slowly. All the others have changed their system of government more than once since the last century as a result of revolutions, civil breakdown or war. France has had five republics, two empires and three monarchical regimes in the last two hundred years. Germany has had an empire, two republics and a dictatorship since its unification in 1870. Italy has experienced constitutional monarchy, dictatorship and a republic. Spain has had two republics, two dictatorships and two monarchies since 1870.

In countries with a history of frequent regime changes, it is not just the policies of the government of the day but the very form of government which becomes a political issue. The present regimes in Germany, France, Italy and Spain command wider acceptance than any of their predecessors and, with the partial exception of Italy, all have passed the critical test of liberal democracy, the peaceful passage of power from one party to another. Yet recent memories exist of dictatorship - until 1944 in Italy, 1945 in western Germany, 1976 in Spain and 1989 in eastern Germany - or the threat of violent overthrow of the constitution - 1958 and 1961 in France, 1981 in Spain. Important anti-system parties survived until quite recently and argument still persists about some of the rules of the political game, such as the electoral system or the extent to which governing parties can monopolize the instruments of power.

Now all have established constitutional liberal democracies. A constitutional regime is one in which the powers of government are specified and the relationships among the various elements in the government system understood. Such specifications and understandings may be codified in law or take the form of unwritten understandings; the important thing is that they be shared and respected. A liberal regime is one in which government is limited and there is freedom of speech, a respect for individual liberties and independent social, political and economic organizations in order that a public life can exist independent of the government of the day. In a democracy, government is elected by and accountable to the people and can be changed. In a stable liberal democracy, the regime will command respect and general acceptance, allowing the government to be changed peacefully from time to time. To permit such alternations in power, it is necessary to have political parties ready to take over, to organize for elections and to engage in peaceful criticism of the government of the day. It is also necessary to have a degree of trust and consensus on basic values so that parties losing elections will accept the result and wait their time in opposition rather than seek to overthrow the system. No significant social, ethnic or political group should find itself effectively outside the constitutional order, unable to play a role in political life or committed to overthrowing the basic regime.

Constitutionalism has become an important issue as regimes stabilize and command wider consensus. So has the role of the judiciary in overseeing it. France, Germany, Italy and Spain have independent courts to oversee their written constitutions and reject laws held to be unconstitutional and, though no European country has as wide a system of judicial review as the United States, the role of the courts in constitutional interpretation has increased considerably over the years.

The State and the Citizen

As well as specifying the powers of government, written constitutions include declarations of citizens' rights to liberty and non-discrimination, enforceable in the courts against governments themselves. In addition, the five states are signatories to the European Convention for the Protection of Human Rights, administered by the Commission and Court of Human Rights at Strasbourg. The state's conceding to the citizen rights against itself, enforceable in law, is a notable evolution of the European state since the second world war, with only the United Kingdom lagging behind. The idea that rights are inherent in citizenship and not bestowed by the state is comparable in some respects to the American tradition of individual justiciable rights. Courts do not have the same scope to strike down statute laws or substitute their own interpretations which they possess in the United States. Complaints about the constitutionality of laws can be made only by certain people and institutions and in restricted circumstances. Yet European courts have been increasingly active in upholding citizen complaints against the state. In sharp contrast to the American experience is the inclusion in many European constitutions and charters of rights of collective rights such as the right to join a trade union or to strike, or specific provision for the public ownership of industries and services. This reflects the larger role for collective institutions in European culture and the power of the labour movement in the postwar settlements. In France, Italy and Spain, the constitution also includes social rights, such as the right to health provision, employment or social protection. These collective and social rights derive from the influence of Social Democratic and some elements of Christian Democratic thought after the war and the belief that purely individual or negative rights on American lines do little to help the poor and the powerless. It also reflects a view of the state as an active promoter of social and economic welfare rather than a mere arbitrator of private social relations.

Also in contrast to American experience is that citizen rights are linked to citizen duties, for example to work, to bring up children, to defend the country or to vote. This reflects the European ideal of nationalism as involving citizen commitments as well as the exaltation of the state and its power to command. In practice, social rights are declarations of principle rather than practical reality, since they are virtually impossible to enforce. Citizen duties, too, merely add force to what is already stipulated in the ordinary law. Yet this broad conception of rights and duties does indicate the larger scope of the European state and the close connection between it and its citizens.

POLITICAL INSTITUTIONS

It is customary to distinguish between presidential and parliamentary systems. In a presidential system, an elected president heads the executive branch of government while a separately elected legislature passes laws, scrutinizes the executive and generally balances presidential power. In a parliamentary system, there is no such division of powers. Instead, the executive is formed from the party or coalition of parties which has a majority of seats in the legislature. Parliamentary systems concentrate governmental power since the executive and legislative powers are brought together. Governments do not usually have to worry about getting their legislation enacted and legislatures are reduced in power and status. Yet while they may be more powerful in office, governments in parliamentary systems have a less secure hold on office. If they do not command a parliamentary majority or lose their majority between elections, they can be removed. Government is controlled not as in the United States by the existence of strong countervailing powers but by the threat of losing office. This is the case in the five countries considered in this book. In France, the parliamentary system coexists with a directly elected executive president. This hybrid of parliamentary and presidential systems is the source of many unresolved constitutional problems.

Relations between the executive and legislative branches and the stability of governments in parliamentary systems vary according to the party system. In two-party systems, governments will by definition command legislative majorities and, in the absence of rebellions within the governing party, will be secure. Where many parties are represented in the legislature and none commands a majority, coalition governments are usually formed. Coalitions are always potentially unstable since a coalition party might withdraw its support at any time. Extreme examples of unstable coalition government are in Italy, which has had more than fifty governments since the second world war, or the French Fourth Republic, which had twenty-five governments in twelve years. Germany, on the other hand, has had rather stable coalitions. The alternative to coalitions in multi-party systems is minority government in which the government must mobilize a parliamentary majority for each item of legislation. Of the five countries surveyed here, France, Spain and the United Kingdom have had minority governments in recent years.

Whether a country has a two-party or multiple-party system will depend on the pattern of political cleavages but also on the electoral system. Europe has a large variety of electoral systems and the five countries considered here present five different varieties. Elections in parliamentary systems serve a number of purposes. Firstly, they select individuals to represent the citizens. Secondly, they allow electors to choose among the political parties by sending their representatives to the legislature. Thirdly, they are about choosing governments. The problem is that these purposes may conflict and each is best served by a different electoral system. There is a bewildering variety of electoral systems available but the basic choices are between majoritarian and proportional representation systems. Majoritarian systems aim to give the leading party an overall majority of seats in the legislature, whether or not it wins a majority of votes. Proportional representation allocates seats to parties in proportion to their share of the popular vote. Majoritarian systems tend to force politics into a two-party mould, since electors are deterred from voting for small parties who stand no chance of forming the government. Two-party politics in turn presents electors with clear alternative governing teams and assures governments once elected of parliamentary majorities. Supporters of strong government thus tend to favour majoritarian systems. Needless to say, so do the leaders of the large parties which benefit! The disadvantage is that minor parties are excluded from the legislature and their supporters unrepresented.

The most common type of majoritarian system is the constituency-based plurality system used in Britain, the United States and Canada. The country is divided into constituencies, each of which elects a single member of the legislature. The candidate with the largest number of votes in each constituency wins the seat. If there are more than two candidates, the winning candidate does not necessarily need an overall majority of votes, merely more votes than the second-placed candidate - this is what a plurality means. Such a method of election, by choosing members from territorial units, preserves the close link between the representative and the constituency which was the basis of the British system from which it originated. In practice, electors in European countries are less interested in voting for individuals than for parties and will tend to vote for the party candidate irrespective of personality. Simple plurality systems make it very difficult for small parties to achieve representation in the legislature since even if a small party wins, say, 20 per cent of the vote in every constituency this may not be enough to allow it to win any individual constituency. Consequently, the system benefits large parties, and those parties whose support is concentrated geographically. It can even cause unfairness between the major parties in a two-party system, with a party gaining fewer votes but more seats than its rival. This perverse outcome, which has occurred twice in Britain since the war, occurs when one party accumulates large majorities in its already safe seats while its opponent spreads its votes more widely, winning more seats by smaller majorities.

The bipolarizing effect is reinforced in the variant used in parliamentary elections for most of the Fifth Republic in France. In this system, if no candidate gains more than 50 per cent of the vote in a constituency there is a second ballot, in which only candidates who have won the votres of more than 12.5 per cent of the eligible voters may stand. In practice, deals are usually done among the candidates to leave only two contenders at the second ballot, in which the candidate with most votes wins. Like the British system, this produces a politics dominated by two large coalitions, on the right and on the left.

The strong government claims of the supporters of majoritarian systems are countered by complaints of unfairness in excluding minor parties. The remedy to these anomalies lies in proportional representation. There is a bewildering variety of forms of proportional representation but all are inspired by the same idea - to match the proportion of legislative seats awarded to a party to its proportion of the popular vote. This treats the small parties fairly by giving a party with, say 10 per cent of the vote, 10per cent of the seats. It does, however, break the link with the constituency since seats have to be allocated according to party lists across regions or the whole country. Germany resolves this issue by having constituency members as well as proportionally elected members, with the latter determining the overall parliamentary balance. Proportional representation encourages the growth of a multi-party system since small parties find it relatively easy to gain seats. Voters in turn may be motivated to vote for small parties in the knowledge that their votes will not be wasted. A multi-party system means that no one party is likely to have a majority in the legislature, requiring parties to come together in coalitions. Coalition government may be unstable, especially where there are several parties in the government, as in Italy. It is also criticized for putting the decision on the formation of governments in the hand of politicians manoeuvring after the election, rather than giving the electorate a direct choice at the election. Critics of proportional representation also note that it may give small parties an influence out of proportion to their votes in the manoeuvring over coalition making. In Germany, the Free Democratic Party has remained in office almost continuously since the 1950s since it is the only available coalition partner for either of the large governing parties. Proportional representation may also encourage extremist parties, as happened in France in 1986.

Plurality and proportional representation are not stark alternatives. Systems may be more or less proportional, depending on the variety used. The Spanish system is much less proportional than the Italian one, while the German system has a rule excluding parties which score less than 5 per cent of the vote. Choosing a system is no mere technical matter since the precise mechanisms chosen can be decisive in shaping the conduct of politics and resolving the central question of democracy - who is to govern. In Europe, where there is a large variety of systems available, they are not surprisingly a matter of intense controversy. France changed its electoral system in 1945, 1951, 1958, 1986 and 1988 and has debated further changes since. In Britain, there is wide support for proportional representation to make the system more democratic. Italy, by contrast, is discussing making its system less proportional to ensure more stability in government.

Territorial Government

There are sharply differing traditions in Europe on the question of centralization and decentralization of the state. In France, the 'Jacobin' tradition emphasises the need for a strong, centralized state in order to safeguard national unity. Since the state is seen as the expression of popular sovereignty, any intermediary authority or division of that sovereignty can only obstruct the expression of the popular will. So democracy and liberty are associated with centralization. This rigidly centralist attitude was exported with varying degrees of success to other countries seeking to forge national unity, notably Italy and Spain. Germany, by contrast, has a federalist tradition, in which power is seen as something shared among territorial governments. In the United Kingdom, the absence of a written constitution has allowed the development of a doctrine of local self-government within the unitary state but subject to the ultimate authority of Parliament. Liberty and democracy are seen to require not a strong centralized state but a loosely organized and decentralized one.

Territorial government in the five countries considered reflects these different doctrines and the there have three distinct traditions of territorial government. Germany is a federal state, reflecting the distinctive German principle that power is not divided, as in other federal systems, but shared. France, Italy and Spain have historically been unitary states with centralized political and bureaucratic systems. These trace their heritage to the early nineteenth century and the imposition of a strong, bureaucratic state by the French emperor Napoleon following his extensive conquests. Centralization was reinforced in the nineteenth century by nation-building elites armed with jacobin doctrines. In France itself, the tradition of centralization goes back further, to the efforts of the monarchy to unite the country. Municipal governments have been rather weak, with few functions and officials of the central state have had extensive responsibilities for supervising them. Many local services are run by field offices of central departments. In practice, centralization has always been extremely difficult to enforce and within the unitary state a variety of devices has emerged to allow local elites to influence national politics. Attempts to impose rigid uniformity fail since conditions differ from place to place and local politicians and centrally-appointed bureaucrats are able to connive in bending the rules. In Britain, there is a unitary state and a rather centralized political system but a strong tradition of local self-administration. The state never established a large centralized bureaucracy on continental lines, preferring to entrust the development of services to local governments. These work largely within centrally-determined rules but the central government is freed from localist pressures since it does not administer most services directly. The United Kingdom has also shown an ability to forge special arrangements for specific territories where there were particular pressures or problems.

The territorial structure of European states has come under a great deal of discussion since the second world war. Most economic management falls to central governments, which are responsible for the overall monetary and fiscal policy, industrial policies and subsidies, nationalized industries and regional planning. As governments extended their economic responsibilities after the war, this led to an increased centralization of the state. As governments have retreated from planning and intervention, subnational governments have to some extent filled the gap but their economic activities are quite strictly controlled in the interests of preserving nation-wide markets and fair competition. The taxing powers of subnational governments are regulated nationally and their powers to incur deficits tightly controlled in the interest of overall financial stability. The welfare state, too has been a force for centralization, since it is based on the notion of national solidarity and the principle that all citizens will be treated equally irrespective of where they live. Party competition has tended to be national rather than local and regional and this has also favoured centralization and uniformity.

Expansion of government responsibilities, especially in land-use planning and the welfare state, has put the issue of local government structures on the political agenda. Centralization has some uncomfortable effects for both centre and localities. Local citizens may be frustrated with uniform rules and services which are ill adapted to their needs. Rising education and political awareness have spawned demands for more participation in decision making. Where central government is responsible for everything, citizen demands rain down upon it, making life miserable for national politicians. Trying to control local administration in detail, central governments find themselves unable to control anything properly. Their own field administrations start to go native, identifying with the local populations rather than the central government. Central government, in extreme cases, can become the prisoner of local interests, unable to impose an overall policy perspective. These problems of central administrative and political overload can make decentralization attractive to central governments.

The weakest form is deconcentration, which involves placing field officials of central government in the territories which they administer and granting them some administrative discretion. Devolution is a stronger form, in which powers are transferred to locally elected bodies, albeit under some form of central supervision, with the national government retaining the authority to step in and over-rule the local bodies. A stronger form again involves giving legal and constitutional guarantees for local and regional governments, restricting the ability of the national government to over-rule them.

At the same time, European states have become conscious of the inadequacy of traditional local governments for the needs of the welfare state and have sought to modernize them, consolidating small units and trying to introduce modern management techniques. The results have been mixed. Britain radically redrew its local government map in the 1970s, reducing the number of local governments to 430, only to return to the issue again in the 1980s and 1990s. In Germany, there was a substantial reduction in the number of units in the 1970s. In France, the weight of local interests in national politics made it impossible to consolidate local units and the country retains over 36,000 local governments. Italy undertook some local government consolidation but, like Spain, it has retained a large number of very small local governments. This is also true of the United States, which has over 80,000 local governments. Consolidation of local government allows national governments to transfer responsibilities to the localities, reducing the political and administrative load on themselves, without surrendering overall control.

An important theme in the restructuring of territorial government has been regionalism. In the 1960s, most European governments adopted regional development policies as an extension of national and sectoral planning. Economically, these were justified in terms of the need to tap underutilized resources in peripheral and declining regions and increase national output.

Politically, they served to enhance national solidarity and secure support from peripheral regions for national parties. They could be presented as a non-zero-sum game in which all could win - the depressed regions through growth, the advanced regions through the relief of congestion and the national economy through additional output and easing of inflationary pressures. Gradually, centralized regional policies were accompanied with more elaborate forms of regional planning. These in due course were institutionalized as governments sought to involve regional political and economic leaders in their elaboration and implementation. So a regional level of administration came into being, primarily concerned with planning and development and issues too large for local governments. This was top-down regionalism, sponsored by the state for its own purposes. It soon encountered another form of regionalism, from the bottom up, which was not always in harmony with it.

For regions themselves were becoming more assertive. In some cases, this was a matter of resistance to change in traditional societies faced with the rapid modernization of the postwar era. In others, new social forces emerged, committed to modernization on a regional basis. Historic claims of regions and smaller nationalities which had been absorbed by the large states were reasserted. The tension between this indigenous regionalism and state-sponsored regionalism became more acute in the 1970s as central governments, giving increased priority to national competitiveness in the global market, found it more difficult to plan their spatial economies and began to reduce regional policy expenditure. At the same time, economic restructuring, following an increasingly global logic, had very diverse impacts on particular territories, creating new coalitions for the defence of territorial interests, be they threatened steel plants, coal fields or traditional sectors of agriculture. The region has thus become a key level of political dialogue and action, where national, continental and global forces meet local demands and social systems, forcing mutual adaptations and concessions.

Some regions have a strong sense of identity, rooted in historical experience, language, culture or political traditions. Some have autonomist or separatist movements and were in the past independent states. Some have distinctive civil societies, with a locally-based business class, an associative life and sense of regional solidarity. Others lack these features or have been reduced to political dependencies of national states or dominant political parties. In some territories, regionalism is confined to culture; in others it is focused on economic development; in others again there is a demand for regional autonomy. In some cases, all three elements are combined.

Regions have become increasingly important as a level of government in the traditionally centralized states of France, Italy and Spain, though the experience varies greatly. In France and Italy, national governments established regions slowly over a period of years, proceeding from mere consultative organs, to indirectly elected, to elected regional councils and then conceding powers and functions. Although regional government is stipulated in the 1948 Italian constitution, it was not until the 1970s that the ordinary status regions came into being. In France, the process, starting in 1972, was not completed until the elections of 1986. French and Italian regions have remained rather weak, overshadowed by other levels of government. In Spain, regions and autonomous communities were established at the time of the restoration of democracy, in response to demands from within the regions themselves. They have stronger constitutional guarantees than those of Italy - French regions have no constitutional guarantee at all. The Spanish system, indeed, may be developing into a semi-federal arrangement for which the special term *Estado de las Autonomías* has been coined. In the United Kingdom, progress towards regional government was later reversed. Electoral pressures from the historic nations of the periphery led the Labour government of 1974-9 to propose elected assemblies in Scotland and Wales, but opposition in Parliament combined with fears of separatism in the peripheral territories themselves to wreck the scheme. An experiment in devolved government for Northern Ireland collapsed in 1972 as a result of sectarian conflict. In England, gradual moves towards the institutionalization of regions in the 1960s and 1970s were later reversed and little remains even at the administrative level.

THE STATE, BUREAUCRACY, INTERESTS AND POLICY MAKING

Political power is one dimension of authority in the modern state. Two other dimensions are important, the power of the professional bureaucracy and the role of organized interests. It is in the interaction among these three dimensions of power that policy is made and implemented.

The State and Bureaucracy

The modern European state is characterized by the presence of an impartial, professional bureaucracy, that is appointed career officials responsible for administration and policy advice. These comprise the permanent personnel of the state, the element of continuity while elected governments come and go. Political and bureaucratic appointees are sharply distinguished. Senior bureaucrats are typically permanent and recruited by competitive examination, and often constitutionally protected. This is in sharp contrast to the American system, whereby several layers of administration may change with the advent of a new president. The permanent, professional bureaucracy is testament to the European notion of the state as an entity beyond the government of the day and able impartially to minister to the needs of citizens.

This model of the impartial state bureaucracy has often been more of an aspiration than a reality. Outside the central departments, in semi-state agencies, autonomous boards and nationalized industries, governments have more discretion over senior personnel and these appointments may be used to nominate sympathetic figures, reward supporters or generally engage in patronage. In southern Europe, the politically neutral legal state conflicts with social norms stressing individualism and social relationships based on personal contact. From this stem the problems of patronage and clientelism. Instead of the state treating all citizens equally, it discriminates. Instead of fulfilling its obligations, the administration fails to deliver services. To compensate for these failings, individuals need to approach politicians who know which strings to pull, how to make things work. Alternatively, they resort to bribery and corruption to get their way. So a gap opens up between the ' legal country', the official rules and procedures, and the 'real country', the way things actually work in practice. Yet the ' legal country', the world of rules and regulations, continues to dominate the university faculties in which students earnestly study constitutional and public law as though it were applied to the letter.

More recently, a further series of issues have put in question the notion of the legally-bound neutral state. The European tradition stresses the separation of political and bureaucratic roles and the personnel of politics and administration are distinct. Yet in practice the roles overlap, since politicians cannot take all decisions themselves and must delegate and, even on major issues, must rely on the advice of career officials. Bureaucracies may be imbued with a sense of mission and mobilizing ideology, regarding themselves as the agents of a higher interest or the promotion of national values; or they may be more pragmatic in attitudes. Questions are therefore regularly asked about the power of the bureaucracy, its representativeness and sensitivity to the needs of citizens and its willingness to follow the orders of elected governments.

In   social background and education, we find considerable differences. British and French senior civil servants are drawn from the traditional upper classes and prestigious educational institutions. This may be both cause and result of the civil service's high status and prestige. In Italy, by contrast, civil servants tend to be drawn from the southern part of the country and lack high social status. German civil servants lie between these two in terms of status. Everywhere, there is an under-representation of people from poor and working-class backgrounds and of women, and this has become a political issue from time to time.

Educational qualifications and orientations also differ. British senior civil servants are usually the product of a generalist liberal arts or classical education. They work as generalists, a style criticized as that of the gifted amateur. German, Italian and Spanish senior civil servants usually have degrees in law and are criticized for treating policy issues in an excessively formal and rule-bound manner, and for mistaking the theory of administration for the reality. French senior civil servants are the products of training schools where they learn the art of government and management. British civil servants are criticized for being excessively pragmatic and unable to see the broader picture. The French, with their intensive training, face the opposite criticism, of excessive abstraction.

All face the challenge of responding and adapting the administration of the state to a changing society, with multiple needs and social and economic problems. Organized on hierarchical lines, they encounter frequent criticism that this deprives them of the flexibility needed to deal with the problems of a rapidly changing environment.

Given the presence of a permanent civil service, its attitudes and its indispensability, the question arises as to the power of the bureaucracy and its relation to elected political authority. Is it the elected politicians who wield power or should we, in seeking to find out who really makes policy, look at the permanent bureaucracy? In the past this questioning extended to the loyalty of the bureaucracy to the liberal democratic regime itself. Postwar Italian civil servants had mostly been recruited and trained under fascism. In Spain the Francoist bureaucracy did not always cooperate with the democratic regime and many of its members hankered after their own privileges. This problem has now largely been overcome and civil service loyalty to the regime is generally secure. The power of bureaucracy, though, remains an issue. On the one hand, a permanent civil service is needed to ensure continuity of the state, professional administration, high quality advice to government and impartial dealing with citizens. On the other hand, this itself may be an obstacle to governments elected to effect change. Civil servants possess scarce resources of skills, knowledge and experience which they may use to press their own policy preference or enhance their own status. In some cases, individual government departments may be so close to outside interest groups with which they work, and who may give them profitable employment on retirement, that they start to identify with them rather than the wider public interest. Politicians, elected to office, may find themselves without alternative sources of advice.

In the unitary French state, most civil servants are employed by the central government, whether their responsibilities are in the capital or in the field. In the German federal system, by contrast, most bureaucratic officials are employed by the *Länder* which administer both federal laws and their own. Britain has a long tradition of local administration, in which more officials are employed by local governments than by the centre. Spain and Italy have had Napoleonic traditions of centralization and great difficulty has been experienced in attempting to transfer staff from national government departments to the regional authorities. Bureaucratic influence thus remains an important factor in centralization and may be an obstacle to reform of the state.

The State and Organized Interests

The final dimension of authority concerns the relationship of government to civil society, that is to the wider array of social and economic actors and associations which exist in modern liberal democracies. These include the main economic interest groups, business and labour, but may also include the military, churches, organized citizens' groups and linguistic/ethnic communities. In different states, government has a greater or less degree of autonomy from organized interests, a greater or lesser ability to impose its will, but in no case is it entirely free to do as it chooses, or to implement policies once chosen.

In a weak state system, such as the United States, interest groups are regarded as legitimate and public policy is seen as properly the outcome of pluralist group pressures. In some pluralist perspectives, indeed, the state almost disappears as an independent actor and instead becomes an arena in which policy is the outcome of competition among interest groups. Government departments, agencies and legislative committees ally or compete with interest groups so that government itself reflects the pluralist world. In strong state societies, such as those of continental Europe, private interest groups have often been regarded as somehow illegitimate, as detracting from the sovereignty and unity of the state.

Elements of pluralism have been identified in European policy-making systems. Interests compete for the attention of government and there is some tendency for government departments and agencies to 'go native,' identifying with their client groups and arguing their case with other departments. It is generally agreed, however, that the European state is too powerful and unified to be assumed away entirely. It may be internally divided, but there is a strong ethos of public power and recognition of the prerogatives of government. Private interests, for their part, are often poorly organized, especially in southern Europe. In many instances, however, private interest groups have grown in importance and gradually come to be recognized as a legitimate part of the policy process. So, in each case, we need to assess the relationship of government to private interests, the relative power of each. We must examine the way in which private interests penetrate the government apparatus and, conversely, how government controls or uses private interests. In other words, how far does government really govern?

Interest Groups

This problem of governing has become more acute as government has extended its scope beyond the traditional functions of law and order, defence and provision of basic infrastructure. The powers and resources needed to solve complex social and economic problems or to make things happen often lie in the private sector of the economy or within the civil society. Managing a modern economy requires more than simply laws and sanctions against offenders. It requires the cooperation of producer groups, and especially of the business community. In any capitalist society, in which the means of production are in private hands, business will have a privileged position since its cooperation is needed to meet national goals of economic growth and rising living standards. This allows business to project itself a, representative of the general interest and not a mere sectional interest group, though it is clearly that as well. Yet the power of private capital in relation to the state varies from one society to another. In the United States, where capitalist values amount to a national ideology, business has not had to struggle to establish its legitimacy. Instead, competition takes place among different business groups within an agreed set of rules. There has been some challenge from groups concerned with environmental and safety issues, but even these have operated within the assumptions of the liberal capitalist order. In Europe, on the other hand, the moral worth of capitalism as well as its efficiency have been challenged historically, by Socialists and even some varieties of conservatism.

The strength and nature of capitalist enterprise has itself varied among countries. In some cases, such as nineteenth-century Britain or postwar Germany, business has developed largely on its own; in other cases, such as France or Spain, it has been dependent on the support and protection of the state. European capitalism also differs from its North American variant in terms of its culture and operating principles.[3] It often tends to be less individualist, more collaborative and more concerned with long-term planning. It organizes itself in business federations, covering sectors of industry or the entire manufacturing class, in order to influence government and confront the labour movement. The rise of business organization parallels and responds to that of the interventionist state and the labour movement. American business, by contrast, has not usually felt the need for centralized organization. In some parts of Europe, business remains fragmented and unable to speak with one voice. So relationships with government vary from one case to another.

Governing also requires cooperation from the other producer group, labour, who can stage strikes, make inflationary wage demands, enforce restrictive practices or engage in political action. European states, more than the United States, have sought to accommodate the working class through legalization of trade unions and collective bargaining, regulation of employment conditions and extension of social and welfare services. The extent of labour organization, through trade unions and labour-related political parties, varies from one country to another. Britain and Germany have traditionally had high rates of union membership compared with France and Spain. Their labour movements have also been allied to national political parties, although willing to work with

Table 1.5 Percentage of workforce in trade unions			
	1970	1980	1988
France	22.3	19.0	12.0
W. Germany	33.0	37.0	33.8
Italy	36.3	49.3	39.6
Spain	n.a.	22.0	16.0
UK	44.8	50.7	41.5
USA	22.8	23.0	16.4

Source: Labour Research Department, Fact Service, 53.31 (1991).

governments of the other persuasion. Union membership has declined in all five countries in recent years, with the decline of traditional heavy industry and the changing composition of the workforce (Table 1.5). Trade unionism has tended to survive in strength only in the public sector where stability of employment and a common employer not usually hostile to unions have encouraged its growth.

Farmers and landowners used to be an important influence in European politics. Large landowners combined economic power with social prestige and political influence. Small farmers were an important and voting force, concentrated into rural constituencies which themselves were often over-represented. This is a declining force, as farming numbers decline (Table 1.6, p.28) but remains an influence in European politics. Other power-holders in society also limit the scope of government. Churches may control the allegiance of voters, possess economic power or retain legal and economic privileges. Of the five countries, France has moved furthest to separate Church and state and reduce religious influence over government. Elsewhere, Catholic and Protestant churches retain a place in the constitution and, at times, have intervened in politics. In the past, the military wielded influence in many European states and there were attempted *coups d'état* in France (1958 and 1962), Italy (1964 and 1970) and Spain (1981). Armies have now been effectively subordinated to the civil authorities, though there are questions raised about control over British army activities in Northern Ireland and some of the activities of Italian senior officers.

Concertation, Corporatism and Consociationalism

In certain sectors one can find close links between governments and producer groups. Elsewhere, these do not exist. Business and unions have been brought in to help run public agencies for economic development, employment matters and social services. On a broader scale, governments have attempted to engage in concertation, bringing in what are sometimes called the social partners to discuss policy and plan for the future. Indicative planning, by which government, business and unions agree on realistic targets for growth and then each undertake their own part confident that the others will deliver theirs, is a good example.

In the 1970s, a substantial literature developed, especially in Britain, to the effect that the modern European state was becoming ungovernable due to the dependence of government on conflicting private interests. Most of the exponents of the ungovernability school concluded that the answer was for governments to reduce public expectations and shed some of their own roles and responsibilities. This was consistent with the theories of the new-right school of political economists who advocated privatization, deregulation and the reduction of government economic responsibilities to management of the money supply. In the 1980s, governments on both sides of the Atlantic were to try to put this into effect.

Another set of observers saw the solution to the problem of governability being worked out in new relationships among government and producer groups. In this perspective the state was neither a strong and authoritative custodian of the general interest nor a mere arbitrator among competing groups. Rather it was a partner with powerful organized interests in concerting policy and ensuring its implementation. This perspective, in which policy is seen as negotiated among the state and powerful groups which are able to make bargains and commit their members, was labelled corporatism. The term originated with the inter-war Fascist movements which believed in a society organized according to occupational groups which would discipline their own members and in turn be controlled by the state. The modern version, sometimes distinguished as neo-corporatism, is less authoritarian. Instead of organized groups being subordinated to the state, they bargain with it as equals. Instead of groups competing with each other as in pluralist theory, they cooperate with each other and the state. They are highly structured and centralized, with near universal membership and thus able to speak authoritatively for their respective sectors and bargain with government. The state, in turn, lends legitimacy to the representatives of the organizations. Policy is made through negotiation, bargaining and compromise, by-passing the mechanisms of parliaments and elections.[4]

Neo-corporatism as a general description of modern government has come in for a lot of criticism.[5] It does not fit any country very well and, like many social science concepts, once it became fashionable, it was stretched by some enthusiasts far beyond its original terms to cover just about everything - and therefore nothing. Its most serious weakness was its lack of an adequate theory of the state. Is the state in a corporatist system an authoritative actor laying down the rules, merely a partner in negotiation, or indeed a series of actors tied to individual industrial sectors?

Another mode of negotiated policy making, which bears more than a passing resemblance to neo-corporatism, is consociationalism. While corporatism is a means of accommodating class conflicts and resolving production problems through negotiation, consociationalism is a way of accommodating religious, ethnic or linguistic divisions. Instead of power being contested through elections in which one side wins and another loses, it is shared. Governing institutions are selected with a view to balance, and jobs and resources distributed proportionally. Policy is negotiated and agreed rather than disputed in an adversary manner. This term, too, has been abused by being stretched too far but it is recognisable as a mode of governing in certain places. It was characteristic of some of the smaller European democracies until the 1970s. It has been tried as a solution to the Northern Ireland problem and in resolving the nationalities question in Spain.

Challenges to the State

Even the milder forms of cooperation have been in decline in recent years as interest group leaders find that they cannot deliver the consent of their members. Agreements reached at the summit are undermined at the base. Nor can the state always deliver its side of the bargain. The European state finds itself under challenge from a number of directions, unable to fulfil many of its traditional functions and with its power and authority eroding.[6]

One challenge is ideological. State nationalism as a doctrine has been to a degree delegitimized in its birthplace, western Europe, by the excesses committed in its name. It is challenged from below by new or re-emerging identities, especially in the historic regions and nations swallowed up in the modern state. It is thus no longer able to present itself as the sole, or even the main framework for liberal democracy and political participation. In some cases, these new or revived regionalisms and minority nationalisms simply represent an alternative nationalism in competition with that of the state, with equally exclusive claims. More often, they represent a challenge to the whole idea that humanity is divided into exclusive nations. Instead they credit individuals with mulitiple identities. Some insist on a new approach to democracy in which individuals relate not just to the nation-state but to a whole range of intermediate and alternative institutions.

More generally, the state has been demystified, its prestige and that of its servants reduced, no longer towering above civil society or imposing its norms and rules everywhere. There have been efforts to strengthen civil societies in continental countries and reduce the weight of the state by means of decentralization, participation and deregulation. Private interests are more accepted as legitimate partners in public policy and pluralism is seen as preferable to state-imposed uniformity.

The role of the state as the guardian of cultural norms, socializing its citizens into a national identity, is facing contrary pressures. There is a globalization of culture, less through merging of national cultures than through American cultural hegemony, imposing similar standards and aspirations and fostering English as a world language. National governments fight against this trend with greater or lesser success through publicly-owned broadcasting media and subsidization and regulation of cultural production. For many Europeans the ultimate symbol of the erosion of European culture by American mass entertainment was the establishment of Euro-Disney in France, to the horror of French intellectuals. At the same time, local, regional and minority languages and cultures have re-emerged in places such as Catalonia, the Basque Country, Brittany and Wales. There is a growing appreciation of tradition and the importance of preserving local culture.

The role of the nation state in economic management is undergoing a threefold challenge, from above, from below and laterally. From above, internationalization of the economy and the mobility of capital have reduced the ability of states to pursue autonomous economic policies. Multinational corporations cannot be regulated and pressured in the way national ones could in the past. International agreements reduce the ability of states to take unilateral actions. Consequently, the large capitalist states have all had to abandon the commitment to full employment and regional balance which they assumed in the postwar years.

At the same time, issues of economic restructuring have come to be seen increasingly in local and regional terms. There is a growing appreciation of the importance of local and regional factors in fostering the conditions for attracting capital and stimulating entrepreneurship. The logic of the multinational corporation, with its global growth strategy, is increasingly divorced from the spatially-bound logic of communities which may be affected by its decisions. So the state is challenged from below by local and regional forms of economic intervention. Laterally, the role of the state in economic management is challenged by the revived faith in markets and privatization. Governments not only of the right but also of the Social Democratic left have abandoned their belief in economic planning, deregulated and privatized and sought to compete in the new global division of labour.

In the area of social solidarity and the welfare state, by contrast, the European nation-state has by and large retained its primacy. There have been some efforts to decentralize the fiscal load of welfare in order to pass down deficits. Fiscal problems of the welfare state are aggravated by unemployment, to which governments do not have answers. Generally, however, the European welfare state remains an important symbol and instrument of national solidarity and cohesion and even rightist governments have had little success in cutting it back.

Internal security too remains the responsibility of the nation state, though terrorism, drug trafficking and other major issues increasingly call for international cooperation. By contrast, external security and defence in western Europe were largely internationalized after the second world war. During the Cold War, defence policy was largely simplified to a confrontation with the Soviet Union and subsumed under NATO. The collapse of the Soviet bloc has raised a whole series of new challenges and forced the western European states to respond to instability in their own backyard. So far, the end of the Cold War has not led to a reassertion of independent national defence strategies in western Europe but to a search for new forms of collective security.

As well as changes in the environment of state autonomy, there have been institutional changes. One is the movement to European integration. In the economic sphere there is the European Community and its associated agencies. For security matters there are NATO, the Western European Union (WEU) and the Conference on Security and Cooperation in Europe. In the sphere of individual rights, there is the Council of Europe whose human rights machinery has separated the definition of human rights from that of national citizenship.

Institutional change is also taking place from below. States have in many cases decentralized government, established regions or handed down powers to federal units. The great exception is Britain, where government centralized over the 1980s. Yet in Britain, too, the central state has transferred responsibilities, in its case to the private sector through privatization and deregulation.

It is not as yet clear what the effect of these processes of devolution upwards to Europe and downwards to regions will be on the strength of the European state. On the one hand, they may weaken it by reducing its functional capacity, resources and decision-making autonomy. On the other hand, they may enhance the autonomy and effective power of state elites by offloading the more burdensome and less gratifying tasks, allowing central states to concentrate on strategic issues. In the case of the smaller states, European integration may be the condition which allows them to continue to exist at all. The European Community has allowed national governments to hive off responsibility for agricultural adjustment, restructuring in coal and steel and, more recently, monetary and fiscal rectitude. Critics have charged that the single market programme of the EC serves to entrench the neo-liberal agenda of deregulation, markets and privatization favoured by existing governing elites, with local and regional communities left to bear the burden of change. Membership of the Exchange Rate Mechanism of the European Monetary System and the need for convergence in the move towards a single currency are presented in France and Spain as imperatives beyond political questioning. In this way, overload is reduced and the problem of governability addressed.

Which of the two outcomes will materialize is a matter on which judgement must be suspended, but certain factors can be identified. In the short term, devolution upwards and downwards may enhance the autonomy and authority of state elites - presumably they would not otherwise engage in the exercise. In the longer term, they may not be able to control the processes they have set in train. New actors and networks may emerge to create a new political game.

The European Community is explicitly intended to provide the basis for a new political order beyond the old state system. Yet the nature of this new order remains unclear. For some, the Community represents a form of internationalism, a transcending of the nation state. Yet in fact the Community is a regional political-economic system set up precisely to enable Europe to compete more effectively against the rest of the world. Others see the Community as the basis for a new state, the culmination of those integrationist and diffusionist trends which are credited with creating the existing states from their component parts. This interpretation is also questionable. The European nation-state as we know it was the product of a specific time and place, in a specific global context. This time and place is not late twentieth-century western Europe, given the erosion of the nation-state described above. Rather, the Community, along with other continental organizations, represents a new form of political order in which authority is dispersed and sovereignty shared. This will be a variegated order of states and regimes with overlapping institutions, responsibilities and memberships.

In this order, the state will cease to be the authoritative determiner of policies. Even where it shares power and makes policy by bargaining with domestic interest groups, such national bargains and social compromises are liable to come unstuck in the face of market and global pressures. States are responding differently to these pressures. Some are experiencing severe tensions from territorial interests. Others are feeling social stresses as governments are unable to respond to domestic demands. Traditional ideas of authority and patterns of politics are coming into question.

PATTERNS OF POLITICS

European politics is marked by divisions of interest, between groups and individuals who compete for the resources of society, and differences in doctrine and ideology. This contrasts with politics in the United States where politics revolves almost exclusively around competing interests. This is not because American politics is bereft of ideology. On the contrary, it is suffused with it; but in the United States the dominant ideology is common to the whole society, so that issues which are the basis of divisions in European nations form part of the very definition of American national identity. Interests, values and ideologies in European politics are linked in complex ways to produce a series of identifiable currents and movements, each with a recognizable social base and common body of doctrine but with a rich variety of national, regional and local variations. So understanding European politics requires an understanding of the main social and political cleavages and of the main doctrinal families. Some of these go deep into history. Others are based on contemporary issues. All are in a process of change and development and are closely interlinked.

Social Cleavages

The most widespread source of political division is social class. Interpretations of society as divided into classes go back as far as the Middle Ages and historians have consistently interpreted changes in European politics in terms of the rise of new social classes, challenging the old ruling elites. Class divisions are themselves complex and change gradually but fundamentally over time. One important one has been between the agrarian/rural world and industrial/ urban interests. In the nineteenth century, this was fought out over issues of tariffs, national representation and regulation. In the twentieth century, competition over subsidies and land use regulations have been added. Economic change, the reduction of the agricultural labour force and urbanization have deprived this division of much of its salience, as the figures in Table 1.6 show. Yet the question has not disappeared. The economic absurdities of the European Community's Common Agricultural Policy can be understood only in relation to the historic and continuing weight of agrarian interests in the politics of modern industrialized European countries like France and Germany.

Within industrial society, the most salient class divide is occupational, pitting the manual working class against the managerial and professional middle classes. The term upper class is hardly used and refers to the remnants of the aristocracy. This of course is a great simplification, since there are many

Table 1.6 Agriculture as percentage of total employment

	postwar *	1970	1988
France	36.6	14.0	6.8
W. Germany	30.0	9.0	4.3
Italy	47.1	19.0	9.9
Spain	52.0	30.2	14.4
UK	4.9	2.8	2.2
USA	12.8	4.5	2.9

* France and Germany, 1946; Italy, 1936; Spain, 1940; UK, 1951; USA, 1950

Sources: Basic Statistics of the European Community (Luxembourg, EC Publishing Office, 1992); International Labour Office, Yearbook of Labour Statistics, Geneva 1952.

intermediate categories such as white-collar clerical workers or skilled craft workers. Yet the working class in western European countries exists not merely as a statistical category but as a culture and way of thinking, and as a set of institutions, including trade unions, political parties, and leisure and sporting organizations. This working-class culture varies from one country to another and the Marxist ideal of international proletarian solidarity has never become a reality. Within nations, however, working-class culture moulds people's political identity and deeply affects voting behaviour and attitudes. Middle class culture is institutionally more diverse but no less well defined.

Class divisions are changing with economic and social transformation. As an occupational category, industrial workers comprise a shrinking proportion of the labour force, as Table 1.7 shows. The changing character of work relations can also be seen in the decline of trade union membership in the 1980s (Table 1.5, p.23). Employment relations have been more individualized and less class-based. New types of occupational differentiation may be becoming more important. For example, white-collar professional workers employed in the public sector may not identify with traditional middle-class values of individualism, the market economy and low taxes. Generations which have benefited from the welfare state may be more attached to it than their parents. There is still considerable uncertainty about whether new class alignments are forming as the result of the transformation of the production process away from the traditional 'Fordist' mode of semi-skilled assembly lines. It may be that class itself is giving way to more individual types of identity in which people choose their own life-styles and political preferences.

Table 1.7 Industry as percentage of total employment

	Postwar*	1970	1988
France	23.8	40.0	30.4
W. Germany	38.0	49.3	41.2
Italy	26.4	42.3	32.6
Spain	22.4	36.6	32.5
UK	49.0	46.0	29.4
USA	36.0	32.5	26.9

*France and Germany, 1946; Italy, 1936; Spain, 1940; UK and USA, 1950.

Sources: Basic Statistics of the European Community (Luxembourg: EC Publications Office, 1992); International Labour Office, Yearbook of Labour Statistics (Geneva, 1951).

The management of class relations and adjustment for much of the postwar period has been considerably eased by the experience of economic growth. As Table 1.8 indicates, the five countries have experienced varying rates of growth, interspersed with short recessions. Where growth has slowed, as in Britain over much of the period and France at various times, social tensions have mounted as governments have struggled to meet expectations of rising living standards while maintaining social and other public expenditure programmes.

Historically, a critical division in European politics has been religion. This takes two forms, the Catholic-Protestant and the Church-Lay division. It was the Reformation of the sixteenth century which first divided Europe into Catholic and Protestant camps, ushering in a hundred years of so-called religious wars - in which power politics were as important as doctrinal

Table 1.8 Average annual percentage growth rates

	1950-60	1960-70	1970-80	1980-90
France	4.3	5.8	3.6	2.3
W. Germany	7.6	4.8	2.9	2.0
Italy	5.9	5.7	3.1	2.4
Spain	n.a.	7.5	3.8	2.7
UK	2.4	2.8	1.9	2.1
USA	3.3	4.0	2.9	2.7

Sources: OECD Economic Outlook, 1990, 1991; Basic Statistics of the European Community (Luxembourg: EC, various years).

differences. The Peace of Augsburg of 1555 enunciated the doctrine of *cuius regio, eius religio,* that is that rulers would each determine the official religion of their dominions and eventually this was generally accepted. England, Scotland, and half of the German states were in the Protestant camp. France, Spain and the various states of Italy remained Catholic. Conflict continued within France, where significant Protestant minorities existed. In Ireland, the British regime never succeeded in converting the indigenous population to the official state Church and eventually abandoned the attempt.

In the nineteenth century, a second religious cleavage developed, especially in those countries which had remained nominally Catholic. This pitted lay and anticlerical forces against the established Church. Anticlericals took their ideas from the rational, secular traditions of the eighteenth-century Enlightenment and the French Revolution. The Catholic Church leadership continued throughout the nineteenth century to condemn the French Revolution, republicanism,

Table 1.9 Religious practice

	% attend church		% believe in God
	weekly	monthly	
France	12	6	62
W. Germany	21	16	72
Italy	36	16	84
Spain	41	12	87
Britain	14	9	76
N. Ireland	42	15	91

Source: S. Harding and M. Fogarty, Contrasting Values in Western Europe (London: Macmillan, 1986).

liberal democracy and socialism. Fierce disputes occurred over the links between Church and state, the use and ownership of Church lands and control of the education system. Since the second world war, there has been a marked secularization in western Europe. This is difficult to measure, since religious practice varies from one denomination to another and it is very difficult to frame questions which have the same meaning in different cultural contexts. Table 1.9 shows the varying levels of religious practice. While strictly comparable data are not available, it does appear that religion is generally a less important factor in the five European countries than in the United States, and that it is more important in the Mediterranean countries than in northern Europe. This is not simply a question of Catholics being more practising than Protestants, since France, a country where most of the population are nominally Catholic, has one of the lowest levels of religiosity. Mapping change across time is even more difficult, but the available evidence indicates a general decline in religious observance in western Europe, though more in some countries than in others. Together with a liberalization of the Catholic Church after the Second Vatican Council in the 1960s, this has taken the heat out of the old secular-lay debates. Yet while religious cleavages now fail, except in Northern Ireland, to provoke the violent confrontations of the past, religious affiliation or non-affiliation continues to affect voting behaviour.

For several centuries, the boundary of Europe, or Christendom, was effectively defined by its contact with the world of Islam. Within Christendom, Islamic influence was expunged even where, as in Spain, it had been very influential. In recent years, immigration has again produced significant Muslim populations in western Europe. Secular states, such as France, which do not recognize any religion in official terms, have difficulty in accommodating Muslim practices and codes. In those states which do recognize religious groups and allow them official privileges, such as the United Kingdom, problems have emerged in adding Muslims to the list of such privileged groups. The most serious difficulties have arisen in relation to religious education. French schools insist on their secular identity and refuse to allow religious symbols to be worn or religious practices to take place on their premises. Britain allows Catholics,

Protestants and Jews to have their own schools, within the state system, but there is great opposition to extending the privilege to Muslims. The fact that Muslim populations are distinct not only religiously but also racially adds another dimension to the problem. Liberals argue that Muslim schools would produce racial segregation, while the extreme right uses religious differences as a code for racial intolerance.

The effect of territory on political cleavages continues to be disputed. Differences in voting and other types of political behaviour are visible from one region to another in all the countries concerned. Yet some observers argue that this can be explained by the varying combinations of other factors - such as class and religiosity - in different places. Ultimately, this may be reduced to an argument about methodology. What is clear is that political patterns vary from one region to another and that the politics of territory itself has been and continues to be an important element in the political life of European nations. Territorial politics may focus on material issues, to do with the allocation of public spending, industrial policy and regional development. It may centre on demands for autonomy for regions; or it may mobilize around cultural demands and the preservation of traditional languages and ways of life in the face of social and economic change. Some states, notably the UK and Spain, contain territories with a strong sense of historic identity where movements exist to secede from the state. Elsewhere, territorial issues are a secondary theme but one which permeates the activities of government and political parties, modifying policy stances and the allocation of resources. This is the case in Italy and France. In Germany, territorial issues are built into the structure itself, through the federal division of powers and the role of the *Länder* in national politics.

In some states, there is a historic division between a dominant capital city, the centre of political, administrative, cultural, economic and religious life, and peripheral territories. This is the case in France and the UK. In Spain, the centre of political power, Madrid, has historically not coincided with the centre of economic power, producing different sorts of tensions. The Federal Republic of (West) Germany was characterized by a dispersion of central functions, with the political capital in Bonn, the financial capital in Frankfurt and the media and cultural activity divided among the major cities. In Italy, the capital is situated between the industrialized, wealthy north and the underdeveloped and poorer south, with the tensions between these two regions deeply affecting politics in the capital.

Until the twentieth century, democracy and universal suffrage were seen exclusively in male terms. Gradually, women were admitted to the franchis: in 1918 and 1928 in Britain; 1919 in Germany; in 1944 in France; 1932 in Spain; and 1946 in Italy. The general tendency at first was for women to vote for the most conservative parties, to the consternation of the liberal and left-wing parties which had supported the female franchise. This can probably be related to the greater religiosity of women and their position in the home outside the paid labour force. Since the 1970s, this gender gap has been closed and has now largely disappeared. As issues of particular concern to women and the whole question of gender equality have been gaining more prominence, so a distinct women's vote is now being recognized again.

Patronage and Clientelism

Modern politics tends to revolve around the competition for the votes of large social categories, such as those discussed above. Yet in many places an older form of politics persists, that of patronage and clientelism. Here politicians are able to build support not through developing comprehensive policy programmes but by doing a multitude of individual favours to electors. The latter, in turn, become dependent on such patronage and hence on the politician, for whom they become clients. Patronage requires large amounts of public resources available at the discretion of the politician and weak bureaucratic structures. Indeed, the more incompetent and less impartial the bureaucracy and the more ineffective the normal policy process, the better since the politician then becomes the indispensable mediator between the citizen and the state. It is through the politician that subsidies, grants, permits, jobs, contracts and other favours can be obtained. This type of politics is often seen as characteristic of modernizing societies, where traditional social roles and values come into contact with the modern, administrative state. Stable, often rural societies, faced with the pressures of change, look to mediators able to protect them or obtain favours from the expanding state. Such was the case in nineteenth century France, Spain and Italy. In the cities of the United States, immigrants from traditional societies relied on the political machine to deal with an administrative and economic system. Yet patronage is also found in industrial society, especially in local government where elected politicians have control over detailed administrative matters such as employment, contracts or access to housing. It may thrive where government is fragmented and complex, with the professional politician the only individual with the ability to draw together the various strands. Once established, customs of patronage and clientelist networks may be difficult to shift.

Patronage and clientelism are strongest in Mediterranean Europe, where individual contacts are highly valued and bureaucratic structure, less well developed. They are usually territorially based, with local politicians able to mobilize votes within a community to get elected to national office and in return obtaining favours for faithful voters. Patronage systems are not only associated with underdevelopment but it is often argued that they themselves are an obstacle to development. After all, if the community develops and modernizes to the point at which it no longer needs handouts, if it acquires its own employment base or if an efficient and impartial bureaucracy is established, then the politician as patron will no longer be needed.

Patronage systems have tended over time to rely less on personal linkages and individual patrons and clients and more on collective entities. The old personal patron with contacts in high places has often been replaced by the party machine, which controls the disbursement of state resources. Favours are done not merely for individuals but for whole social groups or communities.

Values and Ideology

Politics in Europe also centres around values, which cannot always be related directly to material interests or social identity. There is a historic division between authoritarian and libertarian values, crystallized in the nineteenth century by attitudes to the French Revolution and the liberal and democratic movements which followed it throughout the continent. Support for authoritarian values is found across the social spectrum, though appealing more strongly to specific classes at particular historic moments. Another value cleavage is between individualism and collectivism. Individualists stress the autonomy of the individual, oppose big government or other large and powerful social institutions and emphasize competition. Collectivists stress the common interests of people and the need for cooperation and collective institutions. In some cases, this is the state; in others, it is private collective institutions such as churches, communities or trade unions which are emphasized. Much of the value differences in European politics can be understood in terms of positions in relation to these two cleavages between authoritarianism and libertarianism, and individualism and collectivism. While values can be studied independently of class and other interests, they do interact with them in complex ways. Catholicism has been associated with an organic or corporate view of society while Protestantism stresses individual salvation. Working-class culture places a high value on collective action, while middle-class culture tends to be more individualistic. Historical legacies also create clusters of attitudes which may only be broken by traumatic events such as war or revolution, or a gradual and long-term change in social relations.

Some American scholars, surveying the world in the 1960s, announced the end of ideology, the arrival of a world in which political conflict would focus on secondary issues within an overarching consensus on the big questions. At the end of the 1980s, this theme re-emerged as the end of history, the view that the historical process of social change had more or less worked itself out and that henceforth the only available form of society was the American model of : and capitalism.[7] This analysis, brought forward to celebrate the historic victory of liberal capitalism over Marxism and Communism, ironically has a great deal in common with Marxism itself. Marxist analysis, too, sees history as progressing in linear fashion to a defined end. West Europeans of the non-Marxist persuasion, recalling the rise and fall of social systems, empires, states and regimes, from the Roman Empire to the Soviet Union, are sceptical of this idea. For them, history does not move steadily forward to a fixed end point, but consists of phases of change together with elements of continuity based in national and local cultures. So the fall of the Soviet system has not produced the same triumphalism as in the United States. Rather, it has reinforced a scepticism about systems of thought claiming to offer an interpretation of everything and a solution to everything, whether of the Marxist or free-market variety. History continues in the form of politics, though the issues may be changing.

Many of the practical questions of politics in European societies focus on three sets of issues, production, distribution and identity. By production is meant argument about the most efficient means of organizing economic activity, whether through the market, the state or by cooperative enterprise, and about government policies in relation to economic growth. These have aroused passionate debates over the years. In the postwar era, there appeared to be a general consensus on the mixed economy with substantial roles for the public and private sectors. By the 1980s this was under challenge by a revival of neoliberal economic thought, with its belief in privatization and the market. It may be that a new consensus has now arrived, more oriented to market solutions than in the past but not entirely neglecting the role of the state. Yet this is unlikely to be permanent and the boundaries of the public and private sectors will no doubt continue to shift. Some environmentalists even challenge the whole productivist ethos, the very idea that society's aim should be economic growth.

Distribution refers to arguments about the sharing of the social product among classes, regions or generations and between private and public expenditure. These issues will continue to be alive as long as there are differences in wealth, income and opportunity, though the groups in competition are changing. Class structures are being modified profoundly, as the traditional industrial working class declines or becomes affluent. Other have-nots are emerging, such as the urban poor, single mothers and their families or marginalized, often immigrant workers.

Identity refers to issues arising from the presence of religious, ethnic, gender or other identifying characteristics and demands for public policies catering for these. Where cleavages are deep and reinforce each other, we have divided societies, in which there is fixed and permanent opposition between social forces. The compromise and give and take of democratic politics cannot develop and it is difficult to get agreement on the regime, that is the rules of the political game. At one time, it was thought that the advent of mass, consumer society and democracy would make these questions of identity less relevant as everyone was assimilated to the same society. This has not happened. On the contrary, with the exception of religion, they have all become more salient in modern European society. Identities need not necessarily be mutually exclusive, but cross cut, with individuals sharing one characteristic with one group, and a second characteristic with another. Political movements in turn may try to appeal on the basis of more than one social or ideological division, in order to broaden their electoral appeal. The challenge of the modern state is to accommodate these differences while preserving the values of democracy and equity. This has posed severe problems for states whose governing assumptions have been civic equality and uniformity (like France) or ethnic homogeneity (like Germany).

It has been suggested that the contemporary era has seen the rise of a new value set, that of post-materialism. The argument is that a new generation, that of the postwar years, occupationally secure and largely free of material worries, is rejecting the value sets of the past. So attention has shifted to non-material values such as the environment, culture, leisure and quality of life. This is a contentious theory which, at best, explains the orientations of a section of the middle class. It is also questionable whether the term post-material is really appropriate for people whose satisfaction is essentially derived from the satiation of their material wants. What is undeniable, however, is that the environment has become a salient political issue, posing uncomfortable questions to all the old political formulations. Farmers and both sides of the industrial class system find themselves accused of the destruction of humanity's future prospects. Individualists and collectivists, authoritarians and libertarians equally face the question of how to mobilize the collective will to protect the common property and future. It is also true that the fixed political attachments formed in the early years of democratization in the late nineteenth and twentieth centuries are loosening. Voters have become more volatile and parties have to compete harder to gain their support. Far from marking the end of politics, this is merely a new phase.

POLITICAL CURRENTS

Social cleavages, values and historical traditions and experiences have produced political parties, organized groups contesting elections and, usually, seeking governmental power or a share in power. Within individual countries, the form of each party system is also influenced by the electoral system and contingent factors such as historical events, personalities and tactical manoeuvring. This produces party systems of great complexity, and to plunge directly into a description of them would be a recipe for confusion. It is necessary, first, to identify the major political tendencies or currents in European politics, their ideas and their support bases. While it is possible to generalize usefully about these currents at a European level, they do take different forms in the specific conditions of each country. Ideas are combined in different ways; some currents do not exist in all countries; and the names of parties are not always consistent with that of the current to which they belong.

Liberalism

Liberalism is one of the most difficult of European currents to pin down, since many of its ideas have become the common property of almost all parties; and the word itself is used rather differently in different contexts. Liberal parties exist under various names, reflecting diverse elements of the Liberal heritage - Liberal, radical, republican, democratic and combinations of these. Yet, in contrast to the United States, where Liberalism refers to anyone from centre to left of the - admittedly narrow - political spectrum, European Liberalism does have some clear boundaries and central ideas.

Liberalism was born of the eighteenth century -Enlightenment, and developed to become one of the dominant political forces of the nineteenth century. It was marked by opposition to the claims of absolute monarchy and support for constitutional government with a limitation and division of powers as first established in the United States. Individual liberty was emphasized against the claims both of the state and traditional corporations such as the Church. To these political claims were added a set of economic doctrines based on private property, the market economy and, to some extent, free trade. The nineteenth century was an age of nationalism and, along with the emphasis on individual liberty, Liberals supported the collective aims of national self-determination. As is often the case, this produced some inconsistencies, since it is not always obvious just what is the national group which has the better claim to self-determination or where their boundaries lie. Socially, Liberalism was above all a middle class movement, reflecting social change, industrialism and the rise of business and professional groups challenging traditional hierarchies. In the course of the nineteenth century, it often became associated with opposition to established churches. In Catholic Europe this took the form of anti-clericalism. In Protestant countries, it was linked to non-conformist or dissenting Protestant sects. The Catholic Church, and to some extent established Protestant churches, were equally suspicious of the individualistic, rationalist and materialist basis of Liberalism and even of the nation-state itself.

By the late nineteenth century, tensions were emerging in the Liberal family provoked by the rise of working-class demands and the future of the national state itself. While some Liberals favoured a programme of advanced democracy, including universal suffrage, others saw mass democracy as a threat to Liberal values of individualism, constitutionalism and the limited state. While a section of the Liberal movement supported the development of the active welfare state to accommodate working class demands and create a truly equal citizenship, others placed more emphasis on the need to limit government and contain public expenditure. Liberals were further split on colonialism and issues of war and peace. Some favoured colonial expansion to cement national unity and provide new commercial outlets. Others opposed colonialism and military expansion, either on pacifist and libertarian grounds, or because they were a burden on the public purse and squeezed out social expenditures. After the first world war, Liberals faced the further problem that most of their classic demands about constitutionalism, the market economy, national self-determination, secularization and franchise reform had been met. The new agenda, of social welfare, economic development and national defence, divided Liberals themselves and the different policy options of these were more effectively pursued by other formations.

Since the second world war, Liberals have survived or re-emerged as minority parties. Unable to take governmental power alone, they are forced to play varieties of coalition politics. While this is not itself uncongenial to parties which in principle believe in divided power, it produces constant tensions between those wanting to ally with the left, those preferring the right, and those who still consider it possible to carve out an independent niche in the political centre. In the absence of a stable social base, Liberal parties are often reduced to groups of parliamentary notables, well-established locally but owing little to a national party. This makes it difficult to establish party discipline or consistency in the choice of coalition partners at various levels of government. Liberals nonetheless do retain some consistent policy themes such as a belief in constitutionalism and due process in government and in combining the market economy with the welfare state. They have also been among the strongest supporters of European integration.

Socialism and Social Democracy

Socialism is a movement which emerged in the nineteenth century in response to the rise of industrial capitalism and the new working class which it engendered. It contains a complex variety of currents and has spawned a bewildering variety of organizations. Yet the central themes have remained the fight against the social and economic inequalities produced by capitalism and the need for a more collectivist, socially conscious mode of government. Socialism thus contains a strong moral element, criticizing the existing order and believing in the possibility of change. Attracting wide support in the industrial working class, it was also able to recruit progressive middle element who saw a more egalitarian society in which economic privilege was abolished as the logical continuation of the democratic revolution of the century. Organizationally, the working-class movement has contained an industrial wing, based in the trade unions, and a political wing, the Socialist parties. Relations between the two have varied since not all trade unionists have been committed to Socialism and many Socialists regard the trade unions as too limited in their aims. Socialists have differed widely in doctrine, some supporting Marx's critique of capitalism and the need for its overthrow, while others see socialism as a set of essentially moral principles, derived from liberal democratic or religious bases. While socialism as a whole is politically on the left, there is a constant debate on just how far to the left it should go and how far it should compromise with other doctrines.

The most serious divisions in the Socialist and working class movement have concerned methods. Should Socialists seek the overthrow of the existing political and social order by revolution; or work within existing states for the gradual achievement of socialism? Should Socialists support national minorities seeking independence within multinational states like the United Kingdom or the Austro-Hungarian Empire; or regard such issues as a diversion from the class struggle? Should Socialists support their nation in war with other nations; or should the working class regard nations as merely the creation of the feudal and capitalist orders and unite against war? Should trade unions act as the vanguard of political struggle, trying to break capitalism by making impossible demands backed by strikes; or seek to negotiate improvements in wages and conditions within capitalism? A series of tactical questions followed, on electoral strategy, the relationship of the political and industrial wings of the movement and alliances with other social groups such as progressive middle-class elements, the peasantry, or national minorities. Already by the late nineteenth century, this had produced three broad strands of socialism. The Marxist revolutionary strand preached the need for overthrow of the existing order and the dictatorship of the proletariat. Revisionists, who were dominant in Britain and an important element in Germany, argued that the advance of democracy made this no longer necessary and that socialism could be achieved gradually through constitutional means. Anarcho-syndicalists, important in southern Europe, disdained political action altogether and favoured revolutionary action through the trade unions, leading to the overthrow both of capitalism and the state and the achievement of decentralized, self-regulating utopia.

It was the Bolshevik Revolution in Russia which caused a permanent fracture among these traditions, posing the question as to whether Socialists could support the Leninist dictatorship and the Soviet model which developed from it. In 1920, Lenin himself forced the issue, with a demand that Socialists should affiliate to a new international, the *Komintern*, under tight Soviet control. All over Europe, Socialist movements split, with the pro-Soviet elements henceforth known as Communists and the more moderate element as Social Democrats or simply Socialists. Anarcho-syndicalism remained a force in Spain until the Civil War but died out in France and Italy after the 1920s. This broad picture disguises numerous complications. Marxist and revolutionary rhetoric survived in many Social Democratic parties long after it had ceased to have real meaning, and relations between them and their Communist rivals alternated in some countries between hostility and cooperation. There were many attempts to find a third way between the soviet model, increasingly discredited with the reign of Stalin, and social democracy, often regarded as hopelessly timid and ineffectual. In the years immediately following the second world war, there were moves in various countries to bring Communists and Socialists together but these were broken off by the advent of the Cold War in 1947-8. So the left remained divided from the Soviet Revolution in 1917 to its collapse in the 1990s, between those preaching revolutionary overthrow of the state and capitalism, and those seeking their gradual improvement by working within the system.

Social democracy is characterized by mass parties with a large extraparliamentary base of activists and, in principle at least, a democratic structure giving the members control over the party and the party control over its representatives in national parliaments and local governments. Its electoral base is in the industrial working class, though the extent of this varies according to the size of that class and the presence of a Communist party competing for the same votes. Added to this is a progressive middle-class element and a variety of other social groups attracted by the party in particular national cases, for example certain types of farmers, ethnic and religious minorities. Social Democratic parties typically have a link with trade unions though in some countries the union movement keeps a degree of political independence while in others it is divided between Social Democrat and Communist sympathizers or by religion. Everywhere, Social Democratic parties have become integrated into their national political systems, causing some tensions with their ideals of internationalism and working-class solidarity, though they do come together in the Socialist International, an important organization which accredits the Socialist/Social Democratic parties in each country.

The philosophy of social democracy was developed in the 1930s and particularly after the second world war as a programme for the improvement and socialization of society, avoiding either a Soviet-style revolution or Fascist reaction. Instead, the existing state could be captured democratically through the mobilization of the working class and their progressive allies and reforms put in train which in the short term might be modest but which, cumulatively, would be very radical. Social democracy is thus essentially collectivist, wishing to extend the scope of public authority. It is egalitarian in wanting to reduce social and economic distinctions, but parliamentary and gradualist. One aspect of its collectivism is the strong support for the welfare state seen not merely, as with progressive Liberals and Conservatives, as a way of helping society's casualties, but as a contribution to social equality. Another is the need for state management of the economy, to combat what are seen as both the inefficiencies and the unfairness of capitalism. Social Democrats have a limited conception of state intervention, supporting the nationalization of major utilities, basic industries and what used to be called the commanding heights of the economy but with most industry and commerce remaining in private hands. From the 1930s, they were attracted by the new doctrines of planning and Keynesian macro-economic management which seemed to allow a degree of state control and guidance without the need to take the whole economy into public ownership. European unity was seen after the war as a way of resolving old tensions, between internationalism and the state, and Social Democrats have generally been very supportive, with some exceptions on the left and in Britain. On the form of the state, there has been more divergence of opinion, notably between supporters of a strong centralized state which could take firm control of the economy and redistribute resources, and those attached to older traditions of decentralization and participation which have enjoyed new currency since the 1960s.

Social democracy was immensely influential in the thirty-five years after the second world war, when its ideas about welfare and economic planning became part of the national consensus in many countries of western Europe even where Social Democrats were out of office. Aided by strong economic growth, conditions in the working class were improved without provoking a middle-class reaction. Public services, notably free education and health care, were expanded and extended to entire populations, financed through contributions and progressive taxation in different proportions depending on how strong the pressure for social equalization was. The mixed economy, in which public and private ownership coexisted, provided a formula for maintaining basic industries while respecting the processes of the market.

Yet, from the 1970s, social democracy faced a series of crises. Some observers had always noted that the Socialist project contained the seeds of its own destruction since, once the inequities of class society had been removed, it would be redundant. This was known as the embourgeoisement thesis, the idea that the working class would become middle class and vote accordingly. Certainly, the fall in the industrial labour force has weakened the electoral base of Social Democratic parties, while economic and social change mean that the poor are no longer identified with the working class and are no longer the majority. A political strategy focused on redistribution or higher taxation is thus a great deal more risky. Yet, while its traditional working class base was declining, social democracy was able to make new recruits among the expanding salaried professional class, especially in the public sector. These have accounted for an increased percentage of the Social Democratic vote and a considerably larger proportion of its active members and leadership.

The slowdown in growth rates after the energy shocks of the 1970s caused severe problems for the Social Democratic project since further welfare expansion was possible only through tax increases at a time when taxation was meeting increased resistance. Many of the basic industries, such as coal, steel and railways which had been taken into public ownership were themselves in crisis, needing modernization and a reduction in labour. Trade unions, the privileged partners of social democracy, were less and less prepared to subordinate their claims to wage increases to the need for Socialist governments to control inflation and public expenditure. At the same time, a change in intellectual fashion had cast doubt on Keynesianism and planning and favoured a return to monetarism, privatization and a reliance on markets. The realities of the global economy limited the scope for individual states to manage their own economic affairs. Social Democratic governments were often obliged to govern in a fashion not very different from that of their right-wing opponents and, indeed, have usually had to demonstrate additional fiscal and monetary orthodoxy in order to convince naturally suspicious financial markets. So throughout the 1980s Social Democrats were on the defensive, while at the end of the decade, the collapse of the Communist regimes in eastern Europe was used to discredit the whole Socialist ideal, despite social democracy's historic efforts to distinguish itself from the Soviet model.

To match the new reality, Social Democratic parties have taken a series of steps to alter their programme, moving towards the political centre, abandoning much of the old statist model and accepting more fully the market economy. The first to do so was the German Social Democratic Party at its Bad Godesberg conference in the 1950s. In Italy, the shift can be dated to the Socialists' entry into the centre-left coalition in the early 1960s, while in Spain the Socialist leader Felipe González forced a confrontation in 1979 to get the party to accept the new revisionism. In Britain and France the practice of Socialist governments preceded the recognition of the change by the parties themselves, though by the late 1980s both accepted that they were now in the Social Democratic tradition as defined by their German colleagues and dropped the leftist elements of their programmes. With these moves, social democracy has become more of an advanced form of Liberalism and able to appeal more convincingly to the middle classes and upwardly mobile, but risks losing its distinct identity and capacity to inspire idealism and loyalty.

Communism

The Communist parties of western Europe draw their inspiration from Marxism as interpreted by Lenin, believing in revolutionary change and the replacement of capitalist society. They split from the Socialist movement around 1920 over the question of the Bolshevik revolution in Russia and Lenin's insistence that they affiliate to the new Moscow-based international. For the next forty years, western Communist parties followed Moscow's line faithfully and defended both Soviet foreign policy and the Soviet Union as a model of society. This made them outcasts in western politics and Communists did not participate in inter-war governing coalitions except briefly in the Spanish second republic. Even under the French Popular Front of 1936 they gave only external parliamentary support but did not take ministerial office. In Italy and Germany, Communist parties were forcibly suppressed by Mussolini and Hitler, their leaders imprisoned or killed. The pact of 1939 by which Hitler and Stalin agreed to carve up eastern Europe, drove French Communists underground since it put them on the same side as the Germans. Then the German invasion of the Soviet Union, bringing it into the second world war alongside the allies in 1940 changed everything. Communists became part of the anti-fascist resistance and re-established their patriotic credentials. In the period of postwar reconstruction, they participated in coalition governments in both France and Italy. In 1947-8, matters were again reversed with the outbreak of the Cold War. Non-communists were expelled from coalitions in eastern Europe and the Communists were expelled from government in Italy and France. Under the new west German constitution, they were banned along with the Nazi party as undemocratic.

Communism never re-appeared in any force in West Germany, where the example of East Germany served as a permanent reminder of its totalitarian nature. In Britain, it languished and declined, electing only two MPs ever, in the 'little Moscows' of east London and the Fife coalfield of Scotland. Yet communism remained an important force in Italy and France while in Spain Communists were a respected part of the anti-Franco resistance. Communist parties remained committed to revolutionary change through the dictatorship of the proletariat. As interpreted by Lenin, this meant effectively the dictatorship of the Communist Party. They officially rejected what they called bourgeois democracy as a sham and looked to mass action by the workers to achieve their aims. They were highly disciplined internally, making heavy demands on members and operating according to the principle of democratic centralism. In theory, this meant that there was democratic discussion in the party until a decision was taken; from that point all members had to support it loyally. In practice, it meant the subordination of party members to decisions taken by the leadership, often on instructions from Moscow.

At the same time, however, Communists participated in the institutions of liberal democracy, contesting parliamentary elections and in some places winning control of local governments. Their electoral base varied from one country to another. In France and Italy, they had substantial support among industrial workers. They also appealed to sections of the small peasantry. They were also rooted in certain regions and communities, with a tradition of radical dissent, anticlericalism and mass action. Around them, they built not only political parties but whole alternative cultures, including trade unions, cooperative organizations, sports and social clubs, youth wings and newspapers. Individuals thus grew up in the Communist subculture, lived in it and took their cues in politics and social life from it.

From the late 1950s, the monolithic Communist subculture began slowly to fracture. A key event was the leaked secret speech of Soviet leader Khrushchev to the central committee of the Soviet Communist party denouncing the crimes of Stalin. To a generation of Communists brought up to believe that the Soviet Union was a workers' paradise and Stalin the benevolent father of his people, this was a deep shock. It was followed shortly after by the Soviet invasion of Hungary to suppress the democratic uprising there. Large numbers of Communists left the party in protest. By the 1960s younger leftists regarded communism as no more than another oppressive doctrine and tended to move into the libertarian groups of the 'new left'. The events of 1968 in Paris, when the Communists declined to join the student and worker protests, reinforced this view, which was given further confirmation in the same year when the Soviets invaded Czechoslovakia to halt the liberalizing reform programme there. Within western Communist parties, reformist tendencies developed, which came to be know as Eurocommunism. This accepted the need for radical change in society but argued that it could be achieved through peaceful parliamentary means. Eurocommunists also insisted that each national society was different and that the Soviet model was not applicable in the West. Of crucial importance, they came to accept that in a democracy parties should alternate in government so that, if the Communists came to power in elections and were subsequently defeated, they would go peacefully. Abandoning their traditional sectarianism, eurocommunists opened dialogue with other parties and sought cooperation in governing. Where they controlled local governments, they sought to demonstrate their managerial competence and probity.

There were rewards in this strategy, especially in Italy where the Communists steadily increased their vote. Eurocommunism, however, contained some fatal ambiguities. Although much traditional Marxist-Leninist doctrine was discarded, they found it extremely difficult to change the way they ran their own parties and democratic centralism remained the order of the day. This on occasion gave rise to the odd spectacle of the supposedly tolerant Eurocommunists disciplining or expelling old-style Communists for not adopting the new line. There was also ambiguity over the attitude to take to the Soviet Union, obligatory reference point for generations of Communists. Was the Soviet system a basically sound model in need of reform, or was it irretrievably corrupt? If it was the latter, the fault presumably lay in its origins, the 1917 Revolution and Lenin himself. Yet to disown 1917 was to disown communism as a distinct form and would undermine the party's very reason for existence. So apparently arcane historical and ideological disputes about the correct interpretation of the Bolshevik seizure of power and responsibility for Stalinism were in reality debates about the party's very essence and its future. These were never adequately resolved. In Italy, the party moved ever further out of Moscow's orbit. French Communists dallied with eurocommunism, the returned to the orthodox line, expelling its dissidents at every U-turn. Spanish communism split into fragments before coming together in a rather shaky coalition with other left wingers. The small Communist Party of Great Britain divided.

Communist parties also faced a serious erosion of their electoral base. The blue-collar working class declined in numbers, first in northern Europe and later in Italy and Spain. The left-wing peasantry of central Italy and southern France faced a similar erosion of numbers. Social mobility and migration broke up the old subcultures, especially from the late 1960s. Communism as a doctrinal value system declined along with religion while rising educational levels made people more sceptical of the old simplicities. Ideological modernization and eurocommunism helped stem the tide but only for a while.

With the arrival of Gorbachev in power in 1985, the evolution of western communism was overtaken by developments in the Soviet Union itself. Hard-line Communists in France and elsewhere found themselves defending a model of Soviet communism which the Soviet leader himself rejected. In Italy, the response was to press on further, discarding the last remaining elements of Marxist doctrine and abandoning even the party's name. The collapse of the Soviet Union in 1991 removed the last of the external support system for western Communist parties. They continued in the form of a shrunken French Communist Party, a breakaway Italian Communist Refoundation and elements of the Spanish leftist coalition United Left. These may benefit from the rightward drift of Social Democratic parties and provide an outlet for working class frustration in the face of economic restructuring but their support levels by the early 1990s were down into single figures.

The Far Left and New Left

Disillusionment with the Soviet model of communism has produced a large number of dissenting groups on the far left. Some of these are inspired by Stalin's rival Trotsky, who denounced the Soviet Union as a corrupt bureaucratic dictatorship and preached permanent revolution. Some are inspired by libertarian or anarchist traditions. The student movements of the 1960s produced a proliferation of groups on the 'new left', opposed to the social models of both East and West. In 1968 new-left students sparked off a revolt which shook the French Fifth Republic to its foundations. Elsewhere in Europe and North America, student activism made headlines and encouraged the growth of a libertarian left tied to the youth culture and opposed to all forms of established authority. Yet they made few converts outside the universities and few new left groups survived long. They were fractious and ill organized, with little idea of strategy. Apart from some of the Trotskyist groups,they had little contact with the working class, who remained attached to their Social Democratic and Communist leaders. Yet the new left were not totally without influence. In Italy the electoral system has allowed far-left and libertarian parties to gain representation in parliament, where they point to the failings of the established parties. More generally, new-left ideas of decentralization and participation influenced both Eurocommunism and left-wing social democracy. Some new left activists re-emerged in the 1980s in Green parties.

Conservatism

Conservatism is a broad doctrine, with varied currents within it. Its origins lie in opposition on the part of the ruling classes to the Enlightenment and the French Revolution. Since then it has retained its appeal to opponents of change. Traditional conservatism stresses order, hierarchy, natural inequality and the prerogatives of traditional authority in the state, Church and family. It draws on what it sees as a realistic view of human nature which it regards as flawed and in need of firm direction by authority. It is suspicious of radical change, believing that the human mind is incapable of designing grand plans for the future and that the most prudent course is to proceed in small steps. Yet where reform is necessary, the Conservative will accept it as the price for preserving the social order as a whole and of staying in power. Conservatives accept the market economy but the traditional Conservative regards it only as a means rather than an end and will over-ride it where it conflicts with other values. In particular, they are suspicious of the market's potential to undermine traditional authority relationships and its emphasis on material goals.

A key element in conservatism is nationalism in its various dimensions. The Conservative preaches love of country and the promotion of national interests against others. In some cases, this has led to militarism and imperialism. Conservatives also promote the idea of the nation as solidaristic institution or extended family. From this derives a willingness to accept the welfare state, not as a mechanism for social levelling but as a paternalistic obligation to look after the less fortunate members of the national family. Social order is also to be maintained by discipline. Conservatives support strong law and order policies and expanded powers for the police. They place the maintenance of order above the preservation of civil liberties and tend to take an anti-permissive line on moral and social issues.

Conservatism had great difficulty in coming to terms with the rise of industrial society, class conflict and democracy and only in Britain did it manage the transition smoothly. Elsewhere, Conservatives were divided between die-hard reactionaries and more progressive elements prepared to accept social and political reform. Between the wars, conservatism in much of continental Europe was eclipsed by the rise of Fascism which promised a restoration of authority by violent means. Some Conservatives went over to Fascism along with large sections of their upper- and middle-class support base. After the war, conservatism was widely discredited by the experience of the extreme right, just as moderate socialism was later discredited by the experience of communism in eastern Europe. In continental Europe, progressive Christian Democrats or modernizing technocrats appeared more in tune with the needs of the times.

Yet Conservative movements were able to adapt their philosophy and return in force. They ceased fighting the nineteenth century battles against democracy, universal suffrage and republicanism and sought to broaden their social base. During the 1950s and 1960s they governed, alone or in coalition, very much on the same lines as their Social Democratic opponents. Rather than rolling back the welfare state, Keynesian economic management or industrial intervention, they used them as instruments in governing and building political support. This could be justified on classic conservative grounds, the acceptance of what existed and the gradual development of society.

In the 1970s, this began to change as the Social Democratic model of political management came under challenge. Conservatives increasingly adopted the language and policies of the neo-liberal or new-right school which argued for a return to pure market economics and a reduction in the role of the state. Conservatives became exponents of privatization and deregulation, of cutting taxes and reducing public services. While advocating a reduced role for the state in economic management and welfare, they urged a return to strong government in matters of law and order, a reinvigoration of authority in social institutions including the family and the school and a reversal of the permissive society. Rather than the pragmatism on policy which had characterized them since the war, they adopted highly doctrinaire positions on economic and social issues. The most dramatic changes took place in the British Conservative Party which moved sharply to the right under Margaret Thatcher, but similar ideas also took hold in France, Germany, Spain and to some extent Italy. This shift was partly a matter of ideas but also owed much to electoral considerations. Large segments of the middle classes and upwardly mobile workers responded to the appeal of low taxes, attacks on the welfare state and a more individualist message. Privatization offered an apparently painless way to replenish government coffers while reducing expectations on the state. At the same time, the promise of strong law and order policies catered to people's insecurity in the face of change. A tougher line on immigration helped protect Conservatives' flanks from the parties of the extreme right while allowing them, in more or less coded language, to appeal to the racist vote.

Christian Democracy

Christian democracy is a variety of conservative movement which deserves special attention. It had its origins in the nineteenth century when a number of Catholics began to consider how Christianity could be reconciled with the modern world of industrialism, class division and liberal democratic demands. It is an inter-class movement based upon Christian principles, conservative for the most part but accepting the need for reform and change. Its strength lies in the regions of traditional religious observance.

For most of the century, the Church hierarchy had set itself against the legacy of the eighteenth century and Enlightenment and the French Revolution, with their ideas of popular sovereignty, democracy and the secular state. It also condemned socialism and the rise of a left-wing working-class movement. Catholics tended to the conservative and reactionary side in politics or to abstain altogether from political involvement. Fierce struggles pitted the secular state against the Church in Germany, France and Italy. From the 1880s, attitudes began to change as new lay Catholic movements sought to reach out to the working class and to find a place for religious values in contemporary politics. Papal encyclicals began to give them encouragement, accepting elements of democracy and Liberalism and permitting Catholics to involve themselves more in politics. By the first world war, there were Christian Democratic movements in Italy, France and Germany. In Germany and other Protestant countries, a parallel movement of Protestant Christian democracy developed, also aiming to reconcile spiritual values with political and social action.

Between the wars, a substantial section of Catholic opinion sided with the Fascist movements and the papacy aligned itself with the Franco and Mussolini dictatorships. A Christian Democratic tradition, however, survived and, in opposing dictatorship, refined its doctrines and strategy. With the defeat of the dictators it emerged as a powerful force in France and Italy. In Germany, a new Christian Democratic movement, bringing together Protestants and Catholics, became the largest political force. In Spain, Christian Democracy was strongest in the peripheral regions of Catalonia and the Basque Country but had to wait until the fall of the Franco regime in 1975 to emerge as a political force.

Christian Democratic doctrine is broad and complex, varying from one context to another, but it does contain consistent core elements. The most important is that of democracy itself. Christian Democrats reject dictatorship and totalitarianism and accept the idea of universal suffrage and elections at all levels of government. Democracy is seen not merely as a convenient procedure but as a value in its own right. They also believe that political action should be informed by Christian principles and doctrine. This does not mean that they believe in a form of theocracy, or subordination of the state to the Church. On the contrary, they insist on a very clear distinction between the role of the Church in spiritual guidance and the secular activities of government and on several occasions have sharply reminded the ecclesiastical authorities of their place. Politics is a matter for the lay arm of the Christian Democratic movement, not for the clergy; yet this politics should be suffused with Christian principles.

Stress is also placed on the need to reconcile class conflict and to incorporate the working class into political, economic and life. Christian Democrats recognize both a concern, derived from Christian doctrine, with the conditions of the working class and a political need to appeal to them in an era of mass democracy. They have supported the development of the welfare state with its expansive social programmes. Christian Democrats have formed their own trade unions and have on occasion allied with the left in confrontation with employers. Generally, however, they avoid confrontation and promote inter-class collaboration. In the postwar years they promoted worker participation in industry through joint employer-worker councils to reconcile the interests of their middle-class supporters with those of the industrial proletariat.

In the countryside, Christian Democrats traditionally support land reform, the break up of large estates and the creation of a class of peasant proprietors. This they see as the basis for justice as well as social stability and conservatism. They oppose nationalization of the land or the creation of collective agriculture, though they have been involved in the cooperative movement, as a means of allowing small farmers to combine to control the supply of materials or the marketing of their produce.

Christian democracy rejects both the unbridled individualism of Liberalism and the statist collectivism of socialism. Instead, it favours a strong civil society composed of voluntary associations in which the individual can find true expression. These include the family, trade unions, social organizations and local governments. Christian Democrats have put this into action themselves through organizing vigorously in civil society, through Catholic and Protestant lay associations, trade unions, social clubs, youth organizations and sports bodies. The doctrine of personalism stresses individual responsibility within the larger organic society. While accepting the need for the state to organize welfare and regulate social conflict, they emphatically reject the dominant state of German or Jacobin theory. Instead, they invoke the principle of subsidiarity, according to which matters should only be regulated in a larger body if they cannot be resolved in a smaller one. Pope Pius XI stated doctrine thus in the encyclical *Quadragesimo Anno*:

> It is an injustice, a grave evil, and a disturbance of right order for a larger and higher organization to arrogate to itself functions which can be performed efficiently by smaller or lower bodies . . . Of its very nature the true aim of all social activity should be to help

individual members of the social body, but never to destroy them.[8]

So the state should not intrude on private or family life where not necessary. Central governments should not impose on local governments except for good reason. In later years, the principle was to be invoked in discussions about the scope of the European Community. Before the war, the belief in the virtues of intermediate associations between the individual and the state led some Christian Democrats to favour a system of corporatism in which public affairs would be regulated by professional groups and representation in parliament would be on the basis of occupational categories. Experience of this system under Fascism largely discredited it, though a bias in favour of negotiation with groups did remain.

Christian Democrats have always accepted the market economy but seen it more as a means to an end than a rigid point of doctrine. Where appropriate, they have supported state planning and nationalization of industry in the interests of efficiency and social justice. Since the second world war, they have been among the strongest supporters of European integration, pressing for the extension of Community competences and the strengthening of Community institutions.

Religious issues rarely intrude directly into modern European politics but where they do Christian Democrats generally take a pro-Church stance. They favour religious education in schools and public support for churches. They oppose divorce and abortion, though with diminishing success even in countries like Germany, Italy and Spain which have a large Catholic population. Their religious heritage generally leads Christian Democrats to resist racist appeals and they have been more consistent than other conservative parties in resisting the temptation to compete or cooperate with the extreme right.

This is a diverse set of beliefs and different elements are stressed by different elements within the Christian Democrat family. After the war, there was a strong left wing element, emphasizing the welfare state, planning and the needs of the working class. Some of these Christian Democrats were almost indistinguishable from Socialists. The mainstream of the movement, however, has remained staunchly anti-Marxist, criticizing the left for its materialism, its false view of history, its anticlericalism and its subordination of the individual. Most Christian Democrats remain conservative in their orientation, rejecting the idea of social equality or forced levelling. Another element, which has become stronger over the years, stressed the virtues of the market economy and has flirted with the neo-liberal doctrines of the new right. Christian democracy is an inter-class movement, which deliberately seeks a broad social base. It appeals strongly to much of the middle class and rural voters but also has a presence in the working class. This broad base of support is the secret of its success and ability to adapt to changing conditions but it does vary from one context to another. In individual countries, Christian Democrats have had to find an electoral space by appealing to existing social groups and focusing on live issues. So in Germany, Christian Democrats have stressed the virtues of the market economy, albeit combined with an expansive welfare state. In Italy, the Christian Democrats have taken over and perfected a system of clientelism and used their dominant position in parliament to form coalitions around them. In France, christian democracy was practically destroyed by the advent of Gaullism. In Spain it never established a successful mass party. Britain lacks a Christian Democratic party altogether, though traditional, paternalistic conservatism has some elements in common with it.

The Extreme Right

Postwar western Europe has seen the emergence of a number of parties of the extreme right. These draw on a number of legacies. One is the nineteenth century tradition of reaction, the rejection of the Enlightenment, the French Revolution and democracy in favour of pre-democratic forms. Monarchists and absolutists continued to agitate until the first world war, after which many of them threw in their lot with the new Fascist movements. Interwar Fascism was a doctrine of absolute state power adapted to the modern age. It rejected democracy and Liberalism, exalted the nation and placed power in the hands of an all-powerful dictator. Nazi Germany was the most extreme case of a totalitarian regime of the extreme right, in which the might of the state crushed all elements of an independent civil society, including the traditional monarchist right which had helped it to power. In Italy and Spain, dictators had to make compromises with traditional reactionary forces including the Catholic Church, the landowners and the military. These elements of nineteenth-century reaction and twentieth-century revolutionary Fascism co-exist more or less uneasily in the contemporary right. Traditionalists tend to be religious and some have had links with fundamentalist Catholics opposed to the liberalization of the Church after the Second Vatican Council. Other extreme rightists are virulently anti-clerical, proclaiming atheism or dabbling in reinvented pagan cults. The third element on which the contemporary extreme right draws is Europe's legacy of racism. Before the twentieth century, this largely took the form of anti-semitism. Later it was extended to hostility to African and Asian immigrants.

  The extreme right varies from one country to another but a common core of beliefs can be identified. A constant theme is the search for enemies and scapegoats to blame for social problems. In this a central part is played by nationalism, the exaltation of the nation above others and support for an assertive or aggressive foreign policy. Foreigners are the enemy and will, if allowed, damage the national interest. Normally it is the existing nation state which is exalted but extreme rightists are also found in ranks of minority nationalist and separatist movement, for example in the Flanders region of Belgium. Extreme rightists tend to oppose European integration for this reason, though some of them have translated their nationalism to the European plane, regarding all Europeans as belonging to the same national family, albeit in different branches. Among these European nationalists there is often a certain anti-Americanism and a desire to restore Europe's place as the dominant military centre of the world.

A dominant theme over the years has been racism, the search for enemies at home in the form of Jews or, more recently, African and Asian immigrants. Extreme rightists draw on theories of racial superiority to justify the rights of white Europeans and prey on the insecurities of people faced with competition in the labour market. Sometimes, the racism is overt, comprising crude claims to natural superiority. Elsewhere, it is more coded, and takes the form of demands that non-European Community citizens should be denied social benefits or be sent back home in times of unemployment, or that citizenship should be denied to their children. Although inspired by racist considerations, all these policies have been applied at one time or another in various European countries by governments of the democratic parties, enabling the extreme right to claim that they are part of the political mainstream.

Other enemies are found in the political and economic sphere. The extreme right is virulently anti-communist and claims to find Communists and their sympathizers in all manner of unlikely places. It is anti-trade union, though this is moderated in places where extreme right parties have formed their own trade unions to rally native workers against immigrants and ethnic minorities. At the same time, it is opposed to large-scale capitalism, multinational corporations and the banks. These are seen as conspiracy against the nation and an affront to their ideal of independent, small scale business. The anti-capitalist message varies in intensity from one extreme right party to another, as it did in the inter-war years, when some Fascist movements came to terms with big business and abandoned the message.

Great emphasis is placed on the need for a strong state able to enforce social discipline. Civil rights are subordinated to the needs of law and order, with extensive and uncontrolled police powers. An authoritarian state form is envisaged, with limitations on individual and associative rights. Although most extreme right parties declare their belief in electoral democracy, this is probably more of a recognition that overtly anti-democratic parties would stand no chance of gaining power in modern western Europe than a deeply felt belief. On the state's role in economic and social matters, there is a range of views. Some extreme rightists aim for a totalitarian state which controls the economy. Others favour a free-market approach, though with controls on the banks and large monopolies. Like their inter-war counterparts, they have a penchant for large-scale public works and development projects as symbols of the might of the state and the glory of the nation.

There are distinct elements in the make-up of extreme right movements, all of whom have their place. A hooligan, street-fighting or skinhead element creates social disorder to provoke demands for strong state action, and intimidates opponents. Links with terrorist groups are more difficult to prove but a lot of evidence of this has emerged, particularly in Italy. Extreme rightists in some countries have made converts in the police and military and have been linked to coup attempts in France, Italy and Spain since the 1960s. A more respectable-looking leadership group appeals to voters and tries to look like a credible contender for office in a democracy. An intellectual element provides the theories which are used to legitimize the party's attacks on the system. Although the intellectuals of the new right are often not members or activists in the political parties, their work is freely used. Pseudo-scientific theories about racial superiority provide a cover for racist politics. Tendentious revisions of history alter the context of debate by arguing, for example, that the Nazi genocide of the Jews never really occurred. Extreme parties also generate their own literature of magazines, books and tracts in what are, for their size, very large quantities.

The electoral base of extreme right parties is also varied. Lower-middle-class voters, small business people and shopkeepers, finding themselves caught between large-scale capitalism and the unionized working class, are frequently attracted. Upper-middle-class voters sometimes see them as guarantors of law and order and an effective means of keeping the working class in its place. Some working-class voters, for their part, feel threatened by the competition of immigrants and ethnic minorities in the labour market and respond to a racist or nationalist appeal.

Immediately after the war, the extreme right was delegitimated by the defeat of the Axis dictators and the revelations of Nazi atrocities. In both Italy and Germany, constitutional provisions sought to ban a resurrection of the Fascist or Nazi parties. It was not long, however, before the extreme right reappeared in Italy, tolerated by the dominant Christian Democratic Party. In Germany, extreme right activity revived in the late 1960s and again in the aftermath of unification in the early 1990s. The largest extreme right movement is in France, which escaped totalitarian dictatorship between the wars but has a tradition of anti-democratic and racist politics stretching back to the last century. There was a small extreme right movement in Spain after the end of the Franco dictatorship, but this disappeared in the late 1970s. Britain had upsurges of extreme right-wing activity in the 1960s and 1970s and in the 1980s there was some extreme rightist infiltration of the Conservative Party. By and large, however, extremist politics has been contained.

The Greens

Green politics first arrived in Europe in the 1970s in the form of environmental or ecological movements. Initially, these were loose social movements often based on student protest groups of the 1960s and the libertarian new left, and attracting the same followers. They grew as the environment became a salient political issue, especially in the wake of major disasters and the growing body of scientific knowledge about environment degradation. Further impetus was given by the anti-nuclear movement, which targeted both nuclear weapons and nuclear energy, forging an alliance between the established pacifist tradition and the newer green awareness. Local movements protesting against bad development or pollution linked up and made contact with national Green movements. In due course, an international dimension was added as Greens cooperated across national boundaries and addressed issues of global pollution. Some scholars have attributed increased environmental awareness to the growth of 'post-materialist' values. According to this thesis, younger generations of Europeans are turning away from the politics of class and production issues towards quality of life questions including life-style, personal liberty and the environment.[9] Critics of the Greens have charged that it is only those who have already satisfied their material needs who can afford to strike post-materialist postures and that environmentalism is the hobby of the comfortable middle classes.

In the 1980s, environmental movements began to transform themselves into political parties, usually taking the name Greens, and to fight elections. The resulting parties are broad alliances, often known as 'rainbow coalitions', drawing in a wide variety of movements and people. There is a central concern with the environment and the need for a radical change in economic, political and social systems to address the issue. To this is added a strong pacifist element, opposed particularly to nuclear weapons. Greens draw heavily on the 'small is beautiful' theme, opposing large-scale government and big structures of all sorts. They support European unity but oppose the European Community as a bureaucratic and centralized body based on existing states. In its place, they would put a decentralized Europe of the Regions in which nation-states would give way to smaller units loosely federated on a continental basis. This would work in partnership with countries of the Third World, ending their economic and environmental exploitation.

There is a strong belief in participation and in civic equality, especially equality of the sexes. Attitudes towards modernization and high technology differ. Some greens oppose continued economic growth and dream of the simple life in which self-sufficient communities live in harmony with nature. They suspect technology as part of the race for growth and an instrument in the hands of powerful interests. Others want to harness new technologies to promote environmentally friendly growth, free humans from drudgery and allow genuine democracy through instant communication.

With their insistence on participation, equality and decentralization, green parties are necessarily rather loosely organized, if not completely anarchic. Their philosophy is utopian, positing a future world radically different from the present and challenging many of the assumptions on which western societies are built. This creates serious problems for them as electoral contenders in competition with other parties. On their own, they can have only limited impact. Yet if they ally with other parties, seeking compromises and limited reforms, they lose their *raison d'être*, which is to present a radical challenge to the very basis of modern politics. Particularly acute problems are faced in their relationships with the Social Democratic parties. Greens normally see themselves as on the political left and share many ideas with Social Democrats. Many Social Democrats, for their part, have been receptive to green ideas. Yet social democracy is based on the idea of economic growth and depends on a blue-collar electorate often employed in energy industries or heavy manufacturing, whose livelihoods are threatened by the Green agenda. In some local and regional governments, Red-Green coalitions of Social Democrats and Greens have been formed. In other cases, greens insist on their independence, on being neither right nor left and condemn the old production-based parties equally.

Much depends on the electoral system. Where there is proportional representation, Greens can hope to gain seats in national parliaments as well as local and regional councils and use this to bargain over policy. In majoritarian systems, they tend to be shut out, though in the French two-ballot system they are able to bargain their support between rounds. Any bargaining over short-term policy gains, however, weakens their appeal as a radical challenger. There is a tendency consequently for Green parties to split into moderate factions prepared to engage in conventional politics and fundamentalists who will have nothing to do with the established politicians. Greens have often done best in elections for the European Parliament. Except in Britain, these are usually conducted by proportional representation and, as the national government is not at issue, electors feel free to express a protest vote. It may also be that European elections, where national politics are not directly engaged, give greens a chance to put their issues forward more effectively.

REFERENCES

1. I am grateful to Sean Loughlin for clarifying this discussion.
2. A-C. Pereira-Menaut, *El Ejemplo Constitucional de Inglaterra* (Madrid: Complutense University, 1992).
3. M. Albert, *Capitalisme contre Capitalisme* (Paris: Seuil, 1991).
4. Corporatist theory takes many forms. The original modern exposition is P. Schmitter, 'Still the century of corporatism?', *Review of Politics*, 31.1 (1974), pp. 85-131. See also P. Schmitter and G. Lembruch

(eds.), *Trends toward Corporatist Intermediation* (New York: Sage, 1979).
5. M. Bull, 'The Corporatist Ideal-Type and Political Exchange', *Political Studies*, XL.2 (1992), pp. 255-72.
6. G. Peters, *European Politics Reconsidered* (Boston: Holmes and Meier, 1991). M. Keating, 'Regional autonomy in the changing state order: a framwork of analysis', *Regional Politics and Policy*, 2.3 (1992).
7. For example, F. Fukayama, *The End of History and the Last Man* (New York: Free Press, 1992).
8. M. Fogarty, *Christian Democracy in Western Europe, 1820-1953* (University of Notre Dame Press, 1957).
9. R. Inglehart, *Culture Shift in Advanced Industrial Societies* (Princeton: Princeton University Press, 1990).

FURTHER READING

General
Annual Editions, *Comparative Politics, 92/93* (Dushkin, 1992).
Annual Editions, Global Studies, *Western Europe* (1989).
C. Campbell, H. Feigenbaum, R. Linden and H. Norpoth, *Politics and Government in Europe Today* (New York: Harcourt Brace Jovanovich, 1990).
A. Dragnich, J. Rasmussen and J. Moses, *Major European Governments*, 8th edn. (Pacific Grove, Cal.: Brooks Cole, 1991).
M.D. Hancock, D.P. Conradt, B.G. Peters, W. Safran and R. Zariski, *Politics in Western Europe* (Chatham, NJ: Chatham House, 1993).
M. Kesselman and J. Kreiger, *European Politics in Transition*, 2nd edn. (Lexington: DC Heath,1992).
J.E. Lane and S. Ersson, *Politics and Society in Western Europe*, 2nd edn. (London and Newbury Park: Sage, 1991).
Y.Mény, *Comparative Politics* (Oxford: Oxford University Press, 1989).
G. Peters, *European Politics Reconsidered* (Boston: Holmes and Meier, 1991).
G. Smith, *Politics in Western Europe*, 5th edn. (Aldershot, Dartmouth, 1989).
D. Urwin and W. Paterson (eds.), *Politics in Western Europe Today* (London: Longman, 1990).
F. Wilson, *European Politics Today* (Englewood Cliffs: Prentice Hall, 1990).

Parties
L. Cheles, R. Ferguson and M. Vaughan, *Neo-fascism in Europe* (London and New York: Longman, 1991).
A. Day (ed.), *Political Parties of the World*, 3rd edn. (London: Longman and Chicago: James Press, 1988).
M. Dreyfus, *L'Europe des socialistes* (Brussels: Complexe, 1991).
A-M. Duranton-Crabol, *L'Europe de l'extrême droite* (Brussels: Complexe, 1991).
B. Girvin (ed.), *The Transformation of Contemporary Conservatism* (London and Newbury Park: Sage, 1988).
R.E.M. Irving, *The Christian Democratic Parties of Western Europe* (London: Allen and Unwin, 1979).
F. Jacobs, *Western European Political Parties. A Comprehensive Guide* (London: Longman, 1989).
E. Kirchner (ed.), *Liberal Parties in Western Europe* (Cambridge: Cambridge University Press, 1988).
T. Mackie and R. Rose, *The International Almanac of Electoral History*, 3rd edn. (Washington, DC: Congressional Quarterly, 1991).
F. Müller-Rommel (ed.), *New Politics in Western Europe. The Rise and Success of Green Parties and Alternative Lists* (Boulder: Westview, 1989)
W. Paterson and S. Padgett, *A History of Social Democracy in Europe* (London: Longman, 1991).
N. Roussellier, *L'Europe des libéraux* (Brussels: Complexe, 1991).

Territorial Politics
R. Batley and G. Stoker (eds.), *Local Government in Europe: Trends and Developments* (London: Macmillan, 1991).
B. Dente and F. Kjellberg (eds.), *The Dynamics of Institutional Change: Local Government Reorganization*

in Western Democracies (London and Beverly Hills: Sage, 1988).

M. Keating, *State and Regional Nationalism. Territorial Politics and the European State* (London and New York: Harvester-Wheatsheaf, 1988).

Y. Mény and V. Wright (eds.), *Centre-Periphery Relations in Western Europe* (London: Allen and Unwin, 1985).

E. Page, *Localism and Centralism in Europe* (Oxford: Oxford University Press, 1991).

E. Page and M. Goldsmith (eds.), *Central and Local Government Relations: A Comparative Analysis of West European Unitary States* (London and Beverly Hills: Sage, 1987).

S. Rokkan and D. Urwin, *Economy, Territory, Identity. Politics of West European Peripheries* (London and Beverly Hills: Sage, 1983).

J.R. Rudolph and R.J. Thompson (eds.), *Ethnoterritorial Politics, Policy and the Western World* (Boulder and London: Lynne Rienner, 1989).

M. Watson (ed.) *Contemporary Minority Nationalism* (London: Routledge, 1990).

2 The United Kingdom

STATE AND GOVERNMENT IN THE UNITED KINGDOM

Like France and Spain, the United Kingdom was created over centuries by the gradual addition of territories and the consolidation of the state. Although it is a unitary state, it has never been a uniform one like France, nor has the state forged a single, exclusive national identity. The United Kingdom as the name implies, consists of several nations, England, Scotland, Wales and Northern Ireland, united in a single state. Its full name is the United Kingdom of Great Britain and Northern Ireland, often abbreviated to UK. Britain strictly speaking consists only of England, Scotland and Wales, though the term Britain is often used for the whole of the UK. The habit, common in continental Europe and North America, of using the term England to refer to the whole of Britain is geographically incorrect and about as politically tactful as confusing Canadians with Americans. Wales was united with England in 1536, but has retained its national identity and much of its distinctive culture. Scotland was united with England and Wales in two stages. In 1603, James VI of Scotland inherited the English Crown, uniting the monarchies in a single person. Then in 1707 the Parliaments of both states were abolished and replaced with a new Parliament for the unitary state of Great Britain. Ireland was brought into the kingdom over a long period of time, culminating in a formal union in 1800. In 1921, the larger part of Ireland broke away to form what is now the Irish Republic, leaving six counties in the north of Ireland within the UK.

The terms on which the various countries joined the United Kingdom were all rather different. Wales was largely assimilated to England in law and administration, while Scotland kept its own legal system, established Church and local government institutions. Ireland was always administered rather differently and in modern times Northern Ireland is treated as a separate question in British politics. The whole process was complicated by the fact that, as it became a unified state, the UK also became an Empire and a world power and it was not always possible to tell where the home country ended and the colonial Empire began, especially in the case of Ireland. Citizenship was confused and not properly defined until 1981. Even then no less than six categories of British citizens and subjects were recognized, to account for the peoples of the old empire - only one of these has the right to live in Britain !

On the fringes of the British Isles or, as the Irish delicately call them, 'these island'', there are places of indeterminate status, the Isle of Man and the Channel Islands, possessions of the British Crown, yet not formally part of the UK.

This rather haphazard state building illustrates well the British genius for pragmatism in constitutional matters. That is, if they can find a method of governing that works, they care little about abstract principles or legal/constitutional theories. The same applies to the development of the state as an institution and set of practices. There is no theory of the state as an institution separate from and above society in British thought. Nor is the constitution written down in codified form or interpreted by judges. Instead it consists of institutions and practices which have evolved over the years, are generally understood and respected but are capable of change where needed. Central to British practice is the constitutional convention. This is an unwritten understanding as to procedure, hallowed by precedent and practice. So it is understood, but nowhere written in law, that the monarch will appoint as prime minister the leader of the majority party in the House of Commons, or that a government will resign if defeated in a confidence vote in the House. All constitutions rely on conventions and precedents to help interpret them. What is unique in the British case is their preponderance and the absence of any special constitutional law above the ordinary law and changeable only through special procedures. Even those constitutional matters which are written down take the form of ordinary laws which can be changed at the whim of the legislature.

This reliance on an unwritten constitution has historical roots. Britain never experienced revolution or foreign invasion, requiring it to define anew the scope of political authority and the division of powers. Instead, its progress to democracy took the form of gradual, if often conflictual, evolution. Even the union with Scotland in 1707 which abolished both existing Parliaments and established a new one, was interpreted as an evolution, with the new Parliament taking on all the powers and traditions of its English predecessor. In the nineteenth and early twentieth centuries, challenges from the middle class, the working class, religious dissenters and peripheral nationalists were successively accommodated by gradually extending the franchise, bringing the dissenters into the Parliament in London and making *ad hoc* concessions. The whole process was greatly aided by the peaceful and non-revolutionary nature of these challenges themselves. The industrial working class, the first and largest in Europe, rejected Marxist or anarchist ideas of wholesale change in favour of a strategy of gradual reform through trade unions and the Labour Party. Procedural consensus, that is agreement on how politics is to be conducted, was reinforced by substantive consensus, that is a large measure of agreement on the actual issues. So the stakes of politics were reduced and relations of trust established and a practice of peaceful alternation of parties in government established. Only in Ireland did the regime fail, resulting in the secession of 1922 and a continued problem of political authority in Northern Ireland.

The UK is not a state-centred society on the continental mode. Absolute monarchy was defeated in the seventeenth century without ever establishing a strong, centralized bureaucracy and power passed to a parliamentary oligarchy which also preferred to govern through local agents in the counties and cities. Later this evolved into a liberal democracy, while preserving the independent institutions of civil society. The professions are self-regulating, as is the financial centre of the City of London. Even institutions funded largely by the state, like the universities, local government or the BBC (British Broadcasting Corporation) are not formally part of the state apparatus but autonomous bodies, with a degree of independence from political control. Private interests are well organized and traditionally free from state regulation. When the trade unions were legalized in the early twentieth century, they were not given a set of rights and duties under law but it was simply recognized that certain of their activities were beyond the purview of the law and the state. This independent civil society has aroused much admiration from continental observers brought up in the statist tradition[1] but has attracted increasing criticism from those who see it as creating too many vested interests and obstacles to change.

Britain's uncodified constitution and the role of convention can make it difficult to identify the bases of power. The task is not made easier by the national reluctance to abolish institutions which have outlived their usefulness or whose powers have fallen into disuse. Endless debates take place on the role of the House of Lords or the prerogatives of the monarch in the case of a Parliament in which no party has a majority. A nineteenth-century observer, Walter Bagehot, saw this indeed as the very genius of the British constitution. Bagehot made a famous distinction between the efficient elements, those with real power and the dignified elements, the ceremonial ones like the monarchy and the House of Lords which were most visible but least important in practice. The dignified elements, according to Bagehot survived not merely because nobody had got round to abolishing them, but to dazzle the spectator and hide the reality of power. Power itself was continually retreating into hidden places behind the dignified facade.

Yet there is a starting point in exploring the maze, one firm constitutional principle, that of parliamentary sovereignty. This means that, in the absence of a written constitution, Parliament is subject to no higher law and can do whatever it chooses. Technically, Parliament consists of the monarch, the House of Lords and the House of Commons. In practice, democratization has shifted power within Parliament, from the monarch, whose role is now ceremonial and the Lords, whose powers were cut down after a confrontation in 1910, to the elected House of Commons. The rise of disciplined political parties has produced another shift, already noticed by Bagehot in the last century, to the party leaders. As long as a party has a majority in the House of Commons, it controls the full power of parliamentary sovereignty. Since under Britain's parliamentary system the leadership of the majority party forms the government, this gives governments an enormous amount of authority. The non-proportional electoral system sustains two-party politics and usually guarantees governments with parliamentary majorities. The opposition is less interested in restraining the power of government than replacing it and exercising power itself. Some observers have taken this argument further, noting that the government is chosen by the prime minister, so that it is a single person who wields the full power emanating from the constitution. The concentration of political authority remains the striking feature of British constitutional practice.

Yet there are limits on prime ministerial and governmental power. Some of these are derived from the reality of governing in a complex society where policies do not always produce the results expected. Others arise from convention and the strength of civil society rather than formal constitutional provisions. It is this concentration of formal authority together with the practical dispersion of power which is the really distinctive feature of the British constitution. These two apparently contradictory principles could co-exist as long as there was consensus on the broad lines of policy and tolerance for opposition. In recent years, they have come under increasing strain.

At one time, Britain's constitutional arrangements were regarded as a model for the world, combining strong government with liberty, constitutional consensus with flexibility and the capacity to adapt, all underpinned by a culture of tolerance and compromise. The years during and after the second world war marked the high point of British consensual politics. In 1945 the Labour Party was elected for the first time with a majority government and brought in the main provisions of the welfare state, nationalized key industries and assumed responsibility for full employment. Returning to office in 1951 the Conservatives left most of this intact. Decolonization, started under Labour with the independence of India, was continued with the liberation of African possessions so that by the mid-1960s the British Empire was no more. In contrast to France, the British offered little resistance to decolonization and, while leaving severe problems behind, provoked no deep divisions at home. Yet already in the postwar years, Britain faced two serious problems which were to challenge its institutions. First was the question of its international role with the end of Empire and in a world dominated by two superpowers. Successively toying with the idea of a world role through the Commonwealth (the former Empire) and a special relationship with the United States, the UK eventually opted for membership of the European Community but without ever committing itself wholeheartedly to Europe. Second was the problem of economic decline. As early as the 1880s, observers had noted that Britain's industrial might had fallen behind the USA and Germany. By the 1980s, most of western Europe enjoyed higher living standards.

This forced a reappraisal of the British system and a questioning both of its real effectiveness and of its democratic credentials. For all the concentration of power, British governments have been unable to solve the country's economic problems, address social tensions or decide on its place in the world. Interpretations of British decline vary. One school of thought, prominent in the 1960s, blamed it on outmoded institutions. There followed a wave of institutional reform, affecting the Civil Service, organization of central government, economic planning, regional planning, local government, the health service, industrial policy and training. Right-wing commentators have blamed the excessive role of government following the postwar settlement and the power of trade unions. The call for rolling back the state and deregulating the labour market. Left-wing observers blame the failure of British management to develop an entrepreneurial culture, the excessive weight of the financial sector, the rigid class system and the outmoded Civil Service. In the 1980s, radical policy solutions were being canvassed on both left and right, ranging from wholesale nationalization and state control to the privatization of just about everything. Meanwhile, failure to achieve the same levels of growth as its competitors sparked off social tensions, including class conflict, strikes and later urban disturbances. Support for the main parties declined and old territorial tensions re-emerged in Northern Ireland, Scotland and Wales. All of this placed the old substantive and procedural consensus and the conventional mechanisms of government under serious strain.

In the 1980s, the Thatcher government embarked on a radical programme aimed at reducing the role of the state in the economy while reinforcing its authority in other dimensions. Independent institutions of civil society like local government, trade unions, the universities and the BBC found their autonomy reduced. The consensus politics of the old constitutional settlement was explicitly rejected. European integration significantly modified the reality of parliamentary sovereignty though governments were very slow to admit this. A reassertion of nationalist sentiment in Scotland posed questions for the unitary state. Northern Ireland presented an insoluble problem. Large sections of the professional classes had become alienated from the authoritarian style of the Thatcher government and its lack of respect for the institutions of independent civil society in the professions, the media, education and local government. Britain's secretive form of government was under attack as undemocratic and inefficient. All this produced a movement for constitutional reform, in the interests of both efficiency and democracy. The main items involved are a written bill of rights, decentralization to regions, nations and local communities, open government, proportional representation and a more positive attitude to European unity. Both the actions of the right-wing radical administration and the constitutional reform movement which reacted to it have placed a question mark over the British model.

Government and Prime Minister

Like other aspects of the constitution, the structure of British government has developed piecemeal over time, often without clear organizing principles. We can divide the administrative system into three elements, central government departments, local governments and special, or *ad hoc* agencies of various sorts but must remember that this provides only a simplified picture. While the UK is a unitary state with a centralized political system based on Parliament, it has a tradition of decentralized, or indirect administration. So instead of the large centralized bureaucracies found in France and some other European states, there are rather small central departments headed by politically appointed ministers, with administration devolved to local government and agencies of various sorts. This reduces the administrative load on the centre and, by allowing departments to concentrate on policy issues and politically sensitive matters, affects the workings and ethos of central government. Local governments, generally known as local authorities, are elected bodies and will be discussed later. Agencies take a variety of forms. Nationalized industries and public utilities are entrusted to nominated agencies with a degree of operational independence from government, but since the 1980s this category has almost disappeared as a result of privatization. More important now are the agencies which have been hived off from government departments in order to undertake administrative and managerial tasks, a development considered below.

Departments are typically headed by ministers. Senior ministers are known as secretaries of state, though some have ancient titles like Chancellor of the Exchequer, in charge of finance and economic matters, Lord Chancellor, in charge of justice and the courts or Lord Privy Seal, a term of convenience for a minister who may be entrusted with any task. Ministers are assisted by permanent civil servants but are personally responsible to Parliament for anything done by their departments, though this principle has become increasingly difficult to enforce over the years. The most important ministers, including all the heads of departments, sit in the Cabinet which usually has about 20 members. Middle-ranking and junior ministers are not members of Cabinet but assist their senior colleagues within the department and in dealing with Parliament. All ministers must be members of Parliament, in either the House of Commons or the House or Lords. In practice, members of the House of Lords have become much less common in government, except for certain offices where it is obligatory, Lord Chancellor and Leader of the House of

Lords. Ministers are chosen by the prime minister who, by convention, can appoint and dismiss at will. The Labour Party has a rule to the effect that when it comes into government, the members of its elected shadow Cabinet must be appointed to Cabinet, but this does not prevent the new prime minister from dismissing and reappointing subsequently. Politics in Britain is a professional career and a ministerial hopeful must serve a long apprenticeship before making it to Cabinet. Gaining a seat in Parliament may require service in local government or fighting an unwinnable constituency to demonstrate loyalty to the party before finding a 'safe seat'. Then time must be served on the backbenches before promotion to the junior office and finally to Cabinet itself. If the party is in opposition matters will take even longer, awaiting an election victory. In contrast to other countries, it is virtually impossible to drop out of British politics when prospects are poor and then come back again. Anyone with serious ambitions must get into Parliament and stay there until their time comes. Consequently, ministers are typically in their 50s, with some 10 to 15 years in Parliament behind them before promotion to Cabinet. They may not be trained managers or specialists in the work of their department, but they are by definition experienced political survivors.

In principle, Cabinet is the central, directing body of British government credited by the Haldane Committee of 1918 with the roles of determining the policy to be submitted to Parliament, the supreme control of the national executive and the coordination and delimitation of the activities of government departments. This makes the British executive a collective one, a notion reinforced by the doctrine of collective responsibility by which all ministers are responsible for the actions of the government and must support them in public. In practice, this role has become almost impossible to fulfil. Cabinet meets only once or twice a week, and much of its time is taken up with routine business. It is too large to function as a cohesive executive and ministers tend to be absorbed in their own departmental work and ill-briefed on other aspects of government policy. It does not work by voting or counting heads but by discussion leading to consensus, in which the more powerful ministers, if they are supported by the prime minister, tend to get their way. There are occasions when Cabinet comes to life, for example when politically sensitive issues, on which all ministers are expert, come up, or during the annual public expenditure allocation, where they all have a direct interest in defending their own totals. For the most part, the work of Cabinet has retreated into committees comprising the ministers most directly involved. These are chaired by senior ministers or in important cases the prime minister, and their decisions are usually final. In order to preserve the fiction of Cabinet government, their responsibilities and membership were at one time kept secret but in recent years they have been publicly recognized. Some matters do not even make it to Cabinet committee but are handled through less formal arrangements among departments or between the prime minister and the relevant department. Some issues, notably on nuclear defence matters or matters of national security, are not even reported to Cabinet.

Observers have lamented the decline of collective Cabinet government with the consequent tendency for departments to go their own way, a lack of cohesion and a failure to consider government policy as a whole or its long-term implications. A number of solutions have been tried. In the 1960s and early 1970s, departments were amalgamated into giant"superministries', with the intention of reducing the number of ministerial heads and thus the size of Cabinet. With large departments covering whole coherent areas of government, it was thought that issues could be settled within them, freeing Cabinet for the more important matters. Yet the giant departments proved unwieldy and prime ministers were soon tempted to hive off new ones, either as a political gesture to the importance of an issue, like prices or energy, to cut down the power of certain ministers or to satisfy interest groups who wanted to have 'their own' department back. The fate of the Department of Trade and Industry illustrates the process well. Consolidated in 1970, it had been broken down five years later into Trade, Industry, Energy, and Prices and Consumer Protection, with other parts going to the Scottish and Welsh Offices.

Another proposal was to establish a central policy analysis capacity, allowing Cabinet a source of intelligence independent of the individual departments and capable of taking a broad view across government activity and a long view into the future. This was realized in the Central Policy Review Staff (CPRS), set up in 1970 and consisting of a small team of civil servants and outsiders. While the CPRS did some useful studies of policy issues, it aroused resentment among ministers and departmental civil servants and went into decline after its founder, Prime Minister Edward Heath, lost office. Neither Labour Prime Minister James Callaghan nor his Conservative successor Margaret Thatcher were sympathetic to academic analysis offered by the CPRS and shortly after coming into office Thatcher abolished it. They relied instead on a second unit set up in the early 1970s, the prime minister's policy unit, serving not the Cabinet as a whole but the prime minister individually.

Much of the gap left by Cabinet government has been filled by the rise of the office of prime minister. Already by the 1960s observers were debating whether Britain had a prime ministerial rather than a Cabinet system of government and, after the experience of the Thatcher administration the consensus was that it had. This is a complicated issue to resolve, given the secrecy of decision making in Britain and the reticence of former ministers in giving frank accounts of their experiences. Certainly, the British prime minister possesses great powers, but each of them must be qualified in practice to give a balanced picture. In principle, the prime minister has absolute power in the appointment and dismissal of ministers and the allocation of responsibilities.

This would seem to provide unlimited control over Cabinet since close allies could be appointed and dissenters excluded. Yet there are practical constraints. The pool of available ministers, limited to experienced members of the majority party in Parliament, is rather small and not all of these have the required managerial ability or even ambition. A prime minister must ensure a Cabinet majority loyal to his/her own policies but at the same time include powerful individuals or faction leaders within the party, who otherwise might make trouble on the backbenches or in party meetings. Some of these will have prime ministerial ambitions of their own. Geographical and sectoral considerations also arise, especially under Labour, which must balance its rather varied internal factions and sections by giving them places in the government.

A prime minister's freedom to appoint ministers also depends on the government's political standing. After an election victory, it may be possible to reshuffle the government freely and pack the government with close supporters, even sycophants. In mid-term, with the opinion polls unfavourable and government under pressure, a prime minister may be forced to bring in competent and powerful individuals with their own views on policy. The process can be seen under Margaret Thatcher. In 1979, newly elected, she appointed to Cabinet many members of the more liberal wing of the Conservative Party, to whom she herself had given the contemptuous label 'wets'. By 1983, feeling stronger, she had been able to drop Norman St. John Stevas, Ian Gilmour, Mark Carlisle, Christopher Soames and Francis Pym, along with Lord Carrington, who had resigned over the Falklands invasion but had long been suspect by the Conservative right. She ensured that her own supporters held the key offices of Chancellor of the Exchequer and Foreign Secretary and sent the powerful 'wet' ministers James Prior and Peter Walker into political exile in the Northern Ireland and Welsh Offices. By the late 1980s, with the economy deteriorating and the government in political trouble, she was obliged to bring in new ministers who did not share all her own convictions. Eventually it was the resignations of powerful ministers Nigel Lawson and Geoffrey Howe which precipitated her downfall.

A prime minister also wields enormous power through the conduct of government and Cabinet. It is the prime minister who chairs the Cabinet and sums up its conclusions, with ordinary ministers rarely daring to dissent. From what we know of Cabinet proceedings, the style varies, with some prime ministers encouraging free discussion before proceeding to a conclusion and others, more domineering, declaring their position beforehand and inviting ministers to agree. Matters can be taken out of Cabinet altogether and entrusted to ministerial committees or partial Cabinets, also nominated by the prime minister, or simply settled between the prime minister and the minister directly concerned. Ministers who are not trusted but whose presence in the Cabinet is essential for political reasons can be by-passed, as happened with Tony Benn under the Wilson government in the 1970s. Once a decision is taken, whether in full Cabinet, committee or by prime ministerial fiat, all ministers must support it in public or resign. In the British system, resignation from Cabinet is usually a form of political suicide, since ministers rarely come back. Since 1964, only two Cabinet ministers have resigned and subsequently come back to office, Cecil Parkinson, a protégé of Margaret Thatcher whose second coming was short-lived, and Michael Heseltine, whose challenge to Thatcher was the cause of her downfall and who was able to impose himself on her successor, John Major. Resignations and comebacks among junior ministers are slightly less rare and may be useful to mark out a politician as a person of principle, but even these are not common. Collective responsibility makes heavy demands on politicians who may be out of sympathy with a policy but must defend it in public. This rule of secrecy is tempered by the unofficial practice of the leak, in which ministers let it be known through parliamentary journalists that, whatever they may say in public, they are dissenting in private. There is an elaborate code for media stories signalling dissent, with phrases such as 'sources close to the minister' or 'informed sources' indicating to those familiar with the terminology just where the information has come from. Prime ministers regularly denounce leaks as a threat to cohesive government and collective responsibility, but their usual motive is not to stop leaks altogether but to keep a monopoly on leaking for themselves.

Table 2.1 British prime ministers since 1945

Prime Minister	Party	Period
Clement Attlee	Labour	1945-51
Winston Churchill	Conservative	1951-55
Anthony Eden	Conservative	1955-57
Harold Macmillan	Conservative	1957-63
Alec Douglas-Home	Conservative	1963-64
Harold Wilson	Labour	1964-70
Edward Heath	Conservative	1970-74
Harold Wilson	Labour	1974-76
James Callaghan	Labour	1976-79
Margaret Thatcher	Conservative	1979-90
John Major	Conservative	1990-

Prime ministers vary in their activism. Some seek to control the whole of government, intervening regularly in the work of ministers and departments. Examples would be Neville Chamberlain or Margaret Thatcher. Others, such as Clement Attlee, are content to appoint competent ministers and let them get on with the detailed policy work. Yet even the most activist prime minister cannot control all aspects of government. The range of matters is too large and the prime minister does not have the time. Nor does the prime minister possess a substantial department, with advisors to shadow the work of ministers. There is the Cabinet Office, with its secretary, who works closely with the prime minister, but the office is rather small and is also responsible for servicing Cabinet and its committees, preparing agendas, circulating papers and recording minutes. The policy unit already mentioned briefs the prime minister on key issues and may try to second guess departments. Essentially, though, the prime minister depends on the main ministerial departments for information and advice, limiting his/her room for manoeuvre.

British prime ministers also benefit from the personalization of power which has marked modern democracies. Television has concentrated attention during elections on the prime minister and would-be prime minister, who take credit or blame for victory and defeat. Members of Parliament know, and are reminded if they forget, that they owe their seats to the prime minister. Foreign travel and photo-opportunities with world leaders further boost the prime minister's image. Yet not all election campaigns are presidential-type contests between party leaders. The 1992 campaign marked a return to party-based politics as the two main parties realized that their leaders were not their most formidable electoral assets. Even the most powerful prime minister remains dependent on the support of his/her party. It is very difficult to remove a sitting prime minister since dissidents are usually disorganized and potential successors do not want to risk dismissal or accusations of disloyalty by openly plotting; but, if the party considers the incumbent to be an electoral liability, it can usually find a way. In 1990, the Conservative Party and Cabinet demonstrated this to dramatic effect in its ruthless removal of Margaret Thatcher. The whole episode, from declaration of a challenge by Michael Heseltine to the installation of the new prime minister, John Major, took barely two weeks.

Parliament

Parliament is in one sense at the very heart of the British constitution. In the absence of a written constitution, a system of fundamental law or a doctrine of popular sovereignty, it is the monarch, Lords and Commons, collectively comprising Parliament, which is the basis of all authority. Yet in practice, Parliament as an institution plays a more limited role in governing Britain. The monarchy, which is hereditary, has long lost power and become a 'dignified' element of the constitution, a symbol of national unity and a means of providing a head of state outside political controversy. This has the useful effect of preventing government leaders wrapping themselves in the flag and presenting attacks on them as assaults on the nation itself, as can happen where the functions of head of state and government are combined. The corollary of this is that the monarch and the royal family must stay resolutely out of political conflict. The House of Lords, comprising hereditary and appointed members

Table 2.2 Parties Represented in British Parliament, 1992	
Party	Seats
Conservative	336
Labour	271
Liberal Democrat	20
Scottish National	3
Plaid Cymru (Welsh)	4
SDLP (N.Ireland)	4
Ulster Unionist	9
Ind. Unionist	1
Democratic Unionist	3

has also largely been relegated by the advance of democracy to the ceremonial side of the constitution, though occasionally making its voice heard. So the power of Parliament essentially has come to reside in the elected House of Commons. The rise of disciplined parties has in turn taken power out of the Commons as an institution and concentrated it in the hands of the governing majority.

Unlike American legislatures, the House of Commons is not a place where issues are decided by the free votes of members. Nor does it serve as a counterbalance to the power of the executive. Rather it is a forum where government mobilizes a loyal majority to put through legislation, while the opposition mounts a consistent critique aimed not at preventing or changing government proposals but at preparing the way to become the government itself. This system is known as adversary politics, the confrontation of two organized political forces which do not share power but alternate in office. The adversarial nature of the system is symbolized by the chamber itself which is not a hemicycle but a rectangle divided by an aisle with government and opposition facing each other across it. At the front sit the party leaders, known as the front bench; behind them are their followers, the backbenchers.

In fact, there have always been more than two parties in Parliament. In 1992, there were nine, as shown in Table 2.2. Yet the simple plurality electoral system ensures that the great bulk of the seats goes to the two main parties, one of which normally has an overall parliamentary majority. In this case, the governing party controls not only the results of parliamentary votes but the timetable and procedure of the House itself. Party discipline is ensured by a system of whips, members appointed to ensure that their colleagues turn up and vote the party line. Voting is in person and, in a characteristically archaic fashion, involves all MPs trooping through a lobby where they are checked off by the tellers. Members do not need to be in the chamber during debates and the parties have arrangements whereby those with business elsewhere can be paired with a member of the other party to cancel each other out. Those members who have not been paired are summoned to votes by division bells, which sound in the chamber, in the hallways, in members' offices, and even in an adjacent bar patronized by MPs, and must come running. Anyone defying the whip will by summoned to explain him/herself and in extreme cases face withdrawal of the whip, that is suspension from the party caucus. Yet it is not awe of the whips or their disciplinary measures which keeps MPs loyal to the party line but a deep sense of solidarity with their own side. However unhappy an MP may be with the party line, it will rarely justify giving aid and comfort to the enemy by deserting it in a vote. MPs know too that their electors did not really vote for them personally but for the party label which they bear and that indulging their personal preferences in votes is not only breaking this understanding but could put at risk the party endorsement essential for their re-election prospects. Those ambitious for office may call attention to themselves through a few principled rebellions against the party line, but generally will be keen to ingratiate themselves with the leadership. For a large section of both main parties, party loyalty is second nature and needs no further incentives or discipline. MPs do sometimes rebel, especially in matters which divide their parties, such as Europe or devolution in the 1970s, and some observers have claimed that they are becoming a little less disciplined, yet party solidarity is still overwhelming.

A cynic might comment that this makes the British Parliament entirely redundant and that it could be replaced by elections every five years to install the government, after which MPs could return to more useful employment, allowing ministers to carry on. This would be too severe, for Parliament remains central to the British political process, however much it may be criticized. Four principal roles can be distinguished: setting the agenda for public debate, legislation; scrutiny of government; and recruitment of ministers.

As a forum for debate, the British Parliament is at the centre of public life to a greater extent than in most liberal democracies. It is not that most citizens read the accounts of debates published in the record, but a great deal of parliamentary activity does emerge, filtered through the media, in the form of news stories. The effect is most striking when Parliament is not sitting. Then political life slows down, the media filling in with 'silly season' stories such as sightings of the Loch Ness Monster or the mystery of corn circles. Governments themselves recognize the importance of Parliament by trying to issue embarrassing statements or statistics in the recess or at the very end of the session to deprive the opposition of the chance of making political capital. The effectiveness of Parliament as a forum for public debate, however, is questionable. It still has some of the atmosphere of a gentlemen's club, meeting in the afternoons and evenings and sometimes long into the night but resisting morning sessions. Newspaper reporting of parliamentary proceedings was only achieved after a long struggle in the last century and an ancient rule still allows members to cause disruption by crying 'I spy stranger" and calling for the public and press galleries to be evacuated. It took twenty years of argument before television cameras were allowed in 1989, with opponents charging that it would upset the intimate atmosphere of the House, encourage members to perform for the viewers or even scandalize citizens with sights such as MPs lounging with their feet up on the benches in front of them. Even now strict rules govern television coverage, which must focus only on the member speaking at the time and not show the reactions of other members or the empty benches which the orator is often addressing.

The process of legislation in the British Parliament is largely dominated by the government, which initiates the great majority of successful bills and rarely sees its proposals fail. Each bill goes through a series of stages to passage. The first reading is largely formal, merely recording the bill's existence and title. Second reading consists of a set-piece debate on the floor of the House, involving all MPs in which the bill's general principles are presented and criticized. It then proceeds to a committee which, except in the case of constitutional measures like devolution or changes in the competences of the European Community, are taken in standing committees of between 16 and 30 members, chosen to reflect the party balance in the House as a whole. Here the bill is discussed clause by clause and amendments debated and voted upon. Since the format for committee debates is the same as that in the house, with government facing opposition and since the government has a majority, nearly all successful amendments are either proposed or supported by a minister. The bill is then reported back to the House and here further amendments can be taken. In practice, this allows government to mobilize its full parliamentary strength to reverse any defeats it might have suffered in committee. A third reading, largely formal, completes the bill's passage, after which it passes to the House of Lords to go through a similar process. If it is amended in the House of Lords, it must come back to the Commons which decides whether to accept the new amendments or reverse them. In theory, the bill can shuttle between the two Houses until agreement is reached but usually the Lords will give way. If not, then under the Parliament Acts it can be over-ruled.

There has been much criticism of the legislative process for spending too much time in rehearsing familiar party arguments and giving too little time to detailed scrutiny of measures. Even committee stage, which is supposed to examine bills clause by clause, tends to repeat the arguments at second reading, often spending days on the first few clauses and passing the rest of the bill unexamined. Unlike many other legislatures, the British Parliament does not take evidence from outsiders on bills or hire experts to help MPs interpret their complexities. The rigidities of the party system and the rarity of free votes make for strong government and help clarify the choice for electors; but they empty the legislative process of much of its meaning. These rigidities are slightly more relaxed now than twenty years ago. At that time the conventional doctrine that a government defeat on a major legislative issue required it to resign and hand over to the opposition or, more likely, call an election. This was changed under the minority Labour government of 1974-9, which refused to resign after losing votes on issues like devolution, incomes policy or budgetary items, instead calling for a vote of confidence the next day. Only on losing a confidence vote did it feel obliged to resign in 1979. This new convention has now become part of the constitution and has allowed backbench MPs of the governing party to be a little more adventurous in bucking the party line, knowing that the government's existence is not in danger, but it has not broken the party system itself. Critics still call for more genuinely free votes, with the whips removed. The House of Lords serves as a revising chamber and can help improve badly drafted legislation and even make the occasional breach in party solidarity, but its unelected composition is open to serious criticism in a modern democracy.

Parliament's third function is to scrutinize the work of government and hold ministers to account. Governments must retain the confidence of Parliament and can be brought down by a vote of no confidence and the principle that ministers are accountable, individually and collectively to Parliament, is fundamental to the constitution. Ministers are obliged to appear before Parliament regularly to defend their measures and answer questions. The rumbustious atmosphere of these sittings, which can scandalize observers used to the more sedate proceedings in the American Senate or the German *Bundestag*, provides a salutory experience for ministers. It is not possible for a British prime minister to confine public contact to orchestrated press conferences, or snatched questions from a media corps trailing around a golf course or shouting above the din of a departing helicopter. Instead, he/she must descend to the House of Commons to face the concentrated hostile questioning of the opposition's leaders, not to mention the barracking of its backbenchers. The need to answer in the House of Commons also ensures that ministers have a grasp of what is happening in their own departments, since a run of humiliating lapses in the House can mean the end of a ministerial career. Yet ultimately it is government which controls Parliament, rather than vice versa, through its majority and the mechanisms of scrutiny which Parliament possesses have been criticized as more an expression of party warfare than an effective way of probing the details of government activity.

A distinctive British contribution to parliamentary scrutiny, since adopted elsewhere, is the institution of question time. Twice a week in the case of the prime minister and by rota in the case of the others, ministers must come to the House of Commons to answer questions previously tabled by MPs. In appearance this is a powerful tool but in practice the scales are weighted heavily in the minister's favour. With the questions submitted in advance, civil servants are employed researching and framing answers to show ministers in the best light possible. So rather than being a means of unearthing information, questions, at least those for oral answer, are a means of trying to discredit ministers. This requires the questioner either to know the answer to the question already, the aim being to force the minister into an embarrassing revelation, or to use the one unrehearsed supplementary question allowed to follow up. Even here the minister has the advantage, since civil servants are also employed to anticipate supplementaries and have clever responses ready. In recent years, the habit has also developed of ministers planting sympathetic questions to be asked by sycophantic backbenchers on their own side, filling up the order paper and reducing the time available for the opposition. So question time falls into the familiar pattern of ritual struggle between government and opposition. The same is true of the opposition days, on which the opposition chooses the subject for a general debate.

The most promising innovation in the mechanisms for scrutiny has been the system of select committees. These are committees of backbenchers, also chosen to reflect the party balance of the House, with the task of investigating the work of government departments and policy issues. Unlike the standing committees on legislative bills, they are able to commission research, take evidence and call for persons and papers, that is ask ministers, civil servants and others to come and provide them with information. It took a long time for reformers to get investigative select committees accepted as a regular feature of Parliament, since traditionalists regarded them as a distraction from partisan debate while governments feared their potential for embarrassment. After some experiments in the 1960s and 1970s, a set of 14 committees was finally established in 1979 to match the main departments of government. An older institution is the Committee of Public Accounts, which, with the assistance of an official known as the Comptroller and Auditor General, examines past spending to see that moneys have been spent on the purposes for which they were voted and in the most efficient manner. There is also a select committee on European Community legislation and a select committee to consider the reports of the Parliamentary Commissioner for Administration, an official who, at the request of MPs, takes up cases of citizens aggrieved with their treatment by the administration.

Select committees have made a modest improvement in the parliamentary scrutiny of government but have disappointed their more eager advocates who wanted something on the lines of American congressional committees. The basic problem remains that of party loyalty. While some government backbenchers have developed an independent spirit, most are reluctant to embarrass ministers and easily persuaded to tone down critical reports. Able and ambitious MPs do not see select committee service as a route to government office but as a task taking them away from the floor of the house and confining them to detailed and humdrum matters. The more ideologically minded MPs still deprecate the painstaking detailed style of select committee work, preferring the rough and tumble of partisan debate where issues are simple and everything painted in black and white. Select committees by contrast have been favoured more by politicians in the political centre, as a means of promoting consensus politics and breaking down partisan prejudices. Ministers themselves have not encouraged the development of the system. It took reforming Leaders of the

House (the minister in charge of government's relations with Parliament) Richard Crossman and Norman St. John Stevas in the 1960s and 1979 to get the system going at all, but to make it work requires continuing cooperation. Ministers of both parties, however, have refused to appear before select committees, blocked their civil servants from giving evidence and hampered the gathering of information. Committees can request but themselves have no powers to force ministers and civil servants to attend or give evidence. For this they need a resolution of the whole House, which is of course controlled by the government. There is some evidence that select committees are being taken more seriously, especially by the newer generation of MPs, but they remain a minor element in the British system of government.

Parliament remains almost the only means for the recruitment of ministers, apart from a few cases of individuals appointed from outside and then sent to the House of Lords to give them a parliamentary base. As noted earlier, there is long apprenticeship required to rise to the top in British government and Parliament is where most of it is served. It is the parliamentary skills of debate, the ability to present a case or criticize the other side, which first brings promotion to the front bench. Even once in government, further advancement depends on parliamentary performance as well as managerial competence. Critics have asked whether a career spent in parliamentary debate is the best preparation for assuming the administrative responsibilities of a government department and lamented the narrowing of the pool of available ministers which results, but the tradition is extremely strong. On the rare occasions in the past when ministers have been brought in without long parliamentary experience, they have found life very difficult.

Despite the strength of the party system, there is a place for the humble backbenchers who account for about three quarters of the 651 MPs. Some are ambitious for office, planning their careers from the moment of arrival and working their way patiently up the hierarchy. Others are more ideologically minded, seeing politics rather than government as a way of life, unwilling to accept the compromises of office and cultivating followings outside Parliament. Some of these remain rebels all their lives, while others mellow with age and come into government. A substantial group comprises party loyalists, many of whom have come up through local government and entered Parliament rather late, for whom being an MP represents the culmination of a career rather than the beginning. Finally, there are part-time members, pursuing parallel careers in law or the city and staying away from the more burdensome chores like committee service. These members, whose requirements explain a great deal of the character of Parliament, such as the hours of sittings, are becoming much less numerous as politics becomes a full-time profession and career. Backbenchers have occasional opportunities to propose laws, especially in sensitive areas where the parties fear to tread such as capital punishment in the

1960s, divorce law or abortion. Here governments are prepared to step aside, allow free votes and even provide parliamentary time to allow the House to take its own decisions.

All members have demanding roles as constituency representatives, holding regular 'surgeries' at which constituents can come and present their grievances for transmission to ministers. Compared with their counterparts in other countries, British MPs are lamentably ill-equipped for these roles. Only recently have they all been given offices. Until the 1970s they could be seen in the corridors dictating letters to secretaries balancing typewriters on their knees. They have a limited allowance for secretarial and research expenses but do not retain a staff or offices in their constituencies. Any suggestion that facilities could be improved arouses the censorious ire of the popular press and an embarrassed retreat by MPs who, for the most part, are content with their modest lot.

The House of Lords, the upper House of Parliament, is of minor importance. Although volumes have been written on its composition, role and powers its existence can only be explained by the British reluctance to change or abolish institutions which have outlived their usefulness. Certainly, if it did not exist, no-one would imagine inventing such an institution, consisting of hereditary peers, the traditional aristocracy whose title passes in the male line through generations; twenty-six bishops of the Church of England; twenty one judges known as Law Lords; and some 300 members appointed for life and known as life peers. No-one knows for certain how many hereditary peers there are since they never all turn up, though at critical moments there has been a flood of backwoodsmen arriving to vote on some issue about which they are particularly exercised. What is certain is that the vast majority are supporters of the Conservative Party. Life peers are appointed by the monarch on the nomination of the prime minister and there is a convention that the opposition parties should be allowed a share of these. Former Cabinet ministers have a customary right to be appointed. Others are appointed from the business world, the trade unions, education, the arts and even sport. It was the introduction of life peerages in 1958 which allowed women into the House of Lords though, given the existence of the hereditary peers and bishops, they form a very small proportion of the total. After 1964, governments stopped creating new hereditary peerages, and it was thought that the practice was now by convention dead, but in the late 1980s Margaret Thatcher resumed it.

The House of Lords last engaged in a serious struggle with the Commons in 1910, a battle which resulted in its powers being curtailed by the Parliament Act. A second Parliament Act in 1948 limited it further so that now it can delay bills only for one parliamentary session. It has no power to delay or amend money bills. Its powers are rarely used since the Lords recognize that to provoke a new confrontation would threaten their existence. Yet they have remained a minor irritant to Labour governments, especially near the end of the government's term or when its opinion poll ratings are low. Until the 1980s, they had never given Conservative governments any trouble but under the Thatcher government they started to raise some objections about government policy, especially with regard to local government. Numerous proposals for reform have been canvassed, affecting both powers and composition but no government has considered it worth the time and trouble to put them through. They have also been conscious that any reform to make the composition more democratic would give the Lords greater legitimacy and encourage them to use their powers more. It is easier to leave them as a democratic absurdity and trust that they will never feel confident enough to challenge the elected government. The option of simple abolition has its supporters but there are doubts as to whether this could be put through under the Parliament Act and profound differences over what to put in its place. So the upper House survives, more as a dignified than an efficient element of the constitution.

PARTIES AND ELECTIONS

Central to the British political tradition is the two-party adversary system of politics in which the two major political formations contest for control of Parliament and thus government. Because of the simple plurality (that is non-proportional) electoral system, the winning party normally gains an absolute majority of the seats and govern alone. The other main party becomes the opposition, mounting a continual criticism of the government and preparing to assume power in its turn. Britain's entire constitutional arrangements, including parliamentary practice, Cabinet government and the control by ministers over bureaucracy are based on this two-party alternating mode of politics. There has never in fact been a pure two-party system. Between the wars, as Britain moved from the Conservative-Liberal duopoly which had characterized the nineteenth century to the Conservative-Labour duopoly which marked the twentieth century, there was a period of three-party competition. Since the 1970s, there has been a consistent third-party challenge to the duopoly. There are also several minor parties, some of which are sufficiently concentrated geographically to win constituencies. Yet the electoral system penalizes third parties and minority parties heavily, so that even when they gather

Table 2.3 Seats in Parliament at 1992 election and hypothetical results with PR

	Actual Seats	Seats with PR
Conservative	336	275
Labour	271	237
Liberal Dem.	20	101
SNP	3	17
Plaid Cymru	4	3

substantial numbers of votes they find it difficult to break the duopoly of representation in Parliament. Table 2.3 indicates the differences in party representation in Parliament which would have resulted in 1992 if Britain had a system of proportional representation.

Elections are conducted by constituencies, of which there are 651. Officially voters choose not parties or national leaders, but merely their own constituency representative. Until 1970, this fiction was maintained to the point that party affiliation was not given on the ballot paper; parties had to devote a great deal of effort to ensuring that their electors knew the name of the party candidate. Now candidates are allowed up to six words of description in recognition of the fact that it is the party rather than the personality which interests the electors. In each constituency, the ballot papers are taken to a central point, the votes for the various candidates are added up and the one with the largest number is declared elected, irrespective of whether it is an absolute majority. The system produces several distortions in terms of the representation of parties in Parliament. In the first place not all constituencies are of equal size. Impartial parliamentary boundary commissions have the task of revising constituencies every ten to fifteen years to take account of population movements, but they work only on past and not on future movements so that new boundaries are rapidly out of date. Inner city areas which are losing population are thus over-represented and the expanding suburbs under-represented. As this systematically benefits the Labour Party, boundary changes are very controversial. In 1970 Labour Home Secretary Callaghan went so far as to use his parliamentary majority to vote down the boundary commission recommendations, using the impending reform of local government as a pretext. Remote rural areas are allowed lower population minima to prevent them being geographically too large. This is the only electoral provision which benefits the Liberal Democrat Party. There is further differentiation for the four constituent parts of the UK, which have their own boundary commissions and a guaranteed minimum of 71 seats for Scotland and 36 for Wales despite their falling share of UK population, an attempt to assuage nationalist feelings in those territories. At present Scotland has 72 seats, Wales 36, Northern Ireland 17 and England 524.

The over-representation of Scotland and Wales tends to help the Labour Party, and is the occasional subject of criticism from English Conservatives. Within each of the constituent parts of the UK, the boundary commissions have to try and keep constituency populations as close as possible to the average, but even here there are variations among city and rural areas, as already noted. The average parliamentary constituency in Scotland in 1992 had 54,369 voters, while the English average was 69,281. Within England, electorates ranged from 46,855 voters to 92, 913.

Even were all constituencies of the same population, the constituency-based system would still produce distortions in party representation, with only a

Table 2.4 Votes per MP for British parties, 1992 General Election	
Conservative	41, 811
Labour	42, 667
Liberal Democrat	300, 144
Scottish National	209, 852
Plaid Cymru	38, 598

rough correspondence between votes received and seats in Parliament. Since the only way to win seats is to win constituencies outright, small parties can gain a respectable proportion of the total national vote while coming on top hardly anywhere. This is the traditional fate of the Liberal Party. As Table A.2 (in appendix) shows, it has been able to score around 20 per cent in recent elections without gaining a substantial number of seats. In 1983, gaining almost the same proportion of the vote as Labour, the Liberal-SDP Alliance gained just 23 seats to Labour's 207. In 1992, the Welsh nationalists, being more concentrated, were able to win more seats than the Scottish nationalists, though there vote was much smaller. In that year, the number of votes per elected member for the mainland parties was as shown in Table 2.4.

Even for the major parties, distortions arise where a party piles up large majorities in its safe constituencies but falls behind its rival in the key marginal constituencies. In this way a party can gain a larger number of votes but end up with a smaller number of seats. This happened in 1951 and February 1974 when the party with the smaller vote was able to form the government (full results in appendix).

Another feature of the traditional British party model is that both main parties were fairly moderate, one a little left, the other a little right of centre, but with a substantial overlap in their policies and programmes. This reflected the consensual tradition and permitted an alternation of parties in power without upsetting the system of government itself or the neutrality of the Civil Service. It also ensured that there was no place for a specifically centre party, since the Conservative and Labour Parties competed to occupy the middle ground. At the same time, the major parties faced little competition on their extreme flanks. The Communist Party of Great Britain was an insignificant force, winning only three seats in its history, and extreme right wing parties, have been equally unimportant in electoral terms. The injustices of the electoral system were thus rendered more tolerable since few electors could complain that their views were systematically excluded in government. In the 1980s, however, the major parties moved away from the centre, Labour veering to the left and the Conservatives to the right. This opened up the centre ground to a revived Liberal Party, in alliance with a Labour splinter group, the Social Democratic Party. As the major parties moved back to the centre in the late 1980s, the Liberal Democrats, as they had become, were squeezed again.

Given the growth of third-party support since the 1970s it is not surprising that the electoral system has become an issue in British politics. The Liberal

Party and its successor have long supported proportional representation as the only means whereby they can make an impact in politics. They also take comfort from opinion polls showing that, if electors thought that their vote would not be wasted, they would be much more likely to support the Liberals. The large parties have opposed change, though from the late 1980s a section of the Labour Party, who noted that it is the Conservatives who have proved the big gainer from the existing system, was converted to electoral reform. Such a change would have radical effects in British politics. Since no party since the war has ever gained an absolute majority of the vote there would have been no majority governments under proportional representation. Instead, there would be minority governments unsure of their ability to get their legislation through Parliament, or coalitions as in Germany or the smaller European democracies.

Figure 2.1 Percentage vote in general elections, 1945-92

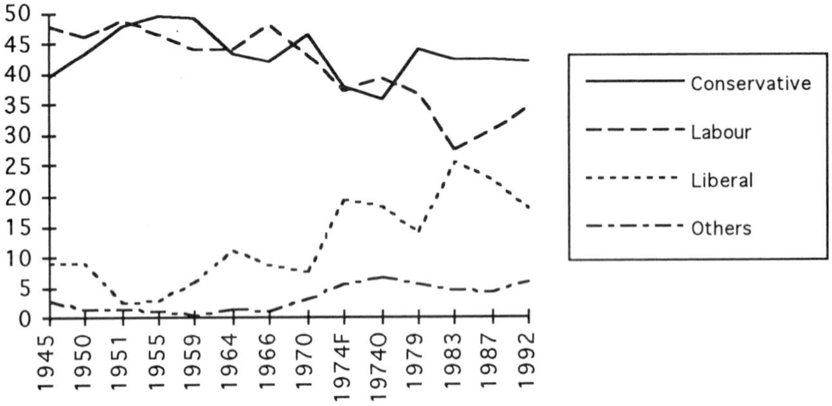

The Conservative Party

The British Conservatives are the most consistently successful right of centre party in Europe, having survived the transition to democracy and industrial society which left many of their continental counterparts behind. The party's secret has lain in its ability to adapt to changing social conditions and ideas while retaining its basic scepticism about change. The traditional British Conservative disdains ideology or grand schemes for social improvement, though an underlying set of ideas does sustain the party and its supporters. These ideas are a complex of elements, different aspects of which are emphasized at different times and which are not always entirely consistent. An essential element is belief in authority and the inequality of human beings. In traditional conservatism this takes the form of respect for order in state and society, support for traditional social institutions like the family, the school and the Church, and a belief in discipline and firm policies on law and order. There is scepticism about the possibility of social engineering or the perfectibility of human nature. Instead, Conservatives aim to manage society as it is, accepting necessary change but not leading it. This is underpinned by an emphasis on the rule of law, the need to obey duly constituted authority and for deviants to be sanctioned. Conservatives thus believe in a strong state, to preserve the existing order, not to change it. Of course, it is a great deal easier for a party which is in favour of the status quo and which has been in power for most of the twentieth century to preach the need to obey the law and respect the constitution. When out of office, Conservatives have occasionally been rather selective in their application of the rule of law. Just before the first world war, its leaders openly called for armed resistance to the legislation for Irish Home Rule and in the 1960s and 1970s many Conservatives openly supported the illegal regime in Rhodesia.

One branch of Conservatism is able to combine this attitude of support for the existing hierarchy with a paternalistic concern for the poor and powerless, derived not, like the socialist vision, from a belief in equality but from an aristocratic conception of social obligation. For true paternalistic Conservative, social policy is not a means of levelling the distinctions in society but a price which must be paid to maintain them. It is this philosophy which allowed British Conservatives to accept the welfare state after 1945, arriving, by a different route, at the same position as many continental Christian Democrats. A conflicting strand of Conservative thought, best described as *laisser-faire* liberalism, believes in the primacy of markets, opposes government intervention in economic or social affairs and is generally antagonistic to the welfare state.

Uniting Conservatives is a British nationalism which allows them to use the national flag as their party symbol and which at one time made the party the strongest supporter of an expanding Empire. This runs in some sections of the party to more or less disguised racism and hostility to immigrants other than those from the old white dominions. In the 1950s, the party leadership accepted decolonization but an old imperial element continually objected to the wind-up of Empire and the withdrawal of Britain from its world military role. In the 1960s, the party was converted to British membership of the European Community over the protests of this group but nationalism has never died away. By the 1990s a substantial section of the party had come out in open opposition to further moves to European integration as a threat to national sovereignty, though this was no longer dressed up in imperialist rhetoric. All sections of the party support a strong line on defence, though Conservative governments have sometimes had to preside over reductions in British military forces. Conservatives have traditionally been the party of the union, opposing home rule in Ireland, Scotland and Wales and insisting on parliamentary supremacy.

Yet until the 1980s, they also supported local government as an expression of traditional values of localism and often attacked Labour governments for their centralization.

These elements are combined in the Conservative Party in complex ways. All profess support for the market, for authority and for the nation yet the emphasis differs as do the proportions in which the elements are combined. Most Conservatives take their policies quite lightly, and the leadership can usually dress up its moves in appropriate language as long as the party is prospering electorally. In 1961-2 Harold Macmillan, who had already purged the party of many imperial illusions, was able to engineer radical changes on economic policy, planning, regional policy and Europe, with scarcely a murmur from the ranks. In 1972, Prime Minister Heath abandoned almost the whole of the programme on which he was elected and espoused a set of policies associated with the Labour opposition. So the party has not traditionally possessed the fixed ideological factions characteristic of more dogmatic parties such as Labour. Dissent within the party is signalled in elaborately coded speeches, invoking one or other of the party's dead heroes to evoke one tradition as against another, and which require careful translation. So a reference to Disraeli meant that the speaker wanted a more caring social policy; a reference to Churchill represented a complaint about Britain's lack of forcefulness in world affairs.

In the 1980s, more factionalism has emerged. For fifteen years the Conservatives were led by a highly ideological leader, Margaret Thatcher, who repudiated not only the postwar consensus but the work of previous Conservative administrations, notably those of Macmillan and Heath. Unlike previous Conservative leaders, Thatcher was a radical who believed that the postwar consensus needed not to be preserved but to be challenged. The conversion of the party to a more dogmatic position was aided by the appearance of a number of right-wing think-tanks in London, feeding ideas to the leadership and seeking to make converts among opinion formers. This emphasis on ideas, on radical change and the power of politics to alter human behaviour was a marked break with Conservative scepticism and opened up a divide between the traditional Conservatives, derided by Thatcher as 'wets' (meaning whimpish bleeding hearts) and the true Thatcherites who inevitably came to be known as 'dries.' Wets believe in a generous welfare state, some government intervention in the economy notably in industrial policy, and tend to support European integration. Dries favour rigorous monetarism in economic management, an aggressive programme of privatization and believe that the European Community should be no more than a free-trade area. Generally, the wets are more tolerant in racial matters. Many Conservatives hoped that the overthrow of Margaret Thatcher in 1990 would allow the party to abandon its ideological crusades and return to its traditional pragmatism. Yet the organized factions which had formed in the Thatcher years continued their efforts to convert the party to their causes. Examples are the Conservative Reform Group (wet), the No Turning Back Group (dry) and the Bruges Group (anti-European Community).

Conservative organization reflects the party's origins within Parliament and its traditions of deference and authority. Strictly speaking the Conservative Party comprises only the parliamentary caucus, with supporters in the country confined to auxiliary organizations. Within the party, the leader is dominant, making policy, appointing the parliamentary front bench and controlling the party organization. So strong is the mystique surrounding the Conservative leader that, until 1965, there was no formal election procedure, the new leader merely emerging from a process dominated by the party barons. After an undignified scramble for the succession in 1963, a procedure was adopted providing for the election of the leader by the Conservative MPs; later provision was made for the leader's removal. The logical consequence of the leader being invested with absolute power is that the party is quite ruthless at dispatching leaders who do not appear to be succeeding. In 1975 Heath was dispatched after losing three elections out of four and in 1990 the Conservatives became the first British party openly to force their own prime minister out of office, installing one of her Cabinet colleagues in her place.

Conservative support organization in the country is divided into two bodies. Central Office, a permanent bureaucracy, which employs constituency agents, organizes campaigns and disseminates policy documents, is headed by a chairman answerable to the leader. The National Association of Conservative and Unionist Associations is the voluntary, activist wing to which ordinary members belong. It holds the annual party conference which has no authority and serves more as a forum for leader-worship than for serious debate on policy. Representatives from constituency parties get the chance to let off steam, especially on emotive topics like race, immigration and capital punishment, and to mingle with the high and mighty. The leadership gets an opportunity for television publicity, boosting the morale of the troops and demonstrating their own popularity. One newspaper has even taken to publishing league tables of the standing ovations given to the leading party personalities, measured in terms of time and decibels! One prerogative, though, is jealously guarded by the constituency activists, the selection of parliamentary candidates. While the leader can purge the approved list of candidates to remove undesirables, selection of an individual from the list is the task of the constituency association and interference from Central Office is greatly resented.

Conservative MPs have always tended to come from upper-class backgrounds, though in recent decades the party has become more middle class. Representation of the titled aristocracy has fallen, along with the military and large landowners, their place being taken by managers and financiers. The last three leaders have all come from relatively modest middle-class backgrounds and have felt less sympathy with the traditional values of inherited privilege and hierarchy. In this way the Conservatives are becoming more of a party of meritocracy, believing in achieved inequality rather than inequality of birth, though this did not stop Margaret Thatcher resurrecting the practice of creating hereditary peerages abandoned by her predecessors.

The Labour Party

While the Conservative Party presents an image of unity behind timeless but flexible values, the Labour Party is self-consciously a coalition of ideologies and interests, in the social-democratic tradition. It was founded at the beginning of the twentieth century by three groups: advanced Liberals disillusioned with their party's inability to pursue a programme of radical reform, trade unions seeking parliamentary representation to reverse anti-union court judgements; and socialists of various sorts, from doctrinaire Marxists to Fabian gradualists. The party's constitution also reflects a coming together of diverse interests: the MPs, or parliamentary Labour Party; the trade unions; and the rank and file members or constituency activists. Certainly these have strong common interests in seeing Labour elected and pursuing policies of social reform, but their priorities often differ. For the parliamentary leadership, gaining power is the main object and since this requires it to appeal to moderate opinion and win over supporters of other parties, it often finds the unions and the activists an embarrassment. The unions have traditionally been concerned with maintaining their freedom to engage in collective bargaining with employers and less with broader aspects of policy. For the activists, the main reward for their work is psychological, the belief that they are creating a better world or constructing the socialist utopia. Were the majority of the electorate trade union members believing in socialism, these three sets of considerations would pull in the same direction and make electioneering rather simple. The problem for Labour is that this has never been the case and so balancing the needs of electability, the trade unions and the activists requires a party structure of Byzantine complexity, apparently highly democratic but in practice open to considerable manipulation.

At the centre is the party conference, the sovereign body which determines party policy and, in conjunction with the parliamentary party, elects the leader. Representation at conference is by affiliated organization, of which there are three types, trade unions, constituency parties and socialist societies. The political activity of trade unions is tightly regulated by law. To affiliate to the Labour Party, they must hold a ballot to establish a political fund and members must be given the opportunity to opt out of paying into the fund. With the fund, the union then affiliates for a given number of members, gaining a corresponding number of votes at conference. Constituency parties affiliate for the actual number of members who have chosen to join the party locally. Socialist societies, such as the Fabians, affiliate for their national membership which is very small and their vote is insignificant. The result is that the great majority of votes at conference are held by the large trade unions, with each union casting all its votes together in a block. Since there is no list of affiliated trade union members or means for them to express their views, the block vote is in practice wielded by the union leaders or the delegation to conference. There is no provision for the parliamentary party to be represented at conference and in theory it is the servant of conference policy, but in practice a leader with the support of the key union leaders can dominate the party. Richard Crossman, a Labour minister of the 1960s, put the matter more cynically:

> Since it could not afford, like its opponents, to maintain a large army of party workers, the Labour Party required militants - politically active socialists to do the work of organising the constituencies. But since these militants tended to be 'extremists,' a constitution was needed which maintained their enthusiasm by apparently creating a full party democracy while excluding them from effective power. Hence the concession in principle of sovereign power to the delegates at the Annual Conference and the removal in practice of most of this sovereignty through the trade union block vote on the one hand and the complete independence of the parliamentary Labour Party on the other.[2]

Between conferences, the party is administered by the National Executive Committee (NEC), itself elected in sections for trade unions, constituency parties, socialist societies and the women's section, with the leader and deputy leader members *ex officio*. Further complexity is introduced at the constituency level where local Labour parties also have the same composition, of trade union delegates, branch members, Socialist societies, and women's sections. So it is, possible, by being a woman trade unionist, and member of a Socialist society and branch party, to be represented four times over at party conference. A policy forum was introduced as part of the organizational reform in the early 1990s. This includes MPs as well as unions and activists and helps develop policy ideas outside the cumbersome mechanisms of the conference.

The leader of the Labour Party is chosen at conference by an elaborate system which gives the trade unions 40 per cent of the votes and the Parliamentary Labour Party (PLP) and constituency parties 30 per cent each. Candidates for the leadership must be MPs and have to be sponsored by a minimum number of fellow MPs. Unlike the Conservative leader, the Labour leader has no powers over policy or party appointments but must build political support in the PLP, among union leaders and in the NEC. In opposition this is a continuous task, depending on the personality of the leader, the balance of forces and the state of the party in the polls. In government, when the leader is prime minister, it is often totally neglected, the government simply ignoring the party and its policies where they are unpopular and seeking to appeal to the public direct. The very fact that the party leader is prime minister or leader of the opposition and thus prime minister in waiting itself gives an immense authority, as do the conventions of parliamentary government give the parliamentary parties a high degree of autonomy. Yet there is little personality cult in the Labour Party; there is more of a sense of shared responsibility and no Labour leader since 1935 has been driven out of office.

Labour is highly prone to factionalism and sustains an internal debate often more vitriolic than that between the party as a whole and its Conservative opponents. A major fault line divides those regarding themselves as the keepers of the socialist conscience on the left, and those who want to trim policy to appeal to the moderate voter to the right. In a deeper sense, this division is less about policy than about culture, between those who see Labour as a crusade, a permanent opposition movement, and those with a culture of government. Patterns of kinship and friendship are also important, with individuals drawn into circles in which they feel at home and adopting policy stances after. So gradually all issues become defined in left-right terms, even those like membership of the European Community, Northern Ireland or Scottish nationalism, which previously cut across it. The traditional Labour Party conference could not present a greater contrast with its Conservative counterpart, marked as it is by fierce debate, plotting in the corridors and laborious attention to the minutiae of resolutions, amendments and composites, that is resolutions from different groups which have been merged.

Between 1900 and 1951 Labour's vote steadily increased at every election but one, peaking at 48.8 per cent. It had a solid base in the organized working class and its collectivist ideas were widely accepted. Labour has never been as ideological a party as its continental counterparts and the influence of Marxism in it has been limited. Despite the views of some of its activists, the leadership has pursued a pragmatic and reformist route, believing in an expanded welfare state and an increased role for government in the economy through limited nationalization. It has portrayed itself as the party of the working class but never preached class warfare and has always been aware of the need to carry middle-class support with it. Between 1945 and 1951 the first majority Labour government laid the foundations of the modern welfare state and nationalized the main utilities and basic industries, changes which were largely accepted by its Conservative successor. In the 1960s it came back to power on a promise of modernization and national planning but was overwhelmed by its economic problems and failed to be re-elected in 1970. Between 1974 and 1979 a weak minority Labour government struggled with further economic crises and was defeated in its turn. These failures caused increasing tension within the Labour movement.

Both in the 1960s and the 1970s, Labour governments came into conflict with the trade unions as attempts to negotiate national agreements on wage limitation broke down and gave way to statutory wage controls. It was a spectacular series of strikes in the winter of 1978-9 which put paid to the Callaghan government's re-election prospects and paved the way for the anti-union policies of the Thatcher government. A new generation of union leaders, more politicized and left-wing, were more demanding in their relations with the party and, even where they made deals with Labour governments, could no longer control their own members. In the constituencies, activists were increasingly alienated by the Labour governments' policies of fiscal rigour, which produced real cuts in public expenditure in the late 1960s and late 1970s, and their subservience to the United States in foreign policy. Many urban constituency parties had atrophied in the 1960s, run by local bosses using the patronage supplied by council house tenancies and local government jobs, and relying more on manipulating union affiliations than attracting active members.

As party membership declined and the machines decayed with the end of patronage, these constituencies were easily taken over by unrepresentative cliques of the left. Trotskyite infiltrators from the Revolutionary Socialist League, insisting that they were no more than readers of the newspaper *Militant,* were joined by those of other minor groups. After the 1979 defeat, this produced a sharp swing to the left in party policy. Radical left-wing policies were adopted by conference and moderates removed from the National Executive Committee. A series of constitutional changes increased the power of the activists and conference at the expense of the Parliamentary Labour Party (PLP), transferring the election of the leader from the PLP to an electoral college constituted from the conference and requiring all MPs to submit to re-selection procedures before each election. Although these changes were put through in the name of party democratization, they really benefited the minority who were prepared to attend endless meetings, manoeuvre in the Byzantine world of constituency policies and secure election to the chain of committees from the local branch to national conference. Proposals which would have genuinely democratized the party by allowing ordinary members rather than constituency activists to select candidates or determine policy, or reducing the block vote, were rejected. In 1980, in the last leadership election under the old system, MPs chose veteran left winger Michael Foot in an effort to hold the party together. A radical election manifesto was put together providing for massive nationalization, state control, withdrawal from the European Community, unilateral nuclear disarmament and an array of issues down to the abolition of fox hunting. In 1981, a group of 35 moderate MPs defected to form the new Social Democratic Party.

The result was the worst election defeat in Labour's history. At 27.6 per cent of the vote Labour was barely ahead of the third party and was only saved from oblivion by the electoral system and its safe seats. Yet this was a turning point. Foot was replaced by Neil Kinnock, an MP with thirteen years parliamentary experience but who, unusually for a major British party leader, had never held government office. He was the only individual who was still able to gain election both to the Parliamentary Committee (elected by the PLP) and the constituency section of the NEC, as well as being acceptable to the trade unions. Like Harold Wilson before him, he was supported by the left and thus well placed to move the party back towards the right. This he proceeded to do, reasserting the independence of the PLP and its leading role in policy making, expelling members of the Militant tendency from constituency parties, and undertaking a major policy review. Nationalization was dropped and the principal privatization measures of the Thatcher government accepted. Withdrawal from the European Community and unilateral nuclear disarmament were abandoned. After the defeat of militant trade unionism in the miners' strike of 1984-5, trade union leaders also agreed to accept much of the legal regulation of unionism brought in under Thatcher. The party's image was changed through the efforts of public relations consultants. Party broadcasts emphasized the party's moderation and Kinnock's qualities as a leader, with soothing images replacing the stridency of the past. Indeed so successful was one Kinnock broadcast that it was plagiarized, down to the personal biography, by a contender for the American Democratic presidential nomination in 1984. Even conference was tamed and by 1990 was almost as stage-managed as its Conservative counterpart. Some genuine democratization was introduced into the party, in the belief that ordinary members would be more moderate than the activists. Parliamentary candidates are now selected by all party members in the constituency, not just the delegates from unions and branches, and the weight of the trade union block vote at party conference has progressively been reduced. Trade union influence has generally declined along with trade union membership. By 1992, they contributed 55 per cent the party's running expenses, down from a peak of 75 per cent. By that time, the largest single source of income was an elite of 28,000 well-off party members who each contributed £5 a week.

The results were a disappointment. As the 1992 election approached, Labour had high hopes, if not of obtaining an overall majority, at least of forming a minority government. In the event, it gained votes back from the Liberal Democrats but made no progress against the Conservatives who were returned for a fourth term. This was despite the fact that there was a serious economic recession, the government had made a series of political blunders, notably over the poll tax, the Conservative Party was seriously divided over Europe and the government in general and Prime Minister John Major, in particular, had fought an extremely uninspiring campaign. Some voices in the Labour Party urged that its whole image was out of date and that it needed to transform itself into a modern, reformist catch-all party, seeking inspiration in the election of Bill Clinton as president of the United States in 1992. The 'Clintonizatio' of the Labour Party would entail the abandonment of any residual reference to socialism and a very sharp turn to the right, though it is doubtful that even the most avid Labour revisionists would share Clinton's enthusiasm for capital punishment. Another group, drawn both from the old left of the party and the traditional centre, argued that by abandoning all ideals and principles, Labour would lose credibility and that, faced with two conservative parties, the electorate would continue to choose the genuine article. They argued that Labour needed big ideas. Some argued that Labour should renew its commitment to social and economic equality. Others emphasized constitutional reform. In particular, they urged that the party, since it appeared incapable of gaining a majority on its own, adopt proportional representation as policy. This would also facilitate an accommodation with the Liberal Democrats on lines already pioneered in the Scottish constitutional convention (discussed below). Others insisted that the party had in two elections brought the Conservative majority down from a hundred and forty to twenty and that one more heave would be enough to put it back in government.

After the 1992 election, Kinnock resigned as leader, and the party chose John Smith, from the traditional right of the party and the only member of the last Labour Cabinet still on the front bench, as leader. This seemed to represent a victory for the 'one more heave' school rather than those looking for a fundamental reform of the party on the lines of the French Socialists in 1971 or the Italian Communists in 1990. Smith continued the Kinnock programme of changing the party constitution, reducing the weight of the trade unions sharply. On other issues, he took a cautiously reformist stance.

The Liberals and the Centre

In the nineteenth century, the Liberal Party was one of the two major parties in British politics but in the interwar period it shrank to minor party status. It was unable to adapt to the rise of class politics, with one tendency pressing for a radical programme to compete with Labour for the vote of the newly enfranchized masses and another preferring to ally with conservatism against the rise of socialism. The party also suffered a series of splits on policy and personal issues and, after its last experience in government, the reforming administration between 1906 and the first world war, was unable to mount a serious challenge. So the Conservative-Liberal alternation gave way to the Conservative-Labour competition, while preserving the essence of the two-party system. The Liberals survived after the second world war as a minor party, effectively allied to the Conservatives who allowed them a free run in half a dozen seats with deep Liberal traditions where they were seen as the best obstacle to Labour. Their strongholds were among the middle class of non-conformist religion and in the Celtic fringe of the Scottish Highlands, rural Wales and south-west England, and parts of Lancashire. From the 1960s, though, they began to revive and, under the leadership of Jo Grimond, moved further to the left and set themselves the goal of reversing history to displace Labour as the natural alternative to the Conservative Party. As the two-party system faltered, there were Liberal revivals in every Parliament between 1955 and 1979, each one larger than the previous, and a series of spectacular by-election victories against both Labour and Conservatives. Yet the simple plurality electoral system prevented them making the breakthrough of which they dreamt at general elections.

On most social and economic issues, the Liberals stood between the Conservative and Labour Parties, a difficult position when the two major parties' own positions were so close. What was most distinctive about the Liberals was their approach to the conduct of politics. They stood for an end to adversary politics in favour of negotiation and compromise. Proportional representation in which they had an obvious self-interest, was presented not only as more democratic but as a means to end one-party dominance of Parliament and force parties to negotiate or form coalitions, compromising on policy matters. Liberals also favoured the dispersal of power through decentralization to elected assemblies in Scotland, Wales and the regions of England, a written constitution and bill of rights limiting the powers of government, and participation by workers in the running of industry. They were the strongest supporters of British membership of the European Community, which they saw as the basis for a federal united Europe. From the 1960s they adopted 'community politics', making progress in local government through their attention to local issues and neighbourhood mobilization which they contrasted with the bureaucratic indifference of Labour city councils. Given their belief in pluralism and democracy and their remoteness from power, Liberal organization had something of an anarchic quality about it. There was none of the deference of the Conservative activists, or the drilled discipline of the Labour Party block vote. Indeed, anyone could join the Liberal Party without necessarily paying a subscription and any member could turn up and vote at the party conference. The party consequently attracted a huge variety of people from the new leftists of the 1960s Young Liberals, through environmentalists and ban-the-bombers, to elderly middl- class elements who might have been at home in the Conservative Party.

Lacking experience in government or well-known leaders, the Liberal Party had long dreamed of splitting off a section of the Labour Party, constituting itself as a major party and letting the rest of Labour fade away as had the Liberals themselves in the interwar years. In 1981 the opportunity came with the defection of a section of the Labour right led by four former Cabinet ministers. By agreement with Liberal leader David Steel, these did not join the Liberal Party itself but sought to tempt the maximum number of Labour MPs and voters by establishing a separate party, the Social Democratic Party (SDP), allied with the Liberals but organizationally distinct. The ploy was only a partial success. Some thirty Labour MPs and one Conservative defected as did a section of the constituency activists but no trade union leaders came, while most prominent leaders of the Labour right remained loyal to their party. Attracting a flood of activists new to politics, the SDP soon acquired a distinctly middle-class, 'yuppy' image, its policies a mix of good intentions and political *naïveté*. Preaching the need to 'break the mould' of British politics by destroying the two-party system, their policies were in fact a recipe for remaking the old mould of consensus, centrist government which the Conservative and Labour Parties, by moving right and left, had abandoned. Although allied to the Liberals, they had differences in policy and emphasis, on defence, devolution and other issues. More importantly, there was a whole cultural gulf between the earnest, disciplined, centralized and well-dressed SDP and the libertarian, pluralist free-and-easy style of the Liberals which made for extremely bad relations at the level of the activists.

Given the polarization between the two major parties, the Liberal-SDP Alliance, representing the centre, did very well at the 1983 election, almost equalling the Labour vote. By 1987, things were more difficult. Voters were confused by the presence of two party leaders, David Steel (Liberal) and David Owen (SDP), and about the strategy of the Alliance. Owen had let it be known that in the event of a Parliament without a majority, he would favour allying with the Conservatives, a move which would be impossible to sell to the more radically-minded Liberal Party. Although the Alliance fell only a little short of their 1983 vote, they had lost their momentum and after the election they fell into acrimonious fighting over whether they should merge into a single party. Membership ballots in both parties favoured a merger but Owen refused to join and led a rump SDP, with three MPs and a diminishing band of activists until 1991 when the party disbanded and Owen called on the electorate to vote Conservative. The merged party, after a baffling series of name changes, decided to call itself the Liberal Democrats. It is arguable that the whole SDP episode was a failure. Labour was not split down the middle and survived as the main opposition party. Those moderates who had remained with it saw their policies triumph, giving the lie to those who said the party could not be reformed and must be destroyed. The Liberal Democrats by the early 1990s were doing no better electorally than had the Liberals on their own in the 1970s. Far from bringing over the working-class vote from Labour, the SDP had merely reinforced the centre's middle-class image. Yet the new party is more than just the old Liberals. It gained from the SDP and the Alliance experience a seriousness which it had lacked and started to think of itself as a party of government and not of permanent opposition. Significant strides forward were taken in local government, with the Liberal Democrats taking control of a number of councils, and holding the balance of power in many more, destroying in the process the Conservatives' hold on English county government. Organization in the new party is more formal and disciplined than in the old Liberal Party but reflects many of its features. It is a federal system, with separate parties for England, Scotland and Wales, and a federal party for the UK. All make policies though the final arbiter of national policy is the federal conference. The leader, who must be a member of Parliament, is elected by a postal ballot of all party members and the election manifesto is prepared jointly by the party executive and the parliamentary leadership.

Electoral Behaviour

For many years, electoral behaviour in Britain was dominated by social class. Labour, which came into being to promote the interests of the working class, took the largest part of the blue collar vote. The Conservatives, for their part, were strongest among the middle classes. Yet, even in the heyday of class voting, in the 1950s, this did not explain everything. There was always a substantial working-class Conservative vote, without which the party could not have won elections; and there was smaller but significant middle-class Labour vote. In recent years, the importance of class in voting in Britain as in other European democracies, has declined further. Fewer people are prepared to identify themselves in class terms or to vote according to their class identity.

Table 2.5 Percentage vote at British General Election, 1992

	Conservative	Labour	Liberal Democrat
Men	41	37	18
Women	44	34	18
18-24	35	39	19
55+	46	34	17
Professional	56	20	22
White-collar	52	25	19
Skilled worker	38	41	17
Unskilled worker	30	50	15
Owner occupier	49	30	19
Council tenant	24	55	15
Trade unionists	30	47	19

Source: C. Rallings and M. Thrasher, Sunday Times, 12 April 1992.

Class does, however, remain an important factor, as Table 2.5, derived from the 1992 election, shows. The Conservative vote declines and Labour's vote increases steadily down the social scale. The Liberal Democrat vote is more evenly spread but is rather stronger among the middle classes.

Another factor of some importance was religion. Members of the established Church of England tended to vote Conservative - the Church was sometimes described by its critics as the Tory Party at prayer. There is a strong Liberal tradition among non-conformists, that is members of the non-established Protestant Churches. In 1987, the Alliance were almost equal with the other parties among non-conformists. Catholics, in contrast to other European countries, have tended to vote Labour, especially in areas with a sectarian tradition such as the west of Scotland or north-west England. Here Catholics are often of Irish origin and have associated the Conservative Party with Protestant unionism and the British establishment. Religion is, however, of declining importance in voting choice as new generations of Catholics are more integrated into British society and less concerned with Ireland or historic wrongs. In the 1960s, Labour could count on the support of two-thirds of Catholic voters. By the 1980s it was well under half.[3] The number of voters declaring no religious affiliation has dramatically increased.[4]

Regional differences are also of importance. Wales and Scotland have long-standing anti-Conservative biases. In Scotland, this appeared to die out in the 1940s but reappeared from the late 1950s. Both Scotland and Wales have nationalist parties which provide a four-party pattern of competition. In Scotland in 1992, the two big parties between them gained less than two thirds of the vote. The "Celtic Fringe' of south-west England, northern Scotland and rural Wales have old Liberal traditions which are still very much in evidence. Sixteen of the twenty seats won by the Liberal Democrats in 1992 were in these areas. Big city politics has increasingly favoured Labour since the 1970s, though this at least partly results from the exodus of middle-class voters to the suburbs and small towns.

Gender, on the other hand, appears to be becoming less important as a differentiating factor. As in other European countries, the changing role of women and their greater involvement in the workforce has changed their political outlook. In the past they tended to be more Conservative in their voting than men, but in recent elections this factor has been moderated. In 1987, there was no gender gap at all in voting, though in 1992 a small bias towards the Conservatives reappeared among women .[5]

One of the key issues in contemporary British politics is the size of the state and the extent of public as opposed to private provision of services. The Conservative government after 1979 embarked on a programme to reduce the public sector which was motivated in part by a desire to reduce the electoral base of the Labour Party. Independent individuals, owning their own houses and having shares in industry would, it was argued, be unlikely to put this at risk by voting Labour. Nor would they be attracted by Labour promises to spend more on public services. It is very difficult to test this theory, since most people continue to use a mix of public and private services and it may be that people who buy shares in privatized industries would be the sort of people inclined to vote Conservative in any case. One sector, however, does provide evidence of the effect of patterns of service provision, that is housing. There is a strong tendency for people who own their own houses to vote Conservative, while those who rent from local councils tend to vote Labour (Table 2.5). Even working-class home owners were more inclined in 1992 to vote Conservative than Labour. This is one reason why the government's programme to sell off council houses at a discount to sitting tenants proved so politically explosive in the 1980s.

Electoral behaviour has become more volatile since the 1960s. The rise of third and fourth parties has given electors a greater choice and confidence in the old parties has diminished. The effects of this are obscured by the workings of the electoral system, which still produces majority party governments, albeit on smaller percentages of the vote. The 42-4 per cent of the vote which allowed the Conservatives to form majority governments in 1983, 1987 and 1992 was lower than that won by any *losing* party between 1950 and 1970. In 1983, the Conservatives won a majority of 140 seats with virtually the same share of the vote which it had had in 1966, the year of its worst defeat since 1945. There is evidence that voters are choosing parties at elections now rather than voting from habit for their usual one.[6] In this choice, an important part is played by perceptions of the performance of the government of the day and the state of the economy. Party leaders are also of importance, their status enhanced by the personalization encouraged by television campaigning. Before the 1992 election, the Conservative Party removed Margaret Thatcher as leader, installed John Major and was able to convince a large part of the electorate that the errors committed since 1987 were all the fault of Thatcher and her Chancellor Nigel Lawson. Major's grey, pedestrian style may have been uninspiring but was a relief after the rigours of Thatcherism. Labour, on the other hand, suffered from the poor image of its leader Neil Kinnock who was not perceived as sufficiently prime ministerial.

There are important changes taking place in the behaviour of the British electorate, but a great deal of academic controversy about where they are leading. Some scholars insist that class voting is in decline[7] while others maintain that it is still important.[8] Matters were not helped in 1992 by the poor performance of the opinion polls which failed to detect the substantial Conservative lead which gave them their parliamentary majority. Even the exit polls taken on the day of the election failed to predict the result within acceptable margins of error. It seems that British electors are increasingly distrustful of all the established parties and inclined to change their minds more easily. They are also confronted with increasingly complex and contradictory signals, without the simple certainties of the past.

THE STATE, ADMINISTRATION AND PUBLIC POLICY MAKING

Britain is characterized by a centralized political system focused on Cabinet and Whitehall - the collective term for central government. Yet there is no tradition of a strong centralized bureaucracy or interventionist state. Central administration is relatively small and concerned with policy matters. Implementation, apart from defence and social security, tends to fall to local governments or *ad hoc* agencies responsible to government. Civil servants tend to be generalists skilled in policy advice and the ways of Whitehall rather than specialists. A large role is played by the independent institutions of civil society which have not come under direct government control but play important public roles. There is a preference for consensual policy making, by negotiation with the parties involved, rather than administrative fiat. Consultation has traditionally been regarded as essential to the policy process, adding legitimacy to it, where in a more state-centred system it might be seen as undermining government authority - though some private interests are more powerful in this process than others. Like other aspects of British government, this approach has come under pressure since the 1960s, as governments have sought answers to Britain's relative national decline in a modernization of institutions.

Government Departments and the Civil Service

The ministerial department is the traditional basis for the organization of British central government. It is headed by a minister, responsible to Parliament for everything which it does, assisted by middle ranking ministers known as ministers of state and junior ministers known as parliamentary secretaries. Most of the day-to-day work is carried out by permanent civil servants, also called officials, who also advise ministers on policy. Ministerial responsibility has been much eroded over the years and it is now rare for ministers to resign over errors made in their departments, but it has profoundly affected the organization of government. Because ministers must answer in Parliament for their department, they must ensure that they are well briefed on what it is doing and, while delegating a great deal, see that important decisions come to their personal attention. This is not merely a matter of separating out routine decisions, which can be taken by civil servants, from important decisions, reserved for ministers, since the most apparently trivial matters may give rise to political embarrassment or set precedents for future decisions.

Senior civil servants in Britain are recruited by competitive examination, out of university and tend to remain in the profession throughout their career, rising through the ranks according to their ability. There is very little movement in and out of the service and no movement between it and the world of electoral politics. Unlike their counterparts in some other countries, Britain's civil servants are generalists, recruited largely with liberal arts or classics degrees and moving between departments as they rise in their career. Their skills are developed through practice and experience rather than intensive training and involve judgement and the ability to appraise advice rather than specialist or technical capacity. They are rigorously neutral in party political matters but must serve elected governments of any persuasion, interpreting their policies and helping put them in effect. They represent continuity in government amid changes of political leadership. During election campaigns, while ministers are our electioneering, they devote their time to analysing the rival manifestos so as to have proposals ready for whichever party wins. If there is a change of government, they alone are allowed access to the old government's papers, which are kept confidential from the new ministers. The British Civil Service is recognized for its competence, sense of duty and absence of corruption. Yet it has also come under a great deal of scrutiny and criticism. These criticisms have focused on their recruitment and training, their alleged excessive power and their lack of modern managerial and specialist skills.

Recruitment into the senior administrative ranks has long been biased to the products of the exclusive private schools, paradoxically known in Britain as 'public schools', and the universities of Oxford and Cambridge. Graduates in classical studies were traditionally over-represented and there was a heavy male bias. Specialists in technical and scientific subjects tended to be confined to advisory or support roles, with little chance to rise to the top. In fact, the Civil Service reflected many of the most criticized features of the British class system.

The most serious criticism has focused on the power of the Civil Service. According to some critics, they constitute Britain's ruling class, an elite which runs the country no matter who is in power. There are three perspectives on this. Critics on the left point to the narrow class background of civil servants and their training in exclusive schools and universities and conclude that they are part of the conservative 'establishment', dedicated to preserving the power and privilege of the rich and upper classes. On the right, critics charge that, given their role in it, civil servants are inherently in favour of expanding the scope of government, not for the public good but to maximize their own power, privileges and pay. According to these critics, who were influential in the thinking of the Thatcher government, the Civil Service tends to the collectivist solutions associated with the left. The third perspective holds that civil servants are biased neither to right nor left but to preserving the status quo against change. These critics, who include left wingers like Tony Benn and right wingers like Keith Joseph, insist that the Civil Service, which prefers continuity and a quiet life, will frustrate radical governments of any persuasion. Individual departments are said to have ingrained prejudices towards certain policy lines through changes of government. As Benn complained in a radio broadcast, civil servants 'are always trying to steer incoming governments back to the policy of the outgoing government, minus the mistakes that the Civil Service thought the outgoing government made.' [9] Richard Crossman's diaries, [10] based on his experience as a Labour minister in the 1960s, tell of continued battles with his civil servants and the popular BBC television comedy series *Yes Minister* pits Minister Jim Hacker against his wily Permanent Secretary Sir Humphrey Appleby.

Civil servants certainly have important resources of power. While ministers remain in office for only a few years and in one department for an average of two and a half years, civil servants are permanent. Although they too move around departments in the course of their careers, they acquire a deep knowledge of the Whitehall system and soon learn to trim their behaviour to the prevailing norms. Ministers come to their departments deeply experienced in politics and the ways of Parliament, but often with no managerial experience or familiarity with the details of the policy issues they must confront. By the time they have learnt what they need to know, they are moved. Most important of all, the civil servants control information and the process of policy implementation. They can present recommendations to ministers tilted towards their own preferences and, if they really dislike a proposed course of action, they can argue that it is impractical, too expensive or needs more study, or agree to it but delay the implementation until the minister has moved. Civil servants have an extremely effective grapevine of communication among departments, while ministers tend to be isolated within them, cut off from their political roots and, given the ineffectiveness of Cabinet, not always in close touch with each other. In extreme cases, civil servants from different departments can agree to brief their ministers in the same way, ensuring that a consensus emerges at Cabinet or Cabinet committee. On the other hand, not all relationships are conflictual and not all conflicts pit the minister against the civil servants. Within a department the minister and civil servants share an interest in defending their common interest and the departmental budget against other departments.

Much depends on the personality of individual ministers. Some come to office with strong ideas on policy and a determination to see them through; others are content to follow the lead of their officials. Some will accept recommendations from the permanent secretary, while others insist on going down the hierarchy to get options from which to choose. When pressed, most former ministers deny that civil servants really run the government and insist that only weak ministers complain of this. There is probably a certain amount of macho posturing in this since to admit to having been bested by the officials would not reflect credit on a politician; but there is doubtless a strong element of truth. Ultimate constitutional authority does belong to the minister and, after all the manoeuvring and complex Whitehall games, he/she should be able to prevail.

The most widely canvassed remedy to the problem of political control over the department is the introduction of political advisors or something on the French *cabinet* model, a team of officials including outside appointees to serve the minister personally. This has never found favour in Britain, where there is a deep fear of politicizing the Civil Service or introducing a spoils system with patronage and corruption. Some ministers have appointed political advisors, either established figures from the academic world to give policy advice, or young political hopefuls who can maintain the minister's links to the political world. The relationships of these outsiders with the regular Civil Service have not been smooth and, while in some cases the experiment has proved useful, it has not had a big impact on the running of government. Under the Thatcher government, a different tack was adopted, with a limited and rather subtle politicization of the higher Civil Service through preference in promotion to those known to share the government's political views. Where governments embark on radical policy changes, such a politicization may be inevitable, since the tradition of Civil Service neutrality is tied closely to that of consensus politics. If politics is to move away from the old consensus, whether to left or right, then the tradition whereby civil servants stay in place while governments change may have to be modified.

There have been many attempts over the years to reform the Civil Service and the structure of government. The most trenchant criticisms of the organization of the Civil Service came in 1969 from the Fulton Committee, charged with investigating it and recommending reforms. In its opening lines, Fulton charged that the Civil Service was 'fundamentally the product of the nineteenth century' while the tasks it faced were 'those of the second half of the twentieth century.' Changes were advocated, to open up recruitment, to promote more specialization, and to improve the management structure. Improved training was recommended in an upgraded Civil Service College which some people saw as a future British equivalent of the elite French *Ecole Nationale d'Administration* (ENA). It was also recommended that the Civil Service open itself up to the wider community, encouraging exchange with industry, local government and academia and where appropriate recruiting experienced managers rather than promoting internally. The impact of the Fulton Report was modest. Senior posts were opened up to specialists and generalists equally, but few specialists have actually made it to the top. More non-civil servants were involved in the final stages of recruitment. An attempt was made to go beyond the public schools and ancient universities, though critics charge that the Civil Service still tends to recruit in its own likeness and looks beyond Oxford and Cambridge only in years when the supply of candidates is poor. By 1991, the representation of women in the senior open structure, the top three grades, was only 4 per cent, though it had risen to 11 per cent in the feeder groups.[11] Of 497 senior civil servants in the twelve large departments in 1992, 44 per cent had been educated at Oxbridge.[12] There has been some increase in contact with the outside world. In 1987, 278 civil servants were on secondment to industry and commerce while 195 were on secondment in the reverse direction.[13] A new Civil Service College was set up but never developed into anything like the ENA and was sharply cut back in the 1980s. Fulton was one of a series of attempts in the 1960s and 1970s to modernize British institutions. Its failure to achieve more was attributed by some to sabotage on the part of the civil servants who were charged with carrying it out.[14] Others criticized the superficiality of its analysis and its failure to consider the more profound problems of British institutions.[15] Its somewhat naive faith in modern management techniques and the failure to appreciate that the generalist plays a vital role in a system such as the British where central government is concerned with broad policy issues rather than implementation, were also criticized.

One set of Fulton recommendations was pursued by the Heath government of 1970-74. This was known as hiving off, the establishment of separate agencies for administrative tasks, leaving ministerial departments to focus on broad policy issues. This was part of a more managerial approach which also involved the creation of giant department and the Central Policy Review Staff. Few of these reforms survived Heath's term of office. Hiving off was confined to a few agencies and petered out in the mid-1970s.

From the late 1970s, attention shifted to cutting back the Civil Service and saving money. Under the Labour government, cash limits were placed on major programmes to ensure that costs did not over-run. If the allocation ran out during the course of the year, the programme would have to be cut back or even closed down. Critics charged that this did not discriminate between programmes which ran out of money for good reasons and those which merely wasted money, and that it was no substitute for proper monitoring. Under Margaret Thatcher after 1979, Lord Rayner was brought in from the successful retail chain Marks and Spencer to advise on cost-cutting. Some success was achieved in improving efficiency but critics charged that cutting expenditure was not necessarily the same as being efficient and that the needs of the public service were not the same as those of a private retail chain. There was also suspicion about the context within which the search for efficiency was being conducted. Thatcher was committed to cutting back the scope of government services, not merely delivering them better and harboured an undisguised hostility to the

Civil Service which she saw as a hotbed of collectivism and social democratic values. More widely supported were the Financial Management Initiative of 1982 intended to give managers in government departments specific targets and responsibility in meeting them; and MINIS system to improve information for ministers about expenditure trends and to take action at the right time.

Potentially the most radical reform in Britain's Civil Service, however, was launched with bipartisan support in the late 1980s. This was the Next Steps initiative to transfer three-quarters of the entire Civil Service from ministerial departments to managerial agencies. These agencies will be given specific targets and budgets and be run by chief executives appointed on fixed-term contracts. They will eventually have flexibility in determining their grade structures, pay scales and recruitment, tailoring these to the needs of the specific task. This represents a revival of the 1970s hiving-off concept and is intended to improve managerial efficiency while freeing ministers and their advisors to concentrate on policy matters. It has, however, attracted some criticism. Some see it as just another excuse for cutting back on public services or introducing commercial values in place of the public service ethos of equity and access. There is also a danger that, as in other countries, agencies could be effectively captured by outside interest groups or at least start to share the assumptions and thinking of the private actors with which they are dealing. Others note that it depends on the discredited idea that one can distinguish between policy, the province of ministers, and administration, the province of civil servants and agencies. In practice, just about any issue may become politicized and MPs spend most of their time chasing up individual cases. It si not always clear just how far ministers will continue to be answerable to Parliament for the work of agencies or what the relationship of managers to MPs will be. As is always the case with British government reforms, a large number of observers predicted that, behind the changes in name-plates, officials would continue to behave much as they always have.

By 1992, about 290,000 officials, more than half the entire Civil Service, had been transferred to agencies. Most of these worked in the field of social security, administering benefits of various sorts. Other agencies were in the fields of economic affairs, land and the built environment and defence procurement.[16] A third of the chief executives had been appointed from outside the Civil Service, earning up to 40 per cent more than the highest salaries available within government departments. There was no sign of the pace of reform slacking, though more difficulties can be foreseen as it goes beyond routine activity like administering social benefits, into areas involving greater discretion and political sensitivity.

Interest Groups and Policy Making

Britain has a long tradition of an independent civil society, an array of groups, interests and orders independent of the state. Many professions, such as lawyers, doctors or accountants, are self-regulating, determining on admission to the profession and policing the respect for professional standards. In other European countries, this would be the responsibility of the state. Even the financial centre, known as the City of London, is largely self-regulating, though since the 1980s a series of scandals has brought this into question. Trade unions , as they were legalized in the nineteenth century, chose to remain outside the scope of the state, demanding and getting a series of immunities from the ordinary law rather than a framework of legal rights and duties. Both sides of industry preferred until recently to keep industrial relations outside the scope of law. British industry, which in the nineteenth century dominated world markets, asked for little other than free trade and *laisser faire* and there was little of the intimate connection with government which existed in the industrializing societies of other European countries.

From the interwar period, however, industry lost its self-confidence and began to look to the state for tariff protection, subsidies and help in reorganization. After 1945, a number of major industries were taken into public ownership and government assumed wide responsibilities for economic management. This more interventionist style drew producer groups into the process of government, providing information, consent and cooperation. In line with the consensual tradition, consultation with affected interests became the norm before governments embarked on new policies.

Both sides of industry are organized. Among employees, levels of trade unionism are among the highest in Europe outside Scandinavia, though precise figures are hard to give and those in Table 2.6 must be taken as approximations.

It is clear that after a decade of historically high unemployment, a hostile government, the decline of traditional manufacturing employment and the growth of new non-union industries, union density has fallen markedly from the 1980 level of 51 per cent and is increasingly concentrated in the public sector and with a continued historic bias to male workers.

The union movement has in the past been fragmented along craft and industry lines rather than according to politics as in France, Italy and Spain and at one time this both weakened the movement and gave rise to disputes between

Table 2.6 Percentage of workers belonging to trade unions, Britain, 1990

All employees	38
Men	43
Women	32
Public Sector	63
Private sector	28

Source: Labour Research Department, Fact Service, 54.23 (1992)

unions. Difficult times in the 1980s forced a series of mergers to create the broader-based unions covering whole groups of workers which had proved so difficult to create in the past. Most trade unions are affiliated to the Trades Union Congress (TUC), founded in 1868. While it is the only trade union central, the TUC has little control over its members and leaves bargaining over wages and conditions to individual unions, though in the 1960s and 1970s it saw its status greatly enhanced when it became the official interlocutor of the trade unions with the state.

The main employers' organization is the Confederation of British Industry (CBI) formed in 1965 precisely to negotiate with government. It is a very broad-based body, its 12,000 members including large private firms, multinationals, nationalized industries and small businesses and consequently has some difficulty in arriving at a common position on specific issues. It can, however, make a powerful claim to be the representative of the business world and its pronouncements are taken seriously. The Institute of Directors, a smaller and rather elitist organization, also represents business interests but takes a more political stance, aggressively promoting the idea of private enterprise. Other organizations such as Aims of Industry, the Economic League and British United Industrialists are explicitly political and campaigning organizations, opposing trade unionism and the Labour Party.

Economic interest groups have various channels of access to decision makers. They all try to maintain links to sympathetic members of Parliament (MPs). The trade unions do this by sponsoring Labour MPs, paying a proportion of their election expenses and sometimes a small retainer, large firms by appointing MPs to their boards of directors. Given the concentration of power in the executive in the British system, this is of limited value and more important are links with the parties and the government. Many trade unions affiliate to the Labour Party, provide it with some 55 per cent of its funding and control the majority of votes at its annual conference. While this gives them a potential controlling interest in the party, unions have, apart from a period in the 1960s and 1970s, limited their influence to matters of direct union concern and to protecting the leadership against challenges. They are also aware that a Labour Party too obviously in the grip of union leaders might be unelectable and have in recent years even acquiesced in Labour's acceptance of some Conservative union legislation. Relationships between business interests and the Conservative Party are less formal but equally important. In 1989, business donations to the party by 38 of the hundred largest British companies amounted to £3.4 million; there are also substantial donations from abroad. Although the reluctance of the party to open its accounts makes it impossible to specify what proportion of total income these constitute, it is estimated at around 50-60 per cent. As in the case of Labour, this does not mean that the interest group runs the party, but it does ensure that they will not be neglected.

More important in terms of policy are the links which certain groups have with government departments. The practice of consultation gives some interests fairly secure access to the department dealing with their field, to the extent that departments are sometimes accused of being captured by the interests they are supposed to be governing. The Ministry of Agriculture has traditionally close ties with farmers, the Department of Trade and Industry is in regular contact with the CBI and the Department of Health must negotiate with representatives of the medical profession. The financial interests of the City of London are represented in the heart of government through the Bank of England, responsible for the implementation of monetary policy and oversight of the financial markets. Although nationalized since 1946, the Bank is not merely an arm of government. It must retain the trust of the financial community, from which its governor is drawn and it is seen as the voice of the City in government as much as that of government in the City. There are frequent complaints that this biases British economic policy in favour of financial interests and away from manufacturing. Interest groups which have close links with government departments gain recognition as trusted insiders, able to influence policy and legislation at an early stage and helping government in turn to frame measures capable of being implemented. They are also represented on the boards of government agencies and boards. Industry and the City are important under any government, since the needs of economic management require the cooperation of the private sector, though they are closest to Conservative governments. The trade unions, for their part are closer to Labour governments though, at least until 1979, they secured a measure of access to governments of both parties.

Non-producer groups, by contrast, have few such privileged links. Some choose to work through public opinion, creating a favourable climate of opinion, though the strength of the party system is such that unless they can convince one of the main parties that their ideas are electorally popular or in line with party ideology, this may not pay off. In a few cases, mainly involving social issues where Parliament does not vote on party lines, lobbying members of Parliament may be effective. This applied for example to the abolition of capital punishment and to the long disputes on abortion law. In a few cases, groups may be able to convince senior civil servants or ministers of the soundness of their arguments but in Britain non-producer groups rarely attain insider status.

From the 1960s, attempts were made in Britain to institutionalize cooperation between government and the main producer groups in order to modernize the economy and increase economic growth. Begun by the Conservative government in the early 1960s, the strategy of tripartite cooperation and planning was pursued, with only a short break in 1970-72, but governments of both parties until 1979. In 1961 the National Economic Development Council or Neddy was set up, bringing together government, employers and unions with independent experts to advise on policies for growth and the way obstacles could be overcome. 'Little Neddies' were established with the same tripartite structure for individual industries, supplemented in the 1960s by sectoral working parties. In 1965 the Labour government produced an indicative National Plan, to give guidelines to government, unions and industry as to how they should work to overcome obstacles to growth. Regional planning councils were set up, including both sides of industry with local government people. Guidelines on wage and price increases were negotiated with the TUC and CBI in the 1960s and again in the 1970s. Regulation of labour relations and training was turned over to the Advisory Conciliation and Arbitration Service and the Manpower Services Commission, on which unions and employers had places.

Many observers saw this as a British form of corporatism in which policy would be made by government in collaboration with the main producer groups. Such was not to be the case and by the 1980s a general disillusionment with this type of policy making had set in. It might be argued that the problems of the British economy and society were too large for such consensual arrangements to handle. Certainly none of the partners proved capable of delivering its side of the bargain. The state was, in comparison with its French counterpart, weak and staffed by generalist administrators rather than dynamic modernizers and governments often treated tripartite consultation as an excuse for inaction. Nor were the CBI or the TUC, both weak federations, able to commit their own members to agreements they might make with the state or even to force them to modernize and adapt. British interest groups proved, again, their power to prevent government doing things but the weakness of the system to make things happen. The Labour government of 1974-9 came in with radical plans for state-led modernization of industry but, under pressure from the CBI and lacking real political will, it quickly backed down.

By the 1980s, corporatism was out of fashion and the Thatcher government rejected it explicitly in favour of privatization, deregulation and a reliance on market forces and business leadership. Privatization of state industries was not a major part of the government's programme in 1979 but picked up considerably in the second term. Between 1980 and 1992, forty-six major enterprises and many smaller ones had been sold off by the government. Privatizations included the telephone system, the aerospace, motor, shipbuilding and steel industries, British Airways, the electricity, gas and water supply industries and substantial holdings in oil. Nationalized industries' share of GDP fell from ten per cent to 3 per cent and over a million jobs were transferred to the private sector. The objectives of privatization were mixed, as were the results.[17] One objective was based on an ideological dislike of state ownership and a belief that it should be reduced. Another was to expose industries to the competitive pressures of the market place. This was only partially achieved. Some industries, like gas and water supply, remained monopolies. In the case of airlines, there

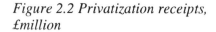

*Figure 2.2 Privatization receipts,
£million*

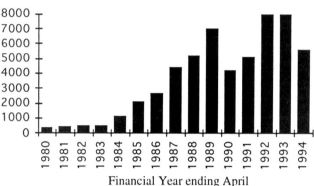

Financial Year ending April
Source: H.M. Treasury

was actually a reduction in competition as the privatized British Airways swallowed its major domestic competitor British Caledonian, created with government encouragement in the 1960s to provide a second national carrier. From the mid 1980s, a major objective of privatization was to raise revenue for government, though critics charged that is was financially imprudent to sell off assets to cover revenue expenditures. Former Conservative Prime Minister Harold Macmillan described it as 'selling off the family silver'. The contribution to government revenues was considerable, reaching some 8 billion pounds a year in 1992. The effect was enhanced by an accounting quirk by which receipts from asset sales were counted not as borrowing or revenue but as 'negative expenditur", that is they were deducted from the spending side of the public accounts. Figure 2.2 shows receipts from privatization. Gaining the maximum price for privatized industries was in conflict with the desire to enhance competition, since they were worth a great deal more as monopolies. It was also necessary, in order to dispose of certain firms quickly, to underprice their assets or to offer 'sweeteners' in the form of hidden subsidies and debt write-offs. This practice came under the critical gaze of the European Commission, which saw it as just another example of government aid to industry and insisted on the return of sweeteners.

Evidence on the efficiency gains from privatizing industries is also mixed. In several cases, the industries had been slimmed down and brought into profitability by government management before they were sold off. Overall, there is no convincing evidence that efficiency is affected either way by an industry being in public or private control.[18] Government relationships with industry, on the other hand, did change radically. It was no longer able to lean on public sector management to pursue policies such as price restraint, keeping plants open or investing in the regions. Instead, a series of large, powerful, internationally-oriented firms came into being. One of these, British Aerospace, created and extended entirely by privatization, came to control almost the entire British-owned aerospace and motor industries and a large part of the defence industries. Such was the scale of the transfer that the Labour Party abandoned any ideas of renationalization.

By the 1990s, the government was thus much less directly involved in the economy and less interested in the instruments of intervention and collaboration. The trade unions were systematically excluded from the counsels of government and a series of laws introduced to curtail their power. Five major pieces of legislation between 1980 and 1990 were aimed at reducing union influence.[19] These stipulated ballots before strike action and limited the activities of pickets. They enforced regular re-election for union officials and gave members more rights in relation to unions, in an effort to secure moderation. They outlawed the closed shop by which unions could insist on membership as a condition of employment in a firm. The overall effect, combined with high unemployment and changes in the composition of the workforce, was to weaken the unions and reduce their influence. Union numbers declined from just over half the workforce to about forty per cent of the workforce.

Some of the reforms, however, had the unintended effect of strengthening unions by modernizing their practices, democratizing them and encouraging participation. A law intended to limit trade union political activity by requiring a ballot before union could establish a political fund had the opposite of the intended effect. All unions with political funds voted to keep them and some which did not have them voted to set them up. A critical turning point in the relations of the unions with the government was in 1985 when, after a year-long strike, the miners were defeated. This trial of strength, which had been sought both by government and by the miners' leadership under the militant Arthur Scargill, showed the weakness of the trade union movement in the face of a determined government. The strike, which in defiance of the miners' own rulebook, had been called without a ballot, had divided the labour movement and its defeat boosted the moderate forces in both the unions and the Labour Party. In due course, the Trades Union Congress accepted nearly all of the trade union reforms introduced by the Conservatives and Labour made it clear that, if it won the election, it would not seek to reverse them.

Business was treated more favourably, being given increased representation on bodies like the Higher Education Funding Council, urban development corporations and training and enterprise councils, while unions were excluded. After the 1992 election, Michael Heseltine, a more interventionist type of Conservative, was appointed Secretary of State for Trade and Industry with a brief to reintroduce some industrial policy. It was made clear that, while the government would be engaged in a dialogue with business about its needs, there would be no place for the trade unions in the discussion. In 1992 the National Economic Development Council was abolished, the Chancellor of the Exchequer declaring that 'the age of corporatism must be put firmly behind us'.

Some attacks were also made on the old privileges of the self-governing professions, bringing the government into conflict with lawyers, doctors and teachers. These were never conducted with the venom which ministers reserved for trade unions and most of the self-regulation of the professions survived. The financial centre of the City of London also survived as a self-regulating system despite several scandals.

The attempt to roll back public spending was only partially successful. The government had started out with the intention of reducing public expenditure. As the practical difficulties of doing this became apparent, the goal was changed to reducing the proportion of public spending in Gross National Product; later again merely to keeping this constant. As Figure 2.3 shows, public spending increased both in absolute terms and as a percentage of GNP until the mid-1980s. Thereafter, it remained steady, but decreased as a proportion of GNP. As the election of 1992 approached, it resumed its steady increase. The government resorted again to Keynesian arguments about the virtues of deficit spending in a recession.

Figure 2.3 Public expenditure in constant terms and as percentage of GNP

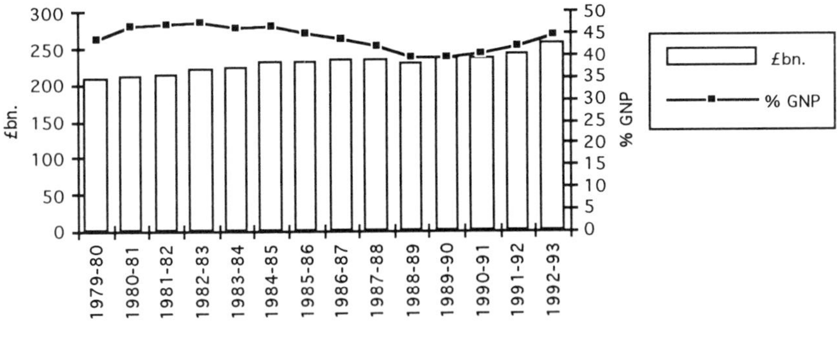

TERRITORIAL POLITICS

The United Kingdom is a multinational state with four principal components, consolidated over time into a union but never entirely assimilated. England is by far the largest, with a population of some 48 million. Scotland has a population of 5 million, Wales about three million and Northern Ireland one and a half million. The Republic of Ireland, whose capital is in Dublin, is not part of the United Kingdom and has a population of 3.5 million.

The United Kingdom is a unitary state, in which authority is concentrated in the Westminster Parliament but politics in the peripheral nations have their own distinct features, requiring constant management by central government to keep them within the fold. In Scotland, the main differences are institutional, a legacy of the Union of 1707 which, while abolishing the Scottish Parliament, left intact many of the institutions of civil society, notably the separate legal system, the educational system, local government and the separate established Church which, in contrast to the Church of England, professes the Calvinist doctrine. Of purely symbolic importance, albeit a source of great confusion, is the fact that the Scottish banks print their own notes. Like those printed by the Bank of England, these are denominated in pounds sterling and so represent the same currency. National pride is evoked by the separate soccer team which participates as a nation in world tournaments, and whose supporters delight in English defeats almost as much as their own victories. More generally, a sense of national identity, permeates the society, expressed through culture and symbols and sometimes in politics. The most obvious political expression is a desire for more control over Scottish affairs shown in every test of opinion since the advent of mass polling. For some this goes so far as a desire for secession, with complete independence from the UK, a policy offered by the Scottish National Party (SNP) whose support since the 1970s has fluctuated between 11 and 30 per cent of the Scottish electorate. The majority of Scots however have traditionally favoured a degree of self-government, or Home Rule within the United Kingdom, much on the lines of American states or Canadian provinces.

Despite these pressures for autonomy, Scotland has remained part of the centralized UK system of government for, while Scots may favour Home Rule they have never given it sufficient priority to abandon their Labour or Conservative preferences and vote in a majority for the SNP. A certain community of values has kept Scots loyal to the state, while the parties have consistently argued that separation would be economically disastrous. Instead, British governments have provided a variety of mechanisms to assuage Scottish discontent without putting the centralized state in question. A special department of central government, the Scottish Office, based in Edinburgh, administers many Scottish domestic matters, including, education, health, local government, police, planning, housing, energy, agriculture and fisheries, social services, and local economic development. It is also responsible for preparing the large amount of separate legislation made necessary by Scotland's distinct legal system though this passes, like all other legislation, through the unitary Parliament at Westminster. By convention the Scottish Office is headed by a Scottish MP of the governing party, the Secretary of State for Scotland, assisted by a number of junior ministers, also Scottish MPs. As part of a unitary system of Cabinet government, the Scottish Office has little discretion on policy matters and mostly adapts common UK policies to the Scottish administrative environment. More important is its role as a lobby for Scottish interests within central government. At times when Scotland has been critical to the fortunes of the governing party, secretaries of state have been able to extract favourable policies on matters of regional development as well as additional financial resources from the Treasury. Overall, Scottish levels of expenditure on domestic services are some 20 per cent higher than English, partly because of special needs but also because of the efforts of successive secretaries of state.

Since the 1970s, these arrangements for conciliating Scotland within the UK have come under increasing strain. In 1974, the SNP, capitalizing on the discovery of oil in Scottish waters, argued that Scotland was now subsidizing England and would be better off on its own. With over 30 per cent of the vote and eleven MPs they were able to force the minority Labour government to return to Labour's historic policy of Home Rule and introduce legislation providing for an elected assembly to take over most of the work of the Scottish Office. The proposals failed because of parliamentary obstruction, much of it from Labour's own ranks, together with confusion among the electorate. Although a referendum endorsed the scheme, it did not reach the qualified majority inserted in the legislation and the incoming Thatcher government in 1979 abandoned the proposals. Since then, a number of factors have served to strengthen Scottish nationalism. Patterns of voting behaviour between Scotland and England progressively diverged, with Labour increasing its majority among Scottish MPs, while the Conservatives dwindled to a quarter of the vote

Figure 2.4 Percentage share of vote, Scotland, 1955-92

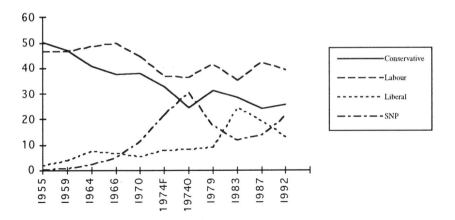

(Figure 2.4). Following the 1987 election, they barely had enough Scottish MPs to staff the Scottish Office and faced something of a crisis of legitimacy. Labour, in opposition throughout the 1980s, became more enthusiastic about devolution, which was also supported by the Liberal Democrats. The Conservatives, who in 1991 fell briefly to third place in terms of seats in Scotland, were the only party opposed to the growing consensus on the need for a move to Home Rule. Opinion poll evidence showed support for separatism to be increasing steadily, especially when it was cast in the more reassuring terms of Scottish independence within the European Community as now favoured by the SNP.

The Scottish Home Rule movement, however, remained divided between moderates wanting a devolved government within the United Kingdom and hard-line separatists. In the mid 1980s, a cross-party group, the Campaign for a Scottish Assembly, organized a Constitutional Convention, with support from the Labour and Liberal Democrat parties, local governments, trade unions, churches and other social organizations. Consciously imitating historical Scottish examples from the seventeenth century to the 1940s, this produced a Claim of Right and a new scheme for a Scottish Parliament within the UK. The SNP, however, refused to participate and the Conservative government dismissed it as self-appointed talking shop. At the 1992 election, the Conservative Party and the SNP sought to polarize the constitutional debate around the options of independence and no-change, with some success. The SNP vote increased by half to 21 per cent. The Conservative revival was a great deal more modest, their vote going up by just over one per cent, to 25.7 per cent. While gaining two seats, they still had great difficulty staffing the Scottish Office. Yet with an overall UK majority they were able to stall again on the constitutional issue, refusing to make any concession.

Scotland has always been a deeply constitutional country without a tradition of political violence in modern times. An explosion of nationalist discontent is not in prospect. Yet the Scottish constitutional issue is unlikely to go away quietly. Increased tensions between a Conservative England and an anti-Conservative Scotland are placing strains on the unitary state and the party system itself. The SNP has proved itself the largest separatist party in western Europe. Labour faces disaffection from neo-nationalist Scottish MPS within its own ranks if it fails to press the issue hard enough. As experience elsewhere shows, the longer the issue is unaddressed, the more severe tensions are likely to be.

Wales, united with England in 1536, has retained less of its distinctive institutions, but does have a national consciousness rooted in history and culture. The Welsh language, once the everyday speech of the majority, is now spoken by some 20 per cent of the population and is the normal mode of communication only in the northern and rural mountains. A distinct Welsh radical tradition, strongly linked to the non-conformist churches, has given support successively to the Liberal and Labour parties, and made Wales a difficult country for Conservatives. In recent decades, a number of conflicting trends have been at work. English immigration and economic change have assimilated much of south Wales and parts of the north to English standards, with traditional Welsh themes dying out and Conservative voting expanding. Yet at the same time, there has been a growing consciousness of Wales as an economic and administrative unit, encouraged by the Welsh Office, established in 1964 in imitation of its much older Scottish counterpart. Even the Welsh language has been stabilized through the creation of Welsh radio and television channels and the fostering of a Welsh-speaking middle class able to monopolize positions in them. The Welsh nationalist party, Plaid Cymru is itself torn by these conflicting trends. Its four MPs represent the old Welsh-speaking heartlands of the north and it has been very weak in the industrial south, undercutting its claim to speak for Wales as a whole. A Welsh assembly was proposed by Labour in the 1970s, along with that for Scotland but with less power and without much enthusiasm. Seen in English-speaking Wales as a concession to the Welsh speaking nationalist element, it was deeply unpopular and was rejected overwhelmingly in the referendum. The weakness of Welsh national identity was illustrated in 1987 when Margaret Thatcher sent as Secretary of State, not a Welsh MP, of which she had precious few but Peter Walker representing an English constituency. Intended as a sharp demotion, even exile, for Walker, the appointment of such a senior politician was seen in Wales not as an insult to national pride but as an opportunity to make their voice heard in London.

In the 1980s, a new form of Welsh identity emerged, less tied to the traditional themes of language and culture and more concerned with economic development issues. The strengthening of Welsh institutions, including the Welsh Office, the Welsh Development Agency, the Wales Trade Union Congress and the Assembly of Welsh Counties, encouraged this. So did the development of the European Community and the need for Wales to find its place in the emerging regional system in Europe. Both among public opinion and political decision makers, support for an elected Welsh assembly grew. Ironically, the very weakness of separatist sentiment in Wales made the idea of an elected assembly there more easily acceptable than in Scotland where critics argued that an assembly would be a slippery slope to independence. Yet the Conservative government, which lost support heavily in Wales at the 1992 election, remained wary of any constitutional change.

Northern Ireland has provided the UK state with its most intractable problem, one with deep historical roots. Although formally brought under the British crown in the Middle Ages when Nicholas Brakspear, the only Englishman ever to become Pope, gave Henry II a bull permitting him to conquer it, Ireland was never assimilated into the United Kingdom. Successive waves of settlers from the mainland were absorbed into the local population until the reformation divided the Irish, who remained overwhelmingly Catholic, from the majority in England, Scotland and Wales. In the seventeenth century, an uprising by the Irish chiefs was crushed and Ulster, the most traditional, Irish-speaking area, planted with Protestant immigrants from Scotland. Unlike previous generations, these never assimilated to the Irish culture and remained strongly attached to the union with Britain. Catholics, for their part, were subject to civil disabilities, could not sit in the Irish Parliament and, with the ruling class divorced from the mass of the people, these gave the state little respect. In 1800 the Irish Parliament was abolished in favour of Irish representation at Westminster and in 1829 Catholics throughout the United Kingdom were allowed to sit in Parliament. Instead of bringing Irish Catholics into the mainstream of political life, this provided the basis for a series of independent Irish parties committed to Home Rule and a break up of the large estates to give the small farmers their own land. Protestants in the north of the country remained largely aloof, suspicious of Home Rule and attached to the union. By the late nineteenth century, rapid industrialization in the north added a new dimension to the division of Ireland as well as exacerbating sectarian problems within Ulster, where Protestants largely monopolized both managerial positions and skilled labour trades.

In 1886, Liberal Prime Minister W.E. Gladstone was converted to Irish Home Rule but his attempt to pass legislation merely split his party and consigned it to opposition for most of the next twenty years. The Conservatives remained adamantly opposed to any measure of self-government, believing that land reforms and firm government would kill off the Home Rule movement. When a new Liberal government found itself dependent on the votes of Irish MPs in 1910, it returned to the Home Rule commitment but by this time the northern Irish Protestants, with the support of the Conservative Party, declared themselves ready to resist it by force. The UK found itself on the brink of civil war, when the first world war intervened to distract attention. Meanwhile, the failure of moderate Irish politicians to gain a measure of Home Rule had radicalized opinion, especially when the British government over-reacted to the glorious failure of a nationalist uprising in Dublin in 1916 by executing the leaders. In the 1918 general election, Sinn Fein candidates, committed to independence, swept everywhere outside the north and, after a period of bitter fighting, the government was forced to negotiate. Its solution was to divide Ireland into two, with elected governments in both parts, within the British Empire. This never worked as intended. After a civil war over the terms of the treaty, the southern part evolved from the Irish Free State into an independent republic, while in the north the Protestant majority retained a stranglehold on power. Yet while the Irish Republic is almost entirely Catholic, the province of

Northern Ireland, consisting of six counties split off from the rest, is only two-thirds Protestant. Declaring themselves 'a Protestant Parliament for a Protestant people', leaders of the Stormont regime, as the Northern Ireland government was known, proceeded systematically to discriminate against their Catholic minority, notably in voting rights, employment and housing.

This system survived until the late 1960s, punctuated by sporadic campaigns of violence by the Irish Republican Army (IRA), a group claiming descent from the independence fighters of 1922 but which, committed to the overthrown of both states in favour of a united nation, was illegal both in Northern Ireland and in the Irish Republic. Catholics in Northern Ireland were largely uninvolved in politics, voting usually for the Irish Nationalist Party, a group of leaders who rarely took their seats either at Stormont or Westminster. From the late 1960s, this began to change under the influence of the civil rights movement. Taking their cue from developments in the southern states of the USA, the civil rights leaders de-emphasized nationalism in favour of claiming their rights as British citizens. Despite the efforts of a reforming Stormont government under Terence O'Neill, this provoked a Protestant backlash, condoned by the Protestant-dominated police force. With the Catholics in danger of a pogrom, the British army was sent in to restore order. Very soon old patterns re-established themselves. The IRA re-formed and targeted the British troops. The latter, untrained in civilian policing, frequently over-reacted. Unwilling to take over direct responsibility, the British government left Stormont in place, so that the army appeared as the defender of the Unionist regime, further alienating Catholic opinion. The introduction of internment without trial in 1971 and the killing of civilians by troops on 'Bloody Sunday' in 1972 produced a greater gulf between Britain and the Catholic minority, allowing the historic animosities to emerge and the historically unusual posture of 1969 - British troops defending Catholics - to be forgotten.

Meanwhile, the civil rights movement had galvanized the constitutional nationalist movement into action and in 1970 the Social Democratic and Labour Party (SDLP) was formed. Though its ultimate aspiration is for Irish unity, the SDLP works within the UK system to improve the lot of the Catholic community, a break in the long abstentionist tradition. On the other side of the sectarian divide, the Ulster Unionist Party progressively disintegrated under pressure for reform from the British government and resistance from Protestant extremists. In 1972, unable to form an administration acceptable both to the British and to Protestant opinion, Stormont was dissolved and direct rule from Whitehall imposed. On top of the political, constitutional and security crisis of the 1970s was then imposed the economic recession, hitting Northern Ireland's old industries particularly hard and creating large-scale unemployment among urban youth, an ideal recruiting ground for the paramilitaries on both sides.

While the Northern Ireland conflict still pits Catholics against Protestants, there are not two but several parties to it. The British government has the legal responsibility for maintaining order in the state, which is discharged through the Secretary of State for Northern Ireland, the rest of the government and most members of Parliament trying to distance themselves as far as possible. Contrary to much nationalist propaganda, there is very little desire in Britain to retain Northern Ireland, which is a costly and embarrassing commitment. The Irish Republic still formally claims Northern Ireland, but has even less desire in practice to take it over and concentrates instead on confining the problem to the north and seeking to help Catholics there in various ways. Politicians in the republic still make the ritual obeisances to nationalist goals but there is no evidence that its citizens would or could pay the sort of price west Germans have done to unify their country. In Northern Ireland, majority Catholic opinion supports the SDLP, committed to unity in the long run by peaceful means. A minority of between 20 and 30 per cent of Catholics supports Sinn Fein, the political wing of the IRA, committed to violence, including attacks on British troops and terrorist activities in Northern Ireland and England. At the beginning of the present troubles, the IRA/Sinn Fein itself split into two sections, the Provisionals, committed to violence and traditional nationalist goals, and the Officials, who had adopted a marxist, non-sectarian stance and progressively played down both violence and nationalism. Later the latter gave up violence altogether and constituted themselves as the Workers' Party, scoring some success in elections in working-class districts in the Irish Republic but making little impact in Northern Ireland. For their part, the Provisionals took up some left-wing themes and involved themselves in community issues in the city to build up support among youth.

On the Protestant side, there are two main unionist parties. The Official Unionist Party and the more intransigent Democratic Unionist Party led by Ian Paisley. There is a paramilitary organization, the Ulster Defence Association, descendant of a long tradition of militia activity on the Protestant side. Unlike the IRA, it long remained legal on the grounds that it is better to have it in the open and under surveillance. It maintains a terrorist wing specializing in sectarian murders, the Ulster Freedom Fighters which, under the thin fiction that they are a separate organization, was banned. In 1992, the British government finally banned the UDA. Another banned Protestant terrorist group is the Ulster Volunteer Force. Finally, there is a small party in the middle, the Alliance Party, committed to maintaining the Union but giving full civil rights to all. Led by middl- class Protestants, its electoral support comes mainly from middle-class Catholics.

Many proposals have been canvassed as a political solution to the Northern Ireland problem. The two limiting cases, integration with Britain and unity with the Republic, illustrate the issues at stake. Full integration is the logical consequence of the oft-stated Unionist belief in their essential Britishness. The problem is that, strictly speaking, Northern Ireland is not British though part of the United Kingdom. Politically, the values of Ulster Protestants seem far removed from those on the mainland, with its traditions of tolerance and secularization, and attempts to introduce the Northern Ireland issue into Scottish politics in the 1987 election by running Unionist candidates came to naught. There is even a problem as to just what integration would mean in institutional terms. Some integrationists call for Northern Ireland to be administered like Yorkshire, that is, as a part of England; but it is not in fact part of England. Most take the model of Scotland; but there administration is in the hands of a Secretary of State who is a member of the ruling party but sits for a Scottish constituency, while the opposition, even when in the majority locally, accept the position. Neither the Conservative nor the Labour Party has local representatives available to do this. Labour refuses to organize there, essentially because of its support for Irish unity but also because of a feeling that its candidates would get no support. Conservative links with the Ulster Unionists were broken in 1972 over Unionist opposition to the suspension of Stormont.

Irish unity is supported in principle by most of the Catholic community and by successive governments of the Republic of Ireland. A large portion of the British Labour Party has long sympathized with the aspiration and in the 1980s it has become official party policy. Some figures on the left of the party have even forged links with Sinn Fein, the political wing of the IRA and have wishfully seen it in the light of Third World national liberation movements. In practical terms, however, Irish unity has not been on the agenda, because of the entrenched opposition of the Protestants who, few can doubt, would resort to armed resistance against it, and because the Republic does not really want to absorb a million hostile Protestants along with the chronic economic problems of the north. In the early 1980s, the electorate of the Republic made clear its lack of concern for an Irish unity which would encompass those of both religions and none by voting down a referendum proposal to allow divorce.

Advocates of both integration and unity illustrate a key aspect of the situation, the ability to assume away the aspirations, indeed the very existence, of the other side. Catholics assume that Protestants will simply accept Irish unity if it comes about. The most liberal Protestants cannot understand why Irish identity would remain important to Catholics even after they had been given all the advantages of British citizenship. Some observers, starting from entrenched hostility between the groups, advocate a re-partition of Ireland to produce homogeneous Protestant and Catholic Jurisdictions. This is less a solution to the problem than an admission of failure and there must be severe doubts about its practicality. Apart from some concentrations along the border, Catholic majority enclaves are spread across Northern Ireland, with the city of Belfast providing insuperable problems of division. Of course, re-partition on religious grounds could be accompanied by forced population movements, as happened in central Europe after the second world war. In those cases, it has not proved to be the basis for stable boundaries and in this instance it would satisfy neither the Catholic, nationalist side, who want a united Ireland, not the Protestant, unionist side, who want a viable province for themselves.

One approach tried in 1974 following the Sunningdale agreement, and pressed on various other occasions, has been the consociational one, of bringing the representatives of both sides together in a power-sharing government to which powers could be devolved, so allowing a gradual withdrawal of direct British involvement. This approach, however, assumes that leaders can bind their followers to power-sharing agreements. Yet, while the SDLP was able to use power-sharing to increase its standing within the Catholic community, each Protestant leader who has tried to share power with Catholics has been overthrown by more intransigent elements. The failure of Sunningdale was followed by a constitutional convention of elected representatives within Northern Ireland, inevitably dominated by the Protestant majority. In the event, its deliberations were fruitless, since the British government refused to accept its proposals for an effective return to Protestant ascendancy. A renewed attempt at a power-sharing assembly faltered on the same problem as its predecessors, the unwillingness of the Protestants to contemplate real power sharing and the inability of the SDLP to settle for anything less.

In the absence of an agreed constitutional model, direct rule has continued, through a Secretary of State appointed in London and representing a British constituency. This is not quite a colonial regime, since Northern Ireland does send representatives to the House of Commons, but it bears some similarity to the nineteenth-century Irish constitution in that the Irish representatives, not being part of either British party, can never form part of the government. By the same token, Northern Ireland electors, having neither Conservative nor Labour candidates, are effectively denied a say in the choice of government. Direct rule involves governing without local collaborators and, if necessary, without consent, though in practice it is widely regarded as the least unacceptable option. Direct rule has been accompanied by repeated searches for a political solution to the problem but also by a preoccupation with the security situation and the war being conducted by the IRA.

At times, this has come near to a belief that the problem is purely a security one and violence simply a criminal matter, to be resolved by tough law and order policies. The problem here is the complex and subtle relationship of political violence to Catholic opinion. Most Catholics will deplore the tactics of the IRA, are repulsed by individual acts of terrorism against civilians and give their electoral support to the constitutional and democratic SDLP. Yet they do not regard IRA violence as purely a criminal matter and are prepared to concede the IRA a degree of legitimacy stemming from historical memories of the 1920s and their own fear of the old Protestant B specials of Stormont days and the Protestant paramilitaries of the present. Above all, they recognize that the IRA, though misguided, are on 'their side'. The IRA are able to play on this complex of beliefs and traditions of resistance to the state by presenting themselves as victims of state policy. Catholic opinion can then swing almost overnight from revulsion at an IRA atrocity to condemnation of the British, the traditional enemy. Failure to understand this has led to some of the worst blunders of British policy, such as internment in 1971 and the reactions to the hunger strikes of 1981. In the latter, a group of IRA prisoners went on hunger strike, in order to win 'political' status as represented by a right to wear their own clothes and not do prison work. The Thatcher government's refusal to give in to the moral blackmail of the hunger strikers was seen in British Conservative circles as a mark of steadfastness in the fight against terrorism. Elsewhere, it was seen as a gift to the IRA of precisely what they wanted - not the concession of their relatively trivial demands, but its refusal so that the hunger strikers would die and join the pantheon of Catholic martyrs. The resulting deaths served to radicalize a large section of Catholic opinion and give an impression that the British government was more concerned with its reputation for not changing direction than the fate of Northern Ireland. Republican extremism and British conservatism proved, as in the past, to be objective allies in polarizing the situation by conjuring up an issue of deep principle which, by more skilful political manoeuvring, could have been avoided.

Direct rule has been accompanied by a return to the 'exceptionalism' which was a feature of nineteenth-century Ireland. In 1976, the Labour government's Prevention of Terrorism Act even allowed the expulsion of British citizens from the mainland to Northern Ireland, an obvious attempt at containment of the province but an extraordinary measure in a unitary state. Another problem with continued direct rule is the effect on the security forces. There have been cases of civil rights abuses by members of the security forces and evidence of collusion with Protestant paramilitaries against the IRA. Civil libertarians have worried that continued direct rule will lead to further erosions of the liberal state, such as the end to the right of accused people to silence or the banning of representatives of Sinn Fein from appearing on broadcast media. Pioneered in Northern Ireland, techniques of civil control may spread to the mainland.

Yet another type of solution canvassed is to tackle the problem of dual identity through some sort of condominium of Northern Ireland by the Republic of Ireland and Britain. The most recent step in this direction is the 1985 Anglo-Irish agreement. Though not providing for joint sovereignty, this involved the Irish government assuming the role of safeguarding Catholic interests, a position largely acceptable to the SDLP but not to the IRA, which opposes both states. It is unacceptable to most of the Protestant community, who feel that no-one speaks for them and resent the interference of a 'foreign state' in Northern Ireland affairs. Indeed, the Anglo-Irish agreement, by recognizing both the reality of the border and the legitimacy of the Republic's intervention in the North, has offended intransigent elements on both sides of the sectarian divide. It is significant in representing the first occasion on which a British government has faced up to Protestant opposition without yielding. There is a provision in the agreement to the effect that it will be progressively phased out as Northern Ireland community leaders agree on new power-sharing arrangements within the province, so providing an incentive for Unionists to cooperate. Despite repeated efforts by secretaries of state, however, such an agreement has not come about.

There have been moves in this direction in the past. In the late 1970s, the idea of an independent Northern Ireland was floated. In practice, this would be extremely unlikely to kill the aspiration to Irish unity and would very likely result in a Protestant-dominated autocracy. If this were to be avoided, there would need to be firm arrangements for power-sharing and civil rights, with international guarantees which could only be enforceable by Britain and the Irish Republic. This would be more like a condominium than real independence.

Northern Ireland thus remains a failure of British policy, a failure rooted in the short-term response to the crisis of 1920-22 but also in more recent mistakes. Economic recession has further exacerbated the problem and allowed the IRA-Sinn Fein to exploit urban discontent, especially among the young. Any advances in opening up job opportunities for Catholics have been overwhelmed by the loss of jobs stemming from the recession and the economic policies of the early 1980s. The political events of the 1970s, too, have polarized opinion on sectarian lines which are likely to leave an imprint for generations. Tragic though it may be, the situation is probably manageable in the long term. The murder rate per million people in Northern Ireland is only two-thirds that in the United States and Belfast's rate is about a tenth that of Washington DC. As long as all-out civil war is avoided and the trouble kept distant from the British mainland, it will remain a side issue in British politics.

Local Government

Britain has a long tradition of local self-government. Unlike the large continental states, it never established a large, centralized bureaucracy to administer its affairs, relying instead on local institutions. Traditionally, these were the city and borough (burgh in Scotland) councils and the justices of the peace in the counties. In the Victorian era, the system was modernized. Elected councils took over in towns and counties and came to play a vital role in the development and administration of the services of the modern state.

While local government has always had large service responsibilities, however, it has had relatively little weight in national politics. Senior local government figures rarely make the transition to leading positions in national government. Local government structure, powers and finances can be changed radically by a determined central government. Elections in local government are dominated by the national parties which gradually extended their presence from the late nineteenth century until the 1970s. Now only the small, rural councils retain a tradition of non-partisan politics. This does not mean that the national parties dictate to their local branches in matters of local politics, but electors are aware of the general stance of the parties on the main issues. Conservatives tend to favour low taxes, privatization and deregulation. Labour favours more service provision and public control. The Liberal Democrats occupy the middle ground on these issues and have a tradition of promoting public participation. Partisanship also affects the conduct of local elections, which are fought out on a national basis and the results largely reflect national rather than local issues. Many a hard-working local councillor has had the uncomfortable and bewildering experience of being thrown out of office in response to the national swing. This is criticized as emptying local politics of much of its meaning. On the other hand, the presence of national parties does give the electors some guidance on the preferences of candidates and opens up local politics to wider issues. It provides an element of responsible party government, since the majority party forms an adminstration, while the losing parties constitute an opposition. The advance of the Liberal Democrats in the 1980s created a large number of councils in which no party had a majority, giving the British a taste of minority and coalition government. Party control in local government may also politicize relations with central government, where this is controlled by the other party. For the most part, relations with central government have been rather consensual but this politicization has led periodically to open conflict, in the 1920s and again in the 1980s.

Since the 1960s, there has been a succession of reforms and reorganizations of local government. In the 1960s and early 1970s, the emphasis was on the

Figure 2.5 Local government structure in the UK

England			Scotland		Wales	N. Ireland
Shire counties			Regions	Islands	Counties	Boards
Districts/ boroughs	Metropolitan boroughs		Districts		Districts	Districts

need for modernization to enable local government to play its role in the expansion of public services and the planning of development. Larger-scale authorities were the fashion and much effort was put into improving and professionalizing management. In 1973-5, the whole system was radically overhauled. The old units were abolished and a new system brought into being. In most of England and Wales, a two-tier system was set up, with counties and districts, or boroughs, both directly elected. The counties have the most important functions and spend most of the money. In the large conurbations, metropolitan boroughs carry out most of the services. Metropolitan counties, responsible for strategic planning and some services, existed above these between 1974 and 1986, when they were abolished by the Thatcher government. Services previously carried out by the metropolitan counties, like fire and policing, are now the responsibility of joint boards of the boroughs. In Scotland, the system is rather different. Nine regional councils discharge the most important local government services. Below them, district councils are responsible for public sector housing, local planning and some other services. The three Scottish islands areas, Shetland, Orkney and the Western Isles, have unitary authorities. In Northern Ireland, local governments were stripped of most of their powers because of their sectarian practices. Important functions like education and social services are discharged directly by central government or through appointed boards, while elected district councils have minimal responsibilities.

The 1970s reform, intended to last for a century, was never universally accepted. The Labour government, before losing office in 1970, had intended to implement the proposals of the Redcliffe-Maud Commission for city regions in England. This would have tended to favour Labour electorally, just as the county-based system which was adopted, tends to favour the Conservatives. Some critics would have preferred a system of large regions in England and elected assemblies for Scotland and Wales, with single-tier local government beneath them. City politicians outside the metropolitan areas resented the subordination of the cities to the county authorities and agitated for a restoration of their lost powers.

Further problems were created by the political polarization of the 1980s which pitted Labour-controlled local governments against a centralizing Conservative government. The Thatcher government after 1979 was committed to reducing the scope of public services, cutting public expenditure, deregulation, privatization and a scaling down of planning. Since local government had developed in the postwar era as an agent of planning and public service provision, this implied a radical change in its role. The Thatcher government was also intolerant of opposition and of independent institutions, whether local government, trade unions or universities, which might nurture such opposition. Local councils were seen not as the basis of local self-government but as entrenched interests promoting collectivist values. On the other side of the fence, the 1980s saw the rise of a new generation of left-wing Labour councils, sometimes referred to as the 'new urban left', committed to expanding the role of local government, politicizing it and not shirking from open conflict with central government. The result was a series of confrontations and a succession of legislative changes as central government sought to reduce local governments to its will. Between 1980 and 1990, some forty pieces of legislation on local government were passed.[20]

A constant preoccupation of government in the 1980s and early 1990s was local government finance. Almost every year new legislation was brought in to reduce local government's discretion in raising and spending revenue, culminating in the ill-fated poll tax. Officially known as the community charge, the poll tax was a fixed sum paid by all adults irrespective of income, apart from some welfare recipients and students, who paid a reduced rate of 20 per cent. It replaced the old system of rates, a property tax on domestic properties. The idea was to force those who vote in local elections to pay for the services in the most painful manner, on the untested assumption that they would then go for low-spending Conservative councillors. Rates on commercial and industrial properties, previously also raised by local government, were taken over by central government, which sets the tax and passes on the proceeds to local governments according to population. The remainder of local government finance comes from central grants determined according to needs. The poll tax proved one of the political own-goals of the century, and the protests at its introduction was one of the causes of Margaret Thatcher's fall from power. Her successor, John Major, abandoned the idea and went back to a form of domestic property tax. Local government's freedom to raise its own revenue, however, remains tightly limited.

Local government has also been changed by legal provisions forcing it to privatize some of its operations, notably the provision of rental housing, and to contract out others to private operators. Its role in planning has been weakened though there has not been the complete dismantling of the planning system which some observers had anticipated. Following the 1992 election, the government confirmed its intentions to move towards a single-tier system of local government in England, Scotland and Wales. The result will be a local government system a great deal smaller and simpler than that of the 1960s. Instead of administering large-scale services directly, it will organize their provision by other operators. Its financial discretion will be limited as will its ability to set its own policy lines.

CONSTITUTIONAL REFORM

Britain's constitutional arrangements were once the envy of the world. It had succeeded in moving from monarchy to parliamentary democracy with no revolutionary upheaval. There was broad consensus on the legitimacy of the state. Governments were restrained by convention and the regular alternation of parties in power. Much administration was decentralized to local government, responsible to local communities. Since the mid-1980s, perceptions have changed and there has been a renewed debate in Britain on the need for constitutional reform. This was prompted by the re-election of Conservative governments with little over 40 per cent of the popular vote, the ease with which the Thatcher government was able to overturn the informal understandings and institutions of Britain's liberal civil society, and a renewed concern with modernization. Its origins, however, lie deeper in Britain's postwar experience. Membership of the EC has brought changes to British government and undermined the doctrine of parliamentary sovereignty, yet governments of both parties have been reluctant to admit this and have continued to fight rearguard actions against each successive move to European unity. The question of devolution to Scotland and also Wales and the regions of England, is another recurrent issue which does not go away, however much governments might hope it will.

Then there is a range of questions relating to citizenship and rights. The rise of citizen rights against the state has been a feature of the west European postwar state, but for years British governments insisted that they were unecessary in Britain's tolerant climate and would be incompatible with parliamentary sovereignty. By the 1980s, these assumptions were being widely challenged, notably by the lobby group Charter 88. Reformers demanded a written charter of rights, or the incorporation of the European Convention for the Protection of Human Rights into British law. Left-wing opponents of jusiticiable rights argued that they would be useless, given the inbuilt bias of the judges who would have to administer it. This might be an argument against a bill or rights - or it could be an argument for reforming the judiciary. Judges are perhaps Britain's least representative social institution. No less than 84 per cent of the judges appointed to the highest courts between 1989 and 1991 were educated at the prestigious 'public' (that is private) schools and 77 per cent were graduates of Oxford or Cambridge.[21] The judiciary has been subject to increasing criticism following a series of miscarriages of justice in Irish terrorist cases.

Another issue is proportional representation, to reduce the power of a single party and change the way that policies are made. This cause, championed for many years by the Liberals, has gained adherents in the Labour Party worried that the alternation of parties in power, which used to restrain governments, no longer seems to work. Many reformers would like to restructure the House of Lords as a regional chamber, or abolish it altogether. The main advocate of constitutional reform has been the Liberal Democrat Party, which makes this one of its main campaign themes. By the early 1990s, however, the cause was making an increasing number of converts in the Labour Party and even a few Conservatives were privately sympathetic. Yet the old order is very resilient and reformers were painfully aware, especially after the election of 1992, that to change the system it is first necessary to win within it.

REFERENCES

1. A-C. Pereira-Menaut, *El Ejemplo Constucional de Inglaterra* (Madrid: Complutense University, 1992).
2. Quoted in R.T. Mackenzie, *British Political Parties* (London: Heinemann, 1964), p. 641.
3. I. Crewe, N. Day and A. Fox, *The British Electorate, 1963-1987. A compendium of data from the British Election Studies* (Cambridge: Cambridge University Press, 1991).
4. I. Crewe, N. Day and A. Fox, *The British Electorate, 1963-1987. A compendium of data from the British Election Studies* (Cambridge: Cambridge University Press, 1991).
5. I. Crewe, N. Day and A. Fox, *The British Electorate, 1963-1987. A compendium of data from the British Election Studies* (Cambridge: Cambridge University Press, 1991). D. Saunders, 'Why the Conservative Party Won - Again', in A. King (ed.), *Britain at the Polls, 1992* (New Jersey: Chatham House, 1992).
6. R. Rose and I. McAllister, *Voters Begin to Choose* (London and Beverly Hills: Sage, 1986). R. Rose and I. McAllister, *The Loyalties of Voters. A lifetime learning model* (London and Newbury Park: Sage, 1990).
7. Rose and McAllister (1986). M. Franklin, *The Decline of Class Voting in Britain* (Oxford: Oxford University Press, 1985).
8. A. Heath et. al., *Understanding Political Change. The British Voter, 1964-1987* (Oxford: Pergamon, 1991).
9. H. Young and A. Sloman, *No, Minister. An inquiry into the Civil Service* (British Broadcasting Corporation, 1982), p. 87.
10. R.H.S. Crossman, *The Diaries of a Cabinet Minister,* vols. 1-3 (London: Hamish Hamilton, 1975-77).
11. A. Hede, 'Trends in the Higher Civil Service of Anglo-American Systems', *Governance*, 4.4 (1991), pp. 489-510.
12. Figures from *Dod's Whitehall Companion* (London, 1992) calculated in Labour Research Department, *Fact Service*, 54.42 (1992)..
13. Treasury and Civil Service Select Committee, Eighth Report. *Progress in the Next Steps Initiative*, HC 481, 1989-90. Treasury and Civil Service Select Commitee, Eighth Report, *Civil Service Management Reform: The Next Steps*, HC 494-1 and 11, 1987-8.
14. P. Kellner and Lord Crowther-Hunt, *The Civil Servants. An Inquiry into Britain's Ruling Class* (London: Macdonald Futura, 1980).
15. These criticisms are discussed in B. Jones and M. Keating, *Labour and the British State* (Oxford: Clarendon, 1985).
16. Treasury and Civil Service Select Committee, Eighth Report. *Progress in the Next Steps Initiative*, HC 481, 1989-90.
17. D. Marsh and R. Rhodes, 'Implementing Thatcherism: Policy Change in the 1980s', *Parliamentary Affairs*, 45.1 (1992).
18. P. Riddell, *The Thatcher Era and its legacy* (Oxford: Blackwell, 1991).
19. D. Marsh and R. Rhodes, 'Implementing Thatcherism: Policy Change in the 1980s', *Parliamentary Affairs*, 45.1 (1992).

20. D. Marsh and R. Rhodes, 'Implementing Thatcherism: Policy Change in the 1980s', *Parliamentary Affairs*, 45.1 (1992).

21. *Observer*, 15 Dec. 1992.

FURTHER READING

General

I. Budge *et. al.*, *The Changing British Political System: into the 1990s,* 2nd edn. (London and New York: Longman, 1988).

J. Dearlove and P. Saunders, *Introduction to British Politics,* (Cambridge: Polity, 1991).

P. Dunleavy, Andew Gamble and Gillian Peele (eds), *Developments in British Politics,* 2nd edn., (LondOn: Macmillan: 1990).

A. Gamble, *Britain in Decline,* 3rd edn. (London: Macmillan, 1990).

D. Kavanagh, *British Politics. Continuities and Change,* 2nd edn. (Oxford: Oxford University Press,1990).

K. Middlemas, *Power, Competition and the State, vol. 3: The End of the Post-war Era - Britain since 1974* (London: Macmillan, 1991).

P. Norton, *The British Polity,* 2nd edn. (London: Longman, 1991).

R.M. Punnett, *British Government and Politics,* 5th edn. (Aldershot: Gower, 1987).

R. Rose, *Politics in England Today,* 5th edn. (London: Macmillan, 1989).

W. Wale (ed.), *Developments in Politics. An Annual Review* (Ormskirk: Causeway).

Constitution and Government

J. Barber, *The Prime Minister since 1945* (Oxford: Blackwell, 1991).

P. Hennessy, *Cabinet* (Oxford: Blackwell, 1986).

P. Hennessy, *Whitehall* (London: Secker and Warburg, 1989).

S. James, *British Cabinet Government* (London: Routledge, 1992).

D. Judge, *The Parliamentary State* (London: Sage, 1993).

P. Norton, *New Directions in British Politics. Essays on the Evolving Constitution* (Aldershot: Edward Elgar, 1991).

R. Blacburn (ed.), *Constitutional Issues* (London: Mansell, 1992).

Institute for Public Policy Research, *A Written Constitution for the United Kingdom* (London: Mansell, 1993).

Parties and Elections

V. Bogdanor, *The People and the Party System. The Referendum and Electoral Reform in British Politics* (Cambridge and New York: Cambridge University Press, 1981).

M. Cunningham and R. Spear, *The Changing Labour Party* (London: Routledge, 1992).

D. Denver, *Elections and Voting Behaviour in Britain* (London and New Yor: Philip Allan: 1990).

D. Denver and G. Hands, *Issues and Controversies in Britihs Electoral Behaviour* (London and New York: Harvester-Wheatsheaf, 1992).

A. Heath *et. al.*, *Understanding Political Change. The British Voter, 1964-1987* (Oxford: Pergamon, 1991).

S. Ingle, *The British Party System,* 2nd edn. (Oxford and Cambridge, Mass.,1990).

A. King *et. al.* , *Britain at the Polls 1992* (Chatham, N.J.: Chatham House, 1992).

R. Rose and I. McAllister, *Voters Begin to Choose* (London and Beverly Hills: Sage, 1986).

R. Rose and I. McAllister, *The Loyalties of Voters . A lifetime learning model* (London and Newbury Park: Sage, 1990).

P. Seyd and P. Whiteley, *Labour's Grass Roots: The Politics of Party Membership* (Oxford: Clarendon, 1992).

Interest Groups and Policy Making

A. Gamble, *The Free Economy and the Strong State. The Politics of Thatcherism* (London: Macmillan, 1988).

W. Grant, *Pressure Groups, Politics and Democracy in Britain* (1989).

B. Hogwood, *From Crisis to Complacency. Shaping Public Policy in Britain* (Oxford: Oxford University Press, 1990).

P. Jenkins, *Mrs. Thatcher's Revolution. The ending of the socialist era*, 2nd edn. (London: Pan, 1989).

A.G. Jordan and J.J. Richardson, *British Politics and the Policy Process* (London and Boston: Allen and Unwin, 1987).

A.G. Jordan and J.J. Richardson, *Government and Pressure Groups in Britain* (Oxford: Oxford University Press, 1987).

D. Kavanagh, *Thatcherism and British Politics. The End of Consensus?*, 2nd edn. (Oxford University Press, 1990).

D. Marsh (ed.), *Pressure Politics. Interest Groups in Britain* (London: Junction, 1983).

D. Marsh and R. Rhodes, *Implementing Thatcherite Politics: Audit of an Era* (Milton Keynes: Open University Press, 1992).

P. Riddell, *The Thatcher Era and its Legacy* (Oxford: Blackwell, 1991).

Territorial Politics

P. Arthur and K. Jeffrey, *Northern Ireland since 1968* (Oxford and New York: Blackwell, 1988).

A. Midwinter, M. Keating and J. Mitchell, *Politics and Public Policy in Scotland* (London: Macmillan, 1991).

B. O'Leary and J.McGarry, *The Politics of Antagonism. Understanding Northern Ireland* (London and Atlantic Highlands, N.J: Athlone Press, 1993).

R. Rose, *Understanding the United Kingdom* (London: Longman, 1982).

G. Stoker, *The Politics of Local Government*, 2nd edn. (London: Macmillan, 1991).

J. Whyte, *Interpreting Northern Ireland* (Oxford: Oxford University Presss, 1990).

3 France

STATE AND GOVERNMENT IN FRANCE

France is one of the oldest nation-states in Europe, built over centuries by the monarchy and succeeding regimes. Some nationalists like to claim that France has natural boundaries - it is often referred to as the hexagon. Certainly, its outlines can be traced in the division of the Holy Roman Empire of Charlemagne at the Treaty of Verdun in 843, but it took several hundred years to become a reality. In the Middle Ages, large parts of the west came under the English crown. The dukedom of Burgundy in the east, almost developed into a separate kingdom. Powerful barons in the south resisted the French monarchy until the late Middle Ages. The Spanish border was laid down in the Treaty of the Pyrenees in 1659 and the eastern frontier established in 1869 with the acquisition of Nice and Savoy. Alsace and Lorraine were annexed by Germany between 1870 and 1914 and between 1940 and 1944.

Having more or less established their frontiers in the seventeenth century, French monarchs sought to build a strong state. A theory of absolute monarchy was fashioned to justify unlimited power for the king, who claimed to rule by Divine Right. The Estates General, or parliament, was not summoned between 1614 and 1789. The landed aristocracy were deprived of political power and brought to the court where they remained under the watchful eye of royal ministers. A standing army was maintained and a central state bureaucracy begun. *Intendants*, personal envoys of the king, were sent into some provinces to administer their affairs directly. This strong, centralized state presents a contrast to Britain where monarchs were forced to govern in partnership with the landed gentry in Parliament and could raise neither taxes nor troops without its permission.

The key event in French history is the Revolution of 1789 which, starting as a reform movement, ended by abolishing the monarchy and executing the king. It took several more revolutions and a century of struggle before the republic was secured against monarchy, but the events of 1789-99 left a permanent legacy. Far from weakening the state, the Revolution and its aftermath strengthened it and gave it a new basis. The doctrine of popular sovereignty, that all power derives from the people, replaced Divine Right. Allied with the doctrine of nationalism, which insisted that the French people are a single entity, it laid the basis for a stronger and more centralized power. All remaining feudal privileges and provincial institutions were abolished as an affront to the indivisible republic. The Church was subordinated to the state; and the Declaration of the Rights of Man announced that all men - but not yet women - were equal. The Revolution, like so many before and since, slid into terror in which its leaders turned on each other and thousands of people of all ranks perished on the guillotine or were shot. Its outcome was a dictatorship under Napoleon Bonaparte in which the power of the state was strengthened still more. A centralized bureaucracy was set up and prefects sent out from Paris to administer the country. In 1804 Napoleon ended the first republican experiment by having himself crowned emperor.

Some of the innovations of the Revolution and Empire were short-lived. Others survived to become part of the institutional fabric of the country. The revolutionary local government system is largely intact. Prefects, while their role has changed, are still there, and the powerful central bureaucracy remains an important element in national life. Other legacies are more contested. Like the Soviet Revolution of 1917, the French Revolution was to serve as a reference point for political arguments both in France and abroad for generations to come. The doctrines of nationalism and popular sovereignty were used to undermine empires and monarchies all over Europe. A battle between republicanism and monarchy was to shape French political debate profoundly through the nineteenth century. A related argument over the role of the Church was not resolved until well into this century. Regional differences of the revolutionary years can still be traced in contemporary voting behaviour, modified by party alignments and new issues but still visible. Only in the late twentieth century have passions died down enough to allow calm and rational debate over the Revolution. Monarchism is now a quaint irrelevance and, with almost everyone now being a republican, aall can claim a share in the revolutionary heritage. On the occasion of its bicentenary in 1989, it was even possible to debate its negative side, the bloodshed, the Terror, the injustices. Polls indicated that, while most people thought the Revolution necessary, they

Table 3.1 French regimes	
Pre-1798	Absolute Monarchy
1789-92	Constitutional Monarchy
1792-99	First Republic
1799-1804	Consulate
1804-15	First Empire
1815-30	Restoration (Bourbon) Monarchy
1830-48	Constitutional (Orleanist) Monarchy
1848-52	Second Republic
1852-70	Second Empire (of Napoleon III)
1870-1940	Third Republic
1940-44	Vichy Regime
1946-58	Fourth Republic
1958 -	Fifth Republic

regretted the excess, the violence and the execution of the king.

History has bequeathed France two major problems from all this: national unity, and regime stability. The preoccupation with unity is reflected in successive efforts to instill a sense of national identity and patriotism into the population and a historic reluctance to decentralize power to the regions. The monarchy sought to centralize power in the name of the king. The Revolution substituted the French people as sovereigns but the creation of a French people from the miscellaneous provinces, language groups and local loyalties was to be the work of the nineteenth century. These efforts were largely successful and separatist movements, while not entirely absent, are of little importance in French politics. The problem of regime stability can be measured by the number of different constitutional systems which France has had since the Revolution of 1789 (Table 3.1).

These thirteen regimes, not counting all the constitutional shifts of the revolutionary periods, fall into four types. Before 1789 there was absolute monarchy. Since then, monarchical regimes have taken the form of limited, or constitutional monarchies. The most recent effort to restore a constitutional monarchy was in 1871 but the awkwardness of the Pretender prevented it succeeding and instead the regime evolved into the Third Republic, the longest regime since the Revolution. There have been five republican regimes including the present one. Finally, there have been three dictatorships, two of which evolved into Empires, under Napoleon Bonaparte and later under his nephew who took the title Napoleon III. Five regimes have ended in revolution, three by *coups d'état*, four in military defeat and one, the Fourth Republic, by a combination of elements. By the late nineteenth century, the republican form of government was largely established, with the defeat of monarchist forces and the ambitions of would-be dictators in the military. 1905 saw the final resolution of the vexed question of the Church, with the separation of Church and State, though echoes of the anticlerical issue could be heard long after.

Yet an important difference remained between supporters of strong government, with a powerful executive or presidency, and advocates of weak government, with power held in Parliament and governments subject to the day to day shifts of public and parliamentary opinion. Supporters of strong government emphasized the need for effectiveness and discipline to overcome the fractiousness of French political life. Their opponents charged them with authoritarian or Bonapartist tendencies and emphasized the needs of democracy, participation and sharing of power. Extremist elements remained on the political fringes looking for an opportunity. Another division was between supporters of centralization and advocates of stronger local government. All these issues interacted with considerations of party advantage, so that often oppositions have demanded weaker and more decentralized government, only to change their tack when in office.[1] Governments have framed the rules to suit themselves and opponents consequently have often challenged not merely the government of the day but the very rules of the political game. Indeed the succession of regime changes in Table 3.1 simplifies matters since, without changing the constitution itself, significant changes are regularly made in the rules of the political game. The parliamentary electoral system, for example, was changed eight times under the Third Republic and has been changed twice under the Fifth. This history of instability and the vulnerability of constitutional regimes to revolution, *coups d'état* and foreign occupation, gives a certain air of impermanence to French constitutional arrangements, which in turn can undermine their legitimacy.

The current regime, the Fifth Republic, can only be understood in relation to these historic problems, and in particular to the failures of its predecessors. France was defeated early in the second world war and its northern part occupied by the Germans. In the remainder of the country, a puppet state known as the Vichy regime existed under Marshal Pétain. Free French forces, refusing to accept defeat, rallied outside France under General Charles de Gaulle while inside the country a resistance movement developed. At the liberation, the resistance forces, including Socialists, Communists, Gaullists and some others, were dominant in politics, grouped in a provisional government under de Gaulle; but they had great difficulty agreeing on a new constitution. Eventually, after two attempts, the Fourth Republic was established. In reaction to Vichy, it was a classic case of a weak government regime, with power in the hands of parliament, to make and break governments. There was a system of fairly pure proportional representation, with a consequent proliferation of parties and an absence of stable majorities. In 1956, there were fifteen party groups in Parliament. With the outbreak of the Cold War, the Communists, the largest single party, were considered to be anti-system and after 1947 they did not feature in coalition-making. Nor did the Gaullists, after their founder had retired from the scene in 1946 in protest at the weakness of the regime and its partisan manoeuvring. The president was elected by the parliament and his office was symbolic. Consequently, government was by shifting and unstable coalitions, with twenty-five governments and eighteen prime ministers in twelve years.

Despite the chronic instability of governments, the Fourth Republic, aided by a powerful modernizing bureaucracy was able to lay the foundations of the French economic miracle and the European Community. Its great failure was in colonial affairs, where it found itself successively embroiled in wars of national liberation in Indo-China and Algeria. Defeated in Indo-China in 1954, France retreated, passing the burden to the United States. Algeria was a different matter. Conquered in 1830, it was regarded as an integral part of France and the million European settlers had a powerful lobby in Paris. Smarting from their humiliation in the second world war and in Indo-China, the military were determined on victory and, as the war became ever more brutal but with no end in sight, it began to undermine the Republic itself. The circumstances by which the Fourth Republic gave way to the Fifth still excite controversy. In 1958, a group of generals in Algeria seized power, defying the government and setting up committees of public safety, a term which recalled the seizure of power during the Revolution. The government temporized while calls went up for a strong man in the shape of General de Gaulle, who had been biding his time at his country retreat. De Gaulle, while not endorsing the generals' action, refused to condemn it either and declared himself ready to assume the affairs of the nation. The outcome was a vote by the parliament installing de Gaulle as prime minister and inviting him to prepare a new constitution. Was this a military *coup d'état*? Or a constitutional transfer of power? It was actually a bit of both. The transfer of power had been peaceful and parliamentary, but the context was one of military intimidation. While most of the political class had been relieved to abdicate in favour of de Gaulle, a section of opinion saw the origins of the Fifth Republic in a military rebellion as an original sin, tainting it from birth and saw de Gaulle as a new Napoleon or military strongman in the mould of Spain's Franco or Argentina's Peron. Others objected to the authoritarian features of the new constitution which they regarded as an affront to republican and parliamentary traditions. De Gaulle, while he had a strong authoritarian streak, proved in the end to be a democrat, leaving office when rejected by the people. Yet questions about the legitimacy of the new regime lingered and were not entirely resolved until 1981, when it proved possible to transfer power peacefully to the opposition parties.

The constitution of the Fifth Republic was intended to provide for a strengthened executive and more stable government than proved possible in the Fourth Republic. This was certainly de Gaulle's preference. Yet he did not have an entirely free hand, and had to compromise with the politicians of the Fourth Republic and France's parliamentary traditions. So an executive presidency was established, to which de Gaulle was duly elected for the seven-year term; but this was an indirect election via a college of parliamentarians and local government leaders. Only in 1962 was direct presidential election by the people instituted. The president appoints the prime minister and government, as in a presidential system; but these are also responsible to parliament, as in a parliamentary system. The result is a hybrid system, with both presidential and parliamentary features Where the president and parliamentary majority are of the same persuasion, united and powerful government is possible. The difficulty arises where these institutions are controlled by different parties, a difficulty made more likely by the fact that the president is elected for seven years but the parliament for five so that every president is faced with the need for a parliamentary election in the course of his mandate.

The Presidency

Article 5 of the constitution defines the powers of the president rather vaguely, declaring that:

> The president of the Republic ensures respect for the constitution. He assures, by his *arbitrage,* the regular functioning of the public powers and the continuity of the State. He is the guarantor of national independence, of the integrity of the territory, of the respect of accords of the (French) Community and of treaties.

Much ink has been spilled on the interpretation of *arbitrage,* which can mean either that the president functions as a referee ensuring that the rules of the game are respected, or that he actively participates in the business of government. Article 20 declares that it is the government which 'determines and conducts the policy of the Nation' while article 21 stipulates that 'the prime minister directs the action of the government'. Under Article 8, the president nominates the prime minister, but this could mean a real choice, or a formal ratification of the party leader commanding a parliamentary majority. Similarly, the president's power to dissolve parliament and call elections could be real or formal. The president chairs the Council of Ministers but this is also open to interpretation. Unlike his American counterpart, the French president does not have a legislative veto and can only send bills back to parliament for reconsideration. Only where government is proceeding by ordinance or decree, does the president possess a veto. Other powers are attributed to both the president and the prime minister, for example in national defence and the nomination of officials. More definite is Article 16, which allows the president in a national emergency when the institutions or territorial integrity of the state are threatened, to function as a virtual dictator, stipulating only that the Constitutional Council must be consulted, that parliament must remain in session and that the powers must be used to restore normal government as soon as possible. These powers have been used only once, by de Gaulle to deal with another military rebellion in Algeria in 1961. Since the 1960s, a firm consensus has developed, embodied in a 1964 decree, that it is the president alone who decides on the use of France's nuclear weapons, underpinned by a doctrine that these are weapons of last resort to protect the national territory itself.

This ambivalence on presidential powers is not peculiar to France but has appeared in other European constitutions, including the new democracies of eastern Europe. It is resolved less by legalistic interpretation of constitutional documents than by custom and convention and the balance of political forces. In the early years of the Fifth Republic, de Gaulle's dominant personality left no doubt as to where power lay and, as long as the Algerian crisis continued, the parliamentary leaders were content to let him rule. His authority was further strengthened by a series of direct appeals to the people through referendums.

Although the constitution envisages a limited use of the referendum for specific purposes, de Gaulle used the instrument in a Bonapartist spirit, as a plebiscite on his own rule, threatening to resign if the electors did not endorse him. It was a failure to gain a majority in the referendum of 1969 which precipitated his own resignation. The most important referendum was that of 1962, providing for the direct election of the president. Although strictly unconstitutional, this is seen in retrospect as validated by the popular will. Thenceforth, the president himself was the product of the popular will, giving him a democratic legitimacy and enormously enhanced status in relation to the parliament.

De Gaulle consistently interpreted the constitution in a presidential manner, choosing his own prime ministers and, although the constitution does not provide for this, firing them - Georges Pompidou is said to have supplied a signed but undated resignation letter at the time of his appointment. Selection of other ministers has also become a presidential prerogative, despite the fact that the constitution give the prime minister the initiative in this. De Gaulle emphasized presidential primacy when in 1962 Pompidou's government was overthrown in parliament. Rather than seek a new prime minister among the parliamentary leaders, de Gaulle delayed accepting Pompidou's resignation and dissolved the parliament to gain a new majority. Major policy decisions were taken by de Gaulle personally, often without consulting the government. In the early years, an attempt was made, largely to manage problems within the Gaullist party, to distinguish a reserved presidential domain involving defence, foreign and colonial affairs. Elsewhere, the prime minister and government would take the lead. This was quickly repudiated by de Gaulle himself in favour of a broader doctrine providing for presidential interventions in any field, but with an assumption that the president would occupy himself with the larger strategic issues, leaving the prime minister the charge of routine administration.

It was the presidential succession of 1969 which determined that the strong presidency would survive. Had the centrist candidate Alain Poher, won, it is likely that the president would have become a national father figure. In the event, the election was carried by de Gaulle's former prime minister, Georges Pompidou (1969-74), who gave his own prime ministers no more leeway than he had enjoyed himself. So the convention of a strong executive presidency was established, to be continued by Valéry Giscard d'Estaing (1974-81). A critical test came in 1981 with the election of the Socialist François Mitterrand (1981-88; 1988-). This was the first major change of governing majority in the Fifth Republic, since previous changes had taken place within the Gaullist and allied camp. Mitterrand had been a consistent critic of de Gaulle and of the dubious methods by which he had returned to power in 1958 and had described the constitution as a permanent *coup d'état*. Many Socialists disliked the strong presidency, the subordinate role of parliament and the generally authoritarian features of the constitutions. Yet over the years Mitterrand had come to accept the permanence of the new institutions and realized that they could be turned to the benefit of the left. On assuming office he declared that while the constitution had not been made for him, it suited him well. The special security court, which had concerned itself with offences against the state and was seen as an instrument of oppression, was abolished. The broadcast media were given more freedom from government direction. More power decentralized to local government. Yet the institution of the presidency was left intact. The fact that the first alternation in power had taken place at the presidential level rather than, as had been widely predicted, through the victory of the left at the legislative elections of 1978 was a critical step in preserving a strong presidency and legitimating it on the left.

Up until 1986, all presidents had enjoyed majority support in Parliament or, where they lacked it, as in 1962 and 1981, had dissolved parliament and obtained a majority. As undisputed leader of a governing formation, they were able to continue the Gaullist practice of hiring and firing prime ministers, with the latter explicitly accepting that they could not continue in office without the confidence of the president. In policy matters, they gradually extended the domain of presidential action but intervening over a wider range of domestic economic and social issues than de Gaulle, pre-occupied with high politics, had regarded as worthy of his attention. On the other hand, lacking de Gaulle's personal authority, they have been bound more closely to the constitution and precedent. They have largely resisted the recourse to the referendum as personal plebiscite. While de Gaulle mounted five referendums, including the ones which brought him to power and removed him, his successors have staged only three. In order to intervene over the whole policy field, presidents have established a substantial staff at the Elysée palace. In 1989, President Mitterrand had fifty-seven *chargés de mission* and counsellors, with their various assistants, to cover the whole range of governmental activity.

Despite its routinization, presidential government is not without its problems. As head of state and the embodiment of national will, all presidents wish to rise a little above the day-to-day squabbles of party politics. They are also able to distance themselves a little from their own governments, putting the prime minister in the firing line of social discontent and political attack and holding back their own interventions until the issues are clarified. They can discreetly signal their support for discontented groups, while keeping their options open, presenting an understanding and sympathetic image. Yet, faced with the five-yearly parliamentary elections, they need to mobilize their partisan forces to ensure a continued majority and freedom to appoint their own government. So Giscard d'Estaing in 1978 and Mitterrand in 1986 had to descend from their pedestals into the political bearpit, at some cost to their prestige. In the event of failure to assemble a majority in the legislative elections, the president loses a large part of his authority and a completely different game unfolds, that of cohabitation (explained below). The choice of prime minister also poses problems even in normal times. A prime minister with his or her own political base or independent ideas may strengthen the presidential coalition but prove a rival to the president. De Gaulle's firing of Pompidou in 1968 has been attributed precisely to the prime minister's success in mobilizing a crushing Gaullist majority at the legislative elections of that year. Serious conflicts led to the dismissal of Prime Ministers Jacques Chaban-Delmas in 1972 and Jacques Chirac in 1976. Yet a prime minister who is a nonentity risks weakening the government as a whole. As Table 3.2 indicates, presidents have used their power to change prime ministers freely, to ensure that they remain faithful executants and to give tired governments a new image, or in response to a change in the parliamentary majority.

Table 3.2 Presidents and Prime Ministers of the Fifth Republic

President	Prime Minister
1958-65 Charles de Gaulle	1958-62 Michel Debré
1965-69 Charles de Gaulle	1962-68 Georges Pompidou
	1968-69 Maurice Couve de Murville
1969-74 Georges Pompidou	1969-72 Jacques Chaban-Delmas
	1972-74 Pierre Messmer
1974-81 Valéry Giscard d'Estaing	1974-76 Jacques Chirac
	1976-81 Raymond Barre
1981-88 François Mitterrand	1981-84 Pierre Mauroy
	1984-86 Laurent Fabius
	1986-88 Jacques Chirac
1988- François Mitterrand	1988-91 Michel Rocard
	1991-92 Edith Cresson
	1992-93 Pierre Bérégovoy
	1993- Edouard Balladur

Government and Parliament

The Fifth Republic did not merely strengthen the presidency; it also reinforced the position of the prime minister and government in relation to parliament. This consists of two chambers, a directly elected National Assembly to which government is responsible, and an indirectly elected Senate, whose powers are largely confined amending and delaying legislation. Abandoning proportional representation had the intended effect of generally producing stable, disciplined majorities in the National Assembly. In case a majority is not found, the president has the right to dissolve the assembly, though this can be done only once in any twelve month period. Government's responsibility to the assembly is strictly defined. It can be removed by a vote of censure but this requires an absolute majority of all members of the National Assembly, not merely of those voting. A censure motion must be signed by 10per cent of the deputies (members of the Assembly) and if it fails those members may not sign another such motion during the session. Further to discourage the sort of coalition break-ups which characterized the Fourth Republic, ministers are not allowed to be members of parliament. On appointment to ministerial office, a deputy or senator must give up his/her seat to a substitute elected at the same time. Although this was intended to ensure government cohesion by depriving resigning ministers of a political base in parliament, the spirit of the law has been undermined by the practice of choosing complaisant substitutes prepared to resign their seats to allow the fallen minister to come back in a by-election. Indeed, ministers have consistently been encouraged to contest parliamentary seats in general elections in order to bolster support for the government, even though they have to give them up immediately. Not that they need much encouragement. A territorial power base remains an important asset in French politics and ministers continue to cultivate their old constituencies even while they are in the temporary care of their substitutes. Nonetheless, the incompatibility rule, by taking ministers out of parliament, shifted the focus of political life and downgraded parliamentary institutions.

Ministers are appointed by the president, officially on the nomination of the prime minister, and collectively form the Council of Ministers. A few ministers bear the honorific title Minister of State, either by virtue of their seniority or because they have been brought into the government to ensure the support of allied parties. Outside the Council of Ministers are delegated ministers and the more junior secretaries of state. Each full minister has charge of a ministry, some of which are always present (Interior, Defence, Foreign Affairs, Education) while others may be changed at will. In the early years of the Gaullist era, there was a preponderance of non-political ministers, brought in from the civil service or the private world, reflecting both de Gaulle's contempt for party politics and his lack of a solid party base. Gradually, as the Gaullist party consolidated, these gave way to career politicians or themselves established political legitimacy by gaining local government office or being elected to parliament - promptly resigning in favour of their substitutes. At the same time, the political class itself came to be dominated by graduates of the prestigious civil service schools. Eight out of eleven prime ministers between 1958 and

1993 had served in the civil service. Three successive prime ministers between 1984 and 1991 were products of the *Ecole Nationale d'Administration* (ENA) who had opted early in life for political careers. Under the Socialists after 1981, there was an increase in the numbers of former teachers in the government, but the civil servants held their place. This colonization of politics by the bureaucratic elite is encouraged by the extremely generous provision for civil servants to take leave (*mis hors cadre*) while they are in politics but come back at any time, with their seniority and pension rights unaffected. Veteran politician Michel Rocard has come back to his civil service post at several points in his political career, most recently after being removed as prime minister in 1991. While there has been a professionalization of the political class since the 1960s, the option of forming a government largely comprising non-politicians remains open to a president without a solid party base in parliament and was used by Mitterrand in 1988 as a means of enlarging the presidential majority and reaching out to civil society.

Certain powers are reserved in the constitution for the prime minister while others are exercised by the Council of Ministers. The prime minister must countersign most presidential acts, a formality in most cases but a potential source of conflict. In the large area reserved for executive action, the prime minister issues decrees, or signs those issued by individual ministers. Unlike in the British case, the prime minister heads a substantial department, which may include substantive functions like the national plan, as well as the government secretariat, which prepares the meetings of the Council of Ministers and liaises with its opposite number at the presidency. Like other ministers, the prime minister also has a personal *cabinet* of assistants to provide information and coordinate the various tasks. In 1990, the prime minister's *cabinet* contained thirty nine members, covering all the main activities of government. There are thus three levels of action for any policy issue, the ministerial department, the Matignon (prime minister's department) and the Elysée (the presidency), a system which allows much routine government to be carried on at the ministerial level but permits the prime minister or president to intervene at will.

Parliament's functions were to be reduced to that of legislation and voting the budget, rather than making and breaking governments. Its rules of procedure are not decided by the two houses themselves but largely contained in the constitution and organic, that is semi-constitutional, laws. Sittings are limited to two sessions of eighty and ninety days, with extra sessions allowed only by permission of the president. The number of permanent committees is limited to six each for the Senate and the National Assembly, with each member sitting on one only; this was intended to avoid specialized committees shadowing departments or falling into the hands of interest groups as happened in the Fourth Republic. The subjects on which it is competent to legislate are enumerated, with other matters falling to the government, and the legislative process itself biased to the advantage of the executive. Laws can be proposed by the government or members of parliament but the vast majority of legislation emanates from the government, whose business has priority. Bills are considered by the appropriate standing committee, which can propose amendments but the parliamentary debate is on the original text, with amendments from the committee, the government itself or members voted on separately. The government further has the right to call a 'block vote'' on all or part of the text, including only its own amendments. It can also stake its confidence on a text; in this case the bill is passed without further vote unless within forty-eight hours a motion of censure is tabled and voted by an absolute majority of all members of the National Assembly. These procedures are useful not only to swamp the opposition but also to cover up divisions in the ranks of the government's own supporters by avoiding detailed debate and amendment of the text. The blocked vote was used only three times between 1981 and 1986 when the Socialists had a majority. Between 1986 and 1988, the cohabitation government of Chirac, with a wafer thin and fractious majority, used it thirty six times. In 1988-9 the minority Rocard government used it sixteen times. Finally, the government can ask parliament to grant it powers to legislate by ordinance in a prescribed field for a specified period. Finance bills must be introduced first into the National Assembly and then the Senate. No amendment increasing expenditure or reducing taxes can be proposed except by the government and if the bill has not been voted within seventy days the government may proceed to implement it by ordinance.

Parliamentary organization is also tightly controlled. Party groups are officially recognized as long as they have twenty-five members and the consolidation of the party system, at least until the mid 1980s, encouraged party discipline in voting. Although the constitution stipulates that voting is in person, this is largely ignored, with party nominees regularly turning members' electronic voting keys for them. The tradition of accumulation of mandates, by which many deputies are simultaneously local government leaders or members of the European Parliament, produces an absentee rate which does nothing for the parliament's prestige or assiduity. The presidential system has moved the focus of political attention away from parliament and this is not, by and large, a place where political reputations are made and broken. So unlike the British situation, in France parliament is in no sense the centre and focus of political life. Even when the government lacks a majority, parliament does not come into its own. On the contrary, governments just use this as a pretext to use the various procedures available to bypass it. This was identified by the late 1980s as one of the reasons for political frustration and the debilitation of political life.

Yet parliament is not to be dismissed entirely. From a very low point in the early years, its role has gradually developed. A question time was instituted in

1974, though it remains a pale imitation of its British counterpart. Parliamentary committees have on occasion played an important role in the development of legislation, for example in the decentralization laws of the 1980s where many deputies had a personal interest as mayors. The 1974 reform allowing sixty deputies or senators to appeal a law in the Constitutional Council before its promulgation gave new strength to the opposition. Research facilities for members have improved and a number of delegations and offices have been established to consider policy in fields like communications, planning and technology. While parliament has ceased to be the centre of French political life, election to the National Assembly is nevertheless considered an important element in building a power base for both national and local politicians.

The status of the Senate has always been controversial. Indirectly elected from local government, it is disproportionately weighted to the small rural communes and to conservative interests; hence the suspicion of it on the part of the left and, for a long time, the Gaullists. Party discipline is looser and the groups do not correspond exactly to those in the National Assembly. Its power is strictly curtailed. Legislation must be approved by both houses of parliament, with provision for a joint committee in case of disagreement, but if no consensus is reached the government can take the bill back to the National Assembly whose decision is final. With its built-in conservative majority, the Senate has caused more problems for Socialist than for right-wing governments, though under administrations of all colours it is vigilant in defence of the local governments from which it is elected.

Presidential or Parliamentary System

Custom and practice since 1958 have largely resolved the issue of where power lies in the Fifth Republic. It is a strong executive system, with a weakened parliament and, within the executive the centre of power is, under normal circumstances, the presidency. Yet the circumstances do matter, in particular whether the presidential and parliamentary majorities coincide. There are three possibilities here: a president with a parliamentary majority; a president faced with a parliamentary majority of opponents; and a parliament with no majority. In the first case, which prevailed between 1962 and 1986, it is clear that the president chooses the prime minister and government and takes the major policy decisions. Parliament is largely reduced to the role of supporting the president and his government. In the second case, where the president's opponents gain an overall majority in the National Assembly, there is potential for a constitutional conflict, since a government nominated by the president could be brought down. In 1962 the government was brought down when elements of the president's coalition deserted him. In this case, the president was able to dissolve the parliament and call on the electorate to return a new presidential majority. Yet this option is not always available. In the course of his mandate, every president has had to face the five-yearly parliamentary election. If this produces a hostile majority, options are limited. A dissolution, with new parliamentary elections, would probably merely produce the same majority, deepening the crisis. It has been suggested that in that case, the president should resign, either retiring or standing for re-election to renew his mandate. This would be to undermine the presidency itself, by suggesting that it was subject to the fluctuation of parliamentary majorities. The spirit of the 1962 reform providing for the direct election of the president is that he has his own power base and a legitimacy independent of parliamentary elections. So there may no choice but to live with the result of the election outcome. If the president is unable to prise apart the hostile majority, winning over some of its members to a new coalition, then he must cohabit, that is appoint a prime minister representing the new parliamentary majority.

In this case, which occurred between 1986 and 1988 and after the 1993 elections, power does shift, not towards parliament which remains as subordinated as ever but to the new prime minister and government issued from the parliamentary majority. It is they who take the major policy decisions, prepare the budget and legislative programme and make appointments to public offices. Yet the president does not lose all power or influence, as Mitterrand showed in the 1986-88 interlude. He remains head of state and, while the doctrine of the presidential domain of foreign and defence affairs was never really established, he does take a particular interest in these matters as the embodiment of France in the world. Mitterrand insisted on personally attending the summit meetings of the European Community and the G7 annual meeting of the main industrial countries along with Chirac, the prime minister. At the outset he let it be known that he had blocked Chirac's nominees as ministers of defence and foreign affairs - though this suited Chirac rather well as the nominees were leaders of his UDF coalition partner whom he had felt obliged to appoint rather than his own followers. It is unlikely that such a coincidence of interests would occur in normal times, and on a number of issues Mitterrand and Chirac clashed on the question of who was really in charge of defence and foreign policy. The issue was only contained by the general consensus in France on the main lines of defence and foreign policy and the absence of major foreign crises during the period, though there were crossed lines in communication with foreign powers and responsibility for some murky dealings with hostage-takers has never been clarified. In domestic matters, Mitterrand was more circumspect but continued to chair the Council of Ministers and made known his views on policy issues, criticizing the government where they were vulnerable and commenting sympathetically on the plight of discontented social groups. When Chirac resorted to ordinances to expedite privatization and the return to the old electoral system, Mitterrand was able to exercise his veto and force the government to use the full parliamentary legislative route instead. Generally, by letting the government take the difficult decisions, placing himself above the fray and cultivating a more understanding, socially-minded image, Mitterrand was able comprehensively to outmanoeuvre Chirac and restore his own public standing. In 1988, Mitterrand beat Chirac decisively in the presidential election, ensuring that cohabitation was merely an interlude in the presidential system. Indeed, the whole period can be seen as an extended election campaign in which the prize was not a parliamentary majority or the prime ministership but the Elysée itself, so strengthening the presidential orientation of the regime. It is now regarded as a serious political error for Chirac, as a presidential aspirant, to have assumed the cohabitation prime ministership at all, rather than entrusting it to one of his more expendable lieutenants. In the second cohabitation, after the 1993 legislative elections, Chirac and Mitterrand were able to agree on the appointment as prime minister of Edouard Balladur, a moderate Gaullist without presidential ambitions of his own.

The third case is one in which no party has a parliamentary majority. This prevailed between 1958 and 1962, but then de Gaulle's personal authority and the Algerian crisis left the president in charge. It was only the end of the Algerian problem together with de Gaulle's challenge to the parliamentary parties in the form of the referendum on direct presidential election which brought an open clash, won by de Gaulle in the referendum and the subsequent parliamentary elections. In 1988, Mitterrand, having been re-elected president, dissolved parliament and, while getting rid of the opposition majority, failed to obtain one of his own. In this case, the president still appoints the prime minister who retains office unless an absolute majority in the National Assembly decide otherwise. The government does not need to be invested by the assembly and, once installed, has access to the full panoply of powers made available by the constitution. For his part, the president can seek to broaden the government's parliamentary base by attracting individuals and groups into the 'presidential majority' a coaliton going beyond his own party. De Gaulle was consistently able to attract elements of the old conservative and centre parties into support. Giscard d'Estaing, while possessing a supportive parliamentary majority, sought to remould it by reducing Gaullist influence. Mitterrand in 1981 took both the Communists and some Gaullist elements into the government even though his own Socialist party had a parliamentary majority on its own. When the president's party does not have a majority, this notion of a presidential majority becomes vital. In 1988 Mitterrand opened up his government to the centre, bringing in some UDF people and non-political personalities, a process continued in local and regional elections into the 1990s. While this serves to stabilize presidential power, however, it has an extremely destabilizing effect on the party system, demoralizing the president's own party and dividing the opposition. In this sense, it works against the strong bipolar tendencies of the regime as a whole.

The cohabitation experience shows that the institutions of the Fifth Republic were solid enough to withstand sharp partisan divisions within them. Opinion polls over the years have shown that the main elements of the constitution, direct election of the president, the right of the president to dissolve the Assembly, the right of the Assembly to overthrow the government, and the Constitutional Council, have broad support, though there is some tendency for attitudes to depend on whether the respondent's own party is in power or not. A poll taken in 1983 on the occasion of the Fifth Republic's twenty-fifth anniversary showed that only among the Communists was there still a lingering hostility to the regime (Table 3.3). Similar attitudes pervade the political parties. Initially seen as the personal instrument of de Gaulle, the regime gained the support of the centrist parties in 1969 and 1974 when they were brought into the governing coalition, of the Socialists during the 1970s when they realized that they could make it work to their advantage, and finally of a large section of the Communists in the 1980s. Polls during the cohabitation of 1986-88 showed the public, after some confusion, wishing the experiment to work so as not to put the regime in danger, and a willingness to sanction any party which should prove disruptive. The knowledge of this proved a strong disincentive for either of the partners to bring the cohabitation experiment to a premature close. Yet cohabitation is an anomaly and suggestions have been widely canvassed for ways in which it could be avoided.

Table 3.3 Percentage considering that the constitution works well or badly, 1983

	All	By party supported			
		Communist	Socialist	UDF (Giscardian)	RPR (Gaullist)
Well or very well	57	40	61	74	65
Badly or very badly	25	49	26	15	18
No opinion	18	11	13	11	17

Source: SOFRES poll, cited in J-L Parodi and F. Platone, 'L'adoption par les gouvernés', in O. Duhamel and J-L. Parodi (eds.), La constitution de la cinquième république (Paris: Presses de la Fondation Nationale des Sciences Politiques, 1988).

One idea is to reduce the presidential mandate to five years so that a president could hold a parliamentary election immediately after arriving in office and not have to face another one in mid-term. A constitutional amendment to this effect was passed by parliament in 1973 but not proceeded with; later the idea was floated by the Socialists. It is opposed by many supporters of a strong presidency, especially in the Gaullist tradition, who argue that the president must have a separate electoral base from the parliament. To elect them at the same time, or in immediate succession, would be to confuse the two elections and reduce the president's status to the equal of parliament. Polls have long indicated that most voters like the idea of a five-year presidential mandate and in the early 1990s the idea gained ground even among Gaullists. A second proposal is to introduce proportional representation for parliamentary elections so that there would normally be no majority in the National Assembly. This would strengthen the presidential element of the regime by giving the president a freer hand in assembling a governing majority, while at the same time making the parliament more representative. Unfortunately, changes in the French electoral system are invariably inspired by short-term partisan considerations rather than a quest for long-term stability of institutions. In 1986, the Mitterrand administration changed the electoral system to a rather impure form of proportional representation in the hope of depriving the opposition of its expected majority, while freeing the Socialists from the need to make second round deals with the Communists. The ploy did not work and, having gained their majority, the parties of the right changed the system back. In 1991, Pierre Mauroy, general secretary of the Socialist party, floated the idea of a new reform, declaring that the party must first determine its general programme, then look for allies among the smaller parties and groups, then design an electoral system for the next legislative elections which could achieve the required results. It seems that the electoral system in France will never be treated as one of the basic rules of the game rather than an instrument in the pursuit of short-term advantage and until it is then it cannot serve to stabilize constitutional practice.

These ideas are to improve the constitution and remove some of the political uncertainty which arises from the constant anticipation of the next presidential or parliamentary election. They do not question the basis principle of presidentialism and strong executive government. After a history alternating between strong and weak government, between republics and monarchies, France has in the Fifth Republic come nearer than ever before to a constitution commanding general acceptance.

Judicial Control

An important contribution to constitutionalism in the Fifth Republic is the establishment, for the first time in French history, of a form of judicial review, taking matters of constitutional interpretation out of the hands of politicians. The Constitutional Council is responsible for determining whether laws and decrees conform to the 1958 constitution and to the 1789 declaration of rights which was re-enacted as the preamble to it, and whether ordinances are valid in terms of the parent legislation. Compared with the United States Supreme Court, the scope for review is limited. Laws can only be reviewed between their passage in parliament and their promulgation by the president of the Republic and it is not possible to challenge the constitutionality of laws in the ordinary courts. Apart from the semi-constitutional organic laws which are automatically reviewed, laws can only be challenged before the Constitutional Council by the president of the Republic, the prime minister, the presidents of the National Assembly or Senate or, since a 1974 reform, sixty deputies or senators. When the president of the Republic exercises the dictatorial emergency powers under article 16 of the constitution, the Constitutional Council gives its advice but cannot rule on the constitutionality of the assumption of the powers or the action taken under them.

Although the Constitutional Council is a judicial body, its composition is politically determined, nominated one-third each by the president of the republic and the presidents of the Senate and National Assembly. The nine members are nominated for nine-year terms, one third retiring every three years, without being eligible for re-nomination. Former presidents of the Republic are members *ex officio* but, as membership involves abstention from political activity, they have tended not to take their places.

In a political culture such as that of France, where institutions have constantly been challenged through history, there was much scepticism about the prospects for a neutral constitutional referee such as the Council. The left saw the new provisions as a prop for the conservative order and a barrier to radical change. The initial rules on reference, confined to the leaders of the government and parliamentary majorities, did little to dispel this. The opening up of the procedure to sixty deputies or senators, which allows the opposition parties to appeal, could merely have brought it further into the party political arena but in fact served to secure its acceptance on the left. Certainly, the 1974 reform led to a huge increase in cases as first the Socialist opposition and then, even more determinedly, the

Table 3.4 Decisions of the constitutional council on ordinary issues

Period	Number	Annual rate of decisions
1958-74	9	0.56
1974-81 (Giscard government)	44	6.3
1981-86 (Mitterrand government)	66	13.2
1986-8 (cohabitation)	26	13.0
1988-92 (minority government)	45	11.0

Source: Les grands textes de la pratique institutionelle de la V République, 6th edn. (Paris: Documentation Française, 1992).

conservative opposition after 1988, made use of the power, as Table 3.4 illustrates.

These were accompanied in both periods by attacks on the integrity of the council as a mere prop to the government but, by developing a constitutional jurisprudence and tending to invalidate sections of legislation rather than whole laws, the council was able to retain its credibility, while extending the field of civil liberties and civic equality, especially in the 1970s. In both 1981 and 1986 it was able not merely to survive the alternation of political power but to smooth the process and give legitimacy to it.

An older mechanism of judicial control is the system of administrative courts, with the Council of State at their summit. These are staffed by professional judges, *maîtres de requêtes* recruited largely from the prestigious *Ecole Nationale d'Administration* (ENA). The Council of State itself is staffed two-thirds by *maîtres de requêtes* promoted from the administrative courts and the rest at the discretion of the government. Although they are civil servants, these officials have a large degree of independence from the government of the day and are able to handle and rule on citizen complaints against agents of public administration. Their independence and status is further boosted by the fact that they comprise one of the most prestigious *grands corps* of the civil service (see below) with all the privileges attached to this, including the ability to move out of their field into other areas of the public and private sectors. The Council of State itself has further responsibilities in advising government on the legal form of laws and certain decrees and, though its advice is not binding, it is taken seriously.

PARTIES AND ELECTIONS

French party politics is traditionally very complex, with parties, factions, clubs and groups fighting, splitting, coalescing in the pursuit of power, personal advantage or doctrinal purity. For a while, the Fifth Republic simplified matters. In the early years, the personality of de Gaulle overshadowed the parties. His movement cut across many of the traditional divisions and the main question in politics was one's attitude to the president. From the late 1960s to the late 1980s, matters further clarified, with the emergence of something like a two-party system of alternating right of centre and left of centre governments. This was encouraged by the direct election of the president since only those parties with credible presidential candidates could henceforth be considered serious contenders. The electoral system also played its part. In presidential elections, it is necessary for candidates to gain the signatures of 500 notables (deputies, senators, local government leaders) representing thirty of the hundred departments and territories. If no candidate gains an absolute majority of votes, a second round is held a week later between the top two candidates or, if either of these drops out, the best-placed remaining candidates. This produces intense negotiation between the two rounds, in which the minor candidates must decide whether to throw their support behind one of the remaining contenders, in the hope of appointments or policy concessions. Such endorsements can be vital. In 1969, in the absence of a left-wing candidate in the second ballot, the Communists advised their voters to abstain rather than vote for the centrist Poher. In 1981, Chirac gave only lukewarm endorsement to Giscard d'Estaing, while the Communist voters rallied to Mitterrand, giving him the edge in the second ballot. The results of the five presidential elections under the Fifth Republic are given in the appendix.

The parliamentary electoral system used for most of the Fifth Republic also tends to consolidate the parties into two camps. This is a two-round system based on single-member constituencies. A candidate gaining more than 50 per cent of the vote at the first round wins but if no candidate does so then any candidate with 12.5 per cent of the electorate may proceed to the second round. This places heavy pressure on the parties to forge coalitions between the two rounds to leave just one candidate each of right and left, presenting the electorate with clear choices of governing teams, rather than leaving coalition making to manoeuvring in parliament as in the Fourth Republic or contemporary Italy. Table 3.5 shows how the discipline of *désistement* or standing down in the second round, has become established over the years so that by the late 1970s there was a two-party contest at the second ballot almost everywhere. As the 1986 legislative elections were conducted by proportional representation with one ballot, the question did not arise. In 1988 and 1993, the number of second ballots and the proportion with more than one candidate increased, as the party system began once again to fragment

The severe penalties of not uniting on the second ballot were felt by the left in the early years of the Fifth Republic. In 1958, the Communists won 19 per cent of the vote at the first round but ended up with just ten seats while the Gaullists with 20.6 per cent of first round votes gained 216 seats. Even

Table 3.5 Second round ballots in legislative elections

Election	Number of second round ballots	Second round ballots with more than two candidates	
		Number	%
1958	426	342	80.3
1962	369	141	38.2
1967	398	69	17.3
1968	316	49	15.5
1973	424	97	22.9
1978	418	3	>1
1981	320	1	>1
1988	453	8	1.8
1993	497	15	3.0

with second round discipline on left and right, the system, like other systems based on single member constituencies, remains non-proportional, exaggerating the advantage of the winning party and excluding small parties. In 1968, the Gaullists won 37 per cent of the first ballot vote but ended up with 62 per cent of the seats. In 1981, the Socialists won 36 per cent of the first ballot vote but 58 per cent of the seats.In 1993, the conservative parties won 40 per cent of the first ballot vote and 80 per cent of the seats.

Since the late 1980s, the bipolar trend has to some extent been reversed. There has been a new fragmentation of the party system, with competing parties emerging at the extremes and attempts to recreate an independent political centre. Voters for their part have become more volatile and, as in other countries, old loyalties are breaking down. Presidentialism itself, while initially encouraging a bipolar party system, has tended to devalue the parties, reducing them to mere circuits in a presidential power system. The relation between presidents and their parties has become asymmetrical since, while parties need credible presidential candidates, presidents themselves are more than mere party figures, deriving their legitimacy from direct personal election. Presidents have all reserved the right to extend their support base by bringing in other forces while insisting on the continued loyalty of their own partisans. Presidents must also be aware of the need to preserve their powers in the event of losing their parliamentary majority and so avoid becoming too closely associated with it. Since the presidency remains the main political prize in the Fifth Republic, parties and coalitions themselves easily break into factions behind the ambitions of the main presidential hopefuls, undermining the discipline which the electoral system imposes on them. By the late 1980s, the main parties themselves had become rather discredited from their recent experience in government. A series of scandals involving party finance had further undermined confidence.

The Gaullists and RPR

The traditional conservative parties emerged from the second world war disorganized and discredited by collaboration with the Vichy regime and, in contrast to other European countries, no mass Conservative party emerged during the Fourth Republic. In the early years of the Fifth Republic, the conservative side of the political spectrum was dominated by Gaullism, under a succession of party labels. While including most of the traditional conservative vote, this extended across a broad social spectrum, with a considerable working-class element, united by de Gaulle's personal appeal an inter-class message. The essence of classical Gaullism was nationalism, an appeal to the idea of a nation beyond class and sectional differences, united in the pursuit of French greatness. Its emphasis on the need for modernization and change if

France was to re-establish her position in the world made Gaullism a form of developmental nationalism and marked it off from traditional conservatism with its emphasis on defending existing positions. Within this set of nationalist assumptions, Gaullism could be flexible on questions of economic and social policy, so that, while it is on the right, it is often difficult to fit into traditional right-wing and conservative categories.

In the pursuit of French greatness, the central role was given to the state. A strong and authoritative state was needed to ensure law and order. There was also a large role for the state in economic management. This inclination on the French right to state intervention, reflecting a lack of confidence in the capitalist class, is often traced as far back as the seventeenth century minister, Jean-Baptiste Colbert, but it was never a fixed point of ideology. For the left, state intervention was a matter of principle; for Colbertistes and Gaullists it was simply a means of furthering the greatness of the nation. An expansive welfare state was another means of strengthening national unity and solidarity. In foreign policy, the emphasis was on furthering French prestige and influence in the world, while recognizing the limits of a second-class power. France remained a member of NATO, but withdrew in 1966 from the integrated military command and removed American bases from its soil. An independent nuclear weapons programme, started under the Fourth Republic, was pursued, though nobody took too seriously de Gaulle's claim in 1968 that the warheads would in future be pointed in all directions, implying that they would be targeted on the United States as well as the Soviet Union. The European Community was founded at the same time as the Fifth Republic and de Gaulle recognized that it was necessary in order to rebuild the French economy and stabilize relations with Germany. He was unwilling, however, to subordinate French sovereignty to the Community and resisted moves to political union. De Gaulle blocked the projected move to majority voting in the Community in 1965 so that the national veto was retained for another twenty years. He was fiercely opposed to American domination of the West and suspicious of Britain's close links with the United States. Fearing that it was a trojan horse for American influence and would undermine the Franco-German axis, he twice vetoed Britain's application for membership of the European Community.

De Gaulle affected to disdain party politics, but ensured that he had capable lieutenants organizing a political party to contest parliamentary elections and give him the necessary support. This went through various name changes but was generally referred to simply as the Gaullist party. De Gaulle's authority, however, was more personal, cemented through direct appeals to the people in presidential elections and referendums. In 1969, weakened by the social explosion of the previous year, he sought to re-establish his authority by a new referendum on regional and Senate reform, aimed directly at the old politicians and their parties. This time the ploy backfired and, losing the referendum, de

Gaulle resigned. His former prime minister, Georges Pompidou, seized control of the party to launch a successful presidential bid of his own. When Pompidou died in office in 1973 his own former prime minister, Jacques Chaban-Delmas, tried to repeat the feat, presenting himself as the Gaullist candidate for the succession. A section of the party under Jacques Chirac, however, threw their support behind Finance Minister Valéry Giscard d'Estaing, an ally but not a member of the Gaullist party. Giscard won and Chirac was rewarded with the prime ministership.

Chirac was unwilling to accept the subordinate role of a Fifth Republic prime minister and, when his request for more power was denied, he resigned. In 1976 he seizing the leadership of the Gaullist party, henceforth called the RPR, and used it as an instrument of his own presidential ambitions. After flirting with a type of left-wing populism in the late 1970s, Chirac moved the party decisively to the right in opposition to the Socialist governments of the 1980s.[2] Borrowing heavily from Ronald Reagan and Margaret Thatcher, he adopted the fashionable neo-liberal rhetoric about rolling back the state, privatization and markets.[3] More consistent with the Gaullist legacy was the call for tougher policies on law and order. So, like the new conservatives elsewhere, the RPR wanted less of the economic and welfare state and more of the gendarme state. On foreign policy, there was a modification of Gaullist positions towards a more pro-European and less anti-American line. Within the limits of its power, this was the policy pursued by the cohabitation government led by Chirac between 1986 and 1988.

Contrary to many expectations, the Gaullist party, in its new form of the RPR survived the death of its inspirer, but at the price of becoming a party like any other. Especially after the death of Pompidou, it became more like a conventional Conservative party. Left wingers who had rallied to de Gaulle in 1940 or 1958 had left the scene or linked up with the Socialists by 1981. References to de Gaulle and his legacy disappeared entirely from RPR rhetoric and were only resurrected in the early 1990s as a means of combating the National Front on the terrain of nationalism.[4] Losing its working-class supporters, it now depends heavily on the upper-middle class, self-employed people and farmers. It must share the Conservative electorate with the UDF while facing serious competition on its extreme right. Figure 3.1 shows how support has fallen from 30-40 per cent in de Gaulle's heyday to around 20 per cent in the 1980s. In 1981 and 1988 Chirac challenged for the presidency without success, though he did lead to government in the cohabitation period of 1986-88. On the other hand, the party did succeed in the 1980s in putting down roots in local government, a task which had defeated it in earlier years.

Another sign that the party has become like any other is the rise of factionalism, especially following the successive defeats in presidential elections in the 1980s. Previously the party was monolithic and united in support of the leadership. Now recognized factions or *courants* are allowed to present motions at the party congress and take issue with official policy.[5] In practice, there are few serious disputes over values. RPR activists are overwhelmingly middle class business and professional people and committed to the values of free market economics, nationalism and law and order and tend to take their detailed policy ideas from the leadership.[6] Yet in the early 1990s, some serious policy differences did emerge. Philippe Séguin led a NO campaign in the referendum on the Maastricht Treaty, against the line taken by Chirac. As president of the National Assemly in 1993, he took a more nationalist, populist and anti-European line than the new RPR-led government. Factions are also moulded by personalities, as presidential hopefuls and power brokers manoeuvre for position. Divisions also opened up over coalition and alliance tactics, in particular relations with the centrist parties and the issue of whether the RPR should make deals with the extreme right National Front.

The UDF

Successive forms of the Gaullist party never monopolized onservative representation in France. Elements of the old conservative, Liberal and Christian Democratic parties survived, allying with Gaullism at one time, going their own ways at another. Giscard d'Estaing was of this world. Finance minister for many years under de Gaulle and Pompidou, he had marked his distance by refusing to support de Gaulle in the referendum of 1969. In 1974 he narrowly won the presidency against the official Gaullist candidate Jacques Chaban-Delmas, but with the support of a section of the Gaullists under Chirac. Rather than call new parliamentary elections, which he was not sure of winning, Giscard decided to govern with the Gaullist-dominated parliament elected in 1973, nominating Chirac as prime minister. In 1976 Chirac resigned and, although the Gaullists remained in the government, Giscard's position was uncomfortable. Facing parliamentary elections in 1978, he needed an independent party of his own. So in 1978, Giscard's supporters founded the UDF (*Union pour la Démocratie française*), a rather loose federation of parties including the Republican Party (Giscard's own moderate Conservative party); the CDS (Christian Democrat); the Radical Party (Conservative/Liberal); the MDSF (a splinter from the right of the Socialist Party); and the *Clubs Perspectives et réalités*.[7] From then, the UDF was able to share the Conservative vote fairly equally with the RPR, with which it remained in alliance. Although the UDF was initially distinguished from the RPR by its emphasis on the market economy, a more liberal attitude on social matters and a greater commitment to Europe, these differences diminished in the course of the 1980s. The UDF and RPR often present joint candidatures from the first round of elections and poll evidence indicates that electors make little distinction between them. In the early 1990s, the main policy differences concerned the European Community, to which the UDF was largely committed, while the RPR contained a nationalist element which opposed political integration and resented France's apparent domination by Germany in the European monetary system. On the other hand, there are sharp divisions between the two allied parties on questions of power. Each insisted on presenting its own presidential candidate at the first round in 1981 and 1988, weakening the conservative side and fragmenting the traditional Conservative vote to their joint disadvantage.[8] There were proposals for a form of primary election to choose a single candidate but it is difficult to see how this might work.

Similar divisions exist within the UDF itself. Its constituent parties have kept their own identities and organizations. They have produced several presidential hopefuls, including Giscard himself who, after his defeat by Mitterrand in the 1978 presidential elections, set himself to work his way back to the top. It remains a party of notables, with the different parties within it rooted in local power structures in various parts of the country. There are sharp differences on tactical issues, with one section of the UDF consistently prepared to do deals with the extreme right National Front while another is tempted by the prospect of a centre-left alliance with the Socialists. Discipline was maintained behind the RPR-UDF cohabitation government of 1986-8 but the UDF decided to present its own candidate for the presidential elections of 1988. This was Raymond Barre, formerly prime minister under Giscard. Although Barre had received the formal endorsement of the UDF, he ran his own personalized campaign, trying to promote a non-party image, which alienated some leading party figures. The candidature was a failure, with Barre coming third in the first round, behind both Mitterrand and Chirac and barely ahead of the National Front candidate Jean Marie Le Pen.

Following the 1988 elections, some UDF figures were lured into the Mitterrand camp with the offer of government posts. The CDS formed their own independent group in parliament, while remaining part of the UDF in organizational terms. This was seen as the beginnings of a resurrection of the independent political centre. Others, such as former minister Michel Poniatowski, sought to forge an alliance with the extreme right National Front. In the 1989 European elections, some UDF figures rallied to the centrist list of Simone Veil, while Giscard himself led a joint list with the RPR. The victory of the Giscard list was a serious blow to those hoping to regenerate the UDF as an independent force. At the 1993 legislative elections, the RPR and UDF presented joint candidates under the banner of the Union for France, led by Chirac and Giscard. Although their total first-round vote remained at the same level as it had been throughout the 1980s, the electoral system produced a crushing parliamentary majority. In the process, the forces for renovation within both parties were silenced.

The Socialists

Left-wing politics in France since the 1920s have been marked by the split between Socialists and Communists, with a variety of splinter groups complicating the picture. France's relatively late industrialization and the weakness of trade unions further reduced the prospects for a strong Social Democratic movement on the British or German model.

Until 1970, French socialism was represented by the SFIO *(Section française de l'internationale ouvrière),* which had broken into two when the Communists seceded in 1920. Under the Third Republic, it was mostly in opposition, though it enjoyed a brief period in office in the Popular Front period in 1936-8. In the Fourth Republic it became an active player in the coalition game, allying with the parties of the centre in both central and local government. Under its leader Guy Mollet, *Molletisme* became a synonym for radical rhetoric, to compete on the left with the Communists, combined with an almost complete lack of principle in government. Both votes and membership declined steadily as the more dynamic elements of the left formed their own small groups and clubs. The events of 1958 found it bereft of policy or strategy and most SFIO deputies voted for the installation of de Gaulle, some no doubt considering that, once the Algerian issue was resolved he would retire and normal politics would resume. In the event, the early years of the Fifth Republic saw the SFIO reduced to irrelevance, falling to just over 12 per cent of the vote in 1962 while membership was largely reduced to local government notables retaining office in 'third force' alliances with the centre parties.

Thereafter, two strategies were open to the Socialists. They could seek to recreate an alliance with the centre against the Gaullists - the centre-left option; or they could seek an alliance with the Communists and others on the left to work for an alternation of power - the left-unity option. The centre-left option was attempted by Gaston Defferre for the presidential elections of 1965 and 1969. In the first case, he did not manage to launch his candidature while in the second he came in with a humiliating 5 per cent of the first-round vote. The left-unity strategy was associated with François Mitterrand, a nonSocialist who had been a minister in several governments of the Fourth Republic. In 1965 he had put together a left-wing alliance which forced de Gaulle to a second round. Following the 1969 debacle, this strategy was revived. The SFIO gave way in 1970 to a new Socialist Party and in 1971 Mitterrand took over as general secretary. In the following years, a variety of the left-wing splinter groups came on board, notably Michel Rocard's *Parti Socialiste Unifié* and a flood of new members transformed the old party of notables. A Common Programme was negotiated with the Communists and the left wing of the Radical Party which had broken away to form the MRG, providing for mutual support in second ballot contests and a coalition government on agreed policies. Third force alliances were broken in local government, resulting in a steady advance in left control of town halls through the 1970s.

Mitterrand's strategy was to bind the Communists into alliance with the Socialists to give the left a chance in the two-ballot electoral system, but he realized that to be electorally palatable such an alliance would have to contain the Communists in a subordinate position. The first success was seen in 1974 when Mitterrand as candidate of the united left was able to run Giscard d'Estaing a close second in the presidential election and by 1978, as the Socialists overtook the Communists in support it was apparent that the united left could win the upcoming parliamentary elections. It was at this point that the Communists broke the alliance, fearing that they were being reduced to irrelevance, attacking the Socialists and demanding revisions of the programme. This worked only to the benefit of the Socialists, since by removing the taint of Communist links it made them more palatable to moderate voters, while Communist voters really had no choice but to continue to support Socialist candidates at the second ballot. In 1981 Mitterrand won the presidential election and an absolute parliamentary majority, allowing him to dispense with Communist support when it became unhelpful. With the decline of the Communists in the 1980s, the Socialists were able largely to monopolize the left. In the 1986 legislative elections, despite losing, they scored their second highest score and in 1988 were able largely to maintain their new voters. Briefly the Socialists dreamed of rivalling the British Labour Party, if they could just raise their vote to 40 per cent, enabling them to come to power on their own with the help of the restored majoritarian electoral system. Soon, however, they realized their limits and were casting about again for allies in the political centre. In 1988 Mitterrand sought with limited success to construct a centre-left government of the type he had rejected in the 1970s.

Socialist Party ideology has developed considerably since 1970. In the early days, there was still a lot of left wing rhetoric and a promise of a 'rupture with capitalism', but this was combined with new themes, such as pluralism, decentralization, participation, environmentalism, feminism and civil liberties, calculated to appeal to the new middle class. Members insisted that they stood for a third road, between the authoritarianism of the Communists and the timid reformism of parties such as the German SPD and British Labour Party. In office after 1981 the Mitterrand government initially pursued a conventional left-wing economic strategy. There was a large programme of nationalization, together with reductions in the working week. To fight the recession, there was an increase in public spending and general reflation. This has since been widely denounced as economically irresponsible, though within two years the right-wing governments of Reagan and Thatcher were pursuing considerably more profligate policies of consumption-led reflation, with similar effects on public and private debt and the balance of payments. The problem for Mitterrand was rather that France was out of synchronization with other western economies. By 1983, it had come up against the international constraints of reflation in one country and was forced by pressure on the franc into devaluation and a more rigorous macroeconomic stance. Thereafter, the party in government has pursued a policy of rigid fiscal and monetary orthodoxy, and maintained a strong franc within the constraints of the European Monetary System. The party itself took longer to come to terms with government, but by the late 1980s had accepted that it was indeed a Social Democratic reformist party and not part of some third road to socialism. Re-elected in 1988, Mitterrand dropped the issue of public ownership, announcing that there would be neither nationalizations nor privatizations, though exceptions to the rule soon had to be made.

Another strand in the refounded Socialist Party was a general libertarianism, a belief in decentralization and pluralism. This was a break in the tradition of the French left, which had always supported a strong, centralized state. It co-existed rather uneasily in the 1980s with the commitment to nationalization and state control of the economy but was to be more influential in the long term. In government, the party relaxed state control of broadcasting and allowed private television stations. Civil liberties made some advances and there was a large programme of decentralization of power to local and regional government.

Despite the rhetoric, the SFIO was never really a party of the working class and nor is the PS. In 1990 just one per cent of the members attending its congress were workers, from a peak of only 5 per cent in the 1970s. 77 per cent of them were professionals or upper/middle-class white-collar employees, including 16 per cent teachers.[9] The electorate of the PS became more working class as it took over the Communist vote but social change has now eroded this and only around a quarter of the Socialist vote in the late 1980s was from blue collar workers. On the other hand, it was able to extend its electorate into the expanding white collar and professional electorate, as well as making headway among liberal Catholics. The abandonment of traditional policies of state control and nationalization and the emphasis on non-material values of individual liberty, decentralization and pluralism further strengthened the party's appeal to the new middle class. This broad appeal, however, was at the expense of depth. Unlike northern European Social Democratic parties, the French Socialists had no solid working-class or trade union base to sustain them through hard times. The new middle class is a fickle and volatile body of voters.

Although the party constitution officially bans factions, the organization of the PS is actually based on them. At the party congress, motions are submitted with names attached and debated and voted upon. Seats on the party executive are then allocated among the names in proportion to the vote attained. The motions are in fact presented by the main *courants* of the party, factions identified with the main leaders and, in some cases, ideological tendencies. In the 1970s and 1980s the most ideological faction was the left-wing group CERES, led by Jean-Pierre Chevènement. Later this renamed itself Socialism and Republic and sought inspiration in the ideals of patriotism and national discipline inherited from the revolutionary tradition. The faction under Michel Rocard preaches the need for modernization of the party's image and a move towards the political centre. While ideological debate persists within the party, factions above all seek to promote the interests of presidential aspirants.[10] Some are based in regional fiefs. In the 1970s and early 1980s, the ascendancy of Mitterrand served to keep factionalism within bounds but, as the struggle for the Socialist presidential nomination heated up, factionalism became more bitter. Mitterrand's dominance of the party proved a mixed blessing, since neither he nor the party managed to provide for a succession at the top.

The failure of the party's ambition to command a parliamentary majority on its own and the consequent search for new allies increased tensions and the end of the left alliance has produced something of an ideological drift. By the early 1990s, signs of the old malaise of the SFIO were unmistakeably reappearing, with attention focused on tactical manoeuvring, the merits of various types of alliance and ways of manipulating the electoral system rather than broad strategy or ideals. As the 1993 elections approached, the party resigned itself to a crushing defeat and started to crumble. Chevènement on the left and Rocard on the centrist wing of the party both announced that the party of Mitterrand and of Epinay (the founding congress in 1971) was finished and that French socialism would have to start anew. 1993 was indeed an electoral disaster, with the Socialists reduced to 17.5 per cent of the vote, their worst result since 1968.

The Communists

The French Communist Party (PCF) emerged from the split in the SFIO in 1920 committed to the Soviet model and for most of its history took its orders from Moscow. Between the wars this involved an oscillation between hostility and cooperation with the more powerful Socialists and culminated in support for the Hitler-Stalin pact of 1939 and opposition to France's entry into the war. Hitler's attack on the Soviet Union caused a sharp change of tack in 1941 and the PCF was to play a marked role in the French Resistance, giving it a national legitimacy at the Liberation. Communist ministers participated in the early postwar coalitions and the party outpaced the Socialists with 28.8 per cent of the vote in 1946. The onset of the Cold War resulted in the expulsion of the Communists from government in 1947 and for the remainder of the Fourth Republic they functioned as an anti-system party, unavailable for coalition building. Rejecting the Fifth Republic, they continued outside the system after 1958, though gaining over 20 per cent of the vote through the 1960s and 1970s.

Communist voting patterns were stable and rooted in local and class cultures, especially in the 'red belt' of working-class suburbs around Paris and the industrial north and in pockets in central and southern France. Here the party formed a political 'ghetto', seeking less to extend its influence in competition with other parties than to defend its positions in local government and parliamentary elections. Its policy stance has been described as that of a 'tribune party' aiming not to conquer power within the system, nor seriously attempting revolutionary overthrow but rather expressing the frustration and anger of its electors while retaining their loyalty. Electoral politics was only one element of its strategy. Equally important was its influence over the largest trade union, the CGT, which at one time it was able to use in political strikes, and its network of social institutions within the Communist subculture. Organizationally, it functioned on the principle of democratic centralism, with members bound to accept the policy line of the moment and no room for dissent. Members of parliament and local elected councillors were regarded as servants of the party, required to hand over their salaries and receiving in return the wage of a skilled manual worker. Unlike its Socialist rivals, the PCF did remain a workers' party, most of its leaders and elected representatives coming from humble backgrounds and lower status occupations. This did not stop the party from appealing to certain intellectuals up until the 1980s but these too were required to accept the party line and its changes - whatever humiliating recantations this involved. Unlike many of its sister parties, it never allowed scope to its thinkers or made any serious contribution to Marxist thought.

Early moves to liberalize the Communist movement found an ambiguous response in the PCF. It supported the Soviet intervention in Hungary in 1956 and greeted Khrushchev's denunciation of Stalin in that year with great suspicion. In the 1960s, eurocommunism made some impact and the PCF was able to issue a muted criticism of the 1968 Soviet invasion of Czechoslovakia. Caught totally unprepared by the student and worker unrest of that year, it sought to turn the events into a purely trade union matter, suppressing all thoughts of revolution. Thereafter, it slid back to a pro-Soviet posture, supporting the invasion of Afghanistan in 1979 and the suppression of Solidarity in Poland in 1981.

From the 1960s, the PCF did begin to accept the need to cooperate with other forces on the left in building an alternative governing alliance but here too their policies were vacillating and contradictory. After the disaster of 1958 when they were almost wiped out, they have always accepted that there should at minimum be agreement with the Socialists on mutual *désistements* (standing down in favour of the better-placed left candidate) at the second round of legislative elections. Beyond that they would support left-wing unity up to the point at which victory was in sight, then pull back. Like Mitterrand, they knew that a left alliance could only come to government under Socialist leadership and feared for their identity and very existence - hence the Communist support for the common programme of government in the early 1970s and their breaking it before the legislative elections of 1978. That year saw the revived Socialists pull ahead of the Communists for the first time since the war, heralding a collapse of Communist support over the next decade as they were comprehensively outmanoeuvred by Mitterrand. By 1981, they were down to 16 per cent of the vote and were taken in to government by the Socialists less for their support, which was not needed, than to tame them and neutralize them. The four Communist ministers, despite behaving in an exemplary manner, had no influence of government policy as a whole and by 1984 the party leadership decided that it was time to move back to opposition. This did them little good for, by changing the electoral system for the 1986 elections, the Socialists were relieved of the need even to agree on second ballot *désistements*. In 1988, the Communist presidential candidate slumped to fifth place with 6 per cent of the vote. With the return of the two-ballot system for the legislative elections, *désistements* were again agreed with the Socialists but such was their fall that the Communists represented the left at the second ballot in only 6 per cent of constituencies, against about half in the 1960s. Since the mid-1980s, their vote in legislative and European elections has been around 10 per cent, which appears to represent a hard core of loyalists.

At the same time, the Communists have suffered an erosion of their electoral base. The proportion of electors identifying themselves as working class halved between the early 1970s to the late 1980s while those remaining were increasingly attracted to the Socialists or even the extreme right National Front which outpaced it among workers in 1988. Its pro-Soviet stance and workerist rhetoric alienated it from the expanding salariat while successive attempts by reformers to renew the party from within were met by suppression of dissent and expulsions. By the late 1980s, the pace of reform in the Soviet Union and the collapse of communism in eastern Europe caught it defenceless, without a strong euroCommunist tradition and unable to reform itself. Only the Socialists' move to the centre and its role in mobilizing opposition to industrial restructuring preserved it a little space on the left and saved it from complete extinction.

The Centre

The political centre, a dominating presence in previous regimes, has been very weak under the Fifth Republic. This can be attributed to the effects of the constitution and to the divisions among the centrist parties. As we have seen, the two-ballot system for parliamentary elections tends to polarize politics, forcing centrists into the right or left camps. The presidential system gives credibility only to those parties with real presidential candidates, which is why there has usually been a substantial candidate representing a centrist position, from Jean Lecanuet in 1965 to Raymond Barre in 1988. With the questionable exception of Giscard d'Estaing, who is more of a conservative than a centrist, however, the centrist candidate has never won.

There are several streams of the political centre but the most important are the Liberal centre and the Christian Democrats. The liberal centre has traditionally been represented by the Radical Party, dominant in the Third Republic but which from the 1950s experienced steady decline, punctuated by revival efforts under Pierre Mendès France in the 1950s and Jean-Jacques Servan-Schreiber in the 1960s. By the 1970s, the party had formally split, its left wing under the title MRG (*Mouvement des Radicaux de Gauche*) allying themselves with the Socialists, while the right wing backed Giscard d'Estaing's 1974 presidential bid and later became a part of the UDF.

The Christian Democratic centre was represented in the Fourth Republic by the MRP (*Mouvement Républicain Populaire*) founded after the war by progressive Catholics issuing from the Resistance. While it scored 28 per cent of the vote in 1946, its position was not solid. Adopting socially progressive and strongly pro-European positions, it rested on a base of Catholics whose politics were well to the right of it. Its early success owed more to the discredit of the traditional Catholic right under the collaborationist Vichy régime than a conversion of Catholics to progressive politics. With the revival of competition from the conservative quarter it was soon in trouble and was eclipsed by the rise of de Gaulle. In 1970, it was refounded as the CDS (*Centre des Démocrates Sociaux*), supported Giscard d'Estaing's 1974 presidential bid and joined the UDF when it was formed in 1978.

By the late 1970s, then, the centre was split between a majority, aligned with the UDF and allied with the right, and a minority allied with the left. After the 1988 elections, with no parliamentary majority and a president seeking an opening to the centre, there were attempts to revive it as an independent force. Raymond Barre, standing as the official UDF candidate in the presidential election, presented himself as the leader of the liberal centre. After the 1988 legislative elections, the CDS moved to sit as a separate group in Parliament, while remaining part of the UDF for extra-parliamentary purposes. The CDS retains its Christian Democratic heritage, which is distinct from the Liberal origins of other elements of the UDF and has been more ready to condemn racism. This, however, has not kept some CDS mayors from the temptation of doing deals with the racist National Front.[11] It suffers from the old problem of French christian democracy, of its leaders being to the left of its traditionalist Catholic voters.

In another attempt to recreate an independent centre, Simone Veil led a centrist list for the 1989 European elections and a number of individuals accepted office under Mitterrand. Yet by this time, the major parties had themselves moved to the centre ground, leaving little distinctive for the centre movements to represent, apart from the ambitions of their leaders to play the swing role in French politics. The revival of the RPR/UDF and their crushing victory in the 1993 legislative elections put paid to the independent centre, at least for the time being. Veil and the main CDS leaders accepted office in the new right-of-centre government.

The Extreme Right

France has several traditions of extreme right-wing politics. Some of these stem back to the late nineteenth century when reactionary and monarchist elements, often supported by the clergy and military, attempted to destabilize the Third Republic, which they portrayed as in the hands of atheists, Freemasons and Jews. Anti-semitism reached a peak in the Dreyfus affair in which a Jewish army officer was falsely convicted of spying for the Germans. This became a *cause célèbre,* dividing progressive republicans from the reactionary right. A minority of liberal politicians and the novelist Zola agitated to reverse the injustice. The army, supported by the monarchists and most of the clergy, refused to revise the verdict, regarding the agitation as a slur on its honour. Despite mounting evidence of Dreyfus' innocence, most high-ranking politicians maintained a prudent silence until Dreyfus was finally vindicated. Between the two world wars, extreme right activity was carried on by *Action Française,* a French variation on the European Fascist parties. After the defeat of 1940 many rightists collaborated with the Germans or were active in the Vichy regime. This destroyed the patriotic credentials of the extreme right and it did not feature prominently in the postwar years. Yet it re-emerged in the 1950s. The *Algérie Française* movement, dedicated to total victory in Algeria, mobilized substantial numbers including elements of the army. In 1956, a right-wing populist movement, the Poujadists, based on small shopkeepers and protesting about larg- scale capitalism, taxes and the welfare state, elected deputies in Parliament. De Gaulle's arrival in power in 1958, however, served to contain the extreme right. The *Algérie Française* people had regarded him as one of their own and, when they realized his plans to grant Algeria independence, it was too late. Certainly, there was the attempted coup in Algeria in 1961 and a terrorist campaign by the OAS (*Organization de l'Armée Secrète*) and the full history of Gaullism's association with extreme right elements is only gradually coming to light, but in the event de Gaulle crushed them and saved the Republic. Gaullism's stress on patriotism, strong defences, an authoritarian style and somewhat brutal police methods, also undercut support for rightist parties.

It was in 1972 that a new extreme right party, the National Front, was formed but it did not make progress until the 1980s. Its leader was Jean Marie Le Pen who had been a paratrooper in Algeria and a Poujadist deputy in the 1950s. The National Front blends right/populist economic values, including opposition to big capitalism and trade unions, with social themes like the traditional patriarchal and authoritarian view of the family and the subordinate role of women. It supports an authoritarian state with stronger police powers and a return to the death penalty and opposes pornography, homosexuality and all signs of the permissive society. There are, however, distinct tendencies within it. Some are committed to neo-liberal economic policies, while others are suspicious of capitalism and inclined to economic protectionism. One strand is linked with the Catholic fundamentalism of Monseigneur Lefèvre, excommunicated from the Church for refusing to accept the reforms of the Second Vatican Council. Another is fiercely secular. Some elements of the party proudly trace their roots to the 1960s right-wing terrorist group OAS, while others are more recent recruits. A unifying theme is opposition to immigration and a deep-seated racism, most of it directed at North African immigrants. These are made the scapegoats for France's unemployment problem, housing problems and crime. Like the traditional extreme right, it also has an anti-semitic tradition - Le Pen has described the holocaust as a mere detail of history - but other elements within the party support the state of Israel which they see as an outpost of western civilization. During the Gulf War of 1991, Le Pen confused many of his supporters by his support for Iraq and opposition to French involvement. This allowed him to play on anti-Jewish sentiment, while signalling that he was not opposed to Arabs as such, only to their presence in France. It also provided an implicit comparison between Le Pen and Saddam Hussein, as patriotic strongmen.

Despite its various strands, the National Front is united by the leadership of Le Pen, who runs the party in a highly centralized and authoritarian fashion. Candidate selection is centrally controlled, dissidents are marginalised or expelled and there is little internal debate. Around Le Pen a cult of personality is sustained.[11]

In 1981, Le Pen could not raise enough signatures from mayors to stand in the presidential election but by the mid-1980s, with the main parties all discredited, the National Front was picking up votes fast. It was regularly able to garner ten per cent of the vote, reaching 14 per cent in the 1988 presidential elections. In the European elections of 1984 and 1989 and the legislative elections of 1986, proportional representation allowed it to translate its vote into seats. In 1988, with the non-proportional system restored, it won just one seat.

The rise in votes was accompanied by a sustained effort to legitimize the National Front as a part of the political system. Le Pen was presented as a presidential figure, the party rhetoric was toned down, it started talking about issues other than race and it sought alliances with the conventional parties. All the traditional parties share some responsibility for the National Front's subsequent success. The Communists had sought to exploit the race issue in the 1970s to rally their working-class electorate in the communes they controlled, legitimizing racial intolerance. The Socialists helped the National Front into parliament in 1986 by changing the electoral system. The RPR and UDF have given the Le Pen's racist rhetoric credibility by trying to compete on the same front, sustaining an anti-immigrant discourse marked by a strong racial bias, with a few honourable exceptions such as Michel Noir, mayor of Lyon, or Bernard Stasi, a CDS leader. Given the dynamics of the two-ballot electoral system used in national and local elections, the conservative parties are under intense pressure to do second-ballot deals with the National Front, and some members have even suggested a common programme on the lines of that agreed between the Socialists and the Communists in the 1970s. Yet the RPR and UDF leaders know that allying with the National Front will lose them the support of more centrist voters than they will gain on the right, as well as undermining their credibility generally. So they have gyrated between condemnation and collusion. In 1983, both Chirac and Giscard endorsed a deal with the National Front in local by-elections in the town of Dreux. By 1985, they had seen the dangers in this and thereafter the national leaders would declare at each election that there would be no deals; but faced with the reality on the ground, local leaders nevertheless continued to deal. Given their looser national discipline and roots in Fourth Republic manoeuvring, it is the UDF local leaders who are most prone to make these accommodations. In a number of regional councils, formal coalitions governments were formed between UDF/RPR leaders and the National Front in 1986. At the 1988 legislative elections, a deal was made in Marseilles whereby the RPR/UDF candidates stood aside at the second ballot in certain constituencies in return for the National Front withdrawing in others. Even at national level, the RPR and UDF conceded key parliamentary committee positions to the National Front in an effort to bolster their precarious majority in the 1986-88 period. At the presidential election of 1988, on the other hand, Chirac refused a second ballot deal with Le Pen, knowing that it would be more damaging than helpful. By the 1993 legislative elections, the RPR/UDF coalition was so far ahead in voting intentions that there was no need for any deals. It is not only the RPR and UDF who have been tempted to dealing with the extremists. Two of the centrist ministers brought in by Mitterrand's opening in 1988, and who doubled as regional politicians, were also suspected of collusion with the National Front following regional elections in 1992.

The Greens

France has not seen the dramatic rise in Green politics which has marked some other European countries. The country's depends on nuclear energy, which supplies 80 per cent of its electricity, and has maintained a staunch nuclear defence policy, yet these have not become important subjects of political debate. Other environmental issues did arise in the 1980s but did not acquire the salience which they had in Germany. French Greens are also penalized by the electoral system, which condemns them to irrelevance or to expedient second-ballot deals with the other parties. The issue of alliances is particularly acute in the French Green movement since they cannot agree on whether they belong on the left, like the German Greens, or whether they should condemn both right and left equally while being prepared to cut deals with either.

In 1981 moderate environmentalist Brice Lalonde scored 3.9 per cent in the presidential election and threw his support behind Mitterrand for the second ballot. Maintaining his links with the Socialists, Lalonde was made minister for the environment in 1988, serving in the governments of Rocard and Cresson before leaving in 1992. In the 1980s, Greens also made some progress in local government, gaining seats on councils and occasionally sharing power with the Socialists or, more rarely, the conservative parties. In 1988, those ecologists who opposed Lalonde's links to the Socialists presented their own presidential candidate, Antoine Waechter, who gained 3.8 per cent of the vote. In accordance with his policy of strict neutrality between the conventional parties, Waechter gave his supporters no advice on the second round of voting but some two-thirds of them moved to Mitterrand, the remainder dividing equally between Chirac and abstention. The European elections of 1989, fought on proportional representation at a time when the electorate was disillusioned with all the old parties, gave the Greens a better opportunity. With 11 per cent of the vote, they gained eight seats. By the early 1990s, they were steadily increasing support at the expense of the Socialists.

Yet the movement remained divided between Lalonde's formation, *Génération Ecologie,* leaning to the left and part of the presidential majority, and the Green Party (*Les Verts*) sticking to their independence but declaring themselves ready to deal with either side. With the Socialists seeking to preserve their position and the RPR/UDF looking for a way to avoid dealing with the National Front, the ecologists of both streams suddenly became much sought after. Jacques Chirac, who as mayor of Paris was known for his pro-car views, donned his outdoor gear and went down to the Landes in south-west France to declare his deep concern for environmental preservation. The Socialists for their part publicly agonized over what changes in the electoral system might enable them to bolster their parliamentary position with the help of either or both environmentalist group. In 1992, a substantial number of Greens were elected to regional councils where they followed highly divergent paths. In some regions, they allied with the left, in others with the right. In many, they simply broke up as a coherent force and individual members and factions went their various ways. The lessons of this disarray explain in large part the determination of the two Green parties to present joint candidates at the legislative elections of 1993. During the campaign, they appeared to me making great progress, at one time equalling the Socialists' in opinion poll ratings. At the elections, however, they scored a disappointing 7.6 per cent and gained no seats in parliament.

Electoral Behaviour

Changes in French regimes and the party system make it difficult to trace patterns of political support over long periods. Many observers have detected a consistency of political alignments on right and left dating back to the last century and persisting through changes in party labels, but these are now tending to break down. Figure 3.1 gives parliamentary elections results for the principal parties during the Fifth Republic.

Support for the left was stable in the 1960s and early 1970s, except for the election of 1968, called in unusual circumstances. It then grew during the 1970s before weakening somewhat in the 1980s. Within the left, the Communists have steadily declined, to the benefit of the Socialists. On the right, the Gaullists dominated in the 1960s. Since the 1970s, they have had to share support with the UDF while losing ground to the Socialists and later the

Figure 3.1 Percentage vote in first ballot, legislative elections, 1958-93

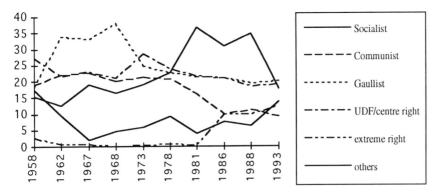

In 1986 the RPR and UDF ran joint lists in most areas and their vote has been divided equally between them. In the appendix, full results are given, with the parties in order from left to right, except for the ecologists who defy this categorization.

National Front. The late 1980s show increased party competition, with neither the Socialists nor the conservative RPR/UDF alliance able to gain a majority. This explains the search by both right and left for new allies in the centre.

Looking at the overall votes for right and left shows slower and more modest changes than we find when looking at the fortunes of individual parties. These long-term changes can be related to the social characteristics of the electorate and generational change. One of the most enduring influences on political attitudes is religion. When modern electoral politics arrived in France under the Third Republic in the nineteenth century, Catholicism was associated with the political right, conservatism, monarchy and authority. On the other side were the heirs of the Revolution, republican, liberal and anti-clerical. Battle lines were drawn over the status and privileges of the Church and especially whether education should be controlled by Church or state. By the end of the nineteenth century, universal, secular education had been established and school teachers became the main agents for the spread of secular and republican values. In 1905 the Church was officially separated from the state, becoming a private organization. Apart from an anachronistic and short-lived row over private Catholic schools in 1983, religious issues have featured little in the politics of the Fifth Republic. The Church has come to terms with the secular state and the conservative parties do not call for a return to monarchy. Yet religion continues to be closely related to voting behaviour, with Catholics leaning to the right and non-religious voters to the left. Table 3.6 illustrates this with figures from the 1988 presidential election. It shows a striking symmetry. The Socialist Mitterrand gained three-quarters of the voters with no religion but only a quarter of Catholics. For the conservative Chirac, the proportions were reversed.

The same survey showed the Communist vote at the first round varying from 0 per cent among practising Catholics to 19 per cent among voters with no religion. As Mitterrand's score shows, the Socialists have been able to make some inroads into the Catholic vote following the arrival of progressive Catholics into the refounded party in the 1970s and the decline of the old anti-clerical themes. There is little religious difference between RPR and UDF supporters, though the CDS does have a special appeal to Catholics in areas with a

Table 3.6 Percentage vote by religion, presidential election ,1988, second round

	Mitterrand	Chirac
Regularly practising Catholics	27	73
Occasionally practising Catholics	44	56
Non-practising Catholics	58	42
No religion	75	25

Source: SOFRES post-electoral enquiry of sample of 2000 electors, in L'état de l'opinion, 1990 (Paris: Seuil, 1990).

Christian Democratic heritage.

Another important influence on voting is social class. The industrial working class has historically supported the Communist Party but since the 1970s has moved strongly to the Socialists. Upper-middle-class voters largely support the conservative RPR and UDF parties, as do farmers. Changes in these social groups explain a great deal of the electoral movement over the years. Farmers, who comprised 17 per cent of the electorate in 1965, were a mere 6 per cent in 1988.[12] The proportion of those identifying themselves as working class also showed a sharp fall. The key group is in the middle of the social scale, white-collar workers and professionals, whose numbers have increased. This group moved to the Socialists in 1981, swung back to the right in 1986 and tended to support Mitterrand in 1988. It is also among this upwardly mobile middle class that the Green vote is concentrated, reaching as high as 22 per cent in the 1989 European elections. Table 3.7 shows in vote in the first round of the 1988 presidential election by social class.

Table 3.7 Percentage vote by social class, presidential election, 1988, first round

Head of household	Lajoinie (Communist)	Mitterrand (Socialist)	Wachter (Green)	Barre (UDF)	Chirac (RPR)	Le Pen (NF)
Farmer	1	23	6	19	35	14
Business, artisan, shopkeeper	3	18	3	15	35	23
Professional, senior white-collar	2	24	7	23	23	17
Junior, intermediate white-collar	8	36	6	19	13	11
Manual	11	42	2	11	10	18
Inactive	6	37	2	17	24	12
ALL	7	34	4	17	20	15

Source: SOFRES post-electoral enquiry of sample of 2,000 voters, in L'état de l'opinion, 1990 (Paris: Seuil, 1990).

Gender has been a factor in voting behaviour since women gained the vote in 1944. As in other European countries, women have in the past been inclined to vote for the more conservative parties and men for the parties of the left. In 1967, the gender gap was 17 per cent but by the 1980s, however, it had largely disappeared.[13] The shrinking Communist vote still had a male bias, but the Socialists had made great progress among women voters. On the right , men were rather more likely than women to support the extreme party, the National Front. Table 3.8 illustrates this with figures from the 1988 presidential elections.

Table 3.8 Percentage vote by gender, presidential election, 1988, first round

	Lajoinie (Communist)	Mitterrand (Socialist)	Waechter (Green)	Barre (UDF)	Chirac (RPR)	Le Pen (NF)
Men	7	32	3	15	20	18
Women	6	36	4	18	20	11
ALL	6	34	4	17	20	14

Source: SOFRES post-electoral enquiry of sample of 2000 electors, in L'état de l'opinion, 1990 (Paris: Seuil, 1990).

Much of French electoral analysis is based on geography, tracing the historic patterns of support in particular cities and regions.[14] These partly reflect the incidence of religious and social structures. So the west of France and Alsace have traditionally been Catholic and conservative, the south anticlerical and leftist. The industrial north and the working-class suburbs of Paris have been strongholds of the left, the prosperous cities of the right. Yet over time, local and regional political cultures have formed which mould behaviour in their own right. In the west and north of the Massif Central, a radical peasantry emerged over time, establishing their own cooperative institutions, penetrating local government and confronting the central state with their own demands. Elsewhere, peasant society was deferential and conservative. The old radical and centre parties were deeply entrenched in parts of France, using their position in local government and client networks to resist the advance of Gaullism. The SFIO, before its transformation into the new Socialist Party, relied heavily on its network of notables and local traditions. In some areas, individuals have established themselves locally through the accumulation of national and local office and have been able to resist national voting trends which might otherwise have swept them away.

These social and geographical patterns have slowly eroded in the course of the Fifth Republic. Gaullism in the 1960s cut across traditional divisions of region, class and religion, reaching into categories resistant to the old conservative parties. Secularization and the more tolerant attitude of the party itself have enabled the Socialists to extend into traditionally Catholic areas like Brittany and Alsace. Presidentialism, by presenting elections as a clash of personalities rather than parties, has loosened old voting habits. In 1988 Mitterrand was able to score an easy victory in the presidential election which eluded his party in the legislative elections held immediately after. As in other countries, voters have become more volatile, concerned with the performance of government and ready to punish politicians who do not live up to expectations. Fragmentation of the party system from the late 1980s, with the emergence of the extreme right, the Greens and an independent centre, further complicate matters by offering voters a greater choice.

GOVERNMENT, GROUPS AND POLICY MAKING

There is a long tradition in France of a powerful and pervasive state, dominating all aspects of national life. This has its roots in the *ancien régime* which sought, with varied success, to consolidate absolute monarchy and use the power of government to develop France, but the idea was carried forward and adapted by succeeding regimes. The Revolution planted the idea of the sovereign people, represented by the state, whose will must be respected. Intermediary institutions, whether territorial, sectoral or corporatist, were seen as illegitimate to the extent that they stood in the way of the popular will. Napoleon added a centralized administration with a bureaucracy modelled on military lines. This idea of the strong, unitary state has been so deeply ingrained that relatively little work was done until recent years on the processes of policy making and the relations of the state to major economic, social and professional interest groups. More recently, the picture has been modified, as a result of reinterpretation of the French experience and of changes in the workings of French government.

It is certainly true that, in comparison with other liberal democracies, the state in France is very important. In contrast notably with Britain and the United States, it enjoys largely positive connotations and a cultural bias exists in favour of state action on social and economic problems. A conception of the public interest as something apart from individual competitive private interests also survives, and the state is seen as its custodian. The French idea of nationalism links French greatness to the performance of its economy and society and gives the state a guiding role in this. Because of the link between the state, national development and nationalism, the right as well as the left have been inclined to government intervention. The state is further enhanced by the weakness of the autonomous civil society, that is of groups, actors and a public life outside the purview of the state. British and North American observers are puzzled for example to see private associations described as registered under the Law of 1901, duly recorded in the *Journal Officiel* - in their own countries these bodies would be unknown to the public authorities. Unlike in the USA, universities are all public institutions. Unlike the public universities of Britain and Canada, these lack autonomous status but form part of the state administration. French private enterprise, too, has historically been relatively weak and has looked to the state for protection, support and subsidy, especially in competition with foreigners.

Bureaucracy

The civil service has always had an important role in French political life. Service in the senior ranks of the state has been regarded as prestigious, many of the most talented students gravitate to it, and it carries with it considerable privilege. While the public service has its roots in the attempts of the *ancien régime* to develop a centralized, obedient administration, it was Napoleon who established the modern bureaucracy as a hierarchical system on military lines. At the summit are the *grands corps,* who may be technically trained, like the engineers of the *Ponts et Chaussées* (Bridges and Roads), or generalist administrators such as the prefectoral *corps,* the inspectors of finance or the Council of State. These are sharply distinguished in terms of status and power from the mass of middle-ranking and junior functionaries.

Recruitment into the *grands corps* is by competitive entry into the elite state graduate schools, the *grands écoles,* followed by an administrative posting corresponding to the grades obtained on examination. For the technical *corps,* the training schools are the *Ecole des Ponts et Chaussées* and the *Ecole Polytechnique,* established under the monarchy and revolutionary regime respectively. Until the Third Republic, selection of generalist administrators was highly politicized but gradually merit selection was introduced here too. In 1945, the *Ecole Nationale d'Administration* (ENA) was added to train entrants to the generalist *grands corps.* It in turn recruits to a large degree from students taking their first degrees at the *Institut d'Etudes Politiques (Sciences Po)* at Paris. The mass of middle-ranking administrators are recruited from the universities, often with law degrees and, while it is possible for them to gain promotion into the higher ranks, this is not easy, so they tend to harbour considerable resentment at the privileges of the *Enarques* (graduates of ENA). Under the Fifth Republic, *Enarques* have enjoyed a steady rise in position and power at the expense of the technical corps.

The higher administration is now a meritocracy, based on academic results rather than political patronage; it is nevertheless an elite. Although examinations are used to ensure objective standards, there is in practice a bias to the Parisian middle class and to some degree to the children of higher civil servants themselves. There is also a historic under-representation of women. It was only in 1970 that the *Polytechnique* admitted women and in 1974-5 that the unwritten ban on women in the *corps* of inspectors of finance and the prefectoral *corps* was lifted. In 1981 the Socialist government introduced a special system of entry to ENA for outsiders and mature students, but this had little success and was discontinued by the conservative government in 1986.

Recruits into the *grands corps* are given a managerial or technical training and are imbued with an ideology of state service. Since the Revolution and particularly the Third Republic, they have come to regard themselves as representative of the 'general interest' of the public, expressed through the state, superior to private, individual interests and which must prevail over them. This ideology contrasts sharply with the pluralistic bargaining characteristic of American administration or the pragmatic approach of the British, though it must be said that the reality often fails to correspond to the theory. Once recruited, officials must spend a minimum of four years in the work corresponding to their chosen *corps* but may then move into other areas of government, with the result that they have succeeded in colonizing large parts of public administration. Their mobility allows them to move into ministerial *cabinets* which have come to be dominated by the *grands corps*. Service in a *cabinet* may become a launching pad for further promotion, or a move to a senior position in a nationalized industry or other public agency. Others move into politics themselves, a tendency particularly marked in the early days of the Fifth Republic, when de Gaulle sought ministers outside the ranks of the old political class, but which has persisted under successive governments of right and left. The main difference between right and left, indeed, is that the latter have been rather more inclined to appoint members of the teaching profession (who also count as civil servants). Most prominent among those moving into politics have been graduates of ENA in the generalist *corps,* including senior figures like Valéry Giscard d'Estaing (President of the Republic), Jacques Chirac, Laurent Fabius, Michel Rocard and Edouard Balladur (prime ministers). Parliament has been colonized by civil servants, their representation increasing from about 20 per cent to some 40 per cent since 1958, with again a tendency for the Socialists to recruit teachers. They are also free to move into the private sector, in a process known as *pantoufflage,* whereby former civil servants take posts in private industry. In contrast to the USA, however, the reverse rarely occurs and the traffic, and hence influence, remains largely one way. All this coming and going is protected by a privileged regime which allows senior civil servants to retain membership of their *corps*, with corresponding pension rights and the right to return to government service, even while serving for long periods in politics or business.

There was much criticism from the left, during the long years of conservative dominance (1958-81), that governments had created a party state, with promotion based on political loyalty. This is a difficult issue to resolve. While entry into the *grands corps* is by merit, placement in senior posts is usually the prerogative of governments. These may choose, either for clientelist reasons or in order to ensure conformity with their policies, to appoint like-minded people to sensitive positions. Both factors are visible in France, but to a limited degree. When governments alternated in 1981, 1986 and 1988, there was a certain amount of movement at the top, especially in politically sensitive areas like the Ministries of Justice and Interior. Rectors - the regional education directors - who are recruited among the academic profession, were changed quite radically. Chiefs of nationalized industries and public agencies, with fixed term appointments at the discretion of the government, were moved. Some senior officials, unhappy at working with the new adminstration, resigned, took leave from their *corps* or transferred to a local government. Generally, however, the senior administration stayed intact, marking a further step in the maturity of the Fifth Republic. Even the officials of the Council of State, who must advise government as well as ruling on administrative law, carried on as before, so establishing their independence.

Interest Groups

Both sides of industry have been relatively weak in France in comparison with northern European countries. Trade unionism has been weakened by the absence of a mass industrial proletariat such as exists in Britain and Germany and by the fragmentation of the union movement on ideological and, at one time, confessional grounds. Unions now represent only some 11 per cent of the labour force, down from some 30 per cent in the 1970s. They are strongest among men, white-collar workers and those inclined to the left. There are no less than six trade union confederations competing for members, largely in the same occupational groups. The largest traditionally has been the CGT (*Confédération générale du travail*), especially among industrial workers. Although there is no formal affiliation, the CGT has long been aligned with the Communist Party, which provides most of its leading figures and has had a strong influence over its activities. It has engaged in industrial militancy and been prepared to confront governments, yet the CGT has followed the Communist line of avoiding revolutionary challenges to the regime. During the May events of 1968, it opposed the revolutionary demands of students and the far left, turning the protest into a conventional argument about wages and conditions. FO (*Force ouvrière*) was formed after the second world war by anti-Communists and has remained free of party ties. The CFDT (*Confédération française démocratique du travail*) was formed in 1964 from the old CFTC (*Confédération française des travailleurs chrétiens*) a Christian Democratic union close to the MRP party. After its transformation into the CFDT its leaders adopted a secular stance, leaving little trace of the old confessional lines and, while officially independent politically, have been close to the Socialist Party. There was at one time a proposal for affiliation on the lines of the British Labour Party but this came to nothing. From the 1970s, the CFDT adopted a distinctive line on *autogestion* (selfmanagement), supporting workers' participation, decentralization and pluralism, together with a moderate line on wage claims.

Two smaller unions are the CFTC, a rump of the former union of that name which did not join the CFDT but retained its confessional stance, and the CGC (*Confédération générale des cadres*), a white-collar union. The teaching union FEN (*Fédération d'éducation nationale*) groups a variety of unions in the education sector, though teaching sections also exist in the general unions. It is also politically independent, though the strong traditions of anticlericalism and republicanism among teachers, together with their left-of-centre tendency, have brought it close to the Socialists.

Given the unreliability of membership figures, union support is best measured by voting in professional elections for the social security committees, the *conseils des prud'hommes* (industrial relations tribunals) and the *conseils d'entreprise* (works consultative committees). These show a steep drop in support for the CGT, while the CFDT has largely held its own and the FO has increased in strength. A rising abstention rate testifies to a decline in union identification, since candidates in these elections are presented by unions, except for the works councils in small firms. The decline in CGT support undoubtedly is related to its links with the Communist Party as well as its vacillating stance on major issues, but also reflects a decline in the industrial labour force where it was strongest. The CFDT has suffered somewhat from its identification with the Socialist Party, in office after 1981, despite its attempts to distance itself from the government. FO, on the other hand, has been able to take a stronger line in opposition to government and even to outflank the CGT in industrial militancy. Table 3.9 shows the changing fortunes of the unions in elections to works committees.

Table 3.9 Percentage vote, elections to works committees

	Abstention	CGT	CFDT	FO	CFTC	CGC	Other	Non-union
1967	27.8	45.0	17.7	7.6	2.1	3.9	3.9	19.9
1989	34.5	25.1	21.0	11.2	4.6	5.5	6.2	26.4

Source: D. Andolfatto, 'Le syndicalisme au miroir des élections professionelles', *Regards sur l'actualité*, 169 (1991).

Despite a more favourable legislative climate since 1981, trade unionism in France has entered a general crisis. Continued austerity and financial rigour since 1983 have limited the scope for large wage increases, while unions have failed to establish themselves as obligatory negotiating partners for government. Public opinion sees them as an increasing irrelevance.

The main employers' organization is the CNPF *(Conseil nationale du patronat français)*, established after the second world war and grouping various sectoral bodies. It is broadly representative of the private sector but faces competition from a variety of bodies dedicated to small business. Within the CNPF there are tensions between large-scale capitalism and the small-firm sector which has traditionally been protected by the French state. Since the 1980s, the CNPF has been more outward-looking, dedicated to free markets rather than protection and supportive of measures of privatization and deregulation. Officially neutral politically, it is in practice much closer to the RPR and UDF than to the left.

Farmers have their own organizations, of which the most important is the FNSEA (*Fédération nationale des syndicats d'exploitants agricoles*). Representing about a third of French farmers, but including all the large ones, this has long had privileged links with the state. Smaller unions represent small farmers, or leftist peasants but exercise much less influence. Economic change has undercut the position of farmers, who now account for just over 6 per cent of the labour force, but they are still able to wield an influence out of proportion to their numbers.

The weakness of associative life in France is matched by a tradition of a strong state, enjoying high status and prestige. In contrast to the United States, where bargaining among private interests is the essence of public policy making, French political culture has tended to regard sectional interests as somehow illegitimate. The state, as representative of the general national interest, is seen as the only legitimate authority. While in English there are separate words for policy, meaning government action aimed at securing specified ends, and politics, referring to the process of argument, pressure, conflict and compromise by which policy is made, the French use the same word, *politique*, for both. This is indicative of a view that policy is made by a unified, purposive state, in contrast notably to American pluralism. Yet this authority is continually under attack. As Gambetta put it in 1881:

> The administration of the state, the government of the state, is neither sufficiently independent nor sufficiently free. It is subjected to a mixture of competition, pressures, influences and solicitations of every sort ... the state and its agents much be given back their rightful prerogatives.[15]

So in practice the state apparatus constantly struggles to free itself from outside pressures. This has prevented the emergence of any general corporatist system in France. Certainly, there is provision for group representation in the policy process. The Economic and Social Council brings together employers' and union representatives with civil servants and outside experts to study and advise on major issues and at one time de Gaulle hoped to convert the Senate into a chamber of sectoral interests. Yet its role is advisory and its influence limited. At local level, chambers of commerce and agriculture are officially recognized, with taxation powers and elections regulated by law. These bodies, which are under-researched, are of increasing importance in the management of infrastructure developments and the implementation of training and local development programmes. For the most part, however, state-group relations are conducted on sectoral lines, with closer or looser links depending on the group in question.

Rather than the incremental adjustment found in countries with strong, stable groups and a pluralist culture, social relations in France have been marked by periods of quiescence punctuated by violent explosions of discontent. These sometimes develop into a 'crisis' in which the state would be forced to make radical policy concessions or the regime itself might collapse. This phase is then usually followed by a reaction in which the policy concessions are eroded or the revolutionary gains dismantled. Tensions then build up to the next explosion. The most serious social explosion of the Fifth Republic was in 1968 when students in Paris took to the streets and fought with police. The *Compagnies républicaines de sécurité* (CRS), a special police force trained to deal with civil disorder, were called in but the unrest spread to the factories where workers came out on strike. For a time it looked as though the regime might collapse and de Gaulle took himself to Germany to assure himself of the loyalty of army units stationed there. In the event a political solution was found. Prime Minister Pompidou persuaded de Gaulle to call a parliamentary election in which the 'silent majority' in the country, frightened at the disorder in Paris, massively returned the Gaullists. Concessions were made to students and workers, who returned to their classrooms and factories and the regime was saved. Later, many of these concessions were eroded but the experience was a salutory one for the authorities. De Gaulle himself lost stature and was to resign a year later when he lost a referendum. Succeeding governments have been more wary of provoking similar social explosions, preferring to negotiate at an earlier stage.

Some groups, with a large potential for disruption, or key voting strength, have managed to establish continuous links with government and a privileged policy position. Others have been excluded and forced to protest from outside. Farmers have long been closely tied into the state, depending on it for protection and subsidies, while exercising a major influence on policy under conservative governments. This cosy relationship is the closest France has come to a corporatist mode, but even here the FNSEA cannot always deliver the consent of small farmers to policy, where restructuring is concerned. Explosions of discontent in the agricultural world occur periodically but governments of both right and left, faced with tractors obstructing the highways or blockading prefectures, or farmers pouring Italian wine into the sea, have usually hastened to make the necessary concessions. Small shopkeepers have been able to extract concessions on the regulation of hypermarkets, producing in the process a vast system of clandestine financing for the political parties through the manipulation of planning regulations. Students still periodically take to the streets to protest against excessive class sizes or selection systems but this is more a sign of their powerlessness than of strength.

The role of the state was further enhanced after the second world war when it took the lead in modernization and change of French economy and society and its adaptation to the new Europe. This was a break with the previous policy of protectionism and preservation of existing positions and required new instruments. The elite corps were strengthened and the *Ecole Nationale d'Administration* established. The technical elite played a prominent role through the national plan and its associated modernization commissions. These laid down the main lines of development, steered subsidies and influenced the allocation of investment funds both for government projects and for major private initiatives. Under de Gaulle, the national plan was described as the 'ardent obligation of the nation' and the state given a leading role in a modernization process to enhance the greatness of France. Business and, to a lesser extent, the trade unions, were involved in this through the various modernization commissions and public-private companies, but the main lines of policy were laid down by the state. Substantial parts of industry and of the financial sector were taken into public ownership after the war and, after the Socialist victory in 1981 nationalization was further extended. In the private sector, state help and guidance was critical in creating a series of national champions, large firms capable of competing on behalf of France in world markets. *Pantoufflage* of senior civil servants into the private sector created parallel business and administrative elites who shared the same values and spoke the same language. The establishment of the Fifth Republic strengthened the technical elite by bringing in non-party figures, often from the bureaucracy, as ministers in place of politicians beholden to private interests. At the same time, Parliament's power was reduced, the permanent commissions which had been prey to interest groups cut back and the electoral system reformed to produce disciplined parties better able to resist group pressures.

The status of the bureaucratic elite was further enhanced by the use of science as a legitimating theme. This idea can be traced to the Third Republic, when national independence and development were seen as requiring a powerful scientific/managerial elite.[16] This technocracy was strengthened during the Fourth and Fifth Republics. The powerful role of the state and the technical bureaucracy in framing choices and mobilizing funds can be seen in the success with which France was able to establish a high-speed train network or a nuclear power programme generating some 80 per cent of electricity, with little effective opposition. It was equally responsible for the Concorde supersonic airliner, a financial disaster from which the British tried to withdraw as early as 1964 but which was seen as a symbol of French technological prowess.

Yet the dominance of the state and its bureaucratic elite in France should not be exaggerated. There may be more inclination to state-centred solutions than in the USA or Germany, but France has never had a command economy. It has remained a capitalist system in which consumer choices and private investment decisions play the major role in allocating resources. In so far as government is committed to economic growth and development, producer groups will have a specially privileged position. Also increasingly recognized is the fact that the state itself is not a unified actor. In the 1960s, observers noted the complexity of centre-local relations, in which the orders of the Jacobin state were in practice negotiated with powerful actors on the ground (see section on local government). Others have noted the rivalries among the *grands corps* and their links with sectoral interests in policy communities, so that the state itself becomes a battleground of vested interests. The Ministry of Agriculture will normally take the farmers' side and under governments of the right the minister was often a virtual nominee of the FNSEA. Other ministries look after their own clients. This very division of the bureaucracy gives enormous power to those bureaucratic and political actors who are in key positions and with the information and skills to play the system. These would include senior scientific and technical managers, members of ministerial *cabinets*, politicians who accumulate office and those responsible for liaison across departments. Many of them would be members of *grands corps*.

Developments in the last twenty years have opened up the French state[17] and may herald the end of the specifically French model of public policy making. The decision in the 1950s to break with the protectionist tradition and open the French economy to international competition made government direction increasingly difficult, while the international economic shocks of the 1970s and 1980s showed the limits of national policies. The national plan was progressively downgraded and, despite attempts to rehabilitate it by the Socialists in 1981 and 1988, is a shadow of its former self. Membership of the European Community has progressively limited the scope for independent state action, first in tariff protection, then in agricultural and industrial subsidies and sectoral policies, more recently in monetary policy. At the same time, decentralization, especially after the laws of 1981-6, has strengthened the local level of decision making and increased the weight of elected politicians in relation to state bureaucrats. Pluralism now has positive connotations and parties of both right and left preach the virtues of a rich associative life independent of the state.

Finally, the fashion for markets and private sector solutions to problems arrived in France in the 1980s, affecting the parties of both left and right. Between 1986 and 1988, the Chirac government privatized a number of enterprises. Although Mitterrand, on his re-election in 1988 promised that there would be no further privatizations nor nationalizations, it was not long before the government was disposing of shares or encouraging state firms to engage in joint ventures with private partners. Both privatization and nationalization have taken a distinctly French form. Chirac's privatization programme, rather than selling off enterprises on the open market, created 'hard cores' of selected shareholders to ensure that the firms remained stable, French and in dialogue with the government. Nationalization under the Socialists created firms which, compared with their British counterparts, have great freedom to raise money on the market, buy and sell subsidiaries and engage in joint ventures. There is a continued passage of personnel between the public and private sectors, though the private sector has become more self-confident and active in lobbying. This represents the residual French model, a business sector increasingly autonomous, operating on the international market, but retaining privileged links with the state. French policies in the European Community show the same tendency, to free-market solutions moderated by a residual inclination to protectionism, to a positive industrial policy and to a preference for national champions.

TERRITORIAL POLITICS

France, sometimes seen as the archetype of the European nation state was in fact moulded into a united country over several centuries, through the action of successive regimes. The monarchy, initially controlling the lands around Paris still known as the Ile de France, gradually expanded to occupy more or less the present 'hexagon'. In the seventeenth and eighteenth centuries, the absolute monarchs sought to unify their kingdom and subject it to a single set of laws. The territorial aristocracy was weakened and brought into the court at Versailles, while *intendants* were sent out into many parts of the country as the administrative agents of the king. Yet by the time of the Revolution of 1789 an extraordinary diversity of culture, language, laws and institutions remained. In the peripheral regions, people continued to speak Breton, Basque, Flemish and German, while over a huge area of the south a variety of Occitan and Provençal dialects, incomprehensible to Parisians, remained in use. The Revolution in turn attempted to secure unity in the name of the French people whose sovereignty it proclaimed. An ideology to which the name Jacobin has subsequently been attached proclaimed the indivisibility of the sovereign nation and rejected all intermediary powers between it and the state. The ancient provinces were abolished, along with the *parlements* (local judicial/ legislative bodies) and law was unified. For the administration of the state, communes were established as the basic unit, corresponding largely to the parishes of the *ancien régime*. Above them, departments were designed in a largely technical manner, such that a citizen could get to the administrative centre and back on horseback in a day. Under Napoleon, centralization was further developed, with the appointment of prefects, central government officials, to run the affairs of the department and supervise the communes. Under the Third Republic from the 1870s, cultural uniformity was promoted through the extension of a centrally controlled education system and compulsory military service in which conscripts were deliberately stationed away from their home regions. Republican governments, fearing the provinces as hotbeds of clerical and aristocratic reaction and a threat to the republican order, were wary about decentralization, though they did gradually allow the free election of mayors in the communes. With the *conseils généraux* (councils) of the departments which had been elected since 1848, these were regarded as soundly republican institutions, as long as they were kept under tight central supervision. Following the second world war, rapid social and economic modernization and migration further undermined local cultures and created a mass consumer society. Yet for all this, territory has remained a vital element in French political life. To understand this paradox, it is necessary to examine the local government system and its relation to national politics.

At first sight, the French local government appears to be highly centralized. There are 36,000 communes, whose boundaries are largely unchanged since the Revolution and which, with some exceptions in large cities, are too small to function as autonomous administrative units. All have an elected mayor and council and identical formal powers. Above them are the 96 departments with *conseils généraux* elected from constituencies known as cantons. Their boundaries too are unchanged since the Revolution, except in the Paris area, and no longer correspond to the facts of contemporary social and economic geography. Then there are 22 regions, established in 1972 but directly elected only since 1986. They consist of groups of departments and, despite their relatively recent foundation, are also generally considered ill adapted to the needs of modern planning and administration, especially in the European context. Most administrative services are provided not directly by local governments but by outposts of the national ministries known as *services extérieurs* (field services in English) which may contract with local governments as well as running services on their own account. In each department there remains the centrally appointed prefect, a figure of great prestige, who is technically in charge of most of the field services as well as supervizing local governments to ensure that they remain within the law. Until 1982, the prefect exercised a *tutelle* (control) over local government, with the right to veto acts of the communes, and acted as the executive of the department and the region. While local governments fix their own tax rates, the money is collected by the central government and expenditure paid out by a central official known as the *trésorier-payeur général* in each department.

Yet there are strong counter forces to the dominance of the central administration. Since the 1960s a large literature has documented the mutual dependence of the prefect and the local elected politicians. In order to secure peace and effective administration, the prefect must make adjustments to the centrally decreed policy, in collaboration with important elected officials. Indeed, such is the tendency of prefects to go native and identify with their department against Paris, that they are moved around about every two years. Similarly, officials of the ministerial field services know that they must get along with local politicians and the rivalry among the various *corps* gives the politicians opportunities to play them off against each other. Another corrective to bureaucratic centralization is the accumulation of mandates, the tradition whereby politicians acquire a string of elective offices at central and local level simultaneously. In 1983, 82 per cent of members of parliament also held local office, while 27.5 per cent of the mayors of large towns sat in parliament.[18] In 1985, half the presidents of the *conseils généraux* were parliamentarians. A *député-maire,* that is someone combining the office of mayor and member of Parliament, is a particularly common and powerful figure. The Senate, elected indirectly from local government, consists almost exclusively of politicians holding a local mandate. Ministers, while having to give up their parliamentary seats, can accumulate local offices. Recent prime ministers, Pierre Mauroy (1981-4), Jacques Chirac (1986-8), Michel Rocard (1988-91), Edith Cresson (1991-2) and Pierre Bérégovoy (1992-3) all retained their office of local mayor. Accumulation works in both directions, from below and from above. Local politicians gaining election to national office will retain their local office as a power base. Individuals elected to parliament or appointed directly to ministerial office will also, if they have serious long-term political ambitions, seek a local mandate as a means of reinforcing their legitimacy. This is especially important for people who have been 'parachuted' into constituencies by the national parties without an existing local base of support. Mayors who are ministers in the government are obviously able to outrank the prefects and other field officials, the phenomenon reaching an extreme in a case like that of Gaston Defferre who in the early 1980s was simultaneously mayor of Marseille and minister of the interior and thus the prefect's hierarchical superior. Even senior opposition figures, especially those who have been in office for a long time, will carry great weight. As well as vertical accumulation, that is holding national and local office, there is a horizontal accumulation of various local offices, in the commune, the department, the region and the various specialized agencies and intercommunal groupings. In a highly fragmented local government system, a politician occupying several offices can also intervene at strategic points and pull together powers and resources from different institutions in order to advance projects. In the long process of conquering power and putting down local roots, such a politician acquires *notoriété,* better translated in English as notability than notoriety. In due course the politician becomes a *notable,* that is an individual deriving power and prestige from the possession of public office and the ability to intervene within the government apparatus and whose power is further strengthened by those very interventions. The most powerful of these, the *grands notables* are veritable bosses of their territories and able largely to dominate the local apparatus of the state.

Some observers have seen in this phenomenon a reversal of the jacobin ideal and concluded that France is really a very decentralized state. The reality is more complicated. Accumulation of offices and the intricate mingling of institutional roles allows policy to be negotiated across the central-local divide and provides coordination in an otherwise fragmented system. It provides for local influence in national politics but where the same politicians occupy national and local office it is difficult to tell whether the localities have conquered central government or the central elite has colonized the localities. The presence of an integrated national-local political elite certainly protects the institution of local government since members of parliament will not vote to undermine their own power bases. Yet this does not necessarily enhance the autonomy of local communities, as opposed to that of the political elite itself. There are potential conflicts of interest among the roles which a politician may hold. There is also a serious incidence of absenteeism which, along with other factors, has reduced the status of the national parliament. The fact that some politicians manage to accumulate powerful offices while others do not leads to considerable inequality in a system where, officially, all local governments at a given level are equal. It is possible for most of the 530 deputies to be mayors, but only a fraction of the 36,000 mayors can be deputies. An individual like Jean Lecanuet who in 1985 was a senator, mayor of Rouen, president of the *conseil général* of Seine-Maritime, member of the regional council of Normandy and member of the European Parliament, as well as holding office in various special bodies, is obviously blocking the route for other people. The accumulation of offices also obscures accountability. If a project succeeds, the local *député-maire* can take credit, but the electors are left wondering whether it is the deputy, the mayor or neither that they should thank. If a project fails, it is easy to blame the centralized administration in Paris. This sometimes reached extreme lengths in the past, when the prefect had the power to veto acts of the mayor. An apocryphal story has a mayor, faced with the classic choice between the popular but imprudent policy and the unpopular but right one, choosing the former, discreetly asking the prefect to veto it and then attacking the prefect for crushing local democracy, so getting the right policy but the credit for the popular one.

From the 1960s, this pattern of central-local relations came under increasing strain. Like other countries, France saw a need to modernize its local government institutions and the issue was given greater urgency by the Gaullists' desire to reduce the power bases of their opponents in local government. Yet such was the power of the territorial notables that little was achieved. There were two principal issues of structure, the problem of fragmentation at the communal level and the need for a regional tier. In 1966, urban communities, grouping communes for various purposes in the large cities, were set up. These have indirectly elected councils and some taxing powers but the communes retain their independent existence. In the early 1990s, legislation was passed to extend the idea to other large towns, but still on the basis of voluntary cooperation. Urban communities have allowed some planning and infrastructure decisions to be taken for metropolitan areas, with some pooling of business tax revenues, but because of their indirect election they have been politically weak, with some tendency to spread resources around equally in a process known as *saupoudrage* rather than concentrate them strategically.

Regionalism proved more complicated but equally difficult for the state to resolve in a decisive manner. Regionalism in France, as in Italy and Britain, had both national and local origins. At national level, the state embarked from the 1960s on a series of regional development and planning initiatives seeking to modernize the industrial infrastructure of France and tap under-utilized resources in the less developed parts of the country. These were delivered directly by state agencies, with little involvement of the local government notables. At the same time, in some regions there emerged dynamic, new leaders in industry, agriculture, trade unions and other organizations, the so-called *forces vives,* challenging the old notables entrenched in the local government system. The combination of protest against state-imposed modernization, the rise of new leaders, the rediscovery of traditional languages and cultures together with the pluralist and libertarian ideas of 1968, produced an outburst of regional political activism. Yet regional mobilization in France was weaker and less sustained than in some other European states. The homogenizing effects of state building had been more effective than in Spain or the United Kingdom and the new regionalists failed to tie the cultural revival or autonomist demands to a project to manage social and economic modernization. While regionalist social movements were of some importance and even gave rise to regionalist parties in Brittany and Languedoc, they made little electoral progress, though they placed the issue on the agenda and forced the mainstream parties to respond. De Gaulle's 1969 project to establish regional councils was partly a response to protests against centralization. Equally importantly, it was an attack on the notables of the left and old centre parties who had resisted the Gaullist advance and who, through their base in local government, controlled the Senate. The attack backfired and resulted in de Gaulle's own demise when the referendum went against him. Pompidou proceeded more circumspectly, setting up weak regional councils in 1972, comprising indirectly elected members from departments and cities together with the national deputies from the region and thus controlled precisely by the notables themselves. The large regional development decisions continued to be controlled by the state itself.

After several false starts, a serious decentralization programme was put in place by the Socialist government which arrived in power in 1981. The Socialists, who had traditionally been rather jJacobin, committed to the centralization of power, had been convinced of the virtues of decentralization by their long period in opposition, during which they had gradually built up a strong position in local government. The new party, as it grew in the 1970s, had absorbed many of the ideas and indeed the people of the regionalist movements, as well as the fashionable notion of *autogestion* (self-management) applied to communities as well as the workplace. Like other parties of the Social Democratic left, the French Socialist Party had in the course of the 1960s and 1970s become more pluralist and tolerant of diversity. Yet there were divisions within the party. As well as a continued jacobin element, there were supporters of strong regions who would ideally have liked to see the departments suppressed. There were notables entrenched in the departments who wanted to see them reinforced; and there was a powerful lobby of big city mayors who were suspicious that powerful regions or departments would exercise a new *tutelle* over them. Given these competing claims and the failure of past governments to get structural reforms accepted, the Socialists abandoned all prospects of abolishing tiers of government, changing boundaries or merging communes and instead decided to strengthen all three levels. Regions were erected into fully-fledged local governments *(collectivités territoriales)* with direct elections as from 1986. Departments were freed from prefectoral control and the president of the *conseil général* assumed the role of executive. The prefectoral *tutelle* over communes was removed and the veto power abolished. It should be said that the latter was less a means of freeing the communes, since the veto had largely fallen into disuse, but more a means of emphasizing the responsibility of mayors and preventing them hiding behind prefectoral authority.

Elected councillors were further strengthened in relation to the bureaucracy by transferring staff or placing them at the disposal of councils and weakening the power of the *trésorier-payeur général* to refuse to authorize expenditure. In the large cities, mayors had already established their own technical services and this continued. The prefects were compensated for the loss of their power over local government by gaining the responsibility to direct most of the other field services, so becoming in theory the unique interlocutor of local governments. In practice, the specialized field services have managed to retain their direct links with Paris and escape prefectoral control. Local governments were also given new responsibilities, with an effort to clarify their respective roles. Regions have the main responsibility in regional planning, economic development and training. Departments concentrate on social services and highway maintenance. Communes are responsible for local planning, environmental matters and local infrastructure. In practice, shared responsibilities remain the norm. All three levels and the central government have responsibilities in education, with the centre retaining the essential matters of the curriculum and the employment of teachers. Low-income housing is similarly shared, with a large role for non-profit housing associations. Large-scale projects continue to be jointly planned and managed, with an intricate pattern of financing and subsidization.

The reforms certainly have strengthened the political class in relation to the bureaucracy. Presidents of departments are now major figures in their own right, able to control resources and determine policy. Big city mayors have continued their steady rise in importance. The regions, while they have gained the enhanced status of direct election and some additional responsibilities, have been rather outflanked by the other two tiers. Regional activists in places like Brittany and Occitania, having put their faith in the Socialist Party, were demobilized and regional agitation has largely died down as the big city mayors came to dominate the scene. Only in Corsica does a serious problem of minority :persist. Despite two statutes giving the island a special autonomy, conflict exists between a minority of extreme separatism moderate autonomists and the clans which have long dominated Corsican public life.

Critics have complained that the reforms have done little for local democracy and participation. This further confirms the power of the central-local political class in France to shape a reform to suit their own interests and resist radical upheaval. Some limitation on accumulation of mandates has been introduced, so that in future politicians will be limited to two significant mandates, that is deputy, senator, member of the European Parliament, mayor of a commune of more than 20,000 or assistant mayor of one of more than 100,000, departmental councillor or regional councillor. No-one can be simultaneously president of a department and region. Ministers are not affected by this, although they are already excluded from parliament, and politicians are still free to accumulate offices in urban communities and special-purpose agencies. As the law on accumulation of mandates took effect, politicians, with some exceptions, tended to abandon their regional mandates, retaining their departmental presidencies and, especially mayoralties which remain the best means of anchoring oneself locally. While some observers saw this as a hopeful sign of the emergence of a new political class at the regional level, it can equally be read as an indication that political heavyweights did not see the region as the important level.

Municipal elections, that is for the communes, are taken very seriously in France. Turnout in 1989 varied from 62 per cent in the largest communes to 82 per cent in the smallest, the average figure of 70 per cent confirming the critical importance of the mayor in political life and vesting mayors in turn with great political legitimacy. In the cantonal elections (for the departments) there is less enthusiasm and the same appears to be true of regional elections. A variety of electoral systems is used in local government. For communes of more than 3,500 population, voting is by lists with two ballots. If a list wins an absolute majority at the first ballot it gains half the seats, with the remainder distributed among all lists, including the winning list, proportionately. If there is no absolute majority, a second ballot is held, and lists can be merged before it to produce broader coalitions. At the second ballot, the leading list gains half the seats, with the rest distributed proportionately. The effect is to ensure that there is a majority on the council while allowing smaller forces to be heard. In the three large cities, of Paris, Marseille and Lyon, there is a ward system of elections, with winning candidates and the best-placed runners up also serving on local neighbourhood councils. In departments, elections are by a two-ballot plurality system with each electoral district or canton returning one member. There is great inequality in the size of cantons and most departments have an inbuilt over-representation of the rural areas. For regional councils, elections are by proportional representation with lists competing in each of the constituent departments. This system, which has been much criticized, tends to reduce regional elections to a series of departmental contests, with a consequent downplaying of region-wide issues and a weakening of regional consciousness. Corsica has a special system, with a high degree of proportional representation, allowing the multitudinous factions to gain representation in the Assembly but making stable government extremely difficult.

Under the Fourth Republic and the early years of the Fifth Republic, there was a great variety of local political coalitions. Socialists were often found in coalition with centrists in what were known as third-force alliances. Radicals and other centrist forces, swept aside in national politics by Gaullism, survived a great deal longer in the localities where notables were well dug in. From the 1970s, however, local politics increasingly took on a national coloration. After the signing of the Common Programme of the left, local Socialists were obliged to break alliances with the centre and forge joint tickets with the Communists. One result was a marked advance for both Socialists and Communists in control of mayoralties, especially in 1977. On the right, the neo-Gaullists of the RPR began to make more headway, with Jacques Chirac winning the mayoralty of Paris and other leading figures winning capturing cities. Local elections reflected national trends and were used by the parties as tests of their overall standing. By the late 1980s, however the crisis of the national party system was felt at local level. RPR and UDF leaders, despite the declared intentions of their parties, repeatedly made deals with the extreme right National Front to cling on to power locally. The Socialists, following Mitterrand's lead, sought new allies in the centre in a return to the old third-force style, or even brought in distinguished outsiders to lead their lists. Both right and left sought to tempt the ecologists. This was less a return to localism in politics than a reflection of the disarray of the party system. Lists and alliances were still largely determined by party headquarters in Paris and openings, whether to the extreme right, the centre or the ecologists, were seen as trials for national realignment rather than forged in response to local needs.

Decentralization has generally been seen as positive in its effects, encouraging responsibility and releasing local energies, but a number of serious problems remain. With 36,000 communes, 96 departments and 22 regions, France has more local governments than the rest of the European Community put together but rationalization has proved impossible. Every local government is somebody's power base and even obvious reforms like merging small communes, realigning department boundaries or merging the regions of Upper and Lower Normandy have proved impossible. Merely encouraging cooperation among communes within the main conurbations has proved a delicate task, given the suspicions and jealousies of mayors. Proposals for larger regions, able to compete in scale and resources with the German *Länder*, have been floated but have come to nothing. The department, once considered functionally redundant, has emerged greatly strengthened and as a key element in the political power structure. Reform of local government finance, too, has proceeded slowly and incrementally. There are large disparities in the fiscal capacity of local governments and, while central government distributes a substantial amount of support to even this out, the formula used is rather crude and outdated. So instead of a radical reform, governments have brought in a continuous series of small changes, new grants, new distribution formulas and modifications to old ones, so that the system has become almost impossible to penetrate. It is clear that, given the power of local notables, the state has not cut back support for local government to the extent that has happened in other countries, and there is not generalized local fiscal crisis, but nor has decentralization produced a clear and transparent system of finance, allowing electors to place responsibility for policy where it belongs.

REFERENCES

1. V.A. Schmidt, *Democratizing France. The Political and Adminstrative History of Decentralization* (Cambridge and New York: Cambridge University Press, 1990).
2. J. Derville, 'Le discours des partis gaullistes', *Regards sur l'actualité*, 165 (1990), pp. 17-29.
3. J. Beaudoin, 'Le "moment néo-libéral" du RPR: essai d'interprétation', *Revue Française de Science Politique*, 40.6 (1990), pp. 830-44.
4. F. Haegel, 'Mémoire, héritage, filiation. Dire gaullisme et se dire gaulliste au RPR', *Revue Française de Science Politique*, 40.6 (1990), pp. 864-79.
5. P. Habert, 'Les cadres du RPR: l'empire éclaté', in O. Duhamel and J. Jaffré (eds.), *SOFRES, L'Etat de l'opinion 1991* (Paris: Seuil, 1991).
6. O. Duhamel and J. Jaffré (eds.), *SOFRES, L'Etat de l'opinion 1991* (Paris: Seuil, 1991).
7. C. Ysmal, *Les partis politiques sous la Vᵉ République* (Paris: Montchrestien, 1989).
8. C. Ysmal, 'La crise électorale de l'UDF et du RPR', *Revue Française de Science Politique*, 40.6 (1990),

pp. 879-98.
9. O. Duhamel and J. Jaffré (eds.), *SOFRES, L'Etat de l'opinion 1991* (Paris: Seuil, 1991).
10. P. Perinau, 'Les cadres du Parti Socialiste: la fin du parti d'Epinay', in O. Duhamel and J. Jaffré (eds.), *SOFRES, L'Etat de l'opinion 1991* (Paris: Seuil, 1991).
11. G. Birenbaum, *Le Front National en Politique*(Paris: Balland, 1992).
12. J. Jaffré, 'Trente années du changement électoral', *Pouvoirs*, 48 (1989).
13. J. Jaffré, 'Trente années du changement électoral', *Pouvoirs*, 48 (1989).
14. F. Bon and J-P. Cheylan, *La France qui vote* (Paris: Hachette, 1988).
15. Quoted in P. Avril, *Politics in France* (Harmondsworth: Penguin, 1969), pp. 135-6.
16. B. Jobert, 'The Normative Frameworks of Public Policy', *Political Studies*, XXXVII.3 (1989), pp. 376-86.
17. Y. Mény, 'The National and International Context of French Policy Communities', *Political Studies*, XXXVII.3 (1989), pp. 387-99.
18. P. Garraud, 'Un maire urbain sur deux est fonctionnaire', *Le Journal des Elections*, 6, Jan-Feb. 1989, p.19.

FURTHER READING

General

M. Duverger, *Constitutions et documents politiques*, 12th edn. (Paris: Presses Universitaires de France, 1989).M. Duverger, *Le système politique français*, 20th edn. (Paris: Presses Universitaires de France, 1990).
H. Ehrmann and M. Schain, *Politics in France*, 5th edn. (Glenview, Ill.: Scott, Foresman, 1992).
P.A. Hall, J. Hayward and H. Machin (eds.), *Developments in French Politics* (London: Macmillan, 1990).
J. Hayward, *Governing France. The One and Indivisible Republic* (London: Weidenfeld and Nicolson, 1983).
J. Hollifield and G. Ross (eds.), *Searching for the New France* (London and New York: Routledge, 1991).
M. Larkin, *France since the Popular Front. Government and People, 1936-1986* (Oxford: Clarendon, 1988).
W. Safran, *The French Polity*, 3rd edn. (London and White Plains, NY: Longman, 1991).
A. Stevens, *The Government and Politics of France* (New York: St. Martin's Press, 1992).
V. Wright, *The Government and Politics of France*, 3rd edn. (London: Routledge, 1989).

Parties and Elections

D. Bell and B. Criddle, *The French Socialist Party. The Emergence of a Party of Government* (Oxford: Clarendon, 1988).
J. Frears, *Parties and Voters in France* (London: Hurst. New York: St. Martin's Press, 1991).
C. Ysmal, *Les partis politiques sous la Vᵉ République* (Paris: Montchrestien, 1989).

Public Policy

Baumgartner, F., *Conflict and Rhetoric in French Policy Making* (Pittsburgh: University of Pittsburgh Press, 1989).
J.W. Friend, *Seven Years in France. François Mitterrand and the Unintended Revolution, 1981-1988* (Boulder: Westview, 1989).
P. Hall, *Governing the Economy* (Oxford and New York: Oxford University Press).
B. Jobert and P.Muller, *L'état en action* (Paris: Presses Universitaires de France, 1987).
S. Mazey and M. Newman (eds.), *Mitterrand's France* (London: Croom Helm, 1987).G. Ross, S. Hoffman and S.Malzacher (eds.), *The Mitterrand Experiment* (New York: Oxford University Press, 1987).
F. Wilson, *Interest Group Politics in France* (Cambridge: Cambridge University Press, 1987).

Territorial Politics

G. Bélorgey, *La France decentralisée* (Paris: Berger-Levrault, 1984).

F. Dupuy and J-C. Thoenig, *L'administration en miettes* (Paris: Fayard, 1985).

M. Keating and P. Hainsworth, *Decentralisation and Change in Contemporary France* (Aldershot: Gower, 1986).

V.A. Schmidt, *Democratizing France. The Political and Administrative History of Decentralization* (Cambridge and New York: Cambridge University Press, 1990).

4 Italy

STATE AND GOVERNMENT IN ITALY

Italy has been recognized since ancient times, but became a united state only in the last century. Following the demise of the Roman Empire, it was divided into a complex patchwork of political units. Some of these were part of the great empires, while others were independent city states like Venice or Genoa, living by trade and commerce. By the mid-nineteenth century, wars, annexations and great power interventions had produced four main units. In the north-west was the kingdom of Piedmont and Sardinia, ruled by the House of Savoy. In the north-east, Lombardy and Venice belonged to the Austrian Empire. In central Italy were the Papal States, governed by the Pope from Rome. In the south was the kingdom of Naples and Sicily, a rather decadent domain ruled by a branch of the Bourbon family. In addition, various small duchies and principalities managed to maintain a more or less precarious independence. To Metternich, the Austrian chancellor, Italy was a mere geographical expression, no more a country than a pile of wood was a ship.

Yet from the early nineteenth century, a new nationalism developed, inspired by the French Revolution. A movement known as the *Risorgimento* called for a renewal of Italy, the overthrow of the old monarchies, for national unification, democracy and a liberal constitution. Liberal nationalism enjoyed a brief moment of triumph in 1848, when revolutions spread across Europe. An Italian Republic was declared in Rome but this was soon defeated in the reaction which followed and the Pope, along with other European monarchs, was restored to his throne. Thereafter the flame of liberal nationalism was kept alive by Guiseppe Mazzini, one of the main theorists of European nationalism and a hero to oppressed peoples across the continent. In Italy, however, liberal nationalism was mainly an affair for intellectuals and middle-class professionals rather than the popular masses and Mazzini was to die a disillusioned man. Unification of the country came about quite rapidly in the 1860s for altogether less idealistic reasons.

The key figures were Camillo Cavour, prime minister of Piedmont and Guiseppe Garibaldi, a military adventurer who had been associated with Mazzini in the brief Republic of 1848. Cavour's aim appears to have been the establishment of a north Italian kingdom, playing on the rivalry of the great powers to expel the Austrians. In 1859 and 1866, Austria was provoked into a war with France and the Prussia. For being on the winning side, Piedmont gained Lombardy and Venice. In 1860, on the pretext of preventing instability and controlling Garibaldi's activities, Piedmont occupied and annexed the Papal States. The Pope himself retreated to the city of Rome under the protection of French troops. Shortly after, Garibaldi led an expedition to the south where he overthrew the Bourbon regime and handed Naples and Sicily over to the king of Piedmont. In 1870, when the French troops were recalled for the Franco-Prussian war, Rome itself was occupied and the Pope shut himself up in the Vatican, from which no Pope emerged until 1929.

The means by which Italy was unified, through political and military manoeuvring rather than popular revolution, left a deep mark on the country's politics. Local loyalties remained strong and as late as the 1930s many country people spoke only their local dialect and could not understand the national Italian language, based on educated Florentine. A t the first meeting of the new Italian parliament, Massimo d'Azeglio declared: 'We have made Italy, now we have to make Italians.' This was to be a long process.

Huge social and economic differences persisted between the industrializing north, part of the European heartland, and the agricultural south, where conditions were closer to Africa than to Europe. Far from attacking this problem, the politics of the unified state tended to perpetuate it. There was an implicit social bargain between the dominant classes in the north and the feudal landowners in the south. Northern capitalists would gain a unified Italian market and tariff protection against competition from other European countries. Southern landowners would be left in peace, with no serious attempt at land reform or modernization. Some of the northern working-class leaders eventually bought into this system, sharing their bosses' interest in tariff protection. The southern landless peasants gained nothing. The early years of unification saw a savage repression of peasant revolts as the full force of the new state was mobilized to maintain the social order. To these social and economic problems was added the development of organized crime in the form of the Sicilian Mafia and its mainland counterparts, who challenged the very basis of the state, the ability to guarantee law and order through the monopoly of force. The failure to mount a social and economic revolution along with political unification was seen by many observers then and since as a fundamental weakness of the new nation. The failure to unify north and south was referred to as the *unificazione mancata*, the missing unification.

The unified state was also shunned by the Church, which seriously undermined its legitimacy given that Italy was an overwhelmingly Catholic country. Outraged by the loss of the Papal States and the secular instincts of the new state, the Pope in 1874 issued the *Non Expedit,* forbidding Catholics to vote or hold office in the state. The response was a series of anticlerical measures on the part of government and a worsening of relations. Only from 1904 was the

Non Expedit relaxed and it was not until 1919 that a Catholic political party was formed.

Rather than introduce a new constitution, Italy made do with the Piedmontese constitution, one of the few lasting gains of the revolutionary events of 1848. It remained in force until 1949. Disowned by the Church and the radical followers of Mazzini, and distrusted by the peasantry, the regime rested on a narrow social base. Formally, it was structured on French lines, with a legalistic constitution, an ordered bureaucracy and centralized administration. In practice, politics revolved around the trading of favours among politicians in Rome. In return for patronage, politicians would deliver the votes of their localities for the government of the day. Rule exemptions, permits, grants and subsidies were used to build up client networks around local bosses. For a time there was an alternation in power of the two wings of the middle-class Liberal Party, the *Destra* (right) and *Sinistra* (left) but by the 1880s these merged into a single party. Even before this, there had developed the Italian custom of *trasformismo*. This involves government through broad coalitions, largely irrespective of ideology. There is no alternation of parties in power. Rather, new opposition movements are invited into the dominant coalition and given their own share of patronage to distribute. Patronage and clientelism were particularly widespread in the south, whose deputies in the national parliament would usually support the governing coalition, whoever it was, to be sure of remaining on the winning side. In the towns and countryside of Italy, little could be done without the support of a patron with connections in Rome.

Reformers in the post-unification years talked of a federal system, with strong regional governments able to manage their own affairs and reducing the burden of centralized government. This idea was rejected then, but has reappeared persistently in Italian politics. After the first world war, there were some reforms. In 1919, all adult males were given the vote. This stimulated the growth of the Socialist Party, which in 1919 gained 156 seats in parliament. In 1919, with the lifting of the papal ban, a Catholic party, the *Partito Popolare*, was founded by a Sicilian priest, Luigi Sturzo, gaining 100 seats in parliament that year. The evolution of the system, however, was stymied by the violent events of the early 1920s. There were strikes and border disputes with Italy's neighbours. In the south landless peasants, many of them demobilized soldiers, staged land occupations on the large estates. Fragmentation of the party system made it ever more difficult to form governments. The Fascist party, formed by former Socialist Benito Mussolini, lost no opportunity to create trouble, engaging in violent confrontations with the Socialists while calling for strong government. In 1922 Mussolini announced a March on Rome by his private army of blackshirts, to sieze power. With only 35 deputies in the parliament and a few thousand members, the Fascists hardly seemed to in a position to seize power but what might have been a piece of comic opera turned into a real *coup d'état* when the king invited Mussolini to form a government. Over the next few years, the parliamentary regime was replaced by a dictatorship under the leadership of Mussolini, who styled himself *Il Duce*. Other parties were banned and trade unions, along with other free associations, suppressed. Instead, there were officially sponsored vertical unions uniting employers and workers. These bodies, which were subordinate to the Fascist Party, were also the basis for the national electoral system. Only candidates proposed by them and approved by the Fascist Party could stand for election, forming a single list, with no opposition allowed.

Mussolini's Fascist regime was a brutal dictatorship with did not hesitate to jail and murder its opponents. Yet it was not as thoroughly totalitarian as Hitler's Germany. The Church was too powerful a force to dominate and instead Mussolini did a deal with it. Under the 1929 Concordat, the Pope recognized the Italian state and gave his support to the Fascist regime. In return, Catholicism became the official religion of Italy and the Church gained valuable privileges in education and financial support. Recognizing that the Papal States were gone for ever, the Pope was given sovereignty over a mini-state consisting of the Vatican and some properties outside Rome. Nor, despite the regime's bombast and the demands of their radical wing, did the Fascists do anything about the problem of the south. Large landowners were left in possession of their estates. Some leading Mafia figures were imprisoned or driven into exile but for the most part, the local political and criminal bosses simply donned black shirts for the duration of the regime.

Mussolini used to muse about establishing a new Roman empire and spent some years trying to conquer Abysinnia. In the Spanish Civil War, Italian troops were sent to fight for Franco. Increasingly, however, his foreign policy came under the influence of Hitler's Germany and at the outbreak of the second world war he joined in on the German side. This sealed the fate of his regime. In 1943, the Allied powers invaded Italy through Sicily and advanced towards Rome. In a bid to save his own throne, the king dismissed Mussolini and joined the Allied side. This precipitated an invasion by the Germans who installed Mussolini as puppet ruler of a north Italian state, the Republic of Salò. A resistance movement, with a military wing, the partisans, and a political leadership grouping the main anti-Fascist forces from the Communists to progressive Catholics, rapidly developed, helping to push the Germans back. Mussolini himself was caught and executed by partisans, suffering the final indignity of being strung up by his heels in a square in Milan.

The postwar Italian regime emerged from the resistance groups but was conditioned by the international context. As it finished the war technically on the winning side, Italy did not experience the prolonged occupation and forced restructuring imposed upon Germany and Japan. The allied powers, Britain and the United States did nevertheless exert an important influence on the shape of the new political order, especially after the outbreak of the Cold War in 1947 when Italy came into the front line against communism. The national resistance council (CLN) was a broad grouping whose principal components were the Communists, the Socialists, the Christian Democrats and the Action Party, a radical liberal grouping. All were initially agreed on the need to break not merely with Fascism but with the corruption and *trasformismo* of the pre-Fascist regime. The monarchy was abolished by referendum and a Republic was declared in 1946. A constituent assembly produced a new constitution, adopted at the end of 1947. This provided for a very democratic system, with a pure system of proportional representation, referendums on important issues and strong regional and local governments. Civil rights were guaranteed as was a series of social rights. A serious dispute arose over the status of the Church. The Vatican, with the support of the Christian Democrats, insisted on retaining its privileges under the 1929 Concordat, against the opposition of the secular parties. Eventually, the Communists broke ranks with the other secular parties and voted to retain the Concordat in the interests of religious peace. They received no thanks from the hierarchy. In 1949 a Vatican decree excommunicated Communists, their voters and sympathizers. The Concordat remained in force until 1985.

The hopes for a modernized, democratic and participative political system were dashed in the years which followed. Proportional representation produced a fragmented party system, with two large parties, the Christian Democrats and the Communists, and an array of smaller ones. The outbreak of the Cold War led to the expulsion of the Communists from the coalition government in 1947. Two powerful external forces, the Vatican and the United States, ensured that they remained outside. Priests called from the pulpit for the faithful to vote Christian Democrat. The United States provided money for the Christian Democrats and warned that in the event of a Communist victory all assistance to Italy would stop. As the Communists were permanently excluded from power, there was no chance of peaceful alternation. Communists and Christian Democrats retreated into their own subcultures, preventing the exchange and compromise needed in a working liberal democracy. Christian Democrats governed through a gradually expanding coalition, in a manner reminiscent of the old *trasformismo* system. The old power brokers, with their habits of clientelism and patronage, returned to influence via the Christian Democratic Party. The bureaucracy was not purged but retained a large number of the servants of the Fascist regime. Fascist laws remained on the statute book even where they were incompatible with the new constitution. Regional government and referendums were not established until 1970.

Since the war, Italy has undergone massive social and economic change. An 'economic miracle' has put it in the first league of industrialized countries. In 1945, 60 per cent of the working population were in agriculture. By the end of the 1980s, this was down to less then ten per cent. Movement from the countryside to the cities was matched by movement from the south to the north. In the mid-1960s, around a quarter of a million people a year were leaving the impoverished south to find work in the factories of the north. Those who remained in the south flocked to the large cities like Naples, Palermo and Catania which sprawled uncontrollably. In the 1980s, the drift to the north halted and, with their higher birth-rate, the southern regions increased their share of national population. The large cities of the north lost population but for the first time in modern history saw significant numbers of foreign immigrants arriving to take the lower-paid jobs.

Rather later than the countries of northern Europe, Italy has begun to secularize. Evidence for this is the decline in Church-going and the referendum majorities to legalize divorce (1974) and abortion (1981). The status of women, traditionally subordinate, has also begun to change since the 1970s.

Yet the country remains bedevilled by a political system which is the despair of thinking Italians. It has survived a number of crises. In the late 1960s and early 1970s, there was an explosion of social protest, in the factories, the streets and the universities. Plots for a *coup d'état* and rumour of plots abounded - it is still not clear what substance there was to all of these. In the 1970s, the 'years of lead', Italy faced terrorism from the extreme left and right, including the bombing of Bologna railway station by a neo-fascist group with the death of 85 people and the murder of Christian Democrat leader Aldo Moro by the Red Brigades. In the 1980s and 1990s the state appears helpless in the face of organized crime. Yet, for all its imperfections, the democratic system survived.

In the 1990s, the Italian political system faces further challenges. Public trust in government is low. The end of the Cold War is hastening the dissolution of the power blocs within Italian society and has removed the main pretext for avoiding reform. Increased concern is expressed about the quality of public administration and the massive budget deficits which are the consequence of Italy's governing style. Above all, the need to compete in the open European market is forcing Italian policy makers and opinion formers to ask hard questions about the viability of their system of government and the need for radical change.

PARTITOCRAZIA

Italy's rather lengthy constitution proclaims the sovereignty of the people, details the rights and duties of citizens and specifies in some detail the legal arrangements for government. In practice, the workings of government owe less to the constitutional provisions than to the manoeuvring of the political parties. These perform many of the classic functions of parties, contesting elections and simplifying electoral choice, recruiting politicians, organizing the legislature and securing the passage of laws; but they do much more than this. They have colonized the public administration and, through an extensive system of state intervention, have extended their reach into the civil society. They have organized their supporters not on the basis of policy programmes but through exclusive subcultures in which loyalty is largely taken for granted. So aspects of life which in other countries might be considered strictly private are in Italy politicized. Politics is less about designing and debating policy alternatives than about sharing out positions of power and the spoils of office, in the form of patronage, favours, grants and exemptions. The bureaucracy rarely works as it should, corruption is rife and political string-pulling is required before the state will respond even on routine matters. This system of government is known to Italians as *partitocrazia,* the rule of the parties.

Yet at the same time, postwar Italy has had a successful economy and managed a period of remarkable social change. Observers have long noted a distinction between these two worlds, the *paese legale*, the legal country of the law, the state and bureaucracy, which does not work; and the *paese reale*, the real country of successful business, social movements and citizens, which somehow manages. Texts on constitutional law still widely used in Italian universities, describe the system in purely legalistic terms and prescribe elaborate administrative reforms to cure the system of its ills. Yet there is a widespread appreciation that the problem lies not in the technical defects of administrative law but in the fact that much of administrative law and the *paese legale* generally is a mere fiction, bearing little connection with the realities of life. Between the two worlds, however, stand the political parties. They are the ones who can make the administration respond to their clients and their power and very existence would be threatened by any reform which would make the bureaucracy responsive and efficient and thus render them redundant.

Italy is a parliamentary system in which government is chosen from and responsible to parliament but the pure system of proportional representation ensures that no party ever wins a majority. All governments therefore have to be coalitions. The main parties, especially the Christian Democrats, are further divided into factions so that governments must balance not only party interests but those of the factions within them. This makes governments very difficult to form and very fragile. Parties and factions withdraw their support regularly, going into opposition or more commonly seeking better terms to enter a new coalition. Between the foundation of the Republic and 1993, there were no less than fifty twogovernments. The longest lived was the Craxi government between August 1983 and June 1986 and the shortest the first Andreotti government which lasted just nine days in 1972. The full list of prime ministers and governments in given in the appendix.

The apparent turbulence and instability of Italian coalitions, however, masks

Table 4.1 Coalition formulas

Formula	Parties
Centre-Right	DC-PSDI-PLI-PRI
Centre-Left	DC-PSI-PSDI-PRI
Pentapartito	DC-PSI-PSDI-PRI-PLI
Monocolore	DC
Historic compromise	DC with external PCI support

DC=Christian Democrat PLI=Liberals
PSI=Socialists PSDI=Social Democrats
PCI=Communists PRI=Republicans

deep continuities in government. Governments may fall every few months, but the new coalitions formed in their wake tend to look very much alike. The same limited number of parties is available and the same faces appear around the table of the Council of Ministers. Even the bewildering variety of coalition arrangements conforms to a limited number of patterns. There are usually about ten parties represented in parliament, but only five of these have been involved in coalition-building. The basic building block of any coalition is the Christian Democratic party (DCI) which has featured in all fifty one coalitions. Within the DCI a politician like Giulio Andreotti served more or less continuously for forty years, being prime minister on seven occasions. During the Cold War, the Communists were excluded from coalition building, leaving the Christian Democrats and four lay parties, the Socialists, the Social Democrats, the Liberals and the Republicans. Until 1963, the Christian Democrats governed in alliance with the Liberals, the Social Democrats and sometimes the Republicans, in a centre-right coalition. From 1963 to 1974, the Socialists joined, in a formation known as the centre-left. From 1976 to 1979 there was the historic compromise, a deal whereby the Communists supported a Christian Democratic government without joining it. This was succeeded for most of the 1980s by a broad coalition known as the *pentapartito,* or five-party government. In the early 1990s, this broke down amid signs of realignment in the party system. The whole period was punctuated by short periods of Christian Democrat single party government, a formula known as the *monocolore.* Table 4.1 gives the constitutional formulas.

The progressive broadening of governing coalitions was a response to a gradual decline in Christian Democrat strength and the difficulties of gaining majorities in the legislature. This was a resumption of the *trasformismo* tradition of the pre-Fascist regime. Rather than alternate in power, the governing party co-opts other parties, giving them a share of the spoils of office and binding them to the system. The entry of the Socialists and the Republicans into the coalition in the early 1960s was seen at the time as a shift in the political power balance and an opportunity for reform. Yet after a few innovative measures, the Socialists were absorbed into the system and behaved much like the other parties. Even the Communists, given a share in municipal coalitions, were not able to resist the temptation to corrupt and clientelistic politics.

Coalition building revolves less around policy issues than around the sharing out of office and patronage. *Lottizzazione* refers to the parcelling out of the spoils of office among the political parties and government crises which precede the fall of coalitions are often provoked by parties wanting a larger share. Allocation of ministerial portfolios is less a matter of finding the best people for the posts than of satisfying party demands and giving them positions which they can use in turn to satisfy their own supporters.

The position of prime minister is therefore a weak one, with little discretion over appointments, little control over policy, and a short life expectancy in office. Powerful politicians have often preferred the office of party general secretary, remaining outside the government, to that of prime minister. This allows them to dictate terms for their party's participation, to nominate ministers and to call an end to the government's term when it suits them.

GOVERNMENT AND PARLIAMENT

Italy's governing institutions are regulated by the constitution of 1948, which provides for a parliamentary democracy. In practice, they have largely been subordinated to the needs of the parties and there has been a growing demand for institutional reform.

The President

The constitution provides for a non-executive president, elected for a seven-year term by a college consisting of members of both houses of parliament and representatives from the regional councils. Voting is secret but largely follows party lines and until 1992 there was an understanding that the regional representatives would be chosen according to the party balance in parliament. In 1992 this understanding broke down and regional electors were chosen by the governing coalitions in the various regional councils. There is an extremely elaborate system of balloting. In the first three ballots, a two thirds majority is required to elect a candidate. If no-one receives this, then from the fourth ballot a simple majority is sufficient. Matters are further complicated by the provision that new candidates can be, and usually are, introduced in successive ballots. The shortest presidential elections were in 1946 and 1985, when there was sufficient agreement to elect a candidate on the first ballot. In 1971, it took twenty-three ballots to elect a president. Oscar Luigi Scalfaro was elected in 1992 as a safe compromise candidate after fifteen ballots. The presidency is a strategic position which in the hands of a strong personality could exercise real influence. Party leaders will therefore strive to keep their main rivals and out. Yet it is not sufficiently important for the major leaders to want it for themselves. It is therefore usually entrusted to a second-ranking, often elderly politician who will recognize the limitations of the role. This does not always work out. Mario Segni (1962-4) was suspected of plans to appoint a non-political government with the backing of the para-military police force, the *Carabinieri*. Francesco Cossiga (1985-92), chosen as a safe, loyal party man, spent his last years lashing out at the parties and the political system, dragging out old scandals and calling for drastic reform, before plunging the political world into chaos by resigning during the legislative election campaign. This merely determined the party leaders to go for a safer choice next time round.

The president is not expected to intervene in day to day politics, but to represent the nation symbolically and ensure the continuity of governing institutions. It is also a presidential responsibility to appoint the prime minister. Since the prime minister must enjoy the confidence of parliament, the president's choice is limited but in the complex manoeuvring to form coalitions there is some scope for presidential intervention. This is another reason why the party bosses like a safe, compromise president

Prime Minister and Government

Government is in the hands of the Council of Ministers, headed by the prime minister - whose official title is president of the Council of Ministers. In Britain, France, Germany and Spain the prime minister or chancellor can usually count on the support of a disciplined party caucus in parliament and a loyal Cabinet of ministers. Italian prime ministers, by contrast, head fragile coalitions. Ministers are nominated not by the prime minister but by the leaders of the coalition parties or Christian Democrat factions. These reserve the right to withdraw at any point, precipitating a government crisis and usually the fall of the prime minister. Someone else is then given the task of trying to construct a new coalition. With such a precarious hold on office, there is little chance for the prime minister to establish a strong personal position to develop policy or pursue long-term strategy.

Seventeen of Italy's twenty prime ministers between 1945 and 1992 came from the Christian Democrat ranks but, since the retirement of Alcide De Gasperi (1945-53), few of these have even been in command of their own party. Factional and personal rivalries ensure that the prime ministership and party leadership are not held by the same person and it is the party leader who is the more important figure. Ciriaco De Mita attempted to ignore this rule in the late 1980s but ended up losing both posts. On three occasions, the Christian Democrats have had to surrender the post of prime minister to other parties, to Giovanni Spadolini of the Republicans (1981-2), to Bettino Craxi of the Socialists (1983-7) and to Giuliano Amato, also of the Socialists in 1992. Both Spadolini and Craxi sought to reform and strengthen the prime minister's office to lessen its dependence on party factions. Spadolini launched a structural reform which was finally put into legislative form in 1988. This reorganized the prime minister's office in the Palazzo Chigi, providing staffing and a budget to the various units and enhancing its policy capacity.[1] As with many Italian reforms, however, this was highly legalistic and formal in its conception and failed to address the essential weakness of the prime ministerial role, that is the party system and the fragile coalition governments which issue from it.

Craxi used his extended period of office to establish an image of strong, decisive government. By skilful manoeuvring he clung on to office for three and a half years, long past the allowance which the Christian Democrats had initially given him. Instead of conciliating and compromising like other prime ministers, he tried to lead from the front. The Communists and their trade union allies were defeated over the *scala mobile,* indexing wages to prices. Confrontations were staged with magistrates, parliament and his Christian Democratic coalition partners. A new Concordat was negotiated with the Vatican. Decrees were increasingly used as a means of by-passing parliament. Yet Craxi's ambitions were essentially tactical, to establish his pre-eminence in the political system, rather than related to a coherent policy programme. His party base remained weak and in due course the Christian Democrats were able to recover the prime ministership.

The Council of Ministers consists of twenty to thirty politicians chosen on the basis of *lottizzazione,* the division of power and patronage among the parties. The needs of coalition making led over the years to an inflation in the number of ministers. In 1948, De Gasperi managed with 22 full ministers and 23 under secretaries. By the seventh Andreotti government in 1991, there were 33 full ministers and 68 under secretaries. Some of these were ministries without portfolio with important patronage functions, or had vague coordinating powers. Certain ministries have effectively become the fief of specific parties or factions. So the minister of agriculture must be acceptable to the *Colidiretti,* the Christian Democrat small farmers' organization. In the 1980s, the Socialists successfully claimed the ministry for the *Mezzogiorno,* in charge of development programmes in the south. Coalition politics mean that there is little collective responsibility for government policy and ministries often go their own way. In economic matters, divisions among the Treasury, the Ministry of the Budget and the Bank of Italy often prevent a coherent line emerging, especially on controlling Italy's large budget deficit.

Parliament

There are two houses of parliament, the Senate, with 315 members and the Chamber of Deputies, with 630 members. Both are directly elected at five-year intervals, but on a slightly different basis. Until 1993, the Chamber was elected by proportional representation by Italians over the age of eighteen; members must be twenty five years of age or over. The Senate was also elected by proportional basis but using the twenty two regions as constituencies. Voting for the Senate is confined to Italians over twenty five and Senators must be at least forty years of age. The idea was to provide an upper house with a more mature, or conservative, view on issues and to provide representation for the regions. In practice, elections for both Senate and Chamber are dominated by the parties and there are only slight differences in the results, reflecting the different voting age or party alliances for senatorial elections in specific regions.

Despite criticisms in the Constituent Assembly, both houses have the same powers. In reality, the Chamber is by far the more important and the one which makes and breaks governments. In the event that a coalition cannot be assembled, parliament may be dissolved early and new elections called. This was never necessary during the 1950s and 1960s but several times in the 1970s and 1980s parliament was dissolved after three or four years. Actual decisions about making and breaking coalitions, however, are made not by members of parliament but by party headquarters or faction leaders. Before 1988, all voting in the Chamber was secret, allowing dissidents or faction leaders to harry the government anonymously or even precipitate its fall. In that year, open voting was introduced for about 90 per cent of issues, producing more discipline within the coalition.

Most of the legislative work of parliament is done in committees. In 1991 there were fourteen standing committees in the chamber as well as special committees of investigation and control. Other committees regulated internal house matters and there were some joint committees between the Chamber and the Senate. It is possible in Italy to delegate legislation to the committees, whose composition reflects that of the house as a whole. This is a matter of considerable importance, since Italy passes a great deal of legislation. Because of the legalistic tradition in public administration, many matters which would be dealt with by executive action in other countries are handled in Italy by law. Other laws are passed as favours to client groups or individuals. These are known as *leggine*, or little laws and take up a considerable amount of parliamentary time. Most of this influence passes through the parties or party factions or powerful party bosses who are more interested in patronage and favours than coherent policy.

The slowness and uncertainties of the legislative process have led governments from the 1970s increasingly to make use of decrees. Intended for use in emergency, these have become routine, accounting for nearly a quarter of government-sponsored legislation in the 1980s. Decrees give immediate effect to government policies but must be confirmed by parliament within sixty days. The idea was to force parliament to address issues but while in the early phase decrees were usually rapidly confirmed, these too have tended to disappear in the parliamentary labyrinth. Even where legislation is duly passed, regulations are usually required to give it effect. These can be a long time coming, given the ponderous pace of the Italian public administration.

Judicial Control

The republican constitution was intended to represent a *Stato di Diritto,* in which the law would be superior to politicians and parties. To this end, a Constitutional Court was provided for, with responsibility for interpreting the constitution. Like the provision for establishing regions, this was a victim of party polarization after the outbreak of the Cold War and the Court was not established until 1956. Meanwhile, constitutional interpretation fell to the Court of Cassation, unpurged after the Fascist era. It proved very reluctant to enforce provisions of the new constitution to strike down old Fascist laws.

The present Constitutional Court consists of fifteen judges appointed for nine-year terms. Five are nominated by the judiciary, five by the president of the Republic and five by parliament according to a procedure giving the opposition as well as governing parties some say. The court has not escaped the politicization of Italian public life and many judges have known partisan affiliations. Yet it has earned a considerable measure of respect. It does not have the sweeping powers to interpret the constitution and disallow laws possessed by the United States Supreme Court but it is able, where a case is brought before it, to strike down laws or parts of them. It is then up to parliament to fill in the void. The Constitutional Court has also played a role in interpreting the social clauses of the constitution to stipulate minimal levels of benefits, in matters of civil liberties and in deciding on the constitutionality of referendums.[2] It has ruled on the powers of regional councils though, in contrast to Spain, it has not become an arena of confrontation over powers between central government and the regions.

PARTIES AND ELECTIONS

Italian elections are conducted by a complicated system of proportional representation, designed to guarantee democracy . and discourage a return to dictatorship. There was not unanimous agreement on this in the Constituent Assembly. Some delegates favoured a constituency-based system to focus elections on individuals rather than parties. Others warned that PR could produce a proliferation of parties and make government impossible, as had happened in 1919-22. Controversy over the electoral system has continued ever since.

Voting is not strictly compulsory but is officially classified as a civic duty and marked on the individual's identity card. Particularly for those seeking public sector employment, this is a strong incentive to turn out, though some electors choose to express their alienation by returning blank or spoiled ballot papers. Turnout levels are consequently high. In 1992, 86.4 per cent of electors voted.

In the system as it existed until 1993, for the Chamber of Deputies, there were thirty-two electoral districts and a national district known as the *collegio unico nazionale*. Most electoral districts had between seven and forty seats, though the Val d'Aosta had just one. An electoral quota was established for each district, consisting of the total votes divided by the total seats. Parties then presented lists of candidates in these districts. Each party gaining the quota of votes was allocated a seat, parties gaining twice the quota of votes got two seats and so on until all the seats were allocated. Any surplus votes, for example where a party gains enough to elect one candidate in a district but not quite enough to elect two, were allocated to the *collegio unico nazionale* (CUN). Similarly surplus seats, for which no party has the requisite quota, were allocated to the CUN. Here there was a further distribution to allocate all the seats. If a party did not gain at least 300,000 votes in the whole country as well as winning at least one district seat, it did not gain representation in parliament at all. Compared with the German 5 per cent rule, this is a very undemanding condition and parties with as little as one per cent of the vote can expect to enter the Italian parliament.

The result was a proliferation of parties. In the elections of 1992, sixteen parties won seats, ten of which had won less than 5 per cent of the overall vote. Since the system is based on party lists, an individual's chances of election depend mainly on his or her position on a party list rather than personal characteristics. Parties are able to bring in new people or recycle old politicians to change their public image or broaden their base of support. The former Communists were in the habit of demonstrating their openness by nominating prominent figures from outside the party to their lists. In the 1970s and 1980s, the tiny Radical Party tried to provoke the conventional parties by outrageous nominations, including a terrorist suspect and a pornographic movie star, Iona Staller, better known as *La Cicciolina*, who served a term in parliament. There was one provision which allowed candidates to make a personal appeal. Electors could choose to give a preference vote to a candidate on a party list. Candidates accumulating preferences could move up the list, so enhancing their chances of being elected. More importantly, preference votes were a means by which politicians could demonstrate their own vote-drawing power, so enhancing their status within their party. Not all electors chose to exercise their preference votes. Those who did were found mainly in the south where it is associated with patronage and the exchange of votes for favours. For this reason, it was a target for reformers and a referendum in 1990 reduced the number of preferences which an elector can express to one.

Elections to the Senate were organized on a similar basis, though the electoral districts are Italy's twenty regions. Results tended to follow those for the Chamber of Deputies quite closely.

The 1993 reforms changed this electoral system. Now 75 per cent of seats in both houses are to be filled on a first-past-the-post, or plurality, system. The remaining 25 per cent will continue to be filled by a variant of the old proportional representation system.

Two large parties dominated Italian politics for most of the postwar era, the Christian Democrats on the centre-right and the Communists on the left. There are four lay parties, so called because they are outside the two big subcultures. The largest of these is the Socialist Party, on the centre-left. The Social Democrats are a breakaway from the Socialists. The Liberal Party stands to the right of the Christian Democrats and is associated with business interests. The Republicans represent the more socially progressive and reforming strand of liberal thought.

Outside the political mainstream, there is an extreme right wing party, the Italian Social Movement (MSI). There is a scattering of small parties, such as

Table 4.2 Parties represented in Italian Chamber of Deputies, 1992

	Seats	Political alignment
Greens (Verdi)	16	Green
Val d'Aosta list	1	Regional
South Tyrol People's Party (SVP)	3	
Communist Refoundation (RC)	35	
Democratic Party of the Left (PDS)	107	Left
Panella list (radicals)	7	
Socialists (PSI)	92	Centre-left
Christian Democrats (DC)	206	
Social Democrats (PSDI)	16	
Network (La Rete)	12	Centre- right
Pensioners	1	
Republicans (PRI)	27	
Liberals (PLI)	17	
Lega Lombarda - Lega Nord	55	Right
Other leagues	1	
Italian Social Movement (MSI)	34	Extreme right

the Radicals, the Greens or the regional party of the Val d'Aosta who elect a few deputies. In 1992, the first serious signs of a break-up of the traditional party alignment occurred. One new element was the election of 56 deputies from the northern Leagues, a regional party with a right-wing populist message. There are also dissidents from the major parties, notably the Communist Refoundation and the Network (*La Rete*), led by a former Christian Democrat. The full list of parties in the 1992 Parliament is given in Table 4.2.

The Christian Democrats

The Italian Christian Democratic Party (DCII) was founded at the end of the war by anti-Fascist Catholics led by Alcide De Gasperi. Like other postwar Christian Democratic movements, it aimed to reconcile Catholicism with liberal democracy and modernity. In Italy, this was a particularly delicate task, given the Church's long hostility to the Italian state and then its collusion with the Fascist regime. The early DCII was a broad coalition. There were figures like De Gasperi, a moderate conservative who had been a leader of the pre-Fascist Popular Party (*Partito Popolare*). There were radical anti-capitalist elements including Catholic trade union and peasant leaders, committed to social equality, planning, land reform and public control of industry; and right-wing elements more in line with traditional Catholic political values. Although some of the early leaders envisaged the party as the secular arm of the Church, most insisted on a separation of roles and the need for the party to be independent. The DCII inherited a collectivist tradition from the Popular Party but also a suspicion of the state and a strong attachment to intermediate institutions including the family, private associations and regional government. This was a formula for a catch-all party, with an appeal across social classes, to town and country, to industry and agriculture. Loosely linking these elements was the search for a third way, inspired by Catholic social doctrine, between market capitalism and socialism. In practical terms, this emerged in support for small-scale peasant proprietorship in the countryside and small business in the industrial sphere. Class cooperation was seen not merely as a practical necessity but as a central element in the creation of an organic, unitary society. In 1946, trying to emphasize both its broad appeal and its progressive edge, De Gasperi described it as 'a party of the centre that leans to the left.' In the late 1940s and early 1950s, this was to change as circumstances and the influence of its powerful sponsors pushed it definitely into the conservative corner.

The first and most important sponsor was the Catholic Church. After the first world war, the Vatican had rather reluctantly allowed Catholics to become involved in politics and given lukewarm support to the Popular Party, but it had soon come to terms with Mussolini. With the defeat of the Axis powers in 1945,

Pope Pius XII realized that the Church's position would have to be safeguarded in a democratic state in which left-wing and anticlerical forces could be important and that this would require a mass Catholic party. So the full weight of Church authority was placed behind De Gasperi. Catholic Action (*Azione Cattolica*), a lay organization, was mobilized behind the party and the parish clergy used their Sunday sermons to instruct their flocks how to vote. The second sponsor was the United States. As the Cold War developed, the Americans saw the DCI as a vital ally in the conflict with communism. Money was supplied to the party, American aid was linked to the party and Italian immigrants in the USA were encouraged to write home urging Italians to vote Christian Democrat to keep the good things flowing. The business community was the third sponsor. It had traditionally looked to the Liberal Party to promote its interests but with the growth of Communist voting many business leaders began to back the DCI as the best way to prevent a left-wing government coming to power. Finally, in the late 1940s and early 1950s, most of the old political brokers of the south, the *notabili* who in pre-Fascist days had found a home in the Liberal Party, moved over to the DCI, bringing their client networks and patronage politics with them. As a result of these developments, the Christian Democrats moved to the right, becoming more like a conventional conservative party. Yet they maintained a broad social base and the progressive, reformist element in the party never died out completely.

A critical turning point was the election of 1948. In June 1947, as the Cold War started, De Gasperi had expelled the left-wing parties from the coalition government and in the following months, with Vatican and American backing, launched a vehement scare campaign against the Communists and their Socialist allies. Threatened with damnation and suffering both in this world and the next should they vote for the left, Catholics turned out *en masse* to support the DCI, which gained 48.5 per cent of the vote and an absolute majority of seats in parliament. Knowing that these unusual circumstances were unlikely to be repeated, the Christian Democrats then sought to consolidate their position by a new electoral law, passed just in time for the 1953 elections. This law, labelled by its opponents the *legge truffa*, or swindle law, provided that any party or coalition of parties winning an overall majority of votes, would be guaranteed 60 per cent of the seats in parliament. The DCI then formed a coalition with the Liberals, Social Democrats and Republicans, confident that they could secure the necessary majority. In the event, the coalition fell just short, at 49.9 per cent of the national vote and the *legge truffa* was repealed. Thereafter, the Christian Democrats have had to govern at the head of more or less fragile coalitions, never sure of a parliamentary majority.

De Gasperi resigned shortly after the 1953 election and the following year Amintore Fanfani seized the leadership of the party, with a promise to revitalize and reform its structure. An attack was made on the southern *notabili* and other opportunists who had come into the party for their own ends. Membership was increased and new branches established. The whole programme was presented as a regeneration of the movement, a reaching out to civil society and a return to the progressive and reformist ideas of the party's early days. The effects were very different. Instead of eliminating patronage and corruption, the Fanfani reforms professionalized it and extended it to the new agencies for welfare and regional development which were being established at the time. While the old-style patronage had been personalized, based on individuals of standing in the community, the new patronage was distributed by the party machine, which reached its tentacles into almost every part of the state and large parts of civil society. The expansion both of the party and the patronage system was particularly spectacular in the south. Early Christian Democracy had its strongest base in the Catholic regions of northern Italy. By the mid-1950s, there were more members and more branches in the south where a party card became an important means of access to government services and favours.

As the Christian Democrats' support base has gradually weakened over the years, it has broadened the coalition governments through *trasformismo*. In the 1950s, it governed in partnership with the Liberals, Republicans and Social Democrats. In the early 1960s, it made an opening to the left, bringing in the Socialists. This move was supported by the progressive elements in the party who saw in this an opportunity for reform and opposed by the conservative wing. Some changes were introduced in government by the Socialists but it is arguable that the main effect was to draw the latter into the patronage system and reduce the prospects for any real change in government. In the 1970s, the party even cooperated with the Communists in an experiment known as the historic compromise. In the 1980s, it forged a broad coalition with four other parties, still remaining the central element in any governing formula, though on two occasions it had temporarily to surrender the prime ministership to other parties.

The DCI is not a unitary party but contains powerful factions within it. These factions are partly based on ideology. Some are further to the left, others to the right. Some identified more closely with the Church, while others want to secularize the party. Some seek reform of the party and government; others wish to stick to the old ways. There is a geographical dimension, with factions based in particular regions or cities. Above all, though, factions are about the distribution of power and patronage

Table 4.3 Votes received by factions, Italian Christian Democratic Congress, 1989	
Faction	% vote
Left	35.0
Forze nuove	7.0
Andreotti	17.8
Fanfani	3.2
Azione popolare	37.0

Source: M. Caciagli, 'The 18th DC Congress, in S. Sabettiand R. Catanzaro (eds.), Italian Politics. A Review, vol.5(London: Pinter, 1991)

among the party powerful. They change shape constantly in response to the manoeuvring of their leaders, but certain constant trends can be identified. For a long time, the dominant faction was the *doretei,* named after a convent where they first met in 1959. By the 1970s, they had broken up into separate groups but could be recognized in the *grande centro,* also known as *azione popolare* in the 1980s. This faction is conservative, opposes radical reform in the state or the party and is the most closely associated with the habits of patronage and power broking for which the party has become famous. There is a left faction, the *Sinistra* identified with reform, broadening the governing coalition and engaging in a dialogue with the former Communists. This is strongest in the north of the country. *Forze nuove* is a group founded by the trade union leader Donat Cattin. In addition there are factions identified with individual leaders, of which the most prominent have been those of Giulio Andreotti, with power bases in Rome and Sicily and, of Amintore Fanfani. At the party congress, positions in the executive are distributed in accordance to the votes received for the motion presented by each faction. In 1989, these were as indicated in Table 4.3. Factions will often hold their own conferences to determine their line on policy matters or power broking. Most have their own journals, press agencies and offices or study centres. Some have special links with outside interests. When a new government is formed, a careful balance is maintained among party factions. Faction leaders are consulted on names and may choose to serve themselves or nominate their followers to key posts. The huge array of appointments to quasi-state bodies and agencies is also distributed according to faction strength. Factions may appear to be a weakness in the Christian Democratic Party, dividing it and dispersing its forces. Yet they are also a source of strength, allowing it to appeal to different constituencies, as a catch-all party. For all their bitter disputes, faction leaders are united on the necessity of gaining and retaining power for the party.

The party is headed by a general secretary but such is the jealousy of the faction leaders that this individual is rarely allowed to accumulate great power. De Gasperi in the 1940s was accepted as the undisputed leader of the party. In the early 1950s, Fanfani amassed influence for a while. Since then, general secretaries have been kept on a short rein. Ciriaco De Mita who served as general secretary for an unusually long term in the 1980s sought to renew the party and enhance his own role but was ultimately forced out. De Mita had also broken the unwritten rule that the DCI general secretary should not also be prime minister. Leadership in the party therefore tends to be collegiate, or shared among the powerful faction barons.

Between 1953 and 1992, the Christian Democrat share of the vote has varied between 42 per cent and 30 per cent of the vote. As Figure 4.1 shows, it held remarkably steady during the 1950s, 1960s and 1970s, and then started to fall in the 1980s and early 1990s. It has continued to be the leading force in every government. Given the chaotic state of much of Italian public administration, the instability of governments and the evidence of massive corruption, the DCI's survival as the principal force in Italian politics needs to be explained. One important factor is the existence of a cohesive subculture based on the Catholic world, which produces the vote of *appartenenza,* or belonging. Belonging is more than merely attending Church services or voting for the DCI at elections. It involves a whole world of Catholic associations in the fields of work, culture, leisure and civic activity. Catholic workers are organized in the CISL trade union federation and the association of Catholic workers, ACLI. Catholic Action is a lay organization under Church control. Founded in the nineteenth century, it was the only non-Fascist national organization tolerated by Mussolini as part of his accommodation with the Church. After the war, it was mobilized in support of the new Christian Democratic Party. Communion and Liberation (*Comunione e Liberazione*), a more militantly active group, was formed in 1969 by young Catholics to propagandize for the faith and pursue Catholic interests in state and society. In 1975, this spawned a political wing, the Popular Movement, which has both campaigned for the DCI and sought to promote Catholic values and combat secular tendencies within it. *Coldiretti* is an organization of independent farmers with close links to the DCI, mobilizing the agricultural vote and gaining policy favours in return. All of this created a sense of solidarity and affective loyalty such that for many people voting for the DCI was less a matter of choice than of affirmation of themselves.

Christian Democratic leaders have all been practising Catholics, many of them recruited through Catholic Action or other lay organizations. The DCI could count on support from the Church at elections, either indirectly through injunctions to the faithful not to vote Communist or, when the Communists looked like doing well, more naked appeals to vote DCI. This did not mean that the party was ever simply the political arm of the Church. Leaders since De Gasperi have realized that a degree of independence was both desirable and politically necessary. An open power struggle took place in 1952 when the Vatican, concerned about possible Communist advances at the municipal elections in Rome, tried to put together a ticket under the aged Luigi Sturzo, founder of the old Popular Party, and including Fascist elements. De Gasperi refused to accept the accommodation with the Fascists and Pope Pius X11 had to back down.

Since the late 1960s, there have been unmistakable signs of the decline of the Catholic subculture. Secularization has reduced the proportion of practising Catholics and the link between religion and voting has weakened. Social modernization and pluralism have lessened people's dependence on Catholic support organizations. Catholic Action's membership declined from over three million in the 1950s to around half a million at the end of the 1980s. It ceased actively campaigning for the DCI in the 1970s. CISL, the Catholic trade union, no longer gives automatic support to the DCI and cooperates more with the secular trade unions. Only Communion and Liberation with its political wing the Popular Movement, have thrived but their enthusiasm and militant activism is not always well regarded by the more cynical power brokers of the party. The *Coldiretti* also continue to support the party but this can be seen more as a client relationship than the result of religious solidarity.

The Church's overt interventions in politics declined in the 1960s, following the Second Vatican Council, though it continued to oppose communism. In the 1970s, a number of progressive Catholics who accepted invitations to run as independents on Communist Party electoral lists were roundly condemned. Several attempts have been made to remobilize the religious vote. In 1974, a group of Catholics sponsored a petition with Church support for a referendum to repeal the divorce law which had been passed by the lay parties in parliament in 1970. Despite the misgivings of the modernizing elements in the party, the DCI leadership threw itself into the campaign, trying to recreate the fighting spirit of 1948 and impose themselves as the essential secular allies of the Church. They failed, as the divorce law was upheld by a large majority. The tactic was repeated again in 1981, in a referendum to repeal the abortion law of 1978, also passed in parliament over the opposition of the Christian Democrats. Again the Catholic-DCI alliance failed, this time by an even larger majority. As recently as 1987, following Communist successes at the European elections of 1984, the Church again lined up behind the Christian Democrats and this, together with the activism of the Popular Movement, has been credited with the slight improvement of their vote. Yet this did not halt the long term trend to a weakening of the Catholic subculture and a steady fall in DCI support. This is especially noticeable in the traditionally Catholic provinces of northern Italy, the 'white belt' where DCI support fell from 61.5 per cent in 1948 to just 34.1 per cent in 1992.[3]

A second source of DCI support has been the extensive system of patronage put in place since the 1950s. Clientelism and patronage are sometimes seen as phenomena typical of modernizing societies. Traditional communities, with value systems rooted in personal contact and continuity, are brought face to face with the modern, impersonal bureaucratic state. In order to deal with this, citizens need intermediaries, politicians with contacts who can obtain resources from the state and distribute them back home, or bend rules to accommodate individual or community needs. In Italy as in much of southern Europe, this function was managed in the late nineteenth century by local notables. After the fall of Fascism, many of these gravitated to the Christian Democrats as the most promising source of resources and favours. The contribution of the party in the 1950s was to modernize this system of patronage and convert it from a temporary mechanism in the transition to modernity into a permanent way of governing. To do this, they displaced the old notables, especially in the south, with the party machine and placed at its disposal the resources of the emerging welfare state together with the new instruments for economic intervention and development. This institutional network, the *sottogoverno*, is discussed below.

Patronage takes both individual and collective forms. Individual patronage is about the distribution of personal favours, such as jobs in the public services, planning consents and licences, exemptions from taxation or regulation, help in dealing with the bureaucracy. Disability pensions are a favoured form of patronage, handed out indiscriminately to sick and healthy alike. This patronage is organized at local level by party officials able to pull strings in Rome. Particularly important is retaining the favour of the *grandi elettori*, local figures of standing who may be able to influence whole villages or neighbourhoods how to vote. Such figures may include priests, community leaders, business and union personalities and mayors. Collective patronage involves handing out favours to supportive groups. The *Coldiretti* have been able to provide their members with benefits and effectively to nominate Christian Democratic ministers of agriculture. Sometimes, benefits are targeted to specific areas to ensure that not only does the party benefit but the individual politician can benefit in a constituency through the accumulation of preference votes. In the 1960s, Andreotti used a long tenure as minister of defence to build 'electoral barracks' around Rome, allowing the troops the luxury of being stationed near the capital with good facilities, and ensuring that, come election time, they knew which party and which politician were responsible for their good fortune.

Among the largest sources of collective patronage are the agencies established for regional development in the poorer south of Italy. Rather than following economic logic, programmes and projects have been bent to suit the needs of parties and politicians. Since these programmes consequently often fail to generate self-sustaining development, the region remains dependent on continuing handouts and interventions, which further boosts the standing of the politicians who obtain them.

As the party seeks to colonize whole areas of society, patronage shades into corruption and often downright criminality. Prominent Christian Democratic politicians in the south are known to have links with the Mafia, which delivers votes and shares in the distribution of largesse. As we shall see, it is precisely these links into the political system which make it so difficult for the state to tackle the problem of organized crime in Sicily, much of the mainland south and now parts of central and northern Italy. The 1992 election campaign was punctuated by the assassination of the prominent Sicilian Christian Democrat Salvo Lima, victim of a Mafia hit. Although Christian Democrat leaders tried to present him as a martyr in the battle against organized crime, the press noted that Lima had been well known as the Christian Democrats' linkman with Mafia bosses and speculated that his death was the result of underworld rivalries.

The declining influence of the Catholic subculture and the increased importance of patronage is one reason for the shift in Christian Democratic strength from the north of the country to the south. Patronage remains a strong influence in southern life while in the north there is increasing resentment at the transfer of their tax revenues into programmes without any long-term pay-off. In 1992, the DCI suffered serious losses to the new Leagues, protesting against the corruption and waste of the system and their vote fell from 32 to 24 per cent. In the south it was unchanged at 40 per cent.[4] As a result southern deputies accounted for over 40 per cent of the party's strength.[5]

From the early 1960s, the Christian Democrats had to share patronage spoils with their coalition partners, notably the Socialists, in a process known as *lottizzazione*. In the 1980s, the fiscal crisis of the state threatened to starve them of resources. Italians have long financed the large government budget deficit with a high savings ratio but the free movement of capital in the European Community gives them other opportunities for investment. European Community targets for deficit reduction are squeezing resources further. Taxing viable industries to pour resources into politically favoured projects becomes more difficult as international competition intensifies.

The third source of support for the Christian Democrats has come from their policies and performance. Despite their own shortcomings, the Christian Democrats have presided over an unprecedented economic expansion in which Italy has gone from being a poor country at the periphery of Europe to a leading industrial nation. Living standards have improved dramatically and opportunities opened. The Christian Democrats may not be associated with detailed policy programmes but their general attachment to a capitalist system moderated by a welfare state has wide support among the middle classes and more recently the working class as well. Their main policy appeal, however, has been anti-communism. For the Catholic world, but also for many of the secularized middle class, they long represented the only obstacle to Communist success. When the Communists have looked to be doing best, the Christian Democrats were able to mobilize support against them. When the Communists appeared in retreat, the DCI has lost support to the lay parties. The reform of Italian communism in the 1970s and its break with the Soviet line moderated but did not eliminate this factor. Communism's collapse at the end of the 1980s, however, cut the ground from under the traditional red-scare message and was an important factor in allowing many middle class voters to desert the party in the election of 1992.

The final element in the Christian Democrats' success has been its strategic position within the political system. As long as the Communists were excluded from governing coalitions, no majority could be formed without the DCI. This attracted to the party many voters and would-be politicians desirous to be on the winning side. As the DCI gradually lost support, it was able, in the process of *trasformismo,* to broaden its electoral coalition, eventually to include five parties. In the process it has been weakened. In the early 1980s, it had to yield the prime ministership successively to the Republicans and the Socialists. Patronage had to be shared around. In the late 1980s, the previously unthinkable happened. Members of the party broke ranks to campaign against the leadership for reform or to run independent candidates in elections. Mario Segni, a Christian Democrat deputy and son of a former president of the state, organized a referendum movement to use the instrument of the referendum to attack the party power structure. The first success, in 1991, was modest yet significant, the reduction of the number of preference votes which electors can express to one. This undercut one of the mechanisms by which party and faction leaders had boosted their personal standing. At the 1992 elections, Segni organized a Pact among candidates of various parties, pledged to work for reforms, especially of the electoral system. A hundred and fifty of these were elected to the two houses of parliament. Half were from the party of former Communists, PDS, but some forty were from the DCI. Another reformer, Leoluco Orlando, who had been removed from his position as mayor of Palermo because of his efforts to root out corruption and confront the Mafia, founded his own party, the Network (*La Rete*). At the 1992 election, capitalizing on Sicilian weariness with corruption and crime, it gained nine per cent of the vote in the island including 24 per cent in Palermo. With much smaller percentages of the vote elsewhere, this gave it twelve seats in the national parliament.

By the early 1990s, signs of decay and crisis in the DCI were unmistakable. The slight recovery in its fortunes in 1987 had been short-lived. In 1993, following disastrous results in local elections, it suffered a series of splits and appeared on the verge of collapse.

The Communists and PDS

From 1946 until it changed its name in 1991, the Communist Party (PCI) was the second largest in Italy, taking up to a third of the vote. Like other European Communist parties, it emerged from a split in the old Socialist Party over membership of the Soviet-led international in 1920. Shortly after, it was banned by the new Fascist regime and existed in exile and clandestinity until 1943. Its leader, Antonio Gramsci, died in a Fascist gaol, but his writings, notably the *Prison Notebooks,* smuggled out and published abroad, represented a major advance in Marxist thought, later taken up by the more anti-Soviet elements of the European left. Among Gramsci's most important contributions were the emphasis on the role of ideas in conditioning political action, and his insistence on the need to each country to take its own road to socialism and communism. In particular, he emphasized the difference between Russia, where the Communists had been able to seize power through capturing the state, and western countries where civil society was more important. In the West, socialism could only come by socialist ideas and practices steadily permeating the civil society, bringing together a historic bloc of progressive forces to achieve change.

From 1943, the Communists joined the anti-German resistance movement and were rewarded with seats in the national unity government which prepared the way for the new Republic. In 1944, their leader, Palmiro Togliatti, returned from Moscow, where he had spent the Fascist and war years as an official of the Communist International, Comintern. Given the nature of Italian society and the presence of allied troops, there was little prospect of a Socialist revolution. Nor, since Italy had been allocated to the western sphere of influence, did the Soviets give this any encouragement. Instead, Togliatti saw his main task as the integration of the party into the new political system and protection of the Republic against a return to Fascism. In the famous *svolta* (U-turn) of Salerno, he accepted the monarchy, effectively putting himself to the right of many Christian Democrats and the majority of the electorate. Later, anxious not to provoke the Church, he also accepted the inclusion of the Concordat in the new constitution. Yet, while making these tactical accommodations, the party firmly adhered to the ideal of a Soviet-type system as their long-term goal and refrained from any criticism of the Stalinist regime.

In 1947, the Communists were expelled from the coalition and in the 1948 general election soundly defeated by the forces of Christian Democracy. Thereafter they remained outside the political mainstream, their participation in government vetoed by a combination of internal and external forces. In the early 1960s, their isolation was completed when the Socialists, who had been allied with them in the post-war years, joined the governing coalition. As a loyal supporter of the Soviet Union, the PCI condemned Italian membership of NATO and the European Community and supported the 1956 Soviet invasion of Hungary to suppress the reform movement.

Like the Christian Democrats, the Communists were more than a party. They were the centre of a whole subculture with a shared outlook on the world and its own patterns of associational life. There were a Communist trade union federation, Communist peasant organizations and cultural and sporting clubs. The party had its own press, notably the daily newspaper *l'Unità,* and later its television and radio networks. Party membership during the 1950s and 1960s was around two million, all paying regular subscriptions. Party activists were trained in short courses and summer schools where they learnt the essentials of Marxist doctrine and how to spread the message. Democratic centralism was rigorously enforced. Motions at party congresses were adopted unanimously, elections to senior party positions were decided by the leadership and Communist representatives in parliament and local government kept under tight control by party headquarters. About two thousand officials worked for the party , not counting journalists in the party press.[6] Support for the party was strongest in the 'red belt' of central Italy, notably in the regions of Emilia Romagna, Umbria and Tuscany. Here they received the votes of industrial workers, peasants and even small business people, drawing on traditions of localism and social solidarity. In the north of Italy, they drew support from industrial workers in the factories. In the 1920s and the immediate postwar years, they had taken the view that the southern peasantry were dangerous, clerical-minded and a potential support base for a new right-wing dictatorship. In accordance with classical Marxism, they believed that change would come from the northern industrial proletariat who would bring the 'wind from the north' to liberate their southern peasant comrades. In the early 1950s, though, the party changed tack and threw itself behind a campaign for land reform, building a new support base especially in Sicily.

In the 1950s and 1960s, this strategy, together with the increase in the blue-collar electorate resulting from industrialization, allowed the Communists to sustain a gradual increase in its vote, outpacing the Socialist Party to become the dominant party on the left. Then, from the late 1960s, it underwent a modernization and transformation which enabled it to expand its support base still further, becoming the foremost exponent of Eurocommunism. This was a liberalized form of communism which shunned violent revolution and believed that the society could be transformed through peaceful, democratic means. Reaching back to Gramscian thought, it insisted on a distinctive Italian road to socialism, quite different from the Soviet model. In particular, the PCI recognized that in Italy the support of the industrial proletariat and some sections of the peasantry would not be sufficient for victory. Instead, the party would have to build a progressive bloc, including lay forces and even progressive Catholics, and work to change the state of civil society. Communists should gradually work their way into the institutions of state and society rather than imposing their will from the top.

In 1968, the party repudiated the Soviet invasion of Czechoslovakia, a sharp contrast to its stance on Hungary twelve years earlier. Thereafter, criticisms of the Soviet regime became more and more vocal. In the course of the 1970s, the party gradually accepted Italian membership of NATO and the European Community. It affirmed its belief in parliamentary democracy and declared that if a future Communist government were defeated at the polls it would go peacefully, a step of immense significance in view of the experience of eastern Europe. Openings were made to the new social movements which were emerging in the late 1960s and early 1970s, notably feminism, pacifism and environmentalism. Public ownership was de-emphasized as an element of party policy and the market economy accepted. This was easier than for other European left-wing parties since in Italy an expansive state was associated with the Christian Democrats and their patronage machine. The Communists also pressed for reform of the state apparatus and decentralization of power to local and regional government. There was an element of self-interest here since Communist local governments, notably in their show-case of Bologna, were demonstrating their ability to provide competent administration largely free of the corruption associated with the national governing parties. This was part of their march through the institutions. Prominent non-Communists were invited on to Communist electoral lists to demonstrate the party's attempts to reach into civil society and broaden its base of support. All this was pushed through by the party leadership, with relatively little dissent. Evidence persisted that the party rank and file was still largely attached to the old ways, regarding the Soviet Union as the home of real socialism and a model to be emulated. Yet the changes were enough to recruit to the Communist cause a substantial number of electors who were not Marxists but merely wanted reform of the political system and saw the party as the best way to achieve it. In all but name, the PCI was becoming a European Social Democratic party. In 1976, the Communist share of the vote peaked at 34.4 per cent (see Figure 4.1), while the Socialists were down to 9.6 per cent.

Communist participation in government, however, remained a distant prospect, effectively vetoed by the Church and the United States, together with sections of Italian business and the military. In 1967, the Greek military had staged a coup, backed by the United States, to prevent a reforming government coming to power. Rumours of coup plots abounded in Italy in the late 1960s and early 1970s. In 1973, the elected Marxist president of Chile, Salvador Allende, was overthrown in a bloody coup inspired by the American government. In France, the left was able to advance under Socialist leadership, with the Communists confined to a subordinate role. In Italy, any left wing government would be dominated by the Communists, increasing its vulnerability to external pressure. So PCI leader Enrico Berlinguer concluded that, even if the left could win 51 per cent of the vote this would not be enough to overcome external opposition. There would have to be a broad bloc of progressive forces.

In the immediate term, there was a need to secure the democratic state itself. Left- and right- wing political terrorists in Italy shared a common aim of overthrowing the liberal democratic regime while the county's economic problems posed a further threat to stability. In these circumstances, Berlinguer decided that the only way for the Communists to come into government would be in partnership with their historic opponents, the Christian Democrats. A Communist-Christian Democrat deal would help to stabilize the democratic regime, defuse American and Vatican fears and allow serious reforms to be addressed. Progressive Christian Democrats, notably Aldo Moro, shared this analysis and wished to bring the Communists within the pale of the constitution. In 1974, the failure to repeal the divorce law weakened the hard-line clerical wing of the DCI. The following year, the Communists, allied in many instances with the Socialists, made sweeping gains in the local elections, gaining control of Rome, Naples and other large cities and demonstrating their electoral muscle. So the Christian Democrats faced increased pressure to deal with the PCI. This was the origin of the 'historic compromise', which lasted until 1979.

Already from 1970, the Communists had agreed to give some support to certain measures of the dying centre-left government. In the early 1970s, family law and the education system were reformed. In 1976, the PCI abstained on the formation of the third Andreotti government in exchange for consultation on policy matters. In the fourth Andreotti government, of 1978, the PCI edged nearer power, becoming part of the government coalition in parliament, though without ministerial positions. Communists were given posts in parliament, including the presidency of the Chamber of Deputies and committee chairs. The final stage, the entry of Communist ministers into the government, never came about. In 1978, Christian Democrat leader Aldo Moro was murdered by the extreme left terrorist group, the Red Brigades, in a successful attempt to disrupt the governing coalition. While all parties united to condemn the killing, the effect was to strengthen those elements within the DCI who were hostile to cooperation with the left. In 1979, the Communists demanded ministerial posts and were rebuffed. The government then fell, and an early general election was called in which Communist support dropped for the first time in a generation, mainly to the advantage of small parties to its left.

For the PCI the experience of the historic compromise was mixed. Some reforms had been achieved, in social matters, education and housing, though no overhaul of state institutions had been attempted. Democracy had been safeguarded against terrorist threats from left and right. As well as a political deal, the historic compromise represented a social contract, a form of consociational agreement between the Communist and Catholic subcultures. Central to this had been wage restraint and an acceptance of austerity on the part of the Communist-controlled unions in the interests of economic stabilization. The party had established itself as a responsible party of government. Yet it had failed to make the breakthrough to a share of national power and its vote at the end of the experience had fallen. Nor had the sacrifices made by the union movement produced a real response. This called for a change of strategy and the Communists now set about trying to build a left-wing alternative to the Christian Democrat coalition, on the lines of Mitterrand's France. The problem with this was that the Socialists were not interested. In the early 1980s, they had re-established their coalition with the DCI and in the 1985 local elections extended this to local level, breaking town hall coalitions with the Communists. Some consolation was taken in the European elections of 1984, when the Communists for the first time overtook the Christian Democrats to become Italy's most popular party. There were special circumstances here, though, notably the death of Berlinguer during the campaign which produced a large sympathy vote.

National elections in 1983 and 1987 suggested that the Communists were in long-term decline. As other countries, the manual working class was declining in numbers and political consciousness. The old centres of peasant communism were being transformed. The reinvigorated Socialist Party under Bettino Craxi was more appealing to the white-collar professional worker. This was starkly brought home in 1985 when the Communists forced a referendum on Craxi's abolition of the *scala mobile*, a system of indexing wages. Like the Christian Democrat referendum initiatives on divorce and abortion, this was intended to rally the faithful and consolidate the vote of *appartenenza* of the unionized working class. Like the Christian Democrat initiatives, it was defeated. The PCI had made great headway in the 1970s with its criticism of Soviet dictatorship. Berlinguer had been particularly harsh in criticism of the 1981 coup in Poland and suppression of Solidarity. Yet from the mid-1980s, the Gorbachev reform programme in the Soviet Union threatened to make even the reformed Italian Communist Party look out of date.

Further change in the PCI required a struggle between party traditionalists and a new generation of leaders. Like the Social Democratic parties of Europe, the PCI had become more middle class in the 1970s and 1980s. Manual workers, who had comprised 33.3 per cent of federal (regional) committee members in 1971, had dropped to 19.3 per cent by 1983.[7] Most elective positions within the party were taken by full-time officials of the party, its support organizations or people technically employed in public administration and local government but effectively working for the party. Party officials were in turn less likely to be former manual workers who had made their way through the party and its summer schools, and more likely to be university graduates. Their attitude tended to be more libertarian and open, much less tied to the closed Communist subculture of the postwar years.

In the late 1980s, factions started to appear in the hitherto monolithic PCI. There was a right-wing element, who wanted to transform the party into something like the northern European Social Democratic parties. A left wing element wanted to open it out to new social movements, including feminists, ecologists and anti-nuclear campaigners. A traditionalist group believed in keeping the Soviet link, putting their faith in Gorbachev's reforms to make communism more palatable. Finally, a centrist element followed the Berlinguer line of distancing the party both from Moscow and from the Social Democratic tradition, seeking a third way between capitalism and communism. After the death of Berlinguer, Alessandro Netta became general secretary and tried to hold the party together but his reign was short-lived. Following the 1987 election defeat, factional rivalries came out into the open; the following year the rules had to be changed to allow them expression at the party congress.

The nomination of Achille Occhetto first as vice-general secretary, then as general secretary in 1988 forced the pace of change. As in most political parties without traditions of internal dissent, much of the early debate was carried on in coded language, by referring to historical incidents. So reformers praised the French Revolution as the foundation of democracy, while the hard-liners spoke more of the Russian Revolution of October 1917. This careful ambiguity was thrown aside when Occhetto dared to criticize the party's postwar hero Togliatti for his subservience to Stalin. This was an attempt to deny the very founding myths of the party and caused a prolonged storm. Occhetto then proceeded to drop references to Marxism from the statement of doctrine presented to the 1989 congress.

It was the fall of the Berlin Wall, the symbolic end of east European Communism, which precipitated the final change. Three days later, in November 1989 Occhetto announced his intention to call a special congress to refound the party, with a new name and all references to communism abandoned. Agreement in principle was gained at a special congress in March 1991. Another one in February 1991 voted finally by two to one to disband the PCI and establish the Democratic Party of the Left (*Partito Democratico della Sinistra*, or PDS). A new insignia of an oak tree was adopted though, in a concession to nostalgia and the opponents of change, a small hammer and sickle was retained at the bottom.

This is perhaps the most dramatic transformation of a political party in modern western Europe, surpassing those undertaken by the French Socialists, the German Social Democrats and the British Labour Party. For the PDS did not represent a move from full-blooded left wing socialism to social democracy. That had effectively taken place in the 1970s. Instead, the PDS has by-passed social democracy to become an advanced Liberal party. References to class politics and collective solidarity, still found in the Social Democratic parties, have given way to an emphasis on democracy, citizenship, individualism and new social movements. The founding myth, the Russian Revolution, has not merely been downgraded. It has been repudiated along with the old party name. It is not surprising, then, that a section of the party found this too much to stomach and formed a splinter group, Communist Refoundation (*Rifondazione Comunista*, RC) which espouses a reform communism of the Gorbachev variety. For its part, the PDS has altogether abandoned democratic centralism and is divided into factions though, in contrast to the Christian Democrats, these factions tend to be organized according to ideological considerations.[8]

It was not expected that refounding the party would lead to a dramatic increase in votes. Rather, with the collapse of communism in the East, it was seen as a necessary step for survival of a progressive force which in due course could form the basis of a non-Christian Democrat coalition. The first test came in 1992, when the PDS scored 16.1 per cent in the general election. This was a sharp fall from the old PCI vote even of 1987. Communist Refoundation did better than expected, taking 5.6 per cent but even if this is added to the PDS vote it still falls short of the old Communist total. On the other hand, the PDS did just manage to retain second position, 2.5 per cent ahead of the Socialists and could hope that, if Communist Refoundation proves short-lived it could yet be the basis for a realignment of the centre-left. It appeared to weather the scandals of 1992-3 a bit better than the other main parties.

The Socialists

The Socialist Party (PSI) traditionally represented the Social Democratic, parliamentary alternative to the Communists. They emerged from the war about the same size as the PCI, gaining 20.7 per cent, to the Communists' 18.9 in the elections of 1946. At that time, they were tied to a strategy of left-wing unity, rather faithfully echoing the PCI's pro-Soviet positions and running a joint list of candidates in the elections of 1948. Unlike the PCI they took a strictly republican line on the constitution, opposing the return of the monarchy and the inclusion of the Concordat in the constitution. Their alliance with the Communists, however, produced a split, with the anti-Communist element, financed by the United States, forming the Social Democratic Party. The split was healed in the late 1960s but opened again soon after and the Social Democrats (PSDI) continue to pick up around 3 per cent of the vote. The Socialists hovered around 12 to 14 per cent in the 1950s and 1960s. Like the French SFIO they combined Marxist revolutionary rhetoric with a rather conservative practice and were ridden by faction fighting. In the early 1960s, their prospects improved when the Christian Democrats sought an opening to the left. After a great deal of tortuous negotiation, they were brought into the coalition. Intended to bring a reformist impetus to the government, this proved yet another exercise in *trasformismo*. Some reforms were introduced, such as the institution of a national health service, some initiatives in urban planning and the belated establishment of regional government. They were also largely responsible, against the opposition of the Christian Democrats, for pushing through the legalization of divorce. Soon, however, the Socialists settled in to enjoy their share of patronage. Reform proposals faltered in the face of Christian Democrat opposition. Whatever gain they made through participating in government was largely lost by defections to the Communists and another splinter group, the Party of Proletarian Unity. By the mid-1970s, they had fallen below 10 per cent of the vote.

It was at this time that a new leadership generation took over under Bettino Craxi, an immensely ambitious politician who became general secretary in 1976. Craxi set about reforming both party organization and programme. The position of general secretary was strengthened and factions brought under control. Any remaining references to Marxist theory, which the party had long ceased to take seriously, were expunged from the programme and the hammer and sickle replaced by a carnation as the party symbol. An image was cultivated of a modern European Socialist party, like that in France, pragmatic, decisive and capable of governing. External support was given by the media magnate Enrico Berlusconi, whose private television channels lean towards the Craxi Socialists.

Strategically, Craxi had three choices, all of which were pursued at one time or another. These were a left-wing unity strategy, in alliance with the Communists to form an alternative government to the old coalitions; a coalition of lay parties against both the DCI and the PCI; or a continuation of the centre-left alliance with the DCI. A left unity strategy would have imitated Mitterrand's achievement in France and represented a decisive change not only for the Italian left but for the political system as a whole. In contrast to France, however, the Communist Party was larger than the Socialist, ruling out the safe alternative of a Socialist dominated coalition with the Communists subordinated to them. Nor was there much prospect of Craxi's party being able to imitate their French colleagues and overtake the Communists electorally, so forcing unity on their own terms. There is not a great deal of evidence, indeed, that Craxi ever took the left alliance alternative seriously. It was emphasized as official party policy only during the period of the historic compromise (1976-9) when the Socialists were out of government and it could be used as a means of embarrassing the Communists for their support of the DCI.

The second strategic possibility was known as the *polo laico,* an alliance of the democratic parties outside the two big subcultures. The rationale was that the old subcultures were slowly dying as voters were secularized and more volatile in their voting behaviour. If the lay parties could expand their combined percentage of the vote from the mid-twenties to the upper thirties, they would become the essential element in a governing coalition. This could provoke a split in the DCI, with the more progressive and secularized elements in it coming over to the new coalition. Breaking up the Christian Democrat monolith proved impossible in the 1980s and by the time it started to happen in the early 1990s the Socialists were in no position to exploit it to their own benefit. Nor were the lay parties able to advance if they remained outside government, unable to demonstrate their fitness to govern or satisfy their voters with policies and patronage. So, in order to prepare for a lay alternative, the Socialists had to re-enter the governing coalition.

This was the third strategic choice, a new coalition arrangement in which the Socialists would strengthen their position. For several years, Craxi used this strategy to brilliant tactical effect. In 1981 the Christian Democrats were forced to broaden their coalition to take in all four lay parties. This was the five-party or *pentapartito* formula. They were also forced to concede the prime ministership to Giovanni Spadolini of the small Republican party. Following the 1983 elections, the DCI were further weakened and Craxi was able to demand the prime ministership for himself. Against all the odds he survived in office for an unprecedented three and a half years, cultivating an image of firm and decisive leadership, or *decisionismo*. The Communists were taken on and defeated over the issue of the *scala mobile* . A new arrangement was made with the Vatican to replace the old Concordat, to which the Socialists had historically been opposed. Decrees were used as a means of by-passing parliament. Proposals for constitutional reform were canvassed, including an elected executive presidency on French lines, with Craxi himself as the obvious candidate for the office. While Craxi saw himself as an Italian de Gaulle, however, the cartoonists liked to present him as a new Mussolini and his decisive style did not go well with the other parties in the system. In April 1987 the Christian Democrats duly claimed back the prime ministership. Elections in June of that year showed that Craxi's governing style had indeed increased support for his party, from 11.4 per cent to 14.3 per cent. In Italian terms, this was a significant gain, but did not represent a breakthrough. It certainly was not enough to allow the Socialists to cast off the Christian Democrats and look for new allies on the left or the lay area. So the five party coalition was reconstituted. Craxi continued to seek institutional reforms and made clear his ambition to be elected president of the Republic with the intention of strengthening the office on Gaullist lines. Yet the Socialists had been sucked back into the old politics of *trasformismo*, getting their share of spoils in return for their votes. In the early 1980s they had wrested the key Ministry for the Mezzogiorno, responsible for development policies in the south and a large source of patronage, from the Christian Democrats.

Their image took a more spectacular plunge when, on the eve of the 1992 elections, a corruption scandal broke in Craxi's power base of Milan. The indictments showed that all the parties had been involved in *tangenti,* rake-offs from public contracts and other forms of corruption but, as the leading party in the city, the Socialists were more implicated than any. As many of Craxi's associates and family members were directly involved, this was a severe blow, destroying his ambitions to become president of the Republic. In the legislative elections, the Socialists, now identified as part of the governing class rather than reformers, saw their vote slip back to 13.6 per cent. This disguises a large shift in the distribution of the Socialist vote, which now looks more like that of their Christian Democrat partners. In the north, they suffered heavily at the hands of the new protest leagues, losing 4.2 percentage points in Milan. In the south, where they had used their time in power to distribute patronage and build up client networks, their vote increased. With half their deputies representing southern constituencies, the Socialists were even more dependent on the south than the Christian Democrats. In the manoeuvring following the election, Craxi failed to gain the prime ministership but was able to impose his deputy,

Giuliano Amato on a weakened Christian Democrat party. This however, was a fragile coalition, far from the strong government for which Craxi had aimed in the 1980s and lasted for only a year. Shortly after, Craxi himself was charged with corruption. In 1993, the Socialist Party's support appeared to be heading for amost complete collapse. In local elections that year, they suffered spectacular setbacks, failing to win a single seat in the city council of Milan, formerly their stronghold.

The Lay Parties

Three small parties, which have participated in coalitions are known as the lay parties because of their secular traditions and position outside the major subcultures. In the immediate postwar era, much was expected of the revitalized, modernizing and secular forces which had emerged from the resistance in the form of the Action Party. Indeed, their leader, Ferrucio Parri, was the first prime minister of liberated Italy. Soon, however, they were squeezed out by the Communists and Christian Democrats and ceased to exist altogether by 1945. In the Cold War climate of the 1950s, there was little place for parties outside the two main camps and none of the small lay parties ever pushed their share of the vote into double figures. Yet their influence has been out of proportion to their size, since they have been able to recruit major personalities as leaders. They have also brought into government coalitions their links with Italy's business community and with the European Community and Atlantic world.

The Liberals are one of Italy's oldest parties and dominated the politics of the pre-Fascist regime, drawing support both from northern industrialists and from southern landowners. In the 1940s, many of their local *notabili* in the south went over to the Christian Democrats, seeing them as the new fount of patronage. They in turn were pushed aside by the party machine in the Fanfani reforms of the early 1950s, though local Liberal patronage networks continue to exist in some parts of the south. Their main support base, however, has been in the business community of northern Italy, especially the large corporations. They are strongly committed to the market economy, privatization and deregulation as well as European integration. This places them in economic matters to the right of the Christian Democrats though they have taken a less conservative line on social issues such as divorce and abortion. The Liberals bring to governing coalitions the endorsement of much of the business community, but only a small number of parliamentary seats. They participated in the early coalitions but withdrew in the early 1960s when the Christian Democrats embarked on the centre-left formula with the Socialists. Placing themselves to the right of the coalition, they were able to increase their vote to a maximum of 7 per cent in 1963. Thereafter, they declined and, after the failure of the historic compromise formula at the end of the 1970s, they re-entered the government. In 1992, they won 2.8 per cent of the vote.

The Republican Party also traces its origins to the last century and the inheritance of the democratic nationalism of Mazzini. Since the war, they have established an image of modernization, seeking an efficient, uncorrupt system of government committed to the European Community and Atlantic Alliance. They tend to the free-market right in economic matters and the libertarian left on social issues such as abortion and divorce. They have attracted to their ranks some prestigious figures from the business community, tired of the Christian Democrats' corruption and inefficiency. They participated in government in the early postwar years, left in the 1950s and came back under the centre-left formula of the early 1960s, which they strongly supported. When in 1981 the Christian Democrats were first forced to concede the prime ministership to another party, it was Republican Party leader Giovanni Spadolini who was chosen. Indeed, apart from the historic compromise period (1976-9), the Republicans were constantly in government from the early 1960s until 1991 when they pulled out in protest against the failure of the other parties to tackle corruption and administrative reform. Their vote increased in 1992 from 3.7 per cent to 4.4 per cent but their reputation for clean politics took a blow when Republicans too were found to be implicated in the Milan affair of the *tangenti*.

The Social Democratic Party (PSDI) was formed in 1947 when Guisseppe Saragat broke away from the Socialists in protest against their alliance with the Communists. Encouraged and subsidized by the United States and business interests, the new party suffered from the image of being a sell-out or a puppet movement and never established a mass base. Its main support comes from the lower middle class and the patronage which it can dispense. For this reason, it makes sure that it is part of whatever coalition is formed, whether centre-right, centre-left or *pentapartito*.

For a time in the 1970s and early 1980s, much was expected of the lay parties as an alternative to the big formations. By the late 1980s, however, their challenge had faded as they came to be regarded as just another element in the old *partitocrazia*. Protest against this system instead took the form of abstention or voting for the new movements, notably the Northern Leagues.

The Crisis of the *Partitocrazia*

From the 1970s, support for the traditional parties, the Christian Democrats, the Communists and PDS, the Socialists and the three lay parties, gradually begand to slip. By the early 1990s, this had become a free-fall and the old party system was headed for collapse. Election turnout, while still high by international standards, slipped from 93 per cent in the 1960s to 88.4 per cent in 1992. The combined vote total for the six parties fell from over 90 per cent to just under

70 per cent. Taking abstentions into account, just under 60 per cent of eligible electors voted for the six parties in 1992. Given the slow rate of change in Italian political alignments, this is very significant.

One important factor has been the decline of the old Catholic and Communist subcultures as a result of secularization, modernization and social and geographical mobility. Young people, in particular, are subjected to a wide variety of influences and no longer automatically follow in the family tradition. The role of women in society has been greatly changed with social and family law reform, secularization and increasing female participation in the workforce. Survey evidence indicates that people no longer seek friends just among members of their own subculture and regard their vote more as a matter of choice than of lifestyle. International surveys showed that Italians were less interested in politics and less trusting of parties than were electors in other west European democracies. Yet more Italians than other Europeans felt themselves close to a political party.[9] This love-hate relationship seems to stem from a feeling that the parties are corrupt and inefficient but that contact with them is still necessary to get anything out of the government or the public administration. In the late 1980s and early 1990s, disillusionment with the parties was greatly accelerated by the end of the Cold War, which had so marked Italian politics. Even faithful Communists found the myth of the Soviet utopia hard to sustain when the leader of the Soviet Union himself was denouncing its shortcomings. The collapse of the Soviet regime finally removed this reference point. Christian Democratic leaders could no longer use the Communist menace as a means of rallying their supporters with the aid of the Church. Corruption scandals and the inefficiency of the public administration alienated voters and engendered a cynicism about politicians and the government in Rome. Increased international competition and the needs of European integration imposed new disciplines on economic management. Subsidies became more difficult to hand out, industries had to be trimmed to meet European competition and the crisis of public finances became a major preoccupation. In these circumstances, the patronage machine was in danger of being starved of resources.

A variety of protest parties came into being. The Greens, while of less importance than in other European countries, made some impact at the 1989 European elections electing seven of Ital''s eighty-one members. In the 1992 national elections, the main Green list, Smiling Sun, scored 2.8 per cent of the vote and elected sixteen members of parliament, mainly from the northern and central regions. The hunting and fishing party, which had made some impact in local and European elections, was less successful at national level, gaining just half a per cent in 1992. Much more serious was the challenge by the Lombard League and its allies, who promised to change the face of Italian politics.

The Leagues

The 1992 national elections saw the biggest movement in postwar Italian history, the eruption of the Northern Leagues, with 8.7 per cent of the vote and 55 deputies. Their origins lie in the Lombard League (*Lega Lombarda*), a right-wing populist protest group founded in the early 1980s under the leadership of Umberto Bossi. Later the movement spread to other northern regions and an alliance of Northern Leagues was created. The Lombard League ties together a complex of different elements in a challenge to the *partitocrazia*, corruption and the organization of the Italian state. It has elements in common with other right-wing populist movements in Europe and North America, such as the Scandinavian anti-tax parties, the Canadian Reform Party or the Ross Perot challenge for the US presidency but places these in a specifically Italian context. Originating in the most advanced region of Italy, it stands both for a reform of the Italian state and for the assertion of the interests of Lombardy. Drawing on discontent with the old politics, it mingles emotive appeals with serious policy proposals and an ambitious, if rather vague plan for reorganization of the state. The end of the Cold War and stumbling of the main Italian parties gave it its opportunity in the late 1980s.

First and foremost, the Lombard League is a protest party, aimed at the politicians in Rome and their wasteful ways. It is anti-taxation but does not call for the slashing of public services. Instead, it claims that taxes levied on the working population are squandered in patronage projects. With clientelism and corruption eliminated and the burden fairly shared, there would be plenty to go round. A strong regional dimension comes into play here since Lombardy, the most advanced of Italy's regions, has to subsidize the development and patronage spending in the south. At times this has extended to hostility towards the large number of immigrants from the south resident in northern Italy. In the late 1980s, this tended to be replaced by hostility to immigrants from non-EC countries. Foreign immigration into Italy is a recent phenomenon and racial prejudice, while it exists, is less widespread than in northern Europe or France. There is much controversy over the question of whether the League is racist and how much of its appeal this would explain. Certainly, the party has not adopted the overt racism of the neo-Fascist right such as the French National Front or German Republicans. Yet it does propose strict limitations on the rights of non-EC nationals to work and settle in Italy and appeals to the insecurity of Italian workers in the face of foreign immigration.[10]

An emotive edge is given to regionalism by the very name, which recalls the mediaeval Lombard League of knights who defeated the emperor Frederic Barbarossa in the twelfth-century battle of Legano. A favoured League symbol represents the Lombard hero Alberto da Guissano with his sword putting his enemies to flight. In the early days, Bossi would talk of the Lombard nation and there was an attempt to promote the Lombard dialect as a separate national language. Rallies are emotional affairs, with members dressed up as medieval knights and waving flags, and there is a general atmosphere of anti-intellectualism. League members are expected to provide loyal support rather than serious policy input. Like many populist movements, it relies on charismatic, personal leadership and at the 1992 election, the League was criticized for the fact that it only possessed two personalities known to the public, Bossi and its house thinker, university professor Gianfranco Miglio. This gives it great flexibility in policy matters and its doctrines have evolved considerably over the years. It also provides a rather authoritarian undertone to the League, with Miglio calling for a government of national salvation led by technocrats and hinting that the alternative would be a strongman like Perón or de Gaulle.[11]

As the League developed, the emphasis on folklore and myth was reduced, although it did not disappear. Lombardy's vocation in Europe was emphasized. Policy positions were developed. In economic matters, the line was to favour market solutions and privatization, both for ideological reasons and as a way of undermining the patronage system. This won the League some support from industrialists, though they later pulled back in the face of League criticism of collusion between big business and the state.

The League's most distinctive position, however, has been on the constitution. From the outset the Lombard League favoured a federal Italy, an idea dating to the last century. By the late 1980s, as Leagues were formed in other northern regions and federated with the Lombard League in the new Northern League, the focus shifted from Lombardy to northern Italy as a whole and from the Lombard to the 'Padano-Alpine' people. They proposed that the country should be divided into three federated republics, the north, which they now call Padania, the centre and the south. Padania would be closely linked to the European Community, while the centre and south would adopt economic policies in keeping with their own needs. The three republics would cooperate in a reformed Italian state, though just how this would operate between strong regions and the European Community is not clear. Nor is it obvious how the three republics could have different economic policies while remaining part of the same federation. At times, Bossi has appeared to flirt with separatism, threatening to declare the Republic of Padania when the Leagues have conquered northern Italy. At other times, the federal message is stronger. Federalism has the added advantage that the League can deny that it is anti-southern. Officially it now supports continued resource transfers from the north to the south, as long as these are not handled by the government in Rome and the north is given a free hand on spending its own allocation. Under federation, the south would be free to adopt its own policies. With the power of the state machine broken along with that of the national trade unions, wages in the south would fall to allow the region to compete in the national and

European markets. This would only be fair, insist the Leagues, since living costs are lower in the south. To demonstrate his lack of prejudice against the south, Bossi himself stood in the 1992 election in Sicily and Rome as well as Milan and has encouraged the formation of southern Leagues with the federal message. Rather than the population of the south, the enemy is presented as the *partitocrazia* and its parasitic bureaucracy in Rome, holding back the productive potential of the country as a whole. The League's performance in the south, however, was derisory, at around 0.2 per cent of the vote. As is customary in the south, the old power brokers had also taken out some insurance against the rise of a new political movement. In 1990 it was reported that money was being offered to those attempting to set up southern Leagues by Mafia figures, some of whom had tried in the 1970s to re-establish the *Uomo Qualunque*, a right-wing populist movement of the postwar years.[12]

The Lombard League's original power base was in the lower-middle classes and small businessmen of Lombardy, the usual basis for right-wing, anti-statist populism. As the movement grew in strength and spread into other regions as the Northern Leagues, it broadened its social base to include more public sector workers, women and some manual workers.[13] It still lacks appeal to immigrants from southern Italy, a legacy of its anti-southerner image, though it claims that Lombards and more generally citizens of Padania are all those who live there, irrespective of origins. The stronghold of the League movement remains Lombardy, where it gained 23 per cent of the vote in 1992, just one per cent behind the Christian Democrats. Elsewhere in the north, the Leagues gained 15-20 per cent, except where rival regionalist movements existed. The three main parties, Christian Democrats, PDS and Socialists, all lost between 5 and 6 per cent of their vote to the Leagues.[14] One in four League voters was a former Christian Democrat and nearly one in five was a former Communist. In local elections in 1993, they strengthened their position still further, winning control of a number of northern cities, including Milan.

The future for the Leagues is at the time of writing uncertain. They have found a response in many sectors of Italian society. Even observers who dislike their right-wing populism and find the pseudo-medieval romanticizing embarrassing recognize that they may have found the weak spot in the system and could be the catalyst for reform. Many of their ideas, for federalism, reform of the bureaucracy and strengthening of civil society against the state, have a long and respectable history in Italy. Yet, in contrast to this liberal legacy, there is an undertow of intolerance and authoritarianism. Their support base is also rather diffuse. Small business people like their anti-tax message and their attacks on the parasitic state bureaucracy. They might be less pleased if the Leagues seriously pursued their policy against tax evasion or really cut off state grants and subsidies. Tactically, the Leagues are still caught in the classical Italian dilemma. They can remain an opposition force, excluded from the political game in Rome like the former Communists; or they can enter in the coalition politics, with the risk of being seduced by the spoils of power in the old *trasformismo* tradition.

The Far Right

The extreme right of the Italian political spectrum is occupied by the Italian Social Movement (*Movimento Sociale Italiano*, MSI). MSI was founded in the late 1940s by former Fascists and named after Mussolini's Italian Social Republic, also known as the Republic of Salò, the puppet regime which lasted from 1943-5 under German occupation. Since the constitution bans the reconstitution of the Fascist Party, there has always been some doubt about the MSI's legitimacy and in 1951 a law was even passed to ban it. Known as the Scelba law after the then minister of the interior, this was never enforced but used by the Christian Democrats to exercise a degree of blackmail over the MSI. In 1972, it merged with the Monarchist Party, also on the extreme right, which had been losing votes rapidly. Despite its admiration for Mussolini, the MSI officially accepts democracy though it argues for a strong presidential role on Gaullist lines and restrictions on civil liberties. It is strongly authoritarian and anti-permissive, and takes a hard line on law and order. It is strongly nationalist and was able to exploit the fears of Italians living in the largely German province of Bolzano to become the largest party there in the 1980s. Although opposed to the left-wing trade unions, it does have its own small union organization, and supports the rights of workers against big corporations. Believing in a strong state and the legacy of Mussolini, it tends to oppose privatization, though at times it has also tried to present itself as a party of the modern market-oriented right on Reagan or Thatcher lines. These ambiguities allow the party to appeal to different audiences but have given birth to serious factionalism and divisions. The MSI has links with other European neo-Fascist parties such as the French National Front and sits with them in the European Parliament.

Because of its extreme views, the MSI has remained outside the coalition game but it was for a time linked to the DCI. After the departure of De Gasperi, it gave external support to Christian Democrat governments of the 1950s, in return for a share of power in local government and some parliamentary privileges. The advent of the centre-left coalition in the early 1960s put an end to this cooperation and the MSI went back into the cold. From the late 1960s until the early 1980s, there was a series of right-wing terrorist attacks, part of what was known as the strategy of tension, a campaign to destabilize the Republic and usher in a right-wing authoritarian regime. In 1969, a bank was blown up in Milan, killing sixteen people. A series of attacks on the railway included the bombing of Bologna railway station in 1980, with eighty five deaths and the bombing of the Naples-Milan express in 1984, which killed twelve people. Although the MSI officially distanced itself from this, it sought to reap the benefit and there were widespread suspicions that some of its leaders were implicated with violence. There was also evidence of collusion by elements of the police, military, security services and magistrature in right wing terrorism. Culprits were rarely found, attempts made to blame the attacks on the left and investigations trailed off inconclusively. Although some sentences were eventually handed down to neo-Fascists in the case of the Bologna station bombing, a series of acquittals was all that emerged from investigations into the Piazza della Fontana (Milan, 1969) and Piazza della Loggia (Brescia, 1974) killings - and these came eighteen years and fifteen years respectively after the events. Some senior officials of the security services were elected to parliament on the MSI and Monarchist tickets after retirement, including Giovanni De Lorenzo, suspected of organizing an attempted *coup d'état* in 1964. Other links connect the MSI to the murky underworld of conspiracies and scandals discussed below.

Support for the extreme right, the MSI and Monarchists combined, peaked in 1953, at 12.7 per cent, then declined. The MSI revived in the early 1970s and reached 9.2 per cent in 1972. By 1992, it was back down to 5.4 per cent, electing thirty-four deputies. These included Alessandra Mussolini, grand-daughter of the *Duce*, elected in Naples with 56 ,000 preference votes as well as in Bologna, who announced that she would occupy her grandfather's old seat in the Chamber. A new generation of leaders in the 1980s tried to improve the party's image and received some response. Efforts have been made by the other parties to bring the MSI back within the pale of the constitution, including representation on parliamentary committees and a small share of patronage spoils. This is seen as a conscious normalization policy intended to separate the parliamentary extreme right from the terrorist fringe, though the success of the strategy is as yet uncertain.

The Extreme Left

In the early 1970s, following the 'hot autumn' of student and worker unrest, a number of groups emerged on the extreme left, dissatisfied with the timid reformism of the Communist Party. They took their political inspiration from a variety of sources, from Mao, to Che Guevara, to the anarchist tradition and the post-1968 new left. Initially they were more concerned with mobilization in the streets, factories and universities but in the early 1970s tried to enter the parliamentary arena. In 1976 a coalition of far left groups, Proletarian Democracy, gained just over one per cent of the vote and elected a handful of deputies. They maintained a small representation in parliament until they broke up in the late 1980s. Another group known as Continuous Struggle tried to maintain mass

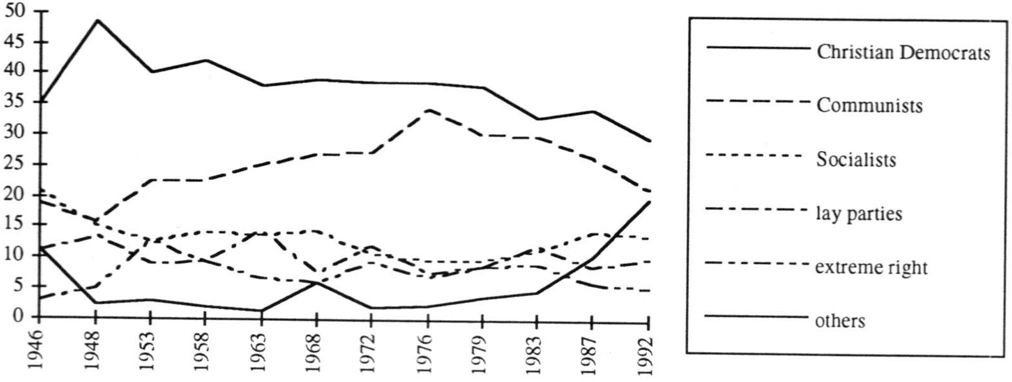

Figure 4.1 % vote in elections for Italian Chamber of Deputies, 1948-92

agitation but folded in 1977.

Beyond the parliamentary left is a violent fringe of terrorist groups, the most prominent of which is the Red Brigades (*Brigate Rosse*), founded in the early 1970s. During the 1970s and 1980s the Red Brigades were responsible for a number of killings of public officials, journalists and people suspected of cooperating with the forces of order. Their most spectacular operation was the kidnapping of Christian Democrat leader Aldo Moro in 1978. Moro was held hostage for the release of Red Brigade prisoners, the idea being to expose the weakness of the state and divide the parties of the coalition. Despite sharp disagreements within the coalition, the decision was taken to stand firm. Moro was killed by his captors and, in a further humiliation to the state, his body dumped in a car mid-way between the Christian Democrat and Communist headquarters. In an unholy harmony with the extreme right, Red Brigades, too, sought to destabilize the Republic, hoping to spark off a revolution. The murder of Moro, however, produced a popular revulsion against them. The police for their party proved more dedicated in tracking down left-wing than right-wing terrorists and by the end of the 1980s the structure of the Red Brigades appeared to have been broken though elements continued to exist.

The Radicals

A more influential group on the new left is the Radical Party. Founded in the 1950s by libertarian members of the Liberal Party, its real participation in Italian politics dates from the early 1970s when it was taken over by Marco Pannella. Although they never achieved more than 3.4 per cent of the vote, the Radicals have played an important role in exposing some of the shortcomings of the system, constantly raising the issue of civil liberties and the need to safeguard proper procedure even in the face of terrorism. They brought on to their lists some unusual candidates, including Toni Negri, a professor suspected of involvement in terrorist activity with the Red Brigades and imprisoned without being brought to trial; television host Enzo Tortora later convicted of Mafia activity; and pornographic film star *La Cicciolina*. They also recruited a number of prominent intellectuals. Radical tactics include parliamentary filibusters, sit-ins and demonstrations but their most important contribution has been the use of the referendum, a constitutional provision brought into force in 1970.

The Radical Party was by definition disorganized and undisciplined and in the 1980s it fell apart. In 1992, Radicals ran under the title Pannella list, gaining 1.2 per cent of the vote and seven seats and pledged to pursue a new series of referendums and constitutional reforms.

Greens

The Italian Green movement has also been disorganized and fractious. Greens ran in the 1987 national elections, gaining 2.5 per cent of the vote and in the 1989 European elections two Green lists gained a total of 6.3 per cent. Disaffected members of the Radical Party and Proletarian Democracy broke away in 1989 to form the *Arcobaleno* (Rainbow) group. This has run joint lists in various elections with another Green formation called *Sole che ride* (Smiling Sun).

THE STATE, ADMINISTRATION AND POLICY MAKING

The Italian state is quite pervasive, reaching into many areas of social and economic life. It is in theory highly structured, legalistic and uniform. In practice, public administration has been captured by political and client interests. Yet its very pervasiveness has inhibited the development of a strong and independent civil society. Much effort is devoted to avoiding formal bureaucratic channels of action.

The Bureaucracy

Italy has suffered since unification from a poor quality of public service. The blame for this is variously attributed to the parties, for their colonization of the state, to the bureaucracy itself, or to a national culture which prefers to bypass formal channels of administration and manages to get by despite the chronic inefficiency of government.

Italy's civil service is, in principle, highly formalized and legalistic, based on the concept of the *stato di diritto*. Nearly all administrative action is governed by regulation, with a jungle of some 100,000 items of administrative law intended to govern any contingency. As in Germany, the relationship of the civil servant to the state is a legal one, with security of tenure as long as the requirements of the job are being fulfilled. Entry is by competitive examination, with three grades, a clerical one, a middle ranking executive one and an administrative one. Promotion through the ranks within these grades is essentially on the basis of length of service.

As in so many matters, there is a large gap between the theory and the practice. Some ministries, like Foreign Affairs or Interior, are run in a manner comparable to northern European norms. In others, a few dedicated civil servants at the top strive to make good the shortcomings of the system. Generally, however, the Italian bureaucracy is slow, ponderous and inefficient.

Civil service careers have a relatively low status and most civil servants are recruited from the south, where the universities produce a surplus of graduates in law and there are few opportunities for local employment. Trained in law, they have a formalistic attitude to work and often lack managerial and policy skills. Low salaries are evaded by extensive overtime and semi-legal or illegal secondary employment. Inefficiency is rife and favouritism, shading into corruption, common, especially in the south - the *bustarella,* an envelope filled with money, is often the best way to clear a bureaucratic blockage. Since the bureaucracy is so inefficient, political intervention and recommendations are required for the most routine matters, providing yet more opportunities for patronage. Regulations on recruitment are evaded by the appointment of temporary civil servants, who often spend many years in the ranks without regularizing their status. The very complexity of bureaucratic regulation not only slows down action. Since the rules are often unenforceable, it encourages evasion and, by allowing officials to play with the tangle of regulations, reduces accountability.

Many laws are unenforced because the requisite regulations have not been produced on time or at all. Money voted for public works and services is unspent because of the bureaucratic rigidities and endless form filling. Despite Italy's enthusiasm for the European Community, it has one of the worst records of implementing Community directives or obeying court rulings. Cynics note that Italy can easily agree to Community proposals, secure in the knowledge that nothing is likely to come of them at home.

Many attempts have been made over the years to reform the civil service. Laws have tried to specify the civil servants' role and responsibilities clearly, in accordance with the *stato di diritto* principle and to avoid capricious interventions by politicians. Provision has been made for better training through a revamped civil service college, the *Scuola superiore de la amministrazione publica,* which reformers wanted to transform on the lines of the French ENA. Proposals have been made for promotion on the basis of competitive examination rather than recommendation and informal assessment. Almost all have either failed to pass through parliament or, having passed, have died in the course of implementation.[15] Politicians in government do not really want to specify civil service roles, so limiting their own discretion. Civil servants themselves to not wish to undergo the rigours of competitive examination or take time out for training courses. Their trade unions have intervened in parliamentary committees and used their links with the parties, especially the Andreotti faction of the Christian Democrats, to obstruct reform. Ministers are rarely in office long enough to take the bureaucracy in hand and administrative reform has never been a political priority.

The *Sottogoverno*

Beyond the ministerial departments, Italy has a further dense network of public agencies. Some of these have their origins in the Fascist regime and its efforts to create a strong interventionist state. Others have been established since the war for the purposes of economic management or as part of the welfare state. Known as the *sottogoverno* (subterranean government), these are a rich source of patronage for the parties.

The oldest are the autonomous administrations, for posts, telephones, railways, road building, forestry and state monopolies. As their name suggests, these are supposed to enjoy an operational autonomy but in practice they are subject to political manipulation. Then there are the state holding companies, which have stakes in a large part of Italian industry. The *Istituto per la Ricostruzione Industriale* (IRI) was founded by Mussolini in 1933 to rescue industries threatened in the Depression. There was some effort to sell off firms in the mid-1930s and again after the war. From the 1950s, however, it was expanded to play a key role in Italian modernization and industrialization. Until the late 1960s, IRI was run by dynamic, modernizing managers and provided a model of effective public-private partnership and efficiency, much admired abroad. Then it gradually fell into the Christian Democratic patronage system, propping up non-viable industries and handing out subsidies for reasons of political advantage. IRI has stakes in a wide range of industrial sectors as well as banks and the state airline Alitalia. In the 1970s, it was used by the state to bail out firms affected by the recession and restructuring. The resulting deficits forced it back to the government for public funds, reducing its operational autonomy further. From the 1980s, however, it sought to re-establish its independence by divesting itself of marginal enterprises and focusing its objectives more clearly.

The *Ente Nazionale Idrocarburi* (ENI) was founded in 1953 to exploit the reserves of natural gas in the Po valley, absorbing the older state oil company, AGIP. Under Enrico Mattei, ENI expanded into a giant holding company and a powerful force both in the economy and in politics. Mattei had his own faction of the Christian Democrat Party and filled the organization with patronage appointees. ENI even had its own daily newspaper, *Il Giorno*.

State participation in the banking system is extensive, from several of the major national banks, through the savings institutions and credit agencies. These handle most banking, loans, credit facilities and investment borrowing, and play a key role in industry, agriculture, services and housing. Altogether, state firms account for some 15 per cent of gross domestic product.

A series of agencies have been established to stimulate local and regional development, especially in the south. The largest, the *Cassa per il Mezzogiorno*, lavished billions in development grants and projects before being formally abolished in 1985. Even after death, it continued a ghostly existence in the form of the agency for southern development, still linked to the old patronage networks.

Then there is a huge sprawl of administrative bodies dealing with welfare administration, industrial advice, agricultural support, health and employment regulations. There are some sixty thousand such bodies, staffed by patronage appointments in the hands of the political parties. Some perform important roles in the welfare state, like the *Unità Sanitaria Locali* (USL), which administer the local health services. Others have long since become redundant but survive in neglected parts of the administrative jungle.

In the early years of the Republic, the Christian Democrats were able to keep most of the patronage plums for themselves. As the coalition was extended through *trasformismo*, they had to share these out, a process known as *lottizzazione*. The Socialists started to share after the constitution of the centre-left in the early 1960s. On their return to the coalition in the early 1980s, they set stiff terms, prising such important sources of patronage as the Ministry for State Sarticipation and the Ministry for the Mezzogiorno out of Christian Democrat hands. As the Communists were brought within the political system, especially during the historic compromise, they too were given a share. The state television service, RAI, has three channels. While in countries like the United Kingdom or Canada, public service broadcasting is obliged to maintain balance by being above and outside party politics, in Italy the question of balance was resolved by giving the large parties a channel each. RAI 1 is the Christian Democrat channel, RAI 2 is the Socialists' and RAI 3 goes to the former Communists, the PDS. These are not used to broadcast crude party propaganda, but news and current affairs items are certainly chosen and presented in ways which reflect party interests. Three private channels are owned by the entrepreneur Berlusconi, who is close to Bettino Craxi and the Socialists.

The *sottogoverno* provides a source of jobs at the disposal of the parties. It allows political control over the administration of benefits such as pensions and subsidies. It gives the parties influence over the implementation of policy; and through the state-owned media it allows them to influence public opinion. The cost is inefficiency, delay and corruption. Highways are aligned with a view to political rather than economic and social benefits. Disability pensions are paid to millions of able-bodied people. Development projects are designed, not to encourage self-sustaining growth but to perpetuate dependence.

Interest Groups

Italy has a pervasive but weak state, colonized by the political parties and extensively penetrated by interests linked to the parties. The autonomous sphere of civil society is correspondingly small. Private business associations have been rather weak since the foundation of the state dependent, as elsewhere in southern Europe, on the support and protection of the state. The experience of Fascism and, after the second world war, the extension of state ownership and the state sponsorship of development in the south further weakened the private sector as an independent actor. Since the late 1970s, though, the private sector has begun to assert itself more forcefully. As in other European countries, the opening of international markets has weakened the ability of the state to plan the economy.

Italian private business is marked by the presence of a small number of very large enterprises, such as FIAT, Olivetti and Montedison, and a large number of small firms. The main business organization is the *Confindustria*, a federation of regional and sectoral associations. *Confindustria* cannot claim to speak for business as a whole since its members account for only about a tenth of the workforce, excluding those in service industries, the public sector, agriculture and very small firms. On the other hand, it does speak for the most dynamic sectors of Italian business, including those in the export sector. For most of the 1950s, *Confindustria* was closely linked to the Christian Democrats which it saw as a guarantor against the left. The extension of state industry under DCI tutelage weakened these links and from the 1960s, Confindustria, under the influence of Gianni Agnelli of FIAT, began to press for a more independent private sector. As many small businesses broke away to form their own association, *Confapi*, the *Confindustria* came under increased domination by FIAT and a few other large firms. In the 1970s *Confindustria* supported national wage bargaining and economic planning and argued for the inclusion of the left and the Communists in national decision making. In the late 1970s it launched an anti-union offensive seeking to roll back the labour force gains of the decade and since then it has taken a strong neo-liberal line. It supported the ending of wage indexation in 1985 and has argued for privatization, deregulation and a reform of the state to enable Italian business to meet the competitive challenge from Europe. Tensions have remained between large and small firms, taking on a territorial dimension as the large firms tend to be based in the north and the small ones in the centre and south. In particular, there is resentment in some quarters about the domination of FIAT.

Large-scale private business together with the small and medium enterprises of central Italy, is one of the few sectors of Italian life able to establish their independence of the state and the *partitocrazia*. Politically, it has often supported the Republican or Liberal Parties or, more recently, the Northern Leagues. Outside the representative structure of the *Confindustria*, the large corporations are able to intervene in politics on their own. Their leaders have access to ministers and senior civil servants and local and regional governments have to pay attention to their needs. They also own large parts of the media, including the major national papers. In the 1950s, much criticism was aimed at the large private electricity monopolies and their nationalization was one of the key items demanded by the Socialists for participation in the centre-left coalition formula. When nationalization came in 1962, however, it took the form of compensation to the companies rather than to their shareholders. The companies were thus left intact and in possession of large financial resources, which they used to maintain their grip on vital economic sectors.

State industries have their own association, the *Intersind*. As appointments in state industries were increasingly filled by patronage, the *Intersind* became associated with the Christian Democrats. In the 1980s, however, problems of restructuring in both public and private enterprises brought leaders of state and private firms in certain branches of industry together in sectoral associations linked with *Confindustria*.

Farmers' organizations are divided on sectoral and political grounds. Large landowners operate through *Confagricoltura*. Small farmers operate through the *Coldiretti* which has close links with the Christian Democrats and thus with the Ministry of Agriculture and the appropriate parliamentary committees. As in other countries, the transfer of agricultural policy to the European Community has diminished the weight of farmers in domestic politics while encouraging them to participate in Community-wide bodies.

Italy's trade union organization is a legacy of the domestic and Cold War divisions which have marked its politics. At the Liberation, a united trade union was set up, the *Confederazione Generale Italiana del Lavoro* (CGIL). Its executive council reflected the weight of the Communist, Socialist and Christian Democrat Parties among the membership and the union was the counterpart of the national government coalition. On the outbreak of the Cold War in 1948, the Catholic element, encouraged by the Vatican and the American Federation of Labour, broke away to form the *Confederazione Italiana Sindicati Liberi* (CISL). Shortly after, the Republican and Socialist elements also left to form the *Unione Italiana Lavatori* (UIL). These three federations now organize most unionized workers, though there is also a small union associated with the MSI, the CISNAL.

During the 1950s and early 1960s, political divisions and the supply of cheap labour from the south kept Italian unions weak, wages low and social benefits limited. From the late 1960s, this changed. The unions began to distance themselves from the political parties and to cooperate among themselves. An increase in worker militancy and strikes culminated in the 'hot autumn' of 1969, an outbreak of social unrest extending to students, neighbourhoods and factories. In the following years, the trade unions made significant gains. Wages were pushed up, working hours regulated and in 1970s a statute of workers' rights enacted. Union pressure was also influential in the passage of a law on public sector housing in 1971. In 1972 the unions signed a pact creating loose federation and although this never became a truly united body, membership of the three components increased dramatically. By 1975 they had secured the *scala mobile*, an arrangement providing for automatic wage rises to compensate for inflation.

In the late 1970s, the unions played a key role in stabilizing Italian democracy, negotiating with the state over a range of issues beyond wages and conditions. So the historic compromise at the level of government was reflected in a series of social compromises between government and unions, bringing the industrial working class into the system of government. This culminated in the EUR line of 1978, named after a suburb of Rome, in which the unions agreed on a broad-based social contract. They would support wage restraint in return for social reforms, job protection and development in the south.

Like the corporatist arrangements in other European countries, this had mixed results. Union representatives were appointed to many state bodies and social stability was restored. Inflation was brought under some control but social reforms were either not introduced or were implemented half-heartedly. By the end of the historic compromise period in the early 1980s, the unions were coming under pressure from various sides. Employers, worried about competitiveness, started to fight back. Work was contracted out to small firms, which could effectively evade labour regulations and unionization. Within the factories, the union federations were under attack from militant shop floor movements known as *comitati di base* (COBAS) uncommitted to national cooperation and interested in pressing immediate claims over wages and working conditions. The final blow was the decision by the Craxi government to end the *scala mobile*, a move which broke the precarious unity of the three union federations. CISL and UIL supported the government while CGIL followed the Communist Party line and backed the 1985 referendum intended to reinstate it. The loss of the referendum vote was a major blow both to the Communist Party and to the CGIL.

Italian trade unionism enjoyed its boom years in the 1970s, when membership increased from 36 per cent to just under half of the labour force. By 1988, it had fallen sharply to just under 40 per cent. This was a higher figure than in France, Germany or Spain and almost the same as the United Kingdom, but the fall reflects a general trend in western Europe. Membership is concentrated in the public sector, in large firms and in the north.

Since Italy is nominally 95 per cent Catholic and is the seat of the Holy See, the Catholic Church is an important influence in politics. The basis of its power is threefold, the formal legal arrangements, the links with the Christian Democratic Party, and the Church's hold over popular opinion. All have undergone major changes since the early days of the Republic.

From 1931 until 1985 the relations between Church and state were governed by the Lateran Pacts, or Concordat agreed between Pope Pius XI   and

Mussolini. This granted the papacy sovereign rights over a state consisting of a small area inside Rome known as the Vatican and the papal properties outside the city. In return, the Pope for the first time recognized the unified Italian state. In addition, the Church was given extensive privileges within the Italian state. Catholicism was officially recognized as the state religion. Clergy enjoyed extensive civil immunities and lapsed clergy suffered civil disabilities. Catholic religious instruction was obligatory in schools. The Church gained financial support from the state, justified as a form of compensation for the Church lands appropriated in the nineteenth century. Although incorporated in the 1947 constitution, the Concordat was long recognized as an anachronism and in the late 1960s negotiations began on its amendment. These were finally concluded in 1985, significantly by a government led by a non-Christian Democrat, Craxi. Under the new arrangement, Church and state are largely separated, each confining itself to its own jurisdiction. Religious instruction in schools is voluntary, though there followed a long controversy over the times and terms on which it would be provided. The Church no longer is supported by the state, though citizens are allowed to deduct from income tax religious contributions up to a certain limit. Finally, other religions are in principle given the same rights; this has been taken advantage of by the small Protestant and Jewish communities.

The close links between the Vatican and the Christian Democrat party have been noted earlier, though this relationship has not always been smooth. The party always insisted on a sphere of autonomous action and party leaders, as hardened politicians, treated religious enthusiasts with a great deal of suspicion. After the Second Vatican Council in the 1960s, the Church liberalized its attitudes and began to distance itself from party politics. Some progressive Catholics even opened a dialogue with the Communists, though this was roundly condemned by the hierarchy. On matters of morality and doctrine, however, the Church insisted on its right to intervene. In 1974, it succeeded in persuading the Christian Democrat leadership to take a gamble on a referendum to repeal Italy's divorce law and lost badly. Again in 1981, they tried and lost with the referendum on abortion. Interest in party and domestic political matters further declined with the election in 1978 of the first non-Italian Pope in four centuries, the Polish John-Paul II. Anti-communism, however, remained a driving force and in 1987 the Church was again mobilized to repel the challenge from the left. Since the collapse of Soviet communism and the transformation of the Italian left, this motive has largely disappeared and the Church has spoken out more often against the corruption of the present governing parties. Links with prominent Christian Democrat politicians, however, remain strong.

The Church's hold on public opinion has weakened as Italy, rather more slowly than other European countries, has secularized. The mass organizations for lay Catholics, such as Catholic Action, have declined sharply, though there has been some growth in the smaller and more militant bodies like Communion and Liberation. A survey of Italians in 1991[16] showed that 90 per cent believed in God and most of them still practised religion. On the other hand, there was a large rejection of Church teaching on divorce, birth control, abortion and clerical celibacy. Most believed that the Church has a role in educating children but not in politics. Few still believed that Catholics have a duty to vote for a Catholic party. So Italians in general now accept a division between religion and politics and see a place for each in its own sphere. There is greater support for broadly-based religious organizations like Catholic Action, which has distanced itself from politics, than for those like Communion and Liberation or *Opus Dei* who believe that they have a political and civic mission. The decline and discredit into which the Christian Democrat Party has fallen have certainly influenced these attitudes, which in turn enhance the prospects for a more secularized state with genuine political competition.

Public Policy Making

Italy has been described as a *partitocrazia*, in which not only the state but large areas of civil society have been colonized by the political parties. Yet, paradoxically, the parties have not been the main agents in determining public policy.[17] They are primarily concerned with issues of power and advantage, with the distribution of spoils and patronage and in these matters they are masters of the art. They are, however, too heterogeneous and factionally divided to formulate and push through consistent policies on substantive issues. Ministers for their part are in office for too short periods of time to make a real impact. Nor does Italy possess a powerful, policy-minded bureaucracy to take the lead in policy making. Its administrative system appears to create a strong, centralized state on Napoleonic lines with wide powers of intervention and regulation. Yet the juridical bent of Italian civil servants and their preoccupation with legal niceties ill qualifies them for policy making and managerial tasks.

In practice, behind the strident tone of partisan debate, much policy making takes the form of consensual negotiation among organized interests, governments and political parties. Even the opposition may contribute to this process. Large business groups such as FIAT have had little trouble getting their way with governments, as policy on highway construction, industrial development and automobile imports shows. Other economic interests have used their links with the relevant ministries to gain policy concessions. In social and environmental fields, policy change has tended to be slow and incremental, with movement taking place when favourable circumstances present themselves. The Craxi governments of the 1980s, with their image of *decisionismo,* tried to break this policy style but the results were more apparent in terms of style than of substance. Even where major policy changes have been put in legislative form, their implementation tends to be delayed or bent to the interests of the bureaucracy or affected parties. Emphasis is placed on distributive bargaining and incremental change. The results have been positive and negative. On the positive side, the regime has been preserved, extremist elements marginalized and democracy entrenched. Italy has also established a modern welfare state, for all its inefficiencies and corruption. On the negative side, major problems have been postponed, reforms have been sabotaged in the implementation, budget deficits have accumulated and a widespread cynicism has developed about politics.

In the 1960s, Italy tried to improve its policy process with indicative planning on French lines. In the Italian context, this was largely a failure. The lack of a modernizing, technical bureaucracy, the inefficiencies of the state and the extent of patronage and corruption in the state sector, prevented it giving a clear lead. Institutional reforms, including the establishment of effective regional governments, did not live up to requirements. In the 1970s, like other European countries, Italy embarked on a period of social concertation, or neo-corporatism, in which business and unions negotiated with government over a range of policy issues. This achieved some results, and may even have saved the Republic from threats from extreme right and left, but could not be sustained. The main evidence of this failure has been the accumulation of budget deficits as the state fails to establish clear policy priorities and the parties use it as an inexhaustible supply of patronage. Between the early 1970s and the early 1990s, Italy's budget deficit averaged 10 per cent of gross domestic product (GDP). In 1992 it was running at 105 per cent of GDP and total public debt amounted to 104 per cent of GDP. The European Community targets are three per cent and 60 per cent of GDP respectively. Until the late 1980s, the deficit could be accommodated by the very high domestic savings ratio. Then the savings ratio started to fall, from 27 per cent of disposable income in the mid-1970s to 16 per cent in 1991, while at the same time the end of exchange controls within the European Community allowed Italians to place their savings abroad. Budgetary discipline became inescapable.

From the mid-1980s, Italy adopted some of the neo-liberal market-oriented policies in current fashion. There was some privatization of the large state sector, supported by the lay parties, reformist Christian Democrats and even the Communists who saw it as a way of reducing patronage. The Bank of Italy was detached from the Ministry of Finance in 1981 in an effort to give it more autonomy and strengthen monetary discipline. Proposals were unveiled in 1992 to sell up to 45 per cent of the equity in the state holding companies, which would be turned into joint-stock enterprises. External pressures have forced Italian governments further down this road than they otherwise might have gone. International capital mobility has lessened their power to control industrial location. European Community directives, though often poorly implemented, have had an impact in areas such as competition and the lifting of exchange controls. The requirements for economic convergence laid down by the Maastrict Treaty were widely regarded as impossible for Italy to meet, given the state of its public finances but each move towards monetary union has imposed more discipline. Italians of nearly all political persuasions are enthusiastic supporters of European unity, which they see as an essential element of social and economic modernization and a means of escaping from the inefficiencies of their own state system. They are also afraid of being left behind if they cannot meet the conditions for convergence with Europe. This may be the external force which, combined with internal change, can succeed in bringing reform to Italy.

TERRITORIAL POLITICS

Italy in the last century was a diverse country, which was unified by leaders steeped in French ideas of centralization. A federal system was advocated in some quarters but the idea was never put into practice. Since then, the country has sought to resolve a variety of territorial issues within the framework of the unitary state. Four questions are particularly important, the question of the south, the integration of culturally distinct minorities around the periphery, the institution of regional government, and the performance of local government.

The Question of the South

Unification in the 1860s brought together two regions which differed radically in economic, cultural and political terms. Northern Italy was becoming a modern, industrialized, secularized European society. Southern Italy, known as the Mezzogiorno, was poor and more religious. Social relationships were based on personal contact and tradition. Its workforce was overwhelmingly agricultural, employed seasonally on large estates whose structure was almost feudal. Unification did little to change this order. Instead, the dominant elites in north and south agreed on mutual support in national politics. Northern industrialists would get tariff protection while southern landowners would be left in possession of their estates. Many of the Socialist leaders of the northern industrial workers also supported this order, since it helped preserve industrial jobs against foreign competition. The southern peasantry regarded the new state as just another set of rulers and engaged in sporadic uprisings which were firmly suppressed. The disentailment of Church lands by the new state authorities was used not to provide land for the peasants but to allow the urban middle class of the south to become landowners. Reformers, such as Guido Dorso, who dreamed of creating a Meridional (southern) political party committed to reform, a redistribution of land and regional autonomy, found that there was no political base for it. Some state investment was made in infrastructure but nothing serious was done to bridge the north-south gap.

At the liberation following the second world war, matters were much the same. About 60 per cent of the workforce were still in agriculture and living standards had fallen further behind the north. Politics was traditional and clientelist, with local notables able to command the vote of whole communities in exchange for patronage favours. A majority of southern voters supported retaining the monarchy in the referendum of 1946. The south had had little experience of the resistance, since it had come under Allied occupation from 1943 and the old pre-Fascist power brokers soon re-emerged. Both Christian Democrats, drawing on the inheritance of the old Popular Party, and the parties of the left, however, had plans for reform in the south involving land redistribution, transfers of funds, development programmes and strong regional governments. This would break the power of the notables and the patronage system, reduce dependence and set the south on a path of self-sustaining growth.

These good intentions fell victim to the politics of the new Republic. There was some land reform but it stalled in the early 1950s as the old notables found their way into the Christian Democrat Party, where they continued their old ways. The Fanfani reforms of the 1950s cut back their influence, only to substitute the party machine as the controller of patronage and favours. Regional governments, except for the special status regions, were postponed until 1970 for reasons of political convenience. A series of agencies was set up to develop the south, of which the most important was the *Cassa per il Mezzogiorno*, established in 1950. In its early years, the *Cassa* concentrated on infrastructure development and agriculture. From the early 1960s, it embarked on a policy of industrialization, sponsoring large industrial complexes. State industries were instructed to place 60 per cent of their new investment in the south until 40 per cent of their productive capital was located there. Unfortunately, many of these developments were poorly integrated into their local economies and they became known as 'cathedrals in the desert'. In the 1970s, there was a return to small-scale, local development and businesses. There was a great deal of criticism of the *Cassa* and its associated agencies from neo-liberal economists who believed that the market should be allowed to solve the problem through a combination of emigration to the north and low wages to attract capital to the south. Others claimed that the problem was not the policy of regional development itself but the way in which it was subordinated to the clientelistic practices of the political parties. Resources were distributed not according to economic logic but according to political considerations. In turn, the failure of the developments perpetuated the dependence of the region on the local politicians to gain more resources from Rome. To these problems were added corruption and the presence of organized crime, which took rake-offs from public works projects and channelled contracts to Mafia-linked companies. There was certainly industrialization and development in the *Mezzogiorno* but its rate of growth lagged behind that of the north, so that over the years the gap in productive capacity actually grew.

The *Mezzogiorno* continues to lag behind the rest of Italy in several respects. In 1987, its gross domestic product per head was some two-thirds of the national average. Unemployment in 1990 was 11 per cent, against a national average of 6 per cent. Secularization has been slower. In the 1974 divorce referendum, most southern regions voted against divorce, which was passed because of the weight of northern and central Italy. Organized crime remains a drag on the region's potential as well as a hazard to its citizens. Subsidies to the south and the waste and corruption which accompany them played a major part in the emergence of the protest Leagues in the north. European integration has greatly exacerbated the problems of the traditional system for managing the south. European Community regulations require budget deficits to be controlled and industrial subsidies limited. The need to compete in the open European market makes it ever more difficult to divert resources into unproductive projects in the south.

Yet politically, this system management in the south became in the 1980s even more important to the dominant parties of the governing coalition as they came under pressure elsewhere. In the 1960s, the south accounted for about 40 per cent of Christian Democratic deputies in parliament. By 1992, this had increased to almost 65 per cent. The Socialists drew about a third of their deputies from the south in the 1960s. During the 1980s, they used their position in government to extend their patronage networks there and in 1992 the south accounted for 60 per cent of their deputies. So more than ever, reform in the Mezzogiorno and reform of the Italian political system as a whole had become inseparable.

The Periphery

Several peripheral and frontier regions of Italy have experienced separatist and autonomist movements and, to accommodate these, special regional governments are established by the constitution. The first of these was in Sicily where a separatist movement briefly flourished in 1943 and 1944, receiving some encouragement from the American and British authorities, who saw Sicily as a strategic military spot should Italy fall into the hands of the left. The main impetus for separatism came from traditional landowners, who also feared a reforming Italian postwar government, aided by the Mafia. Separatism proved to be a passing phase, taken up and abandoned for reasons of convenience, but it alarmed the main political parties enough for them to concede a Sicilian Constituent Assembly which drew up its own statute of autonomy in advance of the Italian constitution.

Provision was made in the Italian constitution for the Sicilian statute and a similar one for Sardinia. In the latter case, a strong autonomist movement had emerged after the first world war and it was generally assumed that the reconstituted *Partito Sardo d'Azione* (PS d'A) would be a powerful force again. In fact, Sardinian regionalism did not take off though the PS d'A has sporadically intervened in elections, making a little progress in the 1980s. Special regional governments were also conceded to two northern border areas. In the Val d'Aosta the population speak French - originally Provençal rather than Parisian - and after the war there was some support for annexation by France. The Alto Adige, known in German as the Sud-Tirol, was annexed from Austria after the first world war and subjected to a campaign of forced Italianization by Mussolini. After the second world war, there was strong support for the creation of a German-speaking region, which the Italian state accommodated in a rather ambiguous way. A special region was set up but it included a large Italian speaking area, so forming the cumbersome Trentino-Alto Adige. Only after considerable agitation, intervention by the Austrian government and some incidents of violence, was a special statute of autonomy, *within* the region, conceded to the German-speaking province of Bolzano. The fifth special status region resulted from a long-running border dispute with what was then Yugoslavia. In 1963, after the status of the city of Trieste was resolved, the special region of Friuli-Venezia-Giulia was set up. The break up of Yugoslavia in 1991 encouraged some neo-Fascist elements to try and create incidents in the area with a view to making gains at the expense of Slovenia and Croatia, but this produced no popular response and the frontier is not an issue in Italian politics. Rather, the collapse of Communist regimes to the north and east is seen as an opportunity to restore cooperation among regions with traditional economic and cultural links. In 1990, the new organization, the *Pentagonale* was established to link Italy, Austria, Hungary and the then republics of Czechoslovakia and Yugoslavia.

The Ordinary Regions

The 1948 constitution also provided for the establishment of 'ordinary status' regions for the rest of Italy. Initially this was supported strongly by the Christian Democrats, who had inherited a preference for regionalism from Sturzo and the Popular Party. Intermediate governments were seen as a way of securing democracy while limiting and dividing government powers and reducing the scope of any future left-wing government in Rome. The

Communists, with their Jacobin traditions and preference for a strong state, favoured only a very weak form of regionalism. In 1948, with the sweeping Christian Democrat victory in the national elections, these positions were reversed. Now the Christian Democrats supported a strong central government, secure in their control of it, while the Communists demanded that regions should be set up. So, although regional governments were stipulated in the constitution, their establishment was continually postponed. Only with the centre-left coalition in the 1960s did the issue come back on the agenda. All the political parties except the Liberals and the MSI were now in favour of regions and the *Confindustria*, which had opposed them in the past, now saw them as a means for improving administrative performance. Even so, it took until 1970 to set up regional councils and the requisite powers were not transferred to them until 1976.

The fifteen ordinary status regions were intended to improve the quality of public administration, reduce the weight of the central bureaucracy in Rome and facilitate economic and land-use planning and the programming of public investments. They have been a mixed success and have not broken the centralist mould of Italian government. The main problem has been their failure to establish real autonomy. The national parties have kept tight control, dictating the composition of electoral lists and coalition strategies. Powers have not been devolved in coherent blocks but piecemeal, requiring complex mechanisms for coordination between central government and regions. This has allowed the central bureaucracy, which has not abandoned its centralist habits, to intervene in detail in regional matters. Regions have virtually no fiscal autonomy. Over 90 per cent of their revenue comes as a grant from central government and most of this is earmarked for specified expenditures, notably on the health service. As was the case with other Italian reforms, the establishment of regions has been marked by excessive concern with legalistic matters, the precise specification of roles and powers, to the neglect of questions of management and coherent policy making. The result is a proliferation of rules and regulations and a tendency to respond to the failures of regionalism by prescribing yet more legalistic changes. Except in Sicily, local governments maintain direct links to Rome rather than passing through the regional government and this has helped sustain local client networks. Indeed, the province's status as a separate tier of local government, not subordinate to the region, was reinforced in the 1980s.

Regions appear to function better in northern and central Italy, where there is a modernized and secularized political culture, than in the south, where patronage and client relationships are the norm.[18] There is greater public support for regions in the north, where they are seen as somewhat better than the national administration. Regions also gave the former Communist Party a chance to demonstrate its governing ability in the Red belt of central Italy and helped its integration into the constitutional system.

As in other European countries, there has been some debate on the best way to equip regions to compete in the new continental market. Few people, however, see the existing regions as the means for reforming the state. The Northern Leagues, who have seized upon regionalism as the way to break the *partitocrazia* and change the whole system, advocate much larger regions, for northern, central and southern Italy and a federal system in which the central administration itself would be largely dismantled.

Local Government

Local government is organized on Napoleonic lines borrowed from France in the nineteenth century. The basic units are the 8,088 communes, ranging from large cities to the tiny *comuni polvere* (speck-of dust-communes) of the north, but all have identical formal powers. Large cities contain neighbourhood councils (*consigli di quartiere*). Small ones are often grouped together in consortia to provide services. Provinces, of which there are ninety-five, function both as a unit for central administration and a tier of local government. As in the case of French departments, their local character has been emphasized in recent years. Prefects, central officials operating at provincial level used to have extensive powers to control local governments but these have largely been taken over by regional committees of control.

Centralization has been reinforced by the bureaucracy, which has maintained an extensive field administration and by the practice of handing down to local governments rather tightly defined tasks rather than whole blocks of responsibilities. Financial powers have been limited since a reform of 1972 which abolished nearly all local tax-raising powers, making communes and provinces almost entirely dependent on central transfers. Like other aspects of Italian government, the whole system is pervaded by party politics. This can be a force for centralization, as the details of local coalition alliances are determined at party headquarters in Rome. On the other hand, the national parties are more concerned with power broking and strategic advantage than with substantive policy issues. Since local government handles large amounts of contract work and issues permits and licences of various sorts, there is ample scope for corruption and scandals have been frequent.

For many years the Communist Party used the city council in Bologna as a show-piece for its democratic and administrative credentials. Urban planning regulations were made and enforced, traffic was controlled so that, unlike in other Italian cities, pedestrians were not obliged to climb over vehicles parked on the sidewalk while being asphyxiated by fumes. Corruption was almost eliminated. As the Communist vote increased in the early 1970s, it was able to forge left-wing coalitions with the Socialists to take over many large cities after the 1975 local elections. This was intended further to demonstrate the left's responsibility and integrity and provide a trial for a possible left-wing national government. The experience, however, was mixed. Left-wing local governments faced serious obstruction, some of them were sucked into the old ways of patronage and corruption and after the 1985 elections the Socialists decreed that local coalitions should reflect that in national government. So local Socialist parties evicted the Communists, who were in any case in decline, and went back into partnership with the Christian Democrats. Recent corruption revelations in Milan have touched all the political parties.

CORRUPTION AND SCANDALS

A principal reason why the Italian state is held in such low esteem by its citizens is the extent of corruption in public administration and the regular scandals which explode into view, frequently linking the worlds of politics, finance, crime and international relations. Italians have developed a worldly cynicism about much of this but in the early 1990s a number of signs emerged of public exasperation and protest. The crumbling of the old *partitocrazia* deprived the politicians of their protection and emboldened honest magistrates to pursue cases of corruption and abuse of power.

Corruption in Government

The extent of corruption in public administration is by definition impossible to measure accurately. It is certainly large and affects the bureaucracy, politicians and the parties. Processing of an application for development permission, a licence, a subsidy of a tax refund will often be expedited by slipping a *bustarella*, an envelope of cash, to a low level official. Political parties finance themselves to a considerable extent from *tangenti*, rake-offs paid to secure contracts for public works projects. Individual politicians without visible means often become suddenly wealthy. In some cases, especially but not exclusively in the south, organized crime is involved in public works contracts, eliminating competition and rigging prices. Major development projects have been the site of some spectacular swindles.

Occasionally, a zealous magistrate would seek to expose corruption and succeed in bringing the perpetrators to justice. More often, the cases were lost in the judicial labyrinth. The magistrature itself was highly politicized and its members tried not to embarrass their party patrons. As the power and prestige of the parties slipped over the years, however, their grip of judicial appointments, promotions and assignments weakened. Magistrates have become more inquisitive and are not always so easily deterred from pursuing their investigations. A major scandal was caused by revelations of corruption in Milan by a persistent magistrate, which punctuated the 1992 general election campaign and fatally weakened Bettino Craxi's chances of emerging from it as prime minister. Investigations in other cities followed. The Milan case also demonstrated what was already widely known but seldom admitted, that corruption was not confined to the backward south but affected the entire Italian state. By early 1993, the prosecution net had widened to over 1000 government officials. Craxi was forced to resign as leader of the Socialist Party, indicted for corruption, and the leader of the Republicans also had to step down. The snowballing revelations of corruption, affecting all the old parties, threatened to strike the final blow to the old *partitocrazia*.

The Mafia and Others

One of the most serious challenges to the state in Italy is organized crime and its large degree of impunity. It is best known in the form of the Sicilian Mafia and its counterparts on the mainland, the Camorra of Campania and the 'Ndragheta of Calabria, but its ramifications reach into other regions and into the heart of the Italian state. The origins of the Mafia lie in the peculiar conditions and social structures of Sicily with its distrust of successive governments imposed from outside and its traditions of personal relationships and close family structures. In the nineteenth century, the Mafia served the interests of the large landowners, suppressing peasant discontent. Yet at the same time they were able to pose as the protectors of the peasantry against the state and the mainland government, establishing their own authority and legitimacy while being used by the political notables for their own purposes. Under Mussolini, there was an attempt to stamp out the Mafia but its roots were left intact, as were the cultural habits of the island. Some mafiosi took refuge in the United States, joining earlier emigrants, and when the Americans needed help in landing in Sicily in 1943 and making contacts in the local society, they turned to them. Lucky Luciano was even released from gaol in New York and brought along. Mafia elements were soon re-established in important positions in the local administration.

During the 1950s and 1960s, the Mafia extended their activities to take advantage of the boom in construction and the development programmes for the south. Contracts were monopolized, works undertaken by non-Mafia firms sabotaged, development permits manipulated and huge profits made from land speculation. They infiltrated the bureaucracy and the political parties, notably the Christian Democrats, and gained key positions in industry and commerce. In 1970, a notorious mafiosi, Vito Ciancimino, was even elected Christian Democrat mayor of Palermo, though normally the Mafia bosses preferred to work behind the scenes. From the 1970s, the Mafia moved into the lucrative drug trade, extending their operations to markets in the cities of the north. The extension of the Mafia to the north was perversely encouraged by the state policy of trying to break the organization by imposing internal exile on members, banning them from Sicily.[19]

The Mafia is organized into territorially-based clans but has an inherently unstable structure. Leaders emerge through a process of several stages, starting with an act of violence or a challenge to an existing leader. The prestige thus gained is reinforced if the perpetrator is charged but acquitted for lack of evidence - this broaDCIasts to the world that he did the deed but that no-one dares testify against him.[20] Gradually, the mafioso earns the status of 'man of respect' and needs to resort less to violence to get his way. He buys his way into legitimate business, uses contacts to trade favours and, if there is violence to be committed, hires others to do it for him. Social legitimation is helped by the fostering of myths about the older generation of mafiosi, presented as honourable outlaws not given to mass murder or immoral activities like drugs and prostitution. This is a recurring theme in Mafia lore down the ages and serves as a mechanism to protect the established leaders, who in their youth were as bloodthirsty as any, from their young challengers who must perpetrate new acts of violence in order to displace them.[21] There is a powerful tradition of *omertà,* the vow of silence, by which citizens do not report to the authorities on Mafia crimes. This is partly a matter of intimidation but it also has roots in historical distrust of the state authorities and the social legitimacy which Mafia leaders have acquired in the community. Further protection is given by the links which the Mafia, Camorra and 'Ndragheta maintain within the state, to politicians, the security services, the bureaucracy and the magistrature. These links are discreet but well known. Attempts to establish a parliamentary committee of inquiry into the Mafia were repeatedly stalled from the late 1940s until 1963 and its work systematically impeded by Christian Democrat ministers thereafter.[22] A reformist Christian Democrat, Francesco Cattanei, who had made some progress in investigation in the 1968-72 parliament, was removed from the presidency of the committee after the next election. In 1992, there occurred the murder in Sicily of the Christian Democrat member of the European Parliament Salvo Lima, obviously the work of the Mafia. While Christian Democrat leaders tried to portray Lima as a martyr to the anti-Mafia struggle, the newspapers did not hesitate to point out that he had been used for years to maintain links between prominent DCI boss Guilio Andreotti and the Mafia and to speculate that he had been caught out in a double game between rival Mafia factions.

As the Mafia expanded their activities into mobile enterprises like drug running, there were increasing territorial clashes between gangs, leading to a spiral of violence. They also increasingly targeted agents of the state, including police and magistrates, for assassination. In 1989 it was recorded that 75 per cent of Italian homicides occurred in Sicily, Campania and Calabria[23] - though for comparison it should be noted that murder rates are still rather low compared with large American cities. A series of tough, anti-Mafia police officers and magistrates, sent down to sort out matters in Sicily, have been murdered. In 1982, Carlo Alberto Dalla Chiesa, a *carabinieri* general who had helped break the Red Brigades, was appointed prefect in Palermo with a brief to stamp out the Mafia. After four months he was murdered. In 1992, the magistrate Giovanni Falcone, known as a relentless opponent of the Mafia, was assassinated in an elaborate car bomb operation which must have required inside information about Falcone's movements and cooperation in digging a hole in the road to plant the explosive. Falcone had in 1988 been ostentatiously passed over for the position of chief prosecutor in Palermo, in favour of a less-qualified candidate. He had also survived an 1989 assassination attempt in Palermo. Falcone had been expected in 1992 to be appointed head of a new anti-Mafia agency and his death was seen as a warning not to proceed with it. A few months after his murder, Paolo Borsellino, favoured as the next choice to head the proposed agency, was also assassinated by a car bomb in Palermo.

Pressure from the state and the fighting among Mafia and related gangs led to some positive results in the 1980s. In 1985, convictions were obtained against a number of Camorra types, including Enzo Tortora, a television host who had been brought on to the Radical Party list and elected to the European parliament. In Sicily, the first real breach of *omertà* occurred when Mafia leader Tommaso Buscetta turned state witness against his former confederates in a massive trial. Although only a few of the hundreds charged were finally convicted in 1987, this marked a step forward in the fight against organized crime. Real progress remained elusive, however, as long as organized crime received protection within the state itself. It was the shaking of the power structure of the state, with the end of the Cold War, the rise of new political forces and the exposures of corruption in 1993 which permitted a new assault on Mafia power. In January 1993, Salvatore Riina, a notorious Mafia boss, was finally arrested. Until that time, the authorities had claimed, with scant credibility, that they did not know where to find him. In March 1993, occurred the most spectacular move of all. Giulio Andreotti, seven times prime minister and the Christian Democrat's leading power broker, was indicted for Mafia connections. This merely confirmed decades of speculation and rumour, but it was an extraordinary step for the judicial authorities to take on someone of Andreotti's political standing. It appeared just possible that the Mafia's increased resort to naked violence against the agents of the state represented, not a show of strength but a measure of desperation at the fact that their political protection was disappearing. The need to resort to murder does appear to indicate that threats and intimidation are no longer effective.

Networks of Secret Power

A series of scandals emerged in the 1980s and 1990s involving an interlinked set of clandestine organizations with ramifications to politics, the Mafia, the financial system, the United States Central Intelligence Agency and the Vatican. These scandals are of impenetrable complexity but three of them give an indication of the problem. These are the P2 masonic lodge, the Banco Ambrosiano and the Gladio affair.

Propaganda 2 (P2) was a secret masonic lodge whose existence was exposed in 1981 after a police raid on the offices of its grand master, Licio Gelli. Its membership list contained hundreds of prominent figures in politics, the military, the police, the judiciary, intelligence services and business and finance as well as the head of the Rome station of the American Central Intelligence Agency (CIA).[24] There were connections to the Mafia and to extreme right-wing coup plotters. Francesco Pazienza, a senior officer in military intelligence and P2, member was later convicted of obstructing justice in the investigation of the 1980 bombing of Bologna railway station by right-wing terrorists.

On the revelation of P2's activities, Gelli fled abroad using an Italian diplomatic passport and was arrested in Switzerland in September 1982. Later he walked free after bribing the guards but after four years in hiding gave himself up and was returned to Italy to face a series of charges on financial matters and implication in the Bologna bombing. In 1988 he was cleared of direct responsibility for the bombing but received a ten-year sentence for obstructing its investigation. A parliamentary investigation into P2 revealed its subversive intentions but the report was gutted of its most sensitive findings after pressure from the parties of the governing coalition.

Banco Ambrosiano was, ironically, founded in the nineteenth century as a Catholic bank which would be free of the corruption then infecting the banking system.[25] In the early 1970s, it started an offshore operation under its director Roberto Calvi, in partnership with Sicilian financier Michele Sindona and the Vatican bank, *Istituto per le Opere di religione* (IOR), headed by Cardinal Paul Marcinkus, a native of Chicago. So close were Calvi's links to the Vatican that he became known as 'God's banker'. He also had connections into the Italian parties, extending credit even to the Communists, and doing favours to businessmen known to be associated with key Christian Democrat faction leaders. His international network was worldwide, with important links in North and South America and the oil-producing countries. Sindona had particularly close connections with the American Mafia and international drug dealers. Both Sindona and Calvi were members of P2 and Gelli received large amounts of money from the *Banco Ambrosiano*. Their friends in high places were used to the full as they pursued a systematic policy of fraud. A 1978 investigation into the bank's dubious activities was stymied when a senior Bank of Italy official who knew too much was arrested on trumped up charges. The governor himself was similarly harassed and only escaped gaol because of his advanced age.

In 1981 Calvi was arrested, sentenced to four years for monetary offences and given provisional liberty pending appeal. In June 1982, *Banco Ambrosiano* collapsed and Calvi fled to Britain. A few days later he was found hanging under Blackfriars Bridge in London. A coroner brought in a verdict of suicide - Calvi had tried to take his own life in prison in Italy - but the family insisted that he was murdered. A new inquest left the matter open. In the ensuing investigation, Cardinal Marcinkus was sought for fraudulent banking practices and for several years remained in the Vatican City, where the Italian police could not arrest him. Later a diplomatic settlement was reached allowing him to go free. Other charges and investigations against the IOR were ruled to be contrary to the Concordat between the Church and the Italian state. The details of the losses sustained by the Vatican in the *Banco Ambrosiano* affair are unlikely ever to be revealed but they were certainly enormous, provoking a crisis in Church finances.

Michele Sindona was convicted in 1986 of the murder of Giorgio Ambrosoli, a Bank of Italy investigator and two days later was poisoned in his cell. The official verdict of suicide was widely questioned.

Rumours long circulated of the existence of another secret network involving the intelligence services and dedicated to stopping the left, if necessary by a *coup d'état*. In 1974 the organization Compass Rose, involving senior military and intelligence officers, was exposed. More sensational was the revelation in 1990 of the organization Gladio. This stemmed from the investigation of a zealous magistrate into right-wing terrorism. Working from clues provided over the years, he forced Prime Minister Giulio Andreotti to admit the existence of an underground organization with its own chain of command, secret arms dumps and plans for taking control of the north of Italy. The official line was that this was a contingency plan linked to NATO for use if the Soviet Union invaded. Critics noted that it looked remarkably like the preparation for a *coup d'état* by right-wing elements in the security services in collaboration with the American CIA.[26] Indeed, Gladio's contingency plans looked suspiciously like the 1964 Solo Plan of General Lorenzo which itself bore a remarkable similarity to the 1967 colonels' coup in Greece. [27] After insisting that Gladio had been wound up in 1972 the government had to admit that it had continued after that. Further strands connected Gladio to Compass Rose and P2.

The truth about Italy's conspiracies and plots may never be known. Some of them have a comic opera air; others are very sinister. The democratic state survived but the revelations further undermined confidence in its institutions.

THE FALL OF THE REGIME

Italy's constitutional system, was devised by the Constituent Assembly in a reaction to Fascist dictatorship and monarchical manipulations. Rather than ushering in a new era of participatory democracy, it allowed many of the historic ills of the Italian state to reassert themselves. These included clientelism, corruption, organized crime and bureaucratic inefficiency. Under the *partitocrazia* , centred on the Christian Democrats, these were developed to new levels of professionalism. The persistence of such a system in a modern liberal democracy is explained by the presence of an internal and an external support system for the regime. By the early 1990s, these supports had been so eroded as to put the regime in question.

One internal support mechanism was the electoral system with its rather pure proportional representation. Intended to promote democracy and prevent the abuse of power, it gave disproportionate influence to small parties which could make and break governments at will. Given the presence of one large governing party and several small ones, it encouraged the politics of *trasformiso* and inhibited responsible opposition. A second internal support mechanism was the Christian Democrat patronage network through the *sottogoverno*, which encouraged electors to support the governing party in hope of individual benefits. This is particularly so in the *Mezzogiorno*, where economic and political underdevelopment favoured patronge relations and where policy was aimed at perpetuating dependence rather than ending it. Another internal support mechanism was Italy's rapid economic growth, which legitimized the system to some degree and provided resources for the patronage machine. The high internal savings ratio enabled governments to finance spiralling deficits through borrowing.

The main external support for the old order was provided by the Cold War. This guaranteed the Christian Democrats the support of the United States and the Vatican against Communism both within and outside Italy. As long as the Communists represented the only serious alternative to the Christian Democrats, many moderate voters just held their noses and voted for the DCI. So, ironically the Christian Democrats, sworn enemies of Communism, needed both the Italian Communist Party and the Soviet Union to remain in power.

For a time, the European Community was also a support mechanism for the system. Italians were able to pass on to Europe difficult problems such as agricultural adjustment, and were a net recipient of Community funds. Europe also provided export markets for the dynamic industries of Italy's north.

By the late 1980s, there were signs of decay both internal and external support systems. The parties' basis of support was weakening and, in order to stay in power, the Christian Democrats were forced to broaden the coalition. The Christian Democrat network had been weakening steadily in northern

Italy, if not in the south. By the late 1980s the patronage machine was being starved of resources. Capital mobility and European competition meant that the state could not finance the huge deficits of the past. The rise of the Northern Leagues made a mortal breach in the old order and indicated that northern voters were not prepared to be held back from full participation in the new Europe simply to feed the corruption in the south. The erosion of support for the established parties was such that by the 1990s, the old four and five party coalition formula was no longer enough to provide a majority government.

The demise of communism in Italy and the collapse of the Soviet Union removed the major external support mechanism. Both the United States and the Vatican were ready to disengage from Italian domestic politics and concentrate on other questions. By the late 1980s, Europe, too, was a force for change. The single market programme increased competition and made a corrupt administration less affordable. Liberation of capital movements meant that Italians could place their money abroad and would not help finance the public deficit unless interest rates were competitive. Business and political leaders realized that, in the new Europe, Italy could be relegated to the second division with Greece and Portugal unless it could bring its public debt under control and improve the state of its administration and infrastructure. If they had not realized, this, the Northern Leagues were there to remind them.

Dislodging the political class remained difficult since the old parties were unlikely to cooperate voluntarily in their own demise. The constitution, however, gave dissidents a weapon in the form of the citizen-initiated referendum. Although it is part of the constitution, the referendum was not introduced in Italy until 1970. The law provides that, if 500,000 signatures are gathered in favour of repealing a law, a referendum must be held. Referendums cannot be used to propose new laws. The procedure was used in the 1970s and 1980s by Christian Democrats opposed to the liberalization of divorce and abortion, but its most assiduous practioners were the Radicals who made up for their parliamentary weakness by promoting referendums. In the early 1990s, a new referendum movement headed by dissident Christian Democrat Mario Segni took aim at the electoral system and the network of corruption and patronage. Given the limitations of the referendum procedure, it was possible only to propose repealing aspects of laws so that, rather than devise a whole new system, so Segni had to proceed piecemeal. First he secured a limitation in the number of preference votes which electors could cast. In April 1993, a referendum overwhelmingly voted to limit proportional representation for the Senate. This gave the clearest signal to the political class that their days were numbered and proved the decisive event in bringing the old system down. In the same referendum, voters agreed to end state financing of political parties; decriminalize many types of drug use; and abolish the Ministries of Agriculture, State Participation, and Tourism. These measures were intended to strike directly at the system of patronage and its links with the underworld.

The success of the referendum of April 1993 gave the signal for change. The four-party coalition resigned and was replaced by a government of national unity to pave the way for constitutional reform and new elections. Headed by a non-party technocrat, Carlo Ciampi, this initially included the PDS and the Greens, though they quit when parliament refused to lift the parliamentary immunity of Bettino Craxi to allow him to be tried on corruption charges. Great hope was held out for reform and many proposals canvassed, from a British, to a French, to a German type constitution.

The most popular proposal was to change the electoral system for both houses of parliament away from proportional representation towards a majoritarian system on either British or French lines. This, it was argued, would break the power of party bosses, stabilize government and favour the alternation of parties in power as against *trasformismo*. Simulations on the basis of the 1987 election showed that this could have produced a real choice between left and right governing coalitions and the possibility of an alternation between them.[28] On the other hand, abolishing proportional representation could exclude from parliament precisely the small parties, such as *La Rete*, pressing for reform. The April 1993 referendum had indicated that the public wanted change; but it was still up to parliament to produce the detailed proposals. The Christian Democrats and the Northern Leagues supported a British-type plurality system with single-member constituencies and one round of voting. This would favour parties with concentrated territorial bases, such as the Christian Democrats in the south and the Leagues in the north. The PDS favoured a two-ballot system such as that used in France, since this could encourage the left and reformist forces to realign, with the prospect of gaining power. In the event, parliament adopted an untidy compromise. For three quarters of the seats, there would be a British-type plurality system based on single member constituencies. The remaining quarter of the seats would be chosen by proportional representation, with a 4 per cent threshold. Few outside observers had anything good to say about this compromise which may simply entrench the old parties (with the addition of the Leagues) without giving stronger or more responsible government. It could also divide the country on geographical lines, given the tendency of the British system to favour parties with strong local and regional bases.

Another proposal widely canvassed is for a stronger presidency, perhaps directly elected. This was associated with Craxi in his *decisionismo* phase and may have been somewhat discredited following his fall from grace. Decentralization and stronger regional government are ideas which go back to the founding of the state but they have been given new currency by the success of the Leagues and the collapse of the old order. Some observers were looking to the establishment of a second Republic, freed from the taint of the first; most saw reform as a long term process. Great hopes were held out for constitutional reform, but observers with a longer historical sense were aware that, without a fundamental change in attitudes and culture, mere institutional tinkering would be unlikely to achieve radical change.

REFERENCES

1. D. Hine and R. Finocchi, 'The Italian Prime Minister', *West European Politics*, 14.2 (1991), pp. 79-96.
2. P. Furlong, 'The Constitutional Court in Italian Politics', *West European Politics*, 11.3 (1988), pp. 7-23.
3. *Mondo Economico*, 2 May 1992.
4. *Il Sole 24 Ore*, 8 April 1992.
5. *La Stampa*, 10 April 1992.
6. P. Ignazi, *Dal PCI al PDS* (Bologna: Il Mulino, 1992).
7. P. Ignazi, *Dal PCI al PDS* (Bologna: Il Mulino, 1992).
8. G.Pasquino, 'Cari estinti: esistono ancora i partiti in Italia?' *Il Mulino,* 1/92, pp. 143-52.
9. R. Biorcio, 'La Lega come attore politico; dal federalismo al populismo regionalista', in R. Mannheimer (ed), *La Lega Lombarda* (Milan: Feltrinelli, 1991).
10. E.g. G. Savelli, *Che cosa vuole la Lega* (Milan: Longanesi, 1992).
11. *La Reppubblica*, 28 April 1992.
12. *L'Expresso*, 18 January 1990.
13. R. Mannheimer, 'Chi vota Lega e perché', in R. Mannheimer (ed.), *La Lega Lombarda* (Milan: Feltrinelli, 1991).
14. *La Reppubblica*, 8 April 1992.
15. G. Capano, 'Le relazioni tra attori politici e burocratici nella politica della dirigenza statale', *Rivista trimestriale di Scienza dell'Amministrazione,* 1 (1991), pp. 3-41.
16. F. Garelli, 'Le diverse Italie delle fede', *Il Mulino*, XL. 337.5 (1991), pp. 859-71.
17. B. Dente and G. Regonini, 'Politics and policies in Italy', in P.Lange and M. Regini (eds.), *State, market and social regulation. New perspectives on Italy* (Cambridge: Cambridge University Press, 1989).
18. R. Putnam, R. Leonardi and R. Nanetti, *La Pianta e le Radici* (Bologna: Il Mulino, 1985).
19. N. Tranfaglia, *Mafia, Politica e Affari. 1943-91* (Rome: Laterza, 1992).
20. R. Catanzaro, 'The Mafia', in R. Leonardi and R. Nanetti (eds.), *Italian Politics: A Review*, vol. 1 (London: Pinter 1986).
21. R. Catanzaro, 'The Mafia', in R. Leonardi and R. Nanetti (eds.), *Italian Politics: A Review*, vol. 1 (London: Pinter 1986).
22. N. Tranfaglia, *Mafia, Politica e Affari. 1943-91* (Rome: Laterza, 1992).
23. F. Sabetti and R. Catanzaro (eds.), *Italian Politics. A review.* Volume 5 (London and New York: Pinter, 1991).
24. G.M. Bellu and G. D'Avanzo, *I Giorni de Gladio. Come morì la Prima Repubblica* (Milan: Sperling and Kupfer, 1991).
25. M.A. Calabrò, *Le mani della Mafia. Vent'anni di finanza e political attraverso la storia del Banco Ambrosiano* (Rome: Associate, 1991).
26. G.M. Bellu and G. D'Avanzo, *I Giorni de Gladio. Come morì la Prima Repubblica* (Milan: Sperling and Kupfer, 1991).
27. G.M. Bellu and G. D'Avanzo, *I Giorni de Gladio. Come morì la Prima Repubblica* (Milan: Sperling and Kupfer, 1991). P. Ginsborg, *A History of Contemporary Italy. Society and Politics, 1943-1988* (Harmondsworth: Penguin, 1990).
28. S. Messina, *La Grande Riforma. Uomini e progetti per una nuova repubblica* (Rome: Laterza, 1992).

FURTHER READING

P. Ginsborg, *A History of Contemporary Italy. Society and Politics, 1943-1988* (Harmondsworth: Penguin, 1990).

D. Hine, *Governing Italy. The Politics of Bargained Pluralism* (Oxford: Clarendon, 1993).

J. Palombara, *Democracy Italian Style* (New Haven: Yale University Press, 1987).

D. Sassoon, *Contemporary Italy. Politics, Economy and Society since 1945* (London: Longman, 1986).

F. Spotts and T. Wieser, *Italy. A Difficult Democracy* (Cambridge: Cambridge University Pr

ss, 1986). *Italian Politics. A review,* published annually from 1986 by Istituto Cattaneo and Pinter Publi

hers (New York an

 London).

P. Farneti, *The Italian Party System (1945-1980),* (London and New York: Pinter, 1985).

R. Leonardi and D. Werthman, *Italian Christian Democracy,* London: Macmillan, 1989.

R. Mannheimer (ed.), *La Lega Lombarda* (Milan: Feltrinelli, 1991).

P. Lange and M. Regini (eds.), *State, market and social regulation. New perspectives on Italy* (Cambridge: Cambridge University Press, 1989).

R. Putnam, R. Leonardi and R. Nanetti, *Making Democracy Work. Civic Traditions in Modern Italy* (Princeton: Princteon University Press, 1993).

E. Santantonio, 'Italy', in E.Page and M. Goldsmith (eds.), *Central and Local Government Relations. A Comparative Analysis of West European Unitary States* (London: Sage, 1987).

Anonimo, *Come fare carriera in politica* (Padua: MEB, 1992).

S. Messina, *La Grande Riforma. Uomini e progetti per una nuova repubblica* (Rome: Laterza, 1992).

5 Germany

STATE AND NATION IN GERMANY

A German nation has long been recognized as one of Europe's peoples. A place called Germany was identified as long ago as the Roman era. Yet endless argument has raged over just who the Germans are and where their boundaries lie. The most widely accepted criterion is language. A standard German language was developed in the early modern period and disseminated after the Reformation through Luther's translation of the Bible, though marked differences in spoken dialects remain. The language was spread eastwards over the centuries by successive waves of settlers, reaching as far as the Volga river in Russia. No German state has ever encompassed all these German speakers. Yet they have claims to be part of the German nation. Defining Germany in terms of boundaries is no easier. Unlike Britain, France, Italy and Spain, it lacks natural or easily defended frontiers in the mountains or the sea.

For centuries, Germany was divided into kingdoms principalities and city states. In 1800 there were some three hundred of these, most of them owing nominal allegiance to a shadowy entity called the Holy Roman Empire. This was a leftover from the medieval Empire of Charlemagne, which in the eighteenth century was described by Voltaire as neither holy, nor Roman nor an empire. Germany's political order was brusquely overturned after 1800 by Napoleon Bonaparte who forcibly reorganized the German states and brought in his train new ideas of nationalism, order and administration forged in the French revolution and the Empire which succeeded it. After the defeat of Napoleon, the Congress of Vienna, attempting to restore the old order in Europe, consolidated Germany into thirty-eight states, but two of these were more powerful than the rest together. In the north, the kingdom of Prussia had established modern state forms in the eighteenth century and now embarked on a period of economic and military expansion. To the south, the Austrian Empire of the Habsburgs evolved as a multinational state, embracing both German and non-German speaking territories.

Ideas of German nationalism can be traced back to the eighteenth century and even earlier, but it was in the early nineteenth century that they crystallized into a demand for a unified state. As in other parts of Europe, including France itself, the French Revolution's ideals of universal brotherhood were turned into a specifically national form. This merged with German romanticism to produce an emotive mixture which could be turned to liberal democratic, or to chauvinistic, expansionist and racist purposes. The first attempts at a united Germany were made by liberal nationalists after the revolutions of 1848 had overthrown the old order in Germany and much of Europe. Meeting in Frankfurt, the liberals declared a unified German state, with a democratic, federal constitution. Although they offered the Crown to the king of Prussia, he had no interest in becoming a constitutional monarch and turned it down contemptuously. Within months, authority was re-established, the Frankfurt parliament dispersed and monarchs returned to their thrones.

With the failure of the liberal revolution, unification came to Germany by a very different route, through military might and diplomatic manoeuvring under the leadership of Otto von Bismarck, chief minister of Prussia. Bismarck engineered successive wars. Victory against Austria in 1866 established Prussia's dominance in Germany. War against France in 1870 united the German states against a common enemy and removed an obstacle to the rise of Germany as a great power. After the defeat of France, the provinces of Alsace and Lorraine were annexed and in 1871 the German Empire was proclaimed in the Palace of Versailles, the symbol of French pride. The Empire was christened the Second Reich - the first being the Holy Roman Empire- and the king of Prussia took the title of Kaiser, or emperor.

Germany's route to unification, through blood and iron, as Bismarck put it, left a deep imprint on the new state. The defeat of the liberals after 1848 and the success of Prussian might inhibited the development of parliamentary democracy. Although the Empire did have a parliament, the *Reichstag*, elected by universal male suffrage, real power lay in the hands of the Kaiser and his chief minister and with the military chiefs. Bismarck sought to assuage working-class grievances through welfare provisions in advance of other European nations, but independent labour organizations were suppressed. The manner of German unification made an implacable enemy of France, which lost the provinces of Alsace and Lorraine to the new Empire and was to fight two more wars with Germany in the next seventy years. Prussian traditions of militarism became a powerful force in politics, especially after the departure of Bismarck in 1890. Less cautious figures came to the fore, pressing for colonial expansion in imitation of other European powers and launching a naval arms race against Britain. The culmination was the first world war and the defeat in 1918 of the four great European empires, the German, the Russian, the Ottoman and the Austrian.

Responsibility for the first world war must be shared among all the great powers, but German militarism and expansionism is certainly a prime culprit. As far as the victorious powers, especially the French and the British, were concerned, the fault was entirely Germany's and they insisted that it be punished appropriately. Under the Treaty of Versailles, land was ceded to France, Belgium, Denmark and the newly created or re-created states of Poland and Czechoslovakia. Austria was reduced to its German-speaking heartland. Punitive reparations were demanded and, when these were not forthcoming, the French re-occupied the Rhineland.

The collapse of the imperial government paved the way for a democratic regime known as the Weimar Republic. Proclaimed in 1918 and led initially by the Social

Democrats and centrist parties, this came under immediate attack from both right and left. The militarist right, who had pitched the country into war, allowed the Social Democrats to take power to negotiate the humiliating peace treaty and then attacked them for stabbing Germany in the back. The revolutionary left sought to spread the Russian revolutionary message to Germany and staged an uprising which was forcibly suppressed. A massive economic crisis hit the country in 1920, with hyper-inflation which took the value of the Reichmark from ten to the dollar in 1919 to four trillion in 1923.

The Weimar Republic was ill-equipped to deal with these problems. It was rejected from the outset by the extreme left, grouped around the Communist Party and the traditional right, with support in the military and upper classes. The constitution was a weak one, with a rather pure form of proportional representation which spawned a large number of political parties. With the extremes of right and left excluded, coalitions revolved around the Social Democrats and the centrist parties. Most powers were vested in the chancellor and government, answerable to parliament, the *Reichstag*, but there was also a directly elected president with wide powers in an emergency. In the declining years of the Republic, there was a drift of power to the presidency. Despite its weaknesses, the Weimar Republic did survive the traumas of its early years, including the hyper-inflation and unemployment and by the mid 1920s appeared to be stabilizing. The economic collapse following the American stock market crash of 1929 which ushered in the Great Depression, however, brought back all the old tensions and paved the way for the rise of Adolf Hitler and the Nazi Party.

Hitler, an Austrian by birth, had served in the German army during the first world war and after the war drifted to Bavaria, then a centre for right wing intrigues. In 1922 he founded the National Socialist Workers, or Nazi party and the following year attempted a *putsch* in Munich intended to precipitate a march on Berlin and seizure of power. The attempt ended in farce and Hitler served a ten-month prison sentence in which he composed *Mein Kampf*, a statement of his ideology and plans. Nazi support was patchy during the 1920s but rose in 1930 to 18 per cent of the electorate, peaking at 37 per cent in July 1932, only to fall to 33 per cent in the second election of that year held in November. By this stage, however, the old ruling classes had decided to use Hitler to further their purposes of suppressing the Communists and Socialists, re-establishing order, accelerating Germany's rearmament and adopting a more assertive foreign policy. Hitler, installed as chancellor in 1933, was to confound them, sweeping aside the old elites as well as all organized opposition and establishing a totalitarian state known as the Third Reich.

Nazi ideology contained a confused mix of elements which the leadership could choose and combine according to purpose. There was a deep-seated hostility to democracy and liberalism and a belief in a strong state led by an all-powerful leader, the *Führer*. Nationalism was exalted and a need asserted for German expansion to the east to create *Lebensraum,* or living space at the expense of the supposedly inferior Slavic races. Racism was a powerful theme within the country, directed especially at the Jews who were blamed for Germany's economic, social and diplomatic problems. Communism was presented as the great enemy, but capitalism was not spared, especially large firms and the banks. One element in the party, indeed, shared ideas with their Communist enemies, wanting to attack capitalism and establish state control of the economy. These were known as 'beefsteak Nazis', brown on the outside and red on the inside.

In government, Hitler put much of his programme into effect. Democracy was abolished and opponents imprisoned or killed. Jews were subject to official persecution from the start, culminating during the war in the systematic and planned murder of some six million of them, together with gypsies, homosexuals, the mentally ill and other minorities. Rearmament was stepped up, Austria was absorbed and Germany's borders extended at the expense of Czechoslovakia and Poland. Public works programmes and state enterprises were established to absorb the unemployed though there was no attack on the private enterprise system. On the contrary, having come to power with the connivance of the big industrialists, Hitler proceeded to liquidate the anti-capitalist elements in his party.

It is a large and important question whether these were merely the continuation and exaggeration of traits and trends already present in German history and culture, or represented an aberration. If the former, then how could Germany hope to establish a viable democracy without building a whole new national personality? If they were an aberration, then it is important to know how they happened and why, so that Germany and other countries could avoid the experience for the future. A related question is the moral responsibility of the German people for Nazi crimes. It is true that Hitler never gained more than 37 per cent in a free vote, but there is little doubt that he was popular at least up until the second world war, and there was little serious resistance within the country to the Nazi regime. Since the second world war, West Germans have proved model democrats, but there are still critics who note that they have not faced up to these questions about their past and the related issues of moral responsibility.

The Third Reich collapsed in 1945 as a consequence of defeat in the second world war. Germany was occupied by the victorious allies, the United States, the Soviet Union and Britain, soon joined by France. Each took an occupation zone and the city of Berlin, surrounded by the Soviet zone, was itself divided into four occupation sectors.

It was not initially clear just what the occupying powers intended to do about Germany. The western powers were fairly well agreed that a punitive peace of the lines of the Versailles Treaty after the first world war would merely fan German resentment and encourage a new Hitler. One proposal was to pastoralize the country, dismantling heavy industry and the capacity to make war. Others suggested breaking it up into the old states. In the event, the western powers concentrated on the four d's, demilitarization, denazification, democratization and decentralization.

The historic state of Prussia was abolished, new regions or *Länder* drawn up and political activity was initially confined to this regional level. In the Soviet zone, there was a more punitive policy. Industrial plant was dismantled and shipped back to the Soviet Union as reparations and the Social Democratic party forcibly merged with the Communist party to make an instrument for Soviet interests.

The outbreak of the Cold War in the late 1940s formalized the division of Germany into western and eastern zones. In 1948 the western powers introduced a currency reform, which had the effect of costing the Soviets heavily. The Soviets for their part tried to force the incorporation of the city of Berlin in their zone by a land blockade which was broken only by an allied airlift. In 1949, the western allies encouraged the *Land* governments to come together to draw up a constitution for a new state. The resulting document was called the Basic Law, intended as a provisional constitution pending the reunification of the country within its 1937 boundaries. In 1949 the Federal Republic of Germany, commonly known as West Germany, came into being, recognized by the western allies and the Soviet Union. Its capital was in Bonn, a small town on the Rhine with no pretensions to grandeur, intended only as a provisional seat of government pending the reunification of Germany.

The Americans soon came to see West Germany as a potentially important ally in the Cold War against the Soviet bloc. So they pressed for the rearmament of the new state. The French, with memories of three wars in seventy years, were not so keen and insisted that Germany could rearm only within a strict alliance structure in which its forces would be effectively under allied control. After proposals for a European Defence Community in which Germany would have been absorbed, failed, the new state was admitted to NATO in 1955. There were similar qualms about the economic potential of the new German state. In 1952 the European Coal and Steel Community was set up to manage these key resources before the Saar coalfield was handed back from French occupation. In 1957 the Federal Republic was one of the signatories of the Treaty of Rome establishing the European Community. So West Germany's re-entry into the community of nations took place through collective international organizations in which its capacity for independent action was strictly limited. With continued occupation of Berlin and the presence of large numbers of troops on German soil, it was sometimes referred to as a semi-sovereign state.

In the Soviet zone, a new state, officially called the German Democratic Republic (GDR) and commonly known as East Germany, was set up in 1949. Its boundary was shifted to the west to give substantial territories to Poland and the Soviet Union and German populations were expelled from the annexed lands. A Soviet style command economy was set up and a monopoly of power placed in the hands of the SED or Communist Party. The GDR was essentially a Soviet puppet state, intended to provide a buffer against the West and a safeguard against a resurgent Germany. On various occasions, the Soviets offered to give it up, allowing German reunification on the condition that the country was permanently neutralized. The western powers and the government of the Federal Republic consistently opposed this option, though it did have some support within West Germany. Meanwhile, the East German regime was maintained by force. In 1953 a rising by workers in East Berlin was suppressed. In 1961, concerned about the number of people fleeing the country for the west, the Soviets built a wall across Berlin, sealing off their sector. Other fortifications sealed the border between East and West Germany.

Neither West Germany nor the western allies was initially prepared to recognize the East German state. West Germany laid claim to all lands within the 1937 boundaries, that is excluding the conquests of Hitler but including the lands annexed by the Soviet Union and Poland. It refused to treat East Germans as foreigners, admitting them to full citizenship rights if they succeeded in crossing the border. It declined to impose tariffs or controls on East German goods, and insisted on a clause in the European Community treaties recognizing East Germany virtually as part of the Community. Under the Hallstein doctrine, West Germany broke off diplomatic relations with any country which recognized East Germany, though for practical reasons an exception had to be made for the Soviet Union itself. The Basic Law both made clear the commitment to a unified Germany and provided a mechanism for the *Länder* in the eastern zone to join in due course.

This rigid attitude began to change after 1966 under the influence of the *Ostpolitik*. Associated particularly with Social Democratic leader Willi Brandt who was successively foreign minister and chancellor, this was an opening to the Soviet bloc intended to defuse tensions and break down barriers. It corresponded to the policy of *détente* pursued by American governments in the early 1970s. Treaties were signed with the Soviet Union and Poland which effectively recognized their annexation and Germany's new eastern border on the Oder-Neisse line. In 1972 a treaty was signed with East Germany which, while falling short of formal recognition, provided for missions from each German state in the other's capital. Finally, the 1975 Helsinki conference on peace and security in Europe, including all the European states, the Soviet Union, the USA and Canada, recognized the inviolability of existing boundaries, implicitly recognizing East Germany's eastern boundary and the existence of two German states. Two years earlier, East and West Germany had been separately admitted to the United Nations.

West Germany developed in the four decades after the end of the war into a stable, prosperous democracy and, while governments and parties made ritual noises about the desirability of reunification, this was generally considered a distant prospect. By the late 1970s, many observers maintained that East Germany, while still effectively a satellite of the Soviet Union, had established a degree of internal legitimacy through its extensive social programmes and its economic performance which, while well behind western standards, compared well with that of other eastern-bloc countries. Yet the essential guarantor of the regime was the Soviet Union. Without Soviet support, the East German Communist regime was extremely vulnerable and, in the absence of the Communist regime, East Germany had no reason to exist as a separate state. East Germany's fate was thus effectively sealed in the late 1980s when Soviet leader Mikhail Gorbachev withdrew his support from the regime.

In 1989, reform agitation, spreading from other eastern-bloc countries, hit East Germany. Hungary, itself moving towards democracy, started to allow East Germans to pass through its territory on their way to the West. Unable to rely on Soviet forces to impose his will, hard-line leader Erich Honnecker was forced to resign. Within months, the GDR, like the rest of eastern Europe, had to concede free elections. At this stage, there was a prospect of an independent East German transition to democracy, and many of those active in the democratization movement, fearing a take-over by the West and the imposition of the harsher aspects of capitalist life, wished to retain a separate state, at least for a period. They were soon overtaken by events. With the opening of the border to West Germany, a flood of refugees, including some of East Germany's most highly trained professionals, began. Under West German law, these were full citizens with every right to stay. In the preparation for democratic elections in the east, western parties moved in with their organization, money and experience, pushing aside eastern reformers. Without an experienced class of democratic leaders and with so many politicians suspected of links with the old regime, East Germany faced a vacuum of political leadership without support from the West. East German citizens, who had marched under banners proclaiming *Wir Sind Das Volk* (we are the people), changed them to *Wir Sind Ein Volk* (we are one people). Instead of reform of East Germany, they were demanding national reunification. Yet this was not so much an expression of national sentiment as demand for western living standards. Reunification was seen as a quick route to prosperity. So the option of an independent East Germany rapidly gave way to a competition over who could best secure reunification.

On the western side, there was a universal commitment to reunification in principle but greatly varying degrees of enthusiasm. Chancellor Helmut Kohl of the Christian Democrats, was determined to push through reunification as quickly as possible to establish his place in history as a modern Bismarck. After suggesting in 1989 a confederation of the two states, he saw the chance for rapid movement in 1990. The opposition Social Democrats worried more about the cost of reunification and preferred a gradual approach, in which East German living standards would first be brought in line with those in the West and political reunification would be postponed to the future. In the event, Kohl showed an uncharacteristic energy and decisiveness in pushing through unity, though the cost was extremely high.

The first stage was to have free elections in East Germany in March 1990. Against expectations, these were easily won by the Christian Democrats with their promises of speedy reunification and economic help. The second stage was an economic and monetary union. Many economists had warned about the dangers of rapid monetary integration and argued for a gradual period of adjustment, but by mid-1990 political pressures, together with the continuing flight of east Germans to the West and the sheer unwillingness of easterners to use their own currency, made this impractical.[1] So monetary union took place on 1 July 1990. The key issue was the rate at which the old East German marks would be exchanged for the western Deutschmarks. For political reasons, Kohl insisted that wages be translated at a one-for-one rate, although this would make most of East German industry uncompetitive. Savings were converted at two-for-one except for the first 4,000 marks for each citizen. West Germany's *Bundesbank* became the central bank for both countries.

The external dimension of reunification proved easier to resolve than expected, despite the potential complications. There was the attitude of the Soviet Union, suspicious of a powerful Germany and its links to the West; it was widely expected that the Soviets would revive their demand for neutralization as a condition of reunification. There was the problem of the eastern frontier. Although both German states had in the 1970s accepted the loss of their territories to the Soviet Union and Poland and the new border on the lines of the Oder and Neisse rivers, Kohl tried for a time to appease right-wing elements in West Germany by suggesting that the issue was still open. Then there was the attitude of the western allies, especially Britain and France, where historic suspicions of a powerful Germany lingered. An elaborate scheme involving the four old occupying powers, Germany and Poland, was proposed, but this was dramatically by-passed by a deal between Kohl and Gorbachev. Faced with economic and political crisis at home, Gorbachev felt in no position to block German unity and even agreed that the unified country should be a member of NATO. In return, he received a considerable package of economic aid from the West German government. The western allies could hardly oppose German reunification, to which they were officially committed but it was understood, at the particular insistence of the French, that the new Germany would be more tightly bound by a strengthened European Community.

In October 1990, reunification of the two Germanies was achieved through the mechanism provided for in the Basic Law. Five *Länder* were recreated in the east and joined the Federal Republic en bloc. In December 1990 the planned West German election was replaced by the first free all-German election since 1933. Kohl's Christian Democrat-led coalition triumphed in the first all-German election and, secure in victory, removed all remaining doubts about the eastern border of the unified state on the Oder-Neisse line. Article 23 of the Basic Law, allowing territories of the 1937 Germany to join the Federal Republic, was repealed to show the world that Germany's boundaries were fixed.

A dispute followed about the location of the national capital, an argument loaded with symbolism. Bonn's government quarter looks more like an industrial estate than the capital of a great power but, until the 1980s, this suited West Germany's modest public image. Before reunification, plans were well advanced for more permanent and prestigious buildings. A purpose-built chamber for the *Bundestag*, to replace the converted water works which had served since 1949, was completed only in 1992, along with a new office building. With reunification, there was a strong sentiment in favour of moving government back to Berlin, the national capital in Germany's days of glory. As Berlin is surrounded by the former East Germany, moving the capital there would also represent a commitment to the new *Länder*. Yet to many people, Berlin symbolized the aggressive past, including the Nazi era. In 1991 the new German parliament did vote to move the capital back to Berlin but the financial burden of unity is expected to delay the implementation of the decision.

Achieving reunification, given the external conditions, proved easier than expected. Making it work was a great deal more difficult. East German industry turned out to be less competitive than was thought and its environmental standards rudimentary. Competitiveness was hampered by the monetary union and the high level of eastern wages in relation to productivity. As had happened in Italy in the 1860s, the rapid monetary integration of two economies at vastly different stages of development had a devastating effect on the weaker partner. Investment in infrastructure and public services in the new eastern *Länder* required a massive transfer of resources from the west and Kohl soon had to break his promise not to increase taxation to pay for unity. Positions of political leadership as well as senior bureaucratic posts in the new *Länder* were almost monopolized by westerners, known as *Wessis*, causing some resentment as easterners felt that they had merely been taken over. Moving the capital to Berlin was seen as a gesture to the east and a commitment of resources, but as the expenses of reunification mounted, doubts grew as to the feasibility of a rapid move. Easterners migrating to the west, known as *Ossis*, experienced contempt akin to that felt by northern Italians for southerners. Reunification, coinciding with the collapse of the Soviet Union itself, was accompanied by a massive influx of refugees, many of them so-called ethnic Germans who have a constitutional right to settle in Germany and assume full citizenship. It also coincided with an influx of refugees from other parts of the world, taking advantage of Germany's liberal laws on political asylum. A series of incidents of extreme right wing and racist violence, directed at incomers, brought a chilling reminder of Germany's past.

Nor did the external effects of reunification proceed as smoothly as hoped. It had been hoped to tie the new Germany tightly into a united Europe and the proposals for European monetary and political union agreed in the Maastricht Treaty of 1991 were designed partly with this in mind. Yet the costs of reunification placed such a strain on German finances that many began to question whether Germany could continue to be the chief financier of European unity or surrender the Deutschmark for a new European currency. The reverberations of reunification will doubtless continue for some years in Germany and we will refer to them again in subsequent sections.

CONSTITUTION AND GOVERNMENT

Intended as a provisional arrangement, the Basic Law has served as the constitution of West Germany and then of a unified Germany since 1949. This represents the only sustained experience of stable democratic government in German history and such has been its success that, rather than design a new constitution after reunification, it was decided to keep the Basic Law largely intact. It is thus possible to describe the German experience of government almost entirely in terms of West Germany's, since East German experience has left little mark on the unified system.

Several factors explain West Germany's transition to liberal democracy after the war. The occupying powers were concerned to avoid a revival of Nazism as well as to contain Communism and undertook a purge of the old political, administrative and judicial elites. Although this was not as thorough as it might have been and some former Nazis ended up working for the United States, it did indicate a new beginning. The old, reactionary military and landed elites who had dominated the Second Reich and helped undermine the Weimar Republic, had been destroyed by Hitler who thus in an ironic way paved the way for the emergence of a democratic culture. The mass of the population, under the impact of defeat and occupation, lapsed into political apathy. Surveys showed that authoritarian and pro-Nazi sentiments survived into the 1950s but most people were content to be good Germans, leaving politics to the new democratic elites who had emerged after the war. From the early 1950s there was rapid growth, known as the *Wirtschaftswunder*, or economic miracle, which raised living standards beyond most people's dreams. Making money was seen as more important than engaging in political confrontation. The new constitution itself provided workable institutions and diffused power while encouraging cooperation and consensus in problem solving. By the late 1950s all the main political parties had come to accept the basic elements of the postwar settlement: a private enterprise economy; a generous welfare state; and West Germany's firm adherence to the Atlantic Alliance and the European Community. Extremist parties did appear from time to time but failed to make headway. Interest groups developed and became an important element in the policy process. In place of the old bureaucratic and military elites, political parties emerged as the prime actors in the new politics.

Consensus was a welcome change from the confrontation of the past, but could at times become almost stifling, so that new social movements have periodically arisen, especially among young people, to challenge it. In the 1970s there was a surge of extreme left-wing terrorism associated with the Red Army Fraction, commonly known as the Baader-Meinhof Gang. Some observers professed to see in this a resurgence of German extremism or a failure to purge the Nazi legacy of violence. Others worried that the reaction of the state to the terrorism posed a threat to civil liberties and the rule of law. Extreme right-wing groups appeared in the 1960s and made some impact in elections. These crises had, however, been overcome by the 1980s. So stable indeed, had Germany become that it had become almost uninteresting as a subject of study.

Reunification and its aftermath have raised a series of new challenges to Germany's institutions and political culture and posed new questions about its ability to cope with change. New extremist movements have emerged, especially in the former East Germany which has not had the democratic experience of the western zones. Strains are placed on the consensus by the need to accommodate the new *Länder* and pay the costs of reunification.

The Basic Law

The Basic Law is a written constitution providing for a federal state with sixteen units or *Länder*. There is a federal president, indirectly elected from the *Land* and national parliaments. The federal parliament, the *Bundestag* is directly elected through a form of proportional representation. The Chancellor, head of the government, is elected by and responsible to the *Bundestag*. The federal council or *Bundesrat* functions as a second chamber of parliament, representing the governments of the *Länder* and with power of veto over certain types of federal legislation. A Constitutional Court exists to rule on interpretation of constitutional powers and responsibilities. The process of government is pervaded by legalism and adherence to legal rules and norms, in contrast to the informal British approach. This is a legacy of the German tradition of the *Rechtsstaat*, or state of law. The constitution is also marked by a separation of powers, in imitation of the American concern with limiting the power of any institution. In the 1940s, this was seen as an essential safeguard for the liberal democratic order against subversion or abuse of power, as happened in the past. Yet separation of powers has worked in a peculiarly German way. Under the Basic Law, the various elements of government must cooperate to produce solutions, placing a premium on moderation and compromise. Practice and custom, evolving since 1949, have reinforced this tendency. While each element in the constitution has its own powers and responsibilities, the workings of government are marked by consensus and compromise and a close interlinking of institutions.

The Basic Law also entrenches a series of civil rights including freedom of expression, of assembly and association, equal rights irrespective of gender, race or religion, freedom of movement and privacy. In contrast to some other Europeans there is no guarantee of social rights, though there were efforts by left-wing parties to insert these in 1949. The right of labour to organize and engage in industrial disputes is, however, guaranteed. The religious settlement is guaranteed by providing religious teaching in schools and allowing churches to levy taxes on their members though no church is established by the state.

Constitutional amendments require the support of two-thirds of the members of both the *Bundestag* and the *Bundesrat*. There is no provision for referendums, a device associated in the German mind with dictatorship and the repression of minorities. The requirement for two thirds majorities in both chambers ensures that constitutional amendments must have the support of the main political parties and broad support from the *Länder*, but where this is present the procedure is simple. Since 1949 there have been many such changes, though none of them have been aimed at the main provisions and institutions.

Reunification did not lead to a radical change in the German constitution. Instead, the Basic Law remained largely intact, with the eastern *Länder* adhering to it. Since then, however, a number of demands have been made for constitutional revision. Some of these involve commitments to rights and obligations, such as a firmer statement of women's rights or a constitutional defence for the environment. The government has pressed for amendments allowing German troops to serve in peacekeeping operations outside NATO, in recognition of German''s new role as a major power. It has also sought to restrict the right of political asylum, to control the influx of refugees. There are demands for a more participative form of government, including a provision for referendums. Some of the *Länder* want a revision of their powers and firmer guarantees for their autonomy, which has been eroded by the expansion of federal power and the effects of reunification. More radical proposals involve redrawing the federal map altogether to create a pattern of fewer and larger *Länder*. As all amendments require a two-thirds majority both in the elected *Bundestag* and in the *Bundesrat*, representing the *Länder*, they need a very broad partisan and social consensus. They have thus tended to be limited to detailed matters, on which the parties and the *Länder* have reached agreement. Radical change is extremely difficult.

The Federal President

The Basic Law carefully restricts the powers of the president, who is elected by a college comprising the members of the *Bundestag* and an equal number of representatives from the *Länder*. Presidential powers are defined and circumscribed in the Basic Law and the office is largely ceremonial and symbolic. Presidential powers are exercised on the initiative of others and the president has no emergency powers. Yet the office is not without importance. A German president has a role in moral leadership whose importance is magnified by the need to make up for the past. President Richard von Weizsäcker has reminded Germans of their obligations, of the dangers of extremism and intolerance and of the need for reconciliation. He strove to calm international fears when Chancellor Helmut Kohl played politics with the issue of Germany's eastern border with Poland. Very occasionally, the president needs to take decisions on procedural or partisan matters, as in 1982 when President Karl Carstens had to decide whether to approve a dissolution of the *Bundestag* after the government had engineered its own defeat (see below). Since 1949 there have been six presidents, all chosen from the ranks of active politicians, though once elected they have risen above party to be the embodiment of the state.

Chancellor and Government

The head of government in Germany is the chancellor. In order to remove the ambiguities over the respective powers of chancellor and president which had bedevilled the Weimar Republic, the Basic Law stipulates clearly that it is the former who proposes government measures. The chancellor is elected by the *Bundestag* (parliament) at the beginning of each legislature. A candidate is proposed by the president and must receive the support of an absolute majority of all *Bundestag* members to be elected at the first ballot. If the president's nominee fails, another candidate may be elected, again by absolute majority. If no individual is elected by a majority within fourteen days, a candidate obtaining the largest number of votes can be elected, or the *Bundestag* dissolved. This in intended to instil a sense of urgency into the *Bundestag* members through the threat of a new election. In practice, the president nominates the candidate of the winning coalition, who has always been elected at the first ballot.

Once elected, the chancellor holds office for the entire term unless removed by a constructive vote of no confidence. Such a vote requires that an absolute majority of all members of the *Bundestag* vote to replace the chancellor with another named individual. This provision, also intended to avoid the instability of Weimar, gives the chancellor considerable security of tenure. The constructive vote of no confidence has been successfully used only once, in 1982 when the Free Democratic Party broke their coalition with the Social Democrats and voted to install Christian Democrat leader Helmut Kohl as chancellor. It is also possible for the chancellor to call for a vote of confidence. If this is not supported by an absolute majority of *Bundestag* members, there is provision for a dissolution of the *Bundestag* and a new election. This has been used on two occasions, in 1972 and 1982 when governments deliberately arranged to lose votes so as to engineer a dissolution and early election. The constitutional provisions have ensured that there has been great stability in the office of chancellor. Between the founding of the Federal Republic in 1949 and 1992, there were just six chancellors, as shown in Table 5.1.

Germany's system of proportional representation has ensured that only on one occasion has a party ever gained an absolute majority and been able to govern on its own. So apart from the years 1957-61, all governments have been coalitions. There have been three coalition formulas in the years since 1949. The centre-right formula groups the Christian Democrats (CDU) with the Free Democrats (FDP). This formula provided governments in the early 1950s, in the early 1960s and since 1982. The centre-left formula groups the Social Democrats with the Free Democrats and provided the government between 1969 and 1982. The grand coalition groups the Social Democrats with the Christian Democrats and governed between 1966 and 1969. Changes in the government in West Germany have come about only through the break-up of coalitions and never as a direct result of elections. Yet the rigorous procedures of the Basic Law and the fact that for most of the time there have

Table 5.1 Governments and Chancellors in the Federal Republic of Germany

Chancellor	coalition		dates
Konrad Adenauer CDU	centre-right	CDU-FDP	1949-57
	singleparty	CDU	1957-61
	centre-right	CDU-FDP	1961-63
Ludwig Erhard CDU	centre-right	CDU-FDP	1963-69
Kurt Kiesinger CDU	grand coalition	CDU-SPD	1966-69
Willi Brandt SPD	centre-left	SPD-FDP	1969-74
Helmut Schmidt SPD	centre-left	SPD-FDP	1974-82
Helmut Kohl CDU	centre-right	CDU-FDP	1982-

Source: Die Bundesregierung, Volkshandbuch, 1988
(Rheinbreitbach: Neue Darmstädter Verlagsanstalt)

been only three parties in parliament have spared Germany the coalition instability found in the Weimar Republic, the French Fourth Republic or contemporary Italy.

The chancellor's status and powers are derived from the Basic Law but are rooted in history, especially the experience of the Second Reich and Weimar and have been further shaped by politics and practice in the years since 1929. The chancellor is responsible for setting the general policy of the government and nominates ministers to take charge of individual departments. Collectively, these comprise the federal government. Successive chancellors have built up their own administrative apparatus in the federal Chancellery in order to direct and coordinate the activities of government. There are over four hundred officials in the Chancellery, supplying information and following the activities of individual ministries. Most federal ministries are quite small, since administration is the responsibility of the *Länder*, which puts them in a weak position. There is collective responsibility so that ministers are jointly responsible for the policy and work of the government, though in practice this is weaker than in some other countries and ministries can easily be captured by the interest groups in their policy field.

Chancellors have varied in ability, strength of personality and the amount of interest they take in policy detail. Some, like Konrad Adenauer or Helmut Schmidt, have been very interventionist, dominating their governments. Others, like Helmut Kohl, have given individual ministers freer rein. In the early years of the Federal Republic, people spoke of a chancellor democracy, so great was the power of the office. In part this stemmed from the status of Konrad Adenauer, the first chancellor. Adenauer possessed not only the formal powers of the office but a secure party base, the support of the western powers, a forceful personality and a favourable political and economic situation. A Catholic conservative, Adenauer had been mayor of Cologne before the Nazi takeover. After the German defeat, he became leader of the new Christian Democratic party and forged close links with the American occupying power. With the establishment of the Federal Republic he secured West Germany's position within the western alliance and the European Community and presided over the economic miracle. Germans by and large retreated from political activity in the postwar years and in the absence of an effective opposition, Adenauer was able to dominate government almost completely. His immediate successors, Ludwig Erhard and Kurt Kiesinger, did not enjoy the same status and were beset by quarrels with their party. Willi Brandt, chancellor from 1969 to 1974 was forced to resign after one of his staff was revealed as an East German spy, but he had already been seriously weakened by tensions within his own Social Democratic Party. Only Helmut Schmidt, SPD chancellor from 1974 to 1982 had the same forceful personality as Adenauer but he too faced increasing opposition from within his own party, especially from the left wing. Helmut Kohl, in office since 1982, soon acquired a reputation for being disinterested in policy detail and for running his government on a loose rein. Only in the reunification events of 1989-90 did he show real drive and leadership.

In theory anyone can be appointed a minister, giving the chancellor great scope to mould the composition and policy of the government. In practice, German politics is dominated by parties and the overwhelming majority of ministers are members of parliament who have risen through the ranks of the governing parties. Control of the government and the ability to hire and fire ministers therefore depends on a chancellor's control of the party and whether powerful individuals within it need to be accommodated. Since nearly all governments have been coalitions among parties, there is a further round of bargaining over appointments and portfolios when a government is formed. Adenauer's successors as chancellor have been unable to hire and fire ministers at will. The Free Democrats have monopolized the position of foreign minister since 1969, in coalition first with the Social Democrats and then with the Christian Democrats. When long-serving Foreign Minister Hans Dietrich Genscher resigned in 1992, the Free Democrats in the *Bundestag* were able to insist on nominating his replacement, against the wishes both of the chancellor and their own party leader. Helmut Kohl has constantly had to balance pressures from his Free Democrat coalition partners with those from the CSU, the independent Bavarian wing of the Christian Democrats. His success in achieving rapid reunification of Germany enormously enhanced his prestige in 1990 and 1991 but tensions soon reappeared within the coalition. Helmut Schmidt's coalition of Social Democrats and Free Democrats came apart in 1982 because he could not reconcile the demands of the two parties. German coalition governments are stable and only occasionally break up, but this stability requires a constant balancing of interests and prevents a chancellor from accumulating excessive power.

Parliament

Parliament in Germany comprises two elements. The *Bundestag* is a directly elected chamber to which the government in responsible. The *Bundesrat* is an intergovernmental committee representing the federal *Länder*, which serves as a second chamber .

Bundestag elections take place every four years according to a hybrid system which provides both for constituency members and for proportional representation. Each elector has two votes, one for a constituency member and one for a party list. Half the members of parliament are elected from constituencies on a first-past-the-post basis. The remaining seats are allocated from the party lists drawn up in the various *Länder* so that the overall balance of parties in the *Bundestag* corresponds to the proportions of votes obtained nationally by the party lists. This provides for overall proportional representation while retaining the principle of the constituency representative. Of course, it does produce two classes of member, those with constituencies and those who owe their seats to their place on a party list. In practice, though, both enjoy the same status. Some prominent party figures contest constituencies but insure themselves by also taking a high place on the party list. There is no stigma attached to losing in the constituency and having to come in via the list.

In order to eliminate very small parties and provide stability in the *Bundestag*, parties which fail to secure 5 per cent of the national vote or win three constituency seats are excluded altogether. This has meant that for most of the time since the early 1950s there have only been three parties represented in the *Bundestag*, which greatly simplifies coalition making. The entry of the Greens in the 1980s and the consequences of reunification in 1990 threatened this stability and may make for more complicated coalition manoeuvring in the future. Table 5.2 shows the balance of seats following the 1990 election, the first

Table 5.2 Parties represented in German Bundestag after 1990 election

Party	Seats
Christian Democrats (CDU)	268
Christian Democrats (CSU)	50
Free Democrats	79
GOVERNMENT COALITION TOTAL	397
Social Democrats	239
Greens	8
Ex-Communists	17
Independent	1
Total	662

after reunification. If it proves impossible to form a government from the parties represented, it is possible to dissolve the *Bundestag* before the end of its term and hold new elections but the Basic Law makes this deliberately difficult in an effort to stabilize governments and force politicians to cooperate.

The *Bundestag*, as the heir of the old German Reichstag, is not the centre of political life in Germany. Chancellor and government are responsible to it but in the German tradition the limits to their powers are set by law rather than by political control. *Bundestag* members are nearly all elected on party tickets and the parties, which are officially recognized, dominate parliamentary life. Procedural matters are determined by the Council of Elders, comprising the leaders of the party caucuses or *Fraktionen*. A great deal of work is delegated to committees on which the parties are represented proportionally and whose reports are usually not challenged in the chamber as a whole. Members on committees must vote and speak according to the party line unless given permission to do otherwise. Votes are closely controlled by the party leadership and the *Fraktionen* and members must seek party approval to place parliamentary questions.

Members have increasingly tended to come from the ranks of the civil service or from interest groups. Civil servants have generous privileges allowing them to take leave of absence to serve in politics and return at any time with no loss of seniority or pension rights. At one time, they were even able to retain both parliamentary and civil service salaries. This colonization of politics by the civil service, an inheritance from the Second Reich and Weimar, has increased steadily over the years. In 1992, 37 per cent of members of parliament, including nearly half the Social Democrats, were public officials. Just 1.2 per cent were manual workers. One in six CDU members was in the union for senior officials.[2] Interest groups have also increased their presence in parliament by getting parties to nominate their spokespersons on to electoral lists. Such members then ensure that they are put on to the relevant parliamentary committees where they can help pursue group interests. In other countries, this might give rise to serious conflicts of interest and loyalty between the member's party and the interest group. In Germany, such conflicts to which this might give rise are moderated by the consensual style of policy making which has developed in postwar Germany, in which group interests are negotiated and compromises made among them.

Among the *Bundestag*'s most important tasks is the election of the chancellor at the beginning of the legislature. Thereafter the provision for the constructive vote of no confidence makes it very difficult to remove the chancellor. In the German tradition, ministers and other public servants are seen as answerable to the law rather than political control, which reduces the status of the *Bundestag*. Scrutiny of government finances, once the *Bundestag* has voted on budgetary allocations and taxes, is mainly carried out by independent auditors rather than parliamentarians. The *Bundestag*, however, has gradually developed mechanisms to scrutinize government. There is a question period in the chamber at which ministers have to answer for their actions. The *Bundestag* can establish committees of investigation.

As a national legislature, the *Bundestag* has the task of passing laws but this role, too, is limited compared with many other legislatures. Most federal legislation is administered by the *Länder* and many federal statutes take the form of framework laws allowing the *Länder* to fill in the details. Much of the work is delegated to committees, where the important work is done and amendments discussed and agreed upon. In contrast to other legislatures, civil servants as well as ministers participate in the work of *Bundestag* committees, explaining the bill to members and generally helping its passage. Generally governments are able to get their way with legislation by using their loyal majorities in the chamber and committees. Yet this is not a system of adversary politics, where majority governments push through matters over the ritual protests of opposition parties. Postwar German political culture has stressed the need for consensus and compromise. The strong presence of interest group representatives among the members serving on committees further forces governments to negotiate over the precise content of laws.

The *Bundesrat*, or federal council, acts as a second chamber of parliament, though in reality it is an intergovernmental committee. It is not directly elected by appointed by the governments of the federal *Länder*, who can send along any member of the *Land* government. Its composition thus changes whenever there is a change in government in any *Land*. Much of the work is done in committees, where *Land* governments can and usually do send civil servants to represent them. *Land* representatives in the *Bundesrat* and its committees are mere delegates of their governments and have to vote as their governments instruct them. Representation is weighted to give more seats to the larger *Länder*, but not in proportion to population. The number of seats per land varies only between three and six, so the biggest *Land*, North Rhine-Westphalia, has just twice as many seats as Bremen, although it has 24 times the population. Table 5.3 gives the distribution of seats among the *Länder*.

All bills proposed by the government are sent first to the *Bundesrat* for scrutiny, allowing the *Länder* to express their concerns before a bill goes to the *Bundestag*. After passage in the

Table 5.3 Population of German Länder and seats in Bundesrat		
Land	Population million	Seats
North Rhine-Westphalia	16.7	6
Bavaria	10.9	6
Baden-Württemberg	9.3	6
Lower Saxony	7.2	6
Hesse	5.5	4
Saxony	5.0	4
Rhineland-Palatinate	3.6	4
Berlin	3.3	4
Saxony-Anhalt	3.0	4
Brandenburg	2.7	4
Schleswig-Holstein	2.6	4
Thuringia	2.5	4
Mecklenburg-West Pomerania	2.1	4
Hamburg	1.6	3
Saarland	1.1	3
Bremen	0.7	3
TOTAL	77.7	69

Source: Economist, 6 October 1992

Bundestag, all bills, whether they are government bills or originate in parliament, are sent back to the *Bundesrat* for approval. Three types of bill can be vetoed by the *Bundesrat* at this stage:

- bills to change the constitution, which require a two thirds majority in each chamber;
- bills affecting tax revenues and finances shared with the *Länder*;
- bills on federal law which would be administered by the *Länder*.

This amounts to about half of all legislation. In 1992, the government brought forward a proposal requiring *Bundesrat* approval for any further transfers of sovereignty to the European Community, whether they affect federal or *Land* competences. This was a response to *Länder* concerns about the implications of the Maastricht treaty on the federal system.

For other bills, the *Bundesrat* can register objections. These objections are sent back to the *Bundestag*, which can over-ride them only by an absolute majority of members. If the objection has been passed by a two-thirds majority in the *Bundesrat*, then a two-thirds majority is required in the *Bundestag* to over-ride it. Most differences between the *Bundestag* and *Bundesrat* are settled in the Mediation Committee, comprising equal numbers from each house. This has no decision-making powers but is usually able to produce compromises acceptable to both sides. Germany's consensual style of policy making comes into play here. *Bundesrat* and Mediation Committee meetings are not dramatic affairs, or marked by oratory. Rather they are business-like committee meetings intended to forge solutions and reach agreement.

The *Bundesrat*'s task is to represent *Land* interests, but as Germany has a national party system, with the same parties operating at both levels of government, there is also a party dimension to the relations between the two legislative chambers. Until 1969, the Christian Democrat-led coalition held a majority in both chambers and relations were quite harmonious. Thereafter, the Social Democrats were in power at federal level, while the Christian Democrats still controlled the *Bundesrat*. A rather conflictual period followed in which the Christian Democrats sought to use the *Bundesrat* in a partisan manner, to frustrate the government in Bonn but, following some court rulings clarifying federal powers, this conflict subsided. After 1982, the Christian Democrats again controlled both levels. By the late 1980s the pendulum had swung back and Social Democrats again controlled the *Bundesrat*. Reunification and the accession of the eastern *Länder* briefly gave control back to the Christian Democrats, but by 1992 they had lost it again as a result of poor *Land* election results in the west. This put the Social Democrats in a powerful position since their consent was required both for changes in the constitution and for a range of policy and financial decisions.

Germany's legislative process is complex. Bills may be introduced by the government or a minimum of 26 members of the *Bundestag*. Government bills go first to the *Bundesrat* to determine if there is a strong *Land* interest or objections.

Then they go to the *Bundestag*, where the Council of Elders, dominated by the parties, determines procedure. There is a formal first reading before the bill is sent to committee. On return to the chamber, it is given a full second reading and a third reading. It then returns, in its amended form to the *Bundesrat*. If there are objections or further amendments here, it proceeds to the Mediation Committee. Finally, the completed bill passes back to the government and thence to the president for signature.

The Constitutional Court

Responsibility for upholding the Basic Law belongs to the Constitutional Court, at Karlsruhe. It resolves jurisdictional disputes between the federal government and the *Länder* or among branches of the federal government and parliament, determines the constitutionality of laws and guarantees citizen rights under the constitution. Jurisdictional disputes can be referred to the Court by the federal or a *Land* government, the federal president, one of the chambers of parliament, the parties or an individual member of the *Bundestag*. Matters concerning the constitutionality of laws can be referred to the Court only in two cases: where the federal Cabinet or one third of the members of the *Bundestag* consider that a law violates the constitution; or where another Court which is hearing a case involving the law requires guidance on the constitutionality of the law. References from *Bundestag* members are made after the law has been passed but before it has been implemented. Not surprisingly, it is invariably the parliamentary opposition which makes such references. Individual citizens can appeal to the Court only where they consider that their fundamental Basic Law rights have been violated by the actions of a public authority.

Members of the Constitutional Court are appointed half by the *Bundestag* and half by the *Bundesrat*. In each case a two-thirds majority is needed, which forces the political parties to agree on a list of nominees. In practice, the parties share nominations among them and many judges have known party affiliations. This has not led to an overt politicization of the Constitutional Court, though patterns of interpretation do differ somewhat according to the political loyalties of judges. The Court does not merely rule on the constitutionality or otherwise of laws. It analyses them in detail to indicate which parts are constitutional and provides guidance on how the law should be interpreted and implemented. In this way, it becomes part of the policy process.

Most references to the Court come from individuals considering that their rights have been violated but very few of these are upheld. Even on serious matters such as the 1972 decree banning radicals from the public service, the Court has tended to side with government, arguing that democracy and the constitutional order must be defended. Between 1951 and 1990, 198 federal laws, or 4.6 per cent of the total, were judged to be unconstitutional.[3] Although this is a small proportion, it includes some important and controversial issues such as abortion law, radio and television and the financing of political parties. Most of these were referred to the Court by the opposition parties in the federal parliament and have attracted criticism that the judiciary is merely an extension of politics. Cases involving the respective rights of elements of the federal government or the division of powers between the federal and *Land* governments have been rather few.

PARTIES AND ELECTIONS

In the early years of the Federal Republic, there was a rather fragmented party system, especially on the conservative side of the spectrum. By the end of the 1950s, however, the minor parties had largely disappeared and fragmentation gave way to a system of two large parties and one small one. Between 1961 and 1983, only the Christian Democrats (CDU/CSU), the Social Democrats (SPD) and the Free Democrats (FDP) were represented in the *Bundestag*. In 1983 the West German Greens won seats for the first time. Although they lost all their seats in 1990, they remain important in some *Länder* and may well come back into the *Bundestag* in future. Reunification brought in some smaller parties from the east, helped by a ruling that, for the 1990 election alone, the 5 per cent threshold should be applied separately in eastern and western Germany. For the most part, however, the western party system was simply transferred to the east and the smaller parties there may not survive long. There have also been recurrent revivals of the extreme right, most recently in the wake of reunification. Although these have so far not posed a serious threat to the party system as a whole they have made inroads at *Land* level and may complicate federal politics in the future.

Parties are recognized and encouraged in the Basic Law as an essential element in democracy. The *Bundestag* is organized on a party basis, with few possibilities for independents, even if they could be elected, to play a part in its work. Parties opposed to the democratic order may be banned by order of the Constitutional Court, though the Communist and neo-Nazi parties banned in the 1950s were able to reconstitute themselves under other names. Parties also receive generous government funding, distributed on the basis of votes to all parties which gain more than 0.5 per cent of the national vote. The Greens, who have a relatively small membership in relation to their vote, benefit greatly from this. Public funding partly frees parties from dependence on private finance, though there have been scandals over business contributions and the exchange of campaign contributions for favours in government. In the early 1980s, a scandal erupted over revelations that the Flick company had made payments to all the main parties in exchange for governmental concessions. State funding enables each major party to operate a *Stiftung*, or foundation, to generate policy ideas and publish literature. German political parties have also been active abroad, providing financial support for their counterparts in countries emerging from dictatorship, such as Spain and Portugal in the 1970s. In 1989, a non-election year, the Christian Democrats and Social Democrats spent 280 million and 275 million Deutschmarks, while the Free Democrats and Greens spent 43 million and 58 million Deutschmarks respectively.[4]

Party competition is dominated by the Christian Democrats and the Social Democrats. Since the 1950s these have functioned as *Volksparteien*, or catch-all parties, seeking to appeal to a broad range of voters and pitching their appeal to the moderate centre. Yet the proportional electoral system ensures that neither of these can usually command a majority on its own and coalition governments must therefore be formed. Unless the two big parties form a grand coalition with each other, as in the period 1966-9, then one of them must coalesce with the Free Democrats. It is the Free Democrats who are the main beneficiaries of the electoral system. They rarely win seats in the constituencies, but consistently pick up seats from the party lists. Their very survival is due to the willingness of many voters to give their constituency vote to the major coalition party and the list vote to the Free Democrats in the belief that this balances their choice. In reality, it does not since the overall balance of seats is determined by the list alone, but this type of split-ticket voting helps keep the Free Democrats alive. In 1990. they won 7 per cent of the constituency vote but 11 per cent of the list vote. Other parties rarely manage to cross the five per cent threshold. The Free Democrats' decisions on coalition making thus determines the composition of governments. Indeed, there has never been a change of government in West Germany following an election. The changes, in 1966, 1969 and 1982, have all followed shifts in coalition patterns among the three parties in the *Bundestag*. Since the 1980s, however, party loyalties have begun to break down and the big parties, especially the Social Democrats, have seen their vote eroded. This may complicate elections and coalition behaviour in the future. Figure 5.1 gives the trend in party support since 1949 for West Germany and, in 1990, united Germany.

Figure 5.1 Percentage vote for parties, national elections,
1949-90

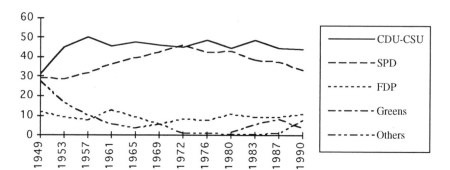

The Christian Democrats

The conservative side of German politics is dominated by the Christian Democratic Union (CDU) and its Bavarian ally the Christian Social Union (CSU). Both were formed in the postwar period so that, unlike their Social Democrat rivals, they lack deep historical roots. Divisions between Catholics and Protestants, agricultural and industrial interests and regions had prevented the emergence of a strong conservative or middle-class party under the Empire or the Weimar Republic. Middle class Catholics had been represented by the *Zentrum* (Centre Party) and the Bavarian Party, while Protestants divided their votes in several ways. After the war, there were efforts in some regions to revive the *Zentrum*, and a Bavarian party survived until the early 1950s. These were, however, eclipsed by the new Christian Democratic Party, which for the first time united both Catholics and Protestants under the leadership of Konrad Adenauer, a former mayor of Cologne and opponent of the Nazis. With the tacit support of the occupying Allies, Adenauer was able to forge a pragmatic, conservative party which by the mid-1950s had absorbed its main rivals on the right.

From the outset, the CDU set out to be a *Volkspartei*, uniting Catholics and Protestants, farmers and city dwellers, and even the middle and working classes. Its ideology was lightly worn, based on rather general Christian Democratic principles about the unity of society, traditional social values, the subsidiary role of government and the need to combine the market with an element of social concern. In the early days, there was an organized left wing around Jacob Kaiser, committed to a more active role for government and a collectivist approach. By 1949, this wing had been defeated and the party rallied round the formula of the social market, associated with Ludwig Erhard, economics minister between 1949 and 1963 and father of the German economic miracle. The social market was based on the primacy of free enterprise in economic matters, combined with government responsibility and a welfare state in social matters. Under Adenauer, the party was also associated with strong anti-communism, support for the United States and the western alliance in the Cold War, and the promotion of European integration.

Under the chancellorships of Adenauer (1949-63) and Erhard (1963-6), these became the basic lines of German policy, eventually accepted by the other parties as well. The party itself played little role in policy making. Its rather small membership followed the lead of Adenauer, content to leave decisions in the hands of the leadership, as was the public at large in the postwar era. Loss of office in 1969 forced a reappraisal of party policy and strategy. Still fervently anti-Communist, the CDU/CSU opposed the *Ostpolitik* of the Brandt government, including the normalization of relations with East Germany and the treaties with the Soviet Union and Poland. There were internal debates over domestic policy, including the welfare state and economic management. Other western conservative parties in opposition in this period adopted neo-liberal economic theories, emphasizing deregulation and privatization and called for drastic cutbacks in public expenditure and the welfare state. German Christian Democrats made only limited gestures in this direction. It is true that Germany did not have a large nationalized industrial sector like Britain or France, so that the scope for privatization was limited. It does, however, have a rather highly regulated labour market, important public monopolies in communications and transport, and an elaborate welfare state. Christian Democrats attacked their Social Democrat successors in government over public spending and called for a rolling back of the state in general terms, but with rather few specific proposals.

In 1982, when the Christian Democrats under Helmut Kohl returned to power in coalition with the Free Democrats, they proclaimed a *Wende*, or turnaround in policy, in the direction of neo-liberalism and deregulation. Some cuts were introduced in welfare services and public spending, but generally change was rather modest. Those changes which did occur were often forced on government by international and European forces or the impact of reunification, rather than stemming from the party programme. In foreign policy, the *Ostpolitik* was continued essentially unchanged even after the United States abandoned *détente*, and Free Democrat Hans Dietrich Genscher remained foreign minister. Against American opposition and the threat of sanctions, the Kohl government proceeded with plans for a natural gas pipeline from Siberia to western Europe.

The CDU's pragmatic, centre-right stance also owes something to the penetration of the party by interest groups which restrain any ideological impulses. Employers are represented through the *Wirtschaftsrat*, which supports market economic principles. A small business organization, the *Mittelstandvereinigung*, is more protectionist in policy.[5] Farmers are highly influential, especially in the Bavarian CSU, and have insisted on maintenance of the European Community's Common Agricultural Policy. As in other Christian Democratic parties, there is a trade union wing but this has declined in influence over the years. Religious groups within the party have also lost influence, though they do help to shape party attitudes on social issues.

In East Germany, the Christian Democratic Party operated as an obedient satellite of the dominant SED. It was generally considered that this would be a disadvantage at the time of reunification, since it would be tainted with its collaboration with the Communist regime. Many observers further assumed that the social democratic traditions of pre-Hitler eastern Germany, which is largely Protestant, would reassert themselves. In the event, the eastern Christian Democratic Party was largely taken over by its western counterpart and was able to distance itself from the old regime. Social democracy was widely rejected as merely half way to capitalism and at the East German elections of March 1990 and the all-German elections of December 1990, Kohl was able to offer East Germans the promise of western standards or prosperity. On both occasions, the Christian Democrats triumphed in the eastern *Länder*. Soon, however, disillusion set in and it is unlikely that the Christian

Democrat's performance in 1990 is an accurate guide to their long-term strength in the eastern regions.

The Christian Social Union (CSU) operates only in Bavaria, where the CDU does not present candidates. In the *Bundestag* they form a single parliamentary group, whether in government or opposition. Yet there are differences between the two. Bavaria is an overwhelmingly Catholic region and the CSU, while it does attract middle-class Protestant support, is more Catholic in leadership and attitudes than the CDU. Under its long-time leader, Franz Josef Strauss, the CSU was more ideological and consistently to the right of the CDU. Strauss' rather forceful nationalism put him at odds with the rest of the German political establishment and he was a strong opponent of *Ostpolitik*. From his Bavarian base, he sought to expand his influence in German politics and to minimize the weight of the Free Democrats in the Bonn coalition. He would threaten regularly to end his alliance with the CDU and to present candidates outside Bavaria but each time his bluff was called when the CDU retaliated by proposing itself to run candidates within Bavaria. Strauss' influence peaked in 1980 when he was able to force himself on to the CDU/CSU alliance as chancellor-candidate. His aggressive personality and right-wing views, however, did not appeal to voters and, after losing the election, he retreated to Bavaria to assume the post of minister-president in the Igovernment. Following Strauss' death in 1988, CSU influence in Bonn declined further. After reunification, it failed in an effort to establish a sister party in the east. As chancellor, Helmut Kohl has been able to play the CSU against the Free Democrats within the governing coalition. Although this had involved a difficult balancing act, it has moderated policy and kept the governing coalition anchored to the centre-right.

The Social Democrats

The German Social Democratic Party (SPD) traces its origins to the nineteenth century. Although persecuted under Bismarck, it benefited from the system of universal male suffrage which existed in the Empire. On the eve of the first world war, it was the largest party in the German parliament. Since power was closely guarded by the Kaiser and his ministers, this did not give it a great deal of power and the Social Democrats tamely supported the war when it came in 1914. They played a more important role in the Weimar Republic, supplying the first president, Friedrich Ebert, and serving in many of the coalition governments. Yet they failed to save democracy from the extremists. Outflanked on the left by the Communists, who had split away after the Soviet Revolution, they combined a marxist rhetoric with a timid reformism in practice. Their vote, which had been as high as 38 per cent in 1919, slumped to 25 per cent in 1930 and 18 per cent in the last democratic election, in 1933. Along with the other democratic parties, they were then banned by Hitler and their leaders imprisoned, killed or driven into exile.

The SPD was refounded after the war under the leadership of Kurt Schumacher and carved out a distinct policy profile in the new Republic. Schumacher was fiercely anti-Communist and opposed the forcible merger of the Social Democratic and Communist Parties in eastern Germany into the new Socialist Unity Party (SED). Fervently nationalist, he supported a united but neutralized Germany and opposed rearmament and entry into NATO. He also opposed German participation in the European Coal and Steel Community, forerunner of the European Economic Community. In domestic policy, the SPD was committed to a fundamentalist Socialist programme, including widespread state control, planning and nationalization and opposed Erhard's social market concept. This proved a political miscalculation and the SPD vote stagnated through the 1950s at around 30 per cent, while the Christian Democrats made steady gains at the expense of the smaller parties.

Schumacher's death in 1952 was followed by a modification of SPD policy, but it was 1959 before the party achieved a radical reappraisal. At its conference that year at Bad Godesberg, it abandoned entirely its marxist legacy and moved into the political centre. Specifically, it dropped proposals for state control and planning in favour of the market economy. It accepted rearmament and membership of NATO and supported moves towards European integration. In due course, it was to become a fervent advocate of European unity through the EC. This policy shift brought it into the mainstream of the German consensus, differing from the Christian Democrats only on matters of emphasis. As a *Volkspartei*, the SPD was now able to reach out to the new middle classes and the party's vote steadily moved up to around the 40 per cent level.

By 1966 it was sufficiently close in policy terms to the CDU to form a grand coalition with them, its first experience in government since the Weimar Republic. Social Democrats took the key ministries of Foreign Affairs, Economics and Justice.[6] Three years later, it formed a new coalition with the Free Democrats, to produce the first real alternation of power in the history of the Federal Republic. 1972 saw its vote share peak at 46 per cent, the only occasion on which it has overtaken the Christian Democrats. The SPD-FDP coalition survived for thirteen years, under the chancellorship first of Willi Brandt (1969-74), then of Helmut Schmidt (1974-82). Brandt's main legacy was the *Ostpolitik,* started when he was foreign minister under the grand coalition. This was a programme to normalize relations with the Soviet Union and eastern Europe and promote contacts between the two parts of Germany. In domestic politics, there were some social reforms and an extension of co-determination in industry. Brandt was forced to resign in 1974 when one of his aides was unmasked as an East German spy, though he continued to be influential as chairman of the Social Democratic Party and later as president of the Socialist International. His successor, Schmidt, was a hard-headed politician with little sympathy for left-wing ideas. Following the world economic crisis of the 1970s, he imposed policies of fiscal austerity and wage restraint, which brought the government into conflict with its natural trade union allies. He supported American proposals to deploy medium-range cruise missiles, a policy fiercely opposed by the party's left wing and a substantial section of German and European opinion. He pressed ahead with the development of nuclear power, against the protests of environmentalists. Yet at the same time he came under pressure from his Free Democratic coalition partners who wanted more cuts in public expenditure and social programmes. In 1982, the coalition government broke up and the Free Democrats joined forces with the Christian Democrats in a new coalition under Helmut Kohl.

In opposition after 1982, the Social Democrats were beset from both left and right. To their left, the Greens made inroads into the youth vote with their programme of environmentalism and pacifism. To their right, the governing coalition offered growth and prosperity to the middle classes. If the party moved to the right, it would alienate these young voters and lose ground to the Greens. If it moved towards the Greens it risked alienating the centrist voters and also the trade unions and blue-collar voters in heavy industry, who supported nuclear power. These traditionally Social Democratic voters were declining in number and would never be enough to put the party back in power but they could not be neglected entirely. In the event, the party moved rather to the left and adopted a number of environmentalist themes in an effort to put together a new broad coalition. Yet it continued to lose votes in 1983 and 1987.

Reunification posed additional problems for the Social Democrats. They had chosen as their chancellor-candidate for 1990 Oscar Lafontaine, minister-president of the Saarland, a member of the younger leadership generation and considered the best candidate to win back support from the Greens. Lafontaine was very cautious on reunification, warning of the costs and advocating a gradual process of adjustment. In the East German elections of March 1990, this message was overwhelmed by Kohl's promises of rapid movement to West German living standards. The Social Democrats managed just over 20 per cent of the East German vote. In the all-German election of December 1990, their vote slumped to 34 per cent, their lowest since the 1950s. As the truth about the costs of reunification sunk in, the SPD made a comeback in subsequent *Land* elections and was soon in control of the *Bundesrat*; but it was still a long way short of regaining national power. It can only hope to come to power in coalition with another party, but has no obvious coalition strategy. A new coalition with the Free Democrats would be difficult to achieve, would risk alienating the party's left wing and might not even be sure of a majority. A coalition with the Greens could alienate the party's trade union supporters and middle class voters and could be unstable, given the Greens' ambiguous attitude to taking power. A grand coalition with the Christian Democrats might be a way back to power, as in the 1960s. Various coalition formulas have been tested at *Land* level, including SPD-FDP, SPD-Greens, the 'traffic-light' formula of SPD-FDP-Greens, and grand coalitions. In the long run, however, the SPD faces the same problem as other European Social Democratic parties, of how to retain and expand its electoral base in the face of the decline of the traditional blue-collar vote and the rise of individualist attitudes.

The Free Democrats

The German Free Democratic Party (FDP) is a liberal party founded after the war but which draws on an old tradition of German liberalism. Its most distinctive feature is its strong commitment to the market economy, free enterprise and private property. This puts it in some respects to the right of the CDU and makes it the party closest to the German business community. At the same time, the FDP supports civil rights, individual liberties and the secular state, and its attitudes on these issues are closer to those of the SPD. There is a social wing which favours the development of the welfare state and government social policy, but the social theme is stressed less strongly than in the other parties. While adhering to the social market formula, the FDP stress the market more than the social. In foreign affairs, the FDP was very nationalistic in the 1950s and opposed European unity. Since then, it has reversed itself. It was a strong supporter of *Ostpolitik*, in which its leader Hans-Dietrich Genscher played a prominent role, and has firmly supported European integration.

These varied ideas allow the FDP to play coalition politics with some success. Between 1949 and 1957 and between 1961 and 1966, it was in coalition with the Christian Democrats. In 1969, after the grand coalition interlude, it entered government again, in partnership with the SPD. This move was made possible both by a strengthening of the FDP's social wing and the SPD's move to the political centre. By 1982, however, strains had developed within the coalition over the FDP's demands for cuts in government social spending to reduce the budget deficit. The coalition broke up and the FDP formed a new government with the Christian Democrats.

The Free Democrats owe their survival largely to their ability to play a balancing role in coalitions. They have rarely gained seats in constituency ballots, but rely on enough voters supporting them in the list ballot to put them over the 5 per cent threshold which gives them seats in the *Bundestag*. Under the centre-left coalitions of 1969-82, some electors gave their list vote to the FDP in order to keep the left wing of the SPD in check. Under the centre-right coalitions since 1982, some electors have similarly voted FDP to prevent the government making concessions to the far right. One of the Free Democrats' best electoral performances was in 1980, when Franz Josef Strauss was chancellor-candidate for the CDU/CSU and many conservative voters sought safety in the political centre. In this way the FDP has not only retained its presence in parliament, but has been in government continuously since 1969. Its former leader, Hans-Dietrich Genscher, was able to keep the post of foreign minister under successive chancellors and coalitions from 1974 until 1992.

The balancing act is not always easy. When the party leadership forged the coalition with the SPD in 1969, there was a heavy loss of voters and members and the party barely managed to cross the 5 per cent threshold. When it changed back in 1982, there was a similar loss, with electors and party members leaving the party and joining the SPD rather than supporting a coalition of the centre-right. On each occasion, however, the Free Democrats were able to recoup their support in subsequent elections. They have also been prepared to form coalitions at *Land* level of a different complexion to the national coalition, so as to keep their options and lines of communication open.

Like the Christian Democrats, the Free Democrats in East Germany were reduced to satellites of the Communist Party. At the time of reunification, though, they showed surprising resilience, helped by the presence of Genscher who was born in the east and was known for his pursuit of the *Ostpolitik* under successive chancellors. In the East German elections of March 1990, they gained over 13 per cent of the vote and eastern votes helped push up their total in the all-German election of December 1990 to 11 per cent.

The Greens

The Greens are an environmentalist party originating in the late 1970s and drawing on a variety of new social movements. The most important theme is protection of the environment and the need for a new economic order less geared to production and growth. Pollution, including the effects of acid rain on the Black Forest, became an increasingly salient issue in the 1980s. So did the issue of nuclear power, as the SPD-FDP coalition embarked on a programme to expand nuclear-generating capacity. The Greens also have a strong pacifist streak, and mobilized support around plans to deploy medium-range nuclear weapons in West Germany as part of the modernization of NATO capacities. Nuclear weapons and nuclear power are linked as twin dangers in the hands of government. The Chernobyl disaster of 1985 gave them a considerable boost. They have drawn from and built on neighbourhood protest movements and the *Bürgerinitiativen* or citizen initiatives of the 1970s, many of which were related to environmental issues. Feminism is an important element and the Greens are committed to social and economic equality and participatory democracy. This puts them firmly on the left, unlike other European Green movements which limit themselves to the issue of the environment and deny the validity of the old left-right distinction. Their support base is among young people and especially students and has been gained largely at the expense of the Social Democrats, who might otherwise expect to have gained these left-leaning young voters.

The Greens first entered the *Bundestag* in 1983 when they just managed to surmount the 5 per cent threshold. In 1987 they increased their vote to 8.3 per cent; they also made progress in *Land* politics. The post-unification election of 1990 was not so favourable to them and, dropping to just under 4 per cent, they lost all their seats. In East Germany, Green activists were part of the protest movement which brought down the Communist regime but they suffered when the western parties moved in and effectively took over the system. Believing in decentralization and direct democracy, they could not import western politicians or money. Campaigning as part of the Bündnis 90 coalition, they just managed to cross the separate 5 per cent threshold set for eastern Germany in the all-German election of December 1990 and gained a foothold in parliament.

In politics, the Greens have tried to continue their principles of direct democracy and accountability. Members of parliament are expected to hand over their salaries to the party, receiving in turn the pay of a skilled worker. Another rule requires them to give up their seats half way through their term which, under the German system, allows the next placed member on the party list to replace them. This was intended to prevent the emergence of a professional political leadership class but proved extremely difficult to apply, since parliamentarians complained that, as soon as they had learnt their job, they were being moved on. Although they de-emphasize the role of individuals and try to avoid any sort of personality cult, some of their leaders, like the late Petra Kelly, have become widely known. Kelly was one of those who refused to observe the rotation rule in the 1980s. While in office, Green politicians are supposed to be subject to the imperative mandate, receiving instructions from the party membership which they must carry out to the letter.

In the protest phase, this style of politics was just about manageable, but as Greens began to attain political office the issue arose of how far they could compromise their principles for the sake of power. Since the German political system is based on negotiation and compromise, this is the necessary price of making any gains in policy terms. A division arose between the *Fundis* (fundamentalists) who refused compromise with other parties and insisted that Greens must stick to their principles come what may, and the *Realos* (realists) who argued that without power Greens could achieve nothing. Power in turn means compromise and a willingness to enter into coalitions with other progressive forces, specifically the SPD. There were short-lived SPD-Green coalitions in the 1980s in Hessen and West Berlin which came unstuck because of policy differences and uncertainty on the part of Greens as to what their role in government was. In the 1990s, such Red-Green coalitions have been formed in Lower Saxony and Hessen and in Bremen the FDP was added to give a traffic light coalition (Red-Green-Orange). This represented a triumph for the *Realos* who by now were in the ascendant and able to make common cause with the younger and more radical elements in the SPD. A division of work has emerged, in which the Greens are given posts relating to the environment, women's issues and social affairs, while the SPD takes the economic and financial portfolios.

Their very decentralized and somewhat anarchic organization, the antithesis of the other parties, makes the Greens liable to splits and defections. The division between the *Fundis* and the *Realos* was followed by a series of quarrels and defections when the Greens failed to gain seats in the 1990 elections. Yet they have recovered in the past and their persistence at national and *Land* level indicates that they will not simply fade away. Their continued presence makes it more difficult for any two parties to form a coalition in national or *Land* politics and greatly complicates politics.

The Extreme Right

Right-wing extremism is a very sensitive subject in Germany, because of memories of the Nazi experience. The Basic Law bans anti-democratic parties and the Office for the Protection of the Constitution (*Bundesamt für Verfassungsschutz*) is responsible for monitoring extremist activity. Extreme right parties never gained mass support in West Germany and survey evidence shows a population committed to liberal democratic values and processes. Yet extremist parties have risen periodically since the war.

In the immediate postwar period, there were various neo-Nazi groups, drawing support from refugees and Germans expelled from the eastern territories lost to the Soviet Union and Poland. In 1952, the *Sozialistische Reichspartei* (SRP) was banned by the Constitutional Court. Although it was then recreated under a new name, it made little impact. In 1964, a new right wing party, the *Nationaldemocratische Partei Deutschlands* (NPD) was founded from a number of smaller groups. During the grand coalition of 1966-9 it was able to exploit the lack of an effective parliamentary opposition and accuse the Christian Democrats of selling out to the left. Although it gained seats in seven *Land* parliaments, it managed only 4.9 per cent of the vote at the 1969 federal election, narrowly failing to cross the 5 per cent threshold required to win seats.[7] Right-wing extremism then faded until the 1980s.

In 1983, the Republicans (*Die Republikaner*) were founded by Franz Schönhuber, a former officer in Hitler's *Waffen* SS. Campaigning against the presence of foreigner immigrants and refugees, it made its first gains in the West Berlin Senate elections of 1989. At the European elections of that year, it gained 7.1 per cent of the vote, giving it five seats in the European Parliament. German reunification under the leadership of the Christian Democrats initially set them back and they won just over 2 per cent of the vote at the all-German election of 1990. During the early 1990s, as disillusionment with the costs of reunification set in, they made further advances at *Land* level. 1992, the Republicans gained 10.9 per cent of the vote in Baden-Württemberg, giving them 15 seats in the *Land* parliament and depriving the Christian Democrats of their majority. Another extreme right party, the DVU (*Deutsche Volksunion*) led by Gerhard Frey won six seats each in *Land* parliaments in Bremen and Schleswig-Holstein. The Republicans seek to project a more respectable image than some of the other extreme rightists groups, trying to appeal to the middle classes, though their support comes disproportionately from working-class voters. Republican voters are former CDU/CSU adherents concerned above all with the presence of foreigners. There is a strong correlation between prejudice against foreigners, Muslims and Jews and the tendency to vote Republican.[8] There is also some tendency for their vote to be higher in areas with more unemployment and with fewer university graduates,[9] suggesting an appeal to the working and lower-middle classes who feel threatened by change.

Another development in the early 1990s was the re-appearance of right-wing violence, led by gangs of skinheads and directed at foreigners and refugees, especially in the former East Germany. Extreme right-wing and racist attitudes tend to be found among the less educated youth and apprentices and have strengthened since reunification.[10] Although the Republicans and DVU officially disavow mob violence, they encourage the xenophobia on which it feeds and exploit it to call for harsh anti-immigrant measures and restrictions on civil liberties. The CDU-led government of Helmut Kohl was widely criticized for its complacent attitude to extreme right-wing violence which contrasted with the vigour with which German governments had stamped out the left-wing terrorism of the Red Army Fraction in the 1970s. Finally, after a particularly horrendous attack in which Turkish immigrants were killed, the government began to act more forcefully. At the same time, it insisted that a change in the Basic Law to restrict the right of asylum was necessary in order to control the influx of foreigners, thus implicitly conceding the right-wing case.

The German extreme right preys on the insecurities of the population in the face of change. It uses immigrants and refugees as scapegoats and promises strong government. It is nationalistic, rails against restrictions on German military capacity and has never accepted the loss of the eastern territories to Poland and the former Soviet Union. This message may appeal to about 10-15 per cent of the west German population. In eastern Germany, which has not had forty years to build a democratic and liberal culture, the danger is more acute. As the promises of economic plenty following reunification are unfulfilled and unemployment mounts, the beneficiaries could, as in the 1930s, be the extreme right. On the other hand, a repeat of the collapse of the Weimar Republic is unlikely. To date the extreme right are divided into factions with different constituencies, different tactics and competing leaders. In contrast to the 1930s, there is no disloyalty among the military and no measurable support for extremist politics among business leaders. Germany has not suffered the humiliation which occurred in 1918 and which gave the Weimar Republic such a poor start. A generation of West Germans has grown up with the habits of democracy and Germany is firmly anchored in the European Community.

The Communists

Under the Weimar Republic, the Communists were a significant political force, gaining around 15 per cent of the vote. Banned under Hitler, many of their leaders went into exile in the Soviet Union and returned in 1945. Campaigning in the western zones as the *Kommunistische Partei Deutschlands* (KPD), they made little electoral headway, especially after the outbreak of the Cold War. In 1952, the KPD was banned by the Constitutional Court and, although it resurrected itself under another name, failed to recover any support. Under Soviet occupation, the Communist Party in eastern Germany was given the leading role. The Social Democrats were forced to merge with it to form the *Socialistische Eihnheitspartei* (SED) or Socialist Unity Party. Other parties, including Christian Democrats and Free Democrats, were subordinated to it.

As the Communist regime crumbled in 1989, the SED was forced to surrender its monopoly of power and allow free, competitive elections. Like other east European Communist Parties, it tried to adapt itself to the new conditions, dismissing its hard-line leaders like party boss Erich Honecker in favour of reformers like Hans Modrow, mayor of Dresden. Changing its name to the Democratic Socialists, it sought to project a moderate, Social Democratic image at the elections of 1990. It was widely assumed that, given its legacy of oppression, the Berlin Wall and subservience to the Soviet Union, this would fail to convince the electorate and the party would disappear. In the event, it did surprisingly well, gaining 15 per cent of the vote in the East German election of March 1990. At the all-German election of December 1990, the Christian Democrats agreed to a separate 5 per cent threshold for eastern Germany, hoping to keep the Democratic Socialists alive and thus damage the Social Democrats. With 9.9 per cent of the votes in the former East Germany, the former Communists did manage to win seats in the *Bundestag*. These votes probably came from former officials of the old regime and individuals worried about the insecurity of the new future. Since they won almost no votes in the western *Länder*, however, their national percentage was just 2.4. If a national 5 per cent threshold is re-established for the next federal elections, the Democratic Socialists could well disappear. On the other hand, the high costs of reunification and the unaccustomed experience of unemployment may push eastern Germans back into the arms of the former Communists.

Electoral Behaviour

A great deal is known about electoral behaviour in West Germany, with studies of voting going back to the 1950s. The eastern *Länder* have experienced democratic and competitive elections only since 1990. These occurred in the special circumstances surrounding reunification and are unlikely to have laid down permanent patterns. Future elections may see new eastern German voting trends as a response to the problems of unity, or a reassertion of older traditions in that part of the country. For the 1990 federal election, many of the analyses report the eastern and western *Länder* separately, so as to enable a comparison over time to be made and this is sometimes done in the analysis which follows. Figures cited are for the second vote, for the party list, since this is what determines the overall allocation of seats.

Table 5.4 compares party support in eastern and western Germany at the 1990 elections. From this it appears that the Christian Democratic lead over the

Table 5.4 Vote share in eastern and western Germany, 1990

	CDU/ CSU	SPD	FDP	Greens/ Bundnis 90	PDS	Repu- blicans	Others
All	43.4	33.8	10.8	4.8	2.6	2.2	4.9
West	43.9	36.4	10.3	4.6	0.3	2.4	4.5
East	41.4	24.1	13.0	5.5	11.5	1.4	4.5

Source: R-O. Schultze, 'Behannte Konturen im Westen - ungewisse Zukunft im Osten', in H-G. Wehling (ed.), Wahlverhalten (Stuttgart: Kohlhammer, 1991)

Social Democrats is higher in eastern than in western Germany. This is a reversal of historic trends. Under the Empire and the Weimar Republic, the eastern areas were among the strongholds of the Social Democrats. The 1990 result, however, is a reflection of the advantage which the Christian Democrats gained from being the party which achieved reunification and promised that it would be almost costless. It provides little guidance as to long-term trends. For that, we need to examine studies of electoral behaviour in democratic Germany and the factors which mould it.

As elsewhere in Europe, voting in Germany is marked by religion and class, which create patterns of party identification persisting over long periods. The Catholic-Protestant division has historically been of great importance in Germany since the religious wars of the sixteenth and seventeenth centuries. It was reinforced under the Empire by the experience of the *Kulturkampf*, in which Bismarck challenged the position of the Catholic Church, leading Catholics to establish their own social and political institutions, notably the *Zentrum* or Centre Party. Division of the country in 1945 left Catholics and Protestants equally divided in the western part and for the first time brought into being a party, the CDU/CSU, which caters for both. As Table 5.5 shows, the CDU/CSU appeals more strongly to Catholics, while the Protestants are attracted to the SPD or FDP. One of the consequences of the Free Democrats' change of coalition partners in 1982 was a sharp loss of Protestant voters who disliked the new alliance with the CDU and particularly the CSU.

Closer analysis shows that, among both Catholics and Protestants, it is the more devout who are drawn to the CDU/CSU.[11] In 1990, three-quarters of regularly practising Catholics and nearly two thirds of regularly practising Protestants voted CDU/CSU.[12] This effect is, however, diminishing as Germany secularizes and the links between religion and voting weaken.[13] It remains strongest among the older generation.

Table 5.5 Vote by religion, West Germany, 1990

Religion	CDU/CSU	SPD	FDP	Greens	Republicans
All	44.3	35.7	10.6	4.8	2.3
Catholic	56.3	26.6	8.8	4.5	2.1
Protestant	39.6	39.7	13.3	4.3	1.7
no religion	25.7	45.0	11.2	11.7	2.5

Source: R-O. Schultze, 'Bekannte Konturen im Westen - ungewisse Zukunft im Osten', in H-G. Wehling, Wahlverhalten (Stuttgart: Kohlhammer, 1991).

Class remains an important factor in voting, as Table 5.6 shows. Manual workers tend to vote Social Democrat, as we would expect. Trade union members are particularly likely to vote SPD. Yet this class alignment is heavily modified by other influences. A substantial proportion of the working class is drawn to the CDU/CSU on religious or other grounds. The middle classes and managerial elements tend to vote for the CDU/CSU. The FDP gains its greatest level of support among independent business people and the self-employed. The class effect in voting behaviour is also diminishing as class identification weakens. Both manual workers and the self-employed have shrunk as a proportion of the electorate and the link between class and voting is not as clear as in the past.

Where class and religious influences operate in the same direction, they can be very powerful, as in the case of non-religious manual workers who are doubly induced to vote SPD, or the Catholic middle classes, stalwarts of the CDU/CSU.

Table 5.6 Vote by class, western Germany , 1990 election

	CDU/CSU	SPD	FDP	Greens	Republicans
All	44.3	35.7	10.6	4.8	2.3
Manual workers	39.0	46.7	6.0	3.2	3.6
White collar workers	43.0	35.9	12.1	5.3	1.6
Managers	46.7	31.9	12.7	6.1	1.7
Self-employed	56.9	17.9	18.1	4.8	1.0

Source: R-O. Schultze, 'Bekannte Konturen im Westem - ungewisse Zukunft im Osten' in H-G. Wehling (ed.), Wahlverhalten (Stuttgart: Kohlhammer, 1991).

Under the Empire and the Weimar Republic, religion, class and associative life combined in particular localities to produce strong subcultures and voting traditions.[14] On the anti-clerical and secular left, the Social Democratic Party and trade union movement rallied the working classes in the cities and industrial areas. On the Catholic side, the Church, the *Zentrum*, lay organizations and Catholic workers' groups showed an equal solidarity. Middle-class Protestants gravitated to secular parties. The Nazi experience and the mass migration after the second world war disrupted these structures and from the mid 1950s the two large parties sought to project themselves as catch-all parties or *Volksparteien*, with an appeal across the class and religious spectrum. Social change, including secularization and the decline of class consciousness has encouraged this process further, loosening the old links. Traditions do nonetheless persist, albeit in weakened form. The Social Democrats have remained a formidable presence in the city-*Land* of Hamburg and parts of industrialized North Rhine-Westphalia. In Bavaria, the CSU, rooted in the local Catholic culture, remains dominant, albeit gradually weakening.

Table 5.7 shows that gender is an influence on voting behaviour in Germany. As in other countries, women have traditionally been more conservative than men. So women are more likely to vote CDU/CSU, men to vote SPD. This effect, too, has weakened over time. In 1957 the gap between men and women was about 9 per cent.[15] By 1990, the bias to the CDU/CSU was present only among older women. Among those under thirty-five, it was reversed, with men more likely than women to vote CDU/CSU.[16] There is no gender difference in voting for the Greens, despite their emphasis on feminist issues. Extreme right voters are slightly more likely to be men than women.

Table 5.7   *Vote by gender, all Germany ,1990*

	CDU/CSU	SPD	FDP	Greens	Others
All	43.4	33.8	10.8	4.8	7.1
Men	42.0	34.1	11.0	4.6	8.2
Women	44.8	33.6	10.6	4.9	6.1

Source: Statistisches Jahrbuch, (Wiesbaden: Statistisches Bundesamt, 1992)

There are some substantial differences in voting behaviour among age groups, as Table 5.8 shows. Older voters are more likely to adhere to the CDU/CSU but the SPD does not now have a corresponding advantage among younger age cohorts. This is a marked change from 1972, when the SPD had a lead of almost twenty points over the CDU/CSU among young voters.[17] Young voters now tend to reject both *Volksparteien* in favour of the newer parties. Green support is heavily concentrated among young voters, particularly students and those with a higher education. Over

Table 5.8 Vote by age, all Germany, 1990

	CDU/CSU	SPD	FDP	Greens	Republicans	Others
All	43.4	33.8	10.8	4.8	2.2	4.9
18-25	35.6	34.4	10.5	10.3	3.6	6.8
25-35	34.7	38.2	9.7	9.7	2.4	4.9
35-45	39.6	34.7	12.6	6.2	2.0	4.0
45-60	46.5	32.1	12.4	2.3	1.9	3.9
over 60	51.7	31.8	9.0	0.6	1.8	4.1

Source: R-O. Schultze, 'Bekannte Konturen im Westen - ungewisse Zukunft im Osten', in H-G. Wehling (ed.), Wahlverhalten (Stuttgart: Kohlhammer, 1991).

60 per cent of Green voters in 1990 were under thirty-five years old. Among working-class youth and those with lower level education, the extreme right-wing parties have made progress.

What all this portends is a marked decline in party identification and habitual voting and an increase in volatility. Parties are forced to compete on the basis of their policies, their leadership and their record. The personality of the chancellor-candidate is a crucial factor. Normally, incumbent chancellors have an advantage since they are able to use the office to their electoral benefit and Germans are unused to the idea of throwing out governments in elections. In 1990, Helmut Kohl, until then regarded as a singularly uninspiring leader, was able to project himself as the hero of national reunification. Social Democratic Chancellors Brandt and Schmidt regularly scored more highly in opinion polls than their opponents. A government's record of economic management naturally influences voters, as does their handling of other critical policy issues.

Values are an important factor in moulding electoral choice. Christian Democratic voters emphasise order and discipline. They tend to take a sterner line on law and police matters. They are materialistic, emphasizing economic progress and the need to raise living standards. Social Democratic voters are somewhat more libertarian. They are materialistic but are often as interested in leisure time as higher living standards. Free Democrat voters tend to side with the Christian Democrats on material and economic issues but are more libertarian and less concerned with social discipline. Green voters are strongly attached to non-material values including defence of the environment, individual liberty and self-expression.[18] Extreme right voters are marked by racist and xenophobic values.

Tactical considerations also come into play, given the two-ballot system and the complexities of coalition politics. No government in Germany has ever changed as a result of an election, so balancing coalition options becomes a delicate and difficult task. The role of the FDP in this is critical. Few voters identify strongly with the Free Democrats[19] but many more will give their second vote to the party in order to restrain the dominant party of the coalition or prevent one party from gaining a majority on its own. Since the Free Democrats hardly ever win any constituency seats, electors tend to regard a vote for them at constituency level as wasted and their list vote is considerably higher. In 1987, when it looked as though the CDU/CSU might gain an absolute majority on its own, there was a swing by moderate voters to the FDP in an effort to limit the influence of the CSU in the governing coalition. By contrast, when the FDP changed coalition partners in 1982, it lost a large swathe of left-of-centre and Protestant voters. With only three parties in contention, tactical voting was relatively simple. When four or five parties are represented in the *Bundestag* and coalition patterns are unknown, it is much more complicated.

THE STATE, BUREAUCRACY AND PUBLIC POLICY

Traditionally, German society was marked by a strong presence of the state. Jerome K. Jerome's humorous *Three Men on the Bummel* captures the spirit of imperial Germany:

> 'You get yourself born,' says the German government to the German citizen, 'we will do the rest. Indoors and outdoors, in sickness and in health, in pleasure and in work, we will tell you what to do, and we will see to it that you do it. Don't worry yourself about anything.'

This tradition of the strong state, encompassing private interests and defining the limits of civil society was heavily discredited by the excesses committed in its name in the Nazi era. The Basic Law, under the influence of the occupying powers, prescribes a balance of powers and a limited state. There has subsequently been a strong growth of civil society and private institutions and a more liberal and pluralistic culture. Yet the German model of liberal democracy still bears its own characteristic traits. There is a strong tendency to collective action and to social solidarity. Participation is highly structured and organized through peak interest groups and strong political parties. Learning the lessons of the Weimar Republic, which was plagued by conflict among groups and parties, these have reverted to traditions of compromise and negotiation. This process, however, is no longer governed and guided by a strong and dominant state standing above society. Rather the state is itself penetrated by parties and interest groups, becoming one of the arenas in which social compromises are reached. These arrangements have been described as 'social corporatism',[20] a system in which peak interest groups negotiate over public policy without being subordinated to a dominant state.

The Bureaucracy

The old Prussian state was noted for its tightly organized, hierarchical bureaucracy, a feature which was carried over in the Empire and Weimar Republic. Max Weber's classic work on bureaucracy as an impartial, hierarchical type of administration, indeed, was derived from observation of the German system. The imperial civil servant was the servant of the state, itself built on a system of law and regulation. Senior officials were trained in university schools of law and enjoyed great social status.

Modern Germany has inherited some of these features but adapted them to the needs of a democratic and pluralist order. With the rise of new industrial and business elites, public service no longer enjoys the same social prestige. Mechanisms exist to ensure that civil servants are accountable to the elected government. Yet the predominance of lawyers and a legalistic attitude to administration remains.

Since, in the German version of federalism, most administration is at the *Land* level, most civil servants are employed by the *Länder* rather than the federal government. Each *Land* organizes its own recruitment, as do the individual federal government departments.

Yet there is a substantial unity because of federal legal regulations on appointment and shared assumptions about the official's role. There are three categories of civil servant. *Beamte*, or officials, are the highest level, occupying senior managerial and policy-related positions. Then there are *Angestellte*, or employees, and *Arbeiter*, or workers. Since teachers at all levels, together with workers in the postal services and railways are classified as civil servants, the total number is rather large. *Beamte* enjoy a special and privileged relation to the state defined in public law. They have security of tenure, pensions and other privileges. They can leave the service to enter politics with the right to return at any time with full seniority. On the other hand, they have no right to strike or to bargain with their employer over pay and conditions.

By and large the German system provides for an impartial and permanent civil service, with appointment on merit and no spoils system. Officials for the most part act according to legal norms and procedures rather than political leadership. Accountability is to the law rather than, as in Britain, to a minister and thence to parliament. At the highest level, however, there is some politicization. Ministers are able to appoint sympathetic officials to policy-related posts and move others aside to less sensitive positions or into early retirement. Generous provisions for security of tenure, pensions and leave ensure that senior civil servants do not suffer unduly in the process. So a class of politicized officials has come into being, identified with one political party or attached to the fortunes of a politician. There is in consequence little sharp distinction between the ministerial and the civil service role at the top of a department. Civil servants will regularly meet with representatives of interest groups and help steer legislation through parliamentary committees. Those working for a long time in the same department will tend to form links with interest group representatives and share their views and assumptions.

Germany has succeeded in producing a largely impartial and efficient bureaucracy, but criticisms are recurrently made about the bias to legal training and legalistic approaches to problems. The bureaucracy is equipped for the impartial administration of law but may not be so well fitted to the tasks of innovation and policy development required by a changing society. They may lack the managerial and technical skills needed in a changing environment. Compared with their French counterparts, they have not taken the lead in economic and social modernization. Instead, that has been the province of the private sector. Yet the new demands stemming from European integration, reunification and industrial and technological change have placed new demands on the civil service and the German model of policy making as a whole.

Interest Groups

Germany possesses an elaborate and highly structured set of interest groups, with close links to the state and incorporated into the policy process. The main employers' organizations are the *Bundesvereinigung der Deutschen Arbeitegeberverbände* (BDA) and the *Bundesverband der Deutschen Industrie* (BDI). Both are organized on a sectoral as well as a decentralized federal basis. They do not compete but share the work of industrial representation, the BDA mainly concerning itself with labour relations and negotiation with unions and the BDI with economic policy and links to government. The BDA is a general employers' association covering all economic sectors, while the BDI represents industry. Both organizations have an extremely extensive membership, with the BDA covering something like 80 per cent of German employers and the various constituent associations of the BDI about 95 per cent of firms in each sector.[21] A third body is the *Deutscher Industrie- und Handelstag*, a federation of local chambers of commerce, which tends to emphasize the needs of small business. As in other continental countries, membership of the local chamber of commerce is compulsory and chambers are able to levy taxes to finance common services and works.

Given the diversity of interests within German business, most of the serious work is carried out by sectoral associations in various industries. Very large firms themselves can maintain direct links with government and seek to influence policy in their own interests. The national business associations are themselves heavily influenced by their large sectoral affiliates and major firms. Yet there is little overt conflict and German business is inclined to cooperation as well as competition.

Trade unions were smashed by Hitler and had to be refounded after the war with the help, notably, of the British Trades Union Congress (TUC). The result was a structure which the British unionists would have liked for themselves, if they had been able to start over again. There is a single trade union federation, the *Deutscher Gewerkschaftsbund* (DGB) with seventeen affiliated unions. These are not divided by politics, religion or craft as in other European states or Weimar Germany; rather there is one union for each industrial sector. Individual unions are independent, leaving the DGB with a rather loose co-ordinating role. Among the unions, by far the largest and most powerful is the metal workers' union, IG Metall. Trade union membership in western Germany at a third of the workforce is lower than in most other northern European countries but higher than France, Spain or the United States. It has fallen from a peak of 37 per cent in 1980, but not as fast as in other advanced industrial countries. It is also significant that trade union density is much lower than that of employers' associations, since the latter include nearly all business firms.

Trade unions tend to identify with the Social Democrats and there is an extensive common membership. Some prominent Social Democrat politicians have emerged from the trade union movement. Yet there are no formal ties between the DGB or individual unions and the Social Democrats and unions have declared their willingness to cooperate with governments of varying complexions. There is also a tradition of Christian Democratic trade unionism which, after the failure of attempts to set up Christian unions in the 1950s, was channelled into the main industrial unions. The union presence within the Christian Democratic Party is a small but significant one and played an important role in persuading the party of the need for expansive social programmes in the 1950s and 1960s. Relationships between the unions and the Social Democrats deteriorated from the late 1970s, as a result of the Schmidt government's austerity policies. In the 1980s, with the Social Democrats in opposition, relationships improved only slightly since the unions were alienated by the Social Democrats' adoption of pro-environmental and anti-nuclear power policies which were seen as a threat to industrial jobs. The new Christian Democratic-led coalition was also less inclined to consult the trade unions, who have therefore lost influence all round. Yet the continued presence, albeit weakened, of a trade union influence within the Christian Democratic Party has modified this neo-liberal stance and restrained the government from launching all-out attacks on the trade union movement such as have occurred in Britain and the United States.

Industrial relations in Germany are highly regulated by law and practice. Wage negotiations are centralized, in the hands of national unions and employers' associations and have tended not be conflictual, especially in times of economic growth. Strikes require the support of 75 per cent of union members in a ballot and are relatively rare. When they do occur, however, they can be bitter and protracted. At the level of the firm, there is a system of co-determination (*Mitbestimmung*) through supervisory boards on which both workers and shareholders are represented. This system, which owes a great deal to Christian Democratic thinking on class co-operation, was put in place after the war. In the 1970s, it was expanded by the Social Democratic government to include medium-sized and small firms. In the classic system of co-determination, which exists in the large heavy unionized industries, workers' representatives have considerable influence, being represented equally on the supervisory board and able to veto the appointment of the personnel director. The version of co-determination extended to smaller firms in the 1970s is much weaker and in the case of the smallest businesses is really an elaborate form of consultation.

Co-determination has reinforced the tendencies to negotiation and compromise of postwar German society. Workers and unions develop an identification with their firm and, in turn, may obtain concessions on working conditions, fringe benefits or the right to notice and a redeployment plan in the event of plant closures. These are substantial gains. On the other hand, critics have suggested, indeed, that it encourages unions to identify too closely with the employers and confuses the roles of cooperation at the workplace and independent bargaining.

Farmers are organized in the *Deutscher Bauernverband* (DBV) whose membership covers over 90 per cent of those involved in agriculture. This is an extremely effective interest group, with close links to the Christian Democratic Party and the Ministry of Agriculture. The Bavarian CSU has been paricularly close to the agricultural lobby. They have been able to preserve Germany's multiplicity of small farms and sustain the European Community's protectionist Common Agricultural Policy. As budgetary, political and international pressure has forced some retrenchment in the Common Agricultural Policy, Germany has reintroduced measures of state support for farmers. Consequently, German farmers are among the most heavily subsidized in the world.

The Churches no longer play an important role in German politics, though their position is safeguarded by the constitution. There is no established Church but, in a provision carried over from the Weimar Republic, Churches levy taxes on their members, collected by the state and passed on to the Church. The Basic Law also stipulates that Sunday shall be a 'day of rest and of spiritual edification.' Church influence is felt also through the Christian Democratic Party, which reflects both Catholic and Protestant interests against the more secular-minded Social Democrats and Free Democrats. This has been an important factor in the battle over abortion law, particularly whether the more liberal East German law should remain in force in a unified Germany.

Policy Making

Policy making in the German Federal Republic has been characterized above all by consensus rather than adversary politics. The basic formula for domestic policy, laid down by Christian Democratic governments in the 1950s, is the social market. This combines a commitment to a market economy with an extensive social welfare system. In the late 1950s, the opposition Social Democrats adopted broadly the same positions and changes of government have not resulted in radical shifts in policy direction.

Productive activity is largely in private hands, with only a small state-owned sector in the railways, post and telecommunications and air transport. Yet, the

German version of the market economy is not quite the same as that found in the United States or Britain. German large firms have a strong corporate culture and tend to concern themselves with stability and long-term growth rather than short-term gains. There is only a small stock market and hostile takeovers of firms are rare. Most finance is raised internally or through banks rather than by floating shares and there is a complex system of cross-nomination of directors to company boards. Negotiation and conciliation rather than confrontation are the rule in industrial relations. Although state ownership of industry is not extensive, various forms of state aid, provided both by the federal and *Land* governments, are quite high in comparison with Britain or the United States (Table 1.2, p.7). In this context, extensive welfare provision has been seen less as a hindrance to economic growth than as a necessary concomitant to building a strong and competitive economy. This is not to deny that arguments have taken place over the appropriate size of the welfare state or taxation levels, but these have taken place at the margin, without questioning the basic model itself.

Several other factors favour a negotiated, consensual policy style. One is the memory of the Weimar Republic with its sharp class and partisan conflicts and a determination not to allow the experience to be repeated. There are also the needs of coalition politics, which require parties to agree on common positions. The federal system, which gives most powers of implementation to the *Länder*, imposes a need for intergovernmental negotiation on policy proposals.

Interest groups are highly integrated into the policy process. In the absence of its own field administration, the federal government often goes to the peak associations rather than the *Länder* for information. Interest groups have been able, through the political parties, to colonize *Bundestag* committees where legislative proposals are negotiated and amended. So the members of parliament discussing an issue are frequently representatives of the very interests concerned with it. Ministries and their civil servants are often equally close to the associations in their area of concern, to the extent that they are sometimes effectively captured by the interests they are supposed to be administering. This is the case, notably, with the Ministry of Agriculture and the farmers' union, the DBV.

The result is a consensual, incremental process in which radical policy innovations are difficult and in which changes in government do not result in extensive changes in policy. Some observers have described this as a variety of corporatism, a system in which policy is negotiated between peak interest associations and the state. In the 1970s, West Germany, like other west European nations, experimented with concerted action, a programme in which government, employers and unions agreed on the main targets for economic policy, prices and wages and sought to coordinate their plans. This, however, was rather short-lived and Germany never established the machinery for peak-level cooperation on economic policy such as existed in some smaller European countries. Instead of such overall national corporatism, Germany has been characterized by sectoral negotiation within individual policy communities. Monetary policy is entrusted to a central bank, the *Bundesbank*, which by law is independent of political control and has the task of pursuing sound money and anti-inflation policies. Fiscal and macroeconomic policies are the responsibility of the federal government, which must negotiate taxation matters with the *Länder*. Policy within individual sectors is negotiated by the relevant ministries, with interest groups and the *Land* governments. Overall coordination is rather weak in formal terms, but the underlying social and political consensus limits the extent of conflict. The independent role of the *Bundesbank* is underpinned by Germans' historic memories of hyper-inflation under Weimar. Conciliation of farmers, the working class and other groups has similarly become part of the German postwar mentality.

In recent years, this model of consensual policy making has come under considerable strain. To some extent, this stems from the decline of political consensus. Christian Democratic-Liberal coalition governments under Helmut Kohl since 1982 have adopted a more neo-liberal economic stance, in rather pale imitation of Thatcher and Reagan's policies in Britain and the United States. On the left, the Greens have raised new issues to challenge the old consensus and found some echo in the Social Democrats. Yet the extent of this should not be exaggerated. Whatever the intentions of some members of the Christian Democrat-Liberal coalition, their efforts to deregulate the economy and roll back the welfare state have frequently been frustrated both by elements within the Christian Democratic Party and by the need to negotiate policy with social and economic interests. There has been a limited amount of privatization in the already small state sector of industry, with the disposal of holdings in the airline Lufthansa and in telecommunications. Deregulation of economic and social affairs has proceeded very slowly. For example, federal law still keeps retail shops closed from mid-day on Saturday until Monday morning.

European integration has modified German policy-making procedures considerably. The influence goes in both directions. Decision-making procedures in the Community owe much to German customs of negotiation and compromise. Yet, since the Single European Act of 1987 a wide range of regulations can be adopted in the European Community by majority vote, forcing Germany to adapt whatever the domestic balance of opinion. More widely, global economic and financial integration and technological change make it difficult for Germany, like other countries, to retain a distinctive style of national policy making in several sectors. In areas exposed to international competition or technological change, like telecommunications and stock markets, Germany has had to accept externally imposed change. In matters without an external dimension, like shop opening hours or health service provision, it has retained a distinctive national system of regulation.[22] Germany's key position in the European and global economies has also made it the target of external pressures. In the 1970s, it was pushed into reflating its economy so as to act as the 'locomotive' for western recovery. During the European financial crisis of 1992 even the fabled independence of the Bundesbank was breached when Germany lowered interest rates in an effort to stabilize the European Monetary System.

Even before reunification, West Germany's consensual and incremental style of policy making, which has been subject to a great deal of admiration, was beginning to be criticized for its inflexibility and inability to adapt to the requirements of a rapidly changing environment. Successful in mobilizing consensus and managing social relations, it is perhaps less successful in purposive policy making and establishing priorities. Reunification imposes further strains on the German style of consensual policy making. It brings in new actors to the policy process and poses serious policy issues. Above all the cost of reunification deprives governments of the fiscal resources which in the past enabled Germany to afford both high private consumption and generous public services. Hard spending choices will have to be made and it is not easy to see how these can always be negotiated consensually. In March 1993, a 'solidarity pact' was negotiated between government and opposition in an effort to resolve the issue through the consensual mechanisms of the past. This provided for tax increases and spending cuts but with the details still to be worked out. The *Land* share of VAT was increased from 37.5 to 44 per cent but the western *Länder* were to pay more to their counterparts in the east. Critics complained that the really hard choices had still be avoided.

TERRITORIAL POLITICS

Despite its late unification, Germany has been a relatively homogeneous country. There are no sharp ethnic, cultural or linguistic differences among its regions and no separatist movements. In contrast to other European countries, it lacks a dominant capital city, monopolizing the main political and economic functions. Instead, these are dispersed among several centres. Bonn has served as the political and administrative capital of West Germany though since reunification the official capital is Berlin and there is a commitment to move the main governmental functions there in due course. Frankfurt is the main financial centre. Corporate headquarters, the media and universities are dispersed among the cities. West Germany also lacked severe economic conflicts among its regions, as it enjoyed a relatively even distribution of wealth and economic activity. In the 1980s, however, a north-south gap began to develop as southern regions like Bavaria and Baden-Württemberg attracted much of the new high-technology industry and older industrial areas in the north faced severe problems of adjustment. Reunification, of course, has posed a massive problem of disparities between the former East Germany and the rest of the country.

Federalism

Germany has a federal system of government, with power divided between the federation, or Bund and the 16 states or *Länder*. This reflects German traditions, since both the Empire and the Weimar Republic were federal in nature. It also owes a great deal to the determination of the Allies and the framers of the Basic Law to prevent undue concentrations of power. Generally, the *Länder* do not correspond to traditional historical units or communities. Only Bavaria and the old Hanseatic city-states of Hamburg and Bremen can trace their roots back to pre-unification states. The Allies were particularly keen to abolish all trace of the state of Prussia, which they regarded as a breeding ground for German militarism. Apart from the three examples mentioned, the present *Länder* owe their existence and borders to the needs of administrative convenience and the boundaries of Allied occupation zones. They vary in size from North-Rhine-Westphalia with a population of 16.7 million to Bremen with just 700 thousand. *Länder* were also established in East Germany after the war but were abolished by the Communists in 1952. They were recreated in 1990 to allow East Germany to join the West through adhering to the Basic Law.

Each *Land* has its own constitution, which must conform generally to the principles of the Basic Law. The larger states, known as areas-states or *Flächenstaaten*, have legislatures (*Landtage*) elected on a similar basis to the *Bundestag* and governments responsible to the legislature, headed by minister-presidents. In the three *Stadtstaaten* or city-states of Hamburg, Bremen and Berlin, the head of government is the mayor, responsible to an elected council or Senate.

The Basic Law formally divides functions between the federation and the *Länder* according to three lists. One list enumerates exclusive federal functions. A second list contains concurrent functions. Here both levels are competent to legislate but federal laws take precedence in case of conflict. The third list is of matters in which the federal level may pass outline laws laying down basic principles, within which the *Länder* can make their own detailed provision. All matters not covered by the three lists are the responsibility of the *Länder*. The Basic Law also provides that the *Länder* should administer most laws, including those within federal areas of responsibility. Direct federal administration is limited to the foreign service, federal financial administration, the railways, postal services, waterways and shipping. This contrasts with the position in most federal systems, where each level of government has its own system of administration. As Table 5.9 shows, most civil servants are employed outside the central departments, giving the *Länder* a significant resource in the shaping of policy.

In practice, the demands of economic management and social intervention in the modern European state have since the 1960s rendered the formal division of powers largely redundant. Nor does the classical federal formula of division of powers between the two levels reflect historic German ideas about the unity of the state and authority. Gradually the federal level has extended its legislative scope so that the *Länder* legislate very little within their areas of responsibility and instead concentrate on administration and influencing federal legislation. Rather than a division of competences between the two levels as in classical American federalism, German federalism is thus characterized by a division of tasks within each policy field. The federal level legislates the broad principles and the *Länder* fill in the details and carry out the administration. Exclusive areas of *Land* responsibility are now effectively limited to local government matters, police and primary and secondary education. This might seem to reduce the *Länder* to a subordinate role in what is effectively a unitary system of government, but such is not the case. As mentioned earlier, the

Table 5.9 Full-time civil servants in West Germany, 1990

All	3,573,308
Federal government	310,119
Länder	1,535,908
Municipalities	1,002,228
Local special purpose bodies	39,747
Railways	246,590
Postal service	230,032

Source: Statistisches Jahrbuch (Wiesbaden, Statistisches Bundesamt, 1992)

Länder enter into the federal legislative process through the *Bundesrat*, whose consent is required for any legislation affecting the *Länder*, including financial matters and laws which they will be required to administer. Federal governments must thus negotiate laws with *Land* governments and cannot simply impose them unilaterally.

Länder are taken very seriously by politicians as power bases. Several of them at any time will be led by politicians of national standing and it is frequently the case that a party's candidate for chancellor at the federal election is not a member of the *Bundestag* but minister-president of a *Land*. In opposition, politicians may choose to return to *Land* politics, where they can serve in government, rather than remain on the opposition benches in Bonn. Party politics in the *Länder* is a reflection of national politics. The same parties operate at both levels and *Land* elections are often regarded as opportunities to reward or censure the federal government rather than to pass judgement on local issues. This can reduce the importance of *Land* politics as an independent arena, but it ensures that the parties take *Land* elections seriously. The parties themselves are also decentralized on a *Land* basis and national leaders must balance *Land* interests in setting policy. *Länder* are also used to test out or balance new coalition arrangements among the parties. So the Free Democrats have generally ensured that, whichever party they are in coalition with at federal level, they have some *Land* coalitions with the other party. *Land* politics has also been a test-bed for coalitions between the Social Democrats and the Greens.

There is an elaborate set of mechanisms to link federal and *Land* levels of policy making. Each *Land* has a permanent mission adjacent to the federal government buildings in Bonn, and in constant contact with the federal ministries. There is a conference of the chancellor and *Land* minister-presidents which meets about every two months.[23] Other conferences bring together specialized ministers at each level. Special provisions exist for joint tasks in which federal and *Land* governments cooperate in matters formally belonging to the *Länder*. This has proved politically sensitive, since it appears to involve serious federal encroachment in *Länder* administrative responsibilities and so it is regulated by a clause added in 1969 to the Basic Law. Joint task programmes themselves are limited to university buildings, regional economic development, agricultural improvement and coastal defences, each of which is subject to a specific law. In the early years of the Kohl government, there was an effort to disentangle federal and *Land* responsibility and cut back on joint tasks. The complexities of policy making in a modern state, however, make this almost impossible and recent years have seen an increase in joint working, including actions in relation to the European Community, German reunification and the refugee problem.

Links are also maintained through the political parties. There are conferences of party leaders at federal and *Land* level and regular meetings of federal members from the various *Länder* with their *Land* counterparts. Party executive committees also handle federal-*Land* issues.

Membership of the European Community has served further to erode the distinction between federal and *Land* competences since the federal government is responsible for seeing that Community laws and directives are applied, whichever sphere they fall into. Gradually, a system has come into being to allow a *Land* input into Germany's negotiating position in the Community. *Land* representatives have been brought into the German delegation and an official known as the *Länderbeobachter* was given the responsibility of keeping the *Länder* informed about developments in the Community. *Land* governments continued to complain about their exclusion from the European process, however, especially after the passage of the Single European Act of 1987. When the Maastricht Treaty on monetary and political union came up for ratification, they threatened to use the *Bundesrat* to hold it up unless they were given more powers in relation to Community matters. In response, the federal government has proposed to involve the *Bundesrat* more fully in European affairs, whether or not they touch on *Land* responsibilities.[24] This further breaks down the federal-*Land* distinction but recognizes the continued importance of the *Länder* in the policy-making process. It also reinforces a tendency to intergovernmental policy making in which both the *Bundestag* and the *Land* legislatures are downgraded in favour of the executive. This is a domestic version of the democratic deficit which arises when national governments decide matters among themselves in the European Community.

The system for financing the federal and *Land* governments is extremely complex and tries to combine the requirements of accountability and fiscal responsibility with the need to share resources between rich and poorer regions.

Redistributing resources from wealthy to poorer jurisdictions, or fiscal equalization as it is technically known, is imposed by clause 106 of the Basic Law. This stipulates that the financial system should serve to ensure 'uniformity of living standards in the federal territory.'

There is a distinction made between joint taxes, which are shared between the two levels, and exclusive taxes, levied by one or other. As joint taxes include income tax, corporation tax and value added tax, they account for most of the revenue, about 70 per cent. Rates for these are set nationally but require the consent of the *Bundesrat*. The federal and *Land* governments each receive 42.5 per cent of the proceeds of income tax, the remaining 15 per cent going to municipal governments. Corporation tax is shared equally between federal and *Land* governments. Value added tax is divided in the ratio of 65 per cent to 35 per cent between the two. The *Land* share of income and corporation taxes is divided among the *Länder* according to where the tax was collected, that is the residence of the individual or site of the business. The *Land* share of value added tax is divided among the *Länder* according to population.

Then the equalization principle is brought into play to redistribute these funds away from the wealthier towards the poorer *Länder*. An equalization formula is determined according to needs, that is the amount required to bring a *Land* up to a nationally determined level of service, and resources, that is the amount which it has available. Then money is taken from the stronger *Länder* and given to the weaker. In addition, the poorer *Länder* receive direct grants in aid from the federal government, whose size is determined as a percentage of value added tax yield.

The system of fiscal equalization has come under increasing strain as the north-south division in Germany has forced prosperous southern *Länder* to contribute

Figure 5.2 Contributions to fiscal equalization, West Germany, 1991

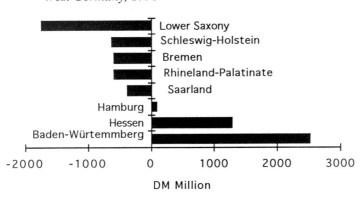

DM Million

Source: German Ministry of Finance, *Finanzbericht* (Bonn, 1993).

more to the older industrial areas. In 1970, the largest contributor was the northern industrial *Land* of North Rhine-Westphalia. Bavaria was a net beneficiary. In the 1980s, North Rhine-Westphalia's contribution dwindled and in some years was negative.[25] The southern states of Baden-Württemberg and Bavaria now contribute by far the largest share while Bavaria has also become a net contributor. The gains and losses from the equalization scheme are summarized in Figure 5.2. In 1986 a group of *Länder*, including both contributors to and recipients from the equalization scheme, brought a case before the Constitutional Court which ruled that the system as is stood was unconstitutional. Later Baden-Württemberg brought a further case against a federal package of aid to depressed regions. Modifications had to be made in both cases.

Reunification presented problems of equalization on an unprecedented scale. Extension of the existing formula would have led to massive transfers away from nearly all the western *Länder* and would have been politically impossible to achieve. So it was agreed to postpone the entry of the eastern *Länder* into the system until 1995. In the meantime, the federal government effectively assumed the responsibility for financing the new *Länder*, with some support from western *Länder*, municipal governments and the EC. A Germany Unity Fund was established for four years, financed by the federal, *Land* and local governments in the west. It was originally intended to phase in the distribution of value added tax receipts to the east, but the fiscal needs of the eastern *Länder* forced a change of view and they now receive their population-based share. As value added tax revenues generated in the east are much smaller than those in the west, this represents a large transfer. Figure 5.3 shows the shares of taxes collected and the share actually received by the federal, *Land* and municipal governments. There are also arrangements for individual *Länder* and local governments in the west to help their counterparts in the east. In 1991, eastern taxes accounted for under 12 per cent of the spending of the new *Länder*.[26] In spite of support from the west, their deficits were rising sharply.[27]

Figure 5.3 Percentage shares of taxes collected and received, 1991

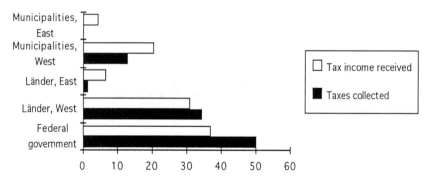

Source: Statistisches Bundesamt, *Wirtschaft un Statistik*, 5 (Wiesbaden, 1992); German Ministry of Finance, *Finanzbericht* (Bonn, 1992).

Increasing pressure on public finances was forcing the federal government to look to ways to cut transfer payments and force costs back onto the *Länder*. Modernization and rationalization of the federal administration itself also threatened the eastern *Länder*. At the time of reunification, East Germany had almost twice as many employees per thousand kilometers of railway track as did West Germany. These will have to be cut back considerably.

Reunification has strengthened the federal government, by allowing it to invade policy fields belonging to the eastern *Länder*, with the support of *Land* governments unable to cope themselves.[28] Some western *Länder* fear that these initiatives might be a precedent for wider incursions of federal power. Federalism has also been affected by the political and administrative weakness of the new *Länder*. Like the East German and all-German elections of that year, the first eastern *Land* elections in 1990 were effectively taken over by the western parties. By 1992, four of the five eastern *Länder* and Berlin were governed by politicians who had come from the west. Senior bureaucratic posts in the new *Land* administrations too tended to be taken by westerners, including retired officials from the older *Länder*. This has caused some resentment in the east, magnified by the fact that the incoming western officials continued to draw higher salaries than their equivalents who had served in the old East German regime.

Reunification has also created new coalitions of *Länder* interests. The new eastern *Länder* cooperate to pursue their common interests as a bloc and sometimes form tactical alliances with the poorer western *Länder*. The latter support them in principle in their demands for more fiscal equalization, but worry that a full extension of equalization to the east would be at their expense. *Bundestag* politics have also been complicated by reunification. Christian Democrat-governed *Länder* in the east make common cause on financial matters with Social Democratic *Länder* in the west. The expansion of the *Bundesrat* to sixteen *Länder*, with a total of 68 votes, has made voting outcomes less predictable. It has also diluted the influence of the large, wealthier *Länder*. Although these have had their voting weight increased from five to six, they account for a smaller proportion of the total. They have enough to block constitutional changes which they do not like, since these require a two-thirds majority, but are vulnerable in financial matters to coalitions of smaller and poorer *Länder*.

German federalism has been described as unitary or cooperative federalism, to distinguish it from systems where there is a clearer division of power. National policy making is the rule but, within this, *Land* interests have an important influence. Conflicts are regulated through the elaborate system of intergovernmental exchange and kept in bounds by the national predilection for consensus and compromise. While the broad lines of policy are agreed nationally, the existence of a decentralized system of politics and administration, together with decentralized economic and media systems, creates a vibrant territorial politics. *Land* governments, in partnership with private business and chambers of commerce, universities, research centres and local governments, have engaged in a wide range of activities to promote regional development.[29] These efforts focus on the promotion of their respective *Länder* in the opening European and global markets.

Yet it has also been pointed out that cooperative federalism and the pursuit of consensus can stifle innovation and needed change. Critics[30] have written of a joint decision trap in which the need to agree produces sub-optimal outcomes and inhibit purposive policy making. This is another example of the inflexibility of German policy-making arrangements alluded to earlier. Joint decision making can also be expensive, since it is difficult to dismantle existing programmes and new ones must be added to them. Priorities may be distorted as governments favour those projects for which the other level will pay part of the cost. At a time of increasing fiscal constraint, with a need to define priorities more clearly, this has become a more serious problem.

A recurrent criticism of German federalism is that the *Land* boundaries, based on the short-term convenience of the 1940s, bear little relationship to the needs of modern government. Even in the old West Germany, there was a gross discrepancy in size and resources between the large area-states like North-Rhine-Westphalia and Baden-Württemberg, and the smaller and poorer ones such as Saarland and Schleswig-Holstein. The city-states of Hamburg and Bremen are confined by the tight borders and cut off from their hinterlands. Only the larger *Länder* were really equipped to compete in the open European market. Reunification has greatly increased these disparities. For reasons of speed and convenience, it was decided to revive the old eastern *Länder* which had been abolished in 1952. Yet Mecklenburg-West Pomerania accounts for less than one per cent of German gross domestic product. There are many proposals for redrawing the map to produce six or seven units, perhaps merging parts of the old eastern *Länder* with western ones. Every *Land*, however, is a power base for a politician or a party and progress is very difficult.

Local Government

Local government structure in Germany is the responsibility of the individual *Länder*. The area-*Länder* are divided into *Landkreise*, or counties, for the rural areas, and *Stadtkreise* for the cities. *Stadtkreise* are responsible for all local government functions within the city. *Landkreise* are further divided into communes, or *Gemeinden*. The latter have a general competence to do anything not specifically prohibited by law, while the *Landkreise* look after matters requiring a larger scale of operation, including secondary education, public assistance and utilities. In the city-states of Hamburg and Berlin, the *Land* government is also the city council. The *Land* of Bremen, for historical reasons, comprises the city of Bremen and the detached port city of Bremerhaven. Those members of the *Land* parliament (the *Senat*) elected in the city of Bremen double up as a city council, though there are also elected neighbourhood councils, or *Beiräte*. Bremerhaven has its own elected council.

As in other European countries, there was a concern in the 1960s and 1970s that municipal governments were in many cases too small to undertake their functions efficiently. So *Land* governments engaged in an extensive process of modernization and consolidation, especially of the small *Gemeinden*. The total number of local governments has consequently come down from over 24,000 to about 8,500.

REFERENCES

1. O. Singer, 'The Politics and Economics of German Unification: From Currency Union to Economic Dichotomy', *German Politics*, 1.1 (1992), pp. 78-94.
2. E-P. Müller, 'Wirtschaftliche und soziale Interessen im XII Deutschen Bundestag', *Zeitschrift für Parlaments fragen*, 1/92 (1992), pp. 5-16.
3. C. Landfried, 'Judicial Policy-Making in Germany: the Federal Constitutional Court', *West European Politics*, 15.3 (1992), pp. 50-67.
4. 'Dokumentation und Kurzanalysen', *Zeitschrift für Parlements fragen*, 2/92 (1992), p. 438.
5. W.E. Paterson and D. Southern, *Governing Germany* (Oxford: Blackwell, 1991), p. 194.
6. S. Padgett and T. Burket, *Political Parties and Elections in West Germany* (London: Hurst and New York: St. Martins Press, 1986), p.57.
7. D. Childs, 'The far right in Germany since 1945', in L. Cheles, R. Ferguson and M. Vaughan (es.), *Neofascism in Europe* (London and New York: Longman, 1991).
8. J. Falter and Schumann, 'Die Republikaner', in P. Eisenmann and G. Hirscher (eds.), *Die Entwicklung der Volksparteien im vereinten Deutschland* (Munich: Aktuel, 1992).
9. J. Falter and Schumann, 'Die Republikaner', in P. Eisenmann and G. Hirscher (eds.), *Die Entwicklung der Volksparteien im vereinten Deutschland* (Munich: Aktuel, 1992).
10. H. Müller and W. Schubarth, 'Rechtsextremismus und aktuelle Befindlichkeiten von Jugendlichen in den neuen Bundesländern', *Aus Politik und Zeitgeschichte*, 38 (1992).
11. G. Mielke, 'Des Kirchtums langer Schatten', in H-G. Wehling (ed.), *Wahlverhalten* (Stuttgart: Kohlhammer, 1991).
12. R-O Schultze, 'Bekannte Konturen im Westen - ungewisse Zukunft im Osten', in H-G. Wehling (ed.), *Wahlverhalten* (Stuttgart: Kohlhammer, 1991).
13. S. Schumann, 'Wertewandel und Wahlverhalten', Politische Studien, 321 (1992), pp. 67-93.
14. K. Rohe, *Wahlen und Wählertradition in Deutschland* (Frankfurt: Suhrkamp, 1992).
15. C.A. Fischer, *Wahlhandbuch für die Bundesrepublik Deutschland* (Paderborn: Schonigh, 1990).
16. H. Rattinger, 'Repräsentative Wahlstatistik, 1990', *Zeitschrift für Parlaments fragen*, 2 (1992), pp. 266-   80.
17. U. Eith, 'Alters- und geschlechtsspezifisches Wahlverhalten?', in H-G. Wehling (ed.), *Wahlerhalten* (Stuttgart: Kohlhammer, 1991).
18. S. Schumann, 'Wertewandel und Wahlverhalten', Politische Studien, 321 (1992), pp. 67-93.
19. M. Jung, 'Der Wechselwähler - das unbekannte Wesen', H-G. Wehling (ed.), *Wahlverhalten* (Stuttgart: Kohlhammer, 1991).
20. D. Hancock, *West Germany. The Politics of Democratic Corporatism* (Chatham House, 1989).
21. W.E. Paterson and D. Southern, *Governing Germany* (Blackwell, 1991), p. 233.
22. D. Webber, 'Kohl's *Wendepolitik* After a Decade', *German Politics*, 1.2 (1992), pp. 149-80.
23. U. Leonardy, 'The working relationships between *Bund* and *Länder* in the Federal Republic of Germany', in C. Jeffery and P. Savigear (eds.), *German Federalism Today* (Leicester, Leicester University Press, 1991).
24. H-G. Gerstenlauer, 'German *Länder* in the European Community', in B. Jones and M. Keating (eds.), *Regions in the European Community* (Oxford: Clarendon, 1993).
25. German Ministry of Finance, *Finanzbericht* (Bonn, 1992).

26. *Der Städtag*, 2 (1992).
27. Statistisches Bundesamt, *Wirtschaft und Statistik*, 5 (1992).
28. R. Sturm, 'The Changing Territorial Balance', in G. Smith, W.E. Paterson, P.H. Merkl and S. Padgett (eds.), *Developments in German Politics* (London: Macmillan and Durham, N.C.: Duke University Press, 1992).
29. J. Esser, 'Does Industrial Policy Matter? *Land* Governments in Research and Technology Policy in Federal Germany', in c. Crouch and D. Marquand (eds.), *The New Centralism* (Oxford: Blackwell, 1989).
30. F. Scharpf, 'The Joint-Decision Trap: Lessons from German Federalism and European Integration', *Public Administration*, 66 (1988), pp. 239-278.

FURTHER READING

History and General

M. Balfour, *Germany. The Tides of Power* (London and New York: Routledge, 1992).
V.R. Berghan, *Modern Germany*, 2nd edn. (Cambridge: Cambridge University Press, 1987).
D. Conradt, *The German Polity*, 4th edn. (London and New York: Longman, 1989).
R. Dalton, *Politics in West Germany* (Glenview, Ill.: Scott, Foresman, 1989).
D. Hancock, *West Germany. The Politics of Democratic Corporatism* (Chatham, N.J.: Chatham House, 1989).
E. Kolinsky, *The Federal Republic of Germany. Innovation and Continuity at the Threshold of the 1990s* (Boulder: Lynne Rienner, 1991).
W.E. Paterson and D. Southern, *Governing Germany* (Blackwell, 1991).
G. Smith, W.E. Paterson, P.H. Merkl and S. Padgett (eds.), *Developments in German Politics* (London: Macmillan and Durham, N.C.: Duke University Press, 1992).

Parties and Elections

P. Eisenmann and G. Hirscher (eds.), *Die Entwicklung de Volksparteien im vereinten Deutschland* (Munich: Aktuel, 1992).
S. Padgett and T. Burket, *Political Parties and Elections in West Germany* (London: Hurst and New York: St. Martins Press, 1986).
H-G. Wehling (ed.), *Wahlverhalten* (Stuttgart: Kohlhammer, 1991).

Policy Making

S. Bulmer (ed.), *The Changing Agenda of West German Public Policy* (Aldershot: Dartmouth, 1989).

Federalism

C. Jeffrey and P. Savigear, *German Federalism Today* (New York: St. Martin's Press, 1992).

Reunification

R. Fritsch-Bournazel, *Europe and German Reunification* (Boulder: Lynne Rienner, 1991).
G. Glaessner, *The German Revolution 1989-1990 and German Unification* (London: Pinter, 1992).
G. Glaessner and I. Wallace, *The German Revolution of 1989. Causes and Consequences* (New York: St. Martin's Press, 1992).
G. Minnerup, *German Question* (New York: St. Martin's Press, 1992).
S. Szabo, *The Diplomacy of German Unification* (New York: St. Martin's Press, 1992).

6 Spain

STATE AND GOVERNMENT IN SPAIN

Spain is one of Europe's oldest states, forged in the late Middle Ages. Yet it has struggled throughout its history with problems of integrating its diverse nationalities and regions and since the early nineteenth century has experienced extreme instability of regimes.

Spanish unity came about through a mixture of conquest and dynastic expansion. The kingdom of Castile, expanded in the Middle Ages to conquer the Moorish (Islamic) fiefs of the south in a process later glorified as the *reconquista*. Dynastic marriages united the kingdoms of Leon, Navarre, Aragon and Portugal to Castile by the end of the fifteenth century but the various territories of the Spanish Crown retained a variety of feudal privileges and institutions. Castile was a unitary monarchical state, with a weak *Cortes* or parliament and a uniform tax system, but in their other territories the powers of the monarchs were limited. In Navarre and the Basque provinces, there were ancient *fueros* to which monarchs were forced to swear, and which provided for separate customs duties and the payment of a lump sum of taxation by the provinces to the Crown, each province being free to determine how this should be raised. The kingdom of Aragon was itself a confederation of Aragon, Catalonia, Valencia and the Balearic islands, each with its own parliamentary institutions, laws and taxes.

The non-Castilian territories were not obliged to raise taxes except for their own administration and defence. On the other hand, the new possessions gained in America in the sixteenth century were attached to the Crown of Castile and only Castilians were allowed to trade and colonize in them. The structure was further complicated by the accession of Charles V to the Holy Roman Empire, creating a multinational European empire within which was a multinational Spain, its component units themselves internally divided. Four languages remained, Castilian, Catalan, Gallego-Portuguese and Basque.

Attempts by the monarchy to create a unitary state on the lines of Louis XIV's France failed and in 1635 Portugal and Catalonia rose in revolt against taxation demands. Portugal's rebellion succeeded but Catalonia was forced back into Spain, apart from its northern province of Roussillon, which was incorporated into France, where it remains. In the war of Spanish succession, support for the unsuccessful claimant Carlos by the Aragonese territories sealed the fate of their representative institutions and in 1714 the victorious Philip V set about creating a unitary state. The *fueros* and the local representative institutions were suppressed in Aragon, Valencia and the Balearic islands, together with the *Cortes* and *Generalitat* of Catalonia. Local customs duties were abolished, the laws unified and, by the decrees of the *Nueva Planta,* modern administrative units created which ignored traditional boundaries. Posts in the Aragonese territories were opened up to Castilians and the American trade to Catalans and others. In the Basque provinces and Navarre, which had supported the losing side, the old foral regime was only dismantled in the course of the nineteenth century. Even with their institutions abolished, though, these regions retained their separate identities which were to re-emerge in force in the twentieth century.

As in the United Kingdom, the creation of the state was immediately followed by the building of an empire. Its imperial possessions in the Americas and Asia made Spain a world power in the early modern period but ultimately sapped its own dynamism. American gold, which had appeared a source of limitless wealth, provoked massive inflation and economic disruption in the Castilian territories while protected colonial markets did little to encourage competitive production. The seventeenth century saw defeats by England and the United Provinces of the Netherlands and the start of a long period of imperial decline. In the early nineteenth century, most of the South American colonies broke away and 1898 saw the last chapter in Spanish imperialism when defeat at the hands of the United States resulted in the loss of Cuba, Puerto Rico and the Philippines.

Imperial decline provided the backdrop for a series of internal struggles. Supporters of the rival dynasty, known as Carlists, staged a series of wars and insurrections during the eighteenth and nineteenth centuries, comparable in many ways to the Jacobite rebellions in Britain. Invasion and occupation by the French in the Napoleonic wars may have helped forge a sense of national unity in the subsequent war of independence but also introduced the ideas of the French Revolution and undermined the old monarchy. Liberals began their struggle against the pretensions of absolute monarchy, with the aim of establishing a constitutional government. By the nineteenth century, a Republican movement had emerged committed to overthrowing the monarchy altogether. Anticlericals fought the powerful position of the Church in the state and education system. Class struggles exploded in the countryside, where an impoverished peasantry sought land reform, and in the emerging industrial centres of the late nineteenth century. A strong presence of anarchist ideology in both cases gave an added political dimension to class strife. The late nineteenth century also saw a re-emergence of regional and nationalist movements, particularly in Catalonia and the Basque Country. Increasingly, the army involved itself in politics, seeing itself as the defender of Spanish national unity and the strong state and the nineteenth and early twentieth centuries saw a series of *pronunciamientos* or military coups.

In 1868 the First Republic was established but lasted only four years until a combination of failures and a new *pronunciamiento* restored the monarchy. The subsequent period, known as the Restoration, saw an attempt to establish a liberal, constitutional monarchy on the lines of contemporary Britain. The exponent of this ideal, Canovas, believed that alternating conservative and liberal governments would win over Republicans and provide a stability which would keep the army at bay, while social and economic modernization could take place. In practice, neither political nor economic modernization proved possible. The constitutional regime, even after the restoration of universal male suffrage in 1890 was merely a cloak behind which electoral manipulation took place.[1] Elections were invariably won by the government of the day through the efforts of local *caciques*, political bosses who traded votes for patronage. The privileges of the army, the Church and the large landowners were untouched. The new industrial bourgeoisie was bound to the system through tariff protection, which maintained their profits, though making industry internationally uncompetitive. The monarch continued to intervene in the political process, nominating governments and dismissing them at will. Serious issues of class conflict and regional discontent remained unattended. The defeat of 1898 produced a shock for the system and a new generation of *regeneracionistas* began to debate the question of Spain, that is the need for reform and modernization. This was linked, then and later, to the question of Europe, the need to join the club of developing industrial democracies to the north, breaking out of the isolationism and stagnation of the old ways. Yet the system, however degenerate, proved resilient and the regenerationist efforts came to little.

Finally the Restoration regime collapsed in 1923 in the face of a new *pronunciamiento* by General Miguel Primo de Rivera. Initially seen as a relief from strife, the new dictatorship eventually fell out with most sections of society. Plans to institutionalize the regime by setting up a system like that of Fascist Italy came to naught and, faced with mounting economic problems and the withdrawal of the support of the king, Primo was forced out of office in 1930. Two years later the monarchy itself collapsed, ushering in the Second Republic. Class, regional and anticlerical tensions continued to mount until 1936 when General Francisco Franco staged a new *pronunciamiento.* This time the constitutional government refused to give way and a three-year Civil War began. This soon became a European issue. The dictators Hitler and Mussolini sent troops to fight with Franco, in a dress rehearsal for the second world war, while left-wing volunteers from Europe and America flocked to the Republican side. Arms, but not troops, were sent from the Soviet Union to the Republican side. The European democracies adopted a policy of official neutrality which, given the pattern of external intervention, worked to Franco's advantage. From an early stage, Franco sought to present the rebellion as a crusade against communism and separatism and for the traditional Spain, enlisting the full-hearted support of the Spanish Church, except in the Basque Country, and the open sympathy of the Vatican. The Civil War produced atrocities in plenty on both sides and, in the Republican camp, a Civil War within the Civil War as the authority of the established government broke down and the Communists sought to establish their hegemony. After three years of fighting, Franco finally triumphed and ushered in a phase of savage repression. No attempt was made at national reconciliation. Over a hundred thousand Republicans were executed, and democratic, regionalist and working-class movements crushed.

While Franco is rightly bracketed with other European dictators of the period, Hitler, Mussolini and Stalin, his regime was not a totalitarian one in which a single party or movement monopolizes power through an all-embracing state. There was a Spanish Fascist Party, the *Falange*, but Franco merely used it as his convenience. Rather, the regime represented the triumph of the most uncompromising right-wing and centralist forces in Spain, the army, the Church and the large landowners. Their power and privileges were left intact and, with the support of the industrial bourgeoisie, these were to be its bulwarks. In the 1940s, repression was accompanied by isolation and an attempt at national self-sufficiency. State-owned corporations were established in imitation of Fascist Italy and industry was protected from international competition. Franco had remained officially neutral in the second world war but made little effort to hide his sympathies for the Axis powers and after the fall of Hitler and Mussolini in 1945, was increasingly isolated. There was support on the part of the British and French left for completing the eradication of fascism in western Europe by taking out the Franco regime and an early resolution of the United Nations condemned it and called for a diplomatic and economic boycott. With the start of the Cold War, however. Spain was increasingly seen as an asset in the confrontation with the Soviet Union. In the late 1940s economic agreements were reached with the United States, Britain and France and, by the early 1950s, the United States extended its protection to the regime in exchange for military bases.

This external support probably saved the regime in the 1950s. The commitment to economic modernization and opening of the economy which followed were in the longer run to undermine it. A series of agreements with the International Monetary Fund, the World Bank and the Organization for European Economic Cooperation, forerunner of the OECD, prepared Spain's entry into the international economy. Within the regime, increased emphasis was put on development and growth to the point that Franco in his annual addresses took to boasting about the increase in GNP rather than the theme of the Crusade as the justification of the regime.[2] The old style military officers and Falangist *apparatchicks* began to give way to modernizers and technocrats, often drawn from the ranks of *Opus Dei* and other Catholic organizations which aspired to combine economic modernization with continued political authoritarianism. The result was a phase of rapid economic growth, based on a very uneven expansion of industry, a boom in tourism, massive shifts of population and an explosion of urban development. Between 1960 and 1970, the proportion of the population employed in agriculture fell from 24 to 14 per cent.

As the 1960s progressed, the combination of economic modernization with political stagnation proved difficult to maintain and the Franco regime looked increasingly anomalous in the context of contemporary western Europe. Under the umbrella of the regime, elements of an alternative order began to form. In the universities, which had expanded to meet the needs of a growing and modernizing economy, students and teachers increasingly rejected the structures of the regime. The official state trade unions were infiltrated by anti-Franco elements, notably Workers' Commissions, which began to negotiate at the workplace with employers in a form of semi-legality. Modernizing elements emerged in industry, though many business leaders were still tied to the old protectionist dogmas and dependent on the regime. In Catalonia and the Basque Country, a rekindled nationalism was pressing for a restoration of self-government. Following the Second Vatican Council (1958-62) the Catholic Church liberalized and began to distance itself from the regime. Younger clergy turned against Franco in large numbers while organizations such as the young Catholic workers' movement sought to reconcile catholicism with social change. By the early 1970s, the bishops too had distanced themselves from the regime to the point that in 1973 the Conference of Bishops asked pardon for the Church's support for Franco in the Civil War. Opposition parties, though still illegal, organized themselves and forged a series of agreements for change, precursors of the pacts through which the transition to democracy was later handled. In 1974, the Communist Party and a small Socialist group, the Popular Socialist Party, formed the *Junta Democratica*, while the Socialist Party (PSOE) together with Christian Democrat, Social Democrat, Basque, Catalan and other groups formed the *Plataforma de Convergencia Democratica*. In 1976, these came together in the *Coordinacion Democratica*, providing a forum for all the main opposition movements. Although Spain was given a preferential trade agreement with the European Community, it was made clear that membership was out of the question until democracy was restored. Yet, while signs of decay were plentiful, the regime refused to admit defeat. A new wave of repression began in the early 1970s, despite international condemnation, and the appointment of the hard-line Admiral Luis Carrero Blanco as prime minister signalled Franco's determination to preserve the regime beyond his own death. Carrero Blanco's assassination in 1973 removed this prop from the system and when Franco himself died in 1975 pressures for democracy were intense.

The Transition to Democracy

A peaceful transition to democracy was not, however, inevitable. Franco had intended to restore the monarchy while preserving an authoritarian regime. To this end, he had by-passed the pretender Don Juan, suspected of liberal and democratic tendencies, in favour of his son Don Juan Carlos, whose education was entrusted to Francoist and military officials. In the later years of the regime, die-hard elements had strengthened their position and democratic forces counted on strong resistance from this Francoist bunker. Large elements of the old bureaucracy and business leaders who had grown rich on protection and state subsidies sought to cling to their privileges. For its part, the democratic opposition was committed to a policy of rupture, a clean break with Francoist institutions and a fresh start with a constituent assembly producing a new constitution. Many assumed that this would entail the declaration of a republic, as a rejection of Franco's legacy and a means of establishing continuity with the legitimate regime which he had overthrown. Most public opinion favoured a transition to democracy but feared the disruption and instability which might accompany it, or a repetition of the 1930s. Matters were not eased by an outbreak of strikes as workers' suppressed expectations exploded to the surface, and an increase in the campaign of violence on the part of the Basque organization ETA.

On ascending the throne, Juan Carlos initially retained the Francoist prime minister, Carlos Arias Navarro who was prepared to make only minimal reforms. Within a few months, it was apparent that this strategy would fail and Arias was replaced by Adolfo Suarez. Although Suarez had held office under Franco, he emerged as a reformer and undertook a transition to full democracy in cooperation with the opposition forces. This required concessions on both sides. The government had to agree to a full parliamentary democracy, pushing aside the hard-line elements. The opposition parties, notably the Socialists and Communists, had to abandon their policy of a radical rupture with Francoist legitimacy and agree to a smooth transition using the Francoist constitution itself.

The main device used was that of the pact, a series of agreements among the main political formations to manage the process of change. In November 1976 the undemocratic *Cortes* was persuaded to accept a law on reform which amounted to its own death sentence. A month later a referendum confirmed this by a 94 per cent majority. The left-wing opposition had boycotted the referendum, calling for abstention on the grounds that it did not provide a clear break with the old order and that they still did not trust the government's intentions. When it nevertheless passed, they recognized the need to cooperate in the transition. Political parties were legalized early in 1977, though fear of the military reaction delayed the legalization of the Communists for some months. In June 1977 democratic elections were held for a new *Cortes*, with the task of drawing up a constitution. These elections were won by Adolfo Suarez, at the head of the *Unión Democrático de Centro* (UCD), a rapidly constructed coalition of reformist elements from the old regime and the more moderate and conservative sections of the opposition. The Socialist Party (PSOE) emerged as the principal opposition formation and partner in managing change. The constitution was negotiated with the opposition parties and accepted in a new referendum in 1978. Meanwhile, a broad-reaching pact, the Moncloa Pact, had been negotiated with the opposition parties, principally the Socialists, for the conduct of further reform and of economic policies. The first elections under the new constitution were held in 1979, resulting in a further victory for the UCD, though without an overall parliamentary majority.

This marked the formal transition to a parliamentary democracy but the new system was far from secure. The transition was a series of elite bargains among party leaders, with little public participation. The institutions of civil society, including mass parties, trade unions and voluntary organizations, remained weak. It coincided with a serious economic crisis, following the oil-price rises of 1973 and 1979, engendering much disillusionment with the new order. The Basque terrorist organization, ETA, far from abandoning the armed struggle with the arrival of democracy, unleashed a new wave of attacks, hoping to provoke a repressive response which would in turn rebound to their political advantage. Even the constitutional Basque nationalists declined to support the new constitution, on the ground that it did not recognize their traditional rights, or *fueros*. Nationalist pressures were strong in Catalonia and demands for autonomy appearing in other regions. Most ominous of all was a threat from the army, who had so often before intervened in Spanish history. In February 1981 a group of officers attempted a coup, holding the parliament at gunpoint and surrendering only after the king had organized a counter-action. The nominal sentences which the plotters received at the hands of the military courts did not reassure public opinion and plots and rumours continued until the mid-1980s. Yet in one sense the effect of the coup attempt was salutary. It showed Spaniards how fragile was their democracy and engendered more enthusiastic support for it than had been apparent before. It also ensured that the party leaders adopted a prudent posture, keeping down the level of rhetoric and pressing ahead with a negotiated, peaceful pattern of change.

Between 1978 and 1980, statutes of autonomy were negotiated with the historic nationalities of Catalonia, the Basque Country and Galicia. In the early 1980s, limited self-government was extended to the other regions of Spain. In 1982, the constitution passed its major test, in the peaceful transition of power from the UCD to the opposition Socialist Party.

Transition also involved normalizing Spain's foreign relations. Entry into NATO was negotiated under the UCD government, at considerable political cost since the move was opposed by PSOE, the Communists and most of public opinion which recalled American support and NATO tolerance of the Franco regime. It was seen as a means of stabilizing Spain's external relations and reinforcing links with the western democracies as well as giving the military a real job, thus discouraging their historic tendency to interfere in politics. After it came into government, PSOE did a policy U-turn and accepted NATO membership, though insisting that Spain would not be part of the integrated military command. Even this reservation was effectively dropped as Spain became a full partner in the alliance. Membership of the European Community was much less contentious since it drew on the historic theme of the Europeanization of Spain as the route to modernization. It was seen as a vital means, not only to stimulate a more competitive economy but to consolidate democracy and modernize socially. The application was made in the early days of democracy by the

UCD government but opposition from French farmers, difficulties with Spain's industrial subsidies and worries about the stability of democracy slowed negotiations. In the aftermath of the coup attempt of 1981, renewed urgency was given to the question and in 1986 Spain and Portugal became the Community's eleventh and twelfth members. Despite the painful economic adjustments required, Community membership has never been seriously questioned. Spain has emerged as a leader of the southern and less advanced member states, insisting on financial transfers from the wealthier members as its price for cooperating in further political and economic integration.

By 1986, with the integration of Spain into the European Community and NATO, the transitional phase was effectively complete. For all the difficulties, the transition was a remarkable one. From being a backward autocracy, Spain is now a modern liberal democracy and for the first time in its history has a stable regime with no substantial element outside it. Yet it still bears traces of its past and both the Spanish state and its democracy face continuing challenges of modernization and change. Political violence continues on the part of ETA. The party system is not symetrical, with a dominant Socialist Party facing a weak and divided right. Nor have the institutions of civil society developed so as to underpin a truly participative democracy. The habits of elite compromise and pact-making, perhaps essential in the transition, have become part of regular political practice, often to the exclusion of truly competitive party politics or open debate.

Constitution and Government

Spain is governed by the constitution of 1978, agreed among the parties in the first democratic legislature and ratified by referendum. This stipulates that sovereignty resides in the Spanish people and that the regime is a parliamentary monarchy. Thus the question of whether Spain should be a monarchy or republic, which had divided the country for over a century, is resolved through the provision that the monarch shall be the head of state while real political power rests in the government chosen through parliamentary elections. Because of its association with Franco, the monarchy was regarded with considerable reserve in many quarters, but the commitment of the restored king, Juan Carlos, to the transition to democracy and, specifically, his role in frustrating the attempted coup of 1981, overcame most doubters. The monarchy is now generally regarded as a factor in promoting governmental stability and removing the dangers of excessive power which might accrue to an elected president. In order to make matters quite clear, the powers of the monarch are carefully defined and limited by the constitution. Article 64 stipulates that his acts must be countersigned by the responsible ministers. Other articles of the constitution stipulate the powers of the various elements of government, the procedures for establishing self-government in the regions and procedures for constitutional amendment. Chapter 2 is a list of citizen rights including free speech, religious liberty, the right to associate and join trades unions and the right to private property. Chapter 3 is more elaborate and altogether more vague, consisting of social and economic rights and duties including the duty of the state to promote sport and culture and the right of the citizen to an adequate environment, housing and consumer protection.

The study of government in Spain tends to focus on minute exegesis of the constitutional document almost to the exclusion of discussion of the realities of political life.[3] It is true that in most systems of government, these realities often differ from the constitutional theory, but in Spain the gap is particularly large. The emphasis on formal constitutional theory is greater than in northern Europe and maintained by the strong position of professors of constitutional law in the universities. Yet Spanish history, with its constant revolutions, *pronunciamientos* and regime changes reveals scant respect for constitutional norms. The constitution of 1978 is significant in being the first time that all Spanish political forces have agreed on the form of a regime and it provides a basic understanding of the framework of government, but to gain an insight into the realities of power we must also look beyond it. Spain is also marked by a tradition of borrowing constitutional and legal theories from other European countries, notably France and Germany, adapting these more or less successfully to its own conditions. Another general feature of the constitution is that, as a negotiated document which had to satisfy diverse political forces in 1978, it is full of compromises, ambiguities and even contradictions. For example, the powers which can or must be devolved to the autonomous communities or regions are confusingly specified, and there is a series of economic and social rights which are almost impossible to define in practical terms or to enforce. Some constitutional theorists, in a spirit of rational improvement, would like to rewrite it, clarify it or remove the ambiguities. Most political forces, however, thankful that Spaniards have at last achieved agreement on their form of government, prefer to leave well alone, relying on practice, interpretation and convention to iron out the difficulties.

Like Britain, Italy and Germany, Spain is a parliamentary system in which there is no sharp separation of powers between the executive and legislature. Instead, the government is formed from the majority party in the lower house of parliament. To emphasize the purely formal role of the monarch and to avoid the governmental instability which plagued the Second Republic in the 1930s, the framers of the constitution made detailed provision for the investiture of the head of government, borrowing freely from the German Basic Law. Officially the head of government is known as the *Presidente del Gobierno* but, to avoid confusion with republican systems, we shall translate this into English as prime minister. After each general election, parliament meets to vote on a prime minister, who must receive an absolute majority of all eligible members. If no candidate receives such a majority, a second ballot must be held forty-eight hours later in which a simple majority of those voting suffices. If this too proves impossible after two months new elections must be called, the idea being to concentrate the minds of members of parliament with the threat of having to face the country and risk their seats. Once invested, a prime minister can be removed during the term of that parliament only by a constructive vote of no confidence, that is a motion which contains the name of an alternative candidate for prime minister and which to succeed must gain an absolute majority of all members of the parliament, not merely of those voting. It is the prime minister and not the government as a whole who is invested and cannot be removed by the head of state.[4] This greatly strengthens the prime minister in relation to parliament. Prime ministerial power is further reinforced by an electoral system which tends to produce majorities for a single party. In 1989, for example, the Socialist Party of Prime Minister Felipe González was returned with a majority, albeit of just one seat, with 39 per cent of the vote. Although a rerun of a disputed election left the Socialist Party with exactly half the seats and thus without a clear majority, González was ensured up to four years' secure tenure of power since to remove him all the opposition parties would have to agree on an alternative.

The prime minister in turn chooses and dismisses the other ministers. These need not be members of parliament, though in practice this is normally the case. It is difficult to generalize about prime ministerial power in Spain, since there have only been three prime ministers and one of these was little more than a stop-gap. Constitutional provision for investiture of the prime minister and the constructive vote of no confidence certainly bolster the power of the office, reducing the danger of parliamentary ambushes and ensuring that the incumbent will normally have a secure term. It is clear, however, that the day-to-day power of the prime minister depends more on the presence of a strong and disciplined party base than on the provisions of the constitution. Prime ministers may be protected from the opposition but, as in other parliamentary systems, a leader who is rejected by his or her own party will not survive. Adolfo Suarez, the first elected prime minister, headed a loose coalition of forces, the UCD, which was to break up altogether in 1982, and his position was weakened as a result. By contrast, Felipe González was able to command a parliamentary majority of tightly disciplined MPs and ensured that as prime minister he kept close control over the party.

Parliament, the *Cortes Generales*, is elected every four years, although the prime minister has the right to call early elections when at least twelve months have elapsed since the last ones. The *Cortes Generales* consists of two houses. The lower house, known as the Congress of Deputies, is elected by a modified form of proportional representation. As is normal in parliamentary systems, it is the more important house and the one to which the government is responsible. The Senate is in principle a chamber of territorial representation. Four members are directly elected in each province. In addition, the parliament of each autonomous community (see below) nominates one member, plus an extra member for each million inhabitants. Senate elections also take place every four years, though where the Congress of Deputies is dissolved for new elections, it is customary to call Senate elections at the same time. There is a general assumption that the Senate should eventually represent the autonomous communities, as in federal systems, but there is as yet no agreement on how to achieve this. In order to ensure governmental stability, party discipline is encouraged by the rules of parliamentary procedure. Official recognition is given to groups which must normally have at least fifteen members, except in the case of regional parties, and there are restrictions on deputies changing groups or forming new ones. Representation on committees is decided by party group and a *Junta de Portavoces*, consisting of party representatives, decides important issues of procedure.

Parliament is responsible for the passage of laws, which are of two types. Organic laws, affecting fundamental rights and liberties, the electoral system and the constitutions of autonomous communities, require the approval of an absolute majority of members of the Congress of Deputies. Other laws require merely a majority of those voting. The Senate can delay legislation but not veto it. Bills can be introduced by the government, in which case they are known as *proyectos de ley*, or by backbenchers, in which case they are known as *proposiciones de ley* and enjoy a lower priority. An unusual feature of the Spanish constitution is that regional governments, the autonomous communities, can also initiate *proposiciones de ley* in the national parliament, as can groups of private citizens if they can must 500,000 signatures to a petition, though without the support of the government they stand no real chance of success. In the third legislature (1986-9) there were 162 *proposiciones de ley*, of which just 13 were successful. These included three of the nine sponsored by autonomous communities but neither of the two sponsored by citizen initiative. There are three stages of legislation. Bills first go to a debate in the whole chamber, where amendments affecting the whole text, proposed by the party groups, are considered. Then it goes to one of the standing committees, whose membership exactly reflects the party balance in the whole chamber. This in turn will usually send it to a subcommittee (*ponencia*) for a report on the text and the detailed amendments which have been proposed. Although this stage is supposed to be completed within two weeks, it rarely is and bills have been known to languish in subcommittees for long periods. After the subcommittee has produced its report, the whole committee considers the bill clause by clause and votes on amendments. It is then sent back to the whole chamber, where debate is led by the minister and the chair of the committee or subcommittee (*ponente*) with only technical amendments allowed. The whole process is managed closely by the government and the party groups and there is little opportunity for intervention by the individual member, or for rebellion against the party line.

Parliament also has the task of scrutinizing government. Oral and written questions are put to ministers, though the time for this is limited and there is nothing like the British Question Time with its charged confrontations between government and opposition. There was a steady increase in questions to ministers, from some three thousand in the first democratic legislature, to eighteen thousand in the third. Investigative committees can be set up to look at specific questions but they have been rather rare with just five in the third legislature (1986-9). In general, parliament has not become an important part of the Spanish political system. Procedural rules designed to promote stability and strong government are reinforced by cultural norms. The habits of debate and scrutiny have yet to develop in a society inured to authoritarian government. The institution of the opposition, critically examining government policy while seeking to demonstrate its capacity to take over, has developed rather slowly, hindered by the disarray of the parties of the centre-right during the 1980s. Party discipline and the existence of a majority freed the PSOE government largely to ignore parliamentary pressures. Members of parliament of the governing party generally consider it their duty to support their leadership and less than 10 per cent of questions to ministers come from their own backbenchers. So ministers find it fairly easy to escape parliamentary scrutiny. Between his investiture for a new term of office in December 1989 and February 1992, Prime Minister Felipe González had attended parliament just eleven times, usually to report on matters of European and foreign affairs. Where government has lacked a majority or where qualified majorities are required, these are usually obtained by deals between the main parties to ensure parliamentary support. More generally, the resort to corporatist deals and social concertation has by-passed parliament as the main form of political representation.

Enforcement of the provisions of the constitution is the responsibility of the Constitutional Court. Members of the Constitutional Court are appointed for nine-year terms, with a third renewed every three years. Four each are appointed by the Congress of Deputies and the Senate, requiring a majority of four-fifths of all the members to be approved. Two are appointed by the government, and two by the General Council of the Judiciary. In practice, this has subjected the appointment of the judges to political patronage. Governments nominate judges known to be sympathetic or, where necessary, do deals with the opposition parties to share the patronage. In 1992, however, the deal broke down when the conservative opposition PP insisted on a deal in relation to coverage on the state television channel as the price of its assent. The, entirely unintended, result was that the minor parties were able to insist on open voting on a list of candidates chosen for their judicial eminence.

Unlike the Supreme Court of the United States, the Constitutional Court is limited to considering laws and acts immediately after their passage and there is a complex system for determining who is eligible to take cases before it. In matters of the constitutionality of laws, these include the prime minister, fifty members of parliament or, where the law affects its own powers, an autonomous community. In practice, it is rare for the parliamentary opposition to appeal the constitutionality of laws and most challenges come from autonomous communities. The ordinary courts are not competent to rule that a law is unconstitutional, though they can in certain cases refer the matter to the Constitutional Court. Where a public body has allegedly contravened the constitutional provisions for citizens rights, ordinary citizens can also appeal. There is an extremely large number of cases brought before the Constitutional Court, over 90 per cent of which involve citizens complaining about breaches of their rights. Between September 1990 and April 1991, there were 1,719 cases brought to the Court, while in the same period 1,979 cases were completed, 1,503 of these being dismissed. This huge workload has led to serious delays, with the average time taken to hear a case rising to over two and a half years. In 1983-5, approval of the abortion law reform undertaken by the PSOE government was held up for a year and a half while the Court decided on an appeal against its constitutionality lodged by the opposition. It was eventually approved subject to detailed changes. The Spanish Constitutional Court has taken a cautious approach to its subject, confining itself to rather narrow issues of constitutionality rather than the merits of laws, and to the case in question rather than general principles. It has also, in the view of many regionalists, tended to favour a rather centralist interpretation of the constitution. In this way it has left political initiative in the hands of politicians, but the absence of definitive interpretations of what is a very complex and sometimes contradictory constitution is one of the factors which has sustained the flood of cases before the Court.

PARTIES AND ELECTIONS

In the initial stages of the transition to democracy, the Spanish party system was highly fragmented. 78 parties presented candidates in the elections of 1977, with 12 gaining seats.[5] By the late 1980s, the system had consolidated considerably and while 58 parties contested the elections, only two of these gained more than twenty seats. The two main parties had absorbed many of their rivals and between them won 65 per cent of the vote and 80 per cent of the seats. So far, however, a truly competitive two-party system has not emerged. Instead, there is a dominant centre-left party, a smaller conservative opposition and a series of centre, leftist and regionalist groups. The reasons for this pattern of competition lie in the electoral system, the historic problems of forming a democratic right in Spain, and the strong regional dimension to the party system.

According to the constitution, elections to the Congress of Deputies are by proportional representation but the effects of this are heavily modified by a provision that the electoral division shall be the provinces and that each province shall have a guaranteed minimum level of representation - three seats according to the current law. In large provinces such as Barcelona or Madrid, this allows a truly proportional distribution of seats.[6] In small provinces, with only three deputies, proportionality is very difficult to achieve. The result is that small parties with support evenly distributed across the country are penalized. Parties with strong regional support, on the other hand, have an advantage. This can be seen from the results of the 1989 election in which the Catalan party, CiU gained eighteen seats for 5 per cent of the vote while the national centre formation, CDS, contesting seats across Spain, won just fourteen seats with 8 per cent of the vote. The biggest gainer of all, however, was the Socialist Party, PSOE which won exactly half the seats with just under 40 per cent of the vote. The provision for a minimum of three deputies whatever the size of the province also biases the system towards the rural areas since the more sparsely populated provinces would not qualify for three seats if these were distributed strictly according to population. The system was designed by and for the large parties, particularly the ruling UCD at the time of the constitution, though ironically the UCD was to prove one of its main victims five years later. Given the weakly proportional effects of the system, small parties, except for the main regionalist ones, have an interest in merging with the larger ones rather than contesting elections on their own and this is precisely what has happened.

The centre-right of the political spectrum was dominated in the early days by the *Unión Democrático de Centro* (UCD), hastily assembled by Prime Minister Adolfo Suarez to contest the first democratic elections in 1977. UCD consisted of a loose grouping of reformists from the Franco era, like Suarez himself, together with conservative opposition elements, Social Democrats, Christian Democrats and Liberals. It was more a collection of notables than a modern political party but its democratic centre-right position carried reassurance to large sections of the electorate who favoured the transition but feared radical disruption. UCD won the elections of 1977 and 1979 but was subject to increasing internal difficulties. In 1981 Suarez was deserted by the Social Democrats, then the Cchristian Democrats and Liberals until finally, unable to govern, he stepped down as prime minister. In the aftermath of the failed coup attempt and difficulties over NATO entry and the LOAPA law on the autonomous communities, the UCD largely disintegrated and in the elections of 1982 was reduced to just 6.5 per cent of the vote and a handful of seats.

To the right of the UCD was the *Allianza Popular* (AP) of Manuel Fraga Iribane, a former Francoist minister. Although he had been considered a reformer under the Franco regime, Fraga staked his position well to the right in the democratic transition, seeking the votes of that section of the electorate who hankered after the old ways. The AP was a collection of parties most of which were little more than projections of individual politicians who had held office under the late Franco regime but who gambled that the majority of the electorate wanted only gradual and modest change. This proved a serious misinterpretation and the attempt was a failure, with Fraga's party gaining just 8 per cent in 1977 and 6 per cent in 1979. The UCD took that section of the conservative vote which was committed to making democracy work. Yet for all its failure as a party the Popular Alliance may well have helped tie the Francoist right to the democratic regime since for all his authoritarianism Fraga never supported a return to dictatorship. It seems that he would have preferred something like France under de Gaulle, a strong government able to impose social discipline and deal firmly with dissent but which at the end of the day would respect the verdict of the ballot box and leave office if it was voted out. From the early 1980s, the party, which became known as the *Partido Popular* or Popular Party (PP), attempted to move towards the mainstream European right, something like the British Conservative Party or the modern French RPR and UDF. It succeeded in absorbing a number of smaller parties and after the collapse of the UCD in 1982 became the main opposition to the new PSOE government. In the early 1980s it also gained the support of the employers' organization the CEOE.

Fraga's Francoist image, however, proved a fatal obstacle since he was considered unelectable as prime minister and the party was seen as the embodiment of the authoritarian tendencies of traditional Spanish conservatism. Opposition to the PSOE government in the early years was exaggerated and alarmist or purely opportunist. In the referendum on NATO membership, for example, the party which supported membership recommended its supporters to abstain in order to deny the government a clear victory, a cynical move which did nothing for its credentials as a serious alternative government. Its programme was a mixture of economic liberalism with social authoritarianism, with promises to see off terrorism within six months, without specifying how. In successive elections of 1982, 1986 and 1989, PP failed to penetrate what became known as Fraga's ceiling, with its vote stagnating at 26 per cent. Fraga was clearly a liability but the party was poorly institutionalized and unable to manage without him as was shown in 1987 when he resigned. The new leader proved a disaster, the party started to fall apart and Fraga had to be called back. Just before the 1989 elections, he again moved aside to become chief minister of the autonomous community of Galicia and José María Aznar took over as leader of PP in an effort to give it a younger image. PP has since sought to project itself as a modern, Conservative party in the European mould, joining the Christian Democratic International and the Christian Democratic/Conservative group in the European Parliament and seeking the centre ground while

Table 6.1 Principal political parties in Spain

Intitials	Full Name	Political Leaning
PSOE	Partido Socialista Obrero Español	Social Democratic
PP	Partido Popular	Conservative
CDS	Centro Democrático y Social	Centrist
CiU	Convergència i Unió	Catalan nationalist and Christian Democratic
IU	Izquierza Unida	neo-Communist
PNV	Partido Nacionalista Vasco	Basque nationalist and Christian Democratic
HB	Herri Batasuna	Basque separatist.

promoting the market economy, deregulation and cutting public expenditure. As these were also the priorities of the PSOE government throughout the late 1980s and early 1990s, it proved difficult to establish a distinct image. The vision of the PP as a modern, reforming party also conflicted with its continued roots in clientelist politics and *caciquismo* inherited from the past and associated with its tenure of power in local and regional government. While lacking Fraga's negative features, Aznar also lacks his predecessor's charisma and was widely discounted as a lightweight. In the general election of 1993, helped by a series of scandals in the Socialist government and a serious recession, he managed to raise the AP vote and pick up many electors from the collapsing CDS. With 35 per cent of the vote, the AP now presented a serious challenge to the Socialists. Yet, given the economic and political conditions, the major opposition party might have been expected to do even better.

The failure to establish a successful Conservative party in Spain also has a historic explanation. In the past, the right distrusted democracy, preferring to call in the army where necessary, and conservative forces were widely discredited by the participation in the Francoist regime. In the Restoration era (1873-1923), business had not felt the need for a political party since both parties could be relied on to deliver what it wanted while the working class had largely taken themselves out of politics. CEDA, a right-wing clericalist group formed under the Second Republic of the 1930s, was the only historic organized party on the political right. Nor, in contrast to other Catholic countries, has Spain ever developed a Christian Democratic party. The Spanish Catholic Church remained loyal to the Franco regime until the 1970s. When it finally abandoned it and supported the transition to democracy, it also decided to abstain from involvement in politics altogether. Christian Democrat movements which did form received no official Church support and made little progress, except in the peripheral regions. Under Franco, most of the business world worked quite happily with the regime. In the early years of democracy, employers spoke out against socialism and showed some interest in establishing a pro-business party in the early 1980s, withdrawing support from the UCD, launching an initiative for a broad right, the *gran derecha,* and intervening in regional and national elections. By the mid-1980s, however, business had little complaint with the policies of the nominally Socialist PSOE government and no need for an independent vehicle. More generally, the Spanish right was delegitimized by the experience of right-wing dictatorship rather in the way the whole left was delegitimized by the Communist regimes in eastern Europe. They were unable to strike the neo-liberal anti-statist line which other European conservatives adopted in the 1980s since in Spain the overbearing state was a right-wing legacy and its reformation was being undertaken by the left. So the PP arouses strong negative feelings from supporters of other parties, preventing it from exploiting weaknesses in its opponents to win over waverers.

The regional question is the final reason for the failure of the Spanish centre right.

In Catalonia and the Basque Country, where the Catholic middle class had been alienated from Franco because of his suppression of regional self-government and culture, strong Christian Democratic movements emerged. The Basque nationalist party, PNV, which dates from the late nineteenth century, was an early adherent to the Christian Democrat international formed after the war. Jordi Pujol's Catalan nationalist group CiU, formed in the transition to democracy is also a party of the christian democrat centre right. Yet their primary commitment is to their own regions, where they have consolidated themselves as the dominant parties in both national and regional elections. In 1986, there was an attempt by the Catalan party to launch a Spanish-wide centre-right movement, spearheaded by its deputy leader Miquel Roca. This was a renewal of an old Catalan ideal, to modernize Spain by 'catalanizing' it but it was no more successful than its early twentieth-century precursors. Thereafter the Catalan party has retained its separate identity as a parliamentary party, prepared to cut deals with the other parties to suit its interests but not to submerge itself in any wider formation. The Basque PNV too has engaged in the politics of parliamentary dealing. Since the 1989 elections, both have been more inclined to deal with the PSOE government than align themselves with the PP, still seen as committed to centralist, anti-regional positions.

The parties of the left are much older than those of the centre-right, with the exception of the PNV. PSOE (*Partido Socialista Obrero Español*), is a Social Democratic party, founded in 1888 and closely linked to the trade union UGT. Yet, in comparison with northern Europe, Spain was not fertile ground for a Socialist worker's movement. The Spanish working class was numerically weak and largely adhered to the anarchist movement with its philosophy of abstention from politics in favour of revolutionary change. So PSOE made little political progress before the Second Republic. Although theoretically committed to Marxism and revolution, it often took a moderate line and in 1920 refused to join the new Communist international, provoking a split and the formation of the Spanish Communist Party (PCE). Under the Second Republic, sections of PSOE moved to a radical, revolutionary stance while the party as a whole played a major role in the popular front government. Its move to the left and the splits in its ranks lost it votes and with the victory of Franco it was banned along with the other constitutional parties. Yet PSOE was able to survive, in clandestine form, both inside and outside Spain. The leadership, based in France, languished until the early 1970s when it was challenged by a younger generation of activists based in Spain. In 1972, the new group held a rival congress in Toulouse and claimed recognition from the Socialist International as the official Spanish party. On achieving this, they held a further congress in France in 1974 at which Felipe González was elected general secretary and the trade union leader Nicolas Redondo organizing secretary. As the Franco regime neared its end, PSOE declared its preference for a radical rupture and in 1976 reaffirmed its position as a Marxist party, rejecting any accommodation with capitalism or simple reform of the system. By 1977, however, the PSOE leadership accepted the strategy of gradual transition using the legal forms of the Franco regime and the constitutional monarchy. It negotiated with the UCD government to secure the Moncloa Pacts on economic policy and the framing of the new constitution. In the elections of 1977 and 1979 it established itself as the principal opposition party and was able to absorb a number of the smaller Socialist groupings. In 1979, in a bid to make PSOE a credible challenger for government, González insisted that it drop its Marxist self-definition and place itself firmly in the European Socialist tradition. When the party conference demurred, González resigned, agreeing to come back later that year only when the party had changed its mind. This both changed the party's public image to a moderate one and established González as the undisputed leader.

Under González and deputy leader Alfonso Guerra, tight central control and rigid discipline were imposed. As in other Social Democratic parties, there is an extremely complex organizational structure which pays-lip service to internal democracy. At the base are over four thousand local party groups, which elect committees and conferences at ascending levels all the way to the Federal Congress which is the supreme body of the party. In practice, the national leadership is predominant. Before 1983, internal party elections were organized on a majoritarian basis, formal tendencies banned and members expelled for speaking out against the leadership line. Since then, internal 'currents of opinion' have been recognized and provision made for representation of the larger minorities in party forums. It was also made possible for organizations to affiliate to the party. As the party became a credible contender for power, it attracted members eager for office, providing the leadership with further opportunities for patronage. In 1982, with the UCD collapsing, PSOE was able to increase its vote to 48 per cent and form a majority government, retaining power in 1986 and 1989 with diminishing majorities. As a government, PSOE abandoned its Socialist past almost entirely. There was one symbolic nationalization, of the RUMASA enterprise. This was later privatized, the episode giving birth to one of the side shows of Spanish politics in the 1980s and 1990s, the efforts of the former owner Ruis Mateus to gain recompense. These included an appeal to the European Court of Human Rights and running lists of candidates in national, regional and European elections some of which, capitalizing on protest vote, were actually elected.

PSOE's general priority proved to be enhancing the competitiveness of the Spanish economy through privatization, running down old heavy industries, attracting inward investment through the promise of low wages and social charges and deregulation of the labour market. In 1986, Spain joined the European Community, a move supported by all parties, and government priorities focused on making Spain competitive in the new Europe. With the peseta linked to the European monetary system, it became essential to keep inflation under control, even at the cost of rising unemployment By the early 1990s, Spanish unemployment levels were running at about 18 per cent, by far the highest among the major countries of western Europe. Foreign capital was being attracted and Spanish growth rates were also among the highest in Europe but increased tensions were appearing as the labour movement complained that the fruits of growth were not being fairly distributed. After 1986 the UGT trade union broke its links with PSOE and in 1989 gave discrete support to its neo-Communist rival, IU.[7] PSOE had opposed the decision of the UCD government to take Spain into the NATO alliance, from which it had been excluded under Franco on the insistence of the European members, and promised a referendum on its return to power. In government, it held the referendum but campaigned in favour of staying in the alliance, with only token concessions to the anti-NATO position in the form of reductions in the American presence. By the late 1980s, PSOE could be better characterized as a party of the European centre-right rather than the Socialist left, further undercutting the prospects of the PP. After it lost its majority following a rerun of the 1989 election in one seat, PSOE preferred to cut deals with the centre-right Catalan and Basque parties rather than the neo-Communists left so that, despite the fall in its support it was able to maintain its key position in the political system.

PSOE's defence of its shift to the centre-right is that the priority in Spain has been the building of democracy and a competitive European economy, bringing the country up to the level already enjoyed by its northern neighbours at which time social questions might be addressed. Nationalization and state planning, policies of the left in northern Europe, were associated in Spain with Francoist authoritarianism and the González government argued that it took a Social Democratic party to liberalize the economy. Unlike other European Socialist movements, PSOE for many years had little serious internal opposition or ideological infighting, in spite of its marked moves to the political right. There was one organized faction, the Socialist Left but it generally accepted party discipline and has not organized parliamentary rebellions. Factions tend to be organized around personalities rather than programmes and to change rather quickly in response to events. Membership is rather small compared with other European social democratic parties but it more than doubled between 1981 and 1988, as newcomers flooded into the new governing party in search of office or position. Like its European counterparts, it has an increasingly middle class membership and working class completely absent from leadership positions. This capacity to attract the ambitious middle class, with the patronage available from office at national and local level and in the autonomous communities, largely explains the leadership's easy control over the organization and the absence of rebellions. After ten years in power without serious opposition, accusations grew of arrogance and remoteness on the part of the leadership and a series of corruption scandals damaged the party's image both at home and abroad. In 1991, Alfonso Guerra was forced to resign from the government, though retaining his position as deputy leader of the party, following a scandal involving his brother and the use of government offices for dubious purposes. Much critical comment focused on the 'beautiful people' (the English expression is used), the new elite who had gained wealth and power from their connections with PSOE and whose flashy lifestyle was deeply resented by people struggling with economic change. By 1993, Guerra, allied with the left-wing, was in open opposition to González who had increasing difficulty asserting his control over the party. Despite this, and the general air of corruption, however, PSOE was able to get back into office at the 1993 election, albeit without an overall majority.

It had been expected that the Communist Party, like its Italian counterpart, would play a prominent role in the democratic regime. It had been active in the developing political opposition in the 1960s and 1970s and, especially in the work place, through the Workers' Commissions. After 1968, its leader Santiago Carrillo, seeing the need for a broader appeal and more attractive image, broke with the Soviet line and became a prominent exponent of Eurocommunism, though retaining tight control over the party itself. In the event Communist strength proved to have been exaggerated, by the party for its own purposes and by Franco to gain western support for his regime in the Cold War. In the first democratic elections in 1977 and 1979, the Communists gained between nine and ten per cent of the vote, but then fell away to 4 per cent in 1982. A series of splits between Eurocommunists and a pro-Soviet element known as Afghans for their support of the Soviet invasion of Afghanistan, and between supporters and opponents of Carrillo, further weakened the party. In 1986, a new alliance was put together of the various Communist factions and other left-wing groups, known as *Izquierza Unida*, or United Left (IU). With the implicit support of the formerly Socialist UGT trade union as well as the usual endorsement of Workers' Commissions, IU was able to capitalize on PSOE's move to the right to capture nine per cent of the vote in 1989. In Catalonia, where it is known as *Iniciativa per Catalunya* and includes some nationalist elements, it has been moving to merge into a single party. Elsewhere, IU remains a very loose coalition prone to infighting and unsure of its future direction.

In the political centre, the main force has been the *Centro Democràtico y Social* (CDS) founded by former Prime Minister Adolfo Suarez in 1982. After a poor start, this gained around 8 per cent of the vote in 1986 and 1989 but has failed to progress beyond this. As a small party with a widely dispersed vote, it is penalized by the electoral system. Nor, with the move of PSOE to the centre-right, is there much room in the political spectrum for an alternative centre party. CDS was further undermined by Suarez's resignation from the leadership in 1991 and consists of a group of notables, with local roots in certain regions rather than a mass programmatic party. In 1993, it lost its last representatives in the national parliament.

The remainder of the political spectrum is filled with a group of smaller regionalist parties, the most prominent of which is *Herri Batasuna*, an extreme Basque Party which supports the violent campaign of ETA and the creation of an independent Basque state in the Basque Country, Navarre and the Basque-speaking parts of France. Although it gains only about one per cent of the national vote, this is tightly concentrated, allowing it to win four seats in 1989. For some years, *Herri Batasuna* deputies, like those of Sinn Fein in Northern Ireland, refused to take their seats in the national parliament, though they do sit in the Basque autonomous parliament and in local councils. In 1993, however, they turned up to the newly-elected national parliament, hoping to exploit the lack of a government majority. Other small regionalist parties winning seats in 1989 included left-wing Catalan and Basque movements and regionalists from the Canaries, Andalusia, Valencia and Aragon.

Parties have played a key role in Spanish democracy, magnified by the weakness of social and economic associations. Yet they remain small in numbers and do not generally encourage mass participation. The lack of mass memberships, together with the opportunities for patronage provided by public office, explains the ease with which leaderships are able to change the policy line in response to the tactical needs of the moment. A significant proportion of the membership of most parties comprises elected or appointed officials at various levels of government. Leadership power is further reinforced by the system of state financing with accounts for over 90 per cent of the income of a party like PSOE. This frees the leadership from the need to build a mass membership or align itself closely with interest groups. Few of the parties have been free of accusations of corruption, or the diversion of public money or bribes into party coffers, a tendency which has brought them into further disrepute.

Electoral Behaviour

Figure 6.1 shows the changing pattern of party support in democratic Spain. The main trend is the consolidation of the two main parties, PSOE and PP and the collapse of the centre. Smaller parties have largely disappeared or been absorbed into the larger formations.

Examining the results in more detail, a regional pattern of support is discernible. As Table 6.2 for the 1989 election shows, PSOE had the most even distribution of support among Spanish regions. Outside the special case of the Basque Country, its support varied between 31 and 52 per cent. Its strongholds remain the southern

Figure 6.1 Percentage vote in legislative elections, 1977-89

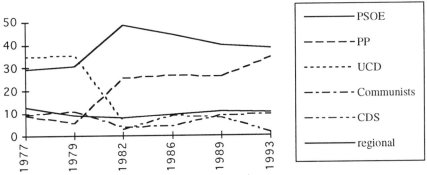

Table 6.2 Percentage vote in 1989 General Election by autonomous community

	PSOE	PP	CDS	IU	Regional
Andalusia	52.2	20.1	4.6	11.9	6.2
Aragon	38.4	27.6	7.6	9.7	11.3
Asturias	40.2	26.3	12.4	15.4	1.0
Balearics	34.1	40.2	9.1	5.0	3.1
Canaries	35.8	19.1	17.4	7.9	13.8
Cantabria	39.6	38.0	9.6	6.3	-
Castile & Leon	35.1	39.8	12.6	6.6	0.1
Castile-LaMancha	47.6	33.5	7.7	6.9	-
Catalonia	35.4	10.6	4.3	7.3	35.2
Extremadura	53.5	24.8	9.5	6.8	1.8
Galicia	34.1	38.7	7.7	3.3	9.0
Madrid	33.1	34.0	10.9	15.3	-
Murcia	45.7	29.8	10.3	9.1	-
Navarre	31.0	35.9	7.0	5.7	19.4
Basque Country	20.9	9.3	3.4	3.0	58.6
Rioja	39.4	40.7	7.1	6.4	-
Valencia	41.2	26.9	7.8	9.0	8.8

Source: Spanish Ministry of the Interior

regions of Andalusia and Extremadura where it was still able to gain over half the vote. Support for the Popular Party was more varied, from just over 10 per cent in Catalonia to over 40 per cent in its best regions. CDS support is very uneven, with its strongest support in the Canary islands and, to a lesser extent, Asturias and Madrid. Asturias, a coal mining region in the north, together with Madrid, also register the highest vote for the neoCommunist IU. Regional variations in voting patterns are partly explained by differences in class structure but also by historical traditions. They are often maintained by clientelist networks established by dominant parties such as PSOE in Andalusia or the Popular Party in Galicia which are able t use the resources of national, autonomous and local governments to reward supporters and oil the party machine. Among the regions, Catalonia and the Basque Country stand out for their support for specifically regionalist or peripheral nationalist parties. In the Basque Country, where several minor nationalist parties compete with the dominant PNV, nearly 60 per cent of the vote went to local rather than Spanish parties. In Catalonia, this phenomenon is less marked since PSOE garners a respectable percentage of the vote. On the centre and right, however, the Catalan nationalist CiU is dominant, reducing the vote which might otherwise be available to the PP or the CDS.

Spain does not possess the rich array of survey evidence on voting available in other west European countries but it is possible to make draw some conclusions about voting patterns since 1977 from opinion surveys conducted by the Centre for Sociological Research in Madrid. This indicates that, as in other Catholic countries, religion remains a significant element in voting choice and that more religious people tend to the right. A 1987 survey found that intentions to vote for the conservative PP varied from 30 per cent of those who attended mass on Sundays and feast days, to just 3 per cent among those who never attended. The neo-Communist IU registered 12 per cent among those who never attend but just one per cent among the regular attenders. PSOE also registered more support among the non-attenders, at 37 per cent, against 16 per cent for those who attend on Sundays and feast days.[9] These differences are not necessarily to be attributed to divisions on the merits of religious issues. In contrast to the past, these have largely disappeared from Spanish public life. The Church does not involve itself in politics apart from matters like abortion and the occasional criticism of excessive social division, and there is no Catholic party. Rather the differences in voting patterns must be seen as the expression of a broader set of values and self-definitions, together with a strong historic legacy. Left and right are still recognizable as political traditions and cultures, even where policy differences have been attenuated or issues like republicanism and clericalism have disappeared. On the other hand, Spain no longer has rigidly defined subcultures such as have marked postwar Italian politics.

Class, too, is an important determinant of voting. The PP's support is skewed to the middle classes and to farmers. PSOE, is correspondingly stronger among workers, though its overall strength in the 1980s allowed it to make inroads into the middle-class vote, giving it a more balanced social profile than the PP. IU is strongest among working class voters and has sought to exploit PSOE's move to the right and conflicts with the trade unions to increase its presence in this sector. It also has a significant level of support among white collar workers. The centrist CDS is best represented among the highest social categories, employers and managers and those with the highest incomes. Gender has little influence on the PP or PSOE vote, but women are much less attracted to the Communist IU than are men, a finding consistent with that of other European countries. Finally, there is the question of ideology. With most of the parties presenting similar policy platforms, it is difficult to attribute voting intentions to these, but it does seem that the PP has failed to shake off the image of the traditional, conservative right. This might help it maintain its vote among farmers, staunch Catholics and elements of the old middle class, but prevents it reaching out to the new professional classes and modernizing elements of society. PSOE, on the other hand, was able in the 1980s to project an image of modernization and Europeanization and so reach into sections of the middle class which otherwise might have been attracted to a more openly conservative or centrist formation. The cost in 1989 was a certain loss of PSOE's working-class vote to the UI but not enough to threaten its dominant position within the political system.

THE STATE, ADMINISTRATION AND POLICY MAKING

During the Napoleonic occupation, Spain adopted many aspects of French state organization and this influence persisted throughout the nineteenth century. In theory, the state was seen as the impartial guider of the nation, run by an enlightened bureaucracy serving the general public interest. It stood above and apart from the civil society. Experience of dictatorship in the twentieth century further enhanced the role of the state, centralized it further, and inhibited the development of an independent organizational life. This dependence on the state has persisted into the democratic era. As Table 6.3 shows, Spaniards were still in the 1980s more inclined to look to the state than Americans or even French people.

Table 6.3 Attitudes to the state, % respondents

	Spain (1988)	France (1985)	USA (1985)
The state is responsible for all the citizens and must concern itself with all of those who have problems	75	44	26
Citizens are responsible for their own wellbeing and must themselves take charge of the situation when they have problems	23	49	74
No reply	2	7	0

Source: M. Beltrán Villalva, 'La Administración Pública y los Funcionarios', in S. Giner (ed.), España. Tomo 1, Sociedad y Política (Madrid: Espasa-Calpe, 1990).

The Bureaucracy

Nineteenth-century Spain was, in theory, run by an impartial, hierarchical bureaucracy recruited by merit. Practice, as in so many aspects of the Spanish political system, was very different. Official appointments were made on the basis of political patronage, sinecures abounded along with inefficiency and corruption. A series of measures during the last century failed to convert theory into reality until the law of 1918 intended to eliminate recruitment by political patronage in favour of competitive examinations and give civil servants security of tenure.[10] The essentials of the system have changed little since then. As in France, the bureaucracy is organized by corps, *cuerpos*, which have proliferated to over two hundred, each dominating a particular branch of administration or ministry. Recruitment and promotion are done by corps, so that there is no necessary relationship between an individual's rank and pay and the task which that individual is performing; two people doing the same job may be of quite different levels of seniority.

Franco left this system essentially untouched while in some respects enhancing the role of the bureaucracy. Unlike other authoritarian regimes, Francoism lacked an effective party organization to recruit political leaders and relied on the civil service even to staff the *Movimiento*, its weak political arm. Professional civil servants filled some 80 per cent of the ministerial and other political posts, 30 per cent of the seats in the undemocratic *Cortes* (parliament) and 50 per cent of national councillors in the *Movimiento*.[11] In the later years of the regime, there was some attempt to reform the bureaucracy, as part of the overall modernization strategy. Technocrats, often recruited through the Catholic lay organization *Opus Dei*, displaced members of the traditional corps in some key ministerial posts. A law of 1964 introduced four new generalist corps intended gradually to displace the old specialized ones, producing a power struggle. Specific job gradings were introduced which were intended to replace corps rankings as the basis of pay and promotion and the government was given more discretion in making civil service appointments outside of the examination-based system of entry into the corps. The main device for this was an increase in the number of temporary postings or appointments made by special contract - as in Italy these 'temporary' contracts could be extended for twenty years or more. Yet the reforms were strongly contested by the old bureaucracy and by the early 1970s had largely run out of steam.

In the transition to democracy, the negotiated and consensual style of proceeding ensured that there would be no purge of the bureaucracy, though some individuals who had been most strongly associated with the repressive aspects of Francoism were discreetly moved aside. All parties, however, were agreed that the ponderous and unwieldy Francoist bureaucracy was in need of reform. The system of corps was regarded as encouraging self-seeking behaviour by civil servants more interested in advancing their collective interests than in impartial administration. The chaotic proliferation of corps and the divisions and rivalries between them impeded coordination of government activity and the flexible deployment of staff. Spanish bureaucracy, as anyone who has had to deal with it knows, had become a byword for inefficiency, delay and red tape, with concentrations of corruption. Training was poor. Few civil servants really worked the hours for which they were paid and many held other appointments incompatible with their duties. Since the Franco regime had not been based on a division of powers, there was a poor specification of political and bureaucratic roles, a critical matter in a liberal democracy where politicians are held accountable by elections and bureaucrats remain outside the political fray.

Finally, the establishment of the autonomous regional communities required a break with the old centralist mentalities and a reduction of the central administration. Tentative efforts by the UCD government to reform the system, however, came to naught and it was left to the PSOE government to introduce change.

In the event, PSOE's reforms were rather limited. A 1982 decree tidied up the organization of government and clarified political and administrative roles. Apart from ministers themselves, who are of course politically appointed and constitute the government of the day, a certain range of civil service positions are recognized as political appointees, changing when the government, or perhaps the minister, changes. These include directors general, in charge of administration in the ministries and the main ministerial divisions but not their deputies, the sub-directors, or any rank below that. In addition, each minister has a *cabinet* on French lines, a politically appointed group of advisors recruited from within and outside the civil service and who help with policy planning, liaison with other departments and relations with the outside world. The 1982 decree also tried to enforce more effectively the existing rules on hours of work and incompatible functions. In 1984 a law was passed intended to weaken the corps by establishing clear job descriptions and relating appointment, promotion and pay to these. At the same time, all posts were opened to members of all corps though in practice branches of administration remain the preserve of specific corps and under 10 per cent of all civil servants are members of the general corps. Greater scope was made for appointment outside the regular system of corps examinations, through open examinations. This was intended to increase flexibility and match people more closely to jobs, but it also has had the effect of encouraging patronage since discretionary appointments and special entry systems can easily be manipulated. PSOE was able to claim when it came to power that the civil service was so associated with the past that it needed to bring in fresh blood and appoint people more sympathetic to its reformist, modernizing ambitions. After ten years in power, its critics were claiming that it had itself colonized large parts of the state apparatus, bringing in party sympathizers or patronage appointees and damaging the impartiality and permanence of the bureaucracy.

The adaptation of the administration to the new autonomous communities (regional governments) was perhaps the greatest challenge which it has faced since the transition. This issue is discussed below in the section on territorial politics. By 1991 the bureaucracy of the autonomous communities had grown to over half a million, with another 350,000 in local government, but the central administration had not been reduced by the equivalent. The field administration of central government had in many cases been transferred to the autonomous communities but headquarters departments in Madrid remained as large as ever and were still imbued with the centralist traditions and habits of detailed intervention. A radical suggestion by Manuel Fraga, chief minister in the autonomous community of Galicia, that Spain should adopt the German model of giving nearly all administrative responsibilities to certain of the autonomous communities, eliminating bureaucratic duplication, was regarded as interesting but politically difficult, given the vested interests involved.

Changing the mentality of civil servants brought up in a centralized, interventionist tradition under an authoritarian state, is a long-term process. So is introducing a culture of innovation and modern management in a system based on legalism, caution and precedent.[12] The programme of deregulation and privatization undertaken by the PSOE government since 1982, together with the requirements of European integration, have gradually reduced the weight of bureaucracy in Spanish life, but it remains considerable. Radical reform of the administrative machine is unlikely to be a priority for any government. Meanwhile, the bureaucratic elite, like its French counterpart, exercises influence beyond the civil service itself, helped by generous provision for absence with the right to return to the corps. More than half the ministers in the government, along with many members of parliament, are civil servants, as are some leading figures in state and private industry.

Interest Groups

Spain has long been notable for the relative weakness of its civil society, that is the network of organized groups and institutions outside the state apparatus. This is reflected in the small number and membership of interest groups and the weakness of most of them. There are historical reasons for this, rooted in the failure to establish stable, democratic government and liberal institutions. In the nineteenth century, the middle class was largely dependent on the state, for employment or industrial protection. The working class, probably the most revolutionary in Europe, was largely isolated from regular political activity, given to violent outbursts of protest which reflected its very weakness. In the early twentieth century, trade unionism was divided between the *Unión General de Trabajadores* (UGT), closely linked to the Socialist Party, and the anarchist *Confederación Nacional de Trabajadores* (CNT), an anarcho-syndicalist group committed to revolutionary change. The client networks of *caciquismo* and the fraudulent electoral system in the Restoration regime allowed parties to win elections without mobilizing social interests and the parties themselves had weak social bases. The higher civil service, modelling themselves on their French counterparts, sought to set themselves apart from society. Two powerful groups, the army and the Catholic Church, had little interest in participative politics. The army retained the right to intervene forcibly to protect its vital interests, with the support if need be of the Church and large sections of the bourgeoisie. In Catalonia, where associative life was best developed, there was more interest in nationalism and autonomy than participation in wider Spanish politics. The Second Republic, far from developing a participative politics of negotiation and compromise, dissolved in violent conflict. A revolutionary seizure of power by workers in the mining region of Asturias in 1934 was crushed by the conservative central government. The left wing government elected in 1936 opted for confrontation with the Church. In 1932 the army had unsuccessfully asserted its traditional right to intervene and in 1936 provoked the Civil War.

Francoism after its victory banned all political activity outside approved channels, without even the mass mobilization under state leadership found in Fascist Italy or Nazi Germany. There was a system of official representation through state-organized associations but, despite the efforts of some of the more enthusiastic Fascist elements, the regime preferred a quiescent and apathetic population. Another distinction between the Francoist state and other 1930s dictatorships is that, while it was undemocratic and authoritarian, it was never totalitarian, that is it never aspired to state control of all aspects of social and economic life. Rather, the state shared power with other dominant groups. The Catholic Church enjoyed wide privileges guaranteed in a Concordat with the Vatican and, except for the last years, was a close ally of the regime. Big business interests, notably the large banks, enjoyed privileged links with the state, gaining protection, subsidies and industrial discipline in return for cooperating with Franco. Large landowners, too, proved powerful enough to stall the land reform efforts of the more radical populist part of the victorious Civil War coalition. The state apparatus was nonetheless very extensive. Large parts of industry were taken into public ownership in the interests of national self-sufficiency and development priorities. Like other authoritarian regimes, the Franco government was given to massive public works projects like hydroelectric schemes, symbolizing the power of the state to achieve development while providing profits for construction companies and banks. The bureaucracy, too, was a vested interest, jealously preserving its privileges even while the various corps conspired and fought against each other. In the later years of the regime, as we have seen, there was some economic liberalization and opening to Europe and the world, but many of the old state and private monopolies remained intact. Social service development lagged well behind the rest of western Europe, creating a mass of expectations for the new democracy.

In the later years of the Franco regime, there had been some social mobilization, which was one factor which allowed the relatively smooth transition to democracy.[13] Although strictly illegal, independent trade union groups, known as the workers' commissions, largely under Communist leadership, had infiltrated the official trade union organizations. The old UGT managed a difficult underground existence, but preferred to boycott the official trade unions structures. Employers' organizations were less well organized outside the official system since business remained largely loyal to the state, but there was an increased willingness in later years to bargain outside the approved state structures. Reformist Church groups emerged and there was a rise in independent activity in the universities. With the transition to democracy, these groups soon came out into the open and organized formally, but remain weak in comparison with their northern European counterparts.

There are two main union organizations, divided on political grounds. Workers'

Commissions (*Comisiones Obreras*) or CCOO, while officially independent, is under Communist leadership. The UGT, founded in 1888 at the same time as the Socialist Party PSOE, has long had close links with the party. Although organizationally separate, party and union were always regarded as wings of a single movement, each with its own sphere of action but linked in membership, leadership and policy. The old anarchist tradition, represented in the CNT, had died out after the failure of the Second Republic and failed to re-emerge at the end of Francoism as union aims shifted from revolutionary politics to collective bargaining. Smaller unions, including the civil service union *Confederación Sindical Independiente de Funcionarios* (CSI), have seen some growth in recent years. Overall, trade unionism remains weak, with only about 15 per cent of Spanish workers belonging to unions.

In the early years of the transition, Workers' Commissions emerged stronger, gaining 34 per cent of the votes in the first elections for works councils in 1978, against 21 per cent for the Socialist UGT. By the early 1980s UGT had moved ahead. This was partly a reflection of developments in the political sphere, where the Communists were declining as the Socialists advanced, but it also reflected on the different union strategies. While both were committed to the transition to democracy, UGT displayed a more moderate image and a greater willingness to negotiate deals with employers and the government. When the Socialists gained power in 1982, UGT appeared to have a very advantageous position, given its organic links with the party and close relationship between its leadership and that of the new government. For example, UGT General Secretary Nicolas Redondo was also a Socialist member of parliament. By 1986, however, the commitment of the González government to neo-liberal economic management and the fall in workers' purchasing power had caused increasing strains in the relationship. Under pressure from Workers' Commissions, the UGT stepped up its demands and in 1985 Redondo became the first Socialist member of parliament to vote against the government. In 1987 he resigned his seat in parliament and UGT began to cooperate more closely with Workers' Commissions in opposition to government policy, convening a general strike in 1988.

Employers felt no need to organize clandestinely under Franco since the government was not anti-business and, especially after the adoption of the modernization strategy, pursued policies favourable to the private sector. Sections of private industry, notably the large banks, had particularly close links with the technical elite in the regime and were able to gain favourable treatment and a considerable influence in major public investment decisions. Large manufacturing and construction firms were able to prosper with the help of tariff protection and state subsidy while relying on the state to repress worker demands. Thus at the transition there was little by way of independent organization, though there were some modernizing elements among employers who bridled at the restrictions of the regime and favoured an end to protectionism, an opening to Europe and a genuine market economy. In 1977, the *Confederación Española de Organizaciones Empresariales* (CEOE) was formed and soon absorbed most of the other emergent business organizations to include firms accounting for some 75 per cent of all employment. CEOE is a federation with a complicated constitution.[14] Business firms do not join it directly. Rather they join sectoral or territorial affiliates, or both and these are represented in the CEOE. Sectoral groups, especially those in metals and construction, tend to be more important than the territorially-based ones in provinces and regions, though the employers' associations of Madrid and Catalonia are an exception. Because of its broad coverage, CEOE sometimes has difficulty representing the diverse interests of its members. Its standing as the voice of the business sector is further reduced by the extensive foreign ownership of Spanish business and the ability of multinationals to deal directly with government without its help. Foreign firms control about 47 per cent of turnover and 43 per cent of employment in the major Spanish industries, which inhibits the development of an indigenous capitalist class.[15]

COEO presses for pro-business policies, reduction of inflation, reduction of social charges, wage restraint and privatization. Particular emphasis is placed on deregulation of the labour market which under Franco had been extremely rigid and remained so under the early UCD governments. Gradually shaking off the historic protectionist instincts of Spanish business, it has supported European integration. It has generally favoured the parties of the right and in 1982 caused a stir with its open campaigning in the regional elections in Catalonia and Andalusia and the national level. However, while the Popular Party officially supports the free-market line of CEOE it cannot credibly present itself as the party of Spanish business, nor as a potential party of government. PSOE, on the other hand, had by the late 1980s adopted most of the free-market deregulating policies advocated by the employers' organization and few important policy differences remained.

In contrast to industry, farming organization is fragmented. There are five major agricultural lobby groups, representing different types and size of farm. Given the sharp differences in interest between wheat producers in Castile or fruit growers in Valencia and milk producers in Galicia, there are frequently disagreements on policies and priorities to be pursued nationally and in the European Community. Together with the highly individualistic tendencies of farmers, this has probably weakened the weight of the Spanish agricultural lobby as a whole.

Two of the most powerful groups in Spanish history, the army and the Church, have seen their political influence sharply curtailed. The army had seen its power gradually reduced in the later Franco years as power was transferred to modernizing technocrats, but substantial sections of it still retained the tradition view that they had a right to intervene to safeguard the essential interests of the state. There were at least five coup plots and attempts in the transition years and the need to placate the military constrained the actions of governments. The military continued to use a Francoist law allowing it to try in military courts anyone accused of insulting the armed forces, including 52 people as late as 1979. Since the early 1980s, the military has slowly been reformed. Strict limits are placed on the rights of military officers to engage in political activity and it is explicitly laid down that soldiers should not obey orders which are contrary to the constitution, such as participating in a *coup d'état*. Spanish entry into NATO gave it a significant external role and turned its interest away from domestic politics. Restructuring has reduced the excessive number of officers in relation to private soldiers and modernization has improved the technical capacity of the armed forces.

The Catholic Church, which had largely detached itself from the regime in the last years of the Franco era, took a decision not to intervene in politics in the democratic system. It supported the transition to democracy, but gave no encouragement to efforts to form a Catholic or Christian Democratic political party. With the support of the UCD and PP it sought a more explicit recognition of Spain's Catholic identity in the constitution but, given the opposition of the left, gained only a vague reference to the Church alongside other religions. It reserved the right to speak out on moral issues such as abortion and divorce but could not prevent the legalization of both. Religious education and state subsidies for it were, however, safeguarded. In the early 1990s, bishops also criticized some of the negative social effects of the PSOE government's neo-liberal economic policies, echoing papal statements against excessive faith in markets alone to solve society's problems. Generally, though, the Church has concentrated on its pastoral mission and has observed strict neutrality in election campaigns. Spain remains a religious country, compared with its European neighbours, with 63 per cent of the population in 1990 considering themselves to be religious. Among young people, though, the proportion was only 46 per cent, indicating a growing secularization, which is gradually eroding the authority of the Church. This has been accompanied by a sharp fall in the number of religious vocations.

Policy Making

Policy making in Spain has traditionally been seen almost exclusively in terms of the state, which is given an exalted role in Spanish political culture. Even if its true power has often been less than that accorded to it in constitutional theory, the state's role has been enhanced by the weakness of civil society, of private institutions and groups. Under Franco, of course, this was taken to an exaggerated degree, with the imposition of an authoritarian state and the subordination of organized activity to it. Within this, privileged groups and sectors enjoyed an advantaged position while others were excluded. The transition to democracy entailed a dismantling of this power structure, a lessened role for the state, decentralization and the creation of autonomous institutions of civil society. This pervasive presence of the state, as we have seen, provided the justification for PSOE, an avowedly Socialist party, to pursue a policy of privatization and deregulation more usually associated with the free-market right. The success of the transition in creating the institutions of a civil society must be regarded as limited, given the continued weakness of groups and associative life but Spain has come a long way since 1977. Policy making styles have evolved gradually, from a first stage of quasi-corporatist bargaining with the newly legalized social partners, through a process of liberalization and deregulation, to a stage in the early 1990s in which policy priorities were set above all by the needs of convergence with the countries of northern Europe within the European Community and Monetary System.

In the early years of the democratic regime governments relied heavily on negotiated accords, or pacts between the political parties and social partners, to the extent that observers began to talk of corporatism as the characteristic policy making style of the Spanish system.[16] In 1977 the UCD government and the PSOE opposition signed the Moncloa Pact, a wide-ranging programme providing for political reform together with wage restraint. The trade unions were not involved in the negotiation of this but supported its provisions. After the 1979 elections, the employers' organization CEOE and the Socialist trade union UGT signed the *Acuerdo Marco Interconfederal*, giving privileged recognition to the UGT over its Communist rival and providing for agreed wage increases. In 1980, this was renewed and broadened to include Workers' Commissions, with the backing of the government. In 1981 an *Acuerdo Nacional de Empleo* was signed between the government and the unions, followed in 1983 by a new *Acuerdo Interconfederal* between unions and employers with the support of the government. In 1985 and 1986 *Acuerdos Económico y Social* were signed among employers, unions and government. These pacts had economic, social and political objectives. The unions promised wage restraint to help keep inflation under control. Employers promised recognition of unions and restraint on prices. Government agreed to expand social benefits in return for restraint on the growth of private incomes. More generally, the whole process was intended to stabilize the new democracy, control unrealistic expectations, modernize the Spanish economy to allow it to enter Europe, and consolidate political structures and the new social partners.

The coming to power of PSOE in 1982 initially gave added emphasis to the negotiated style of policy making, with pacts involving all three partners. By the mid-1980s, however, the trade unions had become disillusioned, especially after the 1983 pact had cut workers' spending power. The González government's commitment to a strategy of market liberalization, privatization, labour-market deregulation and control of public spending brought it into increased conflict with the trade unions. After Spain's entry into the European Community and the later commitment to economic and monetary union, the strategic objective became convergence with Europe in terms of inflation and public sector borrowing, leaving little room for manoeuvre on the part of government or for negotiation of policy with domestic partners. This strategy was generally supported by business, without the need for formal agreements, while the unions were increasingly marginalized.

Pacts have continued to be an important feature of Spanish politics but they tend to involve the political parties rather than organized interests. Pacts have been agreed to manage the transition to full autonomy of the regional councils, to isolate supporters of political violence and combat terrorism. A fully-fledged system of corporatism in Spain, with major issues of social and economic policy negotiated between government and interest groups, however, was never possible. The very word itself was discredited because of its association with the Fascist elements of the Franco regime but even a more benign, liberal type of corporatism faced insuperable obstacles. Spanish interest groups are too weak, unable to negotiate authoritatively or to commit their members, let alone workers or business, as a whole. Another obstacle to corporatism is the European factor. Europe has long been seen as the gateway to political and economic modernization in Spain and after the transition there was almost universal support for an application to the European Community. This was rather quickly agreed and in 1986 Spain and Portugal became the Community's eleventh and twelfth members. Adaptation to Europe has imposed major strains on the Spanish economy and social system. Old, uncompetitive heavy industries have had to be run down, protection and subsidies cut, agriculture and fisheries reorganized and modernized with a heavy loss of jobs. All this is presented as an imperative which allows for no alternative, leaving little room for negotiation. Given the continued consensus on the need to be part of Europe and the almost total absence of opposition to the Community, as opposed to complaints about its effects, government has been able to use this to justify its policy measures. Determined to be in the front rank of the new Europe, the government in 1992 prepared a new plan for convergence intended to ensure that Spain meets the criteria for entry into the single currency embodied in the Maastricht agreements (described in Chapter 7). Worker and farmer discontent has taken the form of cynicism and explosions of social protest, without being able to cohere into a political alternative or force government into real negotiation.

Far from developing in the years of democracy, associational life in Spain appears to have declined, as people retreat from public affairs into the home and private worlds. In 1981, 31 per cent of the population were involved in voluntary organizations, whether religious, artistic, professional, cultural or educational. By 1990, this figure had fallen to 22 per cent. There was majority support in principle for social movements concerned with such modern causes as human rights, ecology, disarmament or feminism, but this did not generally translate into active involvement.[17]

TERRITORIAL POLITICS

Spain has historically been marked by strong regional differences, in culture, language, economic structures and politics. While the effect of modernization, industrialization and social change has in many countries been to break down local distinctiveness, Spanish regions have retained their own characteristics, especially in the cases of Catalonia, the Basque Country and Galicia which regard themselves as historic nationalities comparable with Scotland and Wales within the United Kingdom. Territorial identity was sustained in Spain by a number of factors. While most of Spain speaks the standard form of Spanish correctly known as Castilian, the three historic nationalities have their own languages. In Catalonia and Galicia, these are romance languages related to Castilian and Italian. The Basque language is related to no other known tongue and is of great antiquity, though immigration from other parts of Spain in the last hundred years has reduced its use. Industrial development also differed between Spain's regions, being largely confined in the nineteenth century to Catalonia and the Basque Country. While political power remained at the centre, the economic weight of the country from the nineteenth century shifted back to the periphery. Regional identity was further reinforced by traditions of self-government including the Basque *fueros* or historic privileges which successive kings had to swear to uphold and the memories of self-government in Catalonia before 1714. The failures of the Spanish nation-state in the nineteenth and twentieth centuries further accentuated regional tensions and gave birth to the modern phenomenon of regionalism.

Radically different conceptions of the Spanish state competed throughout the nineteenth and early twentieth centuries. The Bourbon monarchs and right-wing forces, including landowning, aristocratic and military elites, favoured a unified, Castilian-speaking, Catholic state governed on authoritarian principles. The capitalist bourgeoisie, seeking social order, repression of working-class demands and tariff protection against stronger foreign industry, often joined this side. Equally centralist was a strong liberal republican element inspired by French Jacobin ideology. This wanted a democratic, secular, unitary state with a popular and exclusive Spanish national identity, committed to modernization and development. Among the *regeneracionista* generation who emerged following the defeat of 1898, there was a strong commitment to a modernized, European Spain and, again, a presumption in favour of a unitary, uniform state, shedding the archaic peripheral languages and culture. Some elements of the emerging Socialist movement also favoured centralization, partly on grounds of working class unity but also because of the weakness of the Socialist Party PSOE in Catalonia and among the indigenous working class in the Basque Country, who tended to support anarchism or nationalism. At the same time, like other European Socialist parties, PSOE had a decentralist element in its philosophy and throughout its history has displayed a profound ambiguity on the national question.

Decentralization and regionalism were supported from a variety of political perspectives. Carlism, a movement in favour of the dynasty defeated in 1714, was strong in the rural areas of the Basque Country, Navarre and Catalonia. Bearing a strong resemblance to British Jacobitism and some of the provincial monarchist movements in nineteenth century France, Carlism was anti-modernizing, committed to traditionalism, Catholicism and the restoration of traditional privileges and autonomous institutions in the periphery. It thus opposed both Bourbon centralism and liberal, secular republicanism. Regionalism was also favoured by other traditional elements in Catalonia and the Basque Country, who feared that modernization and industrialization threatened old values and the language. From the late nineteenth century, they were joined by sections of the Catalan middle class, frustrated by the inability of the Spanish state to modernize itself. As regional identity strengthened in the early twentieth century, with the continued failure of the Spanish state, the Socialists also began to adopt a regionalist language in order to penetrate Basque and Catalan society.

A third point of view was that of the federalist, Republican movement, which had some influence in the late nineteenth century. Federalists were committed to a modernized, democratic and decentralized federation of the Iberian peninsula. Although such a formula might accommodate the special demands of the peripheral regions, the failure of the brief First Republic, which was to have been federal, discredited the idea and thereafter Catalan and Basque nationalists demanded special treatment within Spain. Federalism never completely died out. In 1918 the Socialist PSOE adopted a resolution, never repealed but long ignored, in favour of a federal republic and federalist ideas have informed the recent debate about the future of regional autonomy.

Organized peripheral nationalism was the product of the late nineteenth century, starting in Catalonia and the Basque Country and spreading to other regions. Catalan nationalism developed from the rather ambiguous position of the local industrial bourgeoisie. In the Spanish context, an advanced and modernizing force, they sought greater influence within the state and an end to the dominance of the landowning, aristocratic, monarchical elite in Madrid. Yet in the European context, they were uncompetitive, requiring a protected Spanish market for their goods. Rejecting the Spanish state, they still called on it to help suppress their own working class in the industrial turbulence of the early twentieth century. Committed to modern industrial values, they were still inspired by a traditional Catholic social ethos. Drawing heavily on the Romantic movement for an emotive element to their nationalism, they also emphasized the defence of language. This provided for an interclass appeal as well as status differentiation, since Catalan has always been regarded locally as of higher status than the Castilian spoken by lower-class immigrants.

In 1892, the *Lliga Catalana* was formed to demand self-government and wider use of the Catalan language. In 1901 this gave way to the *Lliga Regionalista* which, with the aim of establishing a great Catalonia within a great Spain, broke the pattern of centralist, clientelist politics and *caciquismo* at local and national elections in Catalonia, establishing a pattern of separate Catalan parties which has persisted since. At the 1907 elections, the alliance *Solidaridad Catalana* won 41 of Catalonia's 44 seats, with the ambivalent aims of gaining a degree of self-government while seeking the Catalanization of Spain. The fatal mistake of this middle class, conservative nationalism was to collaborate with the dictatorship of Primo de Rivera (1923-31) in the hope that he would grant them autonomy while keeping the working class in order. They were to be disappointed since Primo, true to the right-wing *españolista* tradition, would make no compromises with Catalan nationalism. There were also radical-democratic, republican and leftist varieties of Catalanism, appealing to the lower-middle classes, artisans and sections of the proletariat not won over to anarchism. With the *Lliga* discredited by its collaboration with Primo de Rivera, the nationalist cause was taken over by the left in the form of the *Esqerra Republicana de Catalunya* (ERC) which dominated politics in Catalonia up to the Civil War.

Basque nationalism, also a product of the late nineteenth century, was a very different phenomenon. Basque traditional privileges, the *fueros* had been gradually reduced during the course of the nineteenth century. In 1839 their free-trade privileges were abolished, with the application of Spanish tariffs at the ports and the removal of the customs barriers between Spain and the Basque provinces. Further changes in 1876 left intact only the *concierto economico*, a provision whereby the three Basque provinces and Navarre raise taxes locally and pass on a negotiated amount to the Spanish treasury. These changes stimulated a rapid industrial expansion with a Basque capitalist class, unlike their Catalan counterparts, highly integrated into the Spanish political and economic system. Basque nationalism was a reaction to this, drawing its support from the most traditionalist sectors of society and strongly imbued with Catholicism and Carlism. Sabino de Arana, founder of the Basque Nationalist Party, preached racial exclusiveness appealing to those marginalized by industrial society and threatened by the immigration of non-Basques. Its support was greatest among peasants, fishermen and artisans, with some appeal to the urban lower-middle classes. Basque nationalism never established the same dominance as Catalanism, gaining only around one-third of the vote at elections before the Civil War. Language was always a key element in the Basque movement but one which limited its appeal to the proletariat, a large part of which consisted of immigrants from other regions. Unlike Catalan, Basque is a difficult, non-Latin language, making assimilation problematic. The absence of a written literature or vernacular cultural revival limited the mobilizing appeal of nationalism among the middle classes. For its Catholicism, its racial exclusiveness and its social conservatism, Basque nationalism was regarded with hostility by progressive and left-wing forces in Spain. For its separatism it was detested by the Spanish-nationalist right and the military. Unlike Catalanism, it contained no project for Spain as a whole. Only the advent of the Second Republic produced a tactical accommodation between Republicans and Basque nationalists though this in itself was full of tensions.

Galicia is the third region generally considered as a historic nationality. Yet, despite the existence of a distinct language and culture, there was no significant regionalist movement before the Second Republic. Galicia was a poor country of small farmers without political consciousness and a ruling elite integrated into the institutions of the Spanish state, notably the army and the Court. Political representation took the form of client relationships based on the local *caciques*. Despite some stirrings from the turn of the century, it was not until the Second Republic in the 1930s that a Galician autonomist movement emerged, in imitation of Catalonia. In the early decades of the twentieth century, a movement also developed in Andalusia, focused on land reform, seeing regional autonomy as a means of breaking the landowning aristocracy whose economic power within the region was complemented by their political power in Madrid. Although without great influence at the time, this did create a legacy of Andalusianism identified with progressive and left-wing causes which was to be important in later years.

The Second Republic had to accommodate Catalan and Basque demands while preserving the unity of the state. An agreement of sorts had been reached among Republican forces in the Pact of San Sebastian, which included a recognition of Catalan and Galician demands and, more ambiguously, those of the Basques. On the fall of the monarchy, Republican leaders declared a Catalan Republic as part of a non-existent Iberian federation and had to be persuaded to abandon this in favour of legislated solution. The Basque Country was even more problematic since Republican forces were weak there and Basque nationalism dominated by clerical conservatives. When these proposed special links between the Basque Country and the Holy See, republicans in Madrid, and many Socialists in the Basque Country, feared a 'Vatican Gibraltar'. Eventually, the formula of the *Estado Integral*, loosely based on the Weimar Republic, was concocted to describe a new state which was neither unitary nor federal. From unitary theory, the *Estado Integral* took the sovereignty of the Spanish people as a whole and the need for autonomy statutes to be passed by the national parliament. From federalist and contractual theory, it took the principle of the framing of autonomy statutes in the regions themselves, their negotiation with the centre and approval in a local referendum. Although in theory autonomy was available to all regions, there were provisions which were intended to limit it to the three historic nations. Regions could gain an statute of autonomy only if a majority of the town councils requested it, two thirds of the entire regional electorate approved it in a referendum and the national parliament accepted it. A Catalan statute, approved by Madrid and by local referendum, went into operation in 1932 and the *Generalitat* was restored after two hundred and eighteen years. In the Basque Country, the clerical issue slowed progress and autonomy was conceded only at the onset of the Civil War, a move which committed the Basques to the Republican side - and to Franco's vengeance. By this time, the expectations raised by the Republic, the leftist opposition to the government elected in 1934 and the disintegration of central authority had spawned regionalist demands not only in Galicia where an autonomy statute was conceded in 1936 but in Andalusia, Aragon, Mallorca, Valencia and Asturias. These tended to be left-wing and Republican, confirming the identification of regional autonomy with the left.

It is impossible to say how the autonomy provisions would have operated in a peacetime for the whole process was caught up in the strife and political disintegration which led up to the Civil War. The return of the right in the elections of 1934 halted the autonomy process and the *Generalitat* of Catalonia was suspended. This in turn pushed the Catalan left towards separatism. The restoration of the *Generalitat* by the Popular Front government in 1936 was rapidly followed by the Franco rebellion. Under wartime conditions, Catalonia effectively functioned independently, at least until the Republican government itself moved to Barcelona. In the Basque Country, autonomy was rapidly conceded to ensure Basque support for the Republic.

Franco's victory closed this phase of Spanish regionalism with the triumph of the most intransigent, *españolista,* militarist elements. In the Francoist crusade, regionalism ranked alongside communism and atheism as the deadly enemies of Spain and all traces of regional identity were wiped out. Regionalist leaders like Luis Companys, president of the *Generalitat* and the veteran Andalusian Blas Infante, were executed and speaking Basque or Catalan in public became a crime. Such was the Francoist paranoia about regionalism that no attempt was made to gain regime collaborators among the Basque or Catalan-speaking communities, despite the presence, especially in the former, of rightist, clericalist elements. Franco's persecution certainly crushed the Basque and Catalan movements but, in so doing, reinforced anti-regime solidarity in those regions and ensured that any return to democracy would need a regional dimension.

The repression of the peripheral nationalities under Franco had two conflicting effects. On the one hand, there was some assimilation. Peripheral languages were banned and children educated in Castilian alone. Large-scale immigration brought Castilian speakers from the south so that 37 per cent of the population of both Catalonia and the Basque Country by the late 1970s was born elsewhere in Spain. Sections of the upper industrial bourgeoisie in both Catalonia and the Basque Country collaborated with the regime in return for protection and keeping the working class in its place. On the other hand, the regime was further delegitimized by Franco's identification of Spain and the Spanish nation with the most reactionary, centralist tendencies. This produced broad based opposition movements in the regions, including elements of both right and left, especially from the 1960s.

The first stirrings in Catalonia were cultural, in defence of a language which, while still used regularly by some 60 per cent of the population, was banned in education and the media. By the late 1960s, the language revival had joined with the youth culture and the spirit of protest in the universities linked to the international new left. Religion provided another element in the Catalan revival. The abbey of Montserrat, traditional centre of Catalanism, became a centre of opposition to Francoism as progressive Catholics attacked the links between the Church and the regime and to address current social and economic problems. The economy of Catalonia made great strides forward during the years of expansion, retaining first place among Spanish regions, but there was resentment about subsidizing the rest of Spain and thus sustaining an alien regime. While the large industrialists were integrated into the regime, benefiting from the policies of protection and subsidy, among the professional middle classes there was considerable contempt for the Madrid machine and little inclination to credit it with Catalonia's advance.

The revival of political activity dates from the early 1960s with the emergence of a number of movements and especially of Jordi Pujol. Son of an upper-middle class Barcelona family, a devout Catholic and conservative, Pujol was obsessed with the idea of creating a modern Catalonia. Characteristic of the conservative Catalan nationalist tradition, he combines mystic and spiritual elements and strong religious convictions with a concern with the here and now, the necessity to *fer pais*, that is, to make a modern Catalonia. In the absence of political structures, this would involve culture and economics, with politics coming later. In 1959, he founded the *Banca Catalana*, which became the centre of a vast financial and political movement. His reputation established by a jail sentence, Pujol used the resources of the bank as well as his own to help not only Catalan businesses but a range of cultural and political activities.

The left was more ambiguous about Catalanism. From the late 1940s, the Catalan Communists, the PSUC, following the lead of the Spanish Communists, downplayed the issue and presented the workers' struggle as a Spanish-wide one. The Socialist PSOE, concerned with its position among the non-Catalan immigrant workers, also de-emphasized nationalism. By the late 1960s, though, the success of the new Catalan movements and the ideological rethinking prompted by the emergence of Third World national liberation movements had caused the left to change their line again. In 1965, PSUC resumed its support for Catalan autonomy while PSOE gave more circumspect support. The modernization of Spanish civil society took on a specifically Catalan colour and the demand for autonomy was a central part of the emerging democratic consensus. In 1969 a broad front, the *Coordinadora de Forces Politiques*, was formed, and in 1971 an *Assemblea de Catalunya* demanded liberty, amnesty and a statute of autonomy.

In the Basque Country, repression and immigration combined to reduce the proportion of people speaking the language to a third by 1981. The 1960s, however, saw a cultural revival. A network of voluntary schools, the *ikastolas*, grew up and by the 1970s were enrolling some 50,000 pupils. In the Basque context, such cultural activity was in itself political, bringing new recruits into the democratic resistance. The Basque political movement was divided and ineffective after the Civil War, especially following the failure of a series of strikes in the late 1940s and early 1950s. The Basque Nationalist Party (PNV) continued its line of conservative nationalism but, dropping the exclusive and racist themes of Arana, joined the European Christian Democrat movement. From the 1960s, a militant offshoot, *Euskadi ta Askatasuna* (ETA) began a campaign of violence in pursuit of an independent and united Basque Country, sparking off a cycle of attacks and repression which marked the final years of the Franco regime. In 1974, ETA, like its Irish equivalent the IRA, split into two and in 1976 the politico-military wing renounced violence. The remaining elements carried on their campaign, adapting their ideology to a left-wing national liberation line based on Third World models. Nationalism did not, however, dominate politics as it did in Catalonia. The Socialist Party, PSOE, strongest among the non-Basque immigrant workers, was suspicious of nationalism and gave only lukewarm support to autonomy.

Galicia, as before, lagged in terms of political nationalism, despite having a strong sense of regional identity and a language spoken by around 95 per cent of the population. Gallego remained an oral language, used in the home and the farm but, despite an impressive literary and intellectual tradition, popular levels of literacy were low since the extension of education had taken place in Castilian. Galicia's elites were well incorporated into the regime of Franco, himself a Galician, and in the rural areas political activity was limited to client networks.

In the pacts which formed such an important feature of the transition to democracy, regional autonomy featured strongly. Both the UCD of Prime Minister Adolfo Suarez and the Socialist PSOE recognized the need to make concessions to Catalan and Basque nationalism but, as in the Second Republic, hoped to limit autonomy to the historic nations and prevent a federalization of the whole state. In contrast to the approach in other European countries where regional devolution has been introduced, the initiative for autonomy was to come from the regions themselves, with the statutes being framed locally and negotiated with the central government. To this effect, preautonomous assemblies could be established by the members of the national parliament in a region. At the same time, the state parties insisted that the state was not negotiating association agreements with sovereign regions. Rather, autonomy was to be conceded as a gift of the sovereign Spanish state. It was this claim to sovereignty which led the Basque Nationalist Party (PNV) to recommend abstention in the 1973 constitutional referendum with the result that only 31 per cent of the Basque electorate, though a large majority of those voting, endorsed it. This was to cause problems of legitimacy later on.

The autonomy process can be divided into three phases: an initial phase of concession which accelerated so fast as to threaten to reduce the central state to a residual; a phase of retreat represented by the 1982 LOAPA law and the early years of the Socialist government; and a phase of accommodation from the mid-1980s to the present.

The new regional regime in Spain bears much resemblance to the early *Estado Integral*, as a compromise between federalism and mere regional devolution. The 1978 constitution declares the existence of a plurinational state in a forthright if confusing manner in Article 2:

> The constitution is founded on the indissoluble unity of the Spanish nation, common and indivisible motherland of all Spaniards, and recognises and guarantees the right to autonomy of all the nationalities and regions which comprise it and the solidarity among

them all.

Two routes to autonomy were provided, with the undeclared objective of confining full autonomy to the three historic regions with a capacity to threaten the stability of the state. Article 151 provided for full autonomy for any region but created almost impossible conditions. Autonomy proposals had to be initiated by vote of three quarters of the town councils and an absolute majority of the electors in each province of the region in a referendum. The statute then had to be negotiated and voted by an absolute majority of all the deputies and senators of the region and agreed with the constitutional committee of the national Parliament. The text then had to be submitted to a further referendum where it required a simple majority of those voting in each province. Finally, it had to ratified by an absolute majority of the members of both houses of Parliament. In those regions where autonomy had been voted by referendum under the Second Republic, Catalonia, the Basque Country and Galicia, pre-autonomous assemblies were established and, under a protocol attached to the constitution, these were exempted from the hurdles of Article 151. They could adopt full autonomy statutes by referendum by a simple majority of those voting in each province. Other regions would have to make do with a lesser degree of autonomy under Article 143 of the constitution. Only after five years could they initiate a revision of their statutes to attain full autonomy, though powers could also be devolved by an organic law of the central parliament.

The difference in the two types of autonomy concerns the range of functions devolved. There are two lists, one of powers which are available to all autonomous communities, and one of powers exclusively reserved to the central government. Any powers not featuring in either list may be devolved to those communities enjoying the larger degree of autonomy. In certain fields, the state has the right to lay down basic norms, with the communities filling in the details, or to legislate, with the communities implementing the legislation. This has proved a source of great confusion and contention.

An autonomy statute for Catalonia was negotiated quite rapidly and duly adopted by referendum. The Basque Country proved more difficult because of the question of the historic *fueros* and the claim to Navarre. In the event, while the *fueros* were not accepted as the basis of the new statute, which came as a gift of the Spanish state, much of their substance was incorporated, notably the *concierto economico* which allows the Basque government to collect most taxes and hand over an agreed sum to the national government. Navarre was eventually excluded at the insistence of its own representatives. The Basque statute was approved by a bare majority of the electorate in the face of heavy abstention by immigrant workers and by die-hard separatist supporters of ETA. An autonomy statute for Galicia was approved without great excitement. Thereafter, the autonomy process snowballed to the consternation of the central authorities, with proposals from regions throughout Spain. In Andalusia, a proposal to take the difficult 151 route to full autonomy was launched and, despite obstruction by the UCD government in Madrid and the state-owned media, passed the 50 per cent threshold in every province but one.

The threat of a generalized move to autonomy, with its federalist implications and a weakening of the central state, was enough to push the state-wide parties into a further pact. The attempted military coup of February 1981 reminded politicians of the army's historic image as guardian of a united Spain and provided a further incentive to stabilize the process. PSOE and the UCD, the two main state parties, agreed that Andalusia could proceed with Article 151 but that no other region should be allowed to do so. At the same time, measures were brought forward to harmonize the various types of autonomy, notably the *Ley Organica para la Armonizacion del Proceso Autonomico* (LOAPA). This provoked an appeal to the Constitutional Court by Basque and Catalan nationalists, who insisted that their autonomy statutes derived from their intrinsic national rights and could not be changed in this way. The Court's ruling supported the government's contention that the constitution provides equal rights for all Spaniards and the equality of all groups, but added that this did not entail institutional uniformity. All that was required was that all the autonomous communities were subordinate to the constitution and that their statutes should not enshrine social or economic privileges. Several of LOAPA's key provisions were therefore struck down. This left matters very unclear. The Court's decision would appear to reject the principle of self-determination or of entrenched foral privileges, but in practice to leave considerable scope for political accommodation. The latest phase in the autonomy process has involved just this.

By 1983 autonomy statutes had been agreed for the whole of Spain. In some cases, individual provinces became autonomous communities. Some, such as Madrid, are highly artificial, existing merely to achieve complete coverage. There are now seventeen autonomous communities, with varying powers and functions. The historic nations of Catalonia, the Basque Country and Galicia together with Andalusia, have the largest degree of autonomy, including responsibility for education and the health service of the national social security system. Valencia and the Canaries also have extended powers, granted by organic law, though without health. The remaining autonomous communities have the lesser powers, though Navarre, along with the Basque Country, has retained its foral rights. These include an agreement whereby most taxes are collected locally with the national contribution being passed on to Madrid. The complete list of autonomous communities is given in Table 6.4.

The success of the autonomy programme has to be measured by the degree to which it has resolved the historic nationalities problem in Spain and the extent to which a system of genuine decentralized government has emerged. Polls show marked variations in the enthusiasm of different regions for autonomy with most support for self-government in Catalonia and the Basque Country, together with the island regions of the Canaries and Balearics, as shown in Table 6.5. These, especially the former two, are also the regions which have established their own party systems, reducing their dependence on Madrid leadership.

Table 6.4 Spanish autonomous communities, 1992

Full Powers	Lesser Powers	
	Multiprovincial	Single Provinces
Basque Country	Aragon	Balearics
Catalonia	Castile-La Mancha	Navarre
Galicia	Castile and Leon	Asturias
Andalusia	Extremadura	Cantabria
Valencia		Madrid
Canaries		Murcia
		La Rioja

In Catalonia, the autonomous government has been dominated by Jordi Pujol's *Convergència i Unió* (CiU), with its combination of assertive nationalism and centre-right Christian Democratic politics. Pujol's success is based on beating the nationalist drum and constant demands for more powers and favourable financial terms, combined with something of a personality cult and a network of clientelism within Catalonia. Yet, while CiU wins majorities in the autonomous Parliament, the Socialist Party, campaiging as the *Partit dels Socialistes de Catalunya* and affiliated to PSOE, dominates national elections in Catalonia. As these have a higher turnout, it appears that the difference is made up of immigrant workers who are less inclined to vote in the autonomous elections. Yet immigrants are being assimilated into the Catalan culture. Catalan is the regular language of administration and education, though anyone has the right to conduct official or private business in either Catalan or Castilian. A knowledge of both is required for school graduation. By 1986, 90 per cent of the population could understand Catalan, up ten points in five years. Just 30 per cent could write it but this figure rose to two-thirds among school students. Generous subsidies ensure a large availability of literature, television and radio in Catalan, much of it translated or dubbed. There has been little immigration into Catalonia in the 1980s and 1990s, though there are concentrations of Andalusians in large public housing schemes outside Barcelona who have yet to be assimilated. National identity in Catalonia has also been secularized and broadened. While the number describing themselves as exclusively Catalan has remained around 10 per cent since the 1970s, there has been a substantial increase in those subscribing to a dual Spanish-Catalan identity and a growing tendency to see Catalan identity in terms of residence and voluntary choice rather than race, birth or language.

Separatism has never been a powerful force in Catalonia and it remains weak. In

1992, the Ésqerra Republicana de Catalunya (ERC), a party dating back to the Second Republic, adopted a policy of independence and gained 8 per cent of the vote in the elections to the Catalan parliament. Polls indicate that support for independence fluctuates around 10 per cent. Yet mainstream Catalan nationalists continue to have a rather ambivalent attitude to the state. In 1989, after a series of arguments with the central government, the Catalan parliament passed a resolution insisting on their right to self-determination but in the subsequent uproar Pujol made it clear that this did not imply a desire to separate from Spain. The theme of self-government is now invariably placed in a European context. The slogan *Catalunya, Un Pais d'Europa* both appropriates the European symbol of generations of Spanish modernizers and provides the context for a more autonomous Catalonia. It also marks a break from the earlier nationalist strategy of protectionism within a Spanish market. While the European theme is quite deafening, however, there is little detail on just how Catalonia might fit into the emerging European order; rather an opportunistic search for possibilities.

In the Basque Ccountry, conservative nationalism has been the strongest force in both regional and national elections. PSOE, drawing its support from the non-

Table 6.5 Attitudes to regional autonomy, 1988-9

	Satisfied with autonomy %	Measure of autonomy desired		
		More %	Same %	Less %
Castile-La Mancha	52	-	-	-
Catalonia	48	41	20	15
Basque Country	44	43	27	2
Navarre	43	-	-	-
Murcia	42	9	30	22
Balearics	41	45	27	3
Extremadura	39	50	18	4
Cantabria	37	31	19	6
Castile & Leon	37	31	29	13
Rioja	37	41	14	4
Andalusia	34	11	27	37
Galicia	32	6	24	41
Asturias	28	20	22	2
Canaries	26	49	13	4
Aragon	23	52	2	9
Valencia	-	8	22	29

Source: J.R. Montero and M. Torcal, 'La Opinión pública ante el estado de las autonomías: un visión panorámica', Informe Pi i Sunyer sobre Comunidades Autónomas, 1990 (Barcelona: Civitas).

Basque immigrant workers, is the second party. Around a fifth of the electorate support *Herri Batasuna*, the political wing of ETA It has proved difficult to establish a stable regime in the Basque Country in the context of the autonomy programme. The Basque Nationalist Party (PNV), having recommended abstention in the Spanish constitutional referendum, helped delegitimize the new state. The assumption that the new regime was merely Francoism with a new face was reinforced by the presence of the Spanish national police and civil guard, long distrusted in the Basque Country. ETA refused to abandon its armed campaign and the transition to democracy was marked by a sharp increase in terrorist attacks while the Basque autonomous government under its first leader Carlos Garaicoetxchea pursued a policy of confrontation with Madrid. By the mid-1980s, continued terrorism provoked a political crisis in the Basque Country, a split in the PNV and a political vacuum. After some manoeuvring, a coalition government emerged in 1986 of PSOE and the moderate wing of the PNV, allowing a broad front against ETA and cooperation with the PSOE government in Madrid. Although after the Basque 1989 election, a purely nationalist coalition was formed, cooperation continues, with a pact by the constitutional parties in the Basque Parliament condemning terrorism and a determined effort to isolate *Herri Batasuna*.

As in Catalonia, a modernized regional identity appears to be growing, emphasizing residence and choice rather than race and language and so open to all residents of the Basque Country. Some 30 per cent of the population claim to be exclusively Basque and not Spanish, but the number claiming a dual Basque and Spanish identity has shown a marked increase. Support for independence is around 20 per cent, with most of the population wanting to develop the present system of autonomy without separating from Spain. Some 80 per cent of the population condemn ETA violence without reservation. Nationalists and non-nationalists have tended to come closer as the local Socialists now emphasize Basque themes more strongly and the mainstream nationalists in the PNV now accept the Spanish state. Bilingualism is widely accepted as the answer to the language issue. There remains the intransigent minority represented by ETA and Herri Batasuna. This minority, accounting in recent elections for some 20 per cent of the population, rejects the state, and insists on the unity of all the Basque territories, including the French Basque Country and Navarre, on separatism and on the use of violence even against the will of the majority of the Basque people.

As in Catalonia, Europe provides a context for the assertion of an outward-looking Basque nationalism as an alternative to separatist exclusiveness. The PNV, which was converted to Europe through its participation in the Christian Democratic International, has adopted a symbol of thirteen stars, representing the existing EC twelve and the Basque Country. While the symbol appears to present the Basque Country as a nation-state on a par with the other twelve, the strategic aim is really a Europe of the regions, with forty or fifty components. In the short term, it serves to give Basque nationalism an outward looking and modernist image in contrast with the Arana tradition.

In Galicia, autonomy continues to cause little excitement. Although Gallego and dual identification is strong, it is not politically mobilized or correlated with voting behaviour. Participation in elections is low. The Spanish conservative Popular Party has taken over many of the clientelist networks of the Franco era to establish a *caciquismo* which inhibits political mobilization. Opinion polls show a marked lack of enthusiasm for autonomy (see Table 6.5) together with a widespread view that the autonomous government is marked by clientelism and corruption. In the 1980s, there was an advance by Socialist and some nationalist forces to provide an element of real political competition and a brief coalition government (1987-9) before the conservative Popular Party re-established its majority. In that year the national opposition leader Manuel Fraga returned to his native Galicia to head the autonomous government. Despite his centralist past, Fraga emphasized Galician themes strongly in government, making frequent voyages abroad and establishing Galician 'embassies' in Madrid and Brussels but this represents political posturing more than a real commitment to autonomy, given the Popular Party's national stance. Linguistic normalization has involved extending to official use and education a language already known and used in the oral mode by the vast majority of the population. In Andalusia, the Socialist PSOE dominates elections, with the local nationalist party reduced to minor status. Elsewhere, the autonomous communities are dominated by the Spanish parties, with a sprinkling of regional or nationalist forces.

The 1980s saw a constant recourse to the Constitutional Court to resolve arguments over powers. Between 1981 and 1990 there were 790 such cases, of which 314 concerned Catalonia and 230 the Basque Country.[18] With just 279 cases resolved, a backlog had built up and the president of the court was appealing to the politicians to resolve their differences by negotiation. By early 1990s they were increasingly doing this. PSOE's Basque and Catalan branches had adopted a more local image to compete electorally while the minority national PSOE government turned to the CiU and PNV for support in the national parliament, as an alternative to dealing with the Communist left. Yet while this may take some of the heat out of the autonomy question, the extension of the elite accommodation style of government, with deals between a dominant national party and dominant regional parties, does further reduce political competition and the prospects of a real alternation of power at either level.

Outside the historic nationalities, there has been a slower development of autonomy. In 1992, a new pact was agreed between the PSOE government and the opposition PP for the further development of autonomy in the ordinary status regions, with a view to bringing their powers in line with those of the historic nationalities. More generally, genuine autonomy has been slowed down by the continued weight of centralizing elements within the political system. Most of the field officials responsible for services which have come under the autonomous governments have been transferred, but the central ministries in Madrid have not shrunk accordingly. This has allowed senior officials in the capital to continue laying down detailed policy guidelines. The delay in transferring full powers to the communities in the slow track has provided a further pretext for retaining a large central bureaucracy with detailed rules. Table 6.6 shows the marked growth in administration at the autonomous community and local level, but also shows that the central bureaucracy has not diminished by the same extent. The state has also been criticized for specifying too much detail in the framework laws, restricting the freedom of the communities to vary their application. National norms in matters such as education often leave the communities with little more than the responsibility to pay for the service, rather than control its form.

Table 6.6 Civil servants in Spain

	1982	1986	1989	1991
Central government	1,181,820	946,625	953,268	900,576
Autonomous communities	44,475	326,900	514,273	565,460
Local government	167,045	295,400	333,843	359,877
TOTAL	1,393,340	1,568,925	1,801,384	1,825,913

Source: El País, 22 Feb. 1992

The pre-existing local government units, the provinces and local councils, are guaranteed in the constitution and value their direct links with the centre. While the town councils, *ayuntamientos*, and their mayors, *alcaldes*, are generally well regarded by the population, the provinces represent a rather artificial unit of government originally designed for the purposes of the centralized regime. Their boundaries, like those of the French departments, are often outdated and their functions duplicate those of other levels of government. Some of the autonomous communities consist of only a single province and in these cases the autonomous government has taken over the provincial role. In other cases, there have been conflicts as the autonomous community has sought to expand its power at the expense of the provinces. Catalonia has proposed to abolish its provinces through a law, passed with the cooperation of the national parliament, amalgamating them into a single province. As units of general local administration, it has created *comarques*, smaller bodies reflecting local features. Elsewhere, for example in Galicia, provincial governments are too well entrenched in local systems of clientelism to be moved.

Another problem, in Spain as elsewhere, is the lack of independent revenue-raising powers for subnational governments. The law provides that, along with the transfer of functions there should be a transfer of resources. This is done in a variety of ways. National taxes assigned to the autonomous governments - meaning that they receive the product of the tax without the freedom to set the rate - account for between 8 and 50 per cent of revenues. Catalonia, Valencia and the Canaries have their own independent taxes but, apart from the gasoline tax in the Canaries, the amounts are tiny. The rest comes from transfers from central government. Initially, these transfers were based on the cost of services devolved but later more sophisticated formulas were introduced, the idea, only partially realized, being to allow the autonomous communities more freedom in deciding how to spend the money. For the period 1992-1996 a revised system of transfers was negotiated, which provides for a block grant linked to increases in state taxes, national public expenditure and growth in gross domestic product. In the 1993 budget year, this amounted to 1.6 million million pesetas, about 12 per cent of the national budget. An additional 7 per cent of the national budget is transferred to municipal governments. For poorer regions, there is a special Territorial Compensation Fund intended to transfer money from the rich to the poor regions. Only in the foral communities of Navarre and the Basque Country do local governments collect most taxes themselves, passing on an agreed share to Madrid. A proposal in 1992 to cede the autonomous communities and 15 per cent share of income tax received in each region was supported strongly by Catalonia and other prosperous regions but opposed by poorer regions such as Andalucia and Extremadura who saw it as a threat to national solidarity. Since these regions have great weight in the ruling PSOE party, the proposal ran into trouble. Yet, as the Catalan and Basque nationalist parties were drawn into negotiations about their terms for supporting the minority PSOE government after the 1993 national elections, the proposal was dusted off.

REFERENCES

1. R. Carr, *Spain, 1808-1939*, 3rd. edn. (Oxford: Clarendon, 1975). J. Sanchez Jiménez, *La España Contemporanea, 11. 1875-1931* (Madrid: ISTMO, 1991).
2. J. Sanchez Jiménez, *La España Contemporanea, 111. De 1931 a nuestros días.* (Madrid: ISTMO, 1991).
3. A standard text is E. Alvarez Conde, *El Regimen Político Español*, 4th edn. (Madrid: Tecnos, 1990).
4. P. Heywood, 'Governing a New Democracy: The Power of the Prime Minister in Spain', *West European Politics*, 14.2 (1991), pp. 97-115.
5. R. Gunter, G. Sani and G. Shabad, *Spain After Franco. The Making of a Competitive Party System* (Berkeley, University of California Press, 1986).
6. R. Gunter, 'Leyes electorales, sistemas de partidos y elites: el caso español', *Revista Español de Investigaciones Sociológicas*, 47 (1989), pp. 73-106.
7. R. Gillespie, 'The Break-up of the "Socialist Family": Party-Union Relations in Spain, 1982-89', *West European Politics*, 13.1 (1990), pp. 47-61.
8. *Revista Español de Investigaciones Sociológicas*, 49 (1987).
9. M. Beltrán Villalva, 'La Administración Pública y los Funcionarios', in S. Giner (ed.), *España. Tomo 1, Sociedad y Política* (Madrid: Espasa-Calpe, 1990).

10. M. Beltrán Villalva, 'La Administración Pública y los Funcionarios', in S. Giner (ed.), *España. Tomo 1, Sociedad y Política* (Madrid: Espasa-Calpe, 1990).

11. M. Beltrán Villalva, 'La Administración Pública y los Funcionarios', in S. Giner (ed.), *España. Tomo 1, Sociedad y Política* (Madrid: Espasa-Calpe, 1990).

12. A. Nieto, 'Funcionarios', in E. García de Enterría (ed.), *España; un presente para el futuro. 2 Las Instituciones* (Madrid: Instituto de Estudios Económicos, 1984). J. Subirats, 'La modernizzazione della pubblica ammistrazione spagnola, ovvera la riforma nascosta', *Revista trimestrale di Scienza dell'Amministrazione* 4 (1991), pp. 105-21.

13. V. Perez Diaz, 'Políticas económicas y pautas sociales en la España de la transición: la doble cara del neocorporatismo', in J. Linz (ed.), *España: un presente para el futuro* (Madrid: Instituto de Estudios Económicos, 1984). V. Perez Diaz, *El retorno de la sociedad civil* (Madrid: Instituto de Estudios Económicos, 1987).

14. M. Mella Marquez, 'Los grupos de presión en las transición política', in J.F. Tezanos, R. Cotarelo and A. de Blas (eds.), *La Transición Democrática Español* (Madrid: Sistema, 1989).

15. M. Martinez Lucio, 'Employer Identity and the Politics of the Labour Market in Spain', *West European Politics*, 14.1 (1991), pp. 41-55.

16. V. Perez Diaz, 'Políticas económicas y pautas sociales en la España de la transición: la doble cara del neocorporatismo', in J. Linz (ed.), *España: un presente para el futuro* (Madrid: Instituto de Estudios Económicos, 1984). M. Pérez Yruela and S. Giner (eds.), *El Corporatismo en España* (Barcelona: Ariel, 1988).

17. J.L. Villalaín, A.B. Pérez and J.M. del Valle López, *La Sociedad española de los 90 y sus nuevos valores* (Madrid: SM, 1992).

18. *Conflictos constitucionales de las Comunidades Autónomas. Indices sistematizados 1981-1990* (Madrid: Comunidad de Madrid, 1990).

FURTHER READING

History and Transition

R. Carr, *Spain, 1808-1939*, 3rd. edn. (Oxford: Clarendon, 1975).

R. Carr and J.P. Fusi, *Spain: Dictatorship to Democracy*, 2nd. edn. (London: Allen and Unwin, 1981).

R.P. Clark and M.H. Halzel, *Spain in the 1980s. The Democratic Transition and New International Relations* (Cambridge, Mass.: Ballinger, 1987).

D. Gilmour, *The Transformation of Spain. From Franco to the Constitutional Monarchy* (London: Quartet, 1985).

E. Moxon-Browne, *Political Change in Spain* (London: Routledge, 1989).

P. Preston, *The Triumph of Democracy in Spain* (London and New York: Methuen, 1986).

J. Sanchez Jiménez, *La España Contemporanea, 11. 1875-1931* (Madrid: ISTMO, 1991).

J. Sanchez Jiménez, *La España Contemporanea, 111. De 1931 a nuestros días.* (Madrid: ISTMO, 1991).

J.F. Tezanos, R. Cotarelo and A. de Blas (eds.), *La Transición Democrática Español* (Madrid: Sistema, 1989).

Government and Institutions

E. Alvarez Conde, *El Regimen Político Español*, 4th edn. (Madrid: Tecnos, 1990).

E. Garcia de Enterra (ed.), *España: un presente para el futuro. 2 Las Instituciones* (Madrid: Instituto de Estudios Económicos, 1984).

S. Giner (ed.), *España. Tomo 1, Sociedad y Política* (Madrid: Espasa-Calpe, 1990).

S. Giner and L. Moreno (eds.), *Sociology in Spain* (Madrid: Consejo Superior de Investigaciones Científicas, 1990).

P. Heywood, 'Governing a New Democracy: The Power of the Prime Minister in Spain', *West European Politics,* 14.2 (1991), pp. 97-115.

Parties

R. Garcia Cotarelo and L. Lopez Nieto, 'Spanish Conservatism, 1976-87', *West European Politics,* 11.2 (1988), pp. 80-94.
R. Gillespie, 'The Break-up of the "Socialist Family": Party-Union Relations in Spain, 1982-89', *West European Politics*, 13.1 (1990), pp. 47-61.
R. Gunter, G. Sani and G. Shabad, *Spain After Franco. The Making of a Competitive Party System* (Berkeley, University of California Press, 1986).
P. Heywood, 'Mirror-images: The PCE and PSOE in the Transition to Democracy in Spain', *West European Politics,* 10.2 (1987), pp. 193-210.
M. Ramirez, *Sistema de Partidos en España (1931-1990)* (Madrid: Centro de Estudios Constitucionales, 1991).

Territorial Politics

E. Aja, J. Tornos, T. Font, J.M. Perulles and E. Albertí, *El Sistema Jurídico de las Comunides Autónomas* (Madrid: Tecnos, 1985).
J.P. Fusi (ed.), *España. Tomo 5, Autonomías* (Madrid: Espasa-Calpe, 1989).
M. Hebbert, 'Regionalism: a reform concept and its application to Spain', *Environment and Planning C. Government and Policy,* 5 (1987).
M. Keating, 'Spain. Peripheral Nationalism and the State', in J. McGarry and B. O'Leary (eds.), *Ethnic Conflict in the Western World* (London: Routledge, 1993).

7 European Integration

THE IDEA OF EUROPEAN INTEGRATION

The idea of Europe as a community with common values and institutions is an old one. In the Middle Ages, it was identified with Christendom, its boundaries marked largely by contact with the Islamic world. Its component parts shared a common legacy in the Roman Empire. In the centuries which followed, the religious divisions of the Reformation and the rise of the nation-state seriously weakened this sense of community. The great powers, Spain, France and Britain, successively founded global empires. In Germany and Italy, nation-states were created. The ideal of the nation-state became so entrenched as to appear the natural form of political organization and was exported to other continents until it became universal. Yet, following the two world wars of this century, European unity came back on the political agenda, impelled by a combination of strategic, political and economic considerations.

Strategically, the imperative was to avoid another war between France and Germany after the three devastating confrontations between 1870 and 1945. A Franco-German entente could be the basis for a new security system for the continent as a whole. There was also a need to rehabilitate Germany after the disgrace of the Nazi epoch, encouraging it to join the community of democratic nations while restraining its international role. This problem became acute when the United States pressed for the rearmament of West Germany in the face of the Soviet Union, a policy which the French viewed with grave misgivings. Many Europeans saw integration as the only way to secure influence in a world now dominated by two superpowers with the European states relegated to the second division. For its part, the United States encouraged European unity as a means of strengthening western defences against the Soviets and securing the capitalist system against Communist influence in France and Italy.

Political unity was proposed first by European federalists between the wars and taken up again in the 1950s. Federalism has been an important and contentious theme throughout the debate on integration, right up to 1990s. Some federalists aspire to a United States of Europe, in which the existing nations would be reduced to something like American states or Canadian provinces. Others would settle for something looser, based on strong continental institutions, but with the nation-states remaining in being. Non-federalist supporters of European integration want a system firmly based on cooperation among the nation-states, without strong common institutions.

Economically, European integration rested on the conviction that only with large home markets could European firms compete the their American, and later Japanese, rivals. There was a wide belief that the policies of protection and national autarky which had characterized European responses to the inter-war Depression served to make everyone worse off. According to the theory of comparative advantage, the removal of trade barriers would allow each European country to specialize in those products in which it was most efficient to the benefit of all. Large industrial units could be created to exploit economies of scale and hold their own in the world. Europe itself would represent a major force in world trade and carry much more influence in trade negotiations than any of its individual members.

It was widely believed that these political and economic forces were linked and mutually reinforcing. Before and after the war, a number of prominent Europeans had advocated continental integration on the basis of functionalism, that is the transfer of specific areas of policy and administration to international bodies which could discharge them more effectively than nation-states. With the focus on applied issues in administration rather a frontal assault on national sovereignty itself, it was believed that by very practical steps gradual integration could be achieved. This thinking was to give rise to a series of specialized bodies, as discussed below. Later a more ambitious theory was advanced, under the inelegant name of neo-functionalism. This noted that there were spillovers among areas such that integration in one field would inevitably lead to integration in another. So harmonization of policies in coal and steel might lead to pressures for harmonization in other fields. Removal of tariff barriers might make it more urgent to control exchange-rate fluctuations. These spillovers might occur not only among economic sectors but between the economic and the political world. So economic integration would lead inexorably towards political integration as economic and political decision makers saw immediate advantage in actions promoting unity. To encourage this, institutions would need to be created in which political and business leaders when negotiating would opt for solutions which helped rather than hindered unity. It is this idea which underpinned the otherwise rather strange institutions with which the European Community was to equip itself. This rather optimistic view was based in part on a theory about how the European states themselves were formed, through gradual economic and social integration and the diffusion of common values. European unity would represent the continuation of these trends at the continental level. Critics pointed out that France, Germany, Britain and the other major states were in fact put together by force, dynastic manoeuvring and political calculation, often in conflict with each other ,and that national interests were likely to prove rather resilient in the face of functional logic.

Another key idea was that of supranationality, that Europe would be more than a mere international organization like the United Nations or the General Agreement on Tariffs and Trade, in which members chose whether to cooperate. Instead, it would be a 'supranational' one, with powers to take decisions directly affecting citizens and to force national governments to comply with its directives.[2] Those opposed to supranationality preferred a looser arrangement characterized as 'intergovernmental', in which member states would cooperate voluntarily but not be subject to the overall authority of European institutions.

European politicians and interest groups were divided on the merits of integration but after the second world war the great majority were favourable. A new generation of modernizing elites in business and government were keen to break the protectionist habits of the inter-war era and convinced that modernization, planning and change must go beyond the narrow limits of the nation-state. Large businesses were favourable, seeing opportunities in the wider continental market. Christian Democrats, committed to economic and social modernization while fighting the Communist threat, were strongly pro-Europe. Social Democratic parties were initially more divided, some seeing Europe as a capitalist ploy while others saw it as a step towards international unity. Eventually, Social Democrats were to be among the strongest supporters.

Among nations, the Benelux countries - Belgium, the Netherlands and Luxembourg - tired of their role as battleground for the great powers, were highly enthusiastic, seeing a united Europe as a means to restrain France and Germany and enhance their own influence. In France and Germany themselves, opinion was more divided but the most important political elites saw European unity as a means of overcoming their historic enmity and achieving a more stable and prosperous future. An important external influence, especially in the years of Marshall Plan aid, was the United States, which wanted a united Europe both to form a bulwark against the Soviet Union and to provide an integrated market for its business corporations.

Opposed to European integration was a variety of forces. Nationalists, such as the French Gaullists and both main British parties, disliked the loss of sovereignty and found the whole idea of federalism repugnant. Communists and left-wing Socialists opposed the project which they associated politically with the Cold War confrontation with the Soviet Union and economically as a means to consolidate capitalism. Indeed, the theory of comparative advantage, in which economic activities find their most profitable location, is itself derived from a free-market view of the economy. Large parts of the political left believed that this and other aspects of the project would prevent state intervention and control in economic matters. This opposition persisted until the 1970s when left-wing Socialists and reform Communists began to consider the possibilities of influencing the progress of integration to take account of their concerns rather than trying to block it outright. Trade unions were initially suspicious of integration. British unions and those continental unions under Communist influence were extremely hostile. In time, these too have changed their view and now support integration. Farmers, used to national schemes for protection and subsidy, were also at first suspicious of integration but were bought off with a new subsidy system at the European level. Only recently has this been brought into question. Small business leaders and traders were suspicious of integration, which they saw as favouring their large rivals and this was to cause some problems for the future. Further opposition came from the peripheral regions of Europe, where people feared a further loss of influence as decisions were taken at even greater distance. They also worried that their economic disadvantages, notably remoteness from the major markets, would be exacerbated as investment flowed into the central areas of the new economic union. On the left, some internationalists and sympathizers with developing countries opposed European integration as the creation of a rich man's club, making it easier to exploit the resources of the Third World while keeping their manufactured products and temperate foods out.

The first European institution to be established after the war was the Council of Europe, based in Strasbourg on the French-German border. This is an intergovernmental organization with a Parliamentary forum to discuss common issues and a secretariat which organizes meetings and research projects on matters of common interest. It has an extensive cultural programme and has sponsored conventions on terrorism, data protection and health. It sponsors a Standing Conference of Local and Regional Authorities of Europe and facilitates agreements between local governments in different countries. Attached to the Council of Europe is the European Commission of Human Rights which investigates cases of alleged abuse of human rights in member countries and can send them to trial before the European Court of Human Rights where it believes that there has been a contravention of the European Convention for the Protection of Human Rights. Some member states have incorporated the Convention into their national law, so that domestic Courts can take it into account. Others do not recognize the direct jurisdiction of the Court but usually take steps to rectify any abuses on which the Court has pronounced. A European Social Charter, first signed in 1965, seeks to guarantee minimal social and employment rights but has had less impact. The Council of Europe, which is not to be confused with the quite separate European Community, had 27 members in 1992 and applications pending from the new nations of eastern Europe. The Council of Europe has not aroused great political controversy since its authority is largely moral, but it has been influential in sustaining the democratic ideal in Europe. Greece and Turkey have both at times been suspended for abuse of democratic and human rights and applications from former Soviet bloc countries have been held up pending investigation into these issues.

The next step occurred in the early 1950s, when an attempt was made to establish a unified European defence system, to accommodate a rearmed Germany. The resulting proposals for a European Defence Community, involving France, West Germany, Italy, and the Benelux countries, failed in 1954 when the French Parliament refused to ratify it. Instead, West Germany was admitted to NATO and western European military cooperation took place within this structure, under American leadership. The European members of NATO are united in the Western European Union, a body originally founded in 1948 as the Brussels Treaty Organization and renamed in 1954 when Germany and Italy joined.

The first steps in economic integration came in 1952 with the foundation of the European Coal and Steel Community (ECSC) by France, West Germany, Italy and the Benelux countries. Its occasion was a dispute between France and Germany over the strategic Saar coalfield which neither state was prepared to concede to the other. The ECSC involved common policies for management, modernization and trade in coal and steel and introduced for the first time a supranational element, with a High Authority independent of national governments.

In 1957 economic integration took a massive step forward with the Treaty of Rome, establishing the European Economic Community (EEC) with the same six members. The Treaty provided for the removal of tariff barriers between member states and the establishment of a common external tariff between the Community and the rest of the world; the gradual elimination of non-tariff barriers and other distortions to trade; the free movement of labour and capital around the Community; and a common agricultural policy, this being the price of French support. It also established a system of government enshrining the supranationality principle and intended to develop towards ever greater union. Later, the EEC was merged with the ECSC and the European Atomic Energy Community to form the present European Community (EC). Its constitution remains the Treaty of Rome, as amended by the Single European Act of 1987 and the Treaty on European Union (the Maastricht Treaty) of 1992. In principle the Community is open to all European democracies but, because of its political nature, neutral states, with the exception of Ireland, decided during the Cold War to remain outside.

The original Community comprised just six states. France negotiated its adherence under the Fourth Republic although by the time the Treaty came into effect in 1958 de Gaulle was returning to power. While seeing the need for an economic union, de Gaulle was extremely hostile to the supranational principle and insisted, in contradiction to the Treaty, that member states should retain a veto over Community actions. French farmers, an important interest group, had been conciliated by the common agricultural policy, on the understanding that Germany would be the main financial contributor. Since de Gaulle, French leaders have been more positive about European integration, supporting the major advances, though still wary about the surrender of French sovereignty to Community institutions. They have not abandoned altogether the Gaullist notion of a *Europe des patries,* a voluntary confederation of independent states without a powerful central government. France tends to be more protectionist than other members, often seeking to re-establish at Community level protectionist measures which have been dismantled nationally. West Germany for its part was enthusiastic for membership, seeing it as a means of re-entering the international community and erasing the nationalism of the past, while providing outlets for its industrial production. After their political conversion at Bad Godesberg, the Social Democrats became as enthusiastic as the Christian Democrats. This attitude has persisted and the Germans have supported free trade both within the Community and between it and the rest of the world. In 1990 Germany willingly accepted further moves to political integration as the counterpart to German unification. A Franco-German axis based on mutual interests formed the basis of the Community for many years. Italy has always favoured integration, although the industrial north had more to gain than the underdeveloped south. Italian public opinion generally sees the Community as preferable to its own often ineffective state. In 1989, Italian voters approved by a massive majority a proposition for further integration and strengthening of Community institutions. The Benelux countries saw a united Europe as the only way to survive in the modern world and as a means of restraining the large powers.

Britain, on the other hand, decided against membership. It still saw itself as a global power, at the centre of an evolving Commonwealth of former colonies. Since the nineteenth century, Britain had imported raw materials and food from its Empire while exporting industrial goods and saw no advantage in diverting its trade relations to the continent of Europe. Some even saw the Commonwealth as the basis for a world political and military posture; later this was replaced with the idea that Britain had a special relationship with the United States putting it apart from the rest of Europe. There was much scepticism in Britain about the economic advantages of integration, especially if this would mean substituting expensive European foodstuffs for cheaper produce bought in Commonwealth or world markets. The British left was very hostile to the free-market basis of the Community. It was also concerned about the threat to the new welfare state from integration with less advanced continental countries; in the 1980s this argument was to be stood on its head as British welfare provision lagged behind. Despite the presence of pro-European minorities in both Conservative and Labour Parties, there was massive hostility to any loss of sovereignty and a feeling that British Parliamentary traditions could be prejudiced in a Europe historically prone to revolutions, instability and authoritarianism. Senior civil servants and politicians loftily insisted that the organization would not last. Instead, Britain formed a rival organization, the European Free Trade Area (EFTA), with tariff barriers abolished but no common external tariff or moves to economic or political integration. In 1961, as part of a general reappraisal of strategy, the British Conservative government changed its mind and applied for membership of the EC. By this time, imperial illusions had largely faded and the Community was an economic success. Special relationship or no, the United States had also made it clear that Britain's place was in Europe. In a humiliating rebuff, de Gaulle vetoed British entry, on the grounds that it was not European enough. It appears that he regarded Britain as a Trojan horse for American influence in Europe and feared for the dominance of the Franco-German axis in the Community. In 1967, the Labour government made another application, also vetoed by de Gaulle. Only with de Gaulle's departure from power and death in 1970 did the French give way and in 1973 the United Kingdom, along with the Republic of Ireland and Denmark brought the Community's membership to nine. Britain has remained a rather unenthusiastic member. Although under Conservative governments it has favoured free trade and opening up of markets, it has opposed political integration under governments of both parties.

Following the fall of their dictatorial regimes, the southern European nations of Greece, in 1981, and Spain and Portugal, in 1986, joined the Community. This was seen less as a strategic choice than a necessity in order to stabilize democracy and ensure their membership of the advanced world. With the end of the Cold War, the neutral states abandoned their reservations and applied as well. By the 1990s, the Community had become such a dominant presence that no European state felt it could remain outside.

The Progress of Integration

Economists distinguish among four stages of economic integration. First is a free-trade area, in which tariffs are eliminated among the members but each retains its own national tariffs against outside countries. Second is a customs union, in which there is a common external tariff between members of the union and outsiders. Third is a common market in which there is free movement not only of goods but also of services, labour and capital. Fourth is economic and monetary union, in which monetary policies, and hence much of fiscal policy, are harmonized and there is a single currency, or at least rigidly fixed exchange rates. In the case of the European Community, the intention has been to parallel these stages with moves towards political union. In practice, however, progress has been sporadic, very rapid at times, slow at others, and economic and political integration have not proceeded in harmony.

The first stages of economic integration, the removal of tariff barriers among the original members and the establishment of the common external tariff, was relatively easy and was accomplished by 1970. A common agricultural policy was put in place, though this has since become an object of widespread criticism. The 1970s by contrast, were years of slow progress. Difficulties in adjustment following the oil crises encouraged protectionist tendencies and a reluctance to surrender national power. While free trade existed in principle, a range of non-tariff barriers such as differing product standards, taxation systems and border formalities remained to obstruct the movement of goods. Although there was theoretically free movement of labour, professional qualifications and requirements for citizenship in public employment made mobility difficult. National controls on the movement of capital remained widespread. An attempt in the 1970s to launch an Economic and Monetary Union came to little. Outside agriculture, there were few common policies. Regional and social funds had been set up but operated as mechanisms for redistributing money among member states rather than instruments of Community policy. Political integration was effectively halted in 1965 when de Gaulle vetoed a move to majority voting. Under the Luxembourg Compromise, any nation was permitted to veto a Community policy where it considered that its vital interests were at stake, a provision which was not removed until 1987. Attempts to coordinate foreign policy foundered on the divergent views of Britain and France on defence and the determination of member states to pursue their own interests. Enlargement to include Greece, Spain and Portugal held up integration further, to the satisfaction of the British who had supported their membership precisely for this reason. About the only significant move forward was the direct election of members of the European Parliament in 1979, though without giving them any more powers, a move which was undertaken largely to show that the Community was still moving.

In the 1980s, this changed, with a new political will and more favourable economic conditions. During the economic crises of the 1970s, nation-states tended to be defensive and protectionist, unwilling to risk change. With the resumption of growth in the 1980s, there was a greater willingness to move forward and a feeling that sustained growth would be helped by the dismantling of barriers. Yet there were divergent views on the form which progress should take. A division opened up between broadeners and deepeners.[1] Broadeners wanted to expand Community membership to include EFTA, southern and eventually eastern European countries, even at the cost of cohesion. Deepeners wanted to tie the existing members together more tightly with common institutions and policies, even though this would make enlargement more difficult. A variation on this theme was the line pursued by the French government, which involved broadening the Community to include new members while also adopting new common policies, but without strengthening European institutions. Instead, new policies would be pursued on an intergovernmental basis, through cooperation rather than supranational authority.

In the early 1980s, various proposals for a new political union of a federalist sort were put forward, culminating in the Spinelli draft for a European Union. These gained much support in the European Parliament but made little headway with member states. Proposals for closer integration in defence matters fared no better. With the appointment of Jacques Delors as president of the European Commission, it was decided to proceed again through economic integration, concentrating on issues on which members could agree. With great fanfare, it was announced that by 31 December 1992, the Community would achieve a single market, eliminating all barriers to the movement of goods, workers and capital. Cynics might note that this was really no more than the common market already provided for in the Treaty of Rome and that the single market programme consisted mainly of items already filed in the Community bureaucracy. Yet there was no doubt that the setting of a target date helped galvanize the institutions and the member states. The main items provided for in the 1992 initiative were:
- the elimination of physical and technical barriers to the free movement of goods,
- the alignment of safety and technical standards on goods or mutual recognition of standards;
- the alignment of indirect taxation, notably the Value Added Tax, within fixed limits;
- the opening up of public procurement to contractors from other Community countries;
- free trade in services;
- access to national markets for banks and financial services from any Community country;
- the abolition of exchange controls within the Community;
- the alignment of rules on transportation and the deregulation of road and air transport;
- the improvement of telecommunications and the deregulation of the telecommunications market;
- the free movement of workers and harmonization of professional qualifications, or mutual recognition of qualifications;
- strengthening the competition and anti-monopoly policy,

This programme not only provided for freer trade within the Community. It also represented a move to deregulation and encouragement for the unfettered market, confirming the fears on the left and among trade unions of a business-dominated Europe made for the corporations rather than the citizens. Even governments of the centre-right in the wealthier states worried that the poorer, southern states would be able to undercut them competitively because of their low wage costs and social expenditure overheads. It was therefore proposed that a Social Charter be included ensuring minimal welfare standards and working regulations.

It was also agreed to double the structural fund available for declining sectors and regions to enable them to cope with the effects of the internal market. In order to expedite the progress of this, the Single European Act of 1987 reformed the Community decision-making structures, providing for more majority voting and giving additional powers to the European Parliament.

The 1992 programme succeeded in gaining support from all member states, though with varying degrees of enthusiasm. Britain's Conservative government liked the economic measures for deregulation and freer trade but was adamantly opposed to the Social Charter, which it saw as a means of bringing back the sort of labour market regulation and social protection which it was trying to dismantle at home. Its vehement opposition had the unintended by-product of converting the British trade unions to Community membership!

Eventually, the Social Charter was adopted by a majority of eleven to one against Britain. By 1991 Britain's continued obduracy forced the eleven to adopt the Charter as a parallel measure among themselves rather than putting in the revised Treaty as they had intended. Britain also dragged its feet on the elimination of border controls and free movement of people within the Community, citing fears about illegal immigrants, drug smugglers and terrorists and here the the other members proceeded on their own, establishing the Schengen scheme, a provision for the free movement of individuals initially between France and Benelux, to which other countries have progressively adhered. Other northern countries supported the 1992 initiative wholeheartedly, while the southern countries used their acquiescence as a means of extracting extra transfer payments from the wealthier members. By the target date of 31 December 1992, 260 of the 282 directives which comprised the single market programme had been adopted, though in some cases national governments had

Figure 7.1 Percentage of single market directives implemented,
Aug. 1992

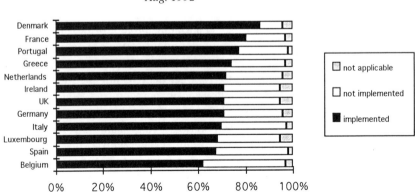

Source: Economist 26 Sept. 1992

not yet translated them into domestic law. Figure 7.1 shows the differences among member states in implementing single market directives.

Even before the completion of the single market initiative, Delors was determined to press ahead with yet more integrative measures. The end of the Cold War and the reunification of Germany gave urgency to new measures to stabilize the continent and contain German economic and political power within a tighter European framework. With countries from EFTA, the Mediterranean basin and eastern Europe seeking membership of the EC, it was widely considered necessary to reform Community institutions and ensure that broadening membership did not result in a weakening of unity. So two intergovernmental conferences were launched, in 1990, to consider further proposals for monetary union and political union. After a great deal of negotiation, the outcome was the Maastricht Treaty, agreed in December 1991 and signed in February 1992.

Maastricht provides for a broadening of the scope of the Community and a strengthening of its institutions. It creates a new umbrella body, known as the European Union. All citizens of Community countries will become citizens of the Union, with the right to move and reside freely in the territory of member states. Under the Union, there will be three pillars. The first is the existing European Community, whose institutions and powers are reformed. The second pillar is for foreign and defence policy and involves intergovernmental cooperation rather than supranational authority. Most decisions under this pillar will have to be unanimous and there is only a vague commitment to building up the Western European Union as a future defence arm of the Union. The third pillar concerns cooperation in police and justice matters. This, too, is subject to intergovernmental cooperation rather than supranational decision making.

Maastricht also provides for monetary union of the Community in a series of stages, leading to a European central bank and eventually a single currency. Community competences were extended in the fields of the environment, research and transport. The social chapter (formerly charter) was incorporated in the Treaty.

Maastricht represented a considerable expansion of Community powers and scope. On the other hand, Community institutions were not strengthened correspondingly. The device of three pillars kept the Commission largely out of the fields of foreign and security policy, which are to be dealt with by cooperation among member states. The elected Parliament saw only a modest increase in its powers. It therefore represented a triumph for the French view of an intergovernmental Community rather than for the federalists. Maastricht was also weakened by the insertion of a series of protocols to allow various members, notably Britain, to opt out of its more important provisions. So Britain was able again to opt out of the social chapter, which would apply only to the other member states. A protocol allowed Britain to opt out of the single currency arrangement. Britain was accordingly given no vote in matters of monetary union and no say in the appointment of directors of the proposed central bank.

Maastricht represented a compromise among different views of Europe's future and proved extremely controversial in several member states. Nationalists assailed it for taking power away from member states and extending Community competences in new directions. On the left it was attacked for emphasizing market integration and monetary discipline at the expense of social considerations. The social chapter was criticized at little more than good intentions. It was widely attacked as undemocratic, taking power away from the nation-state while failing to strengthen mechanisms for democratic control at the European level. Instead of being exercised in an open and accountable manner, the new powers were to be exercised by the appointed Commission, an unaccountable central bank and the intergovernmental council in which ministers could evade responsibility by blaming each other. Anti-Europeans saw this as an attack on the nation-state. Many pro-Europeans saw it as a recipe for a bureaucrats' and businessmen's Europe rather than a democratic Europe.

Denmark and Ireland were obliged by their constitutions to hold referendums on Maastricht. In Denmark, the result was a narrow rejection. Ireland voted by a large majority in favour, encouraged by the proposals for further transfers of funds contained in the Treaty. French President Mitterrand also decided on a referendum, as a way of bolstering his sagging authority and wrong-footing his conservative opponents, who were divided on the issue. After a hard-fought campaign, the YES forces won a very narrow victory in September 1992. By this time, Maastricht was caught up in the anti-politician mood sweeping western countries, including Canada and the United States, where popular votes respectively defeated proposed constitutional changes and threw out the incumbent president. Opposition grew ever stronger in the British Conservative Party, where former Prime Minister Margaret Thatcher came out against the Treaty. In Spain, a country strongly committed to Europe, misgivings grew and the government had to postpone the Parliamentary debate on ratification. In Germany, where the true cost of reunification was just becoming apparent, there was a cooling of enthusiasm for Europe. Germans worried in particular about surrendering the Deutschmark for the proposed European currency and about the costs of transfers to the poorer southern countries of the Community, when they had their new eastern *Länder* to support. More generally, the economic uncertainty of the 1990s, like that of the 1970s, undermined confidence in Europe and made people cautious about large-scale changes. At the Edinburgh summit of Community leaders in December 1992, Denmark was allowed to opt out of most of the important features of the Treaty in the hope that this would encourage the Danes to ratify it in a further referendum. Added to the British opt-outs, this represented a significant breach in the principle that all members of the Community would proceed to integration at the same pace. The details of the Maastricht Treaty are discussed below, under thematic headings.

The development of the Community has been fitful. For a time, as in the 1960s, there is rapid progress. Then, as in the early 1980s, there are periods of stagnation. Much depends on economic circumstances. At times of expansion, the Community thrives but in recession member states revert to caution and national protectionism. External threats, such as the Cold War, may also spur Europeans to cooperation. There is a constant tension between the building of European institutions and national governments' reluctance to surrender powers and frequent disputes occur over the appropriate scope for Community action. It is generally agreed that these should be resolved according the principle of subsidiarity, a complex notion which has its origins in Catholic thinking on the proper role of public authority. As applied in debates on the Community, it has come to mean that matters should be decided at the lowest level practicable. The problem is to agree on what is the appropriate level for each function. Subsidiarity was officially incorporated by an amendment to the Treaty of Rome in 1991 as follows:

> In areas which do not fall within its exclusive competence, the Community shall take action, in accordance with the principle of subsidiarity, only if and in so far as the objectives of the proposed action cannot be sufficiently achieved by the Member States and can therefore, by reason of the scale or effects of the proposed action, be better achieved by the Community.[3]

This represented a warning by certain member governments that they thought that the scope of Community action should be more restricted, though the application of the subsidiarity doctrine and when it should be invoked remain matters for dispute.

COMMUNITY INSTITUTIONS

The Community's institutions are based on the Treaty of Rome as modified by the Single European Act of 1987 and the European Union Treaty of 1991 (the Maastricht Treaty). They were never intended as a final state but rather as a means of ensuring the supranationality principle while building in a dynamic to further integration. Problems in working with them are supposed to lead not to compromises on the lowest common denominator but to solutions representing a further move forward. An analogy is drawn with a bicycle which must keep moving forward if it is to stay upright. A complex interlinking of Community and national elements is intended to ensure that the European ethos penetrates national administrations rather than remaining the exclusive property of EC bodies. When this system is working it is capable of great achievements; unfortunately it is also prone to seize up from the myriad compromises which have to be made.

The key institution is the Commission, located in Brussels. There are seventeen commissioners, appointed by member states for a five-year term, two from the large and one each from the small states, with a president appointed by agreement among the member states. Under the Maastricht Treaty, their appointment is subject to approval by the European Parliament, which also has the power to dismiss the whole Commission. Once appointed, commissioners become totally independent of their home governments, serving only the European interest. Although sometimes referred to as bureaucrats, or Eurocrats, commissioners are highly political animals, usually appointed from the ranks of national politicians and sometimes returning to domestic politics after their terms of office. The Commission has the exclusive responsibility for initiating policy proposals under the Treaty of Rome and the Single European Act, in order to ensure that proposals reflect European and not purely national concerns. This characteristic, of reflecting a European rather than a national perspective is described as *communautaire*, a term with positive connotations when applied to policies or institutions. The Commission further has the responsibility of ensuring that Community policies are implemented working through twenty-three specialized directorates general. Altogether the Commission has a staff of about 12,500. Many of these are translators and the number of administrative staff is smaller than that of most national government departments. Consequently, the Commission cannot implement its own decisions directly and most of the actual work is carried out by national administrations. It also polices the observance of the treaties and laws, taking action against offending persons, firms or states who may be subject to decisions or prosecuted before the Court of Justice. In certain instances, especially under the powers inherited from the formerly separate Coal and Steel Community, it can take action on its own. It represents the Community in international trade negotiations such as those of the General Agreement on Tariffs and Trade and its president has since the late 1970s participated at the annual summits of the seven large industrialized nations, the G7.

On foreign policy and defence matters, the Commission's role is more limited. It does have the power to make proposals, but not sole power. Similarly, on internal security and police matters, it has only an associate role, these matters being handled largely by intergovernmental discussion, with member states able to make their own proposals and amendments.

Legislation in the Community is the responsibility of the Council of Ministers, consisting of one representative of each member state. There is no fixed membership and governments send whichever minister is concerned

Table 7.1 Votes in Council of Ministers	
Country	Votes
France	10
Germany	10
Italy	10
UK	10
Spain	8
Belgium	5
Greece	5
Netherlands	5
Portugal	5
Denmark	3
Ireland	3
Luxembourg	2

with the subject under discussion. Meetings are chaired by the representative of the country which holds the Community presidency, an office which rotates every six months. Preparation of meetings is also the responsibility of the presiding country, though there is also a permanent secretariat attached to the Council of Ministers in Brussels. Except in areas such as defence, foreign affairs and certain security matters, the Council of Ministers cannot initiate proposals and can amend proposals from the Commission only by unanimous vote. In the case of disagreement, the proposal must be sent back to the Commission which may then produce an amended version of its own. There was provision in the Treaty of Rome for the Council of Ministers to proceed to majority voting but, when the time came for this, de Gaulle refused to cooperate, insisting on the Luxembourg compromise under which the veto remained available. In the 1980s, some votes began to be taken by majority and in 1987 the Single European Act formalized matters by providing for qualified majority votes on a large range of matters, including the main items of the internal market. There are seventy-six votes, distributed so as to deny any state a veto but make it difficult to over-rule the large ones (Table 7.1).

A qualified majority requires fifty four out of the seventy-six votes, so ensuring that no major country can be over-ruled as long as it has the support of at least a small one. Some important matters remain subject to unanimous decision, including harmonization of taxation, research, industrial policy and extensions of the Community's own competence. Since the Luxembourg compromise was never formally incorporated into Community law, it has never been repealed and in 1992 France was still threatening to invoke it to veto the GATT agreement on agricultural protection. At Britain's insistence, the implementation of the Social Charter was left out of the formal institutional mechanisms altogether, though the Commission does have a role to play in developing proposals for the eleven participating governments. In most areas, the Council is supposed only to respond to Commission initiatives, but most issues are in fact subject to bargaining and compromise, states trading off gains in one are for losses in another. Marathon sessions have often been necessary to forge these agreements, aided by self-imposed deadlines or crises. Much of the preparatory work is done in the Committee of Permanent Representatives (CORPEPER), consisting of national ambassadors permanently stationed in Brussels, and the Commission engages in extensive consultations with it and with national governments directly before producing proposals. As the

Community's competences have been extended, the Commission's monopoly of policy initiation has been weakened, especially in foreign policy coordination, police and security cooperation and defence matters.

In the 1970s a new institution emerged, the European Council, comprising the heads of state or government of the twelve members. Initially this was regarded with great suspicion by pro-integrationists who saw it as a move towards an intergovernmental rather than a supranational community, a distinctly *non-communautaire* development. In the early years there was a tendency to pass matters where agreement could not be reached at the Council of Ministers up to the European Council, whose procedures were less formalized. As a result its agenda became overloaded and it suffered the familiar problems of international summit meetings, in which leaders invest so much political capital that it is difficult to make the necessary compromises and so resort to posturing rather than action. The Single European Act of 1987 formalized the European Council, limited it to two regular meetings per year, though additional ones can be called as necessary, and specified its powers more clearly. These include the admission of new members and Treaty alterations.

The European Parliament is directly elected for a five-year term, though each member state decides on its own system of elections and no two are identical. There is supposed to be a common system of election, and the Maastricht Treaty reaffirms this goal. This would strengthen the Parliament's unity and democratic credentials and, partly for this reason, member states have never been able to agree on it. The British Parliament decided on a free vote not to adopt proportional representation, fearing that it would set a precedent for themselves. Only in *Northern Ireland* was an exception made, to ensure a seat for the Catholic minority. In France, the Constitutional Council ruled that, as the Parliament was an international organization, only the French nation as a whole could be represented, ruling out a constituency or regionally-based system. Electoral systems are given in the appendix. Each country is given a specified number of MEPs, though not strictly according to population. As from 1993, Germany has 99 members, Britain, France and Italy 87 and the other countries have smaller numbers, though more than a strict population share would warrant.

Intergovernmental wrangling long prevented the Parliament from establishing a permanent home. Its plenary meetings are held in Strasbourg in France, but its secretariat and library are based in Luxembourg. Committee meetings are held in Strasbourg, Brussels or other cities depending on the issue. This all necessitates an extraordinary road-show as staff and documents are moved in convoys from one place to another, following the members. The Parliament itself frequently expressed its wish to establish a single base, preferably in Brussels, next to the Commission and Council but France and Luxembourg refused to concede their loss. Eventually, in 1992 Strasbourg was confirmed as the permanent seat of the Parliament, though it is still permitted to hold a number of meetings elsewhere and the secretariat remains in Luxembourg. Member governments, which made this decision, are not unduly concerned about a system which reduces the effectiveness of Parliament and its ability to scrutinize policy.

In order to encourage a *communautaire* rather than national spirit, the Parliament is organized in cross-national political groups. This is ensured by a rule stipulating that for a group to be recognized it must have at least twenty-three members if all are from one country, eighteen if they are from two countries and just twelve if they are from three or more countries. In fact, in the Parliament elected in 1989 all the groups are multinational, although the British Conservatives had difficulty finding allies and initially had to content themselves with a link to two Danish members. The Conservatives anti-European image and stand against the Social Charter proved obstacles to their joining the christian democrat-led group known as the European People's Party, but eventually they were admitted in 1992. French Gaullists also had some difficulty fitting into the general picture but the RPR has now found a variety of allies. The most homogeneous group is the Socialists, formed by social democratic parties belonging to the Socialist International. The Liberal group, by contrast, represents a variety of ideological perspectives, reflecting the divergences of European liberalism. French Communists and the Italian PDS (Democratic Party of the Left, ex-communist) no longer sit together and have found allies of their own. Greens have their own group. The Rainbow Group is largely a marriage of convenience, including Italian radicals, dissident ecologists and the lone Scottish nationalist. In the case of the French centre and right, further confusion is sown by the fact that members elected on the same party list do not always sit in the same group. Valéry Giscard d'Estaing, elected at the head of a joint RPR-UDF list, became president of the Liberal group, which included members of the rival list of Simone Veil while the RPR members sat separately. The membership of the European Parliament by group and country in given in the appendix.

Under the Treaty of Rome, the Parliament's functions were largely consultative and advisory. It did have power to dismiss the entire Commission by a two-thirds majority representing half the membership but as this was so drastic a step, and there was nothing to stop governments reappointing the same commissioners, no censure motion has succeeded. Nor did it possess the key attributes of legislatures in liberal democratic systems, the power to make laws and control of the purse. Legislation remained in the hands of the Council of Ministers, responsible to their individual national governments and Parliaments. Financial matters were handled by the Commission and Council of Ministers. Gradually, however, the Parliament has increased its powers. Commissioners must be approved by the Parliament before taking office. It can now reject the entire budget, a step which it first took in 1979 as a muscle-flexing exercise following direct elections. It can amend the budget for non-compulsory expenditure, that is expenditure not mandated by existing legislation. This section has progressively been increasing, as explained below. For compulsory expenditure items, mostly concerned with the common agricultural policy, the Parliament can propose reallocations of expenditure which are effective unless the Council of Ministers votes by a qualified majority to reject them. Under the Single European Act and the Maastricht Treaty the Parliament has also entered into the legislative process. In specified matters, the Parliament can veto proposals if agreement cannot be reached with the Council. It is also allowed to amend proposed laws. If the Council of Ministers wishes to reject these amendments, it can do so by a qualified majority if the Commission supports it, or by unanimous vote if the Commission supports the Parliament's view. Even in this case, the Parliament still retains its veto power over the whole proposal. This brings the Parliament in as a third party to the legislative process, especially when it can ally with the Commission against national governments. Under the provisions of the Maastricht Treaty, the Parliament's powers are further extended. It will be able to amend certain types of legislation and veto certain bills outright. This is subject to an extremely complex procedure which includes a conciliation committee, based on the German model, to resolve disputes between the Parliament and the Council of Ministers.

Most of the Parliament's work is conducted in committees, which follow developments in detail and prepare opinions for the Parliament as a whole. Commission members appear before the committees to explain their work and the policies they are presenting to the Council of Ministers. Committees also travel and take evidence from outsiders. Written and oral questions may be put to the Commission, the council and the conference of foreign ministers. The impact of all this is hard to assess and the European Parliament does not make a great impression on public opinion in member states. It has consistently pressed for greater powers and hopes that, like national Parliaments in the transition to democracy, it will gradually enhance its influence.

The evolution of Community institutions has disappointed those who hoped for a strong European level of government. Those institutions which express the supranational dimension, such as the Parliament and the Commission, have been held back at the expense of the intergovernmental institutions, in which member states' interests are bargained, notably the Council of Ministers and the European Council. The result is a unique form of political order. It is more than a mere international organization in that the Community, unlike the United Nations, the OECD or NATO, can make laws directly applicable in member states. Yet, to the disappointment of federalists, it is less than a level of government, in that it is subject ultimately to decisions made by sovereign member states.

Another criticism of European institutions is that integration and consolidation have proceeded faster than mechanisms of accountability and control. This has given rise to a 'democratic deficit'. The Commission is appointed by national governments but not answerable to them during its term of office. Members of the Council of Ministers are individually answerable to their national Parliaments but can claim that they were outvoted or had to compromise in order to reach agreement. The Council as a whole is not answerable. Centralization of power in Community institutions has created feelings of alienation in several member states and consequently has stimulated opposition to further integration. The main suggested remedies to the democratic deficit have centred on the European and national Parliaments and the need to respect the principle of subsidiarity. The European Parliament's powers have been extended to allow it some role in the legislative and budgetary process and in the approval of Commissioners. In some states, notably Denmark, there is provision for the national Parliament to be involved in the preparation for European negotiations. Increased attention has been paid to the principle of subsidiarity, which has now been incorporated into the treaties. The Commission has sought to involve regional and local governments and interests in the framing of programmes for regional development. Yet concern with the democratic deficit remains.

INTEREST GROUPS AND CONSULTATION

Attached to the Commission is an extensive consultative machinery, intended to improve its capacity for policy formulation while drawing interest groups and economic agents into the European process. By encouraging cross-national interest groups, the Commission hopes to foster a *communautaire* spirit while at the same time strengthening its own information network and power base against national governments and the Council of Ministers. The principal consultative body is the Economic and Social Council (ECOSOC), with three types of members, employers, trade unions, and general. These are appointed by national interest groups and organized in specialist committees. There is also a wide range of specialist advisory committees covering the main areas of Community policy.

Many interest groups have set up European-wide federations to lobby the Commission. Although the Commission welcomes this type of cross-national lobbying as strengthening the European identity, the various national components sometimes have difficulty in reaching a common position. By the early 1990s, there were 525 Euro-groups, or lobby groups recognized by the Commission.[4] These include broad umbrella groups like the employers' group UNICE and the trade union group ETUC as well as sectoral organizations. The EC Committee of the American Chamber of Commerce includes US multinationals and carries great weight. The Commission makes a point of being open to all comers. It is easy to approach officials, without going through the formalities often found in national governments and open debate is encouraged. This is a means for the Commission to increase its sources of information, without relying exclusively on national governments. It may also be a device to strengthen its own hand and make friends, as well as coping with criticisms about its unelected status. Given the Community's priorities and the Commission's needs, business groups carry by far the most influence in Brussels, though trade unions, environmentalists and women's advocates have also sought to make their voice heard.

National interest groups also lobby the Commission, though they are less welcome. Their most promising route is generally through their own national governments, once they have persuaded them of the merits of their case. They do, however, go to Brussels to press their concerns and gather information on upcoming developments so as to be able to pursue these with their own national governments through the Council of Ministers. The single market initiative has greatly increased the amount and detail of Community legislation and prompted a corresponding increase in lobbying. There has also been a greater professionalization of the process. It has been estimated that there are about 3,000 professional lobbyists in Brussels. The rise of the professional lobbyist, otherwise much less common in Europe than in North America, attests to the complexity of the decision making process and the lack of familiarity and contacts on the part of many national interest groups.

COMMUNITY POLICY MAKING

Community decision making is a complex process, sometimes described with the French word *engrenage*, referring to the meshing together of European, national and sectoral interests. It is intended to favour solutions representing further integration rather than a mere brokerage among states, hence the key role reserved for the Commission. In practice, matters are often less smooth and national compromises are frequently necessary. National governments are consulted at all stages to ensure that proposals will not be blocked later on. Interest groups are similarly consulted in the framing and refinement of policy. This can make matters very slow. Dossiers can be blocked for long periods in disputes among the various interests and progress may be possible only at the pace of the most reluctant member state. Because of the multiplicity of national and sectoral interests involved, Community policy making is rather compartmentalized, with different interests and policy communities mobilizing around distinct policy fields. In this respect, it resembles the American policy process, with its complex interplay of institutions and interests, its lack of formal cohesion and its need for compromise. It also has affinities with policy making in Germany or the European democracies which have a consociational tradition and are accustomed to proceed by negotiation and consensus. At its best, this can produce solutions which are generally acceptable and which can therefore be implemented. At its worst, it can produce deadlock, or Eurosclerosis, as it was called in the early 1980s. Since the passage of the Single European Act, with its provisions for majority voting and the mandate for the single market programme, policy making has speeded up considerably.

National governments have remained more important in the policy process than was envisaged in the early days. Rather than spring proposals on the Council of Ministers, the Commission undertakes extensive consultations with national governments and does not try to press initiatives when it knows that there is no chance of success. Although the Council of Ministers is not supposed to amend proposals, this is effectively done through consultation and log-rolling among national leaders. It is tempting therefore to dismiss Community policy making as no more than intergovernmental bargaining. Yet there is more than this. Some observers[5] stress the importance of bureaucratic politics, the constant negotiation and refinement of policy in the complex sectoral networks which have grown up around the Commission and its directorates. High politics and major initiatives like monetary union or common foreign policy may be reserved for meetings of national leaders, but a great deal of everyday policy, unspectacular in itself but cumulatively of great importance, comes out of the Commission's directorates and their consultations with European interest groups and individual departments within national governments.

Community legislation takes three forms, all of which have the force of law justiciable both in national and European Courts and, under the supranationality principle, they over-ride national laws which conflict with them. Regulations are Community laws of general effect applying directly as soon as they are adopted. Directives are also legally binding in respect of the ends to be achieved but the means of giving effect to them is left to individual member states. This is necessary since states have different legal and administrative systems and Community law needs to be adapted to this. Although compliance with directives is compulsory, some states, especially in southern Europe, are known to drag their feet in giving effect to them. Figure 7.1 (p. 385) shows how some states have delayed giving effect to directives on the 1992 single market projects. Italy and Belgium, in particular, have come in for criticism for combining enthusiastic support in principle for European integration with an apparent inability to put it into practical effect. Decisions are binding only on the states, companies or individuals to which they are addressed and are often issued by the Commission in pursuance of its duty to implement the treaties and

laws of the Community. Regulations, directives and decisions can be taken by
the Council of Ministers or the Commission, depending on the competence
which each has been given under the treaties or the law.

The European Court of Justice, sitting in Luxembourg, adjudicates on
matters of Community law. There are thirteen judges with staggered terms of
six years to ensure continuity. This is the ultimate court of appeal in matters of
Community law and is a court of first instance in major case, for example where
the Commission is prosecuting a large corporation or a national government.
Rulings of the Court are binding and enforceable in the legal systems of
member states and may be accompanied by orders to cease objectionable
practices or fines. This is effective where individuals and corporations are
concerned but the Court has no effective sanctions against national governments,
relying on their respect for the law and reluctance to upset the European project.
In the Maastricht Treaty, provision was made for fines against member states
but it is difficult to see how these could be collected. In practice, disputes
among states themselves are rarely pursued through the Court but are settled
by political and diplomatic means. Figure 7.2 shows the extent of non-
compliance with Court rulings. Again, the worst offenders are those countries
whose official policy is most enthusiastically European, provoking critics to
note that action comes harder than words.

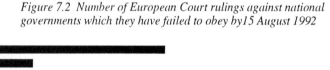

Figure 7.2 Number of European Court rulings against national
governments which they have failed to obey by15 August 1992

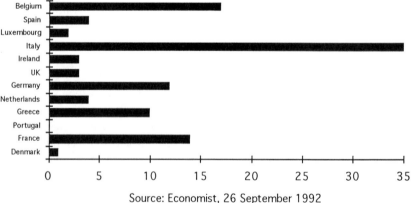

Source: Economist, 26 September 1992

At times the volume of directives and regulations coming out of the
Community has seemed overwhelming. The Commission has often been
criticized for its obsession with 'petty harmonization', introducing European
standards of measurement and quality which often conflict with national
cultural traditions. European regulations have threatened the fine gastronomic

traditions of French cheese making and German brewing as well as the less glorious institution of the British sausage. Symbolic moves such as the common passport cover introduced in the 1980s, while the passports themselves remained national, were intended to promote a sense of European identity. Facing administrative overload in policing common standards and public opposition to petty harmonization, the Community has now retreated. The effort to achieve common standards was largely replaced by the principle of mutual recognition under which products which satisfy legal requirements in any Community country may be sold in any other one. Symbolic proposals, such as the harmonization of car registration plates, have been abandoned in the name of subsidiarity, leaving the Community to deal with matters of substance.

Financing the Community
In the early years, the Community was financed by contributions from member states, based on their relative national wealth. This was considered *non-communautaire* since it did not give the Community its own guaranteed source of income and was replaced by a system of own resources which belong to the EC as of right. This, which consisted of the product of the commons customs duties and agricultural levies together with a share of value added tax (VAT), provoked its own complaints, especially after the enlargement of the Community, since, taking into account contributions and receipts, some members did a lot better than others. Britain led a campaign for changes towards the principle of the *juste retour*, that members should get back what they pay in. The *juste retour* was unacceptable in the Community since it would have reduced its capacity for taking strategic decisions and controlling resources of its own, but mechanisms were put in place to ensure that poorer countries did not have to pay a disproportionate share into EC funds, by linking contributions to gross national product (GNP). There are now four sources of revenue. The first remains the product of the common external tariff on imports from third countries. The second is the agricultural levies which bring imported agricultural produce up to the Community price level. Thirdly there is a proportion of the product of value added tax. All member states are required to have a value added tax, effectively a national purchase tax, and it is intended in due course to bring the various national bases for the tax and rates into line. Meanwhile, the Community works on the basis of a notional common base and requires states to hand over the product of a 1.4 per cent rate on this base. There is a further provision to limit the contributions of certain poorer countries, notably Britain, Ireland and the southern members. The fourth resource is a contribution based on individual members' GNPs. Smaller amounts are provided by a variety of other means including reimbursement of aids, matching contributions to programmes and interest. The proportions of each of these in the 1990 budget are given in Figure 7.3.

Figure 7.3 EC revenues, 1991

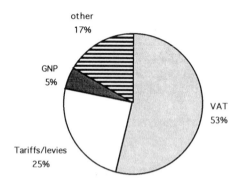

Source: EC Commission

A ceiling is placed on total Community spending, with the GNP percentage contribution adjusted to keep within this. Until 1994, this is fixed at 1.2 per cent of the total Community GNP, rising to 1.27 per cent by 1999, making the EC budget a very small matter in comparison with national public expenditure programmes. It is difficult to determine exactly which countries contribute most to the Community since tariffs and levies are in the last resort paid by the consumer and this might not be a resident of the country into which produce was initially imported. Yet the subject is not surprisingly of critical political importance and caused much argument in the Council of Ministers and the European Council. Richer countries will tend to pay more, given the provisions for VAT and GNP based contributions. Countries with a high propensity to import will also pay more. This has always been the case with the United Kingdom, which continues to import agricultural produce from its traditional suppliers outside the Community. This has made it a net contributor to EC funds and caused a great deal of conflict in the course of the 1980s.

For many years, Community expenditure was dominated by agricultural support, leaving little room for anything else and further affecting the patterns of costs and benefits. Some countries gain heavily from agricultural spending while others, notably Britain, do not. At one time, agricultural spending accounted for over eighty per cent of the budget but over time this has been brought down as pressure has been brought to bear on it, the Community has entered new policy areas and poorer members have insisted on new financial instruments to benefit themselves. The regional fund, introduced to compensate Britain on its entry in the 1970s, has been expanded substantially to accommodate the new southern members and in 1991 a new cohesion fund for transport and communication was agreed as the price of Spanish assent to the European Union proposals. While member states have sought above all to limit their contributions and gain resources to relieve their own financial difficulties, the Commission has consistently opposed the idea of direct rebates, insisting that moneys must be attached to new Community-directed programmes rather than simply handed over to national governments. Even in the 1980s, when special refunds were agreed for Britain, these had to take the form of supplementary programmes within the regional development fund, though this was a thinly disguised fiction, allowing the British Treasury to pocket the money. The main items of expenditure are now the agricultural support system and the structural funds, with an increasing but modest sum for research and development, as shown in figure 7.4.

Figure 7.4 EC expenditure,1992

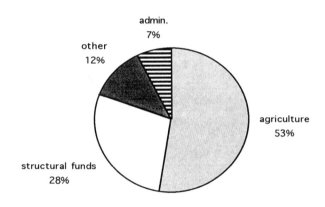

Source: EC Commission

It is difficult to calculate just how much individual states gain and lose from the Community, though this is a topic of intense interest in bargaining sessions at the Council of Ministers. Figure 7.5 shows the percentage of payments from Community funds to each country and the percentage of contributions from each. It covers about 83 per cent of all expenditure. This gives only a general idea of the relative burdens of membership, since it does not include some indirect costs. It is clear, however, that Germany and the UK are the main paymasters of the EC and that Greece, Ireland and Portugal are large beneficiaries. Opinion surveys show that the public in the poorer member states are aware of this advantage and that it has been an important factor in boosting support for the Community in those countries.[6]

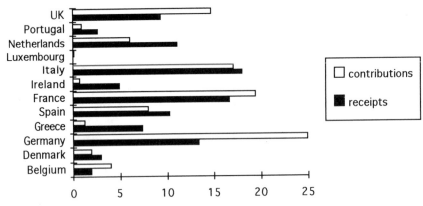

Figure 7.5 EC contributions and receipts, 1989, %

Source: D. Strasser, The Finances of Europe (Luxembourg: EC, 1992)

The Common Agricultural Policy

Under the Treaty of Rome the only real common policy adopted was in agriculture. This is explained by the problems of adjustment in the original states, notably France and the need to gain Community resources to handle this. Farmers were still an important lobby group in France, Germany and Italy and unprepared to expose themselves to the full rigours of international competition as was proposed in the case of industrial modernization. So instead of national systems of protection and subsidy being abolished, they were transferred to the Community level. The highly protectionist regime which resulted, known as the common agricultural policy (CAP), represents a glaring exception to the EC's claims to favour free trade and markets. The centrepiece of the policy is a system of price support to ensure Community producers a given price for their produce irrespective of demand or world competition. Once the price has been set for each commodity, a variable levy is imposed on imported produce to bring it up to that price. This means that, unlike the case of fixed tariffs, it is not possible for outside producers, by cutting production costs, to make themselves competitive since the levy will adjust to bring their selling costs to the European level. At the same time prices within Europe are maintained through intervention in the market whereby the Commission buys up surplus produce to maintain scarcity and therefore prices. This system is liked by farmers since they receive their income directly from sales and so can maintain the illusion that they are not receiving public subsidies.

In fact they are subsidized both by the consumer, who pays higher prices and by the taxpayer, who finances the intervention mechanism. The system produces European prices which generally are higher than those on world markets and leads to periodic surpluses of crops which the Community is obliged to buy up and store. The resulting problem of grain, meat and butter mountains and wine lakes has caused further headaches since these cannot be disposed of within Europe without causing the price to fall again. So they are dumped on Third World markets or sold to overseas governments, notably in the former Soviet Union, at a substantial loss. Levies, shutting out competing produce together with dumping, damage producers in developing countries which the EC is officially committed to helping. Within Europe the policy has tended to favour the wealthy farmers and more prosperous regions. Growing concern about the environment and the effects of intensive farming and over-use of fertilisers had become important political issues as have anomalies such as the Community subsidization of tobacco production when all member governments are committed to reducing smoking.

The absurdities of the CAP and the strain imposed on Community finances have led to increasing pressures for reform. Farmers remain a key element in the CDU/CSU governing coalition in Germany and in France are highly vocal, organized and capable of disruption. Yet their power is waning, as their numbers have fallen and those remaining have modernized and become more market-oriented. Further pressure for change has come from outside, as the Community has fought costly subsidy wars with the United States, Canada and Australia, seeking to dominate third markets. By 1992 the issue of agricultural subsidies was threatening to destroy the General Agreement on Tariffs and Trade (GATT) which had included the question in its latest round of trade liberalization talks, the Uruguay Round.

Internal and external pressures have led to a series of modifications of the common agricultural policy. Quotas have been introduced for products in surplus, limiting the amount which the Community will underwrite. Set-aside schemes encourage farmers to convert land from agriculture. Further proposals in 1991 will reduce guarantees of price support and instead compensate farmers for the acreage under crops, so encouraging a less intensive pattern of cultivation. None of this promises immediate savings in the Community budget since compensation amounts promised to farmers losing protection and price guarantees are generous, but it does herald a gradual transformation of the CAP and in the long run could lead to a reorientation of the Community's activities.

ECONOMIC AND MONETARY UNION

The Treaty of Rome did not provide for common monetary and fiscal policies among member states, but it was widely understood that this would be a logical development from the common market. The first attempt at economic and monetary union took place in the 1970s, with an arrangement tying member state currencies together, so that they floated jointly against the dollar. This was intended as the first step towards a full union, with joint policies on monetary issues and macroeconomic management, but it broke down in the economic disturbances of the 1970s. In 1979, the idea was relaunched in the form of the European Monetary System. The central element of this was the Exchange Rate Mechanism (ERM) by which member state currencies were fixed in relation to each other, with only small fluctuations allowed between them. If a currency is in danger of falling through its floor - the lowest allowable parity - the member state must intervene in conjunction with the others to sustain it. A new unit of account, the European Currency Unit, or ECU, was created, expressed as the value of a weighted basket of member state currencies. The aim of the ERM was to promote trade and factor mobility by minimizing the risk and uncertainty of currency fluctuations and to impose financial discipline on member states so that rates of inflation would converge. In practice, this has meant that currencies are fixed to the dominant European currency, the German mark, to the extent that the EMS has been described as a Deutschmark zone, or a device to impose German standards of monetary rigour on the more feckless members. Membership of the ERM is not compulsory for members but by 1992 only Greece and Portugal were outside it. Britain had joined after much hesitation in 1990. Currencies are not locked together entirely since realignments are possible within the ERM but it is expected that these will become less common as inflation rates converge and member economies adopt parallel courses. Between 1979 and 1983 there were six realignments; between 1983 and 1990 four; and between January 1990 and 1992 just one.

ERM membership is an onerous responsibility, requiring states to increase interest rates and intervene in markets to support their currencies when they are under pressure and ruling out the possibility of devaluation. Monetarist economists regard this as a salutary discipline, forcing governments to adopt prudent policies, or to follow the German *Bundesbank*, which has often amounted to the same thing. They point to the reduction of French and Italian inflation rates as proof of the efficacy of such policies. Critics point to the costs of currency convergence, which forces governments to deflate their economies and raise interest rates, reducing their potential for growth. By the early 1990s, the French Socialist government was receiving high marks from the Community and international financiers for its economic rigour and success in maintaining the exchange rate of the franc, but coming under mounting pressure at home from workers and users of public services who sought a higher growth rate or less restrictive public spending policies. Even Germany found difficulty coping with the demands of membership in the aftermath of unification. By forcing states to respond to disequilibria by changing their monetary and fiscal policies rather than devaluing, the ERM represents a considerable effective loss of national sovereignty.

This could be justified as long as the ERM was serving its purpose. In September 1992, however, the system suffered a serious breakdown as speculators moved against the British pound and Italian lira, its two weakest currencies. Both were forced to leave the ERM and devalue. The Spanish peseta was also devalued, while remaining in the system. Since the very point of the ERM was to instil confidence and reduce inflationary expectations by assuring markets that devaluations would not occur, this was a devastating blow.

In 1990 it was agreed to proceed further with economic and monetary union and an intergovernmental conference was established to negotiate a scheme, finally agreed at the Maastricht summit in 1991. This provides for the establishment of a European Monetary Institute which eventually will evolve into a common European Central Bank (ECB). The ECB will be independent of political control at national or Community level and to ensure this, its directors will be appointed for eight-year, non-renewable terms. It will gradually increase its authority and power. Member states will be required to control their public sector borrowing and gradually monetary and fiscal policies will be aligned. Currencies will be tied more tightly, with no room for fluctuation and no possibility of realignment within the system. Eventually, national currencies will give way to a single European currency, the ECU, but only for those countries which have satisfied the convergence criteria. These are:

- an inflation rate no more than one and a half points above that of the lowest three countries in the Community;
- a budget deficit of no more than three per cent of GDP and public debt of no more than 60 per cent of GDP;
- participation in the narrow band of the ERM with no devaluation for two years;
- long term interest rates no more than two percentage points above those of the three lowest countries.

There are three stages to monetary union. Stage one involves the dismantling of barriers to currency movement, already largely achieved under the single market programme. Stage 2 will see the establishment of the European Monetary Institute and of independent central banks in the member states. The final stage is the establishment of the European Central Bank, replacing the Institute, and a move to a single currency. This is to take effect in 1997 if the Commission certifies and the Council votes that a majority of countries are ready. If not, then those countries which are ready can proceed on their own in 1999.

This programme was accepted by most member states. For the French and smaller northern countries, it was seen less as a loss of sovereignty than an opportunity to convert the EMS from a Deutschmark zone into a genuine European instrument. The Italians showed little reluctance to exchange the lira for the ECU, though the adjustment required in their public deficit will be considerable. While the other southern Europeans worried about the implications of financial rigour and keeping pace with Germany, they again traded their agreement for increases in transfer payments from the richer members. Only Britain held out altogether, insisting on a clause allowing it to opt out of the scheme when the single currency arrives in 1999. The single currency has considerable attractions for governments, allowing them to escape the uncertainties of currency speculation within Europe. On the other hand, it involves a large surrender of national sovereignty. Interest rates, money supply and, by extension, large elements of fiscal policy would escape the control of the nation-state. Public opinion in member states has proved very reluctant to go down this road. Germany, in particular, worries about the effects of losing the Deutschemark, with its assurance of stability and low inflation. Elsewhere, there is concern about handing over such large powers to an unelected and unaccountable central bank, which would use a very narrow set of financial criteria to set policies which would affect everyone.

THE SOCIAL DIMENSION

The Treaty of Rome was primarily concerned with creating an economic common market and the conditions for economic growth. There was a recognition of the need for social cohesion, as one would expect, given the weight of Social Democratic and Christian Democratic ideas in contemporary Europe. It was generally assumed, however, that Europe's contribution would be the creation of wealth, while its redistribution and the building of the welfare state were matters for national governments. The only significant social policy included was the European Social Fund, to assist labour-market adjustment and retrain workers displaced by the effects of the common market. Like the other structural funds, this was largely administered at national level.

The main welfare services remain a national responsibility, but there have been increasing demands for regulation of the labour market and conditions of work at European level. It is this, rather than the broader welfare state, which is meant by European social policy. With the single market initiative of the 1980s, concern was expressed about the effects of economic integration on working conditions and standards. It was feared that firms would seek out the countries with the lowest social charges and the least working regulations and place their investments there. Countries with advanced welfare states and national regulations on conditions of work would be forced to harmonize their standards downwards in order to compete. This process came to be known as social dumping. Concern was also expressed about the neo-liberal basis of the single market initiative, with its emphasis on deregulation, privatization and competition, and about the weight of business interests in shaping its provisions. Trade unions and Social Democrats feared that they would lose the protection of the nation-state, in which they had gained some influence, and be excluded from the building of the new Europe. Even centre-right governments in the wealthier states worried that the poorer, southern states would be able to undercut them with lower wages, less restrictions on employers and fewer social expenditure overheads.

It was to meet these criticisms and make the single market more generally acceptable that Jacques Delors produced the Social Charter. This provided for:
- harmonization of social security and working conditions;
- fair wages, especially for part-time workers;
- paid leave, written employment contracts and provision for lay-offs;
- adequate levels of social protection;
- freedom of association and rights to trade union membership and collective bargaining;
- training and vocational education;
- equal opportunities for women;
- consultation rights for workers;
- health and safety regulations;
- safeguards for young people at work;
- support for the elderly;
- support for the disabled.

This is all consistent with mainstream Social Democratic and Christian Democratic ideology and gained at least the verbal the support of most governments. Yet, even though the Social Charter was merely a statement of good intentions, the British Conservative government refused to endorse it, seeing it as a way of bringing in via Europe the very labour-market and social regulation which it had been abolishing at home. British trade unions, on the other hand, saw it as evidence of the Commission's good intentions and abandoned their long-standing opposition to British membership of the Community. Social policy measures are not subject to majority voting in the Council of Ministers so, given Britain's attitude, the Charter could not be incorporated in the treaties or adopted as a binding element of the 1992 single market programme. Instead the other eleven members agreed to proceed separately on it. The Commission was charged with bringing in measures to ensure its implementation, through a Social Action Programme. Most of these are non-binding and directed only at the eleven members. In a number of cases, however, the Commission has tried to frame social measures as single market items, binding for the Community as a whole and enacted by majority voting.[7]

European employers' groups oppose social regulation at European level or the extension of formal consultation with trade unions. They fear that this may result in European-level corporatism instead of the deregulated market to which they aspire. Britain's Conservative government, too, persisted in its objections during the negotiations for the Maastricht Treaty on European union. To try and accommodate Britain, the Commission's proposals for a social chapter in the Maastricht Treaty were watered down. Yet the British still refused to sign it and again the eleven proceeded on their own. The chapter was incorporated as a protocol to the Treaty, which made clear that it was subordinate to the broader economic goals and subject to national variations. According to the first article of the protocol:

> The Community and Member States shall have as their objectives the promotion of employment, improved living and working conditions, proper social protection, dialogue between management and labour, the development of human resources with a view to lasting employment and the combating of exclusion. To this end, the Community and Member States shall implement measures which take account of the diverse forms of national practices, in particular in the field of contractual relations, and the need to maintain the competitiveness of the European economy.[8]

Some measures can be adopted by a weighted majority vote of the eleven signatories, while others require unanimity. There is a preference throughout the document for voluntary action by states, management and labour and it is likely that the subsidiary doctrine will be invoked to limit further European initiatives in this area. The social dimension to European integration will thus remain much weaker than the market aspects.[9]

POLITICAL UNION

It was the clear intention of the founders of the Community that it should develop as a political as well as an economic union, although this was not specifically provided for in the Treaty of Rome. Over the years, the goal has been controversial and given rise to diverse interpretations. There are those, especially in Britain, who regard the Community as simply an advanced free-trade area, a place in which barriers to trade and commerce are minimized but without eroding the sovereignty of national governments. At the other extreme are European federalists who see in the Community's institutions the embryo of a new level of government, embracing a wide range of functions and effectively reducing national governments to second-tier status. In the late 1980s there was a series of arguments between the 'wideners' who sought to extend the Community as a free trade area to all of Europe, at the cost of cohesion; and 'the deepeners' who wanted to strengthen the unity of the existing Community even if this meant postponing the arrival of new members. By the 1990s, the fall of Communism and the transformations sweeping Europe forced the Community to try and to both at the same time. This opened up a new division. On the one hand were those who saw the Community as a homogeneous whole, centred on a single set of institutions and with all members having the same status, rights and obligations. On the other were those with a less tidy vision, who could envisage a two-speed Community, with an inner circle of tightly integrated members and an outer circle more loosely affiliated. Such a vision might have suited France and Germany, who would be in the inner circle, and Britain, which might have been content to remain in the outer, but other members would certainly complain if they were relegated to second-tier status. Another version, favoured by the French, would involve different arrangements for different purposes, with no single centre of Community power and certainly not a Community level of government.

The issue took on some urgency in the early 1990s for a number of reasons. Changes in the balance of power in Europe were forcing member states to work together in foreign policy matters and consider their defence needs in a post-Cold War world. The single market and economic and monetary union initiatives called into question the effectiveness of Community decision-making procedures and especially the rights of member states to veto progress. With economic integration proceeding so much faster than political, questions were raised about a growing democratic deficit, a lack of accountability of Community institutions. A Community for bureaucrats and business people seemed to be emerging, with important issues of social policy and environmental conservation too often sidelined. Only with a more effective political control and accountability, it was argued, would these issues be addressed. German unification gave an urgency to the issue since many other members were eager to smother the newly united power in a European embrace, a position the Germans declared themselves ready to accept. Yet political union confronts the deep-seated instincts of national governments to preserve their sovereignty and power and can only be approached with great circumspection. Some progress was made in the Single European Act of 1987, which limited the national veto and enhanced the powers of the European Parliament. In 1990 an intergovernmental conference was established, alongside that on economic and monetary union, to consider political union and draft a Treaty, also agreed at the Maastricht summit of 1991.

This appears to entrench the idea of a variegated Community, taking different forms for different purposes not always including all the members and often based upon the sovereign independence of national governments. In some respects, the Community's central institutions are strengthened. More decisions in the Council of Ministers can be taken by majority vote. The Parliament's powers are strengthened, giving it a veto over certain types of legislation under certain conditions. Parliament will also be required to approve the appointment of commissioners. Yet these extensions of Parliamentary control are much weaker than many people had demanded and hardly match the extension of

Community competences. At the insistence of the British, all mention of the Community's federal aspiration was deleted.

European competences are extended into several new areas, including immigration, asylum and visa policies, police and interior ministry cooperation, consumer protection, rights of establishment of professions, some aspects of education, public health and environmental policy, crossborder programmes for transport, telecommunications and energy, research and culture. Governments can agree unanimously to proceed by majority voting in certain foreign policy areas and there are provisions for eventual merging of the Community and the West European Union to form a common defence policy.

Yet crucial aspects of these remain outside the European Community, coming under the umbrella of the new European Union and not all issues are subject to majority voting. Because of Britain's resistance, it proved impossible to include the Social Charter within the new arrangements. Renamed the Social Chapter, this will be carried forward by cooperation among the other eleven, though proceeding by majority votes and with the Commission retaining its initiating role. While all this certainly represents a further move to integration, the Community's new responsibilities in the sensitive matters of immigration, security cooperation, foreign policy and defence will be conducted through intergovernmental means, that is through the cooperation of member states rather than through the unified machinery of the Community. Here the Commission's role will be reduced and that of national governments enhanced. So the extension of the Community has been possible only at the cost of reducing its cohesion, marking a further move away from the idea of a new European state.

FOREIGN POLICY

Movement towards a common European foreign policy has been slow and halting. The first steps in what was initially called European Political Cooperation (EPC) came in 1970 with an agreement among the then six EC members to share information and collaborate on foreign policy issues. This took place outside the institutional framework of the Community and without any common institutions or agencies. The main mechanisms were the meetings of foreign ministers, the European Council of heads of government and a network of contacts among foreign ministries. During the 1970s and early 1980s some common positions were taken on issues such as the Middle East, where the Community did not entirely share the United States' point of view. It is less unconditionally pro-Israel and has long supported the creation of a Palestinian state. The Single European Act formalized European Political Cooperation, bringing it within the Treaty arrangements. It remained, nevertheless, an intergovernmental matter, with the Commission given only a nominal role. Member states have different historic links to the outside world. Britain and France have colonial legacies and special interests in Africa and Asia. Spain has links to Latin America. Germany has revived its historic interest in central and eastern Europe. Greece is concerned more with its regional position than that of Europe as a whole. It has a long-standing quarrel with Turkey over the Aegean and Cyprus. It has objected to European recognition of the former Yugoslav republic of Macedonia, fearing designs on its own province of the same name. Defence and security matters remained largely outside EPC because of objections by neutral Ireland as well as some other states.

Foreign policy and security cooperation received a new urgency in the early 1990s with the collapse of the Soviet bloc and the resulting instability in eastern and central Europe. As the dominant economic power in the region, the EC was expected to take the lead role in economic aid and political support to the new democracies. It was also hoped that a strong Community presence would prevent Germany exercising an effective economic and political hegemony over eastern Europe. A large amount of development assistance has been channelled through the Community. On diplomatic matters, the record has been more patchy. There has been an effort to coordinate recognition of new countries in eastern Europe and the former Soviet Union but this has caused strains within the Community and individual members have their own priorities and historic links with particular regions. Germany insisted on rapid recognition of Croatia, despite the reservations of other Community members and eventually recognized it unilaterally, forcing its partners to respond. Efforts to broker a peace in the former Yugoslavia were hampered by the perception that Germany was not neutral among the warring parties and difficulties in agreeing a common line. EC peacekeepers were sent in to monitor cease-fires but the Community lacked any armed forces to protect them or patrol cease-fire lines. Eventually, the United Nations had to take over the peace-keeping role, though the EC continued, alongside the UN, as a mediator. In 1992, Jacques Delors, president of the EC Commission, called for the United States to take the lead in coordinating possible military responses to the situation in former Yugoslavia, admitting the impotence of the Community.

Nor was the Community able to agree on a common line in the crisis arising from the Iraqi invasion of Kuwait in 1989. Efforts to establish a common position foundered and member states gave varying degrees of support to the American-led military intervention.

The Maastricht Treaty takes EPC a stage further, with its proposals for a foreign and defence pillar of the new European Union. This is still outside the framework of the EC, thus largely excluding the Commission and relying on intergovernmental cooperation. Most decisions will be taken by unanimity, but there is provision for members to agree unanimously to proceed by qualified majority in certain fields.

DEFENCE AND SECURITY POLICY

There are three principal frameworks available for security in Europe in the future, NATO, the Conference on Security and Cooperation in Europe, and a security structure based on the EC and the Western European Union.

During the Cold War, NATO provided a security umbrella for western Europe, backed by the presence of American troops and the American nuclear capability. Although the United States' military presence in Europe was originally seen as short term, the confrontation with the Soviet Union during the Cold War ensured that it remained in place for more than forty years. NATO not only tied the United States to western Europe but also integrated western Europe itself under American leadership. It allowed the rearmament of Germany under close allied control and provided an integrated military command. France preferred a looser arrangement and in 1966 withdrew from the integrated military command and removed the American bases from its soil, while remaining a member of the alliance.

The end of the Cold War and the United States budgetary problems have placed a question mark over the American military presence in Europe and it is likely that it will end in the foreseeable future, or at least be drastically reduced. Britain has indicated that it is opposed to American withdrawal and wishes to retain the existing integrated NATO structure. France, on the other hand, has pressed for more independent European arrangements. Germany's position lies between the two, but in the long run it is likely to side with France. No one seriously advocates a return to independent national security policies for the countries of western Europe. The question then arises as to what new arrangements might be possible.

The Conference on Security and Cooperation in Europe (CSCE) is the product of the Helsinki accords of 1975, themselves the fruit of the *détente* policy pursued by the western powers towards the Soviet Union in the early 1970s. It comprises all the countries of Europe and has the task of reducing tension and enhancing security. Its scope was limited during the Cold War, though the provisions of the Helsinki accords have been credited with encouraging dissent and helping bring down the Communist regimes of eastern Europe. Following the collapse of the Soviet system, the CSCE, has come to prominence again as the basis for a new security system for the continent. It has been strengthened institutionally, with a crisis centre and a centre for the promotion of democracy. It is, however, too large and diverse in membership to become a powerful actor in security matters, as opposed to a forum in which potentially conflicting parties can meet. It has no forces at its disposal and in the Balkan crisis following the break-up of Yugoslavia was sidelined by the EC and the United Nations.

Attempts to forge a European defence community go back to the 1950s. All that was produced in those days was the Western European Union, all of whose members were also in NATO. In the 1980s, as Europe slowly integrated and doubts grew about the American presence, it was suggested that the WEU should be revived as a separate European pillar of the NATO alliance. Meetings of the WEU, which had become virtually moribund, were resumed, and its secretariat strengthened. The WEU now has nine members, all of them in the European Community so it is not surprising that a link between the two has been advocated. This was achieved in the Maastricht Treaty, which indicated, albeit in the vaguest terms, that the WEU would operate as the defence arm of the new European Union.

France has been the strongest supporter of a common European defence policy, based on the WEU and the EC. Britain has been the strongest opponent and insisted on clauses in the Maastricht Treaty which effectively subordinated the defence arrangements to NATO. France and Britain are the only nuclear powers in western Europe so that their decisions on these matters are crucial. Germany inclines to a European defence force and has established some token joint forces with France. In Denmark, on the other hand, neutralist forces are strong and a reluctance to share a common European defence was one reason for the failure of the Maastricht Treaty in the June 1992 referendum. Denmark and Greece, although members of NATO, are not members of the WEU. Ireland is a member of neither and is officially a neutral state. The likely accession of more neutral nations such as Sweden, Austria and Switzerland, will further complicate the search for a common defence and security policy. They may be prepared to surrender their neutrality to a new European security arrangement, as long as this is clearly distinguished from the Cold War arrangements from which they stayed clear. This, however, implies a detachment of Europe from the NATO structure, which would be unacceptable to the British.

EUROPEAN INTEGRATION AND THE REGIONS

European integration has proceeded at the same time as regionalism and a reassertion of subnational political forces. So the nation-state is challenged from above and below simultaneously. There is an apparent contradiction between European integration taking matters to a supranational level, while regionalism is concerned with strengthening the subnational level. Yet there are also elements of consistency and mutual reinforcement of the two movements. Both are inspired by a combination of economic and political factors and a need to rethink the basis of the traditional state. Both carry elements of hard-headed logic together with idealistic commitment. In both cases, states have tried to maintain their own power while using the new institutions for their own ends.

Neo-classical economic theory generally holds that in a free-trade area with capital mobility, less-developed and peripheral regions will be able to exploit their comparative advantages of low cost to attract investment, so producing a convergence in output and living standards. Even if disparities remain, the overall rise in prosperity generated by the open market will raise their incomes alongside everyone else's. This, by and large, was the assumption which underlay the Treaty of Rome. Critics have responded that in the absence of the perfect competition and factor mobility assumed by the neo-classical model, peripheral regions may suffer. Free trade may create pressures to economic concentration, with peripheral regions disadvantaged by their distance from markets, the quality of their infrastructure and technological backwardness. Central regions, by contrast, will enjoy agglomeration economies, building on their existing advantages. So integration will have uneven spatial impacts, exacerbating existing disparities and creating new ones. While in the past nations could intervene to rectify spatial disparities, EC rules on tariffs and subsidies and the inability to manipulate exchange rates within the Exchange Rate Mechanism of the European Monetary System make this more difficult now. Regions may therefore be exposed to the full effects of market forces, without the ability to master them or temper their effects. This created considerable opposition to European integration in peripheral regions and further opposition to Community enlargement with the prospect of more competition. Farmers and wine producers in southern France reacted violently to the arrival of Italian produce in the 1970s and exploded again at the prospect of Spanish entry in the 1980s. Yet in the longer run, regions faced with the inevitability of integration have chosen to play a more constructive game, trying to gain influence within the Community to encourage it to pay more attention to regional problems.

Several Community policies affect regions in differing ways. The expensive common agricultural policy crowds out other possible Community programmes and itself has an uneven spatial impact, serving to reinforce rather than combat existing regional disparities. The competition directorate has become vigilant in rooting out national and local aids to economic development, as distortions of the market and has proved hostile to the development of a community regional policy. Requirements under Economic and Monetary Union to cut budget deficits will have a severe impact on southern European countries depending on government borrowing to finance the infrastructure needed to allow them to compete effectively. Rules requiring governments to open up public procurement have also hit certain regions, traditionally highly dependent on government orders for their economic survival. Deregulation in telecommunications and transport, with the outlawing of various types of cross-subsidy, has caused difficulties in regions like the Italian Mezzogiorno. Environmental regulations have posed severe burdens on the less-developed regions in Spain, undercutting their cost advantage. Sectoral policies in agriculture, fisheries, steel, coal and textiles have all had an uneven regional impact. National states are unable to protect weaker regions through tariffs and subsidies and multinational firms can move their investments around freely within Europe.

European integration has also had political effects in regions. Unable to rely on national diversionary policies, regional governments and movements have started to consider possibilities for indigenous development as well as ways to influence Community policies. Autonomist and separatist movements in Scotland, Wales and elsewhere which in the past often saw the Community as one step more remote, and therefore more objectionable, than national governments, have started to think of Europe in more positive terms. Scottish, Welsh and Basque nationalists now support a policy of independence in Europe as a way of making separation less frightening and costly. If Europe is looking after matters like tariffs, monetary policy and subsidies, it is argued, why do we need the existing national governments? So a movement has begun for a Europe of the Regions in which ultimately national governments would fade away. Elsewhere, in Catalonia for example, Europe is evoked more vaguely, as providing an arena in which the regional personality can be projected and as an alternative frame of reference to the state. In some cases, it merely provides an opportunity for local politicians to engage in diplomatic posturing, trying to create the impression of having their own foreign policy or by-passing the nation-state. Yet even the politics of empty gestures may serve in the longer run to consolidate regional sentiment.

As a result of these trends there has arisen a whole new set of political networks, linking the Community, states and regions. For the most part, regions still have to go to Brussels via their own national governments and those with the best institutions and links into national decision making are the best place to do this. German *Länder* are the obvious example. In centralized states, without regional institutions, it is extremely difficult for regional interests to articulate their demands. At best, the central state may be accessible to local interests through political parties, territorial politicians and clientelist networks. Most national states have insisted that Europe is an aspect of foreign affairs and therefore the exclusive responsibility of central government. This has led not merely to the exclusion of regions from European matters but to the intrusion of national government in regional matters where there is a European policy to be formulated or directive to be implemented. So the Community has proved a force for centralization within states such as Spain and Italy. Regions have accordingly begun to invoke the principle of subsidiarity against member states, arguing that the best level for certain matters to be handled is the regional and local one. In Britain, regionalists and Scottish and Welsh nationalists have made great play of the British government's insistence on subsidiarity in its relations with the Community and its denial of the same principle within Britain itself.

Many regional governments and other interests have accordingly attempted to forge more direct links with the Commission, with a constant succession of delegations and the establishment of offices in Brussels by several regions. Meetings are also convened by the Commission to discuss the implementation of structural fund interventions. There is a great deal of noise created by this regional lobbying and politicians try to extract as much political capital as possible out of a strategy which allows them to project themselves internationally and appear to circumvent the national state. The concrete benefits are more questionable. While the Commission is always happy to talk to regions, thus extending its own information sources, it is rarely able to respond to specific demands, given the rules about funding and programmes. More important is the gradual creation of networks of influence around the Commission, exchanging information, planting ideas and gradually developing policy. The directorates-general responsible for regional and structural policies have to some extent become allies of the regions in promoting a more *communautaire* perspective and maintaining pressure on the Council. For the same reason, the Commission encourages the activities of European-wide organizations of local and regional authorities.

The International Union of Local Authorities and the Council of Communes and Regions of Europe are both wider in scope than the Community and have been closely associated with the Council of Europe which they persuaded to establish a Permanent Conference of Local and Regional Authorities in 1957. In 1986, they opened a joint office to deal with the EC. In 1985, the Council (later Assembly) of European Regions was launched, with 107 members including eleven Swiss cantons and Austrian *Länder*. In 1988, the Commission finally established a Consultative Council of Regional and Local Authorities. In the Maastricht Treaty there is provision for a stronger Committee of the Regions with rights of consultation by the Commission and Council of Ministers and the same status as the Economic and Social Committee. Other regional organizations seeking to influence policy making in Brussels are the Conference of Peripheral Maritime Regions, the Association of European Frontier Regions, the Working Group of Traditional Industrial Regions and three Alpine groups.

One area in which regional, national and European levels interact is in the administration of the Community's structural funds. These have come into being and been expanded gradually over the years in response to complaints from regions and sectors harmed by the integration process. The only regional policy instrument included in the Treaty of Rome at Italy's insistence was the

European Investment Bank. However, as early as the Treaty of Paris establishing the European Coal and Steel Community it had been recognized that exceptions would have to be made to the provision banning subsidies and later regional subsidies were recognized. Since then, European regional policies have developed on three lines: the coordination of national regional policy measures to ensure their conformity to the treaties; the development of Community funds for regional development; and a slow series of moves towards a positive Community regional policy. Initially, the Commission was dependent on national data bases, nationally defined regions and national policy instrument. This has gradually changed.

The Commission also has its own data base of regional conditions and a synthetic index of regional problems. Policing of national regional subsidies is the responsibility of the competition directorate, which fixes ceilings for total permissible subsidies for each region. This is a matter of contention not only with national and regional governments, but also with the directorate for regional policy within the Commission itself.

Moves towards a positive Community regional policy are inspired by the notion of cohesion. This term, more often used than defined, covers economic, social and political issues. Economically, the idea is to permit all regions to compete in the internal market, by endowing them with the necessary infrastructure and skills. Politically, there is a need to demonstrate the value of Community membership in peripheral regions. At the same time, national governments have insisted on a need for a fairer redistribution of Community resources among member states. Unwilling to concede the principle of direct payments among states, the Commission and the more *communautaire* of the members have insisted that they should take the form of Community policy instruments. So the European Regional Development Fund (ERDF) was established in 1975 to accommodate the UK which was about to become a net contributor to the Community. Together with the European Social Fund (ESF) and the guidance section of the European Agriculture and Guidance and Guarantee Fund (EAGGF), it comprises the structural funds of the Community. A related instrument is the European Investment Bank which uses the Community's good credit rating to borrow funds at favourable rates on world markets and lends them for development projects within the Community. The structural funds were doubled as the price for the southern members agreeing to the internal market programme while at the same time there was an effort to integrate the ERDF with the ESF, the agricultural guidance fund and Coal and Steel Community and European Investment Bank moneys. With the needs of the southern countries taking precedence, there was a sharp move of priorities from reconversion of older industrial areas, a policy which favoured the UK, to promotion of underdeveloped areas, favouring Spain, Portugal and Greece. At Maastricht, a further increase in structural fund spending was agreed.

There has been a struggle for the control of these funds among the Commission, member states and regions. In the early years, the funds were largely handed over to states to distribute according to their own criteria to their chosen regions. Most practised a principle known as non-additionality, regarding the money as compensation for their own spending on regional development and so keeping it in their national treasuries. Several states, such as Britain, France and Spain, continue to manage the funds in a centralized manner deciding themselves on how to distribute them internally. Gradually, the Commission has extended its control, moulding the structural funds into an instrument of Community policy rather than a series of compensations to national governments. Eligible regions are determined according to a single Community map, governments are obliged to negotiate over programmes and, where they have failed to demonstrate additionality and transparency, the Commission has held up money. It has further used the funds as an instrument of Community building, strengthening solidarity and demonstrating the benefits of memberships to marginal regions. In this it has found allies in the regions themselves and has insisted on partnership arrangements for Community programmes involving regions themselves within states. These have brought into contact a range of actors at all three levels, strengthening the sense of regional identity and establishing new networks for the exchange of data, ideas and influence. The significance of the funds themselves varies from the purely symbolic to a real contribution to national investment in the cases of Greece and Portugal.

Completion of the internal market, monetary union and global capital mobility are going to increase inter-regional competition. Some regions are better equipped in this respect than others. Southern countries are particularly vulnerable, caught between the technologically advanced states of northern Europe and the low labour cost producers in the non-Community Mediterranean and eastern Europe. Just to bring the less performing regions up to Community average for basic infrastructure would require, according to a Commission study, a tripling of the main regional expenditures between 1994 and 2010. Further transfers to the south will be the price of continued progress to integration and in 1991 proposals emerged for new cohesion funds for transport networks, but there is increasing resistance from northern members to any new expenditure programmes.

There is also a difference in the political capacity of regions, the strength of their business and social networks and their institutional structure. Some states lack regional governments altogether, their regions often lacking internal cohesion or the capacity to mobilize politically or even to use Community financial instruments effectively. A strengthening of the regional dimension of Community decision making at the expense of national governments would not necessarily be in the interest of all regions but could enhance the already privileged positions of the stronger ones. Within the Commission, and in the triangular negotiations among the Community, member states and regions, the debate is likely to continue both on regional policies and the institutionalization of regions within the decision-making process.

ENLARGEMENT

The European Community is in principle open to all European countries, subject to certain conditions. As they have evolved over the years, these are that the prospective member should be a democracy, that it should have a market economy and that it should be ready to assume the economic and financial obligations of membership. New states are also expected to accept the *acquis communautaire*, that is to say the existing body of EC institutions, law and policy, without asking for special derogations. Existing members have insisted on this in order to prevent 'free riders', countries picking the parts of the treaties which suit them while avoiding the costs and responsibilities. As the Community has extended its responsibilities, the scope of the *acquis communautaire* has grown. If the Maastricht Treaty is fully ratified, future members will expected to commit themselves to all three pillars of the European Union - despite the fact the Britain and Denmark have been given derogations! New countries will also be expected to commit themselves to the broader *aquis politique*, the requirement to work together in the framework of common defence and security policies.[10]

Some applicants can quite easily be dismissed. Morocco applied to join in the 1980s and was simply told that it is not in Europe. Turkey poses more difficulties in this respect, raising the question of just where Europe ends. This is partly a geographical question but behind it is an unspoken historical and cultural issue of whether Europe can include Islamic countries. Future applications from Balkan countries and the successor states of the former Soviet Union could raise similar questions.

If a country applies for membership, its application is scrutinized by the Commission which makes a recommendation to the Council of Ministers and the Parliament. The recommendation will take account of the conditions noted above and the state of the applicants' economy. In the case of the early enlargements, to include Britain, Ireland and Denmark, there were no serious problems once the political objections raised by French President de Gaulle had been set aside. In the case of Greece, Spain and Portugal, it was considered that the Community had an obligation to admit these states to assist their transition from dictatorship. Transitional measures were put in place and programmes of adaptation to the European market launched.

While the Community was stagnating in the 1970s and early 1980s, there was no great pressure for expansion. By the early 1990s, however, there was a rush of applications and intentions to apply. These countries can be grouped in three categories. In the first category are the neutral states of Sweden, Austria, Finland and Switzerland, which had stayed out of the Community during the Cold War because of its association with the western and Atlantic bloc. By 1992, all had decided to join the Community, though Switzerland's application was put in doubt when its voters rejected the European Economic Area in a referendum in December 1992. To these can be added Iceland and Norway, which voted by referendum against joining along with Britain, Ireland and Denmark in 1973 but which was reconsidering its position in the early 1990s. These countries are members of EFTA, which already has free trade with the EC; they have advanced economies and are ready in most respects to join the Community. The only obstacles are the neutrality of the first four and the protected agricultural sectors of all the EFTA states. The commitment to a common defence policy in the Maastricht Treaty is part of the *acquis politique* to which they must adhere, though this issue may be effectively fudged. Neutrality has changed its meaning in the wake of the collapse of the Soviet bloc, and the Commission appears to regard this as no longer a serious obstacle.[11] Agriculture in Finland, Austria and Switzerland is even more protected than in the EC and would have to undergo considerable adjustment to fit into the common agricultural policy. Scandinavian countries also have extensive regional policies to benefit communities in remote northern districts, which might fall foul of EC competition rules. These states have found that they are obliged to follow EC regulations in a large range of matters outside the agricultural sector in order to trade with the Community. They have therefore decided that remaining outside simply deprives them of influence of the rules by which they must live. To provide a link between the EC and EFTA, a new arrangement known as the European Economic Area (EEA) was set up in 1992, providing for consultation and joint decision making in some matters. This was held up by objections from the European Court and was in any case soon seen as a bridge to full EC membership rather than a substitute for it. In favour of the admission of the EFTA members is the fact that all would be net contributors to the Community budget.

The second group of countries is in southern Europe and includes Malta, Cyprus and Turkey all of whom had applied to join by 1992. These are all poorer than the Community average and could pose a burden on the budget, especially the structural funds, diverting expenditure away from the existing beneficiaries. There are problems about their political stability and democracy as well as the ability of their economic structures to compete in the single markets. Northern countries are afraid that, with free movement of labour, they would be faced with a large number of migrant workers. Cyprus is disputed by Turkey and Greece, which also have territorial disputes in the Aegean. It is likely that they will be made to wait a considerable time before attaining full membership.

The third group of potential applicants comprises the new democracies of central and eastern Europe. Poland, Hungary and the Czech Republic have indicated their firm intention to join as soon as possible. They are likely to be obliged to wait until their market economies are consolidated and their industrial sectors brought up to competitive levels. Existing members fear that they too might pose a burden on Community finances. For the other countries of eastern Europe, membership is a distant prospect.

A Community of twenty or thirty members could not work in the same way as a Community of twelve. If the existing system of appointments were retained, the Commission would be too large. It has been suggested that only the large states should be allowed to nominate a commissioner each, with the small countries sharing nominations. This has been resisted because it suggests that there would be first-class and second-class members. Smaller countries fear the creation of a directoire of big states taking effective charge of the Community. If enlargement were to leave the existing Council of Ministers intact, it could be impossible to reach agreement. A streamlining of the Community's institutions would be therefore necessary. This might provide for stronger central institutions, or it might apply the subsidiarity principle more fully, confining the Community to essential strategic matters and leaving more to national governments. It is likely that the Parliament will use its right to veto new members to insist on institutional reform as the price of enlargement.

An enlarged Community would be a great deal less homogeneous and might find it more difficult to proceed with tighter monetary, political and diplomatic unity. This is why some observers have noted a potential contradiction between deepening the Community by binding the members closely together, and broadening it by extending its membership. If broadening occurs at the expense of deepening, some observers have predicted a Europe of concentric circles. At the centre would be Germany, France and the Benelux countries, closely integrated. Beyond there would be a second tier of less closely integrated states including Italy, Spain, Britain and the Scandinavian countries. Beyond that would be a third circle of associates, such as Greece, Turkey, Poland and Hungary. On several occasions, the Community has come close to accepting this idea but has in the event insisted on a unified approach. This unified approach, however, had to be stretched a great deal at Maastricht, when Britain and Denmark were allowed effectively to opt out of vital parts of the Treaty. Similarly, the Schengen agreement on open borders applies only to an inner core of member states.

Another scenario is even less tidy. This is the variable geometry Europe, in which there would be a tightly bound inner core but, beyond that, states would have a whole variety of different relationships. All would have free trade and a common market, but not all would adopt common policies. Some might opt into a common defence policy, others in a Social Charter. Some would abolish borders, others would retain controls. This would be a potentially unstable arrangement and create serious problems of transparency and accountability in decision making. It is opposed strongly by the Commission and most member states and has never been admitted as a model for the future. Yet, while denying it in principle, member governments have countenanced it in practice through the special opt-outs allowed for Britain and Denmark in the Maastricht Treaty on European Union. It may reflect the complex and inter-dependent nature of policy making in the contemporary world.

In the 1990s, both governments and the Commission were taking a more hard-headed and instrumental view of the unification process. The Community itself has suffered variations in its fortunes but it is unlikely to fade away. It has become an essential part of the European landscape and there is an enormous political and economic investment in its future. It is even less likely, however, that it will in the foreseeable future displace the nation-state as the basis of political authority.

REFERENCES

1. Among the early academic discussions of functionalism and supranationalism are the works of Ernst. Haas, *The Uniting of Europe* (Stanford: Stanford University Press, 1958) and *Beyond the Nation-state: Functionalism and the Theory of Regional Integration* (Stanford: Stanford University Press, 1964). For a criticism see P. Taylor, *The Limits of European Integration* (New York: Columbia University Press, 1983).
2. N. Nugent, 'The Deepening and Widening of the European Community: Recent Evolution, Maastricht and Beyond', *Journal of Common Market Studies*, XXX.3 (1992), pp. 311-28.
3. Article 3b of the Treaty of Rome as amended by the Treaty on European Union.
4. S. Maizey and J.J. Richardson, 'British Pressure Groups: the Challenge of Brussels', *Parliamentary Affairs*, 45.1 (1992), pp. 92-107.
5. B.G. Peters, 'Bureaucratic Politics and the Institutions of the European Community', in A. Sbragia (ed.), *Euro-Politics: Institutions and Policymaking in the "New" European Community* (Washington DC: Brookings Institution, 1992).
6. *Eurobarometer*, 36 (1991).
7. M. Rhodes, 'The Future of the "Social Dimension": Labour Market Regulation in Post-1992 Europe', *Journal of Common Market Studies*, XXX.1 (1992), pp. 23-51.
8. Article 1 of 'Agreement on Social Policy concluded between the member states of the European Community with the exception of the United Kingdom of Great Britain and Northern Ireland', *Treaty on European Union*.
9. P. Lange, 'The Politics of the Social Dimension', in A. Sbragia (ed.), *Euro-Politics: Institutions and Policymaking in the "New" European Community* (Washington DC: Brookings Institution, 1992).
10. A. Michalski and H. Wallace, *The European Community: The Challenge of Enlargement* (London: Royal Institute of International Affairs, 1992).
11. A. Michalski and H. Wallace, *The European Community: The Challenge of Enlargement* (London: Royal Institute of International Affairs, 1992).

FURTHER READING

C. Archer and F. Butler, *The European Community. Structure and Process* (New York: St. Martin's Press, 1992).

M. Baldassarri and R. Mundell, *Building the New Europe. Vol. I: The Single Market and Monetary Unification* (New Tork: St. Martin's Press, 1992).

EC Membership Evaluated, a series of books on the twelve states (London: Pinter, 1990-2).

J. Greenwood, J. Grote and K. Ronit, *Organized Interests and the European Community* (London: Sage, 1992).

M. Holland, *European Community Integration* (New York: St. Martin's Press, 1992).

L. Hurwitz and C. Lequesne (eds.), *The State of the European Community* (Boulder, Lynne Reimer, 1991).

R.O. Keohane and S. Hoffman (eds.), *The New European Community* (Boulder, Westview, 1991).

A.J.C. Kerr, *The Common Market and How it Works,* 3rd edn. (Oxford: Pergamon, 1986)..

B. Laffin, *Integration and Cooperation in Europe* (London: Routledge, 1992).

R. Leonardi (ed.), *European Community Policies and Politics. An Annual Review* (London: Pinter, 1992).

B. Nelson, D. Roberts and W. Veit, *The Idea of Europe* (New York: St. Martin's Press, 1992).

W. Nicholl and T. Salmon, *Understanding the European Communities* (London: Philip Allan, 1990).

N. Nugent, *The Government and Politics of the European Community,* 2nd edn. (London: Macmillan and Durham: Duke University Press, 1991).

J. Pinder, *European Community. The Building of a Union* (Oxford: Oxford University Press, 1991).

W. Nicoll and T. Salmon, *Understanding the European Communities* (London: Philip Allan, 1990).

S. Serfaty, *The Identity and Definition of Europe* (London: Pinter, 1992).

D.L. Smith and J. Lee Ray (eds.), *The 1992 Project and the Future of Integration in Europe* (Armonk, N.Y.: M.E. Sharpe, 1992).

D. Urwin, *The Community of Europe. A History of Integration since 1945* (Harlow: Longman, 1991).

W. Wallace (ed.), *The Dynamics of European Integration* (Lodon: Pinter, 1992).

STATISTICAL APPENDIX

Table A.1 Basic statistics for five countries, EC and USA

	France	Germany	Italy	Spain	UK	EC	USA
Population, 000	56,893	79,700	57,756	38,993	57,485	344,924	246,329
Area, 1000 sq. km.	544.0	356.9	301.3	508.4	244.1	2, 253.3	9, 372.7
GDP per capita 1989, billion ECUs	16.157	16.954	14.848	10.935	14.582	14.488	19.877

Source: Basic Statistics of the Community (Luxembourg: Official Publication Office of the European Community, 1992).

Table A.2 British General Election results, 1945-92

	Percentage Vote (Seats in Parliament in parentheses)								
Year	Conservative		Labour		Liberal		Others		Government
1945	39.6	(210)	48.0	(393)	9.0	(12)	2.8	(3)	Labour
1950	43.5	(298)	46.1	(315)	9.1	(9)	1.3	(3)	Labour
1951	48.0	(321)	48.8	(295)	2.6	(6)	1.6	(3)	Conservative
1955	49.7	(345)	46.4	(277)	2.7	(6)	1.2	(3)	Conservative
1959	49.3	(365)	43.9	(258)	5.9	(6)	0.5	(1)	Conservative
1964	43.4	(304)	44.1	(317)	11.2	(9)	1.3	(0)	Labour
1966	41.9	(253)	48.1	(364)	8.5	(12)	1.2	(2)	Labour
1970	46.4	(330)	43.1	(288)	7.5	(6)	3.2	(7)	Labour
1974	37.9	(297)	37.2	(301)	19.3	(14)	5.7	(23)	Labour
1974	35.8	(277)	39.2	(319)	18.3	(13)	6.7	(26)	Labour
1979	43.9	(339)	37.0	(269)	13.8	(11)	5.4	(14)	Conservative
1983	42.4	(396)	27.6	(207)	25.4	(23)	4.6	(21)	Conservative
1987	42.3	(376)	30.8	(229)	22.6	(22)	4.3	(23)	Conservative
1992	41.9	(336)	34.4	(271)	17.8	(20)	5.8	(24)	Conservative

Liberals include SDP-Liberal Alliance in 1983 and 1987, Liberal Democrats in 1992.
Since February 1974, Ulster Unionists, formerly counted with the Conservatives, have
sat as separate parties. In 1983 the number of Northern Ireland seats was increased from
12 to 17.

Table A.3 Percentage vote, legislative elections under the French Fifth Republic

1958		1962	
Communists	18.9	Communists	21.9
SFIO (Socialists)	15.5	SFIO (Socialists)	12.4
Left radicals	9.2	Left radicals	7.4
Other left	1.6	Other left	2.0
TOTAL LEFT	45.2	TOTAL LEFT	43.7
MRP (Christian democratD	11.1	MRP (Christian Democrat)	7.9
CNI (conservative)	14.2	CNI (conservative)	7.3
Moderates	5.8	Moderates	4.2
UNR (Gaullists)	18.3	UNR (Gaullists)	33.7
Reformist centre	2.0	RI (Giscardians)	2.3
Extreme right	2.6	Extreme right	0.8
TOTAL RIGHT AND CENTRE	54.3	TOTAL RIGHT AND CENTRE	56.2
1967		**1968**	
Communists	22.5	Communists	20.0
FGDS (Socialists)	18.9	FGDS (Socialists)	16.5
Other left	2.2	Other left	4.0
TOTAL LEFT	43.6	TOTAL LEFT	40.5
Democratic Centre	14.1	Democratic Centre	10.5
Other centre-right	3.3	Other centre-right	2.0
UDR (Gaullists)	33.0	UDR (Gaullists)	38.0
RI (Giscardians)	5.5	RI (Giscardians)	8.4
Extreme right	0.6	Extreme right	0.1
TOTAL RIGHT AND CENTRE	56.5	TOTAL RIGHT AND CENTRE	59.0
1973		**1978**	
Communists	21.4	Communists	20.6
PS (Socialists)	19.1	PS (Socialists)	22.8
MRG (left radicals	1.7	MRG (left radicals)	2.2
Other left	3.6	Other left	4.6
TOTAL LEFT	45.8	TOTAL LEFT	50.2
Centrists and moderates	16.1	UDF (Giscardians)	23.9
UDR (Gaullists)	24.5	RPR (Gaullists)	22.8
RI (Giscardians)	7.2	Extreme right	0.8
Other right	5.3	TOTAL RIGHT AND CENTRE	47.5
Extreme right	0.5	Ecologists	2.0
TOTAL RIGHT AND CENTRE	54.2	Others	0.3

1981		1986	
Communists	16.1	Communists	9.7
PS (socialists)	36.7	PS (socialists)	30.8
MRG (left radicals	1.5	MRG (left radicals)	0.8
Other left	1.3	Other left	2.7
TOTAL LEFT	55.6	TOTAL LEFT	44.0
UDF	21.7	RPR/UDF	42.1
RPR	21.2	Other right	2.9
Extreme right	0.3	FN (extreme right)	9.7
TOTAL RIGHT	43.3	TOTAL RIGHT	54.7
Ec ologists	1.1	Ecologists	1.2
Others	0.1	Others	0.1
1988		**1993**	
Communists	11.3	Communists	9.2
PS (socialists)	34.8	PS (Socialists)	17.6
MRG (left radicals)	1.1	Presidential majority	1.5
Presidential majority	1.6		
Other left	0.4	Other left	1.7
TOTAL LEFT	49.2	TOTAL LEFT	30.0
RPR	19.2	RPR	20.5
UDF	18.5	UDF	19.2
Other right	2.9	Other right	4.6
FN (extreme right)	9.8	FN (Extreme right)	12.5
TOTAL RIGHT	50.4	TOTAL RIGHT	56.8
		Greens	7.7
Others	0.5	Others	5.5

Figures are for first round in all elections except that of 1986 which was conducted by proportional representation

Source: A. Lancelot, Les élections sous la V République (Paris: Presses Universitaires de France, 1988); SOFRES, L'état de l'opinion, 1989 (Paris: Seuil, 1989); Le Monde, 23 March 1993

Table A.4 *Percentage vote in presidential elections under the French Fifth Republic*

1965	Round 1	Round 2	1969	Round 1	Round 2
de Gaulle	43.1	54.5	Pompidou	44.5	58.2
Mitterrand	32.3	45.5	Poher	23.3	41.8
Lecanuet	15.9		Duclos	21.3	
Tixier-Vignancour	5.3		Defferre	5.0	
Marcilhacy	1.7		Rocard	3.6	
Barbu	1.1		Ducatel	1.3	
Turnout	85.5	84.4	Krivine	1.1	
			Turnout	77.6	68.9

1974	Round 1	Round 2	1981	Round 1	Round 2
Mitterrand	43.3	49.2	Giscard d'Estaing	28.3	48.2
Giscard d'Estaing	32.6	50.8	Mitterrand	25.9	51.8
Chaban-Delmas	15.1		Chirac	18.0	
Royer	3.2		Marchais	15.4	
Laguiller	2.3		Lalonde	3.9	
Dumont	1.3		Laguiller	2.3	
Le Pen	0.8		Crépeau	2.2	
Muller	0.7		Debré	1.7	
Krivine	0.4		Garaud	1.3	
Renouvin	0.2		Bourchadeau	1.1	
Sebag	0.2		Turnout	81.1	85.6
Heraud	0.1				
Turnout	81.1	85.6			

1988	Round 1	Round 2
Mitterrand	34.1	54.0
Chirac	19.9	46.0
Barre	16.5	
Le Pen	14.4	
Lajoinie	6.8	
Waechter	3.8	
Juquin	2.1	
Laguiller	2.0	
Boussel	0.4	
Turnout	84.0	81.0

Source: A. Lancelot, Les élections sous la V république (Paris: Presses Universitaires de France, 1988); SOFRES, L'état de l'opinion, 1989 (Paris: Seuil, 1989).

Table A. 5 Percentage vote, elections to Italian Chamber of Deputies, 1946-92

	1946	1948	1953	1958	1963	1968	1972	1976	1979	1983	1987	1992
Christian Democrats	35.2	48.7	40.1	42.2	38.3	39.1	38.7	38.7	38.3	32.9	34.3	29.7
Communists (PDS)	18.9	30.7	22.6	22.7	25.3	26.9	27.2	34.4	30.4	29.9	26.6	16.1
Communist Refoundation												5.6
Socialists	20.7	-----	12.7	14.2	13.8	14.5	10.7	9.6	9.8	11.4	14.3	13.6
Social Democrats		7.1	4.5	4.6	6.1		5.4	3.4	3.8	4.1	3.0	2.7
Liberals	6.8	3.8	3.0	4.6	7.0	5.8	3.9	1.3	1.9	2.9	2.1	2.8
Republicans	4.3	2.5	1.6	3.5	1.4	2.0	2.9	3.1	3.0	5.1	3.7	4.4
Radicals								1.1	3.4	2.2	2.6	1.2
MSI		2.1	5.8	4.7	5.1	4.5	9.2	6.1	5.3	6.8	5.9	5.4
Monarchists	2.8	2.8	6.9	4.8	1.7	1.3						
S. Tyrol People's Party		1.3	0.5	1.0	0.9	1.4	0.5	0.5	0.6	0.5	1.4	0.5
Val d'Aosta list				0.3	0.3				0.1	0.9	0.4	0.1
Sardinian Action Party		0.4									0.9	0.9
Greens											2.5	3.0
Proletarian Democracy								1.1	1.4	1.5	1.7	
Northern Leagues												9.9
Network												1.9
Others	11.3	0.4	2.3	0.3		4.5	3.3	0.3	2.0	0.9	0.4	3.1
TURNOUT	80.0	92.2	93.7	93.0	92.9	93.0	90.1	90.8	89.9	89.0	88.5	86.4

Note: in 1948 Communists and Socialists presented joint lists

Table A. 6 Party percentage vote in German Bundestag Elections, 1949-90

Party	1949	1953	1957	1961	1965	1969	1972	1976	1980	1983	1987	1990
CDU/CSU	31.1	45.2	50.2	45.3	47.6	46.1	44.9	48.8	44.5	48.8	44.3	43.8
SPD	29.2	28.8	31.8	36.2	39.3	42.7	45.8	42.6	42.9	38.2	37.1	33.5
FDP	11.9	9.5	7.7	12.8	9.5	5.8	8.4	7.9	10.6	7.0	9.1	11.0
Greens									1.5	5.6	8.3	3.9
Others	27.8	16.5	10.3	5.7	3.5	5.5	0.9	0.9	0.5	0.5	1.2	7.8
Turnout	78.5	86.0	87.8	87.7	86.8	86.7	91.1	90.7	88.6	89.1	84.4	77.8

Table A. 7 Percentage vote in Spanish national elections for parties
winning seats

Party	1977	1979	1982	1986	1989	1993
PSOE	30.3	30.5	48.4	44.6	39.9	38.6
PSP	4.5	-	-	-	-	
PP	8.4	5.8	25.5	26.3	26.0	34.7
UCD	34.8	35.0	6.5	-	-	
CiU	2.8	2.7	3.7	5.1	5.1	4.9
PNV	1.7	1.5	1.9	1.6	1.3	1.2
Communists	9.4	10.8	4.0	4.5	9.1	9.5
CDS	-	-	2.9	9.2	8.0	1.6
HB	-	1.0	1.0	1.1	1.1	0.9
misc. regional	7.0	3.7	1.5	1.8	3.3	3.3
extreme right	0.6	2.1	-	-	-	
TURNOUT	77.8	68.1	79.9	70.4	69.7	76.6

PSOE = Socialist Party

PSP = Popular Socialist Party

PP = Popular Party, Popular Alliance or Democratic Coalition

UCD= Union of Democratic Centre

CiU = Catalan Nationalists led by Pujol

PNV =Basque Nationalist Party

Communists after 1986 form part of United Left

CDS = Social Democratic Centre

HB = Herri Batasuna, extreme Basque nationalists

misc. regional includes parties from Andalusia, Canaries, Aragon, Navarre and
Valencia as well as minor Basque and Catalan parties

Source: Spanish Ministry of the Interior; T. Mackie and R. Rose,
International Almanac of Electoral History, 3rd edn (Washington:
Congressional Quarterly, 1991).

Table A.8 European organizations and membership, 1993

	EC	WEU	Schengen	EFTA	NATO	Council of Europe	CSCE
Belgium	X	X	X		X	X	X
Denmark	X				X	X	X
France	X	X	X		X	X	X
Germany	X	X	X		X	X	X
Greece	X				X	X	X
Ireland	X					X	X
Italy	X	X	X		X	X	X
Luxembourg	X	X	X		X	X	X
Netherlands	X	X	X		X	X	X
Portugal	X	X	X		X	X	X
Spain	X	X	X		X	X	X
UK	X	X			X	X	X
Andorra							X
Austria				X		X	X
Bulgaria						X	X
Czech Rep.						X	X
Cyprus						X	X
Estonia						applied	X
Finland						X	X
Hungary						X	X
Iceland				X	X	X	X
Latv ia						applied	X
Liechtenstein				X		X	X
Lithuania						applied	X
Malta						X	X
Monaco							X
Norway				X	X	X	X
Poland						X	X
Rumania						applied	X
San Marino						X	X
Slovenia						applied	
Slovakia						X	X
Sweden						X	X
Turkey					X	X	X
Switzerland				X		X	X
Vatican City							X

Table A.9 Political groups in the European Parliament, 1992

	Be	Dk	Sp	Fr	Gr	Ir	It	Lu	Ne	Po	Ge	UK	Total
Socialists	8	4	27	22	9	1	14	2	8	8	31	46	180
European People's Party (Christian Democrat and Conservative)	7	4	18	11	10	4	27	3	10	3	32	33	162
Liberal and Reform Group	4	3	5	9		2	3	1	4	9	5		45
Greens	3		1	8			7		2		6		27
Unitary European left (former Communists)		1	4		1	1	22						29
Rally of European Democrats (Gaullists and others)			2	12	1	6							21
European Right (extreme right)	1			10							3		14
Coalition of the Left (Communists)				7	3					3			13
Rainbow	1	4	2	1		1	3			1	1	1	15
Not in a group			1	1			5		1			1	12
Total	24	16	60	81	24	15	81	6	25	24	81	81	518

Table A. 10 Systems of election to European Parliament

Belgium	Proportional representation by regioin. Separate party lists for Flemish and Walloon communities
Denmark	Proportional representation by party list in single national constituency
France	Proportional representation by party list in single national constituency
Germany	Proportional representation by part list in each Land
Greece	Proportional representation by party list in single national constituency
Ireland	Proportional representation in four multi-member constituencies
Italy	Proportional representation in five regional constituencies
Luxembourg	Proportional representation by party list in single national constituency
Netherlands	Proportional representation by party list in single national constituency
Portugal	Proportional representation by party list in single national constituency
Spain	Proportional representation by party list in single national constituency
UK	Simple plurality in 78 constituencies in Britain. Proportional representation by single transferable vote in N. Ireland

Table A. 11 Italian governments, 1945-93

Prime minister	coalition formula	parties	period
Ferrucio Parri	national unity	anti-fascist parties	June-Nov. 1945
Alcide De Gasperi	national unity	DC-PSI-PCI et.al.	Dec. 1945-July 1946
Alcide De Gasperi	national unity	DC-PSI-PCI-PRI	July 1946-Feb. 1947
Alcide De Gasperi	national unity	DC-PSI-PCI	Feb.-May 1947
Alcide De Gasperi	centre-right	DC-PSDI-PRI-PLI	May 1947-May 1948
Alcide De Gasperi	centre-right	DC-PSDI-PRI-PLI	May 1948-Jan.1950
Alcide De Gasperi	centre-right	DC-PSDI-PRI	Jan.1950-July 1951
Alcide De Gasperi	centre-right	DC-PRI	July 1951-June 1953
Alcide De Gasperi	monocolore	DC	July 1953
Guisseppe Pella	monocolore	DC	Aug. 1953-Jan.1954
Amintore Fanfani	monocolore	DC	Jan. 1954
Mario Scelba	centre-right	DC-PSDI-PLI	Feb.1954-June 1955
Antonio Segni	centre-right	DC-PSDI-PLI	June 1955-May 1957
Adone Zoli	monocolore	DC	May 1957-June 1958
Amintore Fanfani	centre-right	DC-PSDI	July 1958-Jan.1959
Antonio Segni	monocolore	DC	Feb.1959-Feb.1960
Fernando Tambroni	monocolore	DC	March-July 1960
Amintore Fanfani	monocolore	DC	July 1960-Feb.1962
Amintore Fanfani	centre-right	DC-PSDI-PRI	Feb. 1962-May 1963
Giovanni Leone	monocolore	DC	June-Nov. 1963
Aldo Moro	centre-left	DC-PSI-PSDI-PRI	Dec.1963-June 1964
Aldo Moro	centre-left	DC-PSI-PSDI-PRI	July 1964--Feb.1966
Aldo Moro	centre-left	DC-PSI-PSDI-PRI	Feb. 1966-June 1968
Giovanni Leone	monocolore	DC	June-Nov.1968
Mariano Rumor	centre-left	DC-PSI-PRI	Dec.1968-July 1969
Mariano Rumor	monocolore	DC	Aug.1969-Feb.1970
Mariano Rumor	centre-left	DC-PSI-PSDI-PRI	March-July 1970
Emilio Colombo	centre-left	DC-PSI-PSDI-PRI	Aug.1970-Jan.1972
Giulio Andreotti	monocolore	DC	Feb. 1972
Giulio Andreotti	centre-right	DC-PSDI-PLI	June 1972-June 1973
Mariano Rumor	centre-left	DC-PSI-PSDI-PRI	July 1973-Mar. 1974

Mariano Rumor	centre-left	DC-PSI-PSDI	March-Oct.1974
Aldo Moro	centre-right	DC-PRI	Nov.1974-Jan.1976
Aldo Moro	historic compromise	DC	Feb.-April 1976
Giulio Andreotti	historic compromise	DC	Aug.1976-Jan.1978
Giulio Andreotti	historic compromise	DC	Mar. 1978-Jan.1979
Giulio Andreotti	centre-right	DC-PSDI-PRI	Mar.1979-July 1979
Franceso Cossiga	centre-right	DC-PSDI-PRI	Aug. 1979-Mar.1980
Franceso Cossiga	centre-right	DC-PSDI-PRI	April-Sept. 1980
Arnaldo Forlani	centre-left	DC-PSI-PSDI-PRI	Oct. 1980-May 1981
Giovanni Spadolini	pentapartito	DC-PSI-PSDI-PRI-PLI	June 1981-Aug.1982
Giovanni Spadolini	pentapartito	DC-PSI-PSDI-PRI-PLI	Aug.-Nov. 1982
Amintore Fanfani	quattropartito	DC-PSI-PSDI-PLI	Dec. 1982-April 1983
Bettino Craxi	pentapartito	DC-PSI-PSDI-PRI-PLI	Aug. 1983-June 1986
Bettino Craxi	pentapartito	DC-PSI-PSDI-PRI-PLI	Aug. 1986-April 1987
Amintore Fanfani	monocolore	DC	April-July 1987
Giovanni Goria	pentapartito	DC-PSI-PSDI-PRI-PLI	July 1987-March 1988
Ciriaco de Mita	pentapartito	DC-PSI-PSDI-PRI-PLI	April 1988-May 1989
Giulio Andreotti	pentapartito	DC-PSI-PSDI-PRI-PLI	May 1989-Jun1 1991
Giulio Andreotti	quattropartito	DC-PSI-PSDI-PLI	June 1991-April 1992
Giuliano Amato	quattropartito	DC-PSI-PSDI-PLI	June 1992-April 1993
Carlo Ciampi	technocrat/ multi-party		April 1993-

DC   =   Christian Democrats

PSI   =   Socialists

PLI   =   Liberals

PSDI =   Social Democrats

PRI   =   Republicans

PCI   =   Communists

Index